They Came To Fish

A BRIEF LOOK
AT PORTSMOUTH'S
350 YEARS OF HISTORY;
IT'S LOCAL AND
WORLD-WIDE
INVOLVEMENTS
AND THE PEOPLE
CONCERNED
THROUGH THE EYES
OF A REPORTER

BY
RAYMOND A. BRIGHTON

Portsmouth, N. H. / Portsmouth 350, Inc.

Table of Contents

1

The Early Arrivals

[1]. These emplacements housed two 16-inch, all-electric rifles. They were built in 1942-43. In 1944 the guns were installed, and in the spring of that year Battery C of the 22nd Coast Artillery Regiment, fired three settling shots from each gun. The guns were cut up for scrap in 1947. During World War II, the Army acquired more than 100 acres in the Odiorne's Point area, taking over many nice summer homes in the process. It was kept as a military reservation until 1962 when it was bought by the state as a historic site and recreational area with the exception of the part held by the Air Force for a radar station and that, too, has been released to the state.

[2]. U.S. Route 1A, the Ocean Boulevard, was largely the brain child of one man, former Portsmouth Mayor John Pender, who wanted the public to have a scenic road along the ocean. "Old Fuss 'n Feathers", as Pender was known to his political foes, managed to get an appropriation for the road in 1899. He was chairman of the commission charged with laying out the road and ran into a storm of political protest when he tried to get the course of it to run in front of Straw's Point at Rye and across Rye Harbor. Residents in the area, many of them with political connections, managed to get the road moved back from the coast at that point. The road was opened to traffic in 1903. Pender was always one of the stormy petrels of Portsmouth politics. He served as sheriff, postmaster and frequently in the Legislature, besides being mayor in 1902. He was the grandfather of Portsmouth attorney Wyman P. Boynton and Edwin Boynton. Pender was born in Southbridge, Massachusetts in 1843 and died here in 1928.

[3]. This youngster was John Thomson.

[4]. The General Sullivan Bridge was opened to traffic September 1, 1934, built at a cost of approximately $1 million. That it was built at all was due to the persistence of the late Oren V. "Dad" Henderson of Durham, registrar at the University of New Hampshire for many years, who worked for eight years to get it through the Legislature. Finances for the bridge were based on tolls,

and when the time came to free the bridge, Henderson had to fight off attempts to saddle the bridge with still other obligations. The development of Hilton Park, enjoyed by summer picnickers, was the only "free rider" attached to the bridge and it was taken from the toll category November 1, 1949. But much of the beauty of Hilton Park was destroyed when the State of New Hampshire erected a span, parallel to the General Sullivan, on the easterly side, in nearer proximity to the old P & D bridge. This new span has relieved the tremendous pressure of traffic created by the Spaulding Turnpike, which was four lanes funneling down to two to cross the Bay.

[5]. Hubbard in his "History of New England" indicates that the buildings had deteriorated by 1685.

[6]. Sir Fernando Gorges was well connected in English court circles and made several attempts to colonize his holdings in Maine. He had visionary plans for a city at what is now York, to be called Gorgiana.

[7]. Patent was the word frequently used to describe grants of land.

[8]. The Great House near the junction of Marcy and Court Streets might well have been the first permanent structure within the present confines of Portsmouth. Somehow, one pictures it as a combination of home, storehouse and fortification for the little colony at Strawberry Banke.

[9]. Captain John Mason is believed never to have come to his plantation at Portsmouth. While he was engaged in planting the colony, he was also governor of the Castle at Portsmouth, England. It was in his house that the Duke of Buckingham, favorite of James I, was murdered. At one time Mason was in Newfoundland and it seems difficult to believe that he did not visit his New Hampshire grant when he was that near. English sources indicate that Mason's relatively untimely death ended what might have been a successful political career.

[10]. Like many another Englishman of his day, Mason thought of his possessions in America only in terms of the yield, with a particular interest in valuable minerals. He was quite critical of some specimens sent him by Ambrose Gibbins.

[11]. It was this quarrel that gave Bloody Point (the nearer base of the General Sullivan Bridge) in Newington its name. So loud were the prospective combatants in their threats of the blood they would draw, that when they met by appointment and settled their differences without a blow, the settlers derisively tagged it with the name "Bloody Point". Captain Neale, teamed with Henry

Joclyn and Darby Ffield of Exeter, was among the first white men to explore the White Mountains. Ffield later became the first white man to climb rugged Mt. Washington.

[12]. Governor John Winthrop of the Bay Colony recorded Mason's death with the jubilant note: "The last winter Captain Mason died. He was the chief mover of events against us, and was to have sent the general governor, and for this end was providing shipping; but the Lord, in Mercy, taking him away, all of this business fell on sleep...."

[13]. The writer has found at least 20 different spellings of the word Piscataqua as used in the ancient records. Of course, standardized spelling did not come into being until the late 18th Century, and it was every man for himself until then. Throughout the 17th Century, and with the oldtimers until well into the 18th, the name Piscataqua was used to refer to all the towns in the river basin. Men described themselves, even when resident in Kittery, Portsmouth or Dover, as "of Piscataqua". Eventually the town names came to have meaning but old Judge Samuel Sewall, whose diary gives some picture of mast tree operations, throughout his journal used Piscataqua and "the Banke", and when he used Portsmouth, he meant the city in Old England. (Ralph May, "Piscataqua, the correctness of use and meaning of the word," Randall Press, 1956)

[14]. Newichwannock was at Great Falls, South Berwick.

[15]. Warnerton apparently was a rather dissolute character, at least by Puritan standards. In 1644 he gathered up what he could of Mason's property and took it to Nova Scotia to sell to the French. Warnerton was mentioned in the original group of those associated with David Thomson and seems to have been a Bristol man. His trip to Nova Scotia (we have Governor John Winthrop as an authority) ended in his death when he became a little too free in his advances to a woman.

[16]. The Puritan invasion brought the Cutts family to the fore. They were first at the Isles of Shoals, three brothers, John, Richard and Robert. The first two prospered but Robert did not. Their fortunes were based on the fisheries. John lived in the Green Street area and his family cemetery was removed when the railroad laid tracks through it 130 years ago. The remains were re-interred in South Cemetery. Richard was the father of Bridget Cutts Daniel Graffort (so often the town's benefactor) but he never attained the political prominence of his brother John. Robert frequently was beholden to his brothers.

3

2

They Came To Fish

[1]. The Reverend Richard Gibson left little to tell of his time in Strawberry Banke. That he was here by 1640 we know because he is mentioned by name in The Glebe Grant of that year, the part pertaining to him saying that the parishioners had built the "sd Parsonage house, chappell, with appurtenances at their own proper costs and charges, and have made choyse of Mr. Richard Gibson to be the first parson of the sd parsonage...." Twenty men signed that document, including Francis Williams, governor; Ambrose Gibbins, assistant; William Jones, Renald Fernald, John Crowther, Anthony Brackett, Michael Chatterton, John Wall, Robert Puddling-ton, Mathew Cole, Henry Sherburne, John Lander, Henry Taler, John Jones, William Berry (seal), John Pickering, John Billing (seal), John Wolten, Nicholas Row and William Palmer. Thanks to John Winthrop's Journal we do know that Gibson was summoned before the Massachusetts General Court in 1642 for baptizing and marrying by the rites of the Church of England, a crime in Puritan eyes. Winthrop says Gibson came to New England three or four years prior to this to preach at Richman's Island, and then moved to "Pascataquack, and this year 1642 was entertained by the fishermen of the Isles of Shoales to preach to them". Gibson later apparently was mixed up in a juicy scandal that rocked Dover, and so shook the magistrates that he was arrested, leaving the country shortly after that.

[2]. For example they admitted none to the privilege of voting (except in Portsmouth) who were not members of the church, yet everyone had to pay toward support of their minister.

[3]. Bradford in his "Plimouth Plantation" tells of finding some young men idling at football and of his displeasure at the scene.

[4]. The Glebe Grant was made May 25, 1640, to benefit the parish and help maintain the minister. Henry Sherburne and Thomas Walford were named trustees for the property and set up a line of succession for its management. The Glebe was opened to settlement about 1700, and Thomas Phipps, the first schoolmaster,

was first to build about where the Eagle Camera store is today. The parish eventually started letting the land out in lots with 999-year leases. Nominal rents were paid the parish by some, nothing was paid by many more. Ownership of the land has long since passed from the church but there ought to be a good legal hassle around here come the 27th Century when the lawyers try to decide if the church still has a claim.

[5]. There will be many references to the North Church throughout this manuscript. The building we know today was built in 1855, when the church, after long and serious thought, agreed that the "old three-decker" should be torn down. It was the building of the "three-decker", so called because it had a main floor and two successive galleries, that precipitated near civil war in Portsmouth. By 1711, it had become obvious that the church at the junction of South and Marcy Streets was no longer adequate, but there were two schools of thought as to what to do about it. One faction wanted to build "uptown" on the Glebe Land, and the other wanted to stay in the South End. The former were in the majority and they went ahead with their plans and won a vote in town meeting approving it. Sewall cites men who saw it as saying it was 60 x 40 feet. In January, the Reverend Nathaniel Rogers, who was actually pastor for the whole parish, preached the first sermon in the new edifice. and that set off a tempest that was resolved only when the General Court stepped in and ruled that he be accepted as the established minister. Various improvements were made on the building and in 1749, thanks to Daniel Pierce, the town clock was "set agoing" in the church tower.

[6]. Islington Creek flows into the North Mill Pond at Bartlett Street. The Islington Street standpipe is somewhere near the middle of the 38-acre Glebe Grant. In the early days there were mills at the mouth of the Creek.

[7]. St. John's is another of the churches that will figure largely in our story of Portsmouth. The first Church of England edifice was near Court Street, but was taken over for a Puritan parsonage. Opposition to any organized parish for the Church of England was keen among the Puritans. Judge Sewall's diary indicates how bitterly they were opposed in Boston until the weight of the governorship was brought to bear on the town fathers. Long after Boston had one, Portsmouth in 1732 finally saw the erection of a church, known as Queen's Chapel in honor of Queen Caroline. That worthy lady presented a Communion Service that is still in use in St. John's Church. The descendants of Captain John

Mason presented a baptismal font in 1761, and the bell that hung in the steeple was one captured at Louisburg in 1745. That bell, along with the church, was destroyed in the fire of 1806. However, the mass of metal was put in the hands of Paul Revere and he recast it. Revere's work lasted until 1896 when the bell once again had to be recast. St. John's, as the new church was called, was dedicated with full Masonic ceremony in 1807.

[8]. It is from the ancient name of the town that Strawbery Banke, Incorporated, which manages the colonial village project in the Puddle Dock area, takes its name.

[9]. For example, for some reason best known to town fathers long dead, Dr. Renald Fernald, progenitor of all of that name in the Seacoast area, was given what we call Pierce Island. On the basis of that holding, the doctor then was given 50 acres at Islington Creek. The writer once traced the history of the land holdings on Pierce Island from Fernald's day down to its purchase by the city in 1911. That the city was able to buy it at all was due to the alertness of Harry E. Boynton, then on the Council. The city bought the idea of putting it to recreational use, but a sewage disposal plant, in compliance with river clean-up directives, now stands on the southeast corner.

[10]. A time-worn boulder, carefully covered from the weather, still marks the bound used by Governor John Endicott's surveyors at The Weirs. Erosion has obliterated the printing that was once on it.

[11]. These taverns, or "ordinaries" as they were more commonly called, were fairly plentiful. There were two or three at Great Island (New Castle), as would be logical with the provincial government having its seat there for many years. In all probability if there had not been taverns in colonial times, they would have had to create them, because they were indispensable as news centers. With no newspapers, radio, or television, the ordinaries served as information clearing houses. Here came the strangers with word of doings in other places, here men met when they had a chance to swap a word or two. The Isles of Shoals, for instance, was the great informational crossroads of New England.

[12]. Many think the court dockets of our day crowded, but, when the small number of people involved is remembered, 17th Century New Hampshire residents were about at litigious as anyone. They would bring suit over any matter. Thanks to former Judge Elwyn Page of Concord, who utilized his "retirement", to bring order to the early court records, we now have far greater

knowledge of colonial legal proclivities. His book, "Judicial Beginnings in New Hampshire", is well worth reading.

[13]. And well she might be. The hardships of that early day were severe enough to test men, but they must have been even worse for their women. The frequency of death in child birth alone is enough to give moderns the horrors. A man could use up three or four wives in the course of a life-time and longevity was not great. Conversely there were some tough old girls who collected two, three and four husbands over the years, perhaps a manifestation of Women's Lib.

[14]. Captain Bryan Pendleton was a strong figure in the early days of the Massachusetts government in New Hampshire. He was a large property holder and powerful official in the town, representing Strawberry Banke at the General Assembly in Boston and serving as selectman. His title came from his service as commander of a militia company.

[15]. Goodwife Eunice Cole's trials and tribulations as Hampton's official witch were many. At one time a court sentenced her to life in prison, but the sentence had to be shortened when the Town of Hampton refused to pay the expense of her keep in the jail. When the poor old soul finally did die, she was buried in an unmarked grave, a stake through her heart to keep her there. Finally in 1938, as part of Hampton's 300th anniversary celebration, Goody Cole was restored to full citizenship rights. Hers was the only extreme case of punishment for witchcraft in New Hampshire. Charges were hurled at others, but the hearings seemed to come to nothing. Jane Walford is a case in point. She was accused of being a witch and actually won a slander action against her accuser. For some reason the madness that afflicted Salem, Massachusetts, in the 1690s never reached here.

[16]. New Castle was the first town incorporated by the Province of New Hampshire. The excuse for the separate government was flimsy but stood up. The inhabitants argued that having to man the fort made it difficult for them to attend meetings in Portsmouth. So for one peppercorn a year forever, Great Island was set off as a township with its own church.

[17]. This is perhaps a hair-splitting technicality, but the reason is that the original church, built south of the dam, was for the whole community. When the great split came in 1711, the old structure served the South End for a while longer, but in 1731 the South Parish erected a new church on the high ground afterward known as Meeting House Hill. This stood for 130 years, being

7

replaced by the present building. The South Parish built the Stone Church on State Street in 1824. Under the altar of the first church, the parish buried two of its early pastors, the Reverends William Shurtleff and Job Strong. When the building was torn down in 1863, their remains were moved to the South Cemetery. The man who succeeded Strong as pastor, the Reverend Samuel Haven, held the pastorate for 54 years. His successor was the Reverend Nathan Parker who embraced Unitarianism in the 1820s and made it the philosophy of his parish. In more recent years the Unitiarians and Universalists were in close communion, and when the Universalist Church burned in 1947, they came into even tighter union and are known today as the Unitarian-Universalist Church.

[18]. The church-like building atop Meeting House Hill was for years the South Wardroom, the heart of Old Sebastapol. Various religious societies have occupied it and in recent years it has been a clubroom for the Disabled American Veterans. After the DAV vacated it, the building was taken over by Strawbery Banke, Inc. The old clock continues to run. But, at one time the man who tended it refused to do so any more because people were firing bullets through the clock face.

However, within the last five years, John Elwyn Stone on Elwyn Road, and New York City, has put $50,000 into the hands of Strawbery Banke, Inc., for restoration and rebuilding of the edifice. Stone, in letters to the Public Forum of The Portsmouth Herald has expressed his discontentment with the results of his expenditure. Stone, locally at least, is one of the last of the Langdon descendants.

[19]. Owned by the Society for the Preservation of New England Antiquities, the Jackson House is one of the oldest standing in English-speaking America. Richard Jackson built about the accepted date of 1664, although there are some who think the year should be earlier. Richard Jackson owned 26 acres around the site, running down to the North Mill Pond in front and the river to the east. It's interesting to note the similarity of its timbering with Ann Hathaway's cottage near Stratford-on-Avon.

[20]. The English used almost any means of exchange in trading. They even adapted Indian wampum, that is, beads, in some transactions, with black being more valuable than white. Beaver pelts were another medium frequently employed.

[21]. There will be more about doughty old Joshua Moodey in later chapters. He was pastor when the church formally organized on July 21, 1671, with the words in the old records that "The Church Covenant that those who first imbodied did on yt day

publiqly and solemly enter into". That same year the town voted a five-shilling fine "if any shall smoake tobacco in the meetinghouse at any public meeting". And in April that year, "a great storm of driving snow came out of the NW and drove up in drifts about six feet deep". The town also voted that Cotton Cemetery, South Street, be set aside apart for a burying place. It was fenced in 1721.

[22]. A small indication of how long these Puritan divines could run on is found in Sewall's diary. At one time, after he received his master's from Harvard, Sewall entertained ideas of entering the ministry, and a sermon he preached while being considered for a pastorate saw him turn "the glass" twice because he could not find a way to conclude. That means more than two hours of steady lecturing. But then Moodey's listeners were not waiting to get out to Portsmouth Country Club to play golf.

Incidentally, although in Greenland, it should be mentioned that the new Portsmouth Country Club, brought about when the Air Force pre-empted the old one in 1956, is on some of the oldest cultivated land in New Hampshire. And when Francis Champernowne had a farm there in the 17th Century, it was within the bounds of Portsmouth. The original club was founded in 1901 and the course is one of the oldest in New Hampshire. Physically, it has been changed in some respects by the Air Force. Observers can always tell whether or not the commanding officer at Pease is interested in golf by the condition of the Pease golf course.

[23]. What Wallis Sands came to mean to some local people is best told by a story involving the late Garland W. Patch. "Patchy" was a great sunbather, and, after his retirement from the Portsmouth Naval Shipyard, devoted many summer hours to acquiring a tan. On one such excursion to Wallis Sands -- a crowded Sunday -- he moved his towel farther south along the beach to a point where he was in front of one of the cottages.

His siesta was broken by a voice telling him to "get off my beach". Without bothering to honor the intrusion on his slumbers by rising, Patch merely raised himself on one elbow and said, "My ancestors fought Indians on this beach. Do you think you can chase me off?" He then resumed his worship of Old Sol.

[24]. Those killed in the raid included Thomas Onion, 74; Joseph Holmes, 20; Hixon Foss, 17; Peter Moe, 40; James Jaffrey's child, 4; John Jones, 32; William Howard, 30; Richard Parshley, 25; Thomas Meloney, 13; Samuel Foss, Jr., 14; Betsey Babb, 14; Nancy White, 8; William Cate, Jr., 16; and Dinah, the slave of John Brewster. Besides Mrs. Mary Brewster, the injured were

Peggy Jones, 76; William Cate's three children; and Daniel Jackson, 41. That the Plains made a recovery from that horrible morning fairly soon we can gather from Judge Sewall's reference to it in his diary. The entry for May 12, 1714, reads: "Went to Brewster, the Anchor in the Plain; got thither about 11: staid there for Mr. Justice Thomas and Lynde. We din'd there together. Took Joseph Brewster for our guide, and went to town. Essay'd to be quartered at Mr. Knight's, but he not being at home his wife refusd us. I accepted Mr. Penhallow's invitation by his maid. Not being able to get Hay, sent our horses to Kittery side. Waited on His Excellency at Colonel Parker's, who seemed to receive us with passionat respect". The old judge's comments are interesting not only for showing that the Brewsters were still in residence at the Plains, but also that the Plains were in those days so far remote from the town that it was necessary for the party of Massachusetts judges, on their way to the courts of Maine, to be guided into the town. Sewall was still in Portsmouth the next day when a fast was held and heard a sermon by the Reverend Nathaniel Rogers. It is one of the oddities in Sewall's invaluable diary that he would be in Portsmouth at a time when the schism over the building of a new church (North) should be still raging, and yet make no mention of it. Further that he attended services here, heard the Reverend Mr. Rogers, who, according to the "Annals" had been preaching in the new edifice since January 7, 1714, and yet Sewall has to quote someone else as to the size of the church.

[25]. Don't try to find the actual site. Modern-day construction demands have led to destruction of the hill through extensive use as a borrow pit.

3

The Masonian Claims

[1]. Members of this first provincial Council were John Cutts, president; Richard Waldron of Dover, deputy; Richard Martin, active in church affairs; William Vaughan, of Welsh extraction, a wealthy merchant who had been a protege of Sir Josiah Child in London; Thomas Daniel, who left his name for one of our downtown streets; John Gilman, leading citizen of Exeter; and Christopher Hussey of Hampton, one of the first settlers in that town in 1638, and who often represented it in the Massachusetts General Court. He lost his life in a shipwreck along the Florida coast in 1685.

[2]. There is on the records, a long and pathetic letter written by the New Hampshire Council to the Governor and Council in Massachusetts explaining that the separation was not of their doing, but in accord with the command of the King.

[3]. Mason posted notices throughout the province declaring himself as proprietor and demanding that the inhabitants make settlement with him for their holdings. One of these was scornfully torn down by Richard Waldron, who blandly ignored even court proceedings against him, remarking, "If I am cast (lose the court case), then all are cast". Waldron well knew his was a test because of his prominence in the province. When the decision went against him, he continued as he had done until thrown into jail for a time.

[4]. Richard Waldron was the strong man of the New Hampshire of his day. Indomitable Indian fighter, his merchandising ventures were in many places. One of his sons died in Algiers while on a voyage for his father. Waldron was a native of Warwickshire, England, and came to Piscataqua probably as early as 1631. He was one of the first to begin exploitation of New Hampshire's inland resources of trees and furs. He was the key figure in a sham fight with the Indians in 1676 near his Dover garrison in which he disarmed them by trickery and sent some into slavery. That double-cross cost him his life in 1689 when the Indians, under Kancamagus after nursing their grievance for 13 years, took his garrison by a trick and proceeded to torture the old man to death. Waldron's son Richard became prominent in New Hampshire affairs and lived at the

11

Plains in Portsmouth. In fact, some of the most valuable of the early records were destroyed when Richard III's house burned at the Plains in 1745. He was register of probate at the time, and had been province secretary until succeeded by Theodore Atkinson in 1741.

[5]. Former Selectman Kenneth Maxam of New Castle, who made an extensive study of Great Island history, says the Province House stood on Piscataqua Street, across the way from the Portsmouth Yacht Club and up the river from it.

[6]. Fast days were quite common in colonial times, but only New Hampshire has persisted in the tradition, currently setting aside the last Monday in April as Fast Day, but it's one-time religious bent is gone, coinciding as it does with the opening weekend of trout fishing; especially if the Red Sox are playing baseball in Boston; many venture there to see for themselves that pennant hopes are as futile as usual.

[7]. Until 1693, there were only four towns in the province; Portsmouth, Dover, Hampton and Exeter. The two former were the outgrowth of colonizing attempts by commercial interests. Hampton was a purely Puritan outpost in the lands left in doubtful title by the death of John Mason, and Exeter was founded for religious reasons by the Reverend Ebenezer Wheelwright, who was more or less of a refugee from some Puritan beliefs.

[8]. Richard Waldron, outstanding as he was as a leader in provincial New Hampshire, had a blind spot of hatred where Quakers were concerned. In this regard he was in complete accord with the sentiment of his time: Episcopalians, Catholics and Puritans were in agreement that the Quakers were a menace. To Waldron came the chance to demonstrate this fierce hatred and he did so with great venom on the bare backs of three Quaker women. Waldron on December 22, 1662, put into effect the following sentence:

"To the Constables of Dover, Hampton, Salisbury, Newbury, Rowley, Ipswich, Windham, Linn, Boston, Roxbury, Dedham, and until these vagabond Quakers are out of his jurisdiction: "You and every one of you are required in the King's name, to take these vagabond Quakers, Anna Colman, Mary Tompkins, and Alice Ambrose, and make them fast to the cart's tail, and drawing the cart through your several towns, to whip them upon their naked backs not exceeding ten stripes apiece on each of them in each town, and so convey them from Constable to Constable till they are out this jurisdiction, as you will answer for it at your peril, and this shall be your warrant."

That order was carried out to the letter in Dover and Hampton, but between the latter place and Salisbury, the bleeding half-frozen women were rescued by, of all people, Walter Barefoot, in what some claim was one of the few decent acts of his life. Ironically, perhaps inevitably, Dover, where persecution of the Quakers was the worst in New Hampshire, became one of the places where the Friends grew strongest.

[9]. There is a strong reason to believe that Mason mortgaged to Cranfield all that he could realize out of his claims for a period of 20 years.

[10]. It is not certain when Barefoot came to Piscataqua. He is believed to have been a surgeon in the Royal Navy and involved in sharp practices in buying up the warrants for pay given to seamen. Certainly he prospered in New Hampshire, with land and interests not only in Portsmouth and New Castle, but also in Durham and Dover. Barefoot was a persistent litigant, willing to sue anyone, but in his behalf it must be said that if he was fighting the vested Waldron interests in the Dover area, he would really have to battle. We know little about him, except that he was apparently unmarried when here. It is probable that he was first drawn to the Piscataqua because his sister Sarah was the wife of Stratham's second Thomas Wiggin, He died in 1688 or 1689.

[11]. The arrival of James Sherlock and his function as sheriff was the first taste New Hampshire had with this type of law enforcement officer. Actually some such an official was essential to Cranfield's plans because it was a certainty that the town constables would not carry out the evictions of their neighbors.

[12]. Thomas Thurton had the least enviable job in the province. It was his duty to serve the writs issued by the courts. At one time or another he was soaked with boiling water; caned by William Vaughan; and given a fast one-way ride on a horse to the Massachusetts line.

[13]. While people undoubtedly used the main river channel, depending on the tide, much of the traffic flowed along the back channel from the vicinity of Pierce Island to the end of Great Island where the Wentworth Hotel now stands. There in the back water it was easier to pull against the tide and that was the ferry route from Portsmouth. They could also come by road to a point below the Sheldon Krasker house, Little Harbor Road, and then across to New Castle.

[14]. There was no jury, and Walter Barefoot rigged the panel of judges for the trial with Cranfield sympathizers. He

made a mistake in the selection of two of them: Nathaniel Fryer and Thomas Edgerly, which became obvious when they refused to go along with a conviction of Moodey. However, two of the others, Henry Green and Peter Coffin, "saw the light" and voted guilty. Coupled with Barefoot's vote of guilty as chief judge, this gave the attorney general, Joseph Raynes, the conviction Cranfield wanted. Coffin's role is hard to understand. He had been a close associate of Richard Waldron's, shared in the development of the area around Concord with him, was a Puritan and yet he voted against Moodey.

[15]. "The Castle" is what they first called the fortification at New Castle which we know as Fort Constitution. With the advent of William and Mary, the fort took their names, a label which stuck until Revolutionary times, when it became Fort Constitution. The vicissitudes of Fort Constitution's fortunes are a book in themselves, a tale that can be told only fragmentarily here.

[16]. Nothing tells where Amazeen actually came from, but the family name is still a familiar and respected one in Portsmouth and New Castle.

[17]. Elias Stileman owned much of the land in the vicinity of the fort; many of his old deeds figured a few years ago in a court action brought by the Town of New Castle to determine ownership of a strip of land at the beach.

[18]. The part of Hampton in which Gove lived is now Seabrook, and the family still is represented there.

[19]. Thomas Daniel was the first husband of one of the town's early benefactors, Bridget Cutts Daniel Graffort, who was the daughter of Richard Cutts and a niece of the first president, John Cutts. Daniel died shortly after the trial and his widow married Thomas Graffort in 1684.

[20]. The commonly printed version of this sentence is bad enough but the one found by Judge Page during his research is a real twister:

"You Edward Gove shal be drawn on a Sledge to ye place of execution and there you shal be hanged by ye necke and then yet living be cut down and cast on ye ground and your bowels taken out of your body and your privy members cut off, and your body divided in four parts, and your head and quarters shal be placed where our Soveraigne Lord ye King pleaseth to appoint. And ye Lord may have mercy on your soul."

[21]. Records checked at the Tower of London by the writer indicate that Gove was committed to the Tower under warrant

14

of June 6, 1683, addressed to Thomas Cheek, lieutenant of the Tower. And there he apparently waited for nearly three years until set at liberty, in his own recognizance, on March 9, 1686, to await a hearing at Old Bailey. Sometime during that year he returned to his home, claiming to the day of his death, that he had been poisoned while being held in the Tower and that that was the source of the ill health he endured for the rest of his life.

[22]. Cranfield had been some kind of a minor court official before his service as lieutenant governor of New Hampshire. Ordered to return home, he must have found protectors at court because a few years later he was appointed collector for Barbados. Jeremy Belknap says that Cranfield always extended a warm welcome to any Piscataqua mariners visiting Bridgetown. The author was unable in 1970 to find any Cranfield records in Barbados.

[23]. This Thomas Wiggin was the second of the name in New Hampshire. His father was the man who pushed into the seeming "no man's land" around Stratham and settled there. His wife, Sarah, was Barefoot's sister. While Wiggin had no use for Barefoot, he did not refuse to inherit the man's estate through his wife. The Wiggin families in the area generally come down from Thomas and his brother Andrew.

[24]. Judge Page says Mason was encouraged by the home government to push his proprietary claims and returned to New England under Governor Joseph Dudley and Andros for that purpose. The courts set up by Dudley were too honest to lend themselves to his purposes. The claims dragged along after Mason's death and were bought from his heirs by Samuel Allen before Allen became governor. Governor Allen kept pushing to win judgments, using his office as a club over the courts. One of the interesting sidelights is the story back of the records of the province, needed to help Allen's suits. They disappeared with the departure of Richard Chamberlain who had been secretary. John Pickering, son of the builder of the mill dam, got hold of them and kept them out of Allen's hands for two years.

Cases were heard in a tavern at Portsmouth, according to Judge Page, called the King's Armes and kept by another John Pickering. We cannot be sure that this tavern was the original one owned in the 1760s by James Stoodley, but good taverns, for instance the Green Dragon in Boston, had a way of lasting from generation to generation. The cases bogged down despite Allen's machinations. Space forbids exploring all the legal maneuverings but in 1707, one big case was fought between Allen's son, Thomas, and

Richard Waldron, Jr. In spite of the almost direct orders of the judge to find for Allen, the jury found for the defendant, and the verdict was appealed to England but Allen died before it could be reviewed. Allen's heirs had no heart for more struggle. Eventually they sold their claims to the Masonian Proprietors, who set up township grants in the unsettled lands and thus ended the strife of nearly a century.

Eleven Portsmouth men, and one from Dover were involved in the transaction. The selling price, 1,500 pounds, was divided into 100-pound shares, and Theodore Atkinson took three; Mark Hunking Wentworth, two. Nine others held one each; Richard Wibird, John Wentworth, George Jaffrey, Samuel Moore, Nathaniel Meserve, Thomas Packer, Jotham Odiorne, Joshua Pierce, and John Moffat. The Dover man was Thomas Wallingford. The deal was made on January 30, 1746.

4

Moving into the 18th Century

[1]. Among a people as self-reliant as the early Piscataqua colonists there must have been men capable of turning their hands to shipbuilding. Who they were is not now known, but the real genesis of the art of building ships may have come when John Taylor shipped from England to Piscataqua the artisans needed to construct the warships, Falkland and Bedford Galley, in the 1690s. At first some bitterness existed between these men and those already here; that was indicated by the exchange of letters between Taylor and the local government over the way the new men were being treated. Quite probably they were soon assimilated into the community.

[2]. It would be wrong to leave the impression that shipbuilding was confined to Portsmouth. Nothing could be further from the truth. Almost every river feeding into the Great Bay had its shipyards and many of them prospered until really large vessels became the vogue in the 1830s and 40s. For example, in the Portsmouth Athenaeum is a scale drawing of the ship Elizabeth built in 1756 at "Lamprill River" for Captain Nathaniel Adams, one of Portsmouth's more prominent shipmasters in the 1750s. That drawing, by the way, is the earliest of its kind known in the United States.

[3]. As indicated in Note 1, John Taylor had a contract with the British Admiralty to build warships in the colonies. Political pressure may have had much to do with Bedford and Falkland being the last put to such a contract for many years.

[4]. Actual contract for America was given to Sir William Pepperrell of Kittery, hero of the conquest of Louisburg, Cape Breton Island, in 1745. Sir William contracted to build America, with two tiers of guns for 9 pounds per ton. She was launched in May 1749 and went to England with only one tier of her armament. She proved of little value to the Royal Navy, her timbers rotting out quite soon and she was put in ordinary (mothballs we would call it) for a number of years before being broken up. The failure of America is revealing of one unfortunate fact: Much of the oak in

17

New England was not suitable to shipbuilding. In later years, live oak, more similar to the traditional English oak, was imported from Maryland and Virginia for the knees and ribs of vessels, while white oak was confined to planking.

[5]. Described as an "Admiralty Model", the replica of *America* in the Athenaeum is the actual working pattern from which the warship was built. In 1962 the Smithsonian Institute sent an expert to Portsmouth to take off her lines so that a similar one could be built for the Watercraft Collection, and in 1963 the model was loaned to the Smithsonian for a three-year period for restoration and exhibition. Good to the letter of its word, the Smithsonian returned the model from its longest "voyage" in 1966, and on both passages it was insured for $50,000. Construction of the replica, now on exhibit in the museum, was in excess of $10,000.

[6]. The best example is the Warner House, for which see Note 13, this chapter. Only recently has come to light a contract to build a house in the Strawbery Banke area for a Captain John Hill, dated 1698.

[7]. Puddle Dock was a tiny arm of the river, covered in today by Newton Avenue and will be an integral part of the Strawbery Banke village project. At one time Puddle Dock reached back to the very yard of the Langdon House and was spanned in 1727 by Canoe Bridge. Badly in disrepair, in 1768, the bridge was rebuilt by Governor John Langdon and presented to the town. Puddle Dock was filled in by the city in 1895 when it became a silt-filled health menace.

[8]. For many years this highway was known as Divinity Street and so appears in old deeds. It formally became Pleasant Street when the town was mapped in 1778.

[9]. The original manuscript records of town affairs since 1652 are preserved at City Hall. During the 1930s the Federal Writers Project of WPA made excellent copies which save much wear and tear on the originals.

[10]. For this the town was granted a strip of land in what is now Barrington and this was for a time known as New Portsmouth. Captain Archibald MacPhedris was one of the leaders in developing smelters of bog iron ore. How desperately now wealthy Harvard then needed the money is shown by a note in the diary of Judge Samuel Sewall, Class of 1671, taken from Harvard records, which orders that "...and Sir (a title then given to Harvard graduates) Sewall, Fellows of the College, have a half year's salary of their proportion forthwith of the Piscataway gift now in the treasurer's

hands". Sewall at the time was an instructor at Harvard, still trying to decide whether or not to be a minister.

[11]. After being jailed by Cranfield, Moodey left the Province and stayed away for a number of years. His refusal to return promptly brought some bitterness but eventually he came back and died here in 1696.

[12]. Quotations from old records appear in printed matter with punctuation, but the 17th Century writers did not use any. Modern writers have supplied punctuation as they have thought best.

[13]. The Warner House was built between 1715, and 1718. Authentically furnished for the 18th Century, it is now controlled by the Warner House Association, and has been designated as a Historic Landmark by the Department of Interior. MacPhedris, the builder, married Sarah Wentworth, one of the 16 children of Lieutenant Governor John Wentworth. Their daughter Mary married Jonathan Warner in 1754, and it is his name the house bears. The first lightning rods ever installed in New Hampshire were placed on this house in 1762 by Benjamin Franklin, then postmaster general for North America. While here on that visit, Franklin is also believed to have "pulled" some copies of the New Hampshire Gazette on the old and long-lost printing press for New Hampshire's first newspaper.

[14]. New Castle was separated from Portsmouth in 1693. It was the first town incorporated by the General Assembly of New Hampshire. The annual fee charged New Castle for its independence, payable to the British Crown, is two peppercornes. A few years ago, under the aegis of the late Ralph Frobisher, then a selectman, the town sent its payment, which was acknowledged by an equerry to Queen Elizabeth. For more than a century, the town records were missing, gone no one knew where. They were found in a garret in England about 100 years ago and returned to the town.

[15]. The Reverend Arthur Browne by his close association with the Wentworths managed to achieve fame of a sort. He married Benning and the tavern wench Martha Hilton, celebrated by Longfellow in poetry; buried Theodore Atkinson, Jr., and less than 10 days later married Atkinson's widow to Governor John Wentworth, then fell on the church steps and broke his arm. Browne's daughter Elizabeth married the famed French and Indian War hero, Major Robert Rogers, who became a notorious renegade and counterfeiter during the Revolution. His wife Mary died in 1773 and he died June 10 of that year at Cambridge, Massachusetts. Thus he did not live to see the fall of the Wentworth dynasty.

5

The Wentworth Dynasty

[1]. Thomas Wentworth became one of the most powerful men in England and to him was entrusted the task of subduing Ireland, a job that is still proving impossible. Besides generating much enmity in Ireland, he also incurred the wrath of Parliament. Ironically in his early years of public life he was a "Parliament Man", defying the King's wishes. With the agility of a political opportunist, he switched his philosophy when he saw the chance for advancement in royal favor. Ultimately the change cost him his life when Charles I was forced to sacrifice his top-ranking minister in order to placate a cantankerous Parliament and a jealous nobility.

[2]. The name Strafford, associated with the Wentworths, tells where the name of the New Hampshire county of Strafford came from.

[3]. Shifting colonial policy caused confusion for New England in the 17th and 18th Centuries as it does for us today in trying to figure it out. While New Hampshire was split away from Massachusetts in 1679-80 and set up as a separate province, it never had its own governor until Benning Wentworth was given the post. Samuel Shute was one of a long parade of governors who were the chief administrators for the two colonies. Normally they based themselves in Boston, but Judge Samuel Sewall's diary indicates that the governors spent much of their time on the road visiting remote points in their jurisdictions.

[4]. When Brewster was writing the Rambles, no researcher had yet collated all the vast pile of material finally published in a series of volumes known as the Provincial Papers. From that we take the following excerpts to show that Benning Wentworth probably lived for a time in the Warner House: (1) Dated March 1, 1754, "Voted that Clement March Esq. & Henry Sherburne junr be a committee of this House to joyn with such as shall be appointed by the Honble

Council to confer with the owner or owners of the Brick House in Portsmouth in the Province of New Hampr wherein his Excellency lately lived and enquire whether they will put it in Tenantable repair and upon what Rent or Rents yearly they would be willing to lease it, and for how long a time..." (The committee, consisting of Theodore Atkinson, Richard Wibird, Daniel Warner, Meshech Weare, Sherburne and Matthew Livermore, reported on April 26, "...We have Treated with the owners of the Brick House in Portsmo where his Excellency the Governor lately lived (that being the only House in town now to be sold we apprehend suitable for a Government House) who are disposed to sell the sd House with the Lands and Yards adjoining on the South End of the Street". The result of their negotiation was an offer to sell for 9,000 pounds, Old Tenor. On May 4 the committee was authorized to offer 1,750 pounds, New Tenor, which gives us a rough working idea that the new money was worth about five of the old. We can't tell exactly from this when Benning Wentworth vacated the Warner House, but it was a need for a State House, a place where the Council and General Assembly could meet, that prompted the interest of the province. Apparently these negotiations fell through, because the province finally built the structure at the throat of Congress Street which became known as the State House.

[5]. Wentworth had bad luck with some Spanish ventures when England and Spain became engaged in war. He argued successfully at the English court that he should be compensated for his losses, and the way in which it was done was to make him governor. This, coupled with other sinecures such as surveyor of the woods, later vice admiral of New Hampshire, plus all the "fringe benefits" of the office enabled him to recoup financially. At the same time it cost the home government nothing. Readers will recall from their schooldays that William Penn received a grant of land that became Pennsylvania in settlement of a debt owed his father by Charles II.

[6]. When Wentworth took over the old house at Little Harbor, it probably was much as it had been when owned by the Hunkings. The visitor today will notice some odd things about it. For one, it really faces the water, the best avenue of approach in the early days when so much traffic moved by boat. President Washington made his entrance that way when he paid a brief call there. Another is the vast cellar, capable of stabling a troop of horses. And on the landward side grows a lilac, twisted and gnarled into grotesque patterns, which it has every right to be, having grown there perhaps since the days of the Hunkings. Miss Dorothy M. Vaughan says that when the estate was acquired by the Coolidges, they were told by the previous owners of "a

tremendous favor" they had done them by taking a huge mass of papers from the attic to the dump. The reader can spend the rest of his life in idle speculation as to what valuable colonial documants vanished in that misguided benefaction.

[7]. This is one of the least pleasant stories told of Benning Wentworth. Apparently in the lusty days after his wife's death, he became enamoured of a local girl, Molly Pitman by name, who lived with her parents in a house at the corner of Fleet and State Streets which was torn down to make way for the Portsmouth Savings Bank building. Molly Pitman, with the pride of youth and the love of another strong within her, wanted no part of a man who was well advanced in middle age by our standard and an old man in terms of 18th Century life span. Spurning his approaches, she married a man named Richard Shortridge. At that time British frigates were frequent visitors to these ports and whenever short of men, would put a press gang ashore to "recruit" sailors. The story runs that shortly after his marriage to Molly Pitman, Shortridge was impressed under an arrangement between Benning Wentworth and the ship's captain. Impressed men never had shore leave and it was seven years before Shortridge was able to get away and return home to a wife who had remained faithful to him.

[8]. Henry W. Longfellow has immortalized in poetic fancy Benning Wentworth's romance with Martha Hilton. Legend has it that she was a tavern servant and caught the governor's roving eye. Installing her as housekeeper at his mansion, he later determined on marriage and, if the poet is to be believed, ordered the ceremony to be performed one evening while entertaining friends. The New Hampshire Gazette, in the issue of March 21, 1760, simply records, "Last Saturday (March 15) our governor married Miss Hilton of this place". The Reverend Arthur Brown of Queen's Chapel performed the ceremony.

Martha Hilton long survived her elderly spouse, inherited his estate, and then married a distant kinsman of the Portsmouth Wentworths, one Colonel Michael Wentworth. Two sons she had borne old Benning died in infancy, and by the colonel she had a daughter Mary, who, in turn, married another Wentworth, Sir John, who was then practicing law in Portsmouth. Michael Wentworth, as we would say, "lived it up", running through his own and his wife's money and died in New York in 1795, a suicide, supposedly saying on his death bed, "I have had my cake and ate it". His daughter and her husband occupied the Little Harbor mansion until 1816 and in 1817 it was sold to Charles Cushing. The Wentworths moved to Europe and there Mrs. Wentworth died in 1851. The Cushing family sold the property to J.

Templeman Coolidge, whose widow made a gift of it to the state. In 1964 former Governor Hugh Gregg and his Executive Council held a meeting in the old Council chamber, probably the first such in nearly two centuries; and the official party came and went by land, not water.

[9]. Benning had three sons by his first wife, none of whom lived to full maturity. The last of three, John, was buried on November 22, 1759, a few months before Benning married Martha Hilton. By her (see above) he had two sons, but neither lived. His declining years were spent in virtual obscurity, as the "friends" who always collect around a person of a high official shifted their allegiance to the new man. Benning died October 14, 1770, his entire estate going to the widow, probably to the disappointment of his nephew, Governor John. The witnesses to the will included Michael Wentworth, soon to marry the widow, and George Frost, John Lang and a John Saltrige, who made his "X".

[10]. The Mark Hunking Wentworth house was torn down in the early 1850s to make way for the first of Portsmouth's three high school buildings built within the span of a century. Thanks to The Rambler we have some idea of its appearance and learn that it had the gambrel roof familiar to the early 18th Century, of two floors with four large rooms on each floor, and an ell to Chapel Street. The Rambler theorizes that the house was built by Captain Thomas Daniel, but admitted it was open to question, and that Daniel House may have stood nearer to the river. His description of the house indicates a later period than Daniel's time and might well have been built by the father of Governor John. The only date found in the house when it was leveled was 1752, and that was on a wall facing Chapel Street, which probably dates the ell.

Here it was that Governor John was born, and here he spent his first few months as governor of the province. His father, broken hearted by the turn of events in the Revolution, lived out his days quietly and saw the colonies win their independence before he died in 1785. Not that he did not have his trials during the war because, if nothing else, being the father of a royal governor would make it so. Mark Hunking Wentworth and his family were held under close parole until released from it in 1778 by the Committee of Safety. He refused to sign the Association Test, administered locally by his brother Hunking, in 1776.

[11]. Governor John Wentworth made a royal progress through most of the British North American colonies while en route to taking the reins of government. He landed at Charleston, South

Carolina, and in slow stages made his way north. In January 1767, the Gazette reported that some of his baggage and servants had arrived in Boston, but the Governor was coming by way of South Carolina. On June 13, 1767, Governor John Wentworth finally caught up with his baggage, arriving in the province with a roar of welcome in his ears, a far different sound than he would hear when he departed eight years later.

[12]. The story of the old State House would make a chapter in itself. In brief, it is testimony that human nature has not changed much. An earlier note indicates that the General Court was seriously considering buying the Warner House for a government house or capitol, then finally went ahead with plans for a new building. The original committee did nothing about it for several years. There were, as there would be today, wrangles over where to put it, how much to spend and the like. In March 1758 Daniel Warner, Clement March and Henry Sherburne, Jr. were named as a committee to get a State House built. They accomplished the work, and a two-story structure was built on the rocky ledge almost immediately in front of the doors of the North Church, the west end of the building being on a line with the western curb of High Street. The downstairs was divided into three main rooms, the easterly room for the Council, the middle room for the General Court and the western room for the Courts.

Before the building of the State House, the Courts, the General Assembly and the Council met wherever they could, in taverns or private homes. In 1687, for example, Judge Sewall speaks of attending a session of court at Partridge's, obviously an "ordinary". Benning Wentworth often had sessions of his Council at his mansion but there was nowhere for the General Court to go, except a tavern. A balcony, facing east into the Parade (Market Square) was built on the second floor and it was from here that great public documents of the times were read to the people. For years, after the capital shifted inland, it was used for town affairs and until 1836 the county courts met here. In September of that year a subscription was raised to get the building torn down. However, fortunately for us today, part of the old building was kept intact and was moved to Court Street, where it stood midway between Atkinson and Marcy Streets. It is one of the buildings earmarked for restoration in Strawbery Banke, an historic preservation project.

[13]. Governor John Wentworth's marriage to Mrs. Frances Atkinson probably shook colonial society far more than his uncle's marriage to the bar maid. He did not have much choice, as it was obvious to those who could count to nine on their fingers that

time was running out for him and the Widow Atkinson. Frances Atkinson was born Frances Deering Wentworth, daughter of Boston's Samuel Wentworth, and a cousin of the governor. The story goes that she and the Governor had made a twosome in his Harvard days, but after his graduation in 1755 he went to England. His absence from New England grew longer and longer and she married Theodore Atkinson, Jr.; son of New Hampshire's provincial secretary and also a cousin.

Young Atkinson was not a strong man and when the dashing John Wentworth returned from abroad, he was quite ill. Over the months of life left to him, Wentworth was a frequent guest in his home. The governor acquired a house on Pleasant Street which we now know as the Wentworth Home, making frequent walks across the pleasant gardens to the Court Street house where the younger Atkinsons made their home with Theodore, Sr. Young Theodore had married Frances Wentworth on May 13, 1762, and on October 28, 1769, he died at the age of 33. Gossip ran rampant in the town that signals could be seen between the Wentworth and Atkinson houses (in those days there was nothing in between the two houses). Theodore, Jr., was buried on November 1 and within 10 days the widow was the bride of the governor. The Reverend Arthur Browne officiated at both services, and the happy couple took up residence in the Wentworth mansion on Pleasant Street. Tongues clacked again in three or four months when the Wentworths presented a son for baptism at Queen's. That child died shortly afterward. In March 1775, the last unhappy year of his governorship, the governor and his wife had another son, Charles Mary, baptized at the Queen's by the Reverend Samuel Parker of Boston. The son lived his life in England, and a portrait of him is owned by the Portsmouth Athenaeum.

[14]. Governor John Wentworth's sister had occupied this house as a bride. In 1765, her husband, John Fisher, was given the post of collector for the port of Salem and they moved to that town. The new Governor may have taken it over soon after his arrival. Although Loyalist in their sympathies, the Fishers never lost interest in Portsmouth, and were still in possession of the land on which the Indian Head Bank now stands when the town bought it from them in 1800 as a site for a market "forever".

[15]. Governor John Wentworth really pioneered the idea of having a country place and might be said with some justice to have founded New Hampshire's prosperous summer tourist trade. However, when Wentworth built his country place and laid out a road leading to it, still known to some as the Governor's Highway, his main

thought was the development of the interior of the province. Few traces remain of this home on Lake Wentworth, which was destroyed by fire in 1820. It was here that greedy Patriots sold off all Wentworth's cattle and farm property after he was proscribed in the Revolution.

[16]. A bronze plaque on the Church Street wall of the building which now houses the Eagle Photo Shop notes that here, under the guidance of Hunking Wentworth, tough-minded uncle of the governor, who founded the local Committee of Safety during the Revolution. To this house came Paul Revere in December 1774 with word that the British were planning to remove all arms from Fort William and Mary. Perhaps it was within the walls of this building that Hunking Wentworth so bitterly denounced his nephew when he learned that the governor had attempted to hire New Hampshire carpenters to build barracks for the British garrison in Boston.

[17], Indicative of the caste system in early Portsmouth are the titles given these "loving subjects". Wentworth, as lieutenant governor, rated an "Hon." before his name as well as an "esq." after it. Jaffrey and MacPhedris were of sufficient social standing to be esquires, but poor Robert Wilson rated nothing at all.

[18]. Thanks to artists, the average person visualizes the houses in early New England villages as being white, but few, if any, were so painted in colonial times. For example, the Samuel Langdon House, now at Sturbridge Village, Massachusetts, was painted white when it stood here but when it was dismantled the workmen found the basic color was red and it is that color on its new site. In a poem about Ruth Blay, Albert Laighton speaks of

"Our old and quiet town,
With its streets of leafy beauty,
And its houses quaint and brown."

In the spring of 1972, the Portsmouth Historical Society entered into an agreement with Sears Roebuck and Company for the painting of the museum building, the John Paul Jones House. The purpose from the point of view of Sears was to demonstrate a latex paint it was promoting through television commercials and for the society it was a chance to get a free paint job on the house. The actual work was done by Paterson and Getchell, a local firm of painters, with Edward Paterson, and his son-in-law Frederick Getchell, as partners. Before going ahead with the work, the Sears experts, Getchell and Arnold J. Grover, society president, checked and tested the present paint. Sears intended to get back to the base wood, an analysis detected that 40 coats of paint have been put on the house since it was built in 1760. Probably the very first coat of paint, the experts believe, may have been a gray shade. This,it is admitted, could be the result of aging and not the original pigmentation.

John Paul Jones House is almost a courtesy title for this house because, at most, the famed naval captain was only a boarder there. It was built by a Captain Gregory Purcell who married Sarah Wentworth, a niece to Governor Benning Wentworth and acquired the land around 1757. Earliest reference to the lot is found in the recording of a mortgage on September 4, 1714, given to George Jaffrey by John Hunking to secure a loan of 450 pounds. The land is described as adjacent to "ye Highway leading to the Plaines", and would encompass all the land to the corner of Middle and Congress Streets, later occupied by the now demolished Treadwell House, and now a block of stores. Hunking and his wife were granted under the mortgage undisturbed possession for the rest of their lives. The property went to the Jaffrey heirs, and daughter Ann, the wife of Captain Nathaniel Pierce received Mrs. Hunking's orchard, so-called, as part of her share. That was in 1755, and soon after Mrs. Pierce sold to Captain Purcell. It took three deeds to cover the whole transaction, and give Purcell possession of land along the "New Way" (Porter Street) and the "New Street" (State). This gives the time of the establishment of both these streets as 1757 and 1758, at least at their western ends. The grounds took on their present extent in 1857 when Samuel Lord, for many years the owner bought a strip of land between the house and the Rockingham Hotel from Thomas J. Coburn, the hotel's proprietor.

Purcell, who was a mariner, and frequently listed in the maritime notes, gave up the sea in the early 1770s and set up a store. He was prominent socially, being president of the Charitable Irish Society. Another Purcell, Michael, lived in Portsmouth in this time, naming twin sons, Michael and Gregory, perhaps indicative of being a brother to the builder of the Jones House. Captain Gregory died in 1776, leaving a widow and eight children, and shortly thereafter the Sarah Purcell started to take in boarders.

The widow sold it to Woodbury Langdon, and by the time Purcell's creditors had levied their liens, there was not much left except the house and land on which it sat. Henry S. Langdon, son of Woodbury, lived in the house and reacquired the lands from the creditors. He sold to his brother John Langdon, Jr., who, in turn, later conveyed it to his brothers-in-law, Henry and Alexander Ladd. In 1826, the Ladds deeded it to Samuel Lord, and U. S. Senator John F. Parrott was at that time the occupant. Lord lived in it until his death in

1871. The house since 1923 has been the headquarters of the Portsmouth Historical Society.

[19]. This second workhouse also provided space for town offices and Union Hall. It was in this hall that the town fathers collected their year's "pay", by the virtue of an annual banquet with the town footing the bill. In 1834 the Town Farm was built near the New Franklin School -- recent construction in the area has unearthed the bones of unfortunates buried on the Farm at town expense. In 1850 a burial ground for paupers and strangers was authorized at the Poor Farm. The story of the second almshouse and one of its keepers must be told. Clement March ruled it with an iron hand for 36 years. A giant of a man in size, March, at least as far as the inmates were concerned, had never quaffed the milk of human kindness. Brewster relates being told by March's grandson that in his boyhood he could recall that the "keeper was so feared by the inmates, that when any disturbance was heard in any room, he would say, 'Nat, take my cane there'. The boy, shouldering the mysterious wand, and marching through the room, would restore quiet without saying a word". One must admit there wasn't much "creeping socialism" in the 18th Century. Eventually the Courthouse was built on the site and used until a new court building on State Street was opened in 1891.

[20]. Polls at this time were counted only of males over 16.

[21]. An entire chapter could be devoted to slaves and their life in 18th Century Portsmouth. Their numbers increased with the years and the names of some have come down to us. For example, there are those of Prince and Cuffee Whipple, the slaves of William Whipple, the signer of the Declaration of Independence. These slaves enjoyed to limited extent a social life of their own, in their own way. However, there were strict rules for their behavior and woe betide any of them caught out after the curfew, which still resounds in our city. The last resting place of many of them was in the vicinity of Chestnut Street between Court and State Streets, and their bones have often been disturbed by construction work.

[22]. Much of this marshland is in the western part of the city, beyond the Plains and part of the topographical feature known as the Great Swamp.

[23]. Richard Wibird's brick mansion stood on Market Street on the east side about one-third of the way toward Bow Street. Wibird was a powerful man in the town and province. He served on the Council, as judge of probate. After his death, September 25, 1766, the widow, Mrs. Elizabeth Wibird, continued in occupancy of the house,

not being permitted to sell it, although he did allow her to retain ownership of their three slaves, Phillis, Sylvia and Venus, and she was permitted to sell land and buildings at Frame Point, the beautiful residential area which is now circled by Pleasant Point Drive. On the widow's death, the mansion passed to a kinsman, John Penhallow, and the lands held by Wibird were divided in 1802.

[24]. This family, through marriage into the Fernald tribe, became owners of part of Pierce Island in the 18th Century, and one of them, Samuel, signed the Association Test in 1776.

[25]. The Mendums also had a connection with Pierce Island, one part of it taking their family name. This particular Mendum died August 31, 1771, of an "epiliptic fit" at the age of 82.

[26]. Joshua Pierce was the first of the family to settle in Portsmouth, coming about 1700, probably from Newbury. He had a shop at the corner of Market Square and High Street, on a piece of land still held in a family trust. Active in town affairs, he served on the Council and his merchandising enabled him to accrue a valuable estate. He died in 1743.

[27]. The Knight family name was originally Chevalier, but was anglicized at an early date. One of the early Knights operated the ferry between Bloody Point, Newington, and Hilton Point.

[28]. Bradford was probably the father of Captain Thomas Bradford who combined seafaring with shopkeeping first on Spring Hill (the vicinity of Bow and Market Streets), then in a shop just west of High Street on Congress Street.

[29]. The first of the Clarksons here were James and Andrew. The latter had to flee Scotland when but a youth because he had fought under the banner of the Pretender. He came to Portsmouth and found a home with the family of John Cotton, a tanner in the South End. Later his brother James came. The two became highly respected citizens, elected often to public office. They occupied a house that once stood near the Haven School. Andrew married the widow of John Cotton in 1759 and built up a valuable property. James is listed as a "captain" but how long he followed the sea is not clear and the frequency with which he was elected to town office indicates he was usually at home.

He was moderator of the town meeting which the North Parish wardens decided could not be held in the church. After his election on the steps of the church, the citizens found an axe, knocked in the doors and entered to discuss the town business. While a son Walter was buried in Cotton Cemetery in 1789, another son, James, Jr., was the executor of his will which was probated after his death in October 1773 at the age of 74. James, Jr., probably was the sea captain who was reported by the Gazette as having 10 boxes "of Stamped Paper (Stamp Act) aboard when he learned of the unease here and put it ashore". This was on December 31, 1765, and he had managed to get his ship, the King Of Prussia, to the Isles of Shoals. Passengers for Portsmouth, among them Robert Traill, comptroller of customs, and Captain John Cochran, were forced to come into Portsmouth in a small boat because the winds were north, northeast, and Clarkson could not work his ship into port. He finally sailed off to the West Indies and came back on March 21, 1766, having left London the previous fall. Andrew Clarkson died in the summer of 1765.

6

French and Indian Days

[1]. In his diary Judge Samuel Sewall cites a few instances of men who aired opinions of royalty established government that upset the authorities and were summarily dealt with.

[2]. The career of William Pepperrell has been put within the covers of a book. Pepperrell's father was an Isles of Shoals fisherman in the 17th Century. Trading in fish lead to further ventures in a mercantile line and the son, with whom we are concerned, established a prosperous business on the mainland. His Countinghouse and mansion still stand in Kittery Point, in the ownership of a collateral descendant, Joseph W. P. Frost. Built on an acre of ground given to Pepperrell's father by John Bray as a wedding present, the buildings were out of family connection for 167 years until 1945, when they came into the hands of the present owner. In 1949, Frost was able to acquire the original commission given William Pepperrell creating him a baronet. The male line of Sir William Pepperrell died out with the death of his son, Andrew, at 23, but the baronet was not without ideas. He decreed that if the son of his daughter, Elizabeth Pepperrell Sparhawk, would take the name of Pepperrell, he would make him his heir. The young man agreed and when Sir William died in 1759, he inherited the estate but the title itself could not pass to him. However, the wealth and power he commanded in loyalist circles gained him his own baronetcy, but that was all, except personal property, he was able to take with him when he was proscribed at the outbreak of the Revolution. His real estate at Kittery Point was confiscated and at one time housed colonial troops.

[3]. By the Peace of Aix a Chapelle, Britain gave Louisburg back to the French. Colonial indignation ran high at this effront to its venture in arms and even higher with the realization that the peril from French intrusion was again renewed.

[4]. The Reverend Jabez Fitch was the third man to occupy the pulpit of the North Church, that is if the Reverend Joshua Moodey and the Reverend Nathaniel Rogers, both of whom preached at the church south of the mill dam, are counted. His death in 1746 came in the 22nd year of his ministry here and in the 75th

year of his life. His records, if he left any, are kept from the prying eyes of historical researchers by the wardens of the North Church who for years kept them buried deep in the bowels of the Portsmouth Savings Bank, perhaps waiting for Doomsday and a final account of their stewardship. The Reverend Mr. Fitch is known to have published four sermons.

One dealt with a severe earthquake which shook New England on October 29, 1727, and was noted by the New England Weekly Journal in its issue of October 30, as "the most surprizing and awful....; the Noise like Thunder, which lasted for the space of about two minutes, when the Earth trembled and shook to a great degree, the houses rock'd as if they would have fallen down, and many of the Inhabitants being amaz'd ran out into the Streets...." That was published in Boston, but the effect here must have been similar. Another, according to the Annalist, Nathaniel Adams, was on the ordination of the Reverend John Tucke at the Isles of Shoals, July 26, 1732, with his text, "I Will Make You Fishers of Men". Two others were occasioned by the terrible outbreak of diptheria in 1735 when hundreds of persons lost their lives. The Reverend Mr. Titch's widow, Elizabeth, obviously much younger, lived to 1765, dying in her 84th year.

[5]. There will be many references to Theodore Atkinson and many details about his life will be developed in the course of this chapter. However, the Rambler tells of one oddity of history connected with this man that puzzled him when he saw it and is still puzzling today. Atkinson's heirs in Dover, a hundred years ago, had a silver serving tray, or waiter as it was called, on which were engraved the names of 48 persons with the dates of their deaths and their ages. The deaths span a period of 30 years from 1740 to 1771 and are an enigma in that there seems to be no particular pattern or reason behind the recording of them. In some cases wives are listed, but their husbands are not and vice versa. If it was a case of friendships, Atkinson ignored some men who must have been close to him and listed others who were comparative strangers. At the time the Rambler wrote, the waiter was owned by the Freeman family in Dover,, Mrs. Asa Freeman being the daughter of William King Atkinson.

[6]. Samuel Moore was tied into the Pierce family by the fact his wife was a sister of Joshua Pierce. That he had a fine home here is evidenced from the fact that in 1754 that the governor requested the House (Assembly) to meet with him in the Council Chamber at the house of Colonel Moore, deceased. Moore had

commanded the New Hampshire regiment in the 1745 expedition against Louisburg.

[7]. John Moffat has been described as a native of Hertfordshire, England, although this has never been established by investigation. A seaman, he came here first as captain of a mast ship, married Catherine, a daughter of Robert Cutt II, and lived in Portsmouth. His wealth had grown to the extent that in 1763 he was able to build the house we know on Market Street as the Moffat-Ladd House for his son, Samuel. This son failed in business and was forced to flee town, his creditors being eager to throw him in jail as was the custom of the times. Samuel managed to re-establish himself in Eustatia, West Indies, and his father, outbidding all the creditors, took over the Market Street mansion and moved into it from his house on State Street. Samuel's sister, Catherine, married William Whipple, a signer of the Declaration of Independence. Old John Moffat lived to the age of 94, dying in 1786, and on his death bitter litigation went forward for years. The suit was finally resolved in favor of Samuel Moffat's son, Robert C. Moffat, and he sold to Dr. Nathaniel A. Haven, who passed it on to his daughter, Mrs. Maria T. Ladd, wife of Alexander.

[8]. All of these men had extensive holdings in towns throughout the province. For example, these proprietors owned the two eastern ranges in the Town of Peterborough, land that takes in East Mountain and Pack Monadnock. Throughout the province years and into the early day of statehood, their advertisements appear in the pages of the New Hampshire Gazette, calling for meetings of proprietors or urging settlers to move into their holdings.

[9]. Daniel Pierce was the son of Joshua, the first Pierce to live in Portsmouth. He was born in 1709 and graduated from Harvard in 1728. Daniel was engaged in trade but apparently had no liking for it. At one time he studied law but gave up the idea for that occupation as "inconsistent with the character of an honest man". When his father died he was named recorder of deeds, and at the time of his own death, December 5, 1773, his executors had to advertise in the Gazette asking people to make sure their deed had been recorded. Daniel Pierce also served as local magistrate for many years. Three children survived him; Ann, the wife of Thomas Martin; Joseph, who died in 1812; John, who died in 1814.

[10]. Captain Nathaniel Adams was the father of the founder of the Athenaeum and the man who wrote "The Annals of Portsmouth" in 1823. Captain Adams, as did so many other successful mariners, quit following the sea as soon as he could and set

himself up as a merchant with a shop "near the Parade". In June 1760, he advertised, with five other merchants, that the Bohea tea he was selling did not come from damaged cargoes. The year 1762 saw him in England on a business trip and in December of that year he advertised for persons owning packages of goods he had brought from England in the ship Atlantic to come and get them. Captain Adams died October 13, 1768, at the age of 42. His first wife, Deborah, died May 13, 1755, at the age of 20. Elizabeth, his second wife and mother of the Annalist, died November 20, 1814, at 81.

[11]. Robert Stokell came here, probably from Boston, sometime in the 1750s. We find him as master of the brig Penelope in 1760 and trading in the West Indies. He died in 1764 and his widow married William Fernald, also a mariner. Together the widow and her new husband administered the estate which had an inventory of 9,082 pounds. Stokell had a son John, who later sued Fernald for an accounting and his own services as a seaman on Fernald's vessel. A John Stokell became master of his own vessel, the Exeter Galley, during the Revolution, and many of the name lived here until recent times. A Robert Stokell died in a shipwreck on the Essex Bar in 1854.

[12]. Captain Joseph Hixon figured in an 18th Century "Marie Celeste Story" on April 28, 1765. At the time he was master of the ship New Hampshire on passage from London to Portsmouth when he sighted a vessel at Latitude 40, Longitude 30. Hailing her, he received no answer, so he boarded and found no one on a vessel with all sails set, fully loaded with white pine boards and masts. He told the New Hampshire Gazette that the vessel was a pink "North Country built, having no Head or galleries, a very round side". Over the cabin table he said was written: "All Fair Under the Rose". Hixon's account left out more than it told, not even telling whether or not he took the vessel for salvage, or speculating what could have happened to her crew. But Hixon perhaps an unsentimental man, was not given to questioning the mysterious ways of the sea. He died August 20, 1769, on a trading voyage in the West Indies. His widow married George Hart and as late as 1795, the various heirs were still squabbling over the estate, final settlement coming in 1802 on the basis of a map drawn by John Stokell, perhaps a grandson of the Robert Stokell.

[13]. Captain David Horney was another mariner who gave up the sea to follow a less perilous vocation on land, becoming an innholder. He died in June 1757, leaving his house to his widow, Mrs. Hannah Horney. The inn, operated by Mrs. Horney after the

captain's death, apparently was on Court Street, according to an advertisement run in the Gazette by one John Day, a distiller, who in 1763 said he was in business "just below Widow Horney's", and then in 1766 told his customers he had moved up the street (Court) where he has lived for several years opposite Theodore Atkinson's. This is also indicative of the way Court Street was being opened up to house builders.

[14]. This is the same Captain John Cochran who was to command Fort William and Mary the night when the raiders elected to take the gunpowder out of it. Many have thought the title of captain in front of his name was military because of his command of the fort, but that was a political plum handed him by Governor John Wentworth.

[15]. Luke Mills was one of the many Portsmouth captains who experienced the misery of being taken by a French privateer. Mills was captured on August 12, 1757, while on passage from Barbadoes to Portsmouth. The Frenchman, with eight guns and 36 men, kept him and his men prisoner four days before they were released and allowed to go to St. Christopher's. Their vessel was kept by the French. Mills sailed out of here regularly for some years before his death in the summer of 1764, and his widow, Deborah, lived until 1786.

[16]. Captain Nathaniel Sherburne lived near the Swing Bridge (the span across Puddle Dock) and followed the sea through all of his working life. He commanded the snow Amherst in 1761 and advertised for three deserters; in 1762 he had the ship Fox; he died in the winter of 1770 while commanding the sloop Abigail on a voyage to Granada.

[17]. This shipmaster with the odd first name was the 60th Portsmouth captain to lose his life at sea in a span of 13 years. Bunbury, who sailed regularly on the West Indian run, took out the brig Dolphin on January 25, 1772. Four days after the Dolphin sailed she ran into foul weather and Bunbury kept the deck himself to ride out the blow. Deciding the danger was over, Bunbury went below to rest, and the mate, David Welch, kept the helm. Suddenly a huge sea broke over the vessel, putting her on her beam ends; chest and cabinets toppled on Bunbury, killing him. At the same time the sea carried the mate, a Mr. Ritsen, and Nathaniel Barnes overboard. Ritsen alone managed to scramble back on board and by himself managed to work the vessel to the West Indies. Bunbury, who left three small children, was about 35. Eleven years previously, while in command of the snow General Townsend, his vessel had been taken

by a French privateer and ransomed for 300 pounds. The way in which the French would make sure the ransom would be paid was to hold the mate as hostage until the money came. Frequently the mates suffered untold hardships in the French prisons at Martinique and Guadaloupe, and more than one died of tropical fevers while waiting for the ransom. In the case of Bunbury's capture in 1761, Captain Samuel Frost left under a flag of truce to recover not only Bunbury's mate but those of ships commanded by Captain Thomas Leigh and a Captain Wells also.

[18]. Robert Mallard had commanded the St. George for several years before he put her on Hampton Beach. In the summer of 1962, some boys skindiving off the north end of the beach found two ancient cannons and there is some belief that they may have come from the St. George. Mallard also figured, in partnership with Jamed McDonough, in a clever piece of salvage at Great Bay a few months later. The ship Mary upset in the bay and went down. Taking advantage of the thickness of the ice, Mallard and McDonough put 80 youke of oxen on it to raise the vessel while 1,000 persons were reported to have watched, so great was the thickness of the ice. In April, McDonough advertised that the Mary would sail within 30 days. The Hampton Beach wreck, discussed in Dow's "History of Hampton", caused quite a uproar. Jonathan Moulton, the self-anointed overlord of the Hamptons, had been put in charge of salvage, but when he and his men got there, scavengers had cleaned the vessel out. Frantic and not entirely successful efforts were made to recover the stolen goods and charges of riot and rebellion followed a fracas with Hampton residents.

[19]. America rotted out almost as soon as she was delivered to the Royal Navy.

[20]. Nathaniel Meserve founded the shipyard that was later to produce some of the great Clipper ships a century after his death. His home and his shipyard were on the North Mill Pond. Here he built fine vessels used by the sea captains of Portsmouth to bring the trade of the world to the Town's wharves. Key man in Pepperrell's successful attack on Louisburg in 1745, his services were repaid when Pepperrell gave him the job of building the America. That she was a failure was due probably more to the combination of native woods used in her than in Meserve's lack of skill. He fathered three sons, one of whom, Nathaniel, Jr., died with him in the small pox outbreak at Louisburg in 1758; Hanson, a ship's captain, who commanded the snow Stratham, at the time of his father's death, and George, who attained a fame all his own at the time of the Stamp Act. Nathaniel,

Sr., divided his estate among his sons and daughters and Nathaniel, Jr., left his wife to administer his for his son Henry; Hanson, dying two years later, left his estate to his brother George. Sometime after Meserve's death, the house passed into the hands of the acquisitive George Boyd. From his estate it came into the ownership of the master shipbuilder, one of Portsmouth's greatest, George Raynes.

[21]. The record book of the Portsmouth Social Library is preserved at the Portsmouth Athenaeum. It was founded on the principle of a tontine, the last survivor of the original investors would come into ownership of all the books in the collection.

[22]. Former Attorney General William Maynard once pointed out that Ruth Blay was properly convicted under existing law, wrong though that law might have been. The particular law under which Ruth Blay was tried and hanged was not taken off the New Hampshire statute books until 1792.

[23]. Wyseman Clagget was one of the more controversial figures of his times. His zeal, when king's attorney, led to the expression that someone had been "claggeted". Clagget probably arrived here sometime in 1758; that is supported by an advertisement he ran in the Gazette to the effect that he had moved next door to George Jaffrey. He wooed and won for his wife, Miss Lettice Mitchel, a bargain that the poor lady was to spend her life regretting because Clagget was one of those men who had to be consulted on every detail about the household. The Rambler tells a few stories about him and his petty chicanneries.

When fire destroyed James Stoodley's original tavern in 1761, Clagget's residence was badly damaged and he moved to Congress Street and into a house later occupied by the sign painter George Doig. The New Hampshire Gazette gives us no description of how Clagget looked or conducted himself at the Blay trial. But three years earlier Clagget had prosecuted Mrs. Elizabeth Odiorne for the murder of Mrs. Catherine Grant, and the Gazette said, "After a hearing of five hours, the Jury retired for an hour, and then returned with a verdict of Manslaughter only. King's Attorney Clagget and William Parker, Council for the prisoner, were both habited in black robes, the proper dress for the bar and conducted their several parts with such firmness and force of Argument as to reflect great honor on their Fidelity and Abilities".

Poor Mrs. Clagget did get one trip out of her husband; in 1769 with their children, the Claggets embarked on the brigantine Adventure, Ichabod Libbey, master, and sailed for Clagget's old home in Bristol where he had been born in 1721. The Claggets were gone two years and returned to take up an active role in the affairs of those who were tiring of British rule. Despite his post as King's attorney, Clagget early sided himself with those who disliked oppressive taxation. He finally moved to Litchfield, New Hampshire, dying there in 1784. His widow, 20 years younger, died at Bedford at the age of 85.

[24]. Leverett Hubbard was another who managed to move in the "right circles". He was comptroller of the port and active in the little group close to the governors.

[25]. These men, Frederick Martineau and Russell Nelson, were convicted of bringing a man from Rhode Island and killing him near Nashua. Their appeals have been moving through courts for years.

[26]. The death of the son Theodore, whose widow rushed into fast matrimony with Governor John Wentworth, left Atkinson without an heir. He willed his estate to George King who changed his name to George King Atkinson, and it passed from him to a nephew William King Atkinson of Dover.

[27]. On the site of this one-story brick structure once stood the Oracle House. This house sheltered the printing office of Charles Pierce, publisher of The Portsmouth Oracle of the Day, predecessor of The Portsmouth Journal of Literature and Politics. Originally the little house stood south of the North Church and then was moved to Haymarket Square. When the present building was erected, the Oracle House took still another ride, this time to the southeast corner of the intersection of Court and Marcy Streets and is owned by former Governor Charles M. Dale, and occupied by the widow of his son, Thomas M. Dale.

[28]. Daniel Fowle sold copies of a broadside called "Monster of Monsters" by Tom Thumb. He did not print it, but he spent five days in Boston's jail simply because he did not want to tell the General Court that his brother Zechariah, had done the printing. They did get him to admit the sale of two dozen and that he had seen Zechariah in the process of running them through his press. Fowle printed a denunciation of the treatment he had received, protesting that a man could be jailed without a hearing. Still angry at the ill usage, he listened willingly when offered the chance at Portsmouth and came here in the summer of 1756.

[29]. Only recently the Portsmouth Athenaeum acquired two volumes of Province Acts printed by Daniel Fowle and a third printed by his brother Zechariah at Exeter.

[30]. This first hard-cover book was "Good News From a Far Country", printed in 1756, its subject matter a series of seven sermons by the Reverend Jonathan Parsons, minister at Newbury.

[31]. Novelists tend to portray the 18th Century as a society, in which every man was an expert shot, highly skilled in woodcraft, when, in actuality, they were probably no better qualified with weapons than most modern American men and many of the town dwellers were like urban people today.

[32]. Divorce was no light procedure in the 18th Century. It had to be sanctioned by the General Court. The first on record was that of a man named Samuel Smallcorn of Portsmouth who was granted one from his wife, the former Margaret Welch. Mrs. Smallcorn had become involved with a highbinder named John Collier, but apparently it was not a lasting dalliance. Two years after the Smallcorn affair, Moses Brown of Portsmouth posted his wife for having run off with Collier and notes that Collier had been punished before for a like offense.

[33]. George Washington cautioned his officers against having any dealings with Major Rogers, and he was subsequently indicted in Rockingham County for his counterfeiting activities.

[34]. Old Fort No. 4 was at Charlestown, New Hampshire. A project of recreating the old fort, a mile or two from its original location is being carried out. The late Maurice E. Witmer, a local architect, was extensively engaged in the early planning.

7

The Eve of the Revolution

[1]. Henry Sherburne, first of that mighty clan in Portsmouth, was an important man and a wealthy one. When the first meetinghouse was being planned, Henry Sherburne offered to pay for the windows, and the frugal committeemen immediately increased the amount of window space, thus keeping the community's costs for the building that much less.

[2]. Even earlier in the year 1753, January 31, Stoodley had filed a petition in the Assembly asking reimbursement for "the affair of the sloop Speedwell". Stoodley apparently had been hired by the province to go to France with French POWs, and had as his partner in the venture his wife's brother, Nathaniel Doe. Seemingly they lost money (the Province Papers give no previous information on the point) and wanted reconsideration. The records are not clear whether the French were Louisburg prisoners or not, but Stoodley and his partner were voted 30 additional pounds more than a year later. Stoodley was elected overseer of the poor and corder of wood in 1758 and in August the same year became collector of the excise. In 1764, although he does not say where he wanted it built, Stoodley was advertising for the construction of a house 40 feet x 32, the contractor to provide everything except the nails. The town continued to honor him with offices; in 1766 he was auditor, in 1771 named assessor. During the years his tavern prospered; in the third-floor attic hall, Masonic meetings were held and balls frequently staged at which the dashing Colonel Michael

Wentworth often took over the fiddle. Stoodley died June 6, 1779, and in 1785 his widow married a man named Captain William McHurd. The tavern passed to Stoodley's daughter Elizabeth, who married Elijah Hall, one of the Ranger crew who made it his private home until his death in 1830 at the age of 84.

[3]. Collection of taxes was "farmed out" for a percentage to some favored person in the province, and it was his task to get the taverners to pay the taxes due on the liquor they served, far different from our system wherein the state collects the tax when it sells the liquor besides making a profit on the sale.

[4]. James Stoodley I, died in February 1762. His will mentions him as a mariner and lists sons James, William, Thomas and Jonathan, who had died three years earlier. James, Jr., apparently was the chief beneficiary. Captain Jonathan's estate, on which administration was granted in February 1759, was not finally settled until 1791 when there was a division of the house and land which stood at the corner of Deer and Fore (Market) Streets.

[5]. Wyseman Clagget, the king's attorney, was among the sufferers from the fire.

[6]. The Ferry operated between the tip of Market Street and Kittery. Until the first bridge was built in 1820, it was the quickest means for a traveler to get into Maine. In later years, when the Navy Yard became more active, there was a ferry service from the Daniel Street area across to the Yard.

[7]. Some tricky legal maneuvering was involved in this estate. The land being offered for sale was described as being on the north side of Daniel Street, between the houses of Stoodley and the Widow Sherburne. After the auction, John Sherburne of Boston tried to block the sale because Paine's father was living. One of the legal documents indicates that Paine died in Jamaica. Paine had an aunt, Mrs. Lydia Buss, widow of Joseph, a joiner. Her own will was challenged by her son in 1759 on the grounds of mental incompetency. The dutiful son swore that his mother had known that his cousin, John Paine had gone to Jamaica in January of 1758, but in February she had cooked Paine a roast pork dinner because he liked pork and had kept it until "it stunk". And, even though she had been told of Paine's death, she kept waiting for his ship to come in. George Gaines, a cabinet maker who could turn to other trades, testified that while papering a room in her house he had observed that she was childish. Joseph, Jr., was trying to keep his sister, Mrs. Hannah Horney, from getting any part of the estate. As they often do, the old probate records leave us high and dry in this one, except

41

for a small hint in the probate of Joseph, Jr., that he had some of the disputed property in his possession when he died.

[8]. Many citizens of the period, with any wealth at all, indulged in posing for a portrait.

[9]. John Greenleaf was an ancestor of Abner J. Greenleaf, Portsmouth's first mayor.

[10]. Robert Metlin (Macklin) was one of the most remarkable men ever to live in Portsmouth. The property mentioned in the text was where Metlin was burned out of his bakeshop in 1738. He moved across the way, probably somewhere between Winebaum's News Agency and the corner of Chestnut and here conducted his business until he sold out sometime in 1766. What distinguished him in a day when no one had automobiles in which to run down to Sher's bakery, was his ability to walk.

Tradition has it that it was Metlin's custom, when in need of supplies in Boston, to leave his house with the dawn, and head for Boston on foot. In those days the Massachusetts city was 66 miles along a route that took Metlin out to Greenland and down the Old Post Road. At sunset of that day, he would cross the Charles River on the ferry. The next day he would load his purchases onto a coasting vessel, conduct whatever other business he had in Boston, and on the third day he would walk home again. A round trip of 132 miles with some business in between. Perhaps like ex-President Truman, Metlin found that walking leads to a pleasant old age. Metlin lived to be 115 years old.

[11]. Pitt Tavern once had outbuildings, stables and the like, adequate to care for the many guests in the hostelry. These outer buildings fronted on a little thoroughfare known then as Jose Street, which is now Jefferson Street. Renovation of the old tavern will be a difficult and expensive job because owners since Stavers' day have allowed the property to go to ruin. Some have expressed hope that New Hampshire Masons may take an interest in such a project because it was here that the Grand Lodge was instituted in 1790.

[12]. Bartholomew Stavers made his home on Pierce Island, probably in a rented property because Pierce Island deeds show no record of his ownership. Certainly he was there in early 1762 when he advertised that someone had stolen three fat turkeys out of his barn. For about six years, he drove the stage coach on the Boston run and then gave notice in 1767 that he was going to quit to take over as post rider. His notice in the Gazette indicates that the stage coach was for sale at this time, but he would continue to drive

it until sold. Some time after this, Bartholomew drops from sight until 1771 when we find a newspaper note that he has returned from London in a ship commanded by a Captain Bateman. Stavers had a wife and children here, but these he left behind when he returned to England at the outbreak of the Revolution. One son, William Stavers, never saw his father, the latter leaving here in December 1774, a few months before William was born. Another son, Andrew, died young but William became active in mercantile pursuits. The family name was well known in Portsmouth until well into this century, and the line, through females, still survives here. Of John Stavers, the better known brother, there will be more in subsequent chapters.

[13]. This rather strange man left no children to perpetuate his line and the name remembered now only as a street in the North End, where once his orchard stood. But he was the first postmaster in Portsmouth, of whom we have record, although all New Hampshire was included in his delivery area, and, therefore, the predecessor of all the postmasters who have come after him, including the incumbent Alfred V. Cashman. On his mother's side he was connected to the Waldron family, his father having married a daughter of Richard Waldron II, the son of the old Indian fighter. His home was at the end of Market Street, near the ferry, and here he conducted the postal business. His home was also the first Customs House, predecessor to the building now occupied by Halprin's on Daniel Street. Here he lived with four sisters, none of whom ever married. His only brother, Captain Benjamin, died sometime in 1756 in Guinea. Eleazer's ways, according to the Rambler, were precise; nine o'clock was hid bedtime and any guest in the house at that hour was ushered to the door and left on the outside of it. He lived in mortal fear of contracting disease, rampant in those days among the captains and sailors with whom he dealt. Papers of entry he handled with a pair of tongs to escape any possible contamination. So great was his fear, that when the Yellow Fever epidemic of 1798 swept the North End, he shut himself in his house and died within a week, on September 18, 1798, but not of the fever, although two of his sisters contracted it and died in his home. His property went to a nephew, Daniel Waldron, and he was buried in the North Cemetery at the age of 76, having been one of the State of New Hampshire's collectors of taxes and U. S. Naval Officer for the Piscataqua District. These honors came to him in spite of the fact that he refused to sign the Association Test of 1776. In fact, by 1779 he was functioning as naval officer, inspecting vessels to make sure cargo that would aid the British was not getting out of the state.

[14]. Bartholomew Stavers, apparently was replaced on the box of the stage coach by John Noble, who kept at the job for two or three years, until November 1770, when he, too, quit to ride post "from the Post Office in Portsmouth". We cannot help but wonder if he succeeded Bartholomew in this job, too, because by this time Stavers must have been in England. Noble lived at the corner of present-day Vaughan and Hanover Streets. On the stage coach he was succeeded by Benjamin Hart, who had also been a post rider. Hart and John Stavers were in partnership until at least July of 1772, and perhaps as late as January 1773, when an advertisement appeared offering passage to Boston for $1.50. In March of that year Hart and Davis (Theodore) were advertising that the stage would leave "Hart's house near the Ferry" at 8 a.m. each Friday, so it would seem that Stavers had lost the stage line at this time, whether amicably or not we do not know.

[15]. The exact date that St. John's Lodge was organized is not known. There is a possibility that it might have been in existence as early as 1715, but 1736 is the generally accepted date because in February of 1735, Robert Brough, Thomas Colman, John F. Miller, Jonathan Nailer, William Canterbury and William Grogan asked the Massachusetts grand master for recognition as a formally constituted lodge. The charter was granted in 1736 and that is the date used. In its vaults St. John's has a treasure lode of history, ancient records dealing with all but the very earliest years. The most prominent names in the province appear there for one reason or another and the easy informality in which Benning Wentworth could send a man over to a meeting to be made a Mason would shake any modern lodge.

[16]. Even as today among owners of thoroughbreds, a good stallion commanded high fees, and Stavers was not loath to have one standing in his stable. He advertised in 1771 that Haven, "a fine English stallion", was at his tavern.

[17]. In modern day Portsmouth, 15 minutes from the Pitt Tavern to the vicinity of the bandstand in Greenland, would be quite a feat with a car, if all motor vehicle laws are obeyed.

[18]. Hugh Hall Wentworth was a merchant here in 1757, selling miscellaneous goods out of his house. His life here apparently was quiet, dabbling in various business ventures and not getting into the whirl of town affairs. His wife, the former Penelope Jepson of Newport, Rhode Island, died late in 1771 at the age of 30. Two years later, Wentworth was named lieutenant governor of Granada and apparently left to take up his new duties.

[19]. Samuel Livermore was one of the outstanding Portsmouth attorneys of his day. An advertisement in the Gazette indicates that he began practice here in February 1758 with an office in the shop of Elizabeth Paschall, a shopkeeper on Spring Hill (area around the junction of Bow and Market Streets). Probably he made his home with his relative, Matthew Livermore, who had settled here in the 1720s, taught school and then became a lawyer. Born in Waltham, Massachusetts, in 1732, and, by appointment of Governor John Wentworth, Samuel Livermore became King's Attorney, perhaps about 1769 when Wyseman Clagget went to England. Some idea of the struggle a lawyer had to go through in those days to make ends meet before his practice was established can be found in Gazette advertisements. In 1759, Samuel Livermore was a partner of John Beck in the sale of tickets in the Newbury Lottery; the next year was selling a varied line of goods; and in June 1772 we learn that he was selling ladies caps, hats and millinery at his house on Spring Hill. Livermore also turned his hand to farming in Londonderry on two different occasions. Most of the time, however, he spent at the practice of law, and was close to the ear of Governor Wentworth in the days before the Revolution. When the end of royal government came, Livermore, like Postmaster Eleazer Russell and Commissary Jonathan Warner, did not want to sign the Association Test to prove their loyalty to the patriotic cause. Both Warner and Russell refused to sign in 1776 but later made their own peace. Livermore may have gone to Londonderry, at any rate he is not on the list of those who refused to sign, nor one of the signers. Be that as it may, Livermore was moderator of the convention that produced New Hampshire's Constitution, served in the U. S. Senate and in the U. S. House. By that time his sons, Edward St. Loe Livermore and Arthur, had been born. The family made its home in Holderness, New Hampshire, in Samuel's latter years. Edward had three children, Samuel, Caroline and Harriet.

Harriet was the inspiration of the poem "Snowbound" by John Greenleaf Whittier. She became a religious eccentric and died in the Holy Land. Matthew Livermore's house on Livermore Street, now owned by Mr. and Mrs. Ralph Gerth, has passed through many hands since Matthew died in 1776. When Livermore Street was opened up in 1809, Dr. Nathaniel A. Haven acquired the house. Over the years it has been on three different sites, all in the same neighborhood. It was in this house that John Sullivan, one day to be first president of the State of New Hampshire, received his basic training in law.

[20]. In the 18th Century the Plains had a relationship with the downtown like that of a city and its suburb. We have mentioned before that a church was once established there and the residents came within a whisker of making a separate town, which would have compressed Portsmouth's limited acreage still further. That did not come to pass, so the National Little League has a place to play baseball, but it did not prevent the residents of the Plains from living a life of their own. Taverns flourished there. The Globe was one of the better known.

In the years before the Revolution the Globe apparently was in good enough repute to entertain the Masons at regular intervals and yet it changed owners several times. John Parry had it in 1761, and two years later became involved in a domestic row with his wife and a man named George Waldron. Parry advertised in the Gazette, October 21, 1763, that he was not a liar and was innocent of any charges of "profane and atheistic falsehoods". The accuser was Waldron who had said previously in public print that he did not owe Parry any money. That simmered along for a week or two and then Waldron belittled Parry's notice posting his wife for having left his bed and board. Then came an "ad" in the Gazette, couched in language that even newspapers today would find hard to put in print, detailing the relationship between Mrs. Parry and Waldron.

This notice was inserted by one James Hammond of Kittery, who said that Waldron had attacked him while he was in Timothy Fernald's ordinary in Kittery. Waldron's wife had died the year before and it would seem that he did not care what kind of a fracas he was involved in. Daniel Fowle refused to print Waldron's reply to Hammond and said that if he (Fowle) had been in town Hammond's letters would not have been printed either. Other letter writers to the Gazette put in their contributions, siding with Parry. That must have encouraged him because he brought suit against Waldron for "criminal conversation" with his wife, in the sum of 4,000 pounds. Tried in 1766, the jury found for Waldron without leaving the box and gave him his costs. Hard times still faced Waldron, although Parry and his seven children are heard from no more. In 1768, he ran an "ad" asking anyone who owed him money to please bring it to him at "His Majesty's Goal" by March 4. In August, he was still trying to collect and we find no more about him in the Gazette. In March of 1765, the Globe Tavern passed into the hands of John Gotham (Goatum) who had previously lived near the Swing Bridge. Here, in 1763, he had given roof to Henry Golden, an upholsterer, fresh out of London. Gotham described the Globe as being "about two miles from the Town House, on the Great Road to Boston". In May of 1767, Moses Howe took the tavern over from Gotham. Some time before 1773, Howe was succeeded by John King, who was a principal in a tragedy at the tavern. Apparently King was not too successful and debts began to pile up. In the 18th Century one did not brazen it out and dare the creditor to do anything about it. The quickie bankruptcies of our day, just as easy as taking a bath, were 200 years away. The creditor would get a writ of attachment, not only on the property but also on the body of the debtor. The money either was forthcoming or the debtor sat in jail until the obligation was paid. King owed a man $40 (Dollars even before the Revolution were frequently used as money value). Sheriff John Parker of Rockingham County sent a Joseph Moulton, Jr., a deputy, to get the $40 or King. Seeing the deputy coming, the taverner ran, picked up a gun he had nearby, and at a range of 10 feet, let Moulton have a blast of gooseshot. Twelve pellets were taken out of Moulton's head and he was expected to die, but whether he did or not cannot be found in the pages of the Gazette. King fled and the sheriff posted a $20 reward for his arrest and that, too, was never reported. The Globe went through a succession of owners and in 1839, was operated by John H. Jackson, but when the 1851 City Directory came out Jackson was living on Gates Street and the Globe was not listed among the city's hotels. Another tavern at the Plains in the 18th Century was the King George, but it is not clear who was operating it when the Masons met there in 1765, in compliance with a notice posted by Daniel Sherburne, secretary. This Sherburne was a sea captain.

[21]. Families like the Wendells, Sherburnes, Wentworths, Sheafes, Pierces, Harts, Cottons, Brewsters have long association with Portsmouth. It is impossible within the scope of this book to go into genealogical detail and almost unnecessary because family genealogies, complete to the nth remove, have been compiled. Offered here are only highlights in their careers for the most part and so be it with John Wendell. He first made the news in October of 1757 when he offered a $10 reward to any who would tell who started a rumor that he had informed the Customs officers about the smuggling activities of Captain John Frost of New Castle. Wendell apparently was living at that time in Boston, and Captain Frost, master of the schooner Elizabeth, was seized for carrying an illicit cargo. Also protesting that he was not the informer was Charles Paxton, then collector of revenue for the Port of Boston, which seems a bit odd for a sworn official to do. Wendell came here before

1763 when Foster Treferin (Trefethen) and William Jones had him and Hunking Wentworth arbitrate the dissolving of their partnership.

The destruction of the Wendell home two years later we have already mentioned, and we know that in 1767 he was agent for 1,000 proprietors of lands west of the Connecticut, the Hampshire Grants (now Vermont). A year later he advertised that he had been commissioned a notary and Tabellion public with an office in a small building between Samuel Haven's and Matthew Livermore's, about where Livermore Street meets Pleasant today. He sired three sons, Abraham, Isaac and Jacob. In 1776 he signed the Association Test. To digress for a moment, we should say here that the Captain John Frost involved in the smuggling episode was mentioned in the Gazette four years later when the same schooner Elizabeth was wrecked in the October storms of 1760. In April of 1761 an item reports that Mr. Randle, late pilot of the schooner and known as "Old Monk", had returned to town. The crew had spent 15 days on the wreck, been taken off by a French privateer, which in turn was wrecked on the coast of Spain. The item concluded that Captain Frost and his son were daily expected home.

[22]. The late William G. Wendell, whose widow still makes Portsmouth her summer home in the Wendell house at 222 Pleasant Street, had in his possession the notary and tabellion public seal owned by John Wendell. The Wendells made the ancient Warner House their particular project for many years before his death.

[23]. John Abbott lived to the age of 92, dying on January 29, 1768. He sired 11 children, and at the time of his death had 62 grandchildren and 47 great-grandchildren. The Gazette item concludes "most of them now living in town". So it would be safe to conclude that some of the Abbot families in Portsmouth and the area decend from the old fisherman.

[24]. The reader will note the similarity between the surname of Thomas Achincloss and that of Mrs. Aristotle Onassis' mother, Mrs. Hugh Auchincloss. Achincloss had a shop on King (Congress) Street, across from the offices of Continental Cablevision of New Hampshire and near the Marquis of Rockingham Tavern, operated by Captain Jacob Tilton.

[25]. John Adams was the son of William, a mariner, and in 1766 John had a shop, "The Sign of the State House", on the north side of Congress Street near Zechariah Foss' inn. That fall Adams was encouraging the spread of learning by selling tickets, at 24 shillings each, Old Tenor, to two lectures on electricity that were to be given at Foss' inn by David Mason. He moved out of that shop

the next spring and into a house that had been occupied by Pierse Long on Queen Street (Fleet). The dependence to some extent on the Mother Country can be seen from the fact in 1769 Adams advertised garden seeds from London for Sale.

[26]. There were at least two Benjamin Akermans, father and son, and both followed the trade of tanner, a quite common occurrence at the time; the trade of the father being good enough for the son. Benjamin, Jr., held the post of selectman for several years and was in the job when the Revolution came. He also held office as tythingman and overseer of the poor.

[27]. At the age of 25, Henry Appleton was operating a store on Congress Street, near the State House. The building, owned at the time (1762) by Robinson Treferrin of Dover, was on the north side of the street and was described in a "for sale" notice in 1763 as being new. It was in the vicinity of W. T. Grant's. Treferrin sold the property and Appleton moved over to Buck Street (State). In 1764 he had an act passed by the Assembly authorizing him to sell real estate, held by him for his wife, Sarah, who was under 21. Henry did not live long to enjoy the fruits of the sale; he died September 5, 1768, at the age of 31, and was buried with Masonic honors. The inventory of his estate was 261 pounds, according to the appraisers Nathaniel Treadwell and Samuel Penhallow. It was settled by 1770.

[28]. William Appleton is one of the first persons to advertise as a bookbinder. In 1766 he had a shop across State Street from the present site of the old County Courthouse and his subsequent notices indicate that he had a sign displaying a Bible and Crown. Teaming up with Daniel Fowle, and Robert Fowle, Daniel's nephew, both printers, Appleton published the New Hampshire Almanac for 1767. A copy of this almanac was recently sold through the book shop of J. & J. Hanrahan for $1,800. Whether the intellectual appetite of Portsmouth was light, or what happened, we do not know, but Appleton apparently gave up advertising by 1771, and John Sparhawk, who formerly was in Kittery Point, had his old shop. Again in 1775, one Oliver Brewster notifies the public that he has taken still another shop formerly of Appleton. And yet Appleton took the Association Test in 1776 and in 1770 was listed as one of the town's major taxpayers. The secret probably lies in the fact that he married Sarah, the widow of Henry Appleton and she, being a daughter of Jotham Odiorne, a wealthy man who owned the town's largest fishing fleet, might still have had some of that property that her first husband (no relation to the second) was eager to sell off.

Widowed a second time, Mrs. Appleton became Mrs. Daniel Hart, and again widowed. It was in her boarding house on Market Square that the fire of 1802 had its start. At one time she owned the Governor John Wentworth mansion on Pleasant Street, now the Wentworth Home.

[29]. By the time of the Revolution, Portsmouth had moved a long way from the period when each family was sufficient unto itself, making its own clothes and providing its own food. The prosperity of the mid-18th Century brought the service trades to Portsmouth. Among them were men such as Robert Archibald, who had a tailoring business at the west end of Deer Street (near Vaughan); George Sheriff, tailor, with a shop near the State House; Benjamin Pitman, a partner of Sheriff's; John Davis, a Londoner who opened a tailor shop on State Street. There were others, but few of them had the experience of Davis, who advertised that he had gone to Hampton to a vendue (auction) and had been seized and thrown in jail. His creditors thought he was trying to skip town. Pitman, a son of a one-time keeper of the Prison on Chestnut Street, and perhaps a brother of Molly, also had troubles. Some competitors apparently passed the rumor that he had stolen a jacket from them, and he took an "ad" to deny the charge, claiming that they should put the "blame on Sir Richard who at that time had them too much in command", which was a neat way of saying they were drunk. Competing tradesmen in those days were not as superficially polite to each other as are our contemporaries. Daniel Fowle made a pretty penny out of running their disputes as advertising.

[30]. George Ayers was one of several men here who made their livings as cordwainers, a name derived from the famed Spanish leather center of Cordova.

[31]. Philip Bailey is among the first to come to notice who made his living by trading and conducting vendues (auctions). Bailey, much like modern auctioneers, would hold sales on his own premises on Queen Street or at the taverns or anywhere else the goods were available. He was not here many years, being Tory in sympathies. On May 11, 1775, along with Thomas Achincloss and James McMaster, he was forced to make a public plea for forgiveness, through the Third Provincial Congress, of his outspoken opposition to the spirit of liberty that prevailed. Although he declared that he now stood ready to "risk my life and interest in defence of the constitutional privileges of this Continent", Bailey did not sign the Association Test of 1776. Then in 1778, described as a trader, Bailey was one of 76 men "proscribed", that is their properties were

confiscated by the state, and in some cases this meant their wives and families were left to the dubious charity of the times. These proscribed men (another of them was Major Robert Rogers) were barred forever from returning to New Hampshire.

[32]. John Bament was a Londoner who arrived here in 1768, advertising his shop in Queen Street, near Richard Champney's. Champney was a son of the Reverend Mr. Champney, a minister in Beverly, Massachusetts. He moved his shop almost annually for a while, having one place near the Sign of the Hatters Arms, and then to Queen Street where he was selling lemons by the box, hundred or dozen. Champney's sister, Sarah, died in 1771 and he signed the Association Test in 1776, dying in 1810 at the age of 74.

[33]. The presence of an upholsterer in the town meant the people were able to afford better things. Joseph Bass had his shop near Dr. Hall Jackson's, Court Street, and must have been acceptable in a social way almost immediately because three years after his arrival in 1764 we find him on a list of those present when John Sullivan was made a Mason. Like everyone else, he did not stick strictly to his own line of business, but in 1770 advertises the sale of "American Grindstones from Nova Scotia, all sizes". Within a few weeks of the grindstone ad he put in a notice of his intent to leave the province and is selling his house and a pew in Dr. Haven's Church (South). But two years later, March 6, 1772, he had either never left or had returned because he was selling tea next door to the Printing Office on paved Market Street. Bass had two wives, Abigail who died in 1780 four years after he signed the Association Test, and Sarah who died in 1817. He was a commissary officer in the Revolution and apparently lost his shirt in shipping speculations. Later he was postmaster and customs officer, but died a pauper in 1823.

[34]. Caleb Beck was but one of the many local men who followed the trade of shipwright. He lived at Frame (Pleasant) Point.

[35]. John Beck, perhaps a brother to Caleb, was ostensibly a hatter by trade, but he dabbled in everything. For example, in August 1762, while being fitted for a hat you also could have bought a few pounds of salt pork which Beck was selling at his Sign of the Hat. Beck's shop disappeared in the fire of 1813, but was located within a few yards of the northwest corner of Chapel and State Streets on the north side. Beck married the daughter of Mark Chadbourne, another hatter and was the father of John, Jr., and Henry. John, Sr., was active in town affairs, serving as tythingman,

corder of wood, surveyor of highways, measurer of wood at various times. Just before the Revolution the sign on his shop was of "The Hatt and Beaver".

[36]. Portsmouth had two noted schoolmasters in this period. One was Thomas Bickford who died December 18, 1772, in his 58th year, after 40 years a teacher in Portsmouth, and the other, Major Samuel Hale, who died July 10, 1807, at 89. Of Thomas Bickford we know but little. The Rambler spared him not a word in either of his volumes, but from probate records we get a hazy picutre of a diffident man, always of service to his friends and neighbors, highly trusted and well liked. Both Thomas and Hannah, his wife, for instance were witnesses to the will of William Hopkins, blockmaker, and Bickford later went surety on the bond of the execturix, Elizabeth Hopkins. In the case of John Deverson, a joiner, who died in 1751, Bickford made the inventory of the estate. But, while the Rambler and the Annalist had no thought for Bickford, both devoted attention to Samuel Hale. Born in Newbury, Massachusetts, in 1718, Hale graduated from Harvard in 1740. He was in command of troops in the Louisburg operation of 1745, whence came the title he carried the rest of his days. In 1748 he began a teaching career in Portsmouth that lasted nearly 40 years. The schoolhouse that replaced Hale's is now gone, succeeded by Paul V. Brown's block of offices opposite the old Court House lot on State Street. The old building of Hale's day was wooden, one-storied and was erected on land swapped by the town for the lot where City Hall now stands. Hundreds of Portsmouth schoolboys were given the basics of a classical education by Major Hale. For many years he was active with the town's Board of Fire Wards and served as its chairman. Hale also could find time from his school duties to be a judge of the Rockingham County Court of Common Pleas. The father of President Lincoln's Secretary of Treasury, Salmon P. Chase, was Hale's immediate successor as a teacher in the old school. That building was torn down in 1790, partially damaged in the fire of 1813 and then rebuilt. This school was the direct ancestor of the present Portsmouth Senior High School, that multi-roomed structure of brick and concrete, built in 1955. When the first real high school was built in 1855, the old building was turned to other uses and in 1900 served as an office for the superintendent of schools.

[37]. William Blunt, the boat builder, was probably the son of the Reverend John Blunt, fourth clergyman in New Castle. His older brother, John, Jr., a sea captain sired five sea captains, and a sixth son John, III, died at sea during the Revolution. It should be

explained that a boat builder did just that: He built the skiffs, dories and moses boats so useful to a seafaring people; shipwrights built larger vessels. Poor William suffered some bad luck in 1763 when a "terrible gale of wind" flattened a house he was building.

[38]. Moses Boynton must have brought joy to the heart of Daniel Fowle when he moved into town from Stratham in 1761. Boynton had long advertised his shop at Stratham and when he came into Portsmouth his advertising really increased. He announced that he had a shop in Queen Street, (waterfront end), opposite Henry Sherburne's, where he "may easily be found by the Sign of the Buck and Breeches hanging at said Shop". For the times, it must have been a fairly large operation because Boynton said he had six journeymen and apprentices working for him. Before the end of the year he had moved to King Street, "few doors below the Parade", at the Sign of the Buck, Breeches and Glove". Boynton's swath was a wide one while he lasted, but he eventually ran into financial difficulties and disappears from our annals.

[39]. Dr. Joshua Brackett was, with Drs. Ammi Ruhammah Cutter and Hall Jackson, one of the top flight doctors in the Portsmouth of 200 years ago. All three had the same preceptor in the field of medicine, Dr. Clement Jackson, the father of Dr. Hall. Dr. Brackett was born in Greenland in 1733 where many of the name still live. His parents' ambition pointed him toward Harvard and the ministry. He took a degree at Harvard in 1752, studied theology and began on a career in the pulpit, but found it to his dislike. Entering an apprenticeship under Dr. Clement Jackson, he, in the custom of the days before medical schools, soon became a practitioner in his own right. Dr. Brackett dabbled a little at being an apothecary as well and in 1760 was advertising a Venice Treacle of his own manufacture for sore throats, perhaps no better and no worse than some costly concoctions we get today.

In 1783 he was accorded honorary membership in the Massachusetts Medical Society and in 1791 Harvard gave him a medical doctorate. That same year the New Hampshire Medical Society was incorporated with Brackett, Jackson and Cutter among the charter members. Brackett was elected vice president, became president in 1793 and held the post until his health gave out in 1799. On April 14, 1760, Dr. Brackett married Hannah Whipple of Kittery, sister of William Whipple, a signer of the Declaration of Independence. At first he was not enthusiastic about the smallpox inoculation technique introduced here by Dr. Hall Jackson, but later practiced it and so managed to get himself in trouble with the authorities. That was in 1773 when the Governor and Council met to consider a petition from Dr. Clement Jackson asking that his son-in-law, Dr. Stephen Little, be allowed to leave Pest Island, the two patients under his care there being well on the way to recovery from smallpox. The Council was angered enough to note that both Drs. Little and Brackett had been inoculating in disobedience of a Council order to the contrary, and it directed that all doctors post bonds to insure their compliance. A petition from Brackett himself asking permission to bring his wife home from the island where she had recovered from a smallpox inoculation was tabled, the Council being of the sentiment that she should stay there.

Unfortunately the provincial records leave us there and we do not know how long Mrs. Brackett was held on Pest Island, or what she said to her husband when she did get home. Brackett's interests were not confined to medicine. Appointed judge of the Maritime Court at the time of the Revolution, he adjudicated distribution of the prize money from the British ship Prince George, captured in the lower harbor on October 2, 1775, by Captain Thomas Pickering. Loaded with 1,894 barrels of flour, all but 50 were sent to the Army at Cambridge; the vessel itself was sold and there were 71 claimants for a share in the proceeds. Pickering's adventures will be dealt with in more detail later on. In another instance, Brackett signed, with Dr. Hall Jackson, a certificate as to the purity of saltpetre (needed for gunpowder) being made by Dr. Samuel Haven. Active throughout his life, the doctor died in 1802 at 69; his widow died in 1805.

[40]. Robert Calder was perhaps a symbol of a more effete Portsmouth. On October 30, 1767, he advertised himself as from London and "cuts and dresses Ladies and Gentlemen's hair in the genteelest of fashions, either at his house, or attends at the time and place directed by those that will favor him with custom". As an added lure to his shop which was across present-day Marcy Street and to the south of the old Meetinghouse, he had a coffee house going where "may be had tea, coffee or chocolate, served in the best and most agreeable manner". Still another enticement was his promise to have on hand English and American newspapers. We can only surmise at this, but apparently Calder did not find the going too easy. An "ad" published July 5, 1771, announces that he was lately secretary to the governor and is now opening an inn in Newbury Port. It may be there were not enough dandies around Portsmouth to keep him in business.

[41]. John Chapman was not long in business here, but had a shop on King (Congress) Street near the State House.

[42]. John Walter Cook, baker, had his place of business near Canoe Bridge. How prosperous he was is difficult to judge; we do know he was trying to sell out in 1772, but that might have been because he found it difficult to operate under the laws governing the making of bread. In 1769 he had headed a group of bakers petitioning for relief from operation of the act and that the House attempt to ease the burden. For the disillusionment of those who persist in the belief that grandmother, and all her mothers before her, baked their own bread, let us quote briefly from the Bread Act of 1766: "Whereas a just Proportion between the Price of Flour and the Weight and Price of Bread is now a Matter of Importance as many People purchase the greatest part of their Bread of Bakers...."

[43]. Daniel Crockford managed to make a good thing out of his barbering business before his death in 1757. He left an estate inventoried at 1,022 pounds, a goodly amount for those days. His widow Isabella, did not lack for suitors and stayed right with the barbering trade by marrying John Noble, a barber. They sold off Crockford's house so the widow could get out her dower right and by 1763 Noble was also a peruke maker, plying this trade at his shop near the Swing (Liberty) Bridge. They probably sold out before the Revolution because Noble advertised in 1773 that he would sell a house and lot on the street leading from Haven's (Old South) Meetinghouse and the Liberty Bridge. The property fronted 40 feet on the street, 60 feet deep; the house being one story with three rooms. Another John Noble, the post rider, was already in town, but only one signed the Association Test of 1776, so it was probably John, the post rider.

[44]. Peter Curtis brought still a further innovation to Portsmouth by proposing to teach dancing. It's surprising that it took that long for the vogue to reach Portsmouth because Judge Sewall noted the presence of a dancing teacher in Puritan Boston nearly 50 years earlier — not that the judge approved, but he was helpless to do anything because the Church of Englanders, by and large, then held the government. Curtis set up shop in the tavern at one time operated by David Horney, across from The Earl of Halifax, Court Street, in 1767, and claimed he was from Paris. He moved uptown to take room under the Printing Office, Paved Street (Market Street was given its first paving in 1767), and then a year later moved across the street into the house occupied by Captain Bunbury.

[45]. William Davies is another man about whom we know little, yet he carried on his trade in his "own house" about a

quarter-mile south of the Mill Dam, in a property formerly owned by Peter Abbot. There was a Peter Abbot paying taxes here in 1727. Davies, from England, first showed up in 1764, and probably was the same William Davis, silk dyer, who had a black mare stolen from Peter Ball's pasture in 1767.

[46]. Joseph Day was one of the men who earned his livelihood in the manufacture of that end product of molasses so well liked both in colonial and modern times — rum. He first comes to our attention in 1763 when he was in business near the Widow Horney's. In 1766 he suffered a stroke of bad luck when he lost 300 pounds, O.T. "in a work'd pocketbook". And later the same year he moved farther along the street to become a neighbor of Theodore Atkinson.

[47]. John Doane could well have been a traveling clockmaker from Boston as he so described himself. In an "ad" in 1757 he said he was in business at David Griffith's shop, the Sign of the Goldsmith's Arms in Portsmouth. While Doane may have been an itinerant, Griffiths was well known here prior to the Revolution.

[48]. George Doig has been mistakenly described as a house painter, and it is possible that in slack times he would lend his craftsmanship to that trade. But his real line was that of a coach and sign painter and he so called himself when he arrived here from London in 1772. Doig occupied the house that had lately been the residence of Hugh Henderson, who in that same year had married Hannah Sheafe, daughter of the wealthy merchant, Jacob. Doig's "ad" in February 1775 shows a new consciousness of family arms at his shop on King Street. Doig might have been only recently come from England but he quickly adapted himself to the new ways and signed the Association Test of 1776. He early interested himself in Freemasonry and was one of the founders of St. Patrick's Lodge of Masons in 1780. He represented this short-lived lodge at the second meeting of the Grand Lodge in 1789.

[49]. Samuel Evans eked out a precarious living as a post rider and carrier of the New Hampshire Gazette for a number of years. Daniel Fowle had to advertise once that Evans had made collections on his behalf and that he was now unable to get an accounting from him. Poor Evans himself took an "ad" urging his creditors to let him have a letter of license, in other words not throw him in jail, so he could keep on working and somehow retrieve his finances. That pleas apparently did him no good because within a month his house and land were sold on him.

[50]. Perhaps it was the presence of a young, attractive

woman in the governor's mansion that was making Portsmouth's ladies of fashion more conscious of their dress. Anyway, Lucy Fessenden, a mantumaker (cloak or dressmaker) must have thought so because she moved here from Boston in 1770, opening a shop on Queen Street somewhere in the vicinity of William Stanwood's peruke shop. She advertised that she was making negligees, hats, gowns and cloaks.

[51]. Colonel Zechariah Foss was described as innholder as early as 1759. The site where he kept his tavern is now occupied by the Franklin Block. Earlier in life Foss apparently followed the sea because in 1772 he was voted 15 pounds by the Assembly for his services as pilot of the sloop Abigail in the 1744 expedition against Louisburg. Foss married Sarah Waterhouse, daughter of the family with extensive land at what is now Freeman's Point. Foss at one time was so far down on his financial luck that his wife sold some cloth and with the money started a small place of refreshment. From that tiny start they expanded into one of the town's biggest taverns. One of the daughters married Captain John Cochran, the defender of Fort William and Mary; from still another came down the Dennett family which is still with us. Another daughter, Margaret, became the wife of a Captain David Cullam. Cullam's first wife, a Miss Currier, died in August 1774 and, even though he had a young daughter, Cullam gave up housekeeping and moved into Foss' tavern. There he met Margaret and married her. He served under John Paul Jones and made a fortune in prize money. His daughter was brought up by the Daniel Rindge family when too many observed the abuse of her by her stepmother.

[52]. John Fowle was in business for a time at Exeter, moving to Portsmouth in 1761 where he set up as a scrivener in the house of the Widow Lear (of Washington fame) near the South Meetinghouse, also advertising his willingness to teach "most parts of practical mathematics". A scrivener, as the name implies, was a writer, one who pens letters, documents or any other paper work, a quite necessary functionary in a time when many could not read or write.

[53]. George Gaines, as far as management of town affairs was concerned, was "Mr. Portsmouth" throughout the last quarter of the century. In occupation he originally followed that of his father, John Gaines, the famous cabinetmaker. John had his shop and home just east of Fleet Street on Congress; here he lived with his wife, the former Ruth Waterhouse, and fathered George Gaines. Four chairs made by John Gaines are among the proud exhibits of the

Warner House. These chairs were made for his family connections (his wife's sister, Margaret, married Samuel Brewster and his daughter, Mary, married her cousin, David Brewster) the Brewsters. The chairs never left that family's immediate possession until put in the Warner House several years ago. George was born about 1736 and apparently had the usual run of education of the time, then being apprenticed to his father. That he dabbled in other trades, among them that of coffin-maker, we know from his testimony at the hearing into the Buss will. Gaines moved early into town affairs and held the job of selectman for a span of 30 years.

The town also made him its representative to the General Court over much the same time. George Gaines fathered one son, John, who made his home in New Orleans where he died in 1853 at the age of 78. This John Gaines had two sons in mercantile pursuit in the Louisiana city at the time of the Civil War. George Gaines' many achievements for the town will be touched on in later chapters. He was one of the key figures in all Portsmouth's activities during the Revolution, occupying the post of state commissary, an office under the State Constitution which was abolished only in 1950. Gaines reached the title of major by his service with troops at Saratoga. Even before that he had been active in militia circles, and was one of the men who sought permission to drill as a militia company in 1774. The next year he was designated second major of the 1st Regiment of Minute Men. He died April 25, 1809, at the age of 73.

[54]. David Griffith was one of several Griffiths in town during this period. He partnered a man named Samuel Bowles for a while, although that was dissolved in 1771. This partnership paid a tax of 17 pounds to the town in 1770 and stood 13th on a listing of high taxpayers. He apparently was not here at the time of the Association Test in 1776. For a time, he conducted his business on Queen Street and then opened a vendue house on Market Street across from Richard Wibird's. His widow, Sarah, died March 29, 1780 at the age of 42 and it is possible that David Griffith had died before 1776. Another of this family name, and possibly a brother, was Samuel, who, with Thomas Achincloss, were the two paying a tax of 15 pounds in 1770. Like many others among the shopkeepers, his place of business changed several times but was usually in the Queen (State) and Court Street areas. In his shop he sold anything that would yield a shilling or two, such as snakeroot and orange water, gunpowder, shot flints, deer skins. Samuel died December 11, 1773, at the age of 44. His estate was administered by John and Abigail Griffith, with Joseph Whipple and John Sparhawk designated

to receive claims against the estate. Abigail was the widow of Samuel and John may have been a brother. John is another on whom we have little to make a dossier.

Our first notice of him comes through an estate notice in the Gazette for October 21, 1757, posted by him as an executor, with James Moses, to the estate of Captain Daniel Lang, mariner. In the will Lang describes Griffith as his uncle. Moses was his father-in-law. They were granted the right to sell land at Ellin's Point (Pleasant Point). Three years later he was handling the estate of a Captain Robert Lang. John Griffith in 1758 was a busy fellow, serving the town as clerk of the market, corder of wood, town agent and Fire Ward. At one time he was carrying on sort of an express business to Hampton Falls. His wife, Deborah, died in 1771 at 65, but John continued active in town affairs through 1775. However, in 1779, the General Court granted permission for his executors, Samuel Penhallow and William Knight, to sell off real estate rather than divide it among the heirs as required in the will. One of these heirs was David Griffith who predeceased his father by several years.

Another of John's sons was Nathaniel who died in 1771 at the age of 31. Nathaniel's executrix was his widow, Mary; his trade was that of a goldsmith and his shop was approximately on the site where the County Courthouse once stood on State Street. Still another Griffith, Edward, arrived in town in April 1771 from London. He had a store next door to John Griffith where he operated a tailoring business. He offered lappel suits at 1 pound, 8 shillings, and half-trimmed suits at the same price. One William Ward joined Griffith a few days later and set up in business as a staymaker, and another of this family on which we have little information was Gershom Griffith who was witness to the bond of Charles Banfill as administrator of the estate of his father, George Banfill.

One last Griffith deserves some mention. He was Nathaniel Sheafe Griffith, the only one around when the time came to sign the Association Test. Here was one of the real characters of the century. He came to Portsmouth from Hampton in the late winter of 1769 and set himself up in business "almost opposite Dr. Langdon's meetinghouse (North Church) near the Parade where he makes and sells the best of eight-day clocks at the Sign of the Clock and Watch"

While in Hampton, this man had been engaged in a lengthy and bitter correspondence through the pages of the Gazette as to whether or not he was one who had used a Portsmouth man's church pew for latrine purposes. The argument raged hot and heavy and outsiders became involved by taking sides in the matter. That issue died down before Griffith came to town, but he promptly became involved in another argument; this time with a man named John Simnet who had set up in the clock business near the Earl of Halifax Tavern. The year before Simnet had described himself as having 25 years experience in the business and had come here from London.

Within a week after Griffith's first "ad", Simnet launched an attack by warning that "a tinker or smith, near where I dwell, intending to fleece the ignorant and diminish the repute of his neighbors had been telling lies about him and he dares the "watch butcher" to make a watch and display it at Stavers'. The feud raged for a year, to the profit of Daniel Fowle, and an "ad" on June 22, 1770, was a verse which supposedly described Nathaniel S. Griffith:

> *"Near Portsmouth Stocks Sheep Griffith lives*
> *(A Turkey-Legged Youth)*
> *His clocks with both hands give the Lie*
> *His Tongue ne'er speaks the Truth*
> *Stand off, ye Pettyfogging Knaves;*
> *This can you all outdo,*
> *Long Nat, can Filch is of our Time*
> *And of our Money too."*

There the argument ends and we must suppose that "turkey-legged" Griffith had the last laugh. At least he was in town to sign the Association Test and John Simnet was not.

[55]. We include John Haman because his death showed the dangers of the riggers trade. In June 1772, Haman fell from the mizzen top of a ship he was rigging in the North End and he died within an hour.

[56]. We assume that James and Matthew Haslett were brothers. They came here together from Boston in the Spring of 1766 and set up their "factory" at the Sign of the Buck and Glove near Canoe Bridge. In September they scored a "first" using a woodcut of their sign as part of their "ad" in the Gazette, something no other business in town had done up to that time. By November they were expanding, but ran into tough luck when some vandals entered their new building near the Mill Pond and tore it apart. They had the usual adventures of businessmen of the era. One day a George Hall came to them, said his master had sent him and while their backs were turned, he stole a pair of breeches.

They also suffered from one of the recurring complaints of the time: Their servant boy, Samuel Dotey Hamilton, 19, ran away in 1769. It is interesting to note the stature of these runaways and realize how much bigger Americans of 200 years later are. Young Hamilton was listed as five feet tall, and he is not an exception. Most of these descriptions of nearly grown youths range between five feet and five feet, four inches. One man was said to be lusty and big who stood five feet, ten inches, an average height today. The Hasletts lost another boy a year later, Geogre Ulmer, 14, four feet tall. They brought the retail end of their business to King (Congress) Street in the late 1760s, and in 1773 the brothers dissolved their partnership. James Haslett continued the business and was still at it in 1774 when Sarah Winkley and Elizabeth Hill opened a school for young ladies in the house opposite, where they taught sampler working at six shillings per quarter. Before they ended their partnership, the brothers managed to get into an advertising brawl with a doughty sea captain named George Turner. That became one of those name-calling fights so dear to the heart of the 18th Century. Both brothers were in town to sign the Association Test.

[57]. Fresh out of Dublin, Ireland, was John Hickey when he came here in 1761 and set himself up in the silk-dying business. He rented space in the house of Captain Thomas Manning near Swing (Liberty) Bridge at the Sign of the Dove. Hickey moved around quite a bit. He went to Spring Hill, then took quarters in a house owned by Joshua Cate about a quarter mile south of the Mill Dam on the road to his excellency's. In 1763, he took a partner, William Davies from London (see note 45, this chapter), with whom he set up a fulling mill. That lasted only a few months. Hickey stayed in a shop they had near the Town House and Davies ran a dying business in a house formerly Peter Abbot's, about a quarter mile south of the Dam. Hickey moved his household from the Mill Dam area to Canoe Bridge, next door to Captain Mark Langdon, in 1764 and there one Cotton Mather Stevens hung out a sign as a tailor in 1765. Later in the same year he was in partnership with a man named Varney at Cochecho where they had a fulling mill, but that mill was put for lease in 1771. None of these men were around for the Association Test in 1776.

[58]. Charles Hight followed an occupation essential in Portsmouth's economy, that of sailmaking. At one time, he may have been proprietor of an inn called the Bunch of Grapes. He made his home on Church Hill (Chapel Street). Hight amassed a goodly estate of some 9,000 pounds before his death.

[59]. Robert Hughes was another of those itinerant tradesmen who showed up in Portsmouth in the years before the Revolution. He came here from Boston and opened up a shop near the North Church, then moved near the Long Wharf before forming a partnership with James Deacon and opening up still another place near Dr. Hall Jackson's, Court Street. Neither Deacon nor Hughes were around for the Association Test.

[60]. Daniel Humphreys, direct ancestor of the late Cecil C. Humphreys, a former state senator, opened a law office here in May 1774 in a house where he was living next door to Mark H. Wentworth (Daniel Street). Previously, Humphreys had taught an evening school on King Street. Daniel was the brother-in-law of Susanna (Sparhawk) Atkinson. She had married George King, who took the name Atkinson to inherit the estate of Theodore Atkinson the long-time province secretary. To Humphreys in 1796 she left 100 pounds, a house, shop and wharf at Puddle Dock. Two of her nephews, George Humphreys and Daniel Humphreys, Jr., also were remembered in her will. A George Humphreys at the age of 39 signed a scroll commemorating the 200th anniversary of the town in 1823.

[61]. Another accupation essential to a seaport was that of William Jenkins, a caulker, who in 1772 advertised for sale a house lot with water priviledges on Mast Beach. This area was over at the Pool where for a hundred years or more the mast ships came in to load the bulky cargoes.

[62]. Dr. Stephen Little was married to a sister of Dr. Hall Jackson and partnered with Jackson in the selling of drugs and various herbs. He also practiced medicine.

In 1773, on January 25, Little had one of those adventures that can befall a man who had planned only on going on an excursion. Captain James Holmes, master of the ship Loyal Briton, left here with Captain George King as pilot for the trip downriver. Besides Dr. Little, King apparently had with him his son, George, Jr., a Joseph Ward and two Negro men. The trip was uneventful until King and his party had entered their own boat for the return upriver, then the wind came up and drove them to the east five miles and on to rocks. They managed to right the upset boat and in two hours had made their way back to White Island in the harbor mouth.

Nearly frozen, they stayed on the island until 11 p.m. and then made it to Gerrish Island. By this time one of the Negroes had died of exposure and George, Jr., was unconscious. Dr. Little managed to get to a house and brought back help before others died. This George King was the man who inherited the estate of Theodore

Atkinson, but that night he almost never had the chance to change his name. Little was one of those who could not accept open revolt against the Crown. He refused the Association Test and early in 1778 was before the Committee of Safety, along with 14 other Portsmouth men of kindred feeling. They were taken to Exeter under a guard of eight men commanded by a Sergeant Woodward. John Stavers was thrown into prison and James Sheafe, refusing to give his word that he would stay in Exeter until called for, also wound up in jail. Jonathan Warner, Oliver Whipple, Thomas Airmet and James Hickey were allowed to return home until sent for. Peter Pierce, Isaac Rindge, William Hart, Hugh Henderson, Robert Robertson, John Pierce, William Torry, Stephen LIttle and Nathaniel Little all gave their parole to stay in Exeter. James Sheafe recanted after a taste of jail and was allowed to give parole. John Stavers did not find jail to his liking and asked for release, but all he got was the freedom of the prison yard after posting a 500-pound bond that he would stay within it. Most of them, including Stavers, were finally allowed to post 500-pound bonds for good behavior toward the American cause and go home. Little was even granted the extra priviledge of going to York County, and finally fled the country and his property was confiscated under the proscription act. This was no favor to Hall Jackson who had to take on the task of supporting his sister and her children. Little may have returned.

[63]. Daniel Lunt served his town as measurer of wood and followed his trade as tinman.

[64]. Neal McIntyre came here from Boston and promptly set up a tobacco shop in the Spring Hill area. While his specialty was tobacco, McIntyre did not restrict his merchandising to that, but offered any other goods on which he could make a profit. We do not find him in a listing of those who signed the Association Test, but because of his activities on behalf of the local patriots, it's safe to conclude that the "A. McIntyre" on the roster must have been him. In 1775 he was one of those protesting to the absent Governor John Wentworth that the frigate Scarborough had detained two food ships outside Portsmouth Harbor and sent them to Boston. At that time he was also secretary to the local Committee of Safety and signed a receipt for John Akerman of Portsmouth, returned by the Provincial Congress for investigation as a Tory by the Portsmouth Committee. Akerman was exonerated after an examination; it being determined that he had been sent out into the country by Benjamin Hart and John Pierce to see if any armed men might be coming against them, and not to give intelligence to the enemy. Hart and

Pierce were both on the suspect list themselves as Tories and probably had cause to worry about what a mob might do to them. Hart ultimately left the country, and in October 1777 came back to Portsmouth from Newport, R.I., in a truce ship to pick up his family. Hart, described as a ropemaker, was later proscribed. Neal McIntyre stayed in business in Portsmouth, was advertising in 1798 and in 1802 was one of the incorporators of the New Hampshire Union Bank. He died at 68 in 1812.

[65]. Benjamin Mackay lived and carried on his trade in the Spring Hill area. At various times he was clerk of the market, bread weigher and also one of the proprietors of a grant with the optimistic name of Success. The grant was made to Mackay in 1773, but Success, three miles north of Berlin, is still an unincorporated place.

[66]. Just what George Madden, a weaver, did to "blot his copybook" is not known, but in 1774, pursuant to a decree of the court, he was "sold" for seven years. In 1760 Madden had been on war service and was one of those confined at the house of Richard Parsley, near the Pound (Middle Road and South Street) until further order by the Selectmen. It can only be hoped the War for Independence did Madden some good.

[67]. John Meserve, with a house and ropewalk near the house of Colonel Nathaniel Meserve in the North End, did fairly well for himself. He left an estate inventoried at 4,240 pounds; unfortunately there were claims against it of 9,000 pounds.

[68]. Richard Mills perhaps turned out some of the balustrades that still ornament 18th Century homes in this city. He also served his town as constable on different occasions and in 1775 found it necessary to post his wife, Anna. He signed the Association Test in 1776.

[69]. John Nelson had a lively goldsmithing business here just before the Revolution and apparently owned property just west of the Portsmouth Athenaeum building. At one time, a five-foot passageway ran between the Athenaeum and the Nelson property. Nelson was named to the Governor's Council but never served, and was collector at the Island of Nevis after leaving here. He died at Granada in 1785. There were others of the family name here, among them Leader Nelson, Captain Isaac, another John and Joseph. Leader married Abigail, the daughter of Samuel and Margaret (Waterhouse) Brewster. Leader made his living farming and served as a fence viewer. In 1766 a fire damaged his house. The fire "catched through carelessness of carrying hot ashes up into a chamber, of which it is a

pity that People are not more cautious".

[70]. Elizabeth Paschall has been previously mentioned, but she should be included if only to show the hard struggle a woman had to make a living in colonial Portsmouth. Her husband apparently was one of those unlucky souls who was "pressed" into the Navy. In 1763, Mrs. Paschall petitioned for the right to sell land to support her family, her husband, Henry, "being detained more than 10 years beyond the seas in His Majesty's service". The General Court did grant her plea. And with that she disappears from the scene.

[71]. Many shopkeepers are on the list and Benjamin Parker has been included as further illustration of the kind of thing competitors did to each other in the 18th Century. Apparently the "boys" got the rumor going that Benjamin was "non-compos" over money he owed Boston merchants. When the story reached Parker's ears, he had his Boston friends write letters to the Gazette denying the charges and they contended that envious Portsmouth merchants were the cause of the rumors. The local men immediately ran a letter claiming that Parker was unbalanced because about May 1, 1760, he had discarded his "usual and grave garb", donned a laced hat and ruffles, mounted a horse and rode through the streets proclaiming that "Quebec is absolutely taken and what I am doing now is to honor Quebec".

That Parker should do this, long after the battle, was one of several incidents cited by the local merchants to back up their claims. It may have been that they were right about Parker being "off his rocker", but he kept right on in business. And, he was one of the many who had a brush with the high and mighty George Boyd. He advertised that on November 18, 1768, he had given his note to James McDonough for 18 pounds, 12 shillings, fourpence. All but four pounds, 13 shillings, sevenpence of the note had been paid by the time McDonough disappeared from the province, and now Parker said, Boyd, acting for McDonough, refused to accept the balance and would not give up the note. Parker asked that no one accept it in exchange. Parker was still in business in 1774, but not on the Association Test two years later.

[72]. William Smith was engaged in an occupation quite old in New England. Judge Samuel Sewall in his diary quite frequently mentions gifts of chocolate he has made to friends. William was grinding chocolate here two years before the Revolution. When he died, his estate was adjusted by Samuel Smith, also a chocolate grinder.

[73]. Captain Jacob Tilton apparently was one of the long progression of men who managed the famed Bell Tavern. He had previously operated a tavern, the Marquis of Rockingham, near the Hay Market. Here he was in business for at least two years before becoming owner of the Bell. Greenleaf, the founder, had sold out to Gregory Purcell, whose widow later had a boarding house that entertained the famed John Paul Jones. Tilton was proprietor on the tumultuous nights when the raids on Fort William and Mary were plotted. He died in 1776, at the age of 40.

[74]. George Turner was one of those captains who plied two trades. He commanded his own ships and merchandised much of the goods he brought into port. One of the first ships he sailed out of here was the brig Free Mason. Her tonnage we do not know, but three years later Turner was commanding the brigantine Irish Gimlet, and in her, brought word of the repeal of the Stamp Act. In 1767, he came up from the West Indies with news of the severest winter ever recorded there, reporting that men had crossed on ice from the Island of Nevis to St. Christopher's. Within three weeks of this, he was embroiled with the merchants of the town by advertising that he did not water the rum he was offering for sale, and he also took on his pet foes, James and Matthew Haslett, with the information that his shop was a few doors past "Mutton Hall in Broad Street".

Again in 1769, he brought news of the safe arrival of local vessels in the West Indies with the exception of that of Captain Edmund Coffin whose vessel foundered and a seaman named John Broughton was lost. Captain Coffin was 21 days on the wreck of his vessel with nothing to eat except rotten fish and a barrel of apples. Turner decided to go to Ireland in 1770, taking his family with him. While he was gone, the death of his wife in Ireland was reported in the Gazette. Gilliam Butler, music teacher and shopkeeper, took over Turner's old store, but in May 1772 Turner was back in Portsmouth in the Irish Gimlet and selling St. Ubes salt at a store on Sherburne's Wharf. Captain James Guppy took out the Irish Gimlet for him the next month, perhaps while Turner was courting a new wife, Elizabeth (sister of his first wife), who died in 1790.

Turner took out the Irish Gimlet himself in 1773 and reported the loss of Captain Coffin of the ship Hill. Bluff Captain Turner suffered a personal loss in 1774 when his brig Dolphin with his brother, Captain Jeremiah in command, was lost with all hands. A Captain Corbett spoke the Dolphin and stood by to help for three days and three nights, but the seas prevented aid. Corbett watched helplessly as Turner put a yawl over the side only to have it dashed to pieces. Later in the day, they manned a longboat and it, too, was smashed to bits with all hands lost. The Gazette reported that Captain Jeremiah was of the West Indies but had sailed out of here for several years. Turner acquired another vessel that year, the snow Marquis of Kildare, and used her in West Indies trade. His daughter, Polly, married Andrew Sparhawk in 1775.

The outbreak of the Revolution was the bread of life to an Irishman like George Turner. He was active with the Committee of Safety in Portsmouth and interested in the artillery units for the defense of Portsmouth. There being no other enemy to engage, he battled Lieutenant Thomas Pickering over who was top man and the guns were taken away from him but returned in a few days. These he was ordered to emplace at New Castle to defend the island and harbor, and that appears to have been the end of his martial endeavors. After the war, the captain stayed on here and The Rambler tells of the time that his son, George, Jr., was being punished by Salmon Chase, the schoolmaster. The boy ran and told his father and the fond parent, just to show people do not change, went storming in to see Chase. After he had ranted for awhile, Chase ordered him out of the room and, when he did not leave, picked up a ruler as if to give the father a taste of what the son had had. Captain Turner left. His sister married Captain Thomas Thompson in 1772.

[75]. Isaac Williams was another ambitious man who moved here from Boston, hoping to capitalize on the new wealth that Portsmouth was amassing. Williams arrived in 1762 and opened up a shop at the Sign of the Wiggs. The sign and Williams moved around town quite often until he finally settled down for a while at the lower end of Queen (State) Street. Here in 1766, he opened the Crown Coffee House and said he "would serve only the best of liquors". The Peruke business he kept next door and, in connection with it, advertised that he would serve coffee at any hour of the day. The Crown Coffee House was successful enough to warrant St. John's Lodge of Masons marking the Feast of St. John there in 1767. In 1768, he formed a partnership with William Stanwood and in the summer they moved the business to a shop across from the intersection of Penhallow and State Streets. Williams and Stanwood dissolved their partnership in 1775 and Williams moved to Exeter, urging that his customers stay with his former partner. Stanwood apparently prospered and lived to the ripe old age of 80, dying in1827. Williams became very active in state affairs during the Revolution, serving as commissary.

[76]. William Winter made his living as a notary and tabellion public, "by authority of His Grace of Canterbury". He first opened up on Congress Street near Foss' tavern and then moved to a house near Theodore Atkinson on Court Street.

[77]. Smallpox was a frequent and dreaded visitor to New England. Judge Sewall mentions in his diary entry for March 17, 1686, the spread of "yt infectious Disease of Small Pox in some towns in the Countrey (Portsmouth and Exeter)". Again in 1692, the town had experienced smallpox. In 1718, a Captain Robert Almory of the sloop Hawk came into Portsmouth with "ye smal-pox which is still green upon him". Almory and his crew were prevented from landing and finally had to go ashore on Partridge's (Pierce) Island to his father-in-law Partridge's house which had been designated as a pest house, the first reference to such a place in the records. The pattern was a familiar one, and every few years there would be an outbreak. Dr. Joseph Pierce died of it in 1748. In the last outbreak before the Revolution, the town took extreme measures to safeguard itself.

[78]. Even George Washington bore its marks to his grave.

[79]. Various places after Patridge's were utilized as pest houses. One such was at Frame Point where there are now several beautiful homes. In 1748 the town showed its generosity by excusing Ebenezer Crechet of paying a fine because his wife had caught smallpox and also decided to forgive Mary Peacock for contracting the disease. Mary Peacock must have survived because she witnessed Elizabeth Newmarch's will in 1763. The town apparently had acquired an island for the Pest House in 1754 when it contracted with John Fling to be custodian.

The problem of a pest house persisted into this century. In March 1903, Dr. George E. Pender, a graduate of Dartmouth, and son of the former mayor, John Pender, was designated as chairman of the Board of Health, and made a new pest house on city land at Sagamore Creek, an immediate objective. The place was under construction in September.

[80]. Dr. Hall Jackson was the son of Dr. Clement Jackson, born in Hampton, November 11, 1739, and should be a whole chapter by himself. When the family moved to Portsmouth is not known, but Jackson kept his interest in Hampton throughout his life, even bringing suit against that town in 1771. He apprenticed himself to his father and then spent some time in the London hospitals of the day to further his knowledge of his profession. His

struggles with local authorities to win approval of the inoculation techniques he learned in Boston were lengthy. Jackson is credited with being the first man to perform a cataract operation and his surgical skill was often in use in other ways throughout the area. One small example is the case of a Hampton boy who froze both legs in 1768 while crossing the ice of Lake Winnipesaukee. Jackson had to amputate them both. He paid two visits to young Nathaniel Mason to treat the stumps and then tried to get paid. His bill was three pounds for the surgery involved and two pounds, 19 shillings, ninepence for mileage to visit the boy.

The town finally had to pay the bill, as did the Town of Portsmouth when he sued to collect for care given Thomas Card, Harry Card and John Randall in 1774. The bill was nine pounds, seven shillings and threepence, but it took Jackson, even with a court order, five months to collect. A few writers, for reasons best known to themselves, have chosen to regard Hall Jackson as Tory in his sympathies. And that is hard to understand. As soon as Lexington was fought and the troops rallied around Boston he went to the camps to aid the sick. Even before that he had drilled with the local militia company. While in Boston, he tangled with the notorious Dr. Benjamin Church, a highly trusted patriot, who proved to be one of General Thomas Gage's best Spies. The extent of Dr. Church's treachery was not known until this century.

General John Sullivan tells in one of his letters how Hall Jackson was ready to operate on a man's injured foot when Dr. Church came in and forbade it. Church's interference cost the man, a "Mr. Simpson", not only his foot but his life as well. Jackson, it must be admitted, was rather petulant in his dealings with the Provincial Congress in trying to get money and rank in recognition of his status. He came back from the Cambridge camps and threw himself wholeheartedly into the job of building up the harbor defenses of Portsmouth. Jackson was quite close to General Sullivan, although that did not save him from an upbraiding when the testy General thought some of his friends were not doing all they could to promote him politically. Jackson was one of the first to congratulate Sullivan on his achievements when the General returned home in 1780, but in 1785 Sullivan asked John Wendell to find out where Jackson stood on his candidacy for state office.

In the letter, Sullivan bewails the fickleness of Portsmouth politicians. That same year, Jackson had an adventure that nearly cost him his life, 12 years earlier than his actual death in 1797. The roads in March were impassable and he went by sailboat to Sturgeon

Creek to treat a patient. On the return passage, accompanied by Elisha Purrington and William Smith, both of Kittery, a sudden squall upset the stone-ballasted boat, and they were tipped into the water. A daughter of Samuel Ham saw them struggling, from the family home on Ham's Island (Noble's Island), called her father who reached them in a boat. Jackson and Smith were pulled in but by the time they reached Purrington it was too late. He died a half-hour after rescue. Jackson was wearing a heavy watchcoat, two pairs of stockings and heavy boots; when he shed his wet clothing it weighed 50 pounds. Jackson, in 1763, married Mary Dalling Wentworth, daughter of Captain Samuel Dalling who kept a store on Pitt Street near the Long Wharf. Mary Wentworth was the widow of Captain Daniel Wentworth, who died in 1762 of the scourge that Dr. Jackson spent his life fighting — smallpox. They had two children, Theodore, who died at 18, and Mary Elizabeth Symmes who died in 1808. Mrs. Jackson survived her husband by nearly eight years, dying in 1805. Dr. Jackson died from injuries after being thrown from his carriage on September 28, 1797. He was 58. His father, the doughty old Dr. Clement, whose home was on Queen (State) Street opposite a shoe shop, the Crown and Slippers, run by Samuel Foster, had died October 10, 1788, in his 83rd year. He never could collect what was due him. At one time Hall Jackson had to step into the matter and advertise that he would prosecute his fathers's claims against his debtors. The old man served the Patriots' cause faithfully by caring for the soldiers manning the forts along the river and harbor. Dr. Hall Jackson was active in local organizations such as the Federal Fire Society and the Masons. By some fast maneuvering, the Masons worked John Sullivan "through the chairs" in one month and then saw to it he was elected First Grand Master of New Hampshire. Hall Jackson succeeded his old friend in the post.

[81]. "Cuppers" was a nickname given doctors of the time, because they "cupped" a person in order to bleed them. Bleeding a sick person was considered one of the better ways of pepping the patient up in those days.

[82]. Some of these travelers had to sojourn near Joshua Brewster's tavern in the vicinity of South Street and Middle Road for a time before going on into town. Among the names for this tavern was Orange Tree Inn.

[83]. Peter Livius was another man whose life touched closely that of the first president of the State of New Hampshire, John Sullivan. Livius came here with a mandamus to be a councilor and was admitted to the Governor's Council May 23, 1765. He was,

of course, as interested as the next man in turning up a dollar or two. The mills were part of this endeavor and actually stood the town in good stead by providing a handy way of getting to Christian Shore, and opened up the whole Maplewood Avenue area to development. The first mention of Sullivan in connection with Livius was when the latter brought before the Council in 1766 "the Petition of a number of Persons from Durham and other places against Mr. John Sullivan for Evil Practises in him as an Attorney at Law". And from the point of view of the layman, Sullivan had been a little sharp in the way he managed to manipulate foreclosures to his advantage.

The matter was referred to the courts and there disappears from view. Livius was active in Council business, frequently serving on committees to investigate necessary matters such as the condition of Fort William and Mary which he had found badly run down in 1771. But all did not go well between him and Governor John Wentworth. With some justice, at least viewed from the vantage point of two centuries later, Livius complained of the way in which Wentworth stacked the Council and other principal offices with his relatives. The lengthy report presented to the King in 1773 exonerating Wentworth actually would seem to convict him, as the Lords of Trade found him guilty on nearly all counts but thought that the peace and prosperity in the Province was justification for his conduct. A committee from the Privy Council took the Lords report and embellished it up and it "pleased His Majesty to approve thereof". Wentworth did not escape entirely as is obvious from a letter the Governor wrote to a friend in London: "No doubt every person that heard the matter must have been astonished at my adversary's success in prejudicing opinions against me". Livius left here early in 1772 to lay his charges before the court. His grist mills were put up for lease in 1771 and he must havy stayed in England until he lost his suit. In late spring 1774, he came back in a ship commanded by a Captain Hall. He put his mills back in order and then found himself in the same position as his one-time adversary, Wentworth, on the wrong side of a political issue. Livius was proscribed in 1778 and his property confiscated. His loss rankled him and he wangled an appointment in Montreal. It was from there that he wrote a series of letters to General John Sullivan that nearly ruined that worthy's Continental Army career. How far Sullivan went into the spirit of the proposals is a point still being argued by historians and biographers, but he probably was at most indiscreet. Livius died in England in 1795 at the age of 68.

[84]. George Meserve, locally born and brought up,

was one of the many who felt a greater loyalty to the Crown than to the colonial cause. It might have been the years he spent in England that brought it about. Certainly, he came back as Stamp agent with definite ideas as to omnipotence of royal power. His disappointment over loss of the Stamp agency was keen and when the Council turned down his bid for recompense he apparently returned to England. From that trip he returned on March 11, 1768, coming by the way of St. Christopher's. No doubt, repeal of the Stamp Act made it impossible for him to get any redress in England either. Meserve had left London the previous fall but contrary winds kept his vessel from making port and it went on to the West Indies.

So, with Captain John Cochran, he took passage in the first northbound vessel available, that of Captain William Fernald. In the number of his ocean crossings, Meserve must have been like the "International Set" of our time. We have another Gazette note in May of 1770 that Captain Thomas Hart has brought in the ship Ward in eight weeks from London and that George Boyd of Portsmouth and George Meserve, collector for the Port of Boston, were on board. That was the same vessel that brought a doctorate for the Reverend Samuel Haven. Boyd carried the news that Robert Hallowell had been named collector of the Port of Portsmouth. However, Meserve and Hallowell were allowed to exchange posts and Meserve became collector here. The post had been held by John Hughes of Philadelphia who had succeeded James Nevin in 1769.

The job might have been lucrative, but it could no more endear Meserve to the local populace than had the Stamp agency. Seaport people the world over, today and yesterday, regard customs officials as enemies, and George Meserve had long since lost any love Portsmouth might have had for him. When the troubles with England started, life here became untenable. In fact, on November 22, 1775, the Committee of Safety considered issuance of an order that would forbid Meserve from going to Boston. The records are not clear whether he managed to get away then or not. In 1778, he went on the proscribed list and as far as can be determined never returned here. Meserve, who had married the daughter of John Newmarch, lived in the house which used to have the Roma Cafe in its downstairs area. Meserve had a son, George, and two daughters: one, Sarah, married James Sheafe who was to become a U. S. Senator, and Ester, who died May 1, 1799, at the age of 37. Among those who lived in this old house at School and Vaughan Streets, were Daniel Webster and Jeremiah Mason, two of the greatest lawyers New Hampshire ever produced. James Sheafe, like his father-in-law, was a loyalist but did not leave the country, and years later won election to both the U. S. Senate and the House.

[85]. The Parade was a name that covered the wide expanse of street in front of the former Post Office and then later, after the removal of the old State House from the throat of Congress Street, to the whole of Market Square. The name was officially dropped in 1839, but persisted in usage long afterward.

[86]. Debtors had short shrift in colonial times and the custom prevailed of not only taking their property but also putting them in jail until their debts were paid. Portsmouth Gaol usually numbered far more debtors than criminals in its population. The irony of it was that a jailed man could not work off his debt and yet he could not get out until he paid.

In this connection, poor old Sam Bathrick will serve as well as any as an example of what could happen to a guy who got in over his head in those unenlightened days. Sam married Ann Wyman on May 4, 1739, when he was 34 years old. Six years later, without installments to pay on a house, car, TV, stereo or his kids' buck teeth, he was in the Chestnut Street jail for debt. And Sam had been there a while because a petition on his behalf on July 6, 1745, set forth that "he had been of a long time in Prison for Debt & has been for the Greater part of the time be Supported there by Charity having nothing whereby he can either discharge his debts or Support himself in Prison & his Creditors Refusing to Consent to his Enlargement (on any terms he can comply with) and allow any thing toward his Support he has been and still is in a suffering Condition & thereupon Prays that something might be done for his Relief".

This petition, of course, lays bare the stupidity of the whole concept of throwing people in "goal" for debt. If they could not pay before they went in, how could they pay once put beyond the reach of earning money? Apparently the General Assembly was beginning to get some glimmerings of this when it concocted a scheme that would spring Sam Bathrick, and yet hold him liable for his debts. First the legislators decreed that Sam's creditors had to come up with five shillings a week for his support in the Chestnut Street Bastile while he was kept there at their pleasure. If they failed to provide this, then Sam could go free — to enter His Majesty's service at Fort William and Mary. Today's military recruiters, when they are short their quotas for a month, would like to have that kind of leverage.

The General Court, did not overlook the fact that Bathrick's creditors also had rights. It was carefully provided that one half of his meager pay as a soldier (25 shillings a month) in George II's uniform would go toward satisfying the liens upon him. History's dusty pages simply do not tell what choice Bathrick made, but most people, held in a foul, 18th Century jail, would figure that Fort William and Mary, bad though the quarters might have been, was heaven in comparison.

[87]. The jail at present-day Chestnut and Porter Streets was built in the late 1750s. It succeeded a log structure that had been put up on the Glebe Land, west of the North Church, in 1699. Construction of a new "goal" had become a necessity by 1754; men were able to escape the old jail almost at will. The climax came on March 21 when a mob assembled outside the jail and with their trusty axes hacked out the door to let two men, Anthony Bowen and John Morrel, flee. The two were held for the murder of two Indians at Contoocook, a non-criminal offense in the eyes of most English settlers. The Governor and Council did not offer a reward for the detection of any in the mob because "such a number of persons as were supposed to be the authors of the rescous must be many of them known". They did offer 200 pounds for Bowen and Morrel. However, the records do not show that any were brought to book for the crime.

In fact, one account to be found in the Farmer's Monthly Visitor for September 1853, reports that Bowen and Morrel were openly going about their business in the Canterbury area within a month and were never bothered again by the authorities. Governor Benning Wentworth made presents to the relatives of the two Indians, Sabatis and Plausawa, and that was that, despite evidence that Bowen had loaded the two with rum to rob them of their fur catch and then killed them. If it's any consolation to Plausawa's spirit a golf course in his old hunting ground had been named for him.

Even before the well-engineered escape of Bowen and Morrel, a committee had reported the deterioration of the jail. In April of 1754, Peter Gilman of Exeter and Matthew Livermore of Portsmouth had been named by the Assembly to serve with anyone designated by the Council as a committee to look into improvements or the building of a new jail. Again in December of that year, the Assembly took formal recognition of the jail situation and then named the same two men as a committee for the construction of a new one.

Governor Wentworth sent a message to the Assembly that he had appointed two experts on timber to study the jail, because he had learned it was fit for neither criminals nor debtors. Sheriff Thomas Packer brought the matter to the attention of the Assembly, which once again named a committee — Jonathan Lovewell of Dunstable and Richard Jenness of Rye, and voted that funds be taken from a 25,000-pound credit floated by the province. A week later the Assembly formally voted that a new jail be built and that Eleazer Russell "be a Committee of this house to joyn with such as may be appointed by the Honble Council to look out a suitable piece of ground to be build a gaol upon". That same vote was taken again in January 1756.

In December of that year, Thomas Packer again appeared before the Assembly and asked that something be done. The Assembly took note that their vote of January 1756 was not assented to by the governor and again put Eleazer Russell on a committee to meet with the Council. In December of 1757 the Assembly took the same vote and in May 1758, the Assembly repeated its vote, but put Peter Gilman on the committee and decided to build where the old Gaol stood. Finally in May 1759, more than five years after the escape of Bowen and Morrel, the Assembly put Clement March and Peter Gilman on a committee to build a "Gaol". It was assented to by the Governor and was to be built on the site of the old, yet it was not and we do not know why. One thing the above does show is that it took as long, if not longer, to get business done in the old days as it does today. Nor were the troubles of the jail, or Prison as it came to be called, yet over. In 1764, at the request of the governor, it was voted to post an armed guard at the Prison because of "an intent of some ill-disposed persons inhabitants of Kingstown (Kingston) Sandown & parts adjacent to make a breach in the gaol & liberate the prisoners".

Then in 1756, although the vote for a prison six years earlier had stipulated that a well be dug, it was found that one had not been put in and the prisoners were suffering from a lack of water. Jacob Sheafe was given the contract for that at a price of 14 pounds. The Prison apparently kept prisoners confined little better than its predecessor because an Assembly committee found that "sundry breaches (escapes) have been lately made in the Province Gaol which are necessary to be Repaired".

Jacob Sheafe and Sheriff Packer were allowed 119 pounds for the repair work. The repair work did not do much good because in 1766 the province found it necessary to appoint Jacob Sheafe and Richard Jenness a committee to protect its interest in suits being brought against the sheriff for the escape of debtors from the Prison; under the law the sheriff was responsible to the creditors for the safeholding of any debtor put in his charge. The Prison stood where the Portsmouth Savings Bank parking lot now is and provided the town with plenty of excitement at noon on March 15, 1781, when it, along with the mansion of Woodbury Langdon, the house and barn of Nathaniel Treadwell were all burned flat. The little handtubs, by working men in relays because of the heat, managed to save the stately Joseph Whipple House from destruction. A few months later a new jail was built on Islington Street, near the present Knights of Columbus building, and was in service until the new County Jail (the Portsmouth Police Station) on Penhallow Street was opened in 1891. The Whipple House was moved in 1969 to Middle Street, at Park.

[88]. In 1731 the town gave permission to a group of citizens to install a bridge across Puddle Dock with the stipulation that it had to permit the passage of vessels in and out of the cove. Construction of the bridge permitted full extension of the street we now know as Marcy, but which was called Water until a few years ago. Swing Bridge was one of two bridges put across Puddle Dock. At the west end of the cove, on the route of Washington Street, Canoe Bridge was put in. Both of these disappeared when the city filled in Puddle Dock in the late 1890s, closing up one of the most horrendous stinkholes the town had ever known. Swing Bridge became Liberty Bridge on January 9, 1766, when a flagpole was put up to celebrate protest of the Stamp Act. The pole we see today, is maintained by the Liberty Pole Association — first organized July 4, 1912 — and the late Garland W. Patch, Sr., was unofficial custodian for many years. The original pole came down in 1824 and a new one was erected, then another in 1899. Ceremonies were held June 15, 1958, for rededication of the pole. New halyards were strung by Fireman John W. Connors. Officers of the association at the time were Mrs. Marston Fenwick, president; Richard A. Pinkham, secretary-treasurer; Garland W. Patch, Sr.; Thomas H. Berriman and Donald E. Vaughan, trustees.

[89]. Early historians, perhaps because of civic pride, did not see fit to mention it, but this mob went out of control, as most mobs do. We find in the Province Papers a petition from Nathaniel Barrell, Benjamin Hart and four others charging that on "the 1st of November last a number of People were assembled together in a Riotuous manner in the Town of Portsmouth in profess'd design to oppose the Stamp Act taking place, & in a riotuous manner did damage, break & spoil a house built at our expense for the purpose of Worshipping God &c. & Praying redress". What meetinghouse was so damaged is not clear and it is not certain that the General Court ever did anything about it.

[90]. Windmill Hill, which was later to be the site of the mansion of the famed Jerimiah Mason, is now adorned by two churches, the Immaculate Conception — on the site of the first Catholic Church in the city — and the Advent Christian, which utilizes the old Mason house as a parish building.

[91]. Benning Wentworth informed the General Court of the change in administrations by formal message on November 6, 1766: "It having been His Majesty's pleasure to appoint John Wentworth, Esq., to succeed me in the Government, who, I presume may be expected some time in this month, for this reason I thought it necessary to meet you in General Assembly at this Juncture, that you might have an opportunity to provide for his reception, which I flatter myself you will cheerfully engage in". The House sent back a lengthy message to thank Wentworth for his services to the Province and assure him that a reception for his successor was being planned, and concluded: "We have only to add, That we sincerely wish your Excellency all the Ease arising from Retirement from Business and the Pleasure Resulting from a Virtuous, Quiet Life".

8

War Breaks Out

[1]. Wesley Powell, although now a resident of Hampton Falls, is a native of Portsmouth, the son of Mary and Samuel Powell. Educated at Portsmouth High School, the University of New Hampshire and Southern Methodist, Powell is a lawyer by profession, and is currently associated with the firm of Flynn, Powell, McGuirk and Blanchard on Court Street. The offices of the firm are in the old Folsom-Salter House which was moved from its original site at the foot of Chestnut Street, on Court, by Judge Thomas E. Flynn, and West along Court Street to a new site on the north side of the street. The house is noteworthy if only because it once sheltered President James Monroe.

Former Governor Powell made his first attempt for public office in 1950, running against the incumbent U. S. Senator Charles W. Tobey of Temple in the Republican primary. He lost, but made another attempt for the seat after Tobey's death in 1953. In 1956 he was defeated in a bid for the governorship by Lane Dwinell but was nominated and elected in 1958. Re-elected in 1960, he was defeated in 1962 when he tried for an unprecedented third term against John Pillsbury of Manchester. Powell came out for the Democratic candidate John W. King, the ultimate winner, who became the first of his party to hold the post in 40 years.

Before his political campaigns, Powell had served as administrative aide to the late Styles Bridges. Powell named his close friend and aide Maurice J. Murphy, a native of Dover but now a resident of Portsmouth, to fill out Bridges' term. Judge Flynn is a graduate of Portsmouth High School, the University of New Hampshire and Boston University Law School. He has been a close associate of Powell's for many years and was named to the local Municipal Court by him in 1961, and retained the post when it became a District Court. Judge Flynn initiated the wearing of robes by municipal and district court judges in this state. Associated with them are Russell McGuirk and Raymond P. Blanchard. Ex-Senator Murphy now is engaged in the practice of law here in partnership with Judge Gerald Giles of Rye. Mrs. Murphy is the former Marilyn Stocklan of Dover whose father, Louis Stocklan, owns Portsmouth Hardware on Congress Street. They live at 660 Middle Street, the former home of G. Ralph Laighton, who was at one time president of the Portsmouth Savings Bank and also president of the National Mechanics and Traders Bank at 1 Congress Street. Besides Laighton, officials of this now defunct bank were Charles F. Shillaber, cashier; Jackson M. Washburn, teller; John C. Batchelder, bookkeeper; Russell D. Badger, clerk. Laighton's "other bank" had Harry E. Boynton as treasurer; Joseph W. Peirce, D. F. Borthwick, Gustave Peyser, Moses A. Safford and William E. Marvin as trustees. And today Maurice J. Murphy is, himself, a trustee of Portsmouth Savings.

[2]]. Although Benning Wentworth told the General Court in November, 1766 that he expected the new governor within the next month, it was not until June 13, 1767, that John Wentworth ended his long progress through the country and arrived in his own domain.

[3]. The century-long dispute with Massachusetts over the boundary between the two provinces had been settled August 1, 1740, by the King in Council. That was when the southern bound was illogically set at three miles north of the Merrimack River, but extension of the line west to the Connecticut, and beyond, did give the province control of many of the new inland towns that had been springing up under Massachusetts sponsorship.

[4]]. On the site of the present City Hall.

[5]. This was not a new "fringe benefit" for the Governor. Benning Wentworth had been allowed money for house rent in lieu of the province providing a mansion. New Hampshire long failed to provide a mansion for its governors, and they no longer draw any house rent, having to get by on the small salary paid them.

[6]. The Wentworth Home was founded in 1911, the house the gift of Miss Susan J. Wentworth. Much improved over the past half century to fulfill its new function, the Home has an average patient load of 50. Wyman P. Boynton is president, as he has been for a dozen years or more. Vice presidents are Harlan Goodwin and Frank E. Brooks. The treasurer, since 1926, is Charles H. Walker, and he is only the second since the founding; the first was Harry E. Boynton, The clerk is Richard Winslow, and the trustees are the Reverend Jonn N. Feaster, D. D.; Bradford M. Kingman, retired president of Portsmouth Trust; Ralph C. Margeson, Orman R. Paul and Robert M. Simpson.

[7]. When it came to street improvements colonial Portsmouth was no different from the city we know in the 20th Century: Where to get the money for all the projects people wanted

carried out? One way Portsmouth thought of was a lottery. On July 11, 1766, the General Court granted a Portsmouth petition for a hearing on a lottery to improve the local streets. The bill was eventually passed, but there is doubt that the lottery was ever conducted, based on the simple fact that it was never advertised in the Gazette, and that would have been the means of promoting ticket slaes. Why it was not conducted can be seen in the experience of another lottery which was intended to finance the construction of a pier at the Isles of Shoals. Approval of this was sought at the same time and granted, but a year later the managers had to ask for permission to cancel their lottery. They said "by the reason of the scarcity of money there are but few of the said Tickets sold, and they have no prospect of the sale of the Tickets sufficient to carry the Design of the act into Execution". This lottery had George King for one of its managers, the man who, after the death of his son, became the heir to Theodore Atkinson's estate. So the backing was reasonably substantial and yet the lottery did not succeed. The Portsmouth promoters knew this and probably became cautious.

[8]. The old schoolhouse sheltered its last classes in 1935-36, but more on this later.

[9]. Taxation was their primary concern. Here they did not like the tax on sugar products, not that it was new, but just the government decided to enforce it.

[10]. Portsmouth merchants then, and now, had their own ideas about ethical procedures. They could resent the intrusion of a couple of sharpies from Boston, and at the same time be quite upset when local citizens protested to the General Court against some of the merchants' practices in a petition brought by William Shackford and 123 others. The merchants apparently were buying country produce at low prices and retailing at high markups. Their protest brought about the first Merchant Association, long-dead ancestor of our Downtown Associates, an affiliate of the Chamber of Commerce.

[11]. John and James McMasters were here only a short time, although on May 11, 1775, James signed a recantation of all the nasty views he had broadcast on the patriotic movement, which were but natural in a man who had left Boston in order to sell goods. He pledged, "I will risk my life and interest in defense of the constitutional privileges of this Continent". What happened to John is not clear from anything in the records, but James was still around in 1777 when he was given a pass to go to the Kennebec River on business. However, both made the proscribed list in 1778.

[12]. A deep community of feeling apparently existed in earlier days between all the towns of the Country. When one was hit by fire, the others would pitch in with big subscriptions to help the sufferers. In May 1774, the Committee of Safety here sent a message to Boston: "We think the late act of Parliament to shut up the Port of Boston of the most extraordinary nature, and fatal tendency.... We sincerely wish you resolution and prosperity in the common cause...."

[13]. In September 1773, Governor Wentworth was granted a doctorate of laws by the college.

[14]. James Nevin was collector of the port here for nearly 10 years. He was admitted to the Governor's Council April 16, 1759. He disturbed the peace of the smuggling merchants but little, somewhat surprising when it is realized that he was a retired captain in the Royal Navy.

[15]. It is hoped that Samuel Cutt was not typical of Portsmouth merchants of the period. From the Rambler is derived the following unpretty tale of a man's single-minded pursuit of profit that cost another his life in a slow and tortuous death, and drove a second out of his mind over the circumstances. Cutt fitted out a vessel for a trading voyage and put Captain Thomas Leigh in command. William Bennett, a young neighbor of Cutt, whose home was at the corner of High and School Streets, went as first mate. Their passage was supposed to be from here to the West Indies and then into the Mediterranean (entirely illegal under the Navigation Act). They were captured by the Algerians and held for ransom on some flimsy excuse.

Money to pay the tribute would be months in coming and the Algerians offered Captain Leigh the alternative of leaving two men behind as hostages. Bennett and another man agreed to stay, even though they knew the conditions were that they would be allowed certain freedoms only until a reasonable time passed for the ransom to be paid. If the ransom was not forthcoming, they were to be closely jailed for a month, and then cut off without food, to starve to death. Mills (we do not know his first name) could have been a son to Captain Luke Mills, who has been mentioned previously. With the agreement understood by both sides, Leigh sailed for home. On arrival he told Cutt what he had done and received assurances that the matter would be promptly seen to. Months went by but Cutt still stalled.

Bennett's parents put up a note after note in the pulpit (it was the custom of the time when special prayers were wanted to "put up a note", that is, hand the minister a request for the prayers) Cutt did nothing. When the return date passed, Leigh's anger knew no bounds. Mills managed to escape, but Bennettt stayed and died of starvation. Leigh's melancholia over the episode deepened as the years went by, although he was able to sign the Association Test in 1776. He finally went insane and was confined to the Alms House where he stayed the remaining 20 years of his life, dying there Christmas Eve, 1815. Cutt's prosperity continued and he was fervent in the patriotic cause during the Revoultion, which gives cause to hope there is retribution in the Hereafter, if there is one.

[16]. Until 1771, mariners approaching Portsmouth Harbor at night did so more by feel and guesswork than anything else. No welcoming beams from Whaleback or Fort Point lights greeted them. Keating was but one of the many Portsmouth captains who fetched up on the rocks guarding the mouth of the Piscataqua River. The need for some safety device was known for a long time but not until June 18, 1765, did anyone take steps in the matter. A petition, unfortunately lost, went to the General Court, and the next day the signers were given permission to survey the coast up from Odiorne's Point to find a suitable place for the light. Eight men, John Sherburne, Jonathan Warner, Daniel Rindge, Samuel Cutt, Thomas Wentworth, Gregory Prescott, Titus Salter and George Janverin, were delegated the task of finding a site. Here, too, the legislative process was slow.

Not until April 12, 1771, did the General Court decide that "whereas losses frequently happen of Lives and property's of Persons, Arriving and being put upon the Sea coast of this Province in the Night time for want of a proper Light for their direction, and it is thought that large and Suitable Lanthorn to be Lighted and kept upon the Top of the Mast that supports the flagstaff at the fort might be a means of Preserving the lives & property's of many Persons". The fort commander, at this time Captain John Cochran, was charged with the responsibility for the lantern. A schedule of fees, chargeable to vessels entering the harbor, was set up to defray expenses of the light. Sloops and schooners of more than 30 tons were to pay ninepence each and all other larger vessels one shilling, sixpence. That act was to be in effect three years, but in less than a year the lantern on the flagpole proved impractical and a light house was built before January 11, 1772, when a new act was passed increasing the scheduled fees. Vessels between 30 and 100 tons were expected to pay two shillings; 100 to 200 tons, four shillings; 200 and over, eight shillings. Those under 30 tons but more than 15 were to pay six shillings on first entry, which would cover a year of coming and going. These were high prices when the value of money at the time is considered. The rates were increased again a year later and the keeper of the light, to be appointed by the governor, was to get 24 pounds annually for his services. The light proved a lucrative source of revenue for Noah Parker, a local shopkeeper who apparently kept it supplied with oil. He was allowed six pounds, 15 shillings, ninepence in 1772 for oil used in 1771. Daniel Brewster was the contractor who built the light house, and was paid 372 pounds, 11 shillings, one penny for his work. This Daniel Brewster was the son of a housewright, Samuel, who had died in 1752.

[17]. On the surface, at least, Robert Traill appears to have much the same motive as Peter Livius for being in Portsmouth: Exploitation of trade. He became a powerful figure in the province, married a sister (Mary) of William Whipple, the signer of the Declaration, served on the Governor's Council and as comptroller of the Port of Portsmouth. Traill was here at least as early as 1753, an emigrant from Scotland. In 1766 Traill was granted the privilege of a monopoly for the brewing of a "strong beer" in the province in excess of 25 gallons at a time. This brewery he set up in the general area of the present Hobbs Insurance Agency Building at Court and Fleet Streets in the rear of his house which stood in the southwest corner of Fleet and State Streets. Traill probably disappeared from Portsmouth about the time that Royal rule came to an end. Later he was collector of customs at Bermuda. In 1781, William Traill, his son, came to Portsmouth in a ship bearing a flag of truce and the Committee of Safety ordered its port officer, Captain Ebenezer Dearing, to allow him ashore, "he giving his word and Honor he will not say, do or act any thing against the interest of any of the Thirteen United States of America". His widow died here October 3, 1791, at the age of 61. Their daughter, Mary Traill Spence, widow of Keith, died January 10, 1824, at the age of 69.

[18]. Perhaps the records of St. John's Lodge of Masons might yield a clue. The "Indians" who raided the tea ship in Boston, had just come from a Masonic meeting.

[19]. What the British ministry did was turn the tea trade over to the East India Co. as a concession and the company's ships could bring it here, even paying the tax, at prices far below those charged by merchants such as John Hancock of Boston. Hit in the "pocketbook nerve", the merchants, for the first time, came to see that their best interests were with the "rabble" that had been shouting for liberty.

83

[20]. Edward Parry first showed up here about 1771 as agent for the mast trade. Parry was out for a fast cleanup and made a success of both the mast trade and merchandising. The great value of the towering New Hampshire pines is indicated by an ad he ran in 1772 offereing a three-pound reward for each mast recovered from a log raft that had broken up in the Piscataqua. This Edward Parry left here when the troubles started and should not be confused with the Edward Parry who later built "Fort Anglesea" on the South Mill Pond. A power of attorney on record at Exeter shows that the first Edward Parry represented two London men who were mast commissioners.

Edward Parry is useful to today's student in two ways: (1). As a demonstration and reminder that there are probably still undiscovered things about our local history; and (2). as an example of what happened to Tories here in the Revolution.

Parry has been a mystery to local history students, and particularly in his relationship, if any, to another Edward Parry who came here in 1792. A journal written by Parry, covering the period from March 28, 1775 to his leaving the country in 1777, was sold to an English book dealer. This wound up at the Lilly Library, Indiana University, and James Henry Maguire used it in 1970 as part of the requirement for a doctorate. From this journal of Parry's, the student learns much about Revolutionary Portsmouth that The Rambler and others failed to report.

The man suffered indignities, was mobbed, imprisoned, robbed, confined, and shipped 70 miles inland for safekeeping, all for refusal to renounce his King. The oath that the local Committee of Safety sought to impose was a dreadful pledge with more conditional clauses in it than an insurance policy. This Parry rejected outright. Probably his constant foraying up and down the coast, buying masts and other supplies for the Navy, occasioned his troubles. His innocence of wrongdoing in the matter of the tea consignments was obvious to the more enlightened of local residents, although the mob was highly suspicious of him.

The action that might have caused him as much a problem was joining a group known as the Portsmouth Loyalist Associators in March, 1775. By and large, the intent of these men was to protect themselves — through mutual aid — from mob action, and apparently there was good cause to fear such things in Portsmouth. Parry himself was robbed of hundreds of pounds worth of logs and masts as they rested in the waters of The Pool awaiting shipment. These were rafted upriver and hidden. He was arrested in places like

Pownalborough, Maine, and interrogated. Finally, it was decreed that he had to be removed from the coastal areas, so he was taken to Sturbridge, Massachusetts, and there held in more or less close confinement. He was later allowed to return to Portsmouth.

In May, 1777, Parry noted: "During the past three months there have been several mobs in Portsmouth and several persons confined and abused by the rioters. Hitherto, I escaped unmolested, by being Cautious, by keeping at home and employing my time in reading etc. although some persons seemed desirous of pointing me out. Frequently they dig(g)erified the walls of the house with chalked inscriptions of 'TORY HALL' and sometimes 'HOLE' in capitals and other words of similar import such as 'DAMNED TORY' etc. etc. These were frequently rubbed out by the servants and as speedily replaced again by the busy incendiaries. — I thought I could not escape always." He was right. On May 15 the Town Committee sent word to Parry that it wanted him to appear at Union Hall. Parry said the message was delivered by Constable Clement March, but Parry was out, and returned so late that he decided not to appear that day. The next morning he was again summoned and told that he would have to take the oath mentioned above. Parry declined and asked the consequences of his refusal. George Gains, one of the committee, told him that it would mean imprisonment in the "Town Gaol", that there were several others in his predicament and it was suggested that he think it over until morning, staying in his house. Those on the list included Peter Pearse, John Pierce, William Torry, Isaac Rindge, James Sheafe, William Hart, John Stavers, Oliver Whipple and himself.

Parry goes on to say that the afternoon of the day of his appearance before the Town Committee, he met John Langdon on the Parade, and Langdon asked him if he wanted to return to England. Parry left no doubt in Langdon's mind that he did, and Langdon made him a proposal that he go to Halifax, more or less in exchange for Langdon's sister, Abigail, the widow of a Dr. Goldthwaite. Parry told Langdon of confrontation with the Town Committee and expressed doubt that it would let him go. He quoted Langdon as saying, and the impression is that Langdon was impatient with such business, "They be damned. They have no right to meddle with you as you're already a prisoner on parole — they must prove you broke your parole first. However, go to them tomorrow morning and tell them you have been with me and are desirous of returning to England by the flag I shall send to Halifax. And if they start difficulties send for me and I will give them satisfaction".

With some trepidation, Parry went before the tribunal the next morning. There were threats, recrimination, intimidation to the extent that Oliver Whipple and John Stavers knuckled under and took the oath. Parry notes his regret at seeing the "six gentlemen" confined in the Town Gaol, "and I hope to hear that they continue not long in that unwholesome place. The very stench was enough to poison persons with its infectious quality".

Parry quickly went to Exeter and obtained permission to leave. He wound up his affairs and went to Halifax on the sloop Dove, James Miller, Master. At first he had some difficulty convincing the Nova Scotian authorities that he was not a "plant" by the rebelling colonies, but finally was successful.

He arrived at Spithead on August 17, 1777, and the journal concludes: "The 23rd of August being a Saturday I arrived at Carshalton (Surrey), where I saw the family Carriage driving towards London, I desired my postillion to overtake them, and was surprized that neither Mr. John Durand nor any of the family recollected me being so much altered by the Climates, we drove to Vauxhall Gardens where we spent the evening, in most agreeable contrast between that Elisium and the wilds of America".

[21]. Captain Thomas Brown was in and out of this port many times in the years before the Revolution as commander of various mast ships, but never made his home here. This Brown is easily confused with a Captain John Brown who lived here until his death in 1772. As a captain he survived one shipwreck on Bermuda in 1762.

[22]. Governor John Wentworth, in a letter of July 4, 1774, told the Earl of Dartmouth about the tea incident and outlined his role in it. A few excerpts will show his part: "...Hereupon I took effectual precautions to counteract the universal disquiet of America from contravening the acts of Parliament in this instance, or destroying the property.... The town not suspecting any movement until my return from Dover, about 10 miles off, where I purposely staid during this first operation to secure this event....I came to town and passed on horseback through the concourse who treated me with their usual kindness and respect....In this committee of eleven were many principal gentlemen who I knew detested every idea of violating property...."

[23]. Daniel Rindge occupied a large double house where the building that houses Duncan's Jewelry store and the Warwick Club now stands. From him the Town of Rindge gets its name, being incorporated by Governor Wentworth in 1768. Rindge

was admitted to the Governor's Council in 1766 and served until the Revolution brought about its end. He was a merchant by occupation and in his countinghouse were trained, among others, John Pierce and Captain John Langdon, who followed the sea for some years before becoming interested in shore-based pursuits. All three of his grandsons adopted, by legislative act, the name Rindge as part of their Christian names. They were Daniel Rindge Rogers, Thomas Rindge Rogers and Nathaniel Rindge Rogers. Rindge did not sign the Association Test in 1776 and his brother, Isaac, was one of a group of Portsmouth men who had to appear before the provincial Committee of Safety to explain their antagonism to patriotic causes. Isaac had to move 15 miles inland from Portsmouth. Daniel apparently left the province for a time, perhaps in company with Governor Wentworth, but in May 1778, Isaac Rindge and Captain Peter Coues, were given permission to bring home from Connecticut any of their baggage that might have been brought there from Long Island. He was never proscribed.

[24]. John Parker succeeded Thomas Packer as sheriff in 1770. He became the first sheriff of Rockingham County when the province was divided into five counties. John Parker was a son of William Parker and the grandson of a William Parker who had figured in one of the romantic stories of early Portsmouth. This first William Parker in Portsmouth, legend has it, married Zerviah Stanley, a daughter of the Earl of Derby, although she was considerably above him in social station. Their son, William, was apprenticed to his father's trade, but studied law until he was admitted to the bar in 1732. William Parker held various offices under the royal government but took the Association Test. He died in 1781 at 77. John was his third child, second son. One of the daughters, Elizabeth, married Capt. Nathaniel Adams, and became the mother of the "Annalist". John Parker never married, dying October 4, 1791. Although beholden to Governor Wentworth for his job as sheriff, Parker ironically became the man who read the Declaration of Independence from the balcony of the old State House. Parker had even accompanied the Governor on July 6, 1774, into this same State House when Wentworth ordered a meeting there to dissolve the General Court. Those present had met to elect representatives to the Continental Congress. Wentworth naturally saw this act as an attempt to wrest away some of the King's rights.

[25]. For years some writers have persisted in believing that Captain John Cochran's title was derived from the army, although he actually was a sea captain. Port records show him taking

out the sloop Bon Adventure during the 1760s on voyages to the West Indies. At other times he took ships to England and then came back as a passenger in mast ships. (See Note 51, Chapter VII). In 1771, Governor Wentworth appointed him commander of Fort William and Mary, which must have been a restful post after life at sea. John Cochran took his duties seriously, adding his voice to those who wanted fort improvements, a frequent topic for legislative consideration throughout colonial times. As was the custom, Cochran made his home at the fort and in June 1771 entertained the Masons at dinner in the fort to mark the Festival of St. John. His urgent need much of the time was to obtain men for service in the fort. The March 6, 1772, edition of the Gazette carried an "ad" by him for garrison troops. Recruits were offered three dollars a month, one suit of regimentals yearly and five shillings each week for billeting money. When the blowup came, Cochran remained loyal to Governor Wentworth and the Crown. He was host to the Governor when the latter fled his home in Portsmouth and Cochran left New Hampshire for good when Wentworth did, eventually going to Halifax. His wife, Sarah, was allowed to leave for Long Island in 1778.

[26]. John Newmarch was a prosperous citizen here in the years before the Revolution. Around 1740, he bought the lumber of the old Meetinghouse below the Mill Dam and had it fabricated into a house, located approximately 100 feet east of the northeast corner of Fleet and Congress Streets. Next door to him, his son-in-law, a man named Paul March, put up a house that became the Bell Tavern. March's house was framed by his half-brother, a mulatto, Hopestill Caswell by name. March, in conjunction with Newmarch, was an importer of rum, molasses and sugar. Another of Newmarch's daughters married a Richard Billings and they lived in the house to which John Hancock came as a visitor. Billings' wife, Hannah Newmarch, died in 1781, at the age of 45. His second wife, Mary, died in 1815 at 78 and Billings himself, listed as a soldier of the Revolution, died December 19, 1808.

[27]. Samuel Penhallow was typical of the quiet, substantial citizen who seldom appears in the public eye and yet wields great influence with his fellows. His old home stood at the southeast corner of Court and Pleasant Streets. Penhallow kept a shop in part of the house and conducted his court in still another room. It was here the great lawyer Jeremiah Mason came for trial. He was accused of flogging another lawyer, John Wentworth, because of stories Wentworth spread about him. Wentworth's friends gathered outside

the house ready to execute mob vengeance on Mason, but, by the intervention of Captain Thomas Manning, Mason managed to escape to the Greenleaf house which stood on the site of the present Elks Home. Penhallow dispensed the law as he saw it and his activities as clerk of the Portsmouth Social Library indicate his interest in books. But no matter how important his place in the community, it did not deter thieves from stealing 160 pounds out of his house in 1774. Penhallow had kept the money in two bags, one made out of ozna-brigs and the other of white stocking thread. When the Revolution came, Penhallow followed the popular cause and was one of the commissioners appointed in 1777 to take the oaths of civil officers, as to their loyalty to province and country. He was also named postmaster to replace Eleazer Russell. Once a large family here, the Penhallows have disappeared from our ken, leaving only the name of Penhallow Street to tell of their day.

[28]. Colonel John Fenton was another whose loyalties to Governor and King apparently never wavered. We will have more to say about him in later chapters. He was given key county posts when the County of Grafton was established, but still lived in Portsmouth, even serving as representative from Plymouth, although in residence here. Fenton, a retired captain of the British Army, commanded one of the provincial regiments, a post that was stripped from him when it became obvious that his loyalty was to England. From the patriotic point of view he did everything he could to stir up trouble. Still in the records is a letter he wrote to the people of the North Country, urging them to grow all the grain possible because shortages might come. Then, playing on the inland people's old fear of the Indians, he hinted that the Canadians and Indians might attack if the settlers helped their fellow citizens in the southern part of the province, but would not if they were quiet. Asked by the Provincial Congress to explain this letter, Fenton replied that he had no positive information of Indian attack. The Congress decided he was an enemy of the country and ordered him confined. Eventually, because they did not like the expense of keeping him in jail, the Congress turned him over to General Washington and he was allowed to go through to the British lines to return to England — this on the condition that he not take up arms against the American Cause.

[29]. Maine was, until 1820, a district of the Province, later to become the Commonwealth of Massachusetts. So, as today, New Hampshire had no jurisdiction on the Kittery side of the river.

[30]. Daniel Rogers was the apothecary who had his

sons add the name Rindge to their Christian names. Like his father-in-law Daniel Rindge, Daniel Rogers served on the last royal Governor's Council and was suspected of disloyalty to the province. He managed to be in Nottingham when the Association Test was circulated in 1776. A year previously, he had been quizzed on his loyalty but was allowed to go when no specific charges could be brought.

[31]. William Fernald was active in maritime affairs and once operated a packet service to Boston.

[32]. John Langdon was one of the key figures of the Revolutionary period. Born June 25, 1741, his early training was in merchandising and the sea. He captained his own vessel for a number of years and before the Revolution had laid the foundation of a considerable fortune. While he early embraced the patriotic cause, at the same time he would not tolerate mob action, as is shown by his control of the crowd which wanted to smash up the Earl of Halifax tavern. Langdon commanded troops at Bennington and in the Rhode Island campaign. He served in the First Continental Congress, was first president of the state when it formally organized; was the first U. S. Senator and the first man to serve as president pro tempore of that august body. After the Revolution, in 1784, he built the home on Pleasant Street that still bears his name, although it is now owned by the Society for the Preservation of New England Antiquities.

In Langdon's day, it was not considered "degrading" for a man who had served in the U. S. Senate to take a lesser post, and he was elected representative to the General Court, later to the Governorship, a post he held six different times. He was honored by Dartmouth with a doctorate of laws in 1805; and two years later, officiated at the Masonic ceremonies which attended the laying of the cornerstone of St. John's Church. Langdon did not have any sons, although there was a John Langdon, Jr., his nephew, in town. He died September 18, 1819.

[33]. John Sullivan's early story is one familiar to New Hampshire school children. Both he and his brother, James, rose from relatively poor beginnings to become governors of their states, John of New Hampshire and James of Massachusetts. Sullivan came here about 1758 and was employed by Samuel Livermore as a houseboy. Later, in Livermore's absence he undertook to defend a man in Samuel Penhallow's Court and won the case. Livermore helped him with his legal training and on reaching manhood he moved to Durham. Some of his practices there were quite sharp and did nothing to endear him to the public.

Space prohibits full discussion of Sullivan's military career, the success of which is open to question. When he came back to New Hampshire after the war and took up politics, he came into direct opposition with his one-time ally at Fort William and Mary, John Langdon. Sullivan, never quite able to displace Langdon as the state's premier politician, took to the bottle to vent his emotions, and before his death in 1795 was irrational. However, it should be said, to his everlasting credit, that his steadfastness was what brought the rebellion of 1786 to a halt. Disgruntled inlanders, more of a mob than a coherent citizenry, came to Exeter to bend the government of the state to their will. They more than found their match in Sullivan who brought the militia in upon them and broke up the rebellion. Sullivan also should be credited with putting the harbor defenses of Portsmouth in such good shape that no serious attempt was made by British warships to attack the town. To accomplish this, Sullivan had to override the natural procrastination and Toryism of Portsmouth residents and make them do the necessary work.

[34]. These historians believe that the fiery Captain Thomas Pickering was the real leader of the attack at Fort William and Mary. The Rambler tells a tale that puts Pickering at the scene, and as the man who disarmed Cochran. Pickering, who will figure in the story of local activities during the Revolution, accepted Cochran's sword, returned it to him and turned his back. With that, the doughty Cochran took a swipe at him and was then buried beneath a rush of men. A piece of shot, believed from the guns fired at the raiders, has been found in George Pitts' house at New Castle.

[35]. Most writers believe the raid was a night-time affair, but Cochran's letter contradicts this.

[36]. Excerpts from Wentworth's letters: "Yesterday in the afternoon, Paul Revere arrived in this town, express from the committee in Boston...his dispatch to Mr. Samuel Cutt...This day (December 14) before any suspicions could be had of their intentions, about 400 men collected together...This event too plainly proves the imbecility of this government to carry into execution his Majesty's order in Council, for seizing and detaining arms and ammunition imported into this Province, without some strong ships of war in this harbour....The principal persons who took the lead in this enormity are well known...." Governor Wentworth did try to get extra men down to the fort to protect what was left. Colonel Theodore Atkinson, of the 1st Regiment, ordered James Stoodley and John Dennet, captains in the regiment, to get more men. Their report: "Pursuant to the within Warrant we have paraded the streets,

caused the Drums to be beat, & Proclmation to be made at all Public corners & on the Place of Parade, no person appearing to Enlist we wait for further orders". That return was made at 6 p.m. on December 15. No man wanted to get in the way of the fort raiders when they went back for a second time.

[37]. Mark Noble apparently bore Stavers no grudge. A letter over his signature asked the Committee of Safety to let Stavers go free.

[38]. Where St. John's Church now stands.

9

The War for Independence

[1]. Twenty-five of the town's prominent citizens signed a letter, still preserved, in which they told the Governor, "That two vessels laden with Corn, Pork, Flour & other Provisions contracted for by some of the Merchants of this Town for the Supply of the Inhabitants, of which they are in great want, are detained by Scarborough at the mouth of our Harbour — and we are informed are to be sent to Boston the first wind... and beg your Excellency & Honours would Interfere in such a manner as your wisdome shall direct for the liberating of said vessels and Cargoes". Signers were H. Wentworth, Thomas Hart, Pierse Long, Samuel Sherburne, George Hart, Supply Clapp, Henry Sherburne, William Knight, Joshua Wentworth, William Pearne, William Whipple, Jacob Sheafe, Jr., Alexander Morison, George Wentworth, R. Champney, Samuel Penhallow, George Gains, John Penhallow, Elisha Hill and Neal McIntyre.

[2]. This point of land where old Fort Stark still stands in New Castle, at the end of Wild Rose Lane, was first fortified in the earliest days. Historians argue about the name, some contending that it should be 'Jerry's Point". John Albee, who saw this fortification before the Army Engineers built Fort Stark in 1874, described it in his book, "New Castle" as follows: "On this point were probably the oldest defences along the coast. They were of the most primitive construction; six low, semicircular parapets in front of a heavy stone-wall, flanked on the right by a long gully between two ledges, on which were two other, and perhaps more, parapets. Inside was a deep well of good water. They were on the northeasterly side of the promontory, and quite close to the water". Albee also tells of his long and frustrated fight to keep the engineers from leveling the parapets, which were neither in the way nor a source of materials for Fort Stark. They even refused to draw a plan of them for him. On May 31, 1775, Hunking Wentworth informed Matthew Thornton

"that this eight Pieces of cannon were removed from Jerry's Point to this Town & that threats are thereon thrown by the Capt. of the Man-of War that in case he hear of any preparation of Rafts or any other Means being used to annoy him he shall come up with his ship to fire upon the Town....The guns are 6 Twenty-four and two thrity-two Pounders...." Fort Stark, successor to the earlier installation, played a role in the Harbor Defenses of Portsmouth in both the world wars. In the latter, a two-gun battery of 12-inch disappearing rifles was manned by Battery C of the 22nd Coast Artillery and Battery B served a two-gun battery of three-inch barbettes. The Harbor Defense installation in the second war was commanded first by Colonel Harry Pendleton, then Colonel Walter Dunn and finally by Colonel Raymond Watt.

[3]. Many of Wentworth's valuable possessions disappeared at this time. In 1780, Captain Samuel Gilman, trustee for the sale of the Wentworth properties was instructed to "deliver to Mark Hunking Wentworth all the furniture now in his hands at Portsmouth, also the family pictures at Wolfeborough". It's not hard to feel some sympathy for Mark Hunking Wentworth. Too old to tear up his roots in Portsmouth and flee to England, a land he probably had never visited, his was the difficult task of trying to conserve what he could of the family holdings and hope that a fair wind would bring his scattered family back together. In his case the "sins" of the son were visited on the father. The former Governor wrote to him from Flatbush on Long Island, August 3, 1777, to report that Woodbury Langdon, who promised to help get the children of his sister, Mrs. Ann Fisher, out of Portsmouth, had been arrested and restricted to liberty in the City of New York. Wentworth said that what happened to Langdon depended on what happened to a man named Stephen Holland of Londonderry who was high on the provincial list of problem Loyalists. His letter also mentioned that "Mr. (John) Fisher, Mr. (Isaac) Rindge, (Robert) Traill, (George) Boyd, & Thompson were all well 5th to 8th of May last. Captain Cochran and other Gentlemen of New Hampshire are all perfectly well". That letter did the father no good. On September 12, the Committee of Safety decided that Langdon was being held as an exchange for Holland "by the influence of John Wentworth, Esq., late Govr of this State". The committee ordered Sheriff John Parker to take the elder Wentworth's parole "for himself and Family, also the wife and children of John Fisher, Esq., that they do not leave the town of Portsmouth without permit from the Legislative authority of this State...." To this Wentworth agreed on his "Word & Honor".

Holland managed to get away from the jail in Exeter later that year, and Woodbury Langdon apparently was soon back in his native town. M. H. Wentworth never stopped acting in the best interest of his children. He asked permission in 1779 for John Fisher, "now in Great Britain", to return to Portsmouth to live, but it was refused, probably, if for no other reason, because Fisher's property had already been confiscated. Some patriots were nothing if not opportunists.

[4]. Thomas Pickering, he is variously called lieutenant and captain in the records, was a man of action, His exploits against enemy ships in the harbor are detailed in these pages, yet we know little of the man himself. Pickering was of that branch of the family which still owned Pickering's Mills and lived near the dam. His sister was the wife of Samuel Drown. When the Rambler wrote about Pickering's exploit with the barge, a correspondent later embellished on the story, contending that Pickering's fire forced the crew to abandon their craft, that Pickering found it and had it dragged through the streets with himself as teamster. Pickering seems to have been wherever there was anything going on. On October 4, 1777, the Committee of Safety wrote to the Governor of Connecticut to ask that two prisoners they wanted sent to Connecticut be used as an exchange "for one Thomas Pickering a brave young man of this State, commander of a privateer carrying about 16 guns", taken by a British man-of-war and "is now a prisoner at New York". According to the Rambler, Pickering was killed in action when his privateer, Hampden, 20 guns, tangled with a letter of marque (privateer) in March 1779. Certainly Hampden was lost at sea because on October 27, 1779, the Board of War was ordered to deliver to "Mr. Walmsley" of Portsmouth 2 six-pound cannon out of the battery to replace those he had loaned to Hampden. Pickering may have been involved at the time in the grossly mismanaged Penobscot Expedition.

[5]. In the "Annals of Portsmouth", Adams tells of a species of cod caught by the Isles of Shoals Fishermen during December, January and February which was unlike any other. When these catches were cured, they were called dun fish, and were not eaten until the next August, when, after fermentation, the color changed to an earthy hue and the fish could be sold for double the price of any other.

[6]. After the removal of its inhabitants, Gosport still took a century to come to a formal end. Not until 1876 did the New Hampshire Legislature decide to annex it to Rye where the records

of the little island town are now kept. Population figures for the town vary according to the authority consulted. The census made in 1775 shows no return for Gosport, but at the peak, the shoals may have had as many as 300 people, spread across Star and the other New Hampshire islands. Smuttynose and Appledore, two of the bigger ones, are in Maine.

[7]. The Naval Prison first opened its doors in 1907. Despite official frowns, it's known in the service as "The Castle".

[8]. Henderson's Point was a projection into the river that made navigation difficult. Off its tip raged the currents that gave it the name of "Pull 'n Be Damned Point". The point was blasted into rubble in 1905, a story that will be told later.

[9]. Four Tree Island lies to the northwest of Pierce Island, and, despite, its appearance today, once had buildings on it. At one time its reputation for housing women of pleasure was notorious, but after the death of the owner, the property was rented by Daniel Caswell, a lobsterman who lived there with his family and a young helper named Frank Hubley. On March 24, 1907, fire broke out in the house after the Caswells had retired and destroyed the entire property including two of the four big trees from which it took its name. At the time C. E. Gray owned and occupied it, bulkheads were in place all around the island to keep the river from chewing it away as it is doing today. Who lived there in Revolutionary times we do not know, but it was between Four Tree and Pierce Islands that the fire rafts and fireships were assembled. The Committee of Safety's first step was an instruction to William Knight, Joshua Wentworth, Captain William Pearne, Captain Thomas Thompson and Captain Supply Clapp on October 27, 1775, "to take a sufficient number of the meanest vessels you can easily find that will answer the purpose, and fix them in such places and manner above the boom as you shall judge best". The men named reported that they took four vessels, but were soon able to return them to their owners because the fire rafts were ready. These were floated down from Newington where they had been put together over a span of about 10 days. Eighty man days of labor went into the making of the five rafts and an additional 52 days of labor was spent by men and oxen in hauling the materials. Captain William Pearne was another of Portsmouth's merchant-sailors who managed to win a good but precarious living from the sea. In the French and Indian War he was a prisoner nine weeks on an island in the French West Indies; on another voyage he an four men were 20 days on the wreckage of the sloop Sea Flower and kept alive on a half-pint of

water a day. Perhaps younger than Pearne, Captain Supply Clapp was a hardworking seaman. His service in the Revolution appears to have been mainly in land-based capacities, such as commissary. Clapp died March 24, 1811, at the age of 69.

[10]. This pontoon-supported bridge probably went to pieces after the Revolution, and not until the War of 1812 was another built. That War of 1812 span lasted for a while but apparently was gone by 1856 because in March of that year Elbridge G. Pierce was given permission to build a bridge to the island from in front of the Gardner estate for the use of his workmen and suppliers. In 1924, after it bought the island, the City of Portsmouth ripped down whatever was still standing and installed a wooden bridge. Then that, too, was found no longer capable of bearing traffic, particularly the heavy vehicular demands of today, and a new one was constructed in 1958.

Probably this is the time and place to discuss Pierce Island and tell a little of its story which is almost as long as the city's own. What city on the East Coast, or any other coast, would not want such an asset? Pierce Island is really a municipal "jewel" sitting in the mainstream of the Piscataqua River.

Pierce Island was bought by the city in 1923, at the behest of a far-sighted city councilman, Harry E. Boynton, who was so convinced of the propriety of the city buying it, rather than let it fall to developers, that he committed the city to paying $11,000 for it, then had a hard time convincing his fellows of the rightness of his action. He finally did and Portsmouth still owes him a debt.

That purchase by the city marked the first time in 300 years that it had been out of private hands, dating from the original owner, Dr. Renald Fernald, whose progeny still help populate Portsmouth and the entire Seacoast. Fernald was in Portsmouth as early as 1640 because he signed the Glebe Land agreement at that time, and in 1656 he signed an affidavit involving land in the "Mosquito Hall" area of New Castle, indicating that he had been in Piscataqua for 17 years. From him Pierce Island gained its first name, "Doctor's Island". But there is no record to tell how he acquired it, and he was even town clerk for awhile, which would have given him plenty of opportunity to "amend" the minutes. Fernald not only owned Pierce but he also had possession, or got it for his son Thomas, of Puddington's Islands — the site of the Portsmouth Naval Shipyard. He owned Shapleigh's Island and left it to his son, Samuel.

To give a real discourse on the history of Pierce Island would take far more space than available, but the highlights include the transfer, through the female line, to the Waterhouse family, progenitors of the man, Dr. Benjamin Waterhouse, who introduced the kine pox vaccination to this country. This transaction involved a man named Edward Toogood, a bricklayer by trade, who had been the guardian of Sarah Fernald Waterhouse's son (by another marriage) Allen J. Lyde. Unfortunately, Dr. Fernald had another daughter. Sarah had the western (swimming pool half) while Mary had the high land where old Fort Washington still is, or what's left of it.

It was that latter end of Pierce Island that first passed into the hands of the Peirce family, from whom the city acquired it 191 years later. Mary married John Partridge who was in the ferry business to New Castle, and that part of the island was named for him. Joshua Peirce used that time-honored ploy, a mortgage, to get his beach head. Before he was done he had the whole eastern end in his possession, but the family had to wait awhile for the remainder. That part eventually took the name Mendum's Island because a great granddaughter of Sarah Fernald Waterhouse, Frances Lyde, married Nathaniel Mendum. By the time of the Revolution, the western end was known as Janvrin's Island because of a marriage between Elizabeth Mendum and George Janvrin.

During the emergency brought on by the Revolution, the Committee of Safety overrode ownership considerations and went ahead with fortifications, with Captain Ezekiel Worthen of Kensington as chief engineer. But it was General John Sullivan who forced the reluctant populace to throw the first known bridge across to the island from the mainland. Strange things have happened on Pierce Island, but few of them stranger than Sullivan's bridge. For instance, there was the night that the Widow Lyde fought off the attentions of drunken John Harper, an offense for which he was fined. Or the night in 1767 that a 250-ton vessel was blown from its moorings near Liberty Bridge in "as severe a Snow Storm as had been known for many years past....The wind was NNW whereby a ship....taking in her load of oak for Great Britain, lying at the Wharf near the Ferry was drove from thence". Well, if nothing else, it locates the ferry landing near Liberty Bridge.

Sullivan's bridge would not be all that strange to military engineers; it was of the pontoon variety, created by taking "a number of Gundelows", mooring them head and stern, and stringing timbers across them. Sullivan also constructed a boom across to the opposite shore, and anchored fire boats above it.

Troops were mustered to defend the fort, the boom and the bridge. Ten companies of infantry moved in, commanded by

Captains Thomas Berry, Mark Wiggins, Nathaniel Hobbs, Henry Elkins, James Hill, Joseph Clifford, David Copp, Moses Yeaton, Gutting Cielly and Nicholas Rawlings. These were mustered for four months and some men, like an Isaac Pridham or a Thomas Prowse, were stationed on the island throughout the war. There's nothing to indicate that the Committee of Savety ever indemnified John Peirce for its takeover of the eastern, or fort, end of the island, but it did make note that Captain Ebenezer Janvrin had to be compensated for use of his half.

Perhaps payment given Charles Henzell for use of Shapleigh's Island, from which a bridge was also built, will give an idea. Henzell said he was in England when the war came, was unable to get home and had lost the rentals of a warehouse, dwelling and wharf between 1775 and 1783. His agent, Colonel Joshua Wentworth, said the rentals were worth 15 pounds a year, and it was at that rate that Henzell was paid off in 1790.

With unrelenting purpose, John Peirce kept on acquiring parts of Pierce Island; the final plot coming to him from George Long, a Janvrin son-in-law. All that was reserved was 100 square feet, probably a burial plot, but it is not known what little tract the city still does not own on the island. However, Renald Fernald was buried somewhere on his island so it may have been to preserve his rest that the reservation was made.

Daniel Webster, one of American's greatest orators, was the speaker at town meeting in 1813 when the British menace again loomed. Webster's peroration can be found in the Adjutant General's Reports. The thunder of his voice reached crescendo when he urged, "Now I propose that every man who wants these forts repaired, and the Town of Portsmouth defended—appear on the Parade tomorrow morning with pickax, spade and shovel, and that they go these Islands and repair these forts". As mentioned elsewhere, Webster himself, reportedly set an example in this. It may have been the only time in history that a real living congressman caught hold of the business end of a shovel and used it.

They built the fort back to adequacy. Cannon, long stored in the South Street Gun House, were hauled over to Frame Point for testing. One of them blew up, killing Private William Myers outright, and Captain William Vaughan died months later of his injuries. War, of course, ebbed away and in 1816, military gear at Fort Washington was put under the hammer. Who brought the bridge from Pierce to Shapleigh is not known, but a successor was built because it was from there that pictures of the Henderson Point blast were taken in

1905. The original was 130 feet long, three feet wide, with side rails. Also a victim of the auction fever was the bridge from the mainland, which went in bits and pieces.

The shipbuilding and other activities on the island between the War of 1812 and the Civil War are covered elsewhere. The Peirces were left to their island for years until the heirs sold it in 1923. Before World War II, in May of 1941, it was being used as a rest and recreation area for troops. A swimming pool was built by the WPA in the 1930s, and after World War II was put into operative condition by Mayor Mary C. Dondero. Since then, in compliance with the river clean-up program, the city has, over the protests of many conservationists and nature lovers, built a sewage disposal plant on the southeastern end. Old Fort Washington itself continues to disintegrate with the years, although there is occasional talk about restoring parts of it. The lines show clearly, even today, in aerial photographs.

[11]. Many, of course, fled when Governor John Wentworth did, but others stayed on to protect property or because of sheer disbelief that the mighty King of England could be displaced in a system of government. Some eventually fled, but others managed to ride out the stormy days and resume their stations in the community, after the war.

[12]. A case in point is that of George Jaffrey, treasurer of the province under Governor Wentworth and a man of some substance. As soon as Wentworth went out of the province and the government came into the hands of the people, it was decided to get the funds in the treasury away from Jaffrey. A committee went to his house which stood on the high ground in the Penhallow Street parking lot, at the head of Linden Street. No money was forthcoming. That was in June 1775. Later, Theodore Atkinson and Jaffrey surrendered 1,516 pounds, four shillings, eightpence in proclamation money and were given a receipt and the thanks of the Provincial Congress for it.

The Provincial Congress then demanded that Jaffrey come in and explain his accounts as treasurer. Jaffrey apparently stalled for awhile, past two different deadlines and then on October 31, 1775, wrote a letter that shows how men of his class were alarmed by the threat of British bombardment: "I received the vote of Congress requesting me to lay my Treasurer's accounts....had not the alarm of men of war, and other forces coming to destroy this town necessarily prevented — for fear of which calamity I was induced to have my goods pack'd up in order to be removed from the threatened destruction. I began several days later than many of my neighbors, and hastily, before I had engaged a place out of Town, to secure them, and for my Family to retreat, and removed many of my goods out of the Town, which are disposed of in places not secure: That I am necessarily engaged to remove my goods (to a place I am favored with by a gentleman at North Hampton) which are already out of Town in different barns and other places...."

Congress, despite Jaffrey's belief it might understand, took a dim view of his acts and sent the Reverend Elijah Fletcher of Hopkinton, a representative, to tell him so. And the Provincial Congress applied the further sting a few days later of ordering Jaffrey to move 10 miles "at least from Portsmouth". Jaffrey was not singled out alone for this; others on the suspect list were included. Isaac Rindge was told to get 15 miles out of town; William Torry (he had operated a place called the Sugar House for some years where he made lump sugar and refined molasses, which he sold about 1773) was ordered to stay in New Market; William Hart was sent 15 miles out; Nathaniel Rogers was under orders not to leave his own house and farm in New Market and if he moved from there, the location had to be 20 miles from the sea. Jaffrey along with the others was given 20 days to accomplish the removal, but Jaffrey had a powerful friend, John Sullivan, go to bat for him. Sullivan wrote on November 30, 1775: "Since I saw you last I find that George Jaffrey Esq., has assisted much in fixing the works to Defend our Harbour: That being the case I am clearly of the opinion that he ought not in justice be deemed an enemy to his country or treated as such. I therefore consent that he remain at his own house in Portsmouth, if agreeable to you...." Congress found it agreeable to let Jaffrey, Rindge and Hart stay in Portsmouth. Subsequently Rindge did leave the country, but Hart, an instrument maker, lived out his years here, dying January 13, 1812, at 78. Jaffrey lived on here and in 1777 turned over to George King, representing the state, an additional 963 pounds, three shillings, twopence, one farthing.

[13]. Prime came here with his master and served him as pressman for many years, his weekly function being to operate the turnscrew press. He spent so much of his life at the trade that in his late years he was bent at an angle of almost 45 degrees. Slave though he was, Prime was an independent man, and, when, at Mrs. Fowle's funeral, he failed to get in his proper place, Fowle told him to move over. "Go to tudder side ye sef, ye mean jade", he snapped at his master, and Fowle did. Like so many of the Negro slaves here, Prime belonged to their private community, ruled by men like Nero, whose

death was noted in the Gazette, along with that of Pompey, who was described as "governor" of the slave world here. No doubt Nero, Pompey and Prime were each buried in that cemetery along Chestnut Street between Court and State, in which bones are still occasionally found.

[14]. General Gates said, "His Excellency General Washington directs me to acquaint...as the Vessels that were expected to be at Portsmouth, are said to be return'd to Boston. I apprehend they laid aside their design on Portsmouth for the present". Sullivan's departure did shake the Committee of Safety, and in a letter of farewell he gave a report on what had been done and assured the committee that he would get back as soon as he could.

[15]. The New Hampshire Gazette for October 10, 1775, carried the odd note that the subsequent item had been omitted the week before by request: "Yesterday (October 2) morning, the wind blowing strong from the Southward, a ship, which appeared to be a merchantman, was seen off our harbour; Boats were immediately dispatched with a number of men, who boarded her; she proved to be a ship from Bristol, owned by Joseph Glover, Esq., out 11 weeks, commanded by Captain Richard Emms, with 2,000 barrels of flour, consigned to Henry Lloyd, for the use of the ministerial Army at Boston; the ship was brought directly up to the Town, and secured to a Wharf. She had on Board also a small quantity of Beer and Cheese".

[16]. Captain Robert Parker was another who combined the occupations of mariner and shopkeeper. In August of 1775, Parker was on a committee with Titus Salter, George Turner, George Wentworth and George Gains, to inventory the town's artillery. On hand were three 32-pounders; one 24-pounder; nine 4-pounders; three brass, 2-pounder field pieces; one iron, 2-pound field piece; and two howitts (howitzers). That same committee designated the sites later fortified on Pierce Island and at Henderson's Point. Robert Parker also saw service as a master carpenter in the building of the barracks at Pierce Island at a rate of four shillings, sixpence a day. These were the quarters over which Pierse Long later excercised command with the rank of colonel and George Gains was commissary as a major. Parker was put in direct charge of the fire rafts for harbor defense, and on January 9, 1777, he was given permission to take out the ship Portsmouth ("being a private Ship of warr") and to cruise against the enemies of the States of America...."

In his trading days, Parker was in touch with a Frenchman named Begozzat at St. Pierre, Martinique, and it was through that contact that the town and state were able to obtain gunpowder early in 1776. Not that Parker, along with many others, did not have his own troubles with the Committee of Safety. Parker was one of a group of Portsmouth merchants who refused to sell the rum they had in stock to the state for the use of the American Army. These others were Thomas Martin, Neal McIntyre, Mark Hunking Wentworth, Jonathan Warner, Benjamin Austin, George King, Nathaniel Folsom, George Turner, Jacob Treadwell, Ammi Ruhamah Cutter, Robert Furnass, John Hart, III, and Daniel and Samuel Sherburne. Major George Gains tried to induce these people to sell their rum, and on their refusal complained to the committee, which ordered Sheriff John Parker to seize what was needed in specific quantities from each individual.

From Robert Parker, the sheriff took four hogsheads; Daniel and Samuel Sherburne, four; Thomas Martin, three; Nathaniel Folsom, three; Robert Furnass, one; all of which he delivered to Gains. Sheriff Parker said that the following did not have rum in a quantity excess to their own needs: George King, Jonathan Warner, Neal McIntyre, Benjamin Austin, George Turner, Ammi Ruhamah Cutter, Jacob Treadwell and John Hart, III. In political sentiment this was a mixed bag, including Loyalists, patriots and fence-sitters, so the only conclusion we can draw is that the reluctant sellers did not like the price offered.

[17]. John Penhallow was the lesser known brother of Samuel the Magistrate, but served his town well for many years as town clerk. Positions of trust, such as on the Board of War, were held by him. He served two terms on that board, his second election being in 1778, along with Joshua Wentworth and Joseph Gilman. For a living he kept a shop, but we know little about him.

[18]. Stephen Moylan was Commissary General of Musters to the Army and served on the staff of General Washington.

[19]. This Samuel Sherburne was a son of Henry, who had served on the Governor's Council. His brother Edward died of a wound suffered in battle during the Revolution while serving as an aide to General Sullivan. Greatly enriched by being the chief heir to Henry Sherburne, Samuel was able to follow the occupation of a merchant, making one trip to England, 1769, in the same ship that carried Wyseman Clagget and his family. He represented Portsmouth in the General Court many times during the Revolution; his views being substantial enough to warrant his being included on the

103

committee designated to draw up a government for the province in 1776. Sherburne apparently did not remain active in politics after the Revolution and never was elected to office higher than representative. Adams mentions that in December 1804, two barns belonging to Sherburne were destroyed by fire, the work of an arsonist.

[20]. Pierse Long was one of Portsmouth's better contributions to the Revolution, although his early apprenticeship to Robert Traill could have given him a Loyalist bent with equal ease. His father was an Irish emigrant early in the 18th Century, coming here as representative of a merchant in Ireland. The father, also Pierse Long, married into the influential Sheafe family and died a year after his son was born in 1739. Young Pierse had two sisters, one dying young and the other, Mary, died in 1800 unmarried. Besides his service to Traill, Long also followed the sea. As early as 1763, he was sailing out of Portsmouth, master of the ship Isabella. Two years later he had a narrow escape from death when his ship, the Hibernia, piled up on the rocks on Montauk Point, Long Island, while on passage from Antigua to Portsmouth. The ship was lost but no one died. He lived for a time on Water (Marcy) Street and had a shop near Meetinghouse Hill.

Traill's earlier training had little effect on young Long, who was one of the participants in the raid on Fort William and Mary, and from that time forward was in the front rank of the patriots. Portsmouth had chosen him as one of its delegation to the first Provincial Congress, and with the outbreak of war, Long became commander of the first regiment of New Hampshire troops. Garrisoned at Forts Sullivan and Washington, the troops were in provincial service until 1776, when they were discharged, and then re-enlisted in Continental service. Long's outfit was ordered to the Lake Champlain area late in 1776, but in 1777 we find him writing a letter of assurance that he was most willing to make the march but felt that his command was not what many people believed it to be, being at only half strength and that he had a multitude of problems to cope with in the forts at Portsmouth. He speaks of putting his sick into Fort Hancock (New Castle) where they could be adequately cared for. In another letter Pierse Long gives an account of his role in the taking of the schooner George. When he heard a report on the George, Long took a party of men and went down to get her. They found some men already on board, and Long ordered the schooner brought upriver as far as the tide would permit. Long said the 45 prisoners taken were quartered in a public house and that a guard for them was provided by Captain Thomas Thompson of the frigate Raleigh. Long also moved to protect the interests of Captain Richard Pinkham, the man who had brought the George into Portsmouth Harbor and therefore had rights as her captor. Long finally resolved his troubles with the General Court and took his troops to New York where they performed well during the time left in their enlistments. As usual in Revolutionary times, their service period ran out when they were needed most. Burgoyne was on the move down from Canada in June, 1777, but the troops had to be discharged and home they went. However, Long, with some of his staff, went to Saratoga and continued in service until after the capture of Burgoyne. Illness forced him to quit the Army and after his recovery he again took up merchandising. In 1784, he went to the Continental Congress for two years, and then to the Constitutional Convention in 1788. President Washington named him collector of customs here, a post he was prevented from taking by his death April 3, 1789. George Long, prominent merchant and officer of the Portsmouth Aqueduct, was his only son. A daughter, Mary, was the wife of Tobias Lear, Washington's private secretary, and died in Philadelphia in 1795 of yellow fever.

[21]. Raleigh's measurements are known, thanks to the British Admiralty. No local record of them has ever been found, but after her capture by the British, Raleigh was taken to England for refitting and was measured by naval architects. Howard Chapelle in his "History of the American Sailing Navy" says that Raleigh was not precisely the vessel the Congress had in mind when it let out the contracts. For reasons best known to governments through the ages, the design for the Raleigh, as approved by Congress, did not arrive in Newburyport until February 26, 1776, and then took a month or more to get up here. In the meantime, the local builders had decided to go ahead on their own, and the ship was well started when the plan arrived. Chapelle credits William Hackett, cousin to James K. Hackett, as the man who designed the Raleigh. They were in business together at Salisbury, Massachusetts, where William was the master builder and James the business agent. They did do some work at Portsmouth, and William, as a boy, is believed to have seen the building of the America in 1749. Chapelle says that although the cousins did not have the official plans, the dimensions of the Randolph, which was considered the prototype of the class, and the Raleigh are quite close. This is explained perhaps by the fact that William Hackett probably knew in a general way the size of vessel that Congress wanted. The hull lines, however, were different.

Hackett could well have had his information from John Langdon, New Hampshire's delegate to the Continental Congress. The Raleigh was 131.5 feet long on the berth deck; 34 feet, 5 inches, beam; 11 feet, depth of hold; 697 tons; 32 guns. The Raleigh was captured on the ill-starred Penobscot expedition on September 27, 1778, by the ships Experiment, 50, and the Unicorn, 28.

[22]. Controversy has often raged over whether or not Rindge's wharf was also the scene of the building of the Ranger. Historians today are generally agreed that the Ranger was built on Langdon's (Badger's) Island.

[23]. Thomas Thompson will appear again in the narrative, but one anecdote will give some idea of his character. In November, 1774, he was preparing his ship Maria for sea. If the wind was fair, one day was as good as another for sailing as far as Thompson was concerned, and it happened the fair wind blew on Sunday. William Swan, mate of the Maria, was bending some sails on her when one of the town's busy-bodies saw him. When this man, Thomas Hart, moderator of the town meeting, next saw Thompson he told him that he had already reported the matter to Magistrate Samuel Penhallow. Thompson in a subsequent letter to the editor of the Gazette admitted he had cursed Hart "very heartily". Hart filed a complaint, so both Thompson and his mate wound up before Penhallow. Swan was fined one pound, five shiling, fourpence; Thompson, one pound six shillings, threepence.

[24]. The late Richman S. Margeson was one of three brothers who were partners in the present-day Margeson Bros. store, Vaughan Street. He was Portsmouth's second mayor under the Council-Manager form of government, serving 1950-51. Margeson had also served on the first city manager Council, with the title of assistant mayor when Cecil M. Neal was the Council's presiding officer. Also on the first manager Council were the late Mrs. Mary C. Dondero, first woman mayor of the city; the late William J. Linchey, later city marshal; Frank E. Paterson: the late Roland Noyes; the late Judge Thomas H. Simes; and the late Nathan H. Wells.

[25]. Dr. Thayer is only the sixth owner of the Thompson House since it was built. The Margesons now live in New Castle.

[26]. Before Thompson took the Raleigh out for a cruise he was in an argument with the officers commanding the forts because they failed to show colors when she went past the forts. When he asked them, he said, "I was treated with indecent and ungentlemanly expressions, such as I blush'd to hear (Rather hard to

imagine of a man who had been in court for cursing.): I must ask your Honours (Committee of Safety) to make enquiry into this matter.... Colonel (William) Whipple, Colonel (John) Langdon, Major (James K.) Hackett & a number of gentln from the Southward were on board. Messers. John Fernald and Nahum Ward were at the Fort." And there's note that the complaint was directed against Fort Washington. Thompson's letter indicates that the feeling between sailors and soldiers, or Army and Navy, has a long history. Thompson's efforts to get men for the Raleigh were rebuffed by the military when he sought to enlist seamen in the militia companies and by the fact "what most engages seamen's attention is Privateers, not seeing the Wages & other Encouragement given by the Continent far exceeds any other service whatever". The General Court gave him an okay to enlist any man not actually in Continental service. But none of these were problems compared to the dust stirred up over his conduct as commanding officer. Details of the controversy are too involved for this volume, but it should be said that he was relieved of command and never held another in the Navy.

[27]. George Boyd's story would make a play too fantastic even for television. One of Portsmouth's richest and most influential men in pre-Revolutionary days, his success apparently was keyed to the mysterious disappearances of two men. As far as can be determined George Boyd was born in Newington and baptized there on April 23, 1732. The family circumstances were poor and Boyd at an early age was bound out to Henry Sherburne. Not liking his master, young Boyd ran away and did not return here until he attained his majority. A man named Myrick gave him employment in his ropewalk, which was north of Islington Street in the vicinity of Rock Street. Those were good shipping days in Portsmouth and Piscataqua-built vessels had need for rope, so Myrick started to build a house on what is Rock Street. However, only the cellar was ready when Myrick decided to go to England. Whether or not he boarded a vessel bound for England is not known, but he was never seen in Portsmouth again. George Boyd quit the ropemaking business to begin a commercial career that was financed by an abundant but mysterious supply of capital. Still, this did not make him the richest man in town. Another man disappeared before he achieved that.

James McDonough was that man. McDonough came to Portsmouth about 1757 and the next year had improved his lot enough to pay town and province taxes of two pounds sterling. His store on Spring Hill prospered to the point that in 10 years his assessment was 27 pounds. Not only was his business successful but

McDonough was doing well socially. In 1764, he was secretary of St. John's Lodge and by late 1768 was betrothed to Abigail Sheafe, daughter of Jacob Sheafe, one of the town's more affluent citizens.

The wedding day was set, and the appointed time of the nuptials came and went without McDonough making an appearance. What happened to him? That question has never been answered. The bride chose not to mourn him forever, and later married John Pickering, who became in later years chief justice of the Supreme Court. Boyd, by whose approval is unknown, took over administration of McDonough's estate and a year later Benjamin Parker advertised of his attempts. to pay Boyd, as McDonough's attorney, four pounds he owed on a note. Parker said Boyd had charge of McDonough's affairs "when he left the province". It taxes credibility to believe that a man moving up as fast as McDonough would voluntarily leave — on his wedding night at that. But whatever happened, George Boyd by 1770 was by far the town's largest taxpayer, his 67 pounds was above the 30 pounds of Mark H. Wentworth, who was next on the list. And Boyd never looked back.

His prosperity continued; he put his son William into the home James McDonough had intended to occupy with Abigail Sheafe; and bought a splendid mansion for himself near the North Mill Pond. This was the house where Peter Livius had lived, the man who brought to Portsmouth a four-wheeled coach, one of the first seen here, and with it spare wheels, because he doubted the ability of American craftsmen to replace wheels for him. George Raynes, the noted builder of Clippers in the 1850s, later acquired the property, Boyd married Jane Brewster, daughter of Joseph Brewster, a boarding house keeper on Congress Street. The Boyds had 10 children and one of them, Joseph, is mentioned in the will of his grandfather, who died December 4, 1766 at 66. A daughter, Abigail, married a Captain Mackay, then later Captain Samuel Hamm, the man who built the house long familiar to Portsmouth as the Woodbury Mansion, Woodbury Avenue, but which has now gone to make way for a Portsmouth Housing Authority elderly housing project. Submit, the youngest daughter, was born in October, 1774, a few months after her father went to England. He never saw her.

Throughout his years here, Boyd was an enterprising and daring merchant. The retail outlet for his trade was a store near the State House, but the bulk of his wealth was more in the wholesale line. He visited England in 1769 and returned the next year. Some of his ships were built for him at Hampton. One of these was the ship Ann, Captain Robert Hutchins, commander, launched on the 19th of

September, 1772. She was built entirely of white oak and the entertainment after launching was provided by Christopher Toppan. In February, 1774, Boyd advertised his intent to go to England again. While in England on that trip, he was given a seat on the Council. He probably never held the post here, although the Gazette on June 9, 1775, reports that he had been sworn, and in 1777 Governor John Wentworth told his father that Boyd was well, and one gets the impression that Boyd was on Long Island at the time. Why Boyd was sympathetic to the Loyalists is not too hard to understand when it is realized that many men of the merchant class saw war with England as economic suicide.

Boyd, like George Meserve and John Wentworth, had been there and had become convinced that opposition was hopeless. A Gazette note at the time of his departure in 1774 is worth recording: "Last Monday (April 18) sail'd for London ship Felicity, Henry Nutter, commander, Colonel George Boyd, passenger, who perhaps has fixed out more ships, brigs &c in the course of 10 years than was ever before done by any one man in the province in the same space of time--No less than 12 ships, two brigs within a year past---It may be said of him, that he is the most lucky Genius of the present Day in the mercantile Way, though not bred a merchant, & has acquired a handsome fortune. He has gone through life, with a smile, generally laughed at the obstacles that have been thrown in his way--If he met with losses, his Countenance did not discover it, and he has never laid trouble upon interest".

His last known trip home did not come out the way he planned it. Boyd sailed from London in August, 1787, bringing with him a coach and coachman by the name of Charles Harrington. He had sent on ahead an English gardener named John Cunningham. The passage stretched over eight weeks and when the vessel docked here on October 8, 1787, George Boyd was two days dead. The tombstone he had brought with him from England, certainly appropriate to his condition on arrival, can still be seen in the North Cemetery. Several years later, his widow Jane, and Captain Supply Clapp were authorized to bring action against the Weares of Hampton Falls to recover an earlier judgement. Harrington, the coachman, went to work for Woodbury Langdon and Cunningham lived to the age of 94.

[28]. William Whipple was a native of Kittery, born in 1730 and educated in schools there. Like many another Kittery youngster, his formal schooling came to an end when he went to sea, and he became a master before he was old enough to vote. Whipple

became well-to-do in the slave trade, driving his ship on frequent voyages to Africa in a degrading occupation that became known as "blackbirding". When he acquired sufficient wealth in that highly lucrative business, he retired from the sea and became a merchant, with his brother Joseph as a partner. They were advertising their store on Spring Hill in 1763.

William soon began to take an active part in town affairs, and married Catherine Moffatt, daughter of Captain John Moffatt, the man whose name, hyphenated with that of the Ladd family, is still borne by the house on Market Street in which Whipple lived out his life in Portsmouth. Whipple was chosen to represent the province in the Continental Congress of 1775, served on the Committees of Safety for town and state and became a councilor in the state government. He also did his time in the military and was in action at Saratoga. Adams tells the story that Whipple had a Negro slave Prince as a body servant at Saratoga, who, upon being urged to behave bravely in battle, replied that he had no inducement to fight, but if he were free, he would fight to the last drop of his blood. Whipple freed him, then and there. For many years, Prince and his brother Cuffee lived in a house on the grounds of Whipple's home. If Whipple had done nothing else to endear himself to his countrymen, putting his name on the Declaration of Independence would have done it for him. He was sent to Congress in 1778, and in 1782 was named judge on the Supreme Court of Judicature. He served out three years and then suffered a fatal heart attack on November 10, 1785. By his express wish, Dr. Joshua Brackett performed an autopsy that established heart trouble as the cause of death. A desk used by Whipple in his office is in the upstairs library of the Portsmouth Athenaeum.

[29]. John Hancock, whose oversize signature on the Declaration of Independence is familiar to every American, was a frequent visitor to Portsmouth. He not only had business interests in the area, but often called on one of his former clerks, Richard Billings, who lived in a house which stood on the site of the Congress Block, where J.J. Newberry's store in now located.

[30]. Eleazer Russell in a letter to Meshech Weare on August 17, 1776, gives an insight into some of the honest, tortuous doubts that assailed those who were confronted with the Association Test. Excerpts from that letter follow: "On the 4th of May last, Colonel (Hunking) Wentworth of the Committee (of Safety) for the Town of Portsmouth bro't me the Association to subscribe, at a time I was so ill as to be incapable...."

[31]. Few men in colonial America achieved the almost universal fame of Major Robert Rogers. In a way he, too, is symbolic of the agonizing decision many had to make when war with the Mother Country broke out: Loyalty to Britain or to province? Rogers chose the former, but only after becoming highly suspect as a spy during a brief sojourn with the American forces. He turned his hand to counterfeiting and at one time led the Queen's Rangers, a Tory cavalry outfit. After varied adventures he died in France and is buried there, in the capital city of a nation that was the enemy at the time of his greatest exploits.

[32]. Robert Louis Fowle first came to Portsmouth as an assistant to his uncle in the printing business. For a number of years the New Hampshire Gazette carried the imprint of Daniel and Robert Fowle. After his removal to Exeter, he printed a version of the Gazette there and engaged in job printing. After the war he fought bitterly to get back his New Hampshire property but the record is not clear as to his success. He was able to return to Exeter and there married the widow of his brother Zechariah, and died in Brentwood early in 1802.

[33]. Robert Fowle, in printing Rhode Island bills, was merely taking advantage of one of the messier aspects of colonial finances during the Revolution. Each colony had its own plates for printing bills of credit, even before the Revolution, and the outbreak of war only made the counterfeiters' work a little easier in the confused times that followed. Standard banknotes were many years in evolving, and not until the national bank system was created (The First National Bank of Portsmouth was one of the earliest chartered.) did bank bills become of equal value all over the country.

[34]. Daniel Fowle became so exasperated with conditions that he sold the Gazette to Benjamin Dearborn, who brought it out as the New Hampshire Gazette and Freeman's Journal on May 25, 1776. This followed an appearance by Daniel Fowle before the Provincial Congress to explain why he had printed a "letter to the editor" from a writer named Junius who was quite scornful of the idea of independence from England. Fowle took the paper back after a while and was printing it when Robert Fowle ran into counterfeiting trouble. Along with Benjamin Dearborn, Fowle made another trip to Exeter to explain things to the Congress. Apparently he talked himself out of the one, but was right back in trouble when he criticized the Confiscation Act, which applied to nephew Robert. A reprimand was given but he was allowed to continue with the paper and even had printing contracts from the state. For a while he had

Zechariah Fowle, brother of the scapegrace Robert, for a partner, then took in John Melcher. Childless, Fowle let Melcher take over the Gazette in 1784. He died June 8, 1787, at 72.

[35]. Ranger's exact dimensions are not known, although she, like the Raleigh, fell victim to British gunfire. In her case the fire was so effective that she was destroyed in the taking of Charleston, South Carolina. A model, based on well educated guesses as to her lines, is in the John Paul Jones House, home of the Portsmouth Historical Society, next door to the Hotel Rockingham.

[36]. Biographies of Captain John Paul Jones exist in plenty, one of the better being by Samuel Eliot Morison.

[37]. Other Portsmouth men named on the confiscation list were George Meserve, John Cochrane, Benning Wentworth, James McMasters, and John McMasters. Those on the proscription list included Peter Livius, John Fisher, Robert Traill, George Boyd, John Fenton, Samuel Hale, Jr., Edward Parry, Thomas McDonough, Major Robert Rogers, Andrew Pepperrell Sparhawk, alias Andrew Pepperrell, all esquires; Patrick Burn, mariner; John Smith, mariner; William Johnson Rysam, mariner; Stephen Little, physician; Thomas Achincloss, Archibald Achincloss, Robert Robertson, Hugh Henderson, Gillam Butler, George Craigie, all merchants; James Bigby, yeoman; William Pevey, mariner; Benjamin Hart, ropemaker; Bartholomew Stavers, post rider; Philip Bayley, trader; Samuel Holland, esquire; and Jude Kennison, mariner.

[38]. Nathaniel Adams in the form of his"Annals of Portsmouth", left a debt the city can never repay. A chronological account of city history, the "Annals" keeps later writers on the track. Adams was the son of a seafaring man and once occupied a beautiful estate north of Islington Street, where Brooks Motor Sales garage used to be, the grounds extending all the way to Islington Street. A portrait of Nathaniel Adams hangs in the Portsmouth Athenaeum, an organization he helped found in 1817.

[39]. Union Hall was part of the second almshouse, built on the site of the present Central Fire Station. Part of the two-story structure was used by the Selectmen for their meetings and they named one room Union Hall.

[40]. Also destroyed in the fire was the home of Woodbury Langdon, although it is believed that the Langdon Room of the Hotel Rockingham was one of the original rooms of the house and incorporated in the new dwelling Langdon built. The house later became a hotel and to it Frank Jones, Portsmouth's 19th Century tycoon, hauled wood from Barrington as a boy.

[41]. As far as can be determined, only one Portsmouth man was on hand on that day in October 1781, when "The World Turned Upside Down", and a still powerful British army surrendered. He was Thomas Harvey, a Continental soldier throughout the Revolution, who died in 1837 at the age of 84. Colonel Alexander Scammell, for whom the bridge across the Bellamy River is named, was wounded at Yorktown and died a few days before the surrender.

[42]. British intelligence work was so good at the time that an advertisement appeared in a Halifax paper reporting that a privateer, then being built at Portsmouth, would be sold on a certain day in Halifax. Right on schedule, the Hercules sailed, was captured, and was sold in Halifax on the day appointed.

[43]. The Pool is roughly that expanse of water lying between the present road to New Castle and the Wentworth Hotel. Here the mast ships came in to load the tall pine timbers that had been floated down the Piscataqua. Jocelyn makes note of seeing such a huge timber lying on the beach during his visit to Portsmouth in the mid-17th Century.

[44]. Title of New Hampshire's chief executive during the Revolution was president. Meshech Weare held the post for nine years, followed by John Langdon, who was given the title of governor in his second term.

[45]. The Assembly House, once graced by the presence of President Washington, is another old Portsmouth building that no longer stands. Before being leveled it stood in the Vaughan Street urban renewal of Raitts Court, off Vaughan Street. When built by Michael Whidden in 1750, the building was 60 feet long, fronting on the street, 41 feet in depth. Entrance was in the center and the door opened into a hallway 12 feet wide. Upstairs was the Assembly Hall where balls and meetings were held. In 1838 the roof was taken off, the hallway taken out and the south half of the building was moved eight feet in that direction. Reroofing was done at right angles to the street instead of parallel.

10

Return to Peace

[1]. Anyone who doubts the application of Gresham's Law, a monetary theory evolved in the 16th Century, has but to look at the change in his own pocket. Where are the "good" coins dated before 1964? These coins, even with their small silver content, have disappeared in the face of the flood of cheap "sandwich" pieces that now dominate the money marts.

[2]. Theodore Atkinson, Sr., actually died prior to the close of the Revolution, September 22, 1779, at the age of 82, but he was typical of the older men who had served the Province before the Revolution.

[3]. Matthew Livermore, like Atkinson, never knew the outcome of the Revolution, dying in February,1776. He made his mark early in Portsmouth and New Hampshire, becoming attorney general in 1736, 12 years after his arrival here as a school teacher. In May 1753, he collected 80 pounds for his services as attorney general since 1746. His house, now owned by Mr. and Mrs. Ralph Gerth, has been moved several times and is now located on Livermore Street. For many years it was occupied by the family of the prominent attorney, Albert R. Hatch. A notable born in the house was Major General Fitz-John Porter, whose court-martial and dismissal from the Union Army in the Civil War was a long- fought controversy.

[4]. John Parker was a holder of office under royal favor who made the transition without apparent struggle. He was born on November 16, 1732, and acquired a basic grammar school education at the hands of the Reverend Samuel Langdon. From that, he went into the counting house of Nathaniel Sparhawk at Kittery Point, a background which should have given him a Tory slant for life. With the end of his apprenticeship, he went to sea and rose to captain. A business venture with William Rhodes terminated in 1768 when they ran into heavy financial reverses because of the loss of

ships. Governor Wentworth appointed him sheriff to succeed Thomas Packer and he kept right on in the job when the Province became a state. President Washington made him New Hampshire's first federal marshal. He died October 4, 1791.

[5]. John Pickering was a native of Newington, that branch of the family that split away in the 17th Century from the South Mill Dam and farmed along Great Bay. Collateral descendants still live there, including the well-known Pickering triplets. Pickering was educated at Harvard, graduating in 1761. First showing some interest in the ministry, he then read law and opened an office in Greenland after admission to the bar. It was only a short time after that he moved into Portsmouth and became a key figure in local affairs. In 1771 the town elected him its attorney, a post he held for a number of years. The town elected him, along with John Langdon and George Gaines, a delegate to the Second General Court, although Thomas Martin completed his term for him. Such was his high standing that when Phillips Exeter Academy was incorporated on April 3, 1781, he was designated a member of the first Board of Trustees. Pickering also served on the 8th and 9th General Courts, and helped frame the State Constitution in 1783.

After adoption of the Constitution for the state, Pickering served in the first six General Courts held under its terms. While so serving he was chosen a commissioner, along with John Langdon and two others, to represent New Hampshire at the Constitutional Convention in Philadelphia. Nor was he too busy to be a member of a committee to manage a lottery for Dartmouth College, organized in 1784. A grateful Dartmouth later awarded him a doctorate of laws. In 1791, with Langdon and Thomas Martin, he became an incorporator of the New Hampshire Friendly Society which had "formed a fund for friendly, charitable and literary purposes". A year of two later he was one of the incorporators of the Portsmouth Library. He dropped out of the General Court in 1790 when he was named chief justice of the Superior Court of Judicature. In 1795, he gave up that post to become a federal judge. Unhappily, Pickering's last years were clouded by mental troubles, and he had to be removed from office. He died on April 13, 1805, in his 68th year.

[6]. Ira A. Brown, another stormy petrel of local politics, actually once thought (1945) that he had been elected Mayor. A recount showed Mary C. Dondero the winner. He was county commissioner many times. One anecdote about him shouldn't be forgotten and involves the day the late William J. Linchey, deputy sheriff at the time, tricked Brown into entering a cell in the old

County Jail, and locked the gate on him. Brown was kept two or three hours, and it was a little time before he was again on speaking terms with Linchey.

[7]. Other Chief Executives who have visited Portsmouth include John Adams, who had relatives in Newington; James Monroe, who stayed at the old Folsom-Salter House which has been moved to a new site and houses the law offices of Flynn, Powell, McGuirk and Blanchard; James Polk; Ulysses S. Grant; Chester Arthur; Benjamin Harrison, William Howard Taft, Franklin D. Roosevelt and Harry S. Truman. Roosevelt was here in 1932, 1938, 1939, 1940.

Roosevelt's visit in 1939 was prompted by the Squalus tragedy. Truman stayed overnight in the city, aboard his campaign train, on October 15 and 16, 1952 and took one of his famous early morning walks through the streets of the city. Both Herbert C. Hoover and the late John F. Kennedy were here. Kennedy, then a U.S. Senator, stumped the city in March, 1960, in his successful bid for the presidential nomination. He held a press conference in an upstairs room at the Hotel Rockingham, coming here after an appearance at the University of New Hampshire. Like Abraham Lincoln, Dwight D. Eisenhower came no closer than Exeter or Hampton. Lincoln visited Exeter before his election, and Eisenhower came to see his grandson David, a student at Phillips Exeter, both in 1962 and 1963. President Richard Nixon has never been here, but did speak in Hampton prior to the 1968 election.

[8]. Franklin Pierce, 14th president of the United States, was born in Hillsborough, educated at Bowdoin College and came here to read for the bar under Levi Woodbury. During the years he was in Portsmouth, 1824-27, he formed many life-long friendships that stood him in good stead when running for political office. Pierce served in both houses of Congress, and in the Mexican war attained the rank of general. His pro-slavery sentiments while president did not endear him to many of his old colleagues, but they welcomed his coming to Portsmouth after his term expired. There was a sincere hope that he would choose to live in Portsmouth, but in his last years he resided in Concord, dying there October 9, 1869. Pierce was the only President to visit the Isles of Shoals while holding that high office.

[9]. This structure stood on the south end of the Parade, near State Street, and topped a rocky outcropping in the ground. It was put up before the Revolution, built of brick, 10 feet square and one story in height.

[10]. The Rambler, writing years later of his own boyhood, recalled Jonathan Warner as one of the last of the "cocked hats". Warner was born in 1726 in what is known today as the Buckminster House, Islington Street, the son of Daniel Warner. In 1754, he married Mary MacPhedris, daughter of the builder of the house that now bears Warner's name. Warner was on the Governor's Council from June 25, 1766 until the Revolution. When the trouble started he was on the suspect list, and gave bond to the Committee of Safety for his good behavior, but refused to sign the Association Test of 1776. The story is told that he refused to turn over the keys to various storehouses belonging to the government, whereupon a crowd broke in and took the goods away. Warner remarked that he imagined that the marauders would be back the next night, but gave little evidence of any great concern over it. It might be that, because he had taken certain oaths of office, he felt obligated to keep them to the letter and so could not, in his own mind anyway, expouse the patriotic cause. However, judging from his station in life as one of the town's foremost merchants, a royal official, it is more likely his sympathies were with the Tories but never took violent form. Warner prospered in his mercantile pursuits and had his wharf approximately where Memorial Bridge now sits. After the death of his first wife in 1760, he married Mrs. Mary Osborne within a month. His daughter, whose portrait now graces the Warner House, died young. Warner himself died in 1812.

[11]. Contemporary accounts indicate that Washington elected to ride his own horse into Portsmouth and that Lear preceded him in a carriage. The vehicle attracted much attention along the route with Lear bowing in acceptance of the plaudits of the multitude. Lear was a graduate of Harvard College, Class of 1793, and obtained the secretary's post with Washington thanks to General Benjamin Lincoln and the Reverend Samuel Haven. He served Washington until the first President's death in 1799, and was the subject of considerable controversy when some of the general's papers were found to be missing. President Thomas Jefferson made him consul to Santo Domingo, and then later to Tripoli. Kenneth Roberts in his novel "Lydia Bailey" took a dim view of Lear and his activities.

[12]. Colonel William Brewster's Tavern stood where the Elks Home is now. It had previously been the residence of Sheriff Thomas Packer. It was destroyed in the great fire of 1813.

[13]. At least General Sullivan did not make the mistake that the governor of Massachusetts did. John Hancock

maintained that in Massachusetts he was the head of state, therefore, it was President Washington's duty to call on him, instead of Hancock on Washington. This bit of states' rights philosophy, something we have with us still, was neatly squelched by Washington, who refused to fall into the trap. Eventually Hancock capitulated and paid his respects to the President. Hancock was a pompous, conceited man who had thought himself the logical choice for the job given Washington as commander of the army in the Revolution. So some of that old animosity may have been in back of his maneuver. Sullivan had served under Washington in the days of the Revolution long enough to know what few liberties could be taken with that very reserved gentleman, and he thereby had an advantage over Hancock.

[14]. This was old Queen's Chapel, the Episcopal Church here not taking the official title of St. John's Church until February 15, 1791. The building was destroyed in the great fire of 1806.

[15]. The Reverend Joseph Buckminster, for whom the house on Islington Street (now known as the Medical Arts Center) was named, was a native of Rutland, Massachusetts, born there October 14, 1751. He succeeded Dr. Ezra Stiles as pastor of the North Church. Stiles resigned in 1778 to take the presidency of Yale. Buckminster was ordained on January 27, 1779, and ministered to the parish until his death, June 10, 1812. The Buckminster House became his home in 1810 when he married his third wife, the widow of Colonel Eliphalet Ladd. The colonel came here from Exeter, bought the house in 1792, and died in 1806. In the latter months of his life, Buckminster's health failed badly and he was persuaded to travel to Vermont as a cure. He died at Readsborough and was buried in Bennington.

[16]. It is hard to imagine that two old comrades-in-arms, like Washington and Sullivan, could sail down the Piscataqua without Sullivan filling his former commander in on all the work he had done to fortify Portsmouth Harbor in 1775. Sullivan came to Portsmouth on the orders of General Washington, and accounted to him for everything that he did. So he must have had a wonderful chance to explain many of the finer points again. No contemporary account of the trip mentions such a conversation, but old soldiers have always been the same, fond of talking over past campaigns.

[17]. Tradition has it that Washington had no luck with a fish line, and that a local fisherman, Zebulon Willey, hooked a cod, handed the line to the President and let him pull it in. For this

he was handed a silver dollar, probably not one of those supposed to have been thrown across the Rappahannock by the President in the days of his youth.

[18]. The Reverend Samuel Haven, D.D., commenced his ministry here on May 6, 1752, a graduate of Harvard with the Class of 1749. His service to the parish lasted until his death, March 3, 1806, nearly 54 years, although over the latter part he had the assistance of the Reverend Timothy Alden in administering to parish needs. He held at his death, in addition to a master of arts from Harvard, doctorates from the University of Edinburgh and Dartmouth College. The honor from the Scottish university came from his intense interest in map making and his assistance in preparing a map of the province. The diploma for his doctorate arrived here on May 6, 1770, in the ship Ward, with Captain Thomas Hart, who had as passengers the troublesome George Meserve and the daring merchant George Boyd. Haven joyously welcomed the news of Lexington and Concord, promptly setting up a salt petre works on the lot next to his house which stood on what is now the Pleasant Street edge of Haven Park. That he made a good product is attested by the following certificate signed May 13, 1776 by Drs. J(oshua) Brackett and Hall Jackson: "This may certify that we, the subscribers by the request of the Rev'd Dr. Haven, have examined a quantity of salt petre made him, and have weighed off 308 pounds which we judge to be sufficiently pure and dry". On the lot where Haven made his salt petre the second Edward Parry built a house, so he could live in Portsmouth. Haven's account books showed that he never managed to get all the salary due him over the years. The parish was always in arrears, paying him in bits and dabs. For some years he was one of the chaplains to the General Assembly and managed to get a few shillings out of that. However, he raised a family and the house was occupied by his son, Nathaniel A. Haven, and successive generations, until the place was torn down under the will of the last of the Havens. The land, with a gift of $25,000, was given to the city for a park in 1898.

[19]. This badly neglected house is owned today by the Wentworth-Gardner Association. It should be maintained at high standard as only a few buildings that can be connected with Washington's visit here still stand.

11

Looking Inland

[1]. Governor Wentworth early in his administration pushed through a road to land he owned in Wolfeborough. On the shores of Lake Wentworth there are still traces of the house he built and to which he took his bride. Once Wentworth's road linked Portsmouth and Wolfeborough, other settlers in the North Country bombarded the General Assembly with requests for tie-in roads. We have The Rambler for authority that Wentworth's Wolfeborough estate was 2,300 acres with an additional 1,500 in the neighboring towns of Brookfield and New Durham. The house itself was pretentious, with a length of 100 feet and a width of 45. The same source also relates an anecdote of the governor and his lady, Frances Wentworth, which might show a little of the stormy nature of their marriage. While it is difficult to imagine that mighty lady attending such a bucolic affair as a husking party, the story runs that she did and failed to return by the time the Governor was ready for bed. He locked her out. When she did return home, she set up such a tumult that the Governor ran down to find her. Right after he went out the door, she went in, and locked him out in turn. After Wentworth was proscribed, his Wolfeborough property fell under the trusteeship of Captain Samuel Gilman of Newmarket who was ordered to dispose of it to the benefit of the state. Gilman sold the property at public auction June 14, 1782, but not before the General Court had to pass a special act enabling him to sell off the livestock at the farm without advertising it. It seems Gilman had "omitted to mention" that all the cattle and other animals were up for sale. So extensive were Wentworth's holdings that committees were set up in each of the five counties to handle the confiscation and sale. Moreover the state found it necessary to exempt certain lands that Wentworth had acquired by will from the one-time sheriff, Thomas Packer, because the son, Thomas, had been deprived by the then Governor (Wentworth) and Council of his rights to appeal the probate of the will.

[2]. A tradition has grown up that this broad-beamed, utility river boat, with its lateen sail, was unique to the Piscataqua. Joseph W. P. Frost, a collateral descendant of the famed Sir William

Pepperrell and an authority on the old craft, says that such vessels were known on nearly all tidal streams in English America. The earliest reference to gundalows in our records is 1650.

[3]. Edward St. Loe Livermore was a son of Samuel Livermore, born in Portsmouth in 1762. He was educated in local schools and read for the bar here. Too young for service in the Revolution, he was one of the younger men who came to the fore in the decade after it. At one time he served as naval officer for the Piscataqua District, but lost that post in a political upheaval in 1802. Like most of the prominent men of his time, he was a Mason and served the Grand Lodge as its secretary for a while. Livermore made his home at the corner of Daniel Street in the Rindge House, a property Jacob Sheafe later occupied, and then in the now torn-down Treadwell House that stood across from the present Public Library. Three children were born of his marriage: Samuel, Caroline and Harriet. The latter was the heroine of John Greenleaf Whittier's poem "Snowbound". She became a religious eccentric and died in Palestine. Livermore's interests outside of Portsmouth are shown in part by his being granted proprietorship in 1804 of a ferry across the Pemigewasset River between the towns of Holderness and Plymouth.

[4]. Typical of legislative delay on matters of bridge construction was the operation of the 1963 New Hampshire Legislature which was unable to resolve the question of a third bridge across the Piscataqua.

[5]. John Peirce was one of the more influential men of his time. The family name is perpetuated in the Peirce Block and Pierce Island, but John's most beautiful memorial is the stately Peirce House, now used as a parish house by the Middle Street Baptists, which he built in 1799 and which once stood on the edge of the sidewalk. He was the son of Daniel Peirce and grandson of Joshua, progenitor of the family in Portsmouth. Born in 1746, he died June 14, 1814. His business life started in the counting room of Daniel Rindge and he early took over the business of his uncle, Mark H. Wentworth. Basically his career revolved around operating an insurance office and serving as cashier of the New Hampshire Bank, each of which kept him in constant touch with profitable investments.

For years he lived in the vicinity of the present-day Pierce Block, a piece of property that has not been out of the family in more than 250 years. That he had a sense of humor we can gather from the name he gave one of his horses, an animal which he left specifically to his widow, whose maiden name was Mary Pearse. His will provided that she should have the horse named "Secretary Carrigain". A Philip Carrigain served as secretary of state for New Hampshire from 1805 to 1809. It was John's grandfather who put the family into the island business. He acquired pieces of land there, usually through mortgages, until the whole island came under his ownership. That too was in the family for nearly 200 years, being sold to the city in 1923.

[6]. John Hale lived his early years here, where he was born on February 19, 1775, the son of Samuel and Lydia (Parker) Hale. His uncle, who financed his education, was Sheriff John Parker. Hale read law in Portsmouth for a time, then moved to Barrington and on to Rochester where he settled. Perhaps his greatest contribution to New Hampshire history was his famous son, John P. Hale. The son early opposed slavery, represented the state in the U. S. Senate as a Free Soiler and once debated Franklin Pierce on the issues, coming off a winner. Twice he was Free Soil candidate for the presidency, once in 1852, opposing Franklin Pierce. They were probably the only two New Hampshire men who vied at the same time for the presidency. The father was content to live out his days a country lawyer, dying in Rochester October 15, 1819.

[7]. William Gardner was born in Portsmouth in 1751, and at an early age was apprenticed in the mercantile trade to Colonel Joshua Wentworth, whose place of business was at the corner of Hanover and Vaughan Streets. Gardner was one of six brothers, one of whom, Samuel, later published the New Hampshire Gazette. Because of his training, Gardner took over commissary duties during the Revolution and is referred to in the records as deputy clothier. The Rambler tells that the state's credit was once so low that Gardner pledged his own in order to purchase badly needed blankets. The state treasury being bankrupt, the blanket manufacturer came back on Gardner and he was hard put to meet the obligation.

President Washington made him Loan and Pension officer for the state, a post he held until 1798 when President John Adams, eased him out of office to make room for a friend, John Pierce. That turned Gardner into a bitter anti-Federalist and he may have had a financial hand in the establishment of the Republican Ledger, a newspaper that supported Thomas Jefferson. When the latter became President, Gardner was reinstated as loan officer. For some years he made his home on Spring Hill, then moved to the house in the South End we know today as the Wentworth-Gardner House. While a bitter political protagonist, Gardner, who was given the title of Major during the Revolution, was highly thought of in the town. When he died on April 29, 1834, the Portsmouth Journal said of him: "He was one of the most venerable and respectable of our citizens; one distinguished for the integrity of his life, the honesty of his heart, and the purity of his motives".

[8]. Jacob Sheafe was the son of Jacob Sheafe, born in Portsmouth September 6, 1745. His mother was Hannah Seavey, whose father farmed at Seavey's Creek. He had 10 brothers and sisters, one of the sisters being Abigail, who was supposed to have wed James McDonough the night he disappeared from Portsmouth; she later married John Pickering. Jacob, Sr., was a merchant, and Jacob, Jr. followed the same trade. While his brother James remained a loyalist throughout the Revolution, Jacob apparently kept any political sentiments to himself, and continued in trade. The Committee on Safety records show permits to him allowing vessels to leave the harbor, and there is one notation of 89 pounds, 14 shillings paid for molasses supplied by him to the state. His father signed the Association Test in 1776, but brother James did not. Jacob's mercantile ventures made him a rich man, although he was unwise enough from the point of view of local politics to endorse the Jay Treaty. One of his partnerships in a maritime venture was with Matthew Marsh. For them Enoch Bagby built the 380-ton St. Cuthbert in 1802 on Pierce Island. Sheafe was one of the big losers in the fire of 1813, as notes on that chapter will relate. He died on January 25, 1829 at the age of 84.

[9]. Piscataqua Bridge opened to traffic in November, 1794, being about two years under construction. Design for the bridge was by Timothy Palmer of Newburyport and its total length was 2,258 feet, running from Fox Point to Ram (Rock) Island, to Goat Island and then to Durham Point where the granite abutments can be seen today. Palmer innovated an arch between Ram and Goat Islands which permitted water traffic to go on without the necessity of a draw. We do not know for sure the actual cost of construction, but it must have been approximately $50,000 because that is the amount assessed against the 500 outstanding shares. Advertisements in the New Hampshire Gazette tell of dividends being paid shortly after the bridge opened, and yet they had to resort to a lottery to finance repair work in 1804. Again in 1830, when ice crunched out a section, they were put to heavy expense. In 1854 part of the bridge collapsed, but the final blow came on February 18, 1855, when 600 feet of span was ruined. That was never put back by the Frink brothers of Newington, the last owners.

[10]. Arthur Livermore, brother to Edward St. Loe, lived very little in Portsmouth. He was a native of Londonderry where the father Samuel had a farm on which he frequently resided. With his father, he made his home in Holderness and was elected to Congress from that town in 1817.

[11]. Isaac Waldron followed an active business career and was agent for the New Hampshire Turnpike proprietors. He died in 1843, the administration of his estate granted to a son Samuel W.

[12]. Two or three things should distinguish the career of John Goddard in Portsmouth. For one, he was a doctor who chose not to practice his profession but to follow a life of trade instead; and second, he was one of the few New Hampshire men, if not the only one, to refuse to serve in the U. S. Senate after being duly elected — this he did in 1813 when chosen by the Federalists. Goddard's first wife was Jane Boyd, a daughter of Colonel George Boyd. She died in 1790 at the age of 27, and he subsequently married a daughter of Dr. Samuel Langdon, pastor of the North Church. The second wife died June 14, 1808 at the age of 48, but Goddard occupied the Langdon residence for a number of years, a house that has since been taken down and removed to Sturbridge Village, Massachusetts. Goddard was active in town affairs at various times serving as selectman, tythingman, assessor, and in the General Court, both as senator and representative. Perhaps one of his greatest roles was his work on a committee to battle the Yellow Fever epidemic of 1798. In that duty he served both as a doctor and as a citizen. His name is signed to all the public reports on the ravages of the fever and it was he who told the town that the epidemic had run its course. Goddard lost his place of business in the fire of 1802 and moved it into the Sugar House, School Street, until Market Street was rebuilt. His life ended in 1829 at the age of 73.

[13]. The traveler to Concord today, if he slows his mile-a-minute pace between Barrington and Chichester, can spot at least a dozen mile markers for the First New Hampshire Turnpike.

[14]. Franklin City, had it ever come into reality, would have had one distinction, it was planned; other New Hampshire towns, like Portsmouth, have "just growed". Franklin City was the dream of Portsmouth inventor, school teacher and planner Benjamin Dearborn, one of the town's real geniuses. He devised Dearborn's Patent Balances, an extremely accurate weighing scale; devoted hours of labor to designing a power-operated press. His interest in the press most likely was acquired when he published the New Hampshire Gazette in the early years of the Revolution for

Daniel Fowle. However, his idea for Franklin City, as it was to be called, would have been quite a memorial, had it succeeded. What Dearborn did was plan a town to be situated at the Durham end of the Piscataqua Bridge, its main street, Market, carrying all the flow of traffic along the Turnpike to the bridge. Parallel and bisecting streets were laid out exactly and the whole tract was divided into 138 lots. Unfortunately for Dearborn and his two Durham partners, the scheme never became reality, although they did manage to sell a few of their lots. One could almost say they were the first real estate developers in the state.

[15]. George Long was born July 4, 1762, the son of Colonel Pierse Long, who won his rank in the Revolution. Long went to sea at a young age, became a captain and then retired from that life in 1789 to become a merchant. At Portsmouth Pier, he had shop No. 3. There were few ventures in town in which he did not have a share, and he took an active role in the operations of the Portsmouth Aqueduct. Long filled many town offices; served in both houses of the General Court. He was a key figure for many years here but died April 8, 1849 at the Exeter home of his son, Captain John C. Long.

[16]. Martin Parry was one of those unlucky enough to die in the little known Yellow Fever epidemic of 1802. Parry was only 44 when he died on July 29, and was described as a captain, leaving a widow and daughter. That daughter married William P. Jones and they occupied the three-decker house that still stands at the corner of Prospect Street and Maplewood Avenue. Others who died at that time included: Colonel Samuel Adams, surveyor of the port; Mrs. Grace Bayley, wife of Captain Samuel; Adam's daughter, Eliza; Samuel Muchemore at Nathan White's on the road to Little Harbor; Nathaniel T. Sheafe, son of Jacob; and Mrs. John Seawards.

[17]. Clement Storer was a merchant, politician and militia-type soldier. He was born September 20, 1760 and died November 21, 1830. He married the daughter of Dr. Ammi R. Cutter and as general of militia had the privilege of entertaining the commander-in-chief, President James Monroe, on the occasion of the presidential visit in 1817. Storer then was United States Senator. He had previously served in the U. S. House, the State Senate and House, besides holding municipal-level posts. At the time he entertained Monroe, he was living in the Treadwell House, opposite the Public Library. From the sketchings of The Rambler, one gets a picture of Storer as a stuffy, pompous man, who relished his glory as commander of a division of the New Hampshire militia. If The Rambler had the story straight, Storer was once put in his place

rather neatly by Colonel Eliphalet Ladd. Those were days of real political bitterness and Ladd, outspoken character that he was, incurred the enmity of one of the opposition who decided to challenge him to a duel. Storer, one of the challenger's satellites, served as second and as such waited on Ladd with the message. Ladd received the general, who was in full regalia, in the presence of his young son. Storer stated his purpose and Ladd remarked, "Tell Tom ----he is a dirty fellow". The general was quite shaken by the remark and asked if Ladd wanted to insult him, too. To this Ladd replied tartly, "And you are another". As for the challenge, Ladd told his son that it was no day for going to the island (Where the Naval Shipyard is now), being too rough for a river crossing. The duel was never fought. Storer was serving as county sheriff at the time of his death. His executors had a hard time clearing up his estate and were forced to sell real estate to meet his bills.

[18]. Thomas Manning was the man who rousingly proposed changing the name of King Street to Congress when the Declaration of Independence was read from the State House balcony. He has left his name in the form of Manning Street. Although he never quite reached the aristocratic level of the great merchant class that dominated the town, he was always on the periphery of it, more often than not with a sharp needle to jab into complacent hides. His epitaph read, "An honest man" after his death on March 24, 1819 at the age of 72.

[19]. Daniel Huntress died in May, 1820, leaving a fair estate of $9,903. His adopted son, Daniel Hunking Huntress, was executor and inherited $4,000 in cash.

[20]. Elijah Hall spent his years as one of Portsmouth's most revered citizens because he had served under the great John Paul Jones on the Ranger. In the years after the Revolution, he was both a shipwright and merchant, as well as playing an active part in politics. His political service extended to both houses of the Legislature. Hall married Elizabeth, the daughter of James Stoodley, who kept the King's Arms in pre-Revolutionary days. However, the Halls used the old tavern as a private residence, and the gay days when Colonel Michael Wentworth took over the fiddle for dancing in the upstairs room were long gone. The doughty old seaman died on June 22, 1830 at the age of 84.

[21]. Anyone interested can probably find the ancient cobbles underneath the many layers of hardtop above them. When workmen laying a sewer line ripped their way across Bow Street at Ceres Street, in the summer of 1963, the stone surface was exposed.

Also laid bare momentarily that summer was the water-side entrance to the Counting House and warehouse of the Moffatt-Ladd House. This tunnel runs deep under Market Street before the shaft exits in the yard of the old residence.

[22]. Dr. Ammi Ruhamah Cutter was a native of North Yarmouth, Maine, born in 1735, graduating from Harvard College in 1752. He saw service as a medical officer with the Louisburg expedition of 1758, and put the experience to good use in 1777 when he was medical director of the Northern Army in the Saratoga campaign. By 1770, combining his practice with shrewd business ventures, Dr. Cutter had reached the point where he stood 27th on a list of 666 Portsmouth taxpayers. Through the fact he was her son-in-law, Dr Cutter played a role in the life of one of the greatest of Portsmouth's women in the 18th Century. Martha Hilton and Frances Wentworth may catch the romantic attention, but for a real "rags to riches" story and a success achieved by her own work, the life of Mary Treadwell is a better study. Her maiden name was Kelley and prior to her marriage to Charles Treadwell she made her home in New Castle. The Kelleys were an English family, and, having fallen on bad times, made their way to the New World to rebuild their fortunes as best they could. The legend goes that Mary Kelley earned the money to buy cloth for her first dress by mending fishnets, before that she had worn men's clothes. After her marriage she was discontented with her and her husband's slow progress toward economic security and opened a shop in her residence on the southwest corner of Fleet and Congress Streets.

Her business prospered, chiefly because she followed one of the first precepts of smart merchandising: accommodating the customer. When profits accumulated, she acquired a lot of land where the old New Hampshire Electric Company building now is and built a house. This she gave to her daughter Hannah and son-in-law Dr. Ammi R. Cutter.

With the passage of time she bought another lot, across Middle Street from the Public Library and built another house. Her son Jacob became the occupant of this property, acquired in later years by Clement Storer and which was in its last days owned by former Governor Charles M. Dale who tore it down to make way for the business block now located there. Mary Treadwell was not yet done. Soon she purchased another lot, on the northeast corner of State and Fleet Streets, which meant in those days that Treadwell gardens came back to back about the vicinity of present-day Porter Street. Nathaniel, the second son, was given this home. of the three built by Mary Treadwell, only this one still stands, although not on the original site. It is a couple of blocks away at 70 Court Street, the law offices of Boynton, Waldron, Dill, Nadeau and Aeschliman. Before that firm occupied it, the house had been a residence, a boarding house and a headquarters for the YWCA. One would think that Mary Treadwell would have been content to rest from her labors, but not so. Once again, when profit allowed it, she had a vessel built and gave this to her sons for their use in trade. To keep things fairly divided, she deeded her own home and shop to Hannah. Truly a remarkable woman, Mary Treadwell, but we have wandered away from the career of her son-in-law Dr. Cutter, who was a member of the tight little band of determined men who saw the town through the terrible Yellow Fever epidemic of 1798. Teamed with Dr. Joshua Brackett, Dr. William Cutter (his son), George Gains, the Reverend Joseph Buckminster and a few others, Dr. Cutter administered to the needs of the ill all through the sickness. The doctor concerned himself with all facets of community life, belonged to the Federal Fire Society, and the Masons, dying on December 8, 1820, at the age of 85.

[23]. John Samuel Sherburne was a Revolutionary War soldier, losing a leg at Butts Hill, Rhode Island, while serving under the tempestuous General John Sullivan and prior to that he had been aide-de-camp to General William Whipple. The Portsmouth Journal's obituary notice reads in part: "After the peace, he pursued the profession of law with success; was a member of the third and fourth Congress; — and on the election of Mr. Jefferson, received the appointment of U. S. Attorney; and in 1804 was appointed by him as judge of the U. S. District Court of New Hampshire". Less kind was Charles H. Bell in his brief sketch in "The Bench and Bar of New Hampshire". Bell puts squarely on the shoulders of Sherburne the responsibility for forcing the removal of Judge John Pickering as district judge. Bell charged, "Mr. Sherburne's agency in bringing about the removal of Judge Pickering, an unmistakably insane man, by impeachment, always remained in the minds of many a black cloud upon his character He testified strongly against the respondent, but when summoned for further cross examination, he absented himself so he could not be found. The office of District Judge of the United States, from which Judge Pickering was shamefully ousted, largely through his agency, was bestowed on him in 1804, and he occupied it during the remainder of his days." Why Bell should take such umbrage at the removal of an insane man from a post as critical as that of judge is hard to understand, unless it was because Sherburne had learned his profession in Pickering's office and then

used the impeachment process to get Pickering out of the job. The Bell sketch makes it evident that the author thought justice had been served when Sherburne himself suffered mental affliction in his declining years. Sherburne, a graduate of Darmouth in 1776, married Submit Boyd, one of the daughters of Colonel George Boyd. He died August 2, 1830, in the same room of the same house in which he had been born 73 years before.

[24]. The 1839-40 City Directory lists the following banks: New Hampshire Bank — incorporated 1792, Henry Ladd, president; William Haven, cashier; Ladd, Mark W. Peirce, Daniel H. Treadwell, John W. Foster, Edward F. Sise, Alfred W. Haven and George Manent, directors. New Hampshire Union Bank — William Rice, president; John Rice, cashier; George W. Rice, clerk; Rice, Andrew W. Bell, Timothy Upham, Christopher S. Toppan, Henry P. Salter, Samuel Hall and Thomas A. Adams, directors. Portsmouth Bank—Robert Rice, president; Jonathan M. Tredick, cashier; Rice, John L. Thompson, Thomas Tarlton, Joseph B. Upham, John P. Lyman and Joseph G. Sise, directors. Rockingham Bank—John Haven, president, Jacob S. Pickering, cashier; Haven, William Jones, Samuel Sheafe, James Kennard, Edward Cutts, John D. Simes and Charles Cushing, directors. Piscataqua Bank—Samuel Hale, president; Samuel Lord, cashier; James F. Shores, cashier; John M. Lord, clerk; Hale, Ichabod Rollings, Ichabod Bartlett, Ichabod Goodwin, Samuel E. Coues, William M. Shackford, William Stavers, William H. Y. Hackett and Samuel Lord, directors. Commercial Bank—Isaac Waldron, president; George Melcher, Jr., cashier; Waldron, Rufus Kittredge, John Laighton, Meshach B. Trundy, Stephen H. Simes, James H. Kelsey and Thomas P. Treadwell, directors. Portsmouth Savings Bank — James Rundlett, president; Samuel Lord, treasurer; Rundlett, Henry Ladd, John Haven, Nathaniel B. March, Ichabod Bartlett, Edward Cutts, Alexander Ladd, Samuel Hale, Jacob S. Pickering, Ichabod Rollins, Timothy Upham, Daniel H. Treadwell, William Goddard, Robert Rice, S. H. Simes, William Haven, John L. Thompson, William M. Shackford, Ichabod Goodwin and Edward F. Sise, trustees. It is interesting to note that every commercial bank in the town had at least one officer or director on the board of the Portsmouth Savings Bank, which was first bank of its kind in the state, founded in 1823. It should be noted that only Portsmouth Savings survives to this day, although one or two of the others have lineal descendants, such as First National which can trace itself to the old Piscataqua Bank. An oddity is that all seven banks used the same man, Henry Lord as messenger. In 1877, the Directory lists six

banks: First National, National Mechanics and Traders, New Hampshire National, Piscataqua Savings, Portsmouth Savings and Portsmouth Trust. In the past 60 years only National Mechanics and Traders has vanished from the scene; the merger with the First National.

[25]. Dr. Joshua Brackett was one of several local physicians who learned his profession at the side of Dr. Clement Jackson, the father of Dr. Hall Jackson. It can safely be said that Dr. Clement Jackson was Portsmouth's professor of medicine in the 18th Century when practitioners acquired the healing art by what amounted to an apprenticeship system. The doughty old doctor died at 83 in 1788, and could take pride in the skills of men like his own son, Dr. Ammi R. Cutter and Dr. Joshua Brackett. The latter's parents intended him for a career in the ministry, and to this end took him out of the school in his native Greenland and sent him to Stratham where he could be properly tutored for the ministry by the Reverend Mr. Rust. Young Brackett entered Harvard, graduating in 1752, and preached a few sermons.

He soon gave up that calling to study with Dr. Jackson and then practiced on his own. Earlier there has been mention of his work in the field of smallpox innoculation, and in 1783 the Massachusetts Medical Society gave him an honorary membership. When New Hampshire's doctors formed their own society in 1791, he was the first vice president and succeeded to the presidency in 1793. Dr. Brackett, with Drs. Cutter, Hall Jackson and John Jackson were given town approval to open a hospital for small pox innoculation under the old system of using the small pox in controlled doses to build up immunity. All his days, Dr. Brackett kept a keen interest in books and learning. In 1796, he was one of the incorporators of the Portsmouth Library and three years later was named in the charter granted the Greenland Social Library. When the New Hampshire Medical Society was formed, one of its objectives was a useful professional library to which end the doctor contributed more than 100 books. Near the end of his life, he contributed $1,500 toward setting up a chair in natural history at Harvard. He served the state as judge of the Maritime Court during the Revolution and decided the divisions of spoils after the capture of the Prince George. His wife, Hannah Brackett, was the sister of General Whipple on whom he performed an autopsy in 1785. Although only 65, his health began to decline in 1802 and he went to Saratoga to try the waters there as a cure. However, by early July he knew he was dying and returned to Portsmouth where he expired on September 17.

[26]. Probably in the front rank of Portsmouth merchants at this time was Samuel Hill. Apparently he came here from Rochester while still a minor and in 1764, picked Waldo Emerson of Wells as his guardian. By 1773, he was selling a "neat assortment" of coffins through advertisements in the New Hampshire Gazette. Little is known about his activities during the Revolution. He did sign the Association Test in 1776, but seems to have contented himself, as did so many others of the merchant class, with a business-as-usual policy. In May of 1777, he was permitted to send five barrels of powder to Boston for use in a privateer, and no doubt had a hand in financing that one and others. What political affairs he took part in were confined to the municipal level. He was a warden of the North Church in 1792. He teamed with Eliphalet Ladd and Thomas Chadbourne as the first management of the Portsmouth Aqueduct and was a partner of Ladd's in the operation of a rum distillery. Besides some interest in the fur trade, Hill ran two farms in Newington. His death came March 19, 1812 at the age of 67. In his will he made his wife Mary and his son William his chief beneficiaries, but made careful provision for the care of a mentally disturbed son, Samuel, Jr. The will mentions the two farms in Newington, stores and wharves in Portsmouth. The total value of the estate was $82,774. He held 11 New Hampshire Bank shares @ $600 each; 20 shares of the Fire & Marine Insurance Company @ $30 each; 13 shares of the New Hampshire Turnpike (No. 1) at $40; 12 shares of Piscataqua Bridge @ $50; and one share in the Portsmouth Library @ $27.50.

[27]. Joseph Whipple suffered, if that is the word for it, in the shadow of an older brother who played center stage in the most stirring drama of their lifetimes: the struggle for independence. William signed the Declaration, achieved general's rank in the Saratoga and Rhode Island campaigns, and managed to amass wordly goods. It may be that the Whipple brothers elected to follow such a course. Certainly Joseph was busy enough in political and civic affairs at the local level. While he did not represent Portsmouth in the General Court, he had a seat there, being elected by North Country towns in which he had immense land holdings. In Portsmouth he served in capacities such as overseer of the poor. During the Revolution, Joseph Whipple, Committee of Safety Records indicate, was active in the procurement of supplies for the Continental forces and supervising work on a road into the present-day towns of Jefferson and Lancaster. The office of customs collector came his way after the war, and he managed its affairs from a

countinghouse adjoining his home on the northeast corner of State and Chestnut Streets. So quietly did Joseph Whipple live that we get a better insight into his character through his will, more than any other way.

This document reveals a remarkable man with deep interest in the future of his country. Part of his estate he devoted to the establishment of an academy in Jefferson, with the intent that its purpose "be pointed to those studies that tend to improvements in agriculture and natural history....And as it respects political subjects that such studies as tend to a love of peace and an aversion to War, and encouragement and continuance of a Republican form of government as established by the Constitution of the United States, wishing the experiment to be fairly tryed for one century by the termination of which period the practibility I have no doubt will be admitted provided the arts of peace are cherished and adopted and War discouraged and shunned...."

Whipple added the thought that he wanted his money to benefit youth but not in direct fashion because he was "of the opinion founded on long and daily observation that property placed in the hands of young persons operates as a check to their industry and application to useful employment". But Whipple's thinking did not end there. He wanted to encourage industry in the state and to this end set apart funds, the interest of which would go to paying bonuses to woolen cloth and window glass manufacturers who showed the greatest production effort, in the judgement of his executors. The academy was to be financed from the 287 shares of stock he held in the Jefferson Turnpike on which the appraisers of his estate put a value of $3,444. The total value of his property was put at $73,255, a large sum in 1816 when he died. A large part of that valuation rested in the lands he owned in Jefferson, Cockburn (Columbia), Bretton Woods, and Lancaster, more than 23,000 acres. He also had farm land in Washington. In fact, Whipple was fairly typical of the wealthy of his day, much of what they had was tied up in wild lands in remote parts of the state, and they were in effect more land poor than rich. Besides the house on State Street, he owned the lot directly across the street, and, in partnership with John Langdon, had acquired other Portsmouth real estate.

[28]. The Portsmouth Aqueduct went out of existence in 1891, being acquired by the City of Portsmouth. For years complaints had raged over it and there was no Public Utility Commission in those days to make the company do anything about conditions that on occasion premitted lizards to creep out of the

mains. Trustee accounts in the Joseph Whipple estate show that it paid good dividends from the early days and when it was finally bought by the city each of the 100 shares had profitted its holders to a total of $2,954. The city did not get much for the $150,000 it paid, but it did eliminate once and for all private water company operations, except for the system Frank Jones put in for his brewery, for which he dug wells on what is now the Pease AFB Golf Club. That system, too, the city later had to buy. Joseph Whipple had been one of the largest original stockholders in the Aqueduct, owning five shares.

[29]. Islington Street, beyond the intersection with Bartlett Street, was opened to traffic in 1797. Prior to that time the route to the Plains from town led along Islington, then into Frenchman's Lane (a road that ran west in the general direction of the old car barn off Bartlett Street), and then angling across into what we call Spinney Road. Somewhere near the top of the rise on Spinney Road, the highway then turned west and followed a path now bisected by Hampshire Road, Sheffield Road and Essex Avenue, past the old Bates ice pond to the head of Pearson Street. The opening up of Islington Street and the eventual construction of Middle Road did much to shorten the journey between the town and Plains. The Rambler says Frenchman's Lane derived its name from the fact that a French sailor was found stabbed to death on that road one morning. About 2,000 French sailors had the freedom of the town and were given to congregating in the Islington Creek area. One of them was living in a boardinghouse nearby and two men came to see him one afternoon. The trio went for a walk and the Frenchman was never seen alive again. He was buried in the North Cemetery.

The whole episode provokes the thought that mention should have been made earlier of the Marquis de Chastellux who visited Portsmouth at the time the French fleet was here. De Chastellux later published his observations in a book, "Travels in North America", and one or two of his observations are worth noting. "Portsmouth is, perhaps, of all the American towns, the one which will gain most from the present war (Revolution). There is every appearance of its becoming to New England, what the other Portsmouth is to the Old; that is to say, that this place will be chosen as a depot for the Continental Navy....But if a naval establishment be thought necessary at Portsmouth, the quays, the ropewalks, the arsenals, etc., must be placed on the islands, and not on the mainland". And what the Marquis thought has come true, the U.S. Navy's facilities are on the islands, not the mainland.

[30]. The pages of the New Hampshire Gazette are filled with items that show how enterprising merchant seamen from Portsmouth, and all U. S. ports, were subject to harassment from both the French and English throughout the long decade of the 1790s and well into the 19th Century. An example is to be found in the story of a Captain Charles Blunt of New Castle, skipper of the Diana, who sailed out of Trinidad in August, 1799, for Portsmouth. The vessel was taken by a French privateer, and the mate and a seaman put aboard the Frenchman while Blunt and four seamen, by feigning illness, were allowed to stay on the Diana. Under a prize crew, the Diana headed for Martinique, but the French became careless. Blunt got his hands on a cutlass, one of his men grabbed a musket and between them they subdued the helmsmen. Others of Blunt's crew came roaring out and in a matter of minutes Blunt once again commanded the Diana.

About the same time, the ship Rebecca, Captain John Mendum of Portsmouth, was captured by a French privateer under an American renegade James Love. As the Rebecca was not carrying cargo, Love let her go, taking only a barrel of beer. After he let Rebecca go, she was captured again a few days later by another privateer under Captain Lappe. This freelooter took all of Rebecca's stores and dumped 19 American prisoners on her deck. Fortunately, Rebecca fell in with other American vessels and was able to get enough food for the passage home. Earlier in the decade, Captain John Shackford's brig Harmony was taken and the prize crew let her pile up on Bahama Bank. Captain Elijah Hall's will shows that one of the assets of his estate was a claim against the French government of $15,000 for the illegal capture of the ship Fawn before 1800, a vessel owned in three parts by him and one part by John McClintock.

The size of Hall's claim indicates that these were no trifling losses the Portsmouth economy was suffering whenever the French took a vessel. Sometimes, the owners lost everything, cargo, and ship, and at other times they were put up for ransom. In this practice, the mate was usually left behind as the hostage while the captain sailed home to get the ransom money. Many good Piscataqua men died waiting for the owners to send the money. And while the French preyed on the life blood of Portsmouth's economy, the West Indies trade, the British took a heavy toll in able seamen by impressment. George III's warships were always in need of manpower, and what could be handier than using American seamen. Weren't they really English anyway? Certainly few of them could prove American birth so the English captains simply refused to believe that a man they wanted was not English. For example, in February 1796, Edward Nutter, John Libbey and Richard Howes were impressed from the ship Lydia by a 40-gun English frigate. Lydia had put into Jamaica and before she left Captain Robert Blunt found himself short three crewmen. It mattered not to the British captain that Howe had a wife and three children living in Portsmouth. Captain John Seaward lost a hand, William Herrold, while at sea in April of 1796. Joseph Stoodley, of the innkeeping family, was another unlucky one. With Alexander Connell, Stoodley was impressed by HMS Soverign from the brig Union, Captain Charles Treadwell, and was at sea a long time. John Furness, 26, impressed in 1788, was killed in action off the coat of France while on HMS Wolverine. These are a few of the many incidents that can be found in the pages of the New Hampshire Gazette for the period and illustrate the hazards in world trade for Portsmouth merchants, captains and seamen.

[31]. This William Stavers was a son of John, the one-time Tory tavern keeper. When John died September 30, 1797, the bulk of his property went to William and two of his sisters, Mary Frazier and Susannah Appleton. They were left in thirds the land on which the old tavern sat and William also got a house on State Street. At the time of John's death, the old Pitt Tavern and stables were valued at $2,850. When William died in October 1811, his Pitt Street holdings were worth $6,000. Another William Stavers outlived him by many years, dying in 1863. This William Stavers was the son of Bartholomew and cousin to the other. Bartholomew died at Castle Camps, England, in the early 1790s and his widow Martha died in February 1792, leaving an estate of 151 pounds, and three children, William, Sally Hutchings, and Catherine Stavers. Her son was put under the guardianship of Jerimiah Libbey and his cousin William.

[32]. James Sheafe's story is that of a man who opposed, as earlier notes indicate, the struggle for independence, even was jailed briefly in Exeter for his convictions, and yet lived to occupy some of the highest offices the new nation had at its disposal — seats in both houses of Congress. He was a graduate of Harvard in the Class of 1774, married a daughter, Sarah, of George Meserve, who was forced to resign as stamp officer for the province. For a number of years he lived in Meserve's house on Vaughan Street before acquiring a home of his own nearer Market Square. It was his sister Abigail who was supposed to have married the ill-fated James McDonough. He refused to sign the Association Test, and yet, along with Jonathan Warner, another who refused, he was in the delegation that welcomed President Washington to the state and town. He

engaged extensively in trade, as did his brothers Thomas and Jacob, even sending vessels into the new China trade after 1800. At one time, he owned the whole block south of the present Indian Head National Bank, suffering a heavy loss in the fire of 1813. He died December 5, 1829, the same year as brother Jacob, at the age of 74. James' widow put up a memorial to him in St. John's Church, describing him in part as "a venerated merchant of this town, and a cultivated, constant worshipper of this church...."

[33]. Nathaniel Marshall made his home at the lower end of State Street, about in the area where the Esso gas station now is. The amount of his estate — $3,925 — at the time of his death in 1812 forces the conclusion that he was not in the front rank of Portsmouth merchants, but was a reputable citizen.

[34]. Not too much is known about Thales G. Yeaton, except that he was a progenitor of the modern Yeaton families.

[35]. Another man about whom we know little, except that he died in 1807, leaving an estate valued at $6,431.

[36]. William Tredick was a far wealthier man than some of his companions in arrest. His estate was valued at $26,000 when offered for probate in 1806. He lived on Gates Street with his maiden daughter, Grace. Assets of estate were listed in part as 75 percent ownership of the brigs, John Langdon and Anna, appraised at $6,600, plus a cargo of sugar in the John Langdon, Captain Peter Coffin, valued at $5,411.

[37]. The Charles Chauncey referred to here came to the Portsmouth area about 1748 to enter the employment of his uncle Sir William Pepperell at Kittery. He first married Mary Cutts, and after her death, childless, married Joanna Gerrish. They had 12 children. A daughter, Joanna was the wife of Portsmouth's second Edward Parry; a son, Charles, died at the age of 28; another son, Isaac, a sea captain, was lost in a shipwreck off Marshfield, Massachusetts; Samuel, another son, was a sea captain, commanding at one time a ship owned by Eliphalet Ladd, whose daughter Betsy he married. Samuel built a three-story house on Islington Street, the remains of which provide a roof for the Saef Auto Agency. It was later owned by Captain Lewis Barnes. Samuel Chauncey retired from the sea, but his health degenerated and in 1815 he moved to Stratham. However, in 1817 he took the ship Hannah out of Portsmouth for Bremen, and committed suicide while on the passage. The other living children were Elizabeth Hirst and Lucy Yeaton, the wife of Captain William Yeaton. Charles Chauncey made his home a short distance from the present Haven school, in a house owned by

the Clarkson brothers, His granddaughter, Mrs. Eliza Porter, told the Rambler, "I remember my grandfather as a small, very erect old gentleman. of quick movement, wearing a cocked hat, small clothes, and black silk hose, with diamond knee buckles.... I know that he was much interested in political affairs, and with fearless independence expressed his opinion in speaking, and writing for many papers in Boston and in Portsmouth....I felt an unconscious pride steal over my heart when walking with him, as I noticed the respect and reverence with which everyone greeted him. Even the children would cease to play as he approached, saying, 'Here comes the Squire', and stand aside to doff their hats, or bob their courtesies as he passed". Charles Chauncey left an estate of $6,055, part of it being 18 acres of land near the Pound, which was at the junction of Middle Road and South Street. We would like today to be able to buy it for the value set on it after Chauncey's death in 1809, $720. He also held a note of Jonathan Warner's, a successful man of business, with $1,307 still due on it. Another note he held was worth $500, given by Dorothy, George and Abraham Wendell.

[38]. Known early as Rising Castle Island, then Langdon's, it was for a time called Continental Island, and finally after coming into the ownership of the great shipbuilder, William Badger, it took his name.

[39]. Crescent was launched from the "Navy Yard" at Langdon's Island on June 29, 1797. Colonel James Hackett was the master and shipwright and Captain Thomas Thompson had the contract for outfitting her. Josiah Fox of Philadelphia, famed naval constructor, was the designer. She was "raised", as the term for keel-laying went in those days, on October 20, 1796, but little was done, according to the New Hampshire Gazette, until February, but Hackett still beat the contract deadline by several days. Crescent was the fourth ship of war built by Hackett, the previous ones being, Raleigh, 700 tons; Ranger, 300; Bellona, 300; and America, 1,700. The materials for Crescent's sheathing were in Philadelphia 18 days before her launch and yet Hackett got her off the ways as scheduled. A few months later the Gazette carried the note that the Crescent had arrived at Algiers and was highly pleasing to the Dey, following it with a Chamber of Commerce plug for Portsmouth-built products.

[40]. At one time, the U.S. was on the brink of war with her old ally — France. Congress would have figured largely in the sea battles of such a conflict. She was launched on a Thursday, August 15, 1799, at high noon. Governor John T. Cilman was on hand for the occasion, being rowed out to "Continental Island" after

suitable flourishes and greeting on the mainland. Along with the Governor, two Indian chiefs were on hand for the launching, which went off without a hitch. A total of 258 working days went into her with more than 100 different shipwrights, a daily average of 60 being employed on her under James Hackett's direction. The working day, the Gazette said, went from sunup to sundown with a half hour out for breakfast and an hour for dinner. When the launching ceremonies were over, 180 special guests sat down to a dinner replete with toasts. She measured 145 feet at the keel; 41 feet in beam; 26 feet, 7 inches in depth; registered at 1,250 tons. Her armament was 36 eighteen-pounders. Jacob Sheafe had been the inspector on the job and her command was in the hands of Captain James Sever, who had Captain George Turner to assist him as pilot after her launching. Her career was not spectacular. Howard I. Chapelle in his "American Sailing Navy" indicates that she might have been lengthened some time prior to the War of 1812. Most of her years were spent rotting away at "ordinary" and she was broken up at Norfolk in 1836.

[41]. Portsmouth was launched from "the Continental Navy Yard" at Langdon's Island on October 21, 1798, rated at 20 guns. Her commander was Captain Daniel M'Neil of Boston. Other officers included Richard Tibbetts of Portsmouth, first lieutenant; George Turner, Jr., second lieutenant; Lieutenant Robert Oram, sailing master. Colonel Chapelle says her precise measurements are not known and the only hint at them in the Gazette is that she was 93 feet on the keel, which was laid July 4, 1798, and 31 feet in beam. Hackett was the builder and Captain Thomas Thompson agent for supplies. She was sold out of the Navy in 1801.

[42]. Scammel, named to honor Alexander Scammel who died from wounds suffered at Yorktown, was designed as a 16-gun revenue cutter. She was launched shortly before Portsmouth, and saluted the newly launched Portsmouth when she entered the water. Scammel was commanded by Captain John Adams, and dropped down river in company with Portsmouth, at 10 a.m. on January 24, 1799, on their maiden voyages. The two vessels sailed out of the lower harbor the next day for Dominique (Dominica). Later they were reported having arrived there, Portsmouth in 16 days; Scammel in 18. Like Portsmouth, Scammel was sold out of the Navy in 1801.

[43]. The present-day Portsmouth Naval Shipyard had its beginnings, as shown above, at Langdon's Island. There no less than eight ships of war were built, all under the direction of James Hackett. And while it was indicated earlier that a detailed history of

the Shipyard cannot be given here, some of its story must be told. George H. Preble's history of the Yard will give the interested reader more detail. An energetic Secretary of the Navy, Benjamin Stoddard, saw the need for federally owned yards, responsive to the dictates of the Navy. But John Langdon wanted too much money, $25,000, for his island, and another, larger in size, could be had for only $5,500. This was the price William Dennett put on the island, for which he had paid only $1,700 a few years before when he anticipated just such a federal move.

He induced Samuel Sheafe to buy it from the Fernald family for $600, bought it from Sheafe for $1,700, and sold it for $5,500. However, the Navy did not get stung too badly. Fernald's, or Dennett's Island as it was becoming known, had many advantages over Langdon's, in addition to size. This island's 58 acres were mostly wild when the government took it, although in early colonial times it had been the home of several Fernald families. Progress in building a naval installation was slow. Jacob Sheafe, the Portsmouth merchant, as was typical of the times, was put in charge of developing it, and $20,000 was spent in the first year, $5,500 of that for the purchase. The War of 1812 saw the first of the many booms that characterize the story of the Portsmouth Naval Shipyard. The Navy quickly moved to bring the Yard under a Naval officer, Lieutenant Thomas McDonough, later a hero on Lake Champlain. McDonough was relieved by Captain Isaac Hull, an old seadog, and he was in command when the fire of 1813 swept Portsmouth. Hull sent men, officers and machines to help battle the flames, a mutual aid system that still exists between the city and the Shipyard. However, it was not until 1814 that the keel of a ship was laid there, although extensive repair work was done prior to that. It was here that the third Wasp was fitted out in 1813 and recruited her crew from Portsmouth before sailing out to glory and then oblivion. Washington, the first keel at the new yard, was a 74. The Alabama, which stood on the ways for more than 40 years, until 1864, was then launched as the New Hampshire.

Numerous improvements were made at the Yard when the Navy could wring money out of Congress. The Franklin Shiphouse was built in 1838 and lasted until 1936 when destroyed by fire. Seawalls were built; the Navy acquired Seavey's Island in 1866, adding 105 acres to the Yard. The total land holding today is in excess of 220 acres, brought about by filling and the acquisition of other islands. In 1848, the first drydock was built at the Yard at a cost of $732,640. A floating drydock, put together on Pierce Island

and floated to the Yard, was fitted into a basin. The old warship Franklin was the first vessel to use the facility in 1852. After the Navy had thoroughly tested the drydock with the Franklin the old ship was scrapped. The Yard for a time was home port for the famous "Old Ironsides" and she was overhauled and put to receiving ship use.

With the Civil War, the pace again picked up on the Yard. Only 110 men were on the rolls when the war started, but in May, 1865, 2,563 were working there. Perhaps the Yard's greatest contribution to the Union cause was USS Kearsarge, victor over the famed Confederate raider Alabama in the English Channel. The keel for the Kearsarge was laid in May, 1861. Fires were lit under boilers for the first time in December of that year. She was commissioned in January and sailed the next month. Once the Civil War ended the Yard began to take on its normal peace time aspect. Between the end of the war and the beginning of World War I in 1914, only eight ships, none of real significance, went down the ways. However, one great event took place, which will be noted in more detail later on — the war between Russia and the newly emerging Asian power, Japan, was brought to a conclusion with the Treaty of Portsmouth in 1905, the pact being signed at the Yard. When the first World War broke out in Europe, the Navy took a step that has had profound effect on Portsmouth's economic welfare: The Yard was selected to build the first submarine to be constructed in a government yard. And, except for incidental work, submarines have been the Portsmouth Naval Shipyard's major product ever since. That first one was the L-8, whose keel was laid in November, 1914. Her hull was ready within 11 months, but the engines were not available until March of 1917 so she was not launched until April. Since that time, 129 other submarines have followed L-8 into the Piscataqua. More than 100 of them entered the water in the tumultuous years of World War II when the Yard's working force passed the 20,000 point. The inevitable happened right after V-J Day signaled victory over Japan. The Shipyard force dropped below 5,000, but the pressures of the Cold War brought it back to the point where in 1964 it stood at 9,000. With the Cold War came a new wonder, the nuclear powered submarine, capable of months under the sea without refueling. The Navy puts it this way: "From Sails to Atoms". But the more literal minded might phrase it thus: "From Sails to Atoms to Sails", because the superstructure of modern submarines is known as the "sail", although a far cry from the canvas-filled days of Isaac Hull.

However, the impact of the Cold War diminished and in

November, 1964, Secretary of Defense Robert S. McNamara gave orders that the Shipyard should phase out in 10 years. News of the blow to Seacoast economy was brought here by Senator Tom McIntyre and announced by him in a room at the Rockingham Hotel. McIntyre's displeasure was obvious to all and he never stopped working to get the order killed.

The closure order signaled the start of a long hard battle to keep the Shipyard going. It brought into full bloom the Kittery-Portsmouth Armed Services Committee, which inaugurated the "Man in Washington Plan", actually the engagement of a full-time lobbyist on behalf of the Shipyard. The congressional delegations of the two states held a hearing at Portsmouth Senior High School, and an all-out effort to change Portsmouth's industrial direction was begun with Thomas Prentiss, then executive officer at the Newington Simplex plant, as chairman. A multitude of interested people put much hard work into winning recision of the closure order, and that was finally won in 1971, with U. S. Representative Louis C. Wyman getting a large measure of credit for his efforts in getting President Nixon to allow the Shipyard to stay open. Since then the Shipyard has been slowly cutting back in personnel as the whole course of existence is being changed. As of this writing, the Yard is to be charged primarily with the overhaul and renovation of nuclear submarines, and there will be no more new construction. In keeping with this, a reduction in force (RIF) was ordered in March of 1972 which brought the work force down to 5,000 men.

[44]. The Downtown Associates, as the name implies, was formed in 1962 as a combination of merchants to counter the threat posed by the shopping centers being built, such as Lafayette Plaza, on the outskirts of the city. Combinations of merchants to achieve definite objectives are not new here. As early as 1760, six local merchants headed by Nathaniel Adams, father of the author of "The Annals of Portsmouth", banded together to advertise that the Bohea tea they were offering for sale did not come from damaged cargoes. In 1789, Benjamin Dearborn, inventor, printer, teacher and scholar, was secretary to an association of tradesmen and manufacturers.

[45]. The Spring Market stood approximately where John Newick's former lobster restaurant rests on its ancient pilings. The cobwebbing to anchor the old pier came to light in the summer of 1963 when workmen were trenching for the new city sewer lines along Ceres Street. Some of the old timbers looked in as good

condition as when laid down nearly 200 years ago. Originally, the Spring Market was built on the corner of Market and Bow Streets; that was in 1761. Thrity-five years later it was moved to a position out over the river. All the country traders came to it, many by water, from Eliot and Kittery, bringing in their produce. But the Great Bay had been bridged and a turnpike built into central New Hampshire, so the merchants wanted a better located market.

[46]. John Fisher married the sister of Governor John Wentworth and held property here even after he moved to Salem, Massachusetts, as Customs Officer. His wife's kinship to the royal governor and his own political leanings helped Fisher win a place on the proscribed list in 1778, although he did not flee immediately to England or Nova Scotia as so many Tories did. For a while he was with his brother-in-law, the Governor, on Long Island, New York, when the latter was vainly trying to find some place for himself in the British Army. It's still a moot point as to whether or not Fisher ever returned to Portsmouth to live. If he did, there was a conspiracy of silence in which even The Rambler joined because nothing in newspapers or books indicates it. However, one small clue indicated that for a time he may have returned. In 1905, the Federal Fire Society, organized in 1811 as a mutual aid group in case of fire, published sketches of some of its early members, and among those on the list is John Fisher, "admitted in 1797", more than 20 years after he was forced to leave. The society's history says that he lived on State Street and lost his home in the fire of 1813, moved back to England and died in Kensington in 1838 at the age of 74.

[47]. Richard Billings attracted our attention earlier as the former clerk of John Hancock, who was frequently host in his Congress Street home to his former employer. Billings died December 19, 1808, at the age of 74 and his tombstone notes him as a Revolutionary soldier. His estate was valued at $7,204, $6,500 of which was his house.

[48]. Captain John Flagg cannot be blamed for the epidemic. He had no more knowledge than his fellow citizens that mosquitoes carried Yellow Fever. He was a highly respected member of the community and served on the Relief Committee formed after the fire of 1813. His home was on Vaughan Street and he died December 23, 1814 at 50.

[49]. Thomas Sheafe, middle brother between the better known Jacob and James, was born April 16, 1752. Like his brothers, he was heavily engaged in trade with ventures to Russia, the West Indies and the Orient in a ship captained by Charles Coffin.

Also like his brothers, both of whom he outlived, Sheafe lived to a fine old age, dying September 4, 1831 at 79.

[50]. Dr. William Cutter was a dedicated man of medicine who contracted Yellow Fever himself and had a hard time recovering from it. He apparently never married, or if he did, his wife predeceased him, because there is no mention of a wife in his will which he signed May 16, 1817, only six days before his death. Life interest in his estate, including the "Creek Farm", was left his parents with his brother Daniel, who died October 26, 1832, at 65. He named the brother and brother-in-law, Daniel R. Rogers, as executors. Dr. Cutter was only 48 when he died. The Gazette said of him, "This man was formed in no common mould; as a man, benevolence and rectitude marked his footsteps; as a Physician, his scientific knowledge in the healing art was acknowledged". He had had a good tutor, his father.

[51]. Dr. John Jeffries was the grandson of George Jeffrey of Portsmouth, but born in Boston, February 5, 1744. Father was David Jeffries and mother was Sarah Jeffrey. He was adopted by his uncle John Jeffries at an early age. He attended Harvard and was early engaged in the study of smallpox, with special attention to the effects of cooling the body. His sentiments were Tory during the Revolution but he returned to the United States in 1789...He made his first aerial crossing of the English Channel with Blanchard on January 7, 1784.

[52]. From the time in 1800 that the federal government decided that the Piscataqua should have a Navy Yard, no other single thing has had as great an impact on Portsmouth, and the area towns, as the establishment of Pease Air Force Base. The base is named for Captain Harlan Pease, Army Air Corps, a native of Plymouth, New Hampshire, who was killed in the South Pacific while on a World War II bombing raid. That it was built here at all is a standing memorial to the power wielded in Washington by the then senior senator from New Hampshire, the late Styles Bridges. For more than two decades he was one of the most influential men in government. Much more will be said about Pease later on.

[53]. However, balloon ascensions will again be familiar to Portsmouth, if Dr. Paul Tessier, local urologist, has his way. Dr. Tessier is an enthusiast, and not long ago had as one of his passengers, Norman Kent, a conservative banking type, who confessed that a balloon ascension at midnight—even when the whole apparatus is tethered, does something for the adrenalin flow, especially when the gas valve does not operate quite as expected.

12

The Great Fires

[1]. From the early days of the Puritan invasion of New Hampshire until comparatively late in the 19th Century, Portsmouth generally did not observe Christmas in our extravagant way, either materially or religiously. With the Puritans the word "Merrie" did not exist in the phrase "Merrie Christmas". To them such festivals smacked of Papism and that belief was abhorrent. The few Church of Englanders in the community undoubtedly kept Christmas on the sly and that there was some sentiment for it is obvious in the law passed by the Massachusetts Assembly in 1659 and in force here: "For puenting disorders arrising in seuerall places wthn ys jurisdiccon, by rason of sum still obseruing such ffestiualls as were supersticiously kept in other countrys, to ye grate dishonner of God & offence of others, yt it is ordr'd by ys Court... that whosoeuer shal be found obseruing any such day as Xtmas...euery pson so offending shal pay for euery offence five shillings...." Restrictions against celebration of Christmas eased as royal governors or royal authority began to make itself felt in New England, but the majority of the population in most towns was Congregational in faith or sympathy and it was not until the middle 1850s that the Portsmouth Morning Chronicle began an editorial campaign which led eventually to the closing of local shops on the great Christian holy day.

[2]. The Brick Market had proved immensely popular with the public and the out-of-town traders. The large room above the open air market place was soon known as Town Hall, and then in 1801 was given the name that stuck to it ever after — Jefferson Hall. The original plan called for a roof of tar and gravel for protection against fire, but shingles were used instead and when the fire came they quickly ignited. The Brick Market was gutted but the walls withstood the terrific heat and were used in the rebuilding that took place in 1804. Few changes were made in the original design when it was rebuilt. The upper hall rested on the open arches of the market, which in winter meant it was a chilly place for the selling of goods.

These arches were closed in and windows substituted in 1826. While used for many activities, the hall was not used for elections until 1818, the voters having cast their ballots for years in the old State House near the North Church.

[3]. The first local tradesmen to occupy stalls included Joseph and Isaac Shepherd, Asa Dearborn, John French, Amos Sheldon and Captain Edward Gove. The latter had the misfortune to go through bankruptcy shortly after the fire. Many a stormy town meeting took place within the walls of Jefferson Hall, including the wild night, of which more will be told later, when the Democrats tried to outlast the Whigs. Finally in 1864, November 10, the hall was dedicated as the seat of the city government. Here city business was conducted for nearly half a century until the present City Hall building became available with the construction of a new high school in 1905 on the George W. Haven land west of the Public Library. The market beneath City Hall was closed in 1875. The city finally disposed of the property, the "market place forever", to the then New Hampshire National Bank. That was in 1912. Before its walls came tumbling down, the old hall had been the scene of many exciting local events. Here the town celebrated its 200th anniversary. To it came Daniel Webster in the last years of his active life to receive the plaudits of his former fellow townsmen, telling his audience, "Your fathers were my friends". Political rallies were staged in the hall and the Masons used it for some of their festivities. Appropriately enough, The Rambler, Charles W. Brewster, was the speaker when the Jefferson Hall became City Hall. The New Hampshire Bank was incorporated in 1792, the first in the city, for 50 years. The charter wasn't renewed in 1842.

[4]. John Nelson was the member of the family who settled here before 1756. Besides his goldsmithing, he dabbled in trade, at one time handling a shipment of salt brought by the snow Mary and Jane, Captain Thomas Tallant. Other ads indicate his interest in selling cloth. He eventually was named to the Governor's Council, being sworn in on March 2, 1763. However, he did not stay here long after that but became collector for the Island of Nevis. Nelson made his home on the lot occupied today by the Portsmouth Athenaeum. In the early years of the Athenaeum an alley ran through to Ladd Street along its west wall. When the Masons held meetings in the upstairs rooms of the Athenaeum, they used an outside staircase rising up from the alley. Other Nelsons lived in the town. Isaac was a mariner; Leander a farmer who lived in the vicinity of the Plains, served as a fence viewer and tythingman and whose

house "catched" fire in January 1766, through carelessness in carrying hot embers to an upstairs chamber; Matthew, a cordwainer, whose daughter Lucy married George Ham; Mark, a goldsmith, who had his place of business across the street from John; Joseph, a farmer, and father of Leander, William and Benjamin.

[5]. The New Hampshire Fire and Marine Insurance Company was incorporated on June 10, 1803, by Samuel Ham, John Wardrobe, a sea captain; James Rundlet, a merchant and Gilman Leavitt. The act provided for a minimum capital stock of $200,000, maximum $400,000, and issuance of 2,000 shares. First meeting of the corporation was called for July 12, 1803 at Colonel William Brewster's Tavern (Elks Home) by the incorporators. In August they were advertising that $50,000 was subscribed and that the company would underwrite fire policies on houses, stores, goods, wares and merchandise; also on vessels, freight, money, goods, against captivity at sea. The office was in the home of Richard Billings near the Parade and Samuel Ham was president. The young company suffered some losses in the fire of 1806, more in the War of 1812 and in the fire of 1813, and by the 1820s was in sad financial straits. Part of this was due to losses, and part to what was then believed were the embezzling tactics of one of the officials who issued stock without bothering to make a record of it. Actually the poor devil involved made good, over the years, on what people thought he had stolen. Many years later, when the safe, still functioning in the Athenaeum, was cleaned out, the missing stock was discovered. To the writer, the irony of discovering this was quite real. Years ago he learned during the early days of his proprietorship in the Athenaeum, that the late A. B. Duncan, then president, issued orders that "Brighton is not to see the New Hampshire Fire and Marine records because he would only make a story out of an old scandal". Actually such an article would have cleared a man's name. The writer hopes he has time to do it some day.

The company's charter expired in 1823 and was not renewed. Settlement of its affairs took many years and Daniel Webster was instrumental in getting back some money on losses when he was U.S. Secretary of State by pushing claims against foreign governments for illegal capture of insured vessels. The Portsmouth Athenaeum acquired the building in 1817 when the insurance company was struggling to get out from under its indebtedness. Complete records of the New Hampshire Fire and Marine are owned by the

Athenaeum, and would be well worth study by a history student in search of a master's thesis.

[6]. This property bears the names of two families who occupied it, Moffat and Ladd, but ignores the more famous man, William Whipple who made it his home. The house is now owned by the Society of Colonial Dames. It was built by Captain John Moffat in 1763 for his son Samuel, a 1758 graduate of Harvard. Where the Moffats came from has become, among historians, an increasingly interesting point of discussion. Usually, it is contended that Captain John came from Hertfordshire, England. However, attempts by researchers to establish this have been in vain. In 1963, an Englishman, John W. Whiteman, from Hertfordshire, but a reporter for The Portsmouth Herald, did an article for The Hertfordshire Countryside Illustrated on the house and two or three theories have been advanced. One of them is that the house is similar to a house in North Mymms, Hertfordshire, and known as "Moffatts". Various spellings of the name confuse the matter: Moffett, Muffett, Moffatt, Mouffet. Dr. Thomas Moffet is believed to be the man whose daughter was "Little Miss Muffet" of Mother Goose fame.

Be that as it may, Captain John Moffat came here fairly early in the 18th Century as skipper of a mast ship.

He was born in 1692 and before 1725 had married Katherine, daughter of Robert Cutt, II. His mercantile operations were successful. His son, John, died in 1736, but Samuel married on February 1, 1764, Sarah, the daughter of John Tufton Mason. Young Samuel rapidly became a leading merchant in his own right, but, by overextending himself, he had to flee from the country to keep out of jail for debt. The father, to whom the son owed much of the money, attached his property and bid it in himself at auction. He then moved into the house from his old home on State Street. When his daughter Catherine married William Whipple, the couple made their home there, along with Samuel's wife and children. Samuel Moffat drifted around the West Indies and finally got into a business in Dutch Guiana, where his wife went to live with him. Their second daughter, Mary Tufton, lived with her grandfather and married Nathaniel Appleton Haven in 1786. Bitter litigation developed after John Moffat died in 1786 at the age of 92. Samuel's son, Robert C. Moffat retained the noted Jeremiah Mason, as his lawyer and managed to win his case. Afterwards, he sold the property to N. A. Haven, who left it to his daughter, Maria Ladd, the wife of Alexander Ladd. One of the unusual and intriging features of the property is the tunnel which still connects this property with the waterfront, although it has been many years since anyone has ventured through it.

[7]. Along this side of Market Street, Benjamin Dearborn had his school, the prosperous Daniel Rindge made his home and numerous shops were in operation.

[8]. James Rundlet left his mark on the town in the form of one of its more stately homes, still occupied in 1972 by a descendant, Ralph May. This Middle Street house is the only one in the city for which there is a complete record of its construction. In 1946, Ralph May published a lengthy article on this detailed account book. The house is now owned by the Society for the Preservation of New England Antiquities.

May is a graduate of Harvard and past president of the Portmouth Athenaeum, an institution in which he has a deep interest. He was born in the John Paul Jones House, one of two persons now living, 1972, able to make the claim. The other is Mrs. Thelma Carpenter of Middle Road. May was honored at a cocktail party in the garden of the Jones House and Mrs. Carpenter was also in attendance. This was in July, 1970 and arranged by the president of the Portsmouth Historical Society, Arnold J. Grover. Governor Walter Peterson attended and spoke briefly during the program, which had former Society President John H. DeCourcy as master of ceremonies. Mrs. Grover is the senior hostess at the Jones House and is assisted by Mrs. Ruth Call and Mrs. Bernice Downing.

[9]. A listing of those who lost property in the fire of 1802 reads almost like a "Who's Who" of the town: Enoch Thompson; Stephen Pearse; Peter Pearse; William and Daniel Treadwell, printing office; Peter Pearse, Sr., house; Mrs. Daniel Pierce, house; Samuel Sprague, barber shop; Mrs. Samuel Bowles, house; Charles Pierce, house and brick store; William Hart, house, occupied by Captain Samuel Pearse; store, owned by Mrs. Hart, occupied by Cazneau Bayley; William Hart, shop; Jacob Walden, house and store; Captain Elijah Hall, a store; Captain Keyron Walsh, house, occupied by George Dame, John Frothingham, house, Samuel Elliot, house and bakeshop, also occupied by Mr. Folsom, bakery; Mr. Newhall, shoe store, and Mrs. Seavey as dwelling; John Badger's shop, tinman; house and barn of Jacob Sheafe, occupied by Richard Evans, James Rundlet, Samuel Haven, Jr., Oliver Briard, Nathaniel Dean, merchants; Henry Haven, house and outhouses; Judge (John Pickering's house; John Penhallow, house and buildings; new hardware store owned by H. & B Penhallow; William Boyd, store house and barn, occupied by James Henderson, J. B. Sewall and Nathan Folsom,

English and West India goods and as dwelling by William and Daniel Treadwell; Daniel Austin, house; George Jaffrey estate, two rows of stores, occupied by Daniel Eaton, Stephen Little, Benjamin Leverett, Clement Jackson, Mr. Noble, Ebenezer Chadwick, Robert Mendum (shoes), Nutter Coleman, Ball, Jenkins, Beck etc.: store owned by underwriters in Mr. Pierce's insurance office and occupied by William Seavey; row of small houses owned by Jaffrey estate and occupied by a number of poor families; Mr. J. Day, pot ash store; Mr. Rymes' shop; store owned by Mr. Ebenezer Thompson of Durham; Isaac Rindge, store; fish market; brick stores owned by Joseph Haven, James Sheafe, and Keyron Walsh and occupied by Peter Coffin, Joseph and Joshua Haven, Henry Ladd; N. A. and J. Haven, Samuel Jones, William Jones, Theodore Furber, Nathaniel Dearborn and part of the middle story as a custom house; stores owned by Samuel Hill and occupied by himself, Jonathan Clark, Alexander Ewen, Joseph Gavet and Nathaniel White; stores owned by heirs of late Jonathan Hamilton; store of George Cutts; store of Woodbury Langdon, occupied by Abel Harris; Miss Ann Alcott's store, occupied by George Cate; a house owned by John Langdon and occupied by Captain William Rice; late Samuel Cutts house; Neil M'Intire, house and store; John Langdon, house and store, occupied by Ebenezer Chadwick; Martin Parry estate, house and store, occupied by Captain Samuel Larkin and Captain Henry McClintock; house of Alexander Ewen; Nicholas Rousselet, house occupied by James L. Giles, Mr. Hooper and Mr. Carter; house owned by Mrs. Furness, occupied by Nathaniel and Washington Pierce as dwelling; Joseph Whipple, store occupied by Benjamin Brierley; house with two shops, owned by Clement Storer, occupied by Colonel Nathaniel Folson as a dwelling and one shop by Benjamin Sweetser; house and two shops, owned by Simes estate, occupied by William Simes, goldsmith and two of his sisters; house, two shops in front, estate of Deacon John Noble, occupied by Oliver Briard and shops by a daughter of Noble and Dr. Josiah Dwight; store, two shops in front, owned by Edward Parry, occupied by himself and Joshua Blake; brick store, owned by John Goddard, occupied by brother Jonathan as hardware store; row of three-story brick stores owned by Eliphalet Ladd, occupied by himself, James Foster, Samuel Thompson, N. Wire; Mr. Hasty, widow Hardy, Mr. Gordon, Richard Perry, Mrs. Winkley; Isaac Smith, house; Goerge Simes, workshop; Jeremiah Libbey's store, with William Walker: house, large store with six shops, owned by John Melcher, "late Printer", occupied by himself as dwelling and Henry Burley, William Garland, Robert M'Cleary, N.S. & W. Pierce, print shop,

John Gains, and Isaac Stanwood; store, two shops in front, owned by Widow Nelson, Mrs. Harris and Mehetable Man, occupied by John Nelson, Job Jarris; also house of Widow Nelson; house and shop, owned by John Pierce, occupied by Benjamin Swett and Henry Burley, as dwelling and John Man as shop; house and shop, owned by Widow Warner and occupied by herself and children.

[10]. One man who resisted this tide of migration was Edward Parry who built the brick building now used by C. F. Pearson & Son, as a clothing store at 46 Market Street.

[11]. At this time the firewards were equipped with much of the power now resting with Fire Chief Ernest Weeks. For instance we find a law in 1803 (after the fire, naturally) charging that it "shall be the duty of the fire wards, or the major part of them, within the Town of Portsmouth...To make such Rules and Regulations not repugnant to any Law of this State, For preventing fires — or for clearing away shavings, chips, or any combustible materials that may be thought dangerous...."

They were given power to levy fines and half of the fine collected was to go to the prosecutor and the other half to support the fire engines in the town. Under an act passed in 1781, the fire wards were each to have a staff, five feet long, painted red, with a "bright brass spire at the head" as a badge of office. There was a fire ward in each of the several districts of the town and it was his duty to take charge of a fire in his locality, assisted by his brother fire wards. The first of the acts providing for fire wards was put on the books in 1758. And it was a job not voted on lightly by the electorate, as some towns are apt to do today in electing men to the office of hog reeve.

[12]. Over the years the fire wards were among the town's more responsible citizens. We find such names as that of Major Samuel Hale, the school master; and Jonathan Warner, member of the Governor's Council, in the days before the Revolution. During the fire of 1802 the fire wards were Samuel Chase, Clement Storer, George Long, John McClintock, William Ham, Samuel Jones, Joseph Whipple, William Gardner, Neil McIntire, Clement Jackson, Thomas Manning, Samuel Hall and Edward Cutts, everyone of them a citizen of the first order, although business reverses shortly after forced Clement Jackson to go into bankruptcy. Nathaniel Adams with his "Annals of Portsmouth" left a memorial to his life that is now irreplacable. His name would endure if only because of his intense interest in books, the two libraries he was instrumental in founding, the Athenaeum and the Portsmouth Library. His father, Nathaniel,

was a sea captain.

[13]. Mark Simes died October 7, 1834, at the age of 59. His home was on Court Street.

[14]. Jonathan Goddard was a brother to Dr. John Goddard and a partner to him in various business enterprises. He died March 4, 1807 at the age of 37. His widow later became the wife of Robert Rice, a highly successful merchant and manufacturer here in the mid-19th Century. She was the mother of Arabella Rice, who left the funds for the Rice Memorial Library in Kittery. During Goddard's life-time he lived in the house that had been the property of John Fisher, about where the Piscataqua Savings Bank is today. The Rambler says that it was a gambrel roofed house, similar in appearance to the John Paul Jones House and end to the street, with gardens stretching to State Street. Dr. Josiah Dwight was living in it at the time of the 1813 fire.

[15]. This apparently is the same Stephen Little who was forced to leave the country at the time of the Revolution.

[16]. This was the old building known for many years as Queen's Chapel and the place where Washington worshipped at the time of his visit. In the belfrey hung the famous Louisburg bell. The original Episcopalian chapel was approximately in the northeast corner of the First National store parking lot on Pleasant Street. That structure passed into the hands of the North Churchers. Queen's Chapel was built in 1732 and named in honor of Queen Caroline who donated a communion service, still in use. When the old building fell victim to the flames, plans for a new one were immediately begun. On January 27, 1807, Benjamin Brierley, Matthew S. Marsh and Thomas Brown advertised that they were agents for contracts to supply bricks, hewn stones and lumber for the new structure. Corner-stone laying took place on St. John's Day, June 24, 1807, Captain Thomas Thompson, grand master of New Hampshire Masons, officiating. The ceremonies involved a Masonic parade through the streets and Governor John Langdon was in attendance. The Louisburg bell, badly damaged by fire, and its fall from the steeple, was recast by Paul Revere of Boston, no stranger to Portsmouth, and was hung in 1808 when the construction was completed. After nearly 90 years, in 1896, the bell was again recast with 300 pounds of new metal added.

[17]. The fire of 1806 was the least damaging of the three holocausts, but its toll was heavy enough. The Gazette listed the losses thus: "The principal sufferers are N.A. & J. Haven, Abel & Robert Harris, Ebenezer Thompson, Edward and George Cutts,

Nathaniel Adams & Son, James Day, Stephen Little, Benjamin Hill and Washington Pierce". Christopher Rimes and Samuel Cotton, lost dwelling houses; the church (St. John's) and parish house, three stories tall, new and nearly completed. Four houses were pulled down to stay the spread of the flames, those of John Staples, the Widow Tuttle, Mark Simes and George Wendell and the workshop of Mr. Giles. Suffering losses when their goods were moved were Jeremiah Libbey, William Walker, Daniel Brown, B & J. Weare, George and Jacob Wendell, William, Thomas and Charles Neil.

[18]. The writer remembers at the time the Frank D. Perkins Tire and Rubber Company building on Market Street was destroyed on a sub-freezing day in 1948. He accompanied Fire Chief George T. Cogan, now deceased, into the attic of the building next door. A double brick fire wall stood between the structures and no heat could be felt on the side opposite the raging blaze next door. That old fire partition performed its duty perfectly that time.

[19]. J. Smith, of course, was John Smith, and the crippled leg he suffered with for the rest of his life was a constant reminder of the fire.

[20]. Again we go to the Gazette for a listing of the losses in the fire of 1813: Broad (State) Street — Mrs. Woodward's house and barn; late John Sheafe's house, improved by M. S. Blunt ("Improved by" was a polite way of saying "occupied"); late Major (Joseph) Bass', improved by R. Henderson, Mrs. Furniss; house of Miss Hale, improved by herself, Mr. Remick, Judge (John S.) Sherburne and Mr. Freeman, in this building the Portsmouth Library was burnt up: Judkin's and Senter's shop; A. Greenleaf's shop; S. Barker's store. Jaffrey (Part of Court) Street --- Benning Adams' house; house occupied by James Danford. Court (Part of present-day Pleasant) Street -- Honorable D. Webster's house; T(homas) Haven's house; Deacon Clark's; Union Bank; Miss Wentworth's shop; G(eorge) Wentworth's store, improved by Joseph Clark and the collector of customs; Widow Adams' house, improved by herself and Colonel (Timothy) Upham; Honorable James Sheafe's house, improved by Dr. Dwight; E(benezer) Chadwick's house. Daniel Street -- S(amuel) Fernald's shop; Samuel Pierce's house; Colonel Walback's house; houses of Benjamin Wentworth, Jonathan Walker and T. S. Lewis; Widow Sparhawk's house; Thomas Roach's House, improved by John Gookin and others; Andrew Clark's house; Jonathan Warner's store; house owned by Jonathan Warner and occupied by Daniel Humphreys; Widow Shackford's house, house of William Tredick, Jr.; John Seaward's house; George Plaisted's house

and shop; house of William Badger, Jr.; Mrs. Sherive's two houses; Judge Sherburne's house, improved by C. Rinaldi; D(aniel) Huntress' house, improved by T. King; J. Frothingham's tallow chandlery; S. & J. Gardner's store; G(orge) Dennett's shop; B(enjamin) Hall's shop; Samuel Cotton's shop; six stores on Langdon's Wharf, improved by Colonel Harris for the navy agent and others. Buck (Eastern end of State Street) Street -- Mrs. Adams' buildings, improved by L. Brucex, I. Chapman and M. Janvrin; Honorable James Sheafe's two houses, improved one by himself and the other by Dr. (J.H.) Pierpont and Widow (Abraham) Isaac; George Wentworth's house; Widow Marsh's house; middle schoolhouse and watch house; Captain (William) Cox' house; E. Wyatt's house; Davenport's Tavern; W(illiam) Stanwood's shop; William Ham's three houses and shop; Jacob Sheafe Esq.'s house; shop improved by T. S. Bowles and T(homas) G. Moses; store improved by Mr. Wiggins; house of William Jones, Jr.; Widow Christie's house; J. Johnson's house; S(amuel) Fernald's house; late Samuel Griffiths' house; T(hales) G. Yeaton's house; M. Beck's house; Widow Edwards' house; Widow Dimsey's house; John Seaward's house, improved by G. Forrester; Thomas Brown's two houses and store, improved by John Place and others; Widow Jackson's house; George Ham's house, improved by himself and D(aniel) P. Drown; Drown and Treadwell's store; Deacon Drown's house; Mrs. Gregory's house; Peter Cow(u)es' house; Samuel Tripes's house; Daniel Eaton's house; Robert Yeaton's house; house and store late of N(icholas) Rousselet, improved by L. Serratt; Abner Blaisdell's four houses, improved by himself, Blaisdell and Bennett and others; Joseph Amazeen's house; Thomas Jackson's house; house of Abner Blaisdell, Jr.; N. Merriam's house; J. Pierce's house, improved by Widow Shapley; four shops of S. Balch, S. Rand, N(athaniel) S(heafe) Griffity, and others; William Tredick's house; block of houses of John Seaward, improved by N. Seaward, B. Woodbury and John Yeaton; R. Ham's house; N. W. Fernald's house; Widow Stoodley's house; house of Newton, improved by Mitchell; J.D. Seaward's house; a store improved by Abel Harris; a block of 16 stores on Portsmouth Pier, improved by William and Theodore Chase, John McClintock, B(enjamin) Holmes, Jr., Thomas Manning and others. On cross streets -- Joseph Low's house, improved by W(illiam) Fernald, and others; Joseph Gavett's house; Daniel Melcher's house; Andrew Lynn's house; Samuel Pierce's house; S(amuel) Gerrish's shop. Water Street -- New Hampshire Hotel; Block improved by Jacob Cutter and others; James Shapley's house; Widow Champney's house, improved by Joseph Bartlett Esq.; E(dmund) M.

Quincy's house; James Shores' house; Widow Talpey's house; house of late J. Wendell; James Orne's house; Elisha Whidden's store; house improved by T. Johnson; D(aniel) Austin's house, improved by Widow Dixon. Sheafe's Wharf — A block of stores owned and improved by Jacob Sheafe, Esq. Shapley's Wharf — A block of stores owned and improved by A(braham) Wendell, R. S. Randell, R(euben) Shapley, T(homas) Pierce, et al. Driscoe's Wharf — Three stores, improved by R(obert) Rice, J. Low, Jr., and others; Pitt (part of Court Street) Street — Widow Dalling's house, improved by B(enjamin) Hart; Thomas Moulton's house and shop; Stephen Foye's house; house improved by Samuel Hutchings, Jr.; house of late S(amuel) Dalling; P. Clement's house. Washington Street — James Tarlton's house; two houses late of Dr. Hall Jackson. Atkinson Street — John P. Ross' house, improved by James Ladd.

[21]. Daniel Webster, a native of Salisbury, New Hampshire, who attended Phillips Exeter and graduated from Dartmouth College, came to Portsmouth in 1807. Within a short span of years he rose to great popularity with the people of his adopted town. He was the son of Ebenezer and Abigail (Eastman) Webster, born January 18, 1782. In 1808 he married Grace Fletcher of Hopkinton, and with her made his home here. Webster quickly mastered many of the tricks of the trial lawyer and early in his career was described by Jeremiah Mason, a great lawyer himself, as one of his toughest opponents. He went to Congress as a representative from 1813 to 1817. One of the homes he occupied while in Portsmouth, has been moved to Strawbery Banke, Inc., for preservation. It stood originally at High and Hanover Streets.

Webster attained his greatest fame as a pleader in arguing the celebrated Dartmouth College case but that was after he had moved to Massachusetts, a state he represented in the national legislature many times. Although he and Mason· were frequently antagonists at the bar, they were warm personal friends, and at Mason's home, a pair of slippers and a pipe were always reserved for Webster. As indicated by the anecdote, Webster was an able man with a bottle and his capacity was remarkable. Mason preceded Webster as a tenant in a Vaughan Street house that had been owned and occupied by George Meserve, the one-time Stamp officer. Webster was followed by Timothy G. Upham and in turn he was supplanted by James Sheafe, who came back to the house to live after his property was destroyed in 1813. Webster moved from there to the house that was burned and then into the house that is preserved by Strawbery Banke. Webster and his wife were back in Portsmouth to help the town celebrate its 200th anniversary on May 21, 1823. Their names are signed to the scroll used to record those present at the festivity, a document which is preserved in the Portsmouth Athenaeum. Webster's last visit to Portsmouth came 21 years later, almost to the day, May 17, 1844. He was entertained royally, both at Jefferson Hall in the afternoon and at the Cameneum, a building which stood toward the western end of the Vaughan Street parking lot and was the scene of many local meetings. Eight years later "Black Daniel" was dead.

[22]. Portsmouth Pier represented in its very being, the zenith of Portsmouth as a deepwater port. It was part of the logical pattern of developing a straight line of communication between inland New Hampshire and the sea. Located as it was at the foot of State Street, where C. E. Walker Company's old wharf was, the flow of traffic came almost straight to it from the New Hampshire Turnpike and Piscataqua Bridge. The incorporation took place January 8, 1795, with Samuel Sherburne, Richard Hart and Elijah Hall as key people in the organization. The articles of incorporation give hint that some kind of a company was already in business, consolidating the holdings of those concerned. In 1796, they built the pier, 340 feet long, 65 wide. Where the Walker Company had its office was the site of the New Hampshire Hotel, owned by Portsmouth Pier, although it probably was nearer the center of the street than the present building. Widening took place at this point after the fire of 1813. The hotel building itself was an old structure and believed to have been the first brick house in the town. Samuel Penhallow, a member of the Governor's Council who died in 1726, built it and lived in it with his wife the former Mary Cutts, daughter of President John. Later it was bought by Henry Sherburne who was a brother-in-law to Lieutenant Governor John Wentworth. Henry and his son Henry, both members of the Governor's Council, lived in the house and here the Masons frequently met. The Sherburnes sold it to the pier company and the 1813 fire destroyed it. The company struggled as best it could to shake off the terrible blow of the fire, the pier was rebuilt to some extent, and the company stayed in existence for years, but Portsmouth's day as a major port was nearing a close for other reasons.

[23]. Edward Cutts was a prominent merchant here for many years. He built the house that stands high on the slope above the corner of Maplewood Avenue and Cutts Street in 1810. The house is now the property of Dr. Peter Beck, who makes his home at 43 Austin Street. The house was lived in for some years by Hampden

Cutts, an attorney who left Portsmouth for Vermont in 1833 and where he died in 1875. While he lived here, he gained note as a public speaker and as the editor of a newspaper, "The Signs of the Times". Another Edward Cutts, this one a native of Kittery, made his home here at about the same time Edward the merchant was prospering. This Edward occupied the house east of the Rockingham Hotel at the corner of Chestnut and State Streets, a property once owned by Abraham Shaw, a noted backer of privateering ventures. This Cutts was a lawyer and was for a time president of the United States Bank here. It was his widow, Mary H. Cutts, a daughter of Jacob Sheafe, who left $14,000 for the improvement of Richards Avenue.

[24]. John Haven was a leading merchant who for some years lived in a house that stood approximately where the Esso station on State Street is, not at the corner of what was called Mulberry (Wright Avenue) and State. The property was also occupied for a time by Nicholas Rousselet, who operated a museum on the site. While Rousselet was in occupancy, he changed the name of Mulberry Lane to Demerara Street. Rousselet came here from Demerara and married Catharine, a daughter of Samuel Moffatt, which made him a brother-in-law to Dr. Nathaniel Haven. After Rousselet's death in Demerara shortly after 1800, Dr. Haven acquired the property, although as one lawyer put it not long ago while searching titles in the area, "by what right he did it, I don't know". John Haven left the house to move into one he had built on what is the site of the Farragut School, Islington Street. This property stayed in the Haven family until acquired by the city in 1904.

[25]. Daniel Austin built the first three-story store in the city. That is the building, now shorn of its upper level, that stands at the southern end of the North Church. Austin put up the building in 1800, and there were only 15 three-story houses in the town, most of them less than five years old. Austin sold the property to General Asa Dearborn in 1811. Later it came into the possession of Joshua Wentworth.

[26]. The Widow Woodward, referred to by both the Gazette and The Rambler, was Mrs. Moses Woodward whose husband Captain Woodward was bringing the sloop Amity from Grenada to Georgetown, South Carolina, when he ran into a heavy storm. Woodward himself took the helm and a tremendous sea washed him overboard. He made a desperate effort to get back and managed to get his hands on the main sheet. No one could reach him to give him a hand and an injury he must have suffered when being washed over

the quarter rail hampered his own efforts. Finally with a desparing cry, "I must go", he disappeared into the ocean. The barn owned by his widow stood where the Stone Church is now.

[27]. John Gains was a son of George, who was so much in the forefront of town affairs for more than 30 years.

[28]. The Isaacs had their shop on the site of the old Rockingham County Courthouse building. Abraham Isaac began advertising in the Gazette in the 1790s and some years was quite busy as an auctioneer in addition to operating his shop. The Rambler is the authority that they were the first Jewish residents of Portsmouth. However, with a strong Jewish colony at Newport, Rhode Island, Jewish traders must have been here at various times. Rebecca Isaac, after her husband's death, February 15, 1803, continued to operate the shop until the fire. Wiped out, she went to New Ipswich, New Hampshire, to live with an adopted son, Henry Isaac, who was married to the daughter of a prominent Boston minister. The Isaac family was well known in the town, engaged in manufacturing and merchandising for many years.

[29]. The story goes that John Davenport kept the body of his wife three weeks. When the fire put him out of business, Davenport bought the house on the northeast corner of State and Fleet Streets, the site of the First National Bank, and adapted it as a boarding house. In all his years of business, Davenport never sold liquor in his houses and hence they cannot be regarded as hotels. The first Mrs. Davenport was not long in her grave when the bereaved husband found a new wife. She was a waitress in a hotel in Haverhill, Massachusetts. His new location kept for him his old patrons and his business prospered to the day of his death, March 28, 1842, at the age of 90. His widow Sarah managed to get him into the ground within three days, so business may have been a little slack. Sarah survived him by a year, dying at 81. Davenport was active in Masonry, was master of St. John's Lodge and Davenport Council of Select Master Masons was named in his honor.

13

Prelude to War

[1]. Woodbury Langdon's activities have been touched upon, and at one point only his brother's political power saved him from serious trouble when there was a move to impeach him and remove him from the state judiciary. His home was on the site of the Rockingham Hotel, and he also owned the John Paul Jones House to the west.

[2]. The Portsmouth Bath was a real going concern. It was founded at a time when only those of wealth enjoyed the luxury of a bath in their own home. And then such an item would not be part of the plumbing, but handfilled and drained by servants. The John Paul Jones House has one of these — wooden — on display.

The bath stayed in business either publicly or privately owned for better than a century because plumbing was not as common a feature of Portsmouth homes as it would be thought. There were frequent ads in the columns of the newspapers telling of the services offered by the bath. Sometimes in storms and high tides, floating on the river as it did, the Bath House would go adrift. In the 1850s it was caught in an ice pack and smashed.

In 1891, the Bath House Commission had a new buliding constructed, letting the contract to Warren Keene for $2,600. This "salt water dipping tank" as The Herald irreverently called it, was usually located on Mechanic Street near the City Landing. Customarily, it was taken to Four Tree Island for "winter quarters", out of harm's way from rough weather and ice. But for some reason, the commission was late in getting it taken care of in 1907, and on November 16, the high tide swept it from its moorings near the Portsmouth Yacht Club. Along with it went three boats, one belonging to John P. Holman, a machinist at the Navy Yard; another to Dr. Joseph Boyle, a dentist; and the third to Richard Crocker. A member of the Yacht club went out and untangled the boats, but the Bath House continued on a majestic cruise upriver. Finally, as any such unshapely and unguided craft would have to do, it came to rest against the Portsmouth Bridge. Efforts by tugs from the North End proved unavailing in the strong current, plus the fear that too great a strain would pull the building apart, so it was left there to come down with the tide. The chairman of the commission, a man named Wendell, insisted that the lines had been tampered with because he had personally increased them only a few days before.

[3]. Thomas Moses was connected to the "Dr. Moses" celebrated by The Rambler as one of the great practical jokers of the 18th Century. One of the first women to serve on a Portsmouth City Council — the late Ellen Moses — was descended from this family. The Rambler has several delightful tales to tell of "Dr. Moses" and the pranks he played.

[4]. If there's a criticism to be leveled at the Reverend Timothy G. Alden, Jr., for his discourse on local religious societies it would be under the heading of brevity. His service here began with an assistantship to the Reverend Samuel Haven in the South Parish. He was ordained on November 20, 1799. In 1808, Alden authored a treatise entitled, "An Account of the Several Religious Societies in Portsmouth", and it's still a valuable work.

14

The War of 1812

[1]. Henry S. Langdon was the son of Woodbury Langdon. His mother was Sarah, the daughter of Henry Sherburne. In 1839 his home was on Islington Street. In March of 1814, Langdon, as Navy agent, acknowledged receipt of $50,000 for the Yard: $15,000 for the "74", $12,000 for provisions; $3,000 for contingencies; $20,000 for the Navy Yard. That Langdon should hold such a lucrative sinecure can be explained quite easily by the fact that his uncle, John Langdon, was a former President, Governor and U. S. Senator.

[2]. Langley Boardman built the Boardman-Marvin House on Middle Street. At the time of the privateer Fox venture, Boardman was 38 years old. Later he served on the Governor's Council, dying in 1833 at the age of 58. Boardman was one of the partners in the building of the original Franklin Block which burned May 8, 1879. A cabinet maker, Boardman's memorial, and reminder that he once lived amongst us, is the house that stands on the west side of the double bricked building put up by the Parrotts. It stayed in the family, through Boardman's son, Dr. John, until 1900.

[3]. William Gardner, owner of the Wentworth-Gardner House, Mechanic Street, died April 29, 1834, at the age of 83. During the Revolution he was a commissary, getting the job of loan commissioner under Washington, a post from which he was fired by John Adams, but later reappointed. Many notes about him are available in The Rambles. His home is presently owned by the Wentworth-Gardner House Association, headed by former Governor Charles M. Dale. This organization also owns the Tobias Lear House.

[4]. Abraham Shaw, a sharp-witted financier of privateering, or anything else that would make a dollar, lived in the house on State Street, east of the Rockingham, owned by Andrew Jarvis. These ventures included those by his brother, Captain Thomas M. Shaw. Abraham Shaw died October 14, 1828, at 53, and his portrait, by the courtesy of former Mayor Jarvis, hangs in the Portsmouth Athenaeum.

161

[5]. John Parrott, born in Devon in 1742, sired two sons, John F. and Enoch G. A grandson, Enoch G., invented the Parrott rifle, an artillery piece that had a direct bearing on the outcome of the Civil War. The grandson lived out the last days of his life, a retired rear admiral, at the Hotel Rockingham, dying May 10, 1879, at 63.

His grandfather came to North America with General James Wolfe's expedition in 1759, which resulted in the capture of Quebec and Canada. That Parrott, who is on the church register as "Parrett", according to Gerald D. Foss, came down here and settled. In the Revolution, he guarded Portsmouth Harbor. His home was on the site of the present-day Kearsarge Hotel.

[6]. Henry Salter followed the sea for many years, and an 1839 listing had him as a mariner. He lost two wives while in his 20s, not abnormal for that day, when childbirth was woman's greatest enemy.

[7]. George Long, Jr., a grandson of the Revolutionary leader, Colonel Pierse Long, died in Havana, June 28, 1819.

[8]. One of the more successful investors in privateers, William Rice no doubt would be pleased to know that his Deer Street home still stands, despite urban renewal. That it will house, some time in the future, the offices of the Greater Portsmouth Chamber of Commerce, which might not be Rice's idea of fame, cannot be helped. In the course of his privateering gambles, Rice once accumulated so much calico that his wife's friends came to the house and cut pieces from the bolts, taking as much as they wanted. Rice lived to enjoy his profits, dying in 1851.

[9]. Abel Harris died December 22, 1829, at 67. Rooksby, his wife, died July 6, 1833, at 73. Associated with Robert Harris, he owned the Bristol-Packet and they used her in a freighting business with Europe.

[10]. Thomas W. Penhallow, then at the mellow age of 39, signed the Bicentennial Roll on May 21, 1823. He took a girl from Gloucester, Massachusetts, Miss Mary Beach, as his bride. His native town had his services in the Legislature of 1822. Penhallow lived to the age of 92, dying on September 22, 1876.

[11]. Tradition, and probably fact, has it that German U-boats used the Wentworth Hotel as a landmark in World War I. Certainly guests sat on the famed verandas, and, using their binoculars, claimed that they could see a school of the German craft sort of "sunning" themselves in the early summer of 1918 between the Shoals and the mainland. Naval vessels moved into the area, but the

U-boats managed to make a killing of shipping heading for Europe.

[12]. This Enoch G. Parrott died June 13, 1828, aged 47. At the end of the War of 1812, Parrott bought in the privateer Fox at auction for $2,400, seemingly a small sum for a vessel that had made many hundreds of times that amount for her owners. Perhaps a clue to this lies in a news item at the time which indicated that Fox was a "wet vessel", meaning that everything had to be kept battened down in a heavy sea. In other words, she would not be a success as a merchant vessel.

[13]. William Jones, Jr., became one of the town's more prosperous businessmen in later years.

[14]. John Melcher, who has had more obsequious worship from latter-day sycophants than he warrants, acquired the New Hampshire Gazette from the aging Daniel Fowle.

[15]. As an auctioneer, Samuel Larkin, during the War of 1812, became the Parke-Bernet of Portsmouth. Something over $2 million in prizes (Remember this was in 1812-14) passed under his hammer. One of Fox' prizes alone brought $334,415 in one part of a sale, and another $132,673 in the cleanup. One of the most beautiful homes on Middle Street, exterior anyway, is the brick mansion at No. 180, which was built by Larkin. It's now occupied by Mrs. Arthur H. Rice.

A house lived in by Colonel Joshua Wentworth had stood on the site, but was removed to make way for the house built by Larkin after he purchased the property from Wentworth's estate. Mrs. Larkin was a daughter of Joshua Wentworth, and she, with the assistance of her husband, provided her father with 22 grandchildren. Later the property passed to a man named Hurd of Exeter. One of Hurd's daughters married the merchant Henry Ladd, who thus came into the property. Larkin attained the age of 76 before dying on March 10, 1849.

[16]. Robert Rice, brother of William, became a leading merchant and manufacturer. His house on Islington Street, long since supplanted by commercial buildings, was struck October 2, 1847, by a piece of the roof of the Portsmouth Steam Factory, blown off by a small, local tornado. The Steam Factory later became Kearsarge Mills. Rice, who married a daughter of Captain Thomas Martin, had an only daughter, Arabella, who never married. Kittery's Rice Public Library, named and funded in honor of her father, still stands.

[17]. With romantic historians and novelists, one of the more popular stories of the War of 1812 is the battle between HMS

Boxer and the USS Enterprise. Boxer met defeat and was taken into Portland Harbor, but, from the pages of Preble's "History of the Navy Yard", we glean a shameful little tale that clouds the idealism of those who refuse to accept ancestral perfidy. The story's not often told but it involves HMS Boxer, and Preble had it from Charles Toppan, brother of Christopher Toppan, a frequent speculator in privateer vessels — U.S. that is. Toppan put this in a letter about 60 years after the War of 1812:

"At the commencement of our war with Great Britain in 1813, the United States had but few if any factories for the manufacture of woolen cloth and blankets. It was understood that no captures would be made of British goods owned by citizens of the United States, and many American merchants imported via Halifax and St. Johns, New Brunswick, their usual stock of goods. In 1813, I went with others in the Swedish brig Margaretta to St. John, New Brunswick, and filled her with British goods, intending to take them to Bath, Maine, and enter them regularly and pay the lawful duties thereon. All we had to fear was American privateers, and we hired Captain Blyth, of HMS Boxer, to convoy us to the mouth of the Kennebec River, for which service we gave him a bill of exchange on London for 100 pounds. We sailed in company, and in a thick fog off Quoddy Head the Boxer took us in tow. It was agreed that when we were about to enter the mouth of the river two or three guns would be fired over us, to have the appearance of trying to stop us, should any idle folks be looking on. Captain Burrows, in the United States brig Enterprise, lay in Portland harbor, and hearing the guns got under way and, as is well known, captured the Boxer after a severe engagement in which both captains were killed. Our bill of exchange, we thought, might in some way cause us trouble and we employed Esquire Kinsman to take 500 specie dollars on board the captured ship and exchange them for the paper, which was found in Captain Blyth's breeches pocket".

Well, Toppan must be given credit, he and his associates could just as easily have stolen the 100 pounds out of the dead man's pocket. This is probably more typical an incident along the New England coast during the War of 1812 than many historians like to admit. Remember New England adamantly opposed the War of 1812 because it was injurious to its trade.

[18]. For those who tend to glamorize wars, especially those of long ago, a letter written by a Portsmouth man from Dartmoor Prison may be an antidote. Captain Henry Trefethen's letter appeared in The Morning Chronicle and was contributed by

Thomas Spinney of Boston. Lack of space dictates using only excerpts: "This prison or depot is situated in the County of Devon, and lies about 15 miles northeast of Plymouth, and 26 miles northwest of Exeter, the capital town...The country around, as far as the eye can reach, is an uneven, barren and dreary waste....The climate here is rather unhealthy. The prisoners are almost continually affected with colds....This Depot consists of seven prisons, each being calculated to contain from 1100 to 1500, who are under the care of an agent appointed by and under the control of the Transport Board. Here are stationed as guard 2,000 well disciplined militia, and two companies of Royal Artillery. The prisons are all strongly built of stone, and are surrounded by two circular walls. The outer wall measures one mile in circumference, and on the inner wall are military walks for sentinels....There are three separate yards, which communicate with each other by a passage....Opposite this passage is the Market Square....

"The first yard contains three prisons; Nos. 1 and 3 only are occupied by American prisoners. The inside of the prisons present a melancholy and disagreeable appearance. One would imagine they were calculated more for the reception of cattle than for human beings....To enter either of the prison yards from without, you must pass through five gates. Fronting the outer gate is a reservoir of water, which is brought the distance of six miles by a canal....The hospital is under the superintendents of a physician....Dr. Magrath is the present Superintendent and a gentleman of eminence and skill in his profession; and will ever be remembered by the American prisoners with esteem and respect....Many hardships have the prisoners suffered in this depot, more especially in the winter of 1813....Many of the prisoners almost naked, no fire allowed them.... The prisoners on many occassions have received harsh treatment from the Governor of this depot....

"The recent massacre which took place by his orders ought forever to stamp the name of Thos. G. Shortland with barbarity infamy and disgrace....On the 6th day of April 1815, as a small party of prisoners were amusing themselves at a game of ball, someone of the number hitting the ball with too much violence, it flew over the wall fronting the prison yard into the soldiers' barracks. The sentry on the opposite side was requested to heave the ball back, but refused; upon which the party threatened to break through and regain their ball....A hole was made sufficiently large for a man to pass through, but no one attempted to do it. Soon after the alarm bell and the militia beat to arms. The prisoners, surprised at the alarm, ran into the passage fronting the Market Square, where appeared Captain Shortland at the head of about 500 military, the front rank of whom were ordered to fire, and soon after did the same with considerable execution....

"The scenes of barbarity and horror that were witnessed on this day were indescribable. Seven were killed and 38 wounded, some of whom have since died of their wounds....A man by the name of John Washington being severely wounded and overtaken by the military, begged for his life; but these ruffians, deaf to the voice of pity, deliberately pointed their muskets within six inches of his head and blew his brains out. A young lad of 14 years was run through by an officer of the military...."Captain Shortland endeavors to justify his conduct by saying that the prisoners were attempting to break out. So far from being the case, the prisoners were in momentary expectation of being drafted on board cartels for their own country; and had the gates been swung open to them, scarce a single person out of 5,000 would have left the prison. It was a notorious fact that Captain Shortland has long sought for a plausible pretext to glut his revenge and hatred against men whose principles and manners are so uncongenial with that of his own countrymen in general...The 6th of April, 1815, will be long remembered with emotions of horror at the savage ferocity of the military headed by Thos. G. Shortland..."

And it should not be forgotten that the War of 1812 was over; that fact was even known by then in the United States, let alone England.

[19]. On January 14, 1814, Navy Secretary William Jones wrote Commodore Hull, after the Yard commander had expressed fears on the security of the 74: "When the intention of the Government to built the 74's was known all the intelligent men from the vicinity of Portsmouth represented the place to be so strong by nature as to require very little protection from art; but to create and maintain the force contemplated in your letter would be an effectual bar to building at Portsmouth, as the expense of defending the ship while building, if the means of defense, natural and artificial, are really so feeble as represented, would cost more than the ships would be worth when built. This is a subject which I wish distinctly to understand before further expense is incurred on the establishment, for had I conceived the situation to be so vulnerable and exposed as it is stated to be, I should certainly not have authorized the great expense already incurred...."

Probably Captain Elmer T. "Tom" Westfall, the present day shipyard commander, would not have to dig far into his files before finding a note from Washington that might sound the same. However, the Secretary said he would take the security problem up with the President and Secretary of War, and he must have done so, because, in his next letter he told Hull that the defenses would be beefed up and Colonel John Walbach had been ordered to take command at the lower forts. Hull still wanted to speed up the launch and move the vessel upriver but again was overruled. The Secretary in September ordered the ship to be named Washington, but it was not until July of 1815, and the war over, that she took to the water.

[20]. An excellent article on Wasp appeared in the February, 1961, issue of the United States Naval Institute Proceedings. There would be nothing more enjoyable than to quote the whole article which was written by a highly competent news reporter, James M. Perry, but it cannot be done. Suffice to say that Wasp came to the Navy Yard for fitting and did the last of her recruiting in Portsmouth. She was built in Newburyport, which, as any loyal Puddle Docker knows, hardly rates as a seaport. Actually, the Wasp had so much draft that she was sent to Portsmouth without guns because she could not cross the sand bar at the mouth of the Merrimack with them aboard. By one of those ironies with which life is filled, Wasp's skipper was a man named Johnston Blakeley, who had the misfortune to be relieved of command of USS Enterprise 16 days before her fight with HMS Boxer. Lieutenant William Burrows, the captain who relieved Blakeley on Enterprise was killed in the engagement with Boxer; but then, Blakeley never came back from his cruise with Wasp. Before she disappeared forever, Wasp left definite impressions as to her ability to fight. Thirteen times she laid it on the line with various craft, not the least of which was HMS Reindeer, and that was right in the English Channel. Reindeer was smashed to bits and her captain, William Manners, received the usual two-cannon-balls-at-the-feet burial at sea. What happened to Wasp? Who knows? Best bet is Jim Perry's conjecture that she was weakened after so many fights and succumbed to a storm. The log of the Swedish brig Adonis would seem to confirm it because she met her in Latitude 18 degrees 35' North, Longitude 30 degrees, 10' West in October 1814. Whatever her fate, there were many homes in Newburyport and Portsmouth which waited a long time for news and never had it.

[21]. According to Yard historian Preble, various British warship skippers let word get ashore as to their plans. And one big spy scare came at the time of Washington's launch when it was rumored that a British agent had been present. The war was over but that did not make any difference, the hunt was on until it was

learned that the "spy" was the brother of the man in charge of the launching, Commodore Isaac Chauncey. The commodore had quite an interest in the proceedings because Washington was to be his flagship. Thousands were on hand for the launching. But getting Washington to sea was another story because the Yard workers went on strike. Benjamin W. Crowninshield had succeeded William Jones as "SecNav" on December 19, 1814, and was as direct and tough as his predecessor in saying on August 21, 1815: "If the work of the ship is suspended in consequence, measures will be taken to equip the ship in order to proceed to New York, where the payments in Treasury notes are equal to those in gold and silver. This will eventually drive all the naval operations and equipment from the Northern to the Middle and Southern States. You will be pleased to report to me the present state of the ship and time necessary to fit her for sea, so as to proceed for New York." The Yard workers had a point. Their wages were being devalued because of the depreciation of Treasury notes, as indicated in the Secretary's letter, but the matter was resolved. Washington sailed for Europe and became the flagship of that squadron until 1818. Then she returned to New York, was laid up in ordinary (mothballs) and finally broken up in 1843.

[22]. On the gate to the old fort on Fort Point, set into the brick work, is a simple chisled stone saying 1808. That indicates, in all probability, the first real federal effort to put the fort into what could be called an operative status. Colonel John Walbach was the soldier commanding; he had come here from Germany, and probably was more a military engineer than a tactical commander. But the story of Fort Constitution and Walbach Tower is not really pressing on a history of Portsmouth. Today, a Task Force, really an auxiliary to the Revolutionary War Bicentennial Commission, is trying to determine the fort's place in history. Among the members are Mrs. Edward G. Wood of North Hampton, Joseph Copley of New Castle, Mrs. Shirley Merrill of Hampton, Mrs. Dorothy Wilcox of Durham, Raymond A. Brighton of Portsmouth and former Parks Director Russell Tobey of Concord.

[23]. That a Yard commander could so blithely do this, without budgetary considerations, is horrifying to modern thought. Captain Elmer T. Westfall, today would have to explain such an action through 17 pages of original with five copies, to each pertinent division, plus twice replying by endorsement, "hereon", and then all the paper would be warehoused somewhere west of the Mississippi.

[24]. The Navy Yard, a few years ago, had several of these, but some, if not all, disappeared when one of the officers retired and have not been seen since.

[25]. If C. S. Forrester, a prolific writer on this period in the British Navy, is to be believed, one would have expected a midshipman to be doing this dirty detail. But fourth lieutenants were not far up the ladder either.

[26]. Preble says, "On another occasion the Sally was chased by Tenedos frigate, when loaded with knees and other timber for the Washington 74. The chase resulted in Tenedos striking upon some rocks, which so exasperated her captain that he opened fire on Sally with his broadside guns, 18 pounders, none of which, however, struck the little craft, but Captain Fernald went ashore and picked up one of the balls, which on his arrival at the Navy Yard, he presented to Commodore Hull as a token...."

[27]. Sark End is an old Englishism meaning the "shirt" end, or, as far as uptown Portsmouth was concerned, the South end of town.

15

Aftermath of War

[1]. The following figures on the Port of Portsmouth were printed in The Portsmouth Journal on March 9, 1850: Imports — in U.S. vessels, $54,616; foreign vessels, $30,233. Exports — in U.S. vessels $5,376; foreign vessels, $170. Bank and cod fishery: Tonnage at Custom House, 2,445; 315 men and 45 boys employed; fish cured, 27,848 cwt., valued at $61,413; oil, 1,147 gallons, value $5,376, for a total of $66,789, which meant a net to each hand of $185. In the mackerel fishery 874 tons were registered, employing 102 men and 19 boys; value of the catch was $13,122, net to each hand of $108. These figures become all the more shocking when set against those reported by "The Annalist" at the end of this chapter for the year 1823.

[2]. Samuel Sheafe lived on Market Street, and died in 1857 at the age of 72.

[3]. Samuel Lord, a South Berwick native will figure often in the narrative of the next few years. For nearly six decades he was a local Rothschild, closely associated with the city's major banks (Portsmouth Savings and even into the First National era) and an insurance broker. He made his home in what is familiar today as the John Paul Jones House, the museum operated by the Portsmouth Historical Society, which was known as the Lord House as recently as 70 years ago. As early as 1813, Lord was active in banking, helping to organize the Rockingham Bank. Lord was on hand for the incorporation of the First National in 1864, staying on as cashier until 1871. The Morning Chronicle said of him after his death in that year:

"Fifty years Mr. Lord had left his home and proceeded to his daily avocation with more than the regularity of clockwork, never swerving from the most exact punctuality except in case of sickness, a rare thing indeed with him".

[4]. John Langdon, Jr., was not the son of Governor John. He was a nephew. He married one of the daughters of Eliphalet Ladd. In 1818, he was in the State Senate.

[5]. Jacob S. Pickering made his home on Vaughan Street, and was cashier of Rockingham Bank.

[6]. Rockingham Bank voted to go out of business March 30, 1905, and a dividend of $135 was declared on the stock. The 885 shares at the annual meeting were unanimous. Causes for closing were that there were too many other banks in the city and low interest rates. In 92 years it had never passed a semi-annual dividend. Four men served as president: John Haven, 1813-45; Jonathan M. Tredick, 1845-75; John J. Pickering, 1876 to death in 1904; and William A. Peirce, who was in charge of liquidation. The cashiers were Jacob S. Pickering, 1813-49; John J. Pickering (son of Jacob S.), 1849-76; John P. Hart to the close. Hart served the bank 35 years. The Peirce family had three generations in the bank, Joshua, beginning in 1824; his son, William A., and his grandson, J. Winslow Peirce. When the bank closed the directors were J.S.H. Frink, Frederic M. Sise, J.W. Peirce, George G. Frink and Hart.

[7]. Andrew W. Bell had his place of business on Portsmouth Pier and lived on State Street. He was a selectman in 1822.

[8]. Reuben Shapley died January 10, 1825. His tombstone in St. John's includes the sentiment that his good works demanded such a monument.

[9]. Nathan Priest died September 30, 1822, at the age of 38.

[10]. The deaths of a New Castle couple when their convertible plunged into the waters through the rails of the first bridge, precipitated action in rebuilding the bridges into the safe spans we know today. The unfortunate victims of bureaucratic shuffleboard were Professor Merrick Dodd of Harvard and his wife, Winifred. That was in 1953, and Harlan Talbott of New Castle recalls the Dodds well. As Talbott says, the car, driven by Mrs. Dodd, skidded on the ice-over planked surface and it went into a spin she could not control. A portable crane was brought from the Naval Shipyard to pull the wreckage out of the water in the dawn hours.

[11]. Shapleigh's Island was where those who were undergoing smallpox "this season" would go for the period of their illness. From The Rambler we see a copy of a letter of July 8, 1776 (Liberty was only four days old) from Joseph Barrell, a merchant of Boston, addressed to Colonel Joshua Wentworth, with the following as a postscript: "Mr. Storer had invited Mrs. Martin to take the smallpox at his house: if Mrs. Wentworth desires to get rid of her fears the same way, we will accommodate her the best way we can". The Rambler goes on to tell of a time in 1797 when young ladies and gentlemen went to Shapleigh's Island for smallpox vaccination. Many

years later a local woman told The Rambler the summer she was vaccinated was one of the happiest times of her life. Apparently even in the 18th Century it was recognized that there were two sexes (Gloria Steinem, notwithstanding) and "a greater amount of that species of amusement known as "lovemaking", was, probably, never concentrated within a briefer space or more limited period". Who knows but perhaps some nights when the Dr. Tom Conroys or the Bill Marconis think they are hearing waves lapping along the shore of the island, the sounds might really be the laughter of those long-ago young people still echoing on the beach. Well, anyway, it's fun to think it might be true.

[12]. The Goat Island Club is a tightly knit social group, whose membership is never a matter of record, but, with certain people, you are "in" if you are one of the fraternity that frequents that little cluster of buildings on the west end of the New Castle causeway. While the island's known a lot of fun and laughter, it's also known tragedy, such as the time when one of the foremost members, owner of the island and former Portsmouth mayor, took his own life there. Robert Marvin, well known attorney, was said to have been in a mood of depression at the time.

[13]. A map in the Public Record Office, London, shows a bridge at the foot of the slope at the end of Little Harbor Road near the Sheldon Krasker home. That was dated early 18th Century, and the map indicates the bridge was already in a state of disrepair.

[14]. The name was taken from the Ham family which was long in possession of the island. The toll house was located there. It was one of the Ham girls who saw a boating mishap involving Dr. Hall Jackson, and gave the alarm that saved his life.

[15]. Edward Cutts built the mansion that stands on the high ground at the intersection of Maplewood Avenue and Cutts Street about 1810. Cutts was a lawyer. At the time of the 1823 celebration he was 59 years old. In recent times the house was owned by Harry Jones, then Harry Winebaum, and now Dr. Peter Beck.

[16]. Jeremiah Mason, it's agreed by many professionals, was the greatest lawyer ever to plead at the Rockingham County bar. He was so considered by the man with whom he often locked horns — Daniel Webster, no mean advocate himself. He built a house on Windmill Hill which now serves the Advent Christian Church as a parish hall. The Rambler tells a tale of the time Mason and a friend literally whipped a lawyer named John Wentworth because of allegations made by him in a news article. Politics quickly

entered the affair and the Republicans had Mason arrested. There was even some chance of mob action, but it was handled quite smoothly by Captain Thomas Manning, a Republican, who had no desire to see a prominent Federalist roughed up. The crowd hissed Mason liberally and he hid out in the house — burned in 1813 — that stood on the site where the Elks home is. Mason, a giant of a man, especially for the early 19th Century, stood six feet, six inches tall, and sired several children.

[17]. Dr. Nathaniel Haven was an acquisitive soul who devoted his life more to the mending of his fortunes than people's bones. One of the places in which he lived was the Livermore House, and then he was on Pleasant Street. The Livermore House is now the property of ex-City Councilman Ralph Gerth.

[18]. John F. Parrott was the son of Captain John Parrott who had a home on the Kearsarge Hotel site. He served in the State Senate, 1830-31, and succeeded Daniel Webster in the U.S. House in 1817.

[19]. Henry Ladd, for a generation or more, was one of Portsmouth's most important merchants and business men. He was a son of Colonel Eliphalet Ladd, shipbuilder, but whose lasting memorial was Portsmouth's first water system. For years Henry Ladd was closely associated in business with his brother, Alexander, and Samuel Chauncey, a ship's captain who married a Ladd sister, Betsy. The house which Chauncey used for a home used to be the offices and showrooms of Coleman Rambler. This was the house occupied by Captain Lewis Barnes, and, even today, it is used in "horror film" as to what can happen to fine old houses, if preservationists can not save the day.

Ladd's estate was large, and the late Charles Gouse once had in his extensive collection an inventory of the holdings of this man. Among the items was a share in the Portsmouth Marine Railway and that leads to an interesting sidelight into the way Portsmouth businessmen made their money 120 years ago. The Marine Railway had no locomotives; its very name is misleading. Ladd was probably only a stockholder, and the organizers were men like Andrew W. Bell, farmer Charles Cushing and Christopher S. Toppan and Samuel Hale, merchants. The service the Marine Railway offered — to those willing to pay its rates — was to haul vessels, up to 650 tons burden, out of the water and enable workmen to scrape their bottoms, recopper, or do other work below the waterline. In sailing days foul bottoms were really a major problem, slowing vessels and encouraging rot. The Railway had two sets of tracks which provided the skidding surfaces for both large and small vessels. It was sited where the old Allied Gas Company tanks used to be, now a flower garden financed by Prescott Trust Funds. Before going on, it should be explained that in 1833, when the Marine Railway was built, Water (Marcy) Street was much nearer the river. Filling has done much to change the terrain in that area and the Portsmouth Marine Railway Company bought out a wharf owned by the Ayres family as a site for its venture.

Vessels were dragged up the railed ramp literally by two-horse power involving utilizing the leverage of block and tackle. Ladd payed $100 for his share and in his estate it was valued at $150 in 1841. But troubles beset the Marine Railway almost from the beginning. Nothing is clear in the records — preserved at the Portsmouth Athenaeum — as to when steam horsepower was substituted for living engines. By 1855, a three-man committee — Jonathan M. Tredick, William L. Dwight and Samuel Hale — were trying to decide what to do. The committee reported in May that the tracks and cradle were beyond repair except at great expense; that the company was $2,000 in debt, with litigation still pending over damage done the bark Hannah. It was decided to get out of the business and a price of $6,000 was asked. Again the records are not clear, but apparently the company's business was wound up in 1857, with a $14 dividend.

[20]. The Piscataqua gundalows, despite a local tradition, were not unique to this river. Joseph W. P. Frost, of Kittery, long a student of this subject, debunks the myth completely. More than 20 years ago, the author had the pleasure of being a member of a party that went upriver on a Portsmouth Navigation Company vessel — then owned by the late John E. Seybolt and others — to attend a launching at Adams Point, of probably the last gundalow--type vessel. It was built by old Captain Adams as a hobby, and launched near the family place. The post-launching ceremonies were a little damp and also a little much for the old craftsman, who enjoyed one of the best days of his life. On this river, the gundalow was designed to clear the Portsmouth Bridge with a minimum of difficulty. In recent times, the Interstate Bridge Authority has found it necessary to design and install a sliding span for the railroad tracks that are slung under the bridge. This installation has saved several hundred lifts a year for the main span. The Interstate Bridge paid off its bonds by 1967 and the tolls have since been intended to establish a trust fund that will provide for maintenance of the bridge in the years after this when it becomes toll free in October, 1972.

[21]. An Alexander Rice of Kittery operated a fully licensed ferry and he was given $4,000, payable from toll fees, to compensate him for his loss of business.

[22]. The tide flips through Memorial Bridge and past Fisherman's Pier Restaurant, owned by Jimmy Canty, at about seven miles an hour. Arnold J. Grover, formerly with New England Telephone, told the writer of a time when divers were inspecting phone cables across the river, and these underwater men reported seeing large boulders rolling like marbles along the river floor as the tide carried them along.

[23]. Even before the end of World War I, it was becoming recognized that the old Portsmouth Bridge was no longer adequate to cope with the burgeoning automobile traffic. The Boston and Maine Railroad was now operating that old span, still a toll bridge. Contracts for what would become the Memorial Bridge were let in November 1920, for the foundation work, which was completed on March 1, 1922. The last span was placed on December 20, 1922. Piers for the spans went down as much as 82 feet to bed rock in some places. Six thousand tons of sand and 14,000 barrels of cement went into their construction. After the ribbon was cut by five-year-old Helen I. Dondero, the draw was lifted and Maine's Governor Percival Baxter held the little girl in his arms.

This was the first public appearance by one of present-day Portsmouth's best known and popular women — Eileen Dondero Foley. That was on August 17, 1923, and everyone assumed that the mighty new span would be adequate for another hundred years as its predecessor had been. So much for the foresight of mere men. Before Eileen (the given name she now uses) Dondero finished her college career at Syracuse University, the bridge she had opened could not cope with the traffic.

Mrs. Foley entered the Women's Army Corps after graduating from college, and, on her return to civilian life, became the first woman city clerk a year after her mother was sworn in as the first woman mayor. Since then she has served on the School Board, in the House of Representatives, in the State Senate, and presided as mayor for four years, yielding the gavel to Arthur F. Brady, Jr. in January, 1972. Independently of her own political activities, she currently works for Senator Tom McIntyre as "field representative" with an office in the new federal building. On February 4, 1972, an "Eileen Foley Night" was held at the National Guard Armory, Circuit Road, with a capacity crowd on hand to honor a prominent citizen and decent person. Her husband is John J.

Foley, himself a POW in Italy in World War II; long employed at the Portsmouth Naval Shipyard, he is now retired. They are the parents of two sons and a daughter.

Because Memorial Bridge is such a dominant feature of the intown landscape, a few more details about it might be pertinent. Built by the American Bridge Company, it's of the Waddell-vertical lift type, 1,200 feet in length with four 300 foot spans. The two towers are 200 feet above high tide level and vessels have 150 feet of clearance at high tide. The draw was originally counter-balanced by two 400-ton weights, but these have been lightened because the paving of the draw span was opened up with a lighter grill deck.

Two 100 h.p. electric motors are used to wind the 16 one-inch wire ropes which activate the draw. With the exception of the span that connects the bridge to Badger's, the spans were prefabricated at Union Wharf and floated into position with the high tide on barges. When first opened, the vessels desiring to go upstream had to make prior arrangements for their passage, but now they come up freely.

[24]. The Interstate Bridge opened for traffic on November 8, 1940 at 2 p.m. The Reverend Maxwell Gantner, rector of St. John's opened the ceremonies with a prayer, and then two little girls — Deborah Cole, daughter of Hollis B. Cole of Kittery, and Joan Everett, granddaughter of Frederic E. Everett of Concord, cut the ribbon. Among Portsmouth people attending the ceremony were Frank E. Brooks; Wallace F. Purrington, executive secretary of the Maine-New Hampshire Interstate Bridge Authority; Rear Admiral John W. Wainwright of the Portsmouth Navy Yard; Kennard E. Goldsmith, mayor of Portsmouth, and the youngest man ever to serve in that role; Francis P. Murphy, Governor of New Hampshire; Carroll Sterling, chairman of the Kittery Board of Selectmen.

Here are some of the statistics: Over-all length of the project, 4.4 miles; length of the bridge between the abutments, five spans, including the 224-foot lift, 3,798 feet; length of the bridge approach, New Hampshire side, 15 spans, 2.55 miles; Maine side, six spans, 1.34 miles; Width, three lanes, 33 feet; width of highway, two double lanes, 44 feet; concrete pavement, 100,000 square yards; steel, 7,300 tons. Cost - $3,155,000. Construction time - Two years.

History: On his inaugural as mayor in 1930, Fernando W. Hartford said, "One bridge to the great State of Maine is not sufficient". While mayor, the late Robert Marvin had surveys done of traffic over Memorial Bridge. It's only 35 or so years ago and many can remember the crush of traffic summer weekends brought to

Portsmouth. The writer recalls coming through Portsmouth on a Sunday afternoon in 1937, and taking more than an hour to go from Kittery to the Route 101 exit off Middle Street. On such afternoons, long-time residents say, Middle Street could not be crossed. The two states came to an agreement, Congress approved it and the authority held its first meeting in June, 1937. The first earth was turned in the open land back of former Mayor Cecil M. Neal's Spinney Road home. That was in December, 1938.

[25]. The new high-level bridge, seen as a major escape route into Maine, will cost in excess of $20 million when completed. When it opened for traffic in 1972, it marked the end of nearly a dozen years of agitation to relieve the traffic congestion on the Interstate Bridge. Ninety per cent of the funding is from the federal government, the rest from the two states. The proposal was defeated in the New Hampshire Legislature in 1963, but approved in Maine. New Hampshire finally gave its okay in 1965, and Governor John W. King (now a Superior Court judge) signed the bill into law on April 16.

Rising 130 feet above the river, the bridge is 3,900 feet long, and the main span runs 670 feet. The construction, with its complex new system of approaches, has displaced many families. At one point in 1968, it appeared as though the bridge would not be built because of a "freeze" in federal funding. By 1969, engineer Frank Foster reported that the work was ahead of schedule, part of which included the erection of 13 approach piers in Maine and 18 on the New Hampshire side, and four river piers. Work actually began in May, 1968, and on August 1, 1969, The Herald reported that 70 trucks were hauling 18,000 yards of fill each day. The borrow pits were in Greenland, North Hampton and beyond Durham. At that time, a little more than half of the fill work had been done.

On June 24, 1970, came one of the great tragedies in the building of the new bridge. Four construction workers fell to their deaths when a platform slung under the approaches in Kittery collapsed. Four other men who tumbled to the ground were seriously injured, and another hung for more than an hour by one hand awaiting rescue. Dead on arrival at Portsmouth Hospital were Carl Koski, 20, of 91 Lafayette Road; George Dinsmore, 28, of Bucksport, Maine; Michael Wood, 23, of Locke Road, Rye; and Noel A. Dube of Rollinsford.

[26]. There is some sentiment, first really finding public voice in the summer of 1971, to curb this vacation-recreation and general escapism into Maine. Many Mainers are beginning to see

it as a peril to the very enviornment that is the lure for the thousands who want to get out of the seemingly unsolvable urban problems of today.

[27]. John Bowles died July 8, 1837, age 72, and is buried in the North Cemetery. He was in the Legislature and a selectman.

[28]. Colonel Gideon Walker, buried in the North Cemetery, died May 2, 1829, at 63. He came down in the line of Gideon Walkers, one of whom signed the Association Test in 1776.

[29]. This man is probably the Mark Laighton listed in the 1839 Directory as a mariner and boarding at 5 Green Street, and was an uncle to Celia Thaxter.

[30]. Ephraim Dennett was probably the son of Jeremiah Dennett, the grandson of the Ephraim Dennett who inhabited the Dennett House, Christian Shore, later known as the "Bee Hive".

[31]. "Sugar House" was one of the first to really advertise its products and the place was operated by William Torrey, a man who refused to sign the Association Test of 1776.

[32]. William Stavers was the son of the first stage coach driver, Bartholomew. He never knew his father.

[33]. Ichabod Rollins, in 1840, was one of three Ichabods in town and all of them were directors of the Piscataqua Bank. The other two were Ichabod Goodwin and Ichabod Bartlett. Rollins was partnered with Samuel Hale, the son of the old schoolmaster, as a merchant. As might be suspected, Rollinsford was his home town. Born there on January 12, 1792, Rollins came here as a clerk. Early in the next century, such are the odd quirks of fate, he was sent on a trading mission to the Baltic as a supercargo and was away during most of the War of 1812. When he did return, he settled into the familiar Portsmouth business groove, including his partnership with Hale. His son, William H. Rollins, was born in Portsmouth, September 7, 1822, and in 1896 was a past president of the Portsmouth Athenaeum, and once secretary-treasurer. William C. Harris in the 1851 Directory listed as teaching at a private school at 1 Islington Street (Portsmouth Academy), tutored Rollins for Harvard, to which he was admitted in 1837, graduating in 1841, and going on to Harvard Law. Before being allowed to practice law, Rollins also studied under Ichabod Bartlett.

William C. Harris, incidentally, was the man known and referred to as "Master Harris", and was revered by Portsmouth people for years to come as the greatest teacher ever engaged here.

Harris taught in the Portsmouth Academy.

[34]. Isaac Waldron was in business at 5 Bow Street and made his home at 44 Congress. He attended the 1823 anniversary ball and signed his age as 49. He was on the Governor's Council, 1840-41.

[35]. The plant was set up at the end of Pearl Street, in the building vacated by Brady Ford, and what was, in far earlier days, the site of the Nathaniel Adams place. Later the Steam Factory became Kearsarge Mills and, after the fire of 1880, the property was sold and became the Portsmouth Machine Shop. Later it sheltered Brooks Motors.

[36]. Ichabod Goodwin was a North Berwick boy who came to the "big city" and made good. He was born in 1796 and died July 4, 1882. There will be frequent mention of Goodwin throughout this narrative and his career reached its peak when he became the state's first Civil War Governor.

[37]. Thomas B. Laighton was the father of Celia Thaxter, the Isles of Shoals poet, who was born on Daniel Street, near Penhallow. While she was quite young, her father decided to remove to the more secluded life of lightkeeper at the Isles of Shoals. It was her life on the islands, and the salon she held on Appledore Island each summer, that brought to her cottage all the famous of the world of arts and letters. Celia Thaxter died on her beloved islands. On November 15, 1888, she came back to Portsmouth to spend her winters but always her thoughts were:
"I but crave
The sad, caressing murmur of the wave
That breaks in tender music on the shore".
Her brothers, Oscar, born June 30, 1839, and Cedric, born September 4, 1840, grew up on the islands and managed hotels there.Celia, four years Oscar's senior, married Lincoln Levi Thaxter, a summer visitor to the islands. Thomas B. Laighton died in 1886. He had been active, even after going to the Shoals, in Portsmouth political life and was a selectman as late as 1843, also serving in the State Senate. He took command of White Island Light in 1839. Oscar was the last survivor of the three, dying in 1939, at the age of 99 years, nine months. Cedric died in 1929. A painting of Oscar, by Edmund Tarbell, is in the John Paul Jones House.

[38]. Alfred W. Haven was a practicing lawyer with a home on Congress Street, a little diagonally across the street from the Kearsarge Hotel where the Worth Corporation has a block of new stores. Worth Corporation has Arnold Fishbein, manager of

Hudson's, as president and is the developer since the Vaughan Street Urban Renewal project leveled all the buildings along that side, except the former YMCA, now Goodman's Store, owned by Melvin H. Goodman. The YMCA building was preceded on the site by the mansion of W.H.Y. Hackett, which was moved back across the old Vaughan Street parking lot when the "Y" was built. Hackett, one of the town's leading attorneys for years, remarked in 1876, on his golden wedding anniversary, that he had lived in the same house for 50 years, practiced law in the same office and sat in the same pew in the South Church. He presided over the State Senate in 1862.

[39]. Charles Cushing was owner of the Wentworth-Coolidge House after the Wentworths. He bought the property in 1817. Cushing came here from South Berwick, and his widow, the youngest daughter of Thomas Wallingford of Somersworth, who lived near Salmon Falls, survived until 1855 when she was nearly a century old.

[40]. The Rockingham House originally was the mansion acquired from the Woodbury Langdon estate and converted into a hostelry in 1830.

[41]. One of the rugged, shrewd financiers of the mid-19th Century generation, Mark W. Peirce was the son of John, community leader and sharp businessman in the late years of the 18th Century. John Peirce died June 14, 1814. His son Mark married Margaret Sparhawk. Peirce signed the Bicentennial Roll at the age of 50.

[42]. The Navy Yard's log for August 15, 1820, recorded, "Yard men at the Isles of Shoals in pursuit of pirates". And before passing on, let's note the type of disciplinary action handed sailors in those days: A man named "Dyas" received 12 lashes on the naked back agreeable to the rules and regulations of the Navy, for smuggling spirituous liquors on the Yard. Dickson received the same number in consequence of Striking the Gunner".

[43]. The similarity of names between this vessel and the privateer in the War of 1812 is probably coincidental. "Packet" was a fairly common appellation.

[44]. Even as today, Uncle Sam occasionally steps in and exercises clemency. The Portsmouth Journal, out of New York, reported on April 13, 1822: By the last Savannah papers we learn that eight pirates who would have been executed in Savannah on the 2nd of April were respited in the pleasure of the President of the United States. We shall probably next hear of their pardon and then of their return to their old trade and possible afterwards of their

capture and probably the tale will again wind up with further executive clemency".

In September of 1815, the National Journal reported that piracy had virtually been wiped out. Commodore Warrington, commander of USS Constellation, was the source and he was quoted, "The pirate hordes along the coast of Cuba have been completely broken up. The fact that these deprecators can no longer exhibit themselves in such force as to cause any serious alarm will give new confidence to those engaged in the peaceful pursuits of commerce; and the energy which has been exercised in the extermination of the corsairs will and still more to the favor which our gallant Navy already enjoys from the people of the United States".

In this connection it should be noted that at about this time, Lieutenant James Ramage, original commander of Porpoise, stood trial on charges brought by one of his officers, Lieutenant Frederick G. Wolbert. Ramage was acquitted and the charges "themselves have been pronounced malicious". The Journal added, "The gallant officer who was the object of this groundless prosecution will now return to his duty, more firmly established in the confidence of government and his country from the investigation, unpleasent as it was in its process, which his conduct has undergone". Captain James Barron was president of the court martial which was held in Washington, D.C. Lieutenant Wolbert was subsequently cashiered and dismissed from the service, a sentence approved by the President.

[45]. In 1792, Neil McIntire was one of the incorporators of this bank. He was a tobacconist by trade, according to his ads in the New Hampshire Gazette. He died April 7, 1812, at the age of 68. McIntire served as a private in the Rhode Island campaign of 1778 under Colonel John Langdon. Commanding all the troops was General John Sullivan.

[46]. John Wardrobe occupied the house of Matthew Livermore. Among the other owners and occupants at various times were Nathaniel Sparhawk, Colonel Edward J. Long, Captain John Porter, USN, Captain Samuel Ham and Jean Toscan, the French Consul. Dr. Nathaniel A. Haven acquired it in 1813 after Livermore Street was opened up.

[47]. For a more detailed account of this old savings institution, see "The Portsmouth Savings Bank", by Ray Brighton.

[48]. Brother of "The Signer", Joseph Whipple made his home on Broad Street (State) on the northeast corner of the Chestnut Street intersection. He died February 26, 1816, at the age of 78. His house is now on Middle Street, at Park Street, and the

original site has been leveled for additional bank parking and driveway.

[49]. Samuel Elliott Coues was the son of Peter. Among his civic functions was heading the American Peace Society for several years and he was also president of the Lyceum in 1840, having Charles W. Brewster as secretary and George Manent as treasurer. It was formed about 1833. Coues was, for a conservative businessman, a bit of a free thinker, and in one treatise of his own writing tried to upset Newton's Theory of Gravity. For a long period he was in the Patent Office in Washington, returning to Portsmouth in 1866, and dying July 3, 1867. Many of his business ventures saw him associated with Ichabod Goodwin.

[50]. The son of Langley, a practicing physician in 1840 at 94 State Street, but moved to the Boardman House on Middle Street before 1851.

[51]. The Reverend David Millard was pastor of the First Baptist, later Middle Street Baptist Church.

[52]. George Doig and John Dennett, wardens of St. Patrick's, attended a meeting of the Grand Lodge in 1789, but that is the only note of the lodge in the record. Doig was a sign painter by trade with a shop on Congress Street somewhere in the vicinity of the present-day Athenaeum building. In the Portsmouth Aqueduct Company list of customers, George Doig is reported as having 10 persons in his household on Congress Street in 1800. Which one of the John Dennetts was in St. Patrick's is now obscured by time.

[53]. The founders of Pythagorean Lodge were Daniel D. Akerman, Asa Young, Daniel Story, Hanson M. Hart, Michael Wise, Daniel P. Drown, John K. Gilman, John Gregory, Thomas Clapham, James Wildes, Samuel Shackford, John Mendum and Joseph E. Robinson. The last was a farmer in 1840 with his home given as the second house above the bridge on Creek (Bartlett) Street.

[54]. Charter members of St. Andrew's were George W. Towle, Thomas L. Pickering, John S. Locke, Hanson M. Hart (he was also an incorporator of Pythagorean), John E. H. Barnes, Joseph Perry, Benjamin Weeks, Ebenezer Runnells, Aaron L. Rand, Joseph M. Edmunds and Jethro Locke. Edmonds was publisher of the 1840 City Directory. One of the officers of the new lodge was John Christie, who was, at the same time, grand master of New Hampshire Masons.

[55]. Gerald D. Foss, more than 40 years a Mason, has authored "Three Centuries of Freemasonry in New Hampshire". Foss is a past master of St. John's (1945) and an authority on Masonic

lore. For quite a few years as historian of St. John's, he had written sketches on local Masonry for the monthly Trestleboards. The book came out in May 1972.

[56]. Only a couple of months before President James Monroe had visited here. He stayed for a few days in a house that now shelters the Powell, Flynn, McGuirk law firm on Court Street. To many local people it's still known as the Folsom-Salter House and in the years after World War II was operated as a gracious restaurant by Earl Philbrook, whose son, Robert D., is presently a member of the Portsmouth School Board. It was removed from the site to make room for the high-rise housing for the elderly, known as the Feaster Apartments. This structure, built with federal funds, was named in honor of Capt. William Feaster, son of the Rev. John N. Feaster, pastor of the North Church and Mrs. Feaster. The younger Feaster was killed in Vietnam while serving as chaplain. "Billy" was the victim of what many ex-GIs know as the "short round". That is, an artillery shell fired from our own guns which landed in our troop deployments. For years, he was active in local scouting, went to Harvard College with a bent toward archeology, and then gravitated toward the profession of his fahter. He was a captain at the time of his death, and his wife, Lieutenant Judith Feaster, serving in Korea as an Army nurse, was flown to Vietnam to be with her husband before he died of his wounds.

[57]. It's doubtful that Portsmouth, ever before or since, has enjoyed such a teary bout with nostalgia as on September 1, 1824, the occasion of Lafayette's visit to the town. Shortly after the General arrived in Boston, a special town meeting was held and the selectmen were directed to invite him to come here. A committee was appointed by the selectmen, consisting of Levi Woodbury, Colonel Timothy Upham, Alexander Ladd, and Jacob Wendell. They immediately left for Boston and called on Lafayette on Tuesday morning. He promised an immediate reply, after Woodbury had told him that "time has since robbed her (Portsmouth) of her Langdons, her Whipples and indeed most of the contemporaries on whose memory your image was indelibly engraved". Wednesday evening the deputation was still waiting, and so it called once again on the General. Woodbury had made the point that "the citizens of Portsmouth feel anxious to welcome you again to their hearths and their altars. They wish to mingle their sympathies with the prisoners of Olmutz, and to cherish as their guest the patriot who in one hemisphere shed his youthful blood in the triumphs of liberty, and in others endured 30 years of persecution and disappointed hopes...."

Lafayette, apparently on a tight time schedule, hemmed and hawed, but finally agreed to make the trip to Portsmouth, via Marblehead and Newburyport. However, Lafayette laid down the stipulation that he would have to be back in Boston by noon on Thursday, September 2, because he intended to leave for New York that afternoon. Then the schedule was outlined: Lafayette would "breakfasted at Marblehead, at 8 a.m. on Tuesday next, 31st August. He will Dine at Salem at 2 p.m. — sleep at Newburyport — Breakfast at Newburyport on Wednesday — Dine in Portsmouth and return to Boston by 12 o'clock on Thursday". His stay would be all too brief as far as the Portsmouth people were concerned, but it was better than nothing.

Once the word came back to Portsmouth, the Selectmen asked the following to serve as a committee: Timothy Upham, Levi Woodbury, John F. Parrott, James Sheafe, Jeremiah Mason, Clement Storer, Nathaniel A. Haven, Hunking Penhallow, Langley Boardman, James Shapley, Titus Salter, John Haven, Jacob Cutter, Samuel Larken, Henry Ladd and Ebeneezer Wentworth.

Probably the proximity of General Lafayette had nothing to do with it, but as the town fathers prepared for the big reception, a party of Penobscot Indians were encamped at Kittery near the Portsmouth Bridge. A second party pitched camp just above the bridge on the Portsmouth side. They had arrived by canoe from Penobscot River and intended to stay five or six weeks. The Journal said, "They have excited much curiosity in our citizens; and those who have visited them at their wigwams have expressed much pleasure in witnessing their modes of life. Their deportment thus far has been very civil and if not indulged in spirituous liquors they will doubtless prove to peaceable neighbors".

The Portsmouth Police Board, through an ad, let its concern be known over the crowds Lafayette's visit would attract. It expressed hope there would be no disorderly conduct and "to promote this object the Board of Police give notice that all firing of guns, squibs, crackers or any preparation of gunpowder (except such as may be authorized by the Committee of Arrangements) is hereby strictly prohibited; and all improper conduct on said day will be duly noticed and the perpretrators prosecuted according to the law".

Everyone was eager to take part, even to the extent, as the Portsmouth truckmen did, of posting a notice to meet and discuss plans. Signing it were Oliver Nowell, William Dame and John Oxford, Jr.

The first note of Lafayette's reception in Portsmouth is one on the national salute fired in his honor by the gun crew at the Navy Yard. But the day was one really swinging with emotion and action. Let The Journal tell it:

"The promised visit of General Lafayette to this town was paid on Wednesday and his arrival was hailed by all our citizens with pride and exultation. We shall give a brief account of the interesting scenes of the day but the deep feelings produced by the presence of this early and devoted friend of our country can not be adequately described. There was a glow of unaffected delight on every countenance which gave an honest and heartfelt welcome. General Lafayette was received at Hampton Falls by the Committee of Arrangements who accompanied him through Greenland to the limits of the town, where the Selectmen of Portsmouth were waiting to receive him. He proceeded from thence under the escort of a party of citizens on horseback, and followed by a long train of our most respectable inhabitants in carriages. The procession extended nearly two miles. On reaching Wibird's Hill, a national salute was fired by a detachment of the Portsmouth Artillery, and the bells in town began to ring. The General took his seat in an open barouch attended by the honorable William Ham, chairman of the Selectmen. He entered the compact part of town under a military escort followed by the Strafford Guards from Dover, the Rockingham Guards and the Gilman Blues. A short distance below the Hill upwards of a thousand children from the several schools, generally dressed in uniform, and wearing the badge of Lafayette, were arranged on each side and formed a most interesting part of the show. Though the weather was unfavourable, and many of them wore only chaplets of flowers on their heads, neither clouds nor rain could drive them from their station. As the procession advanced, their shouts of "Welcome, Lafayette"! was distinctly heard above the music of the military band and the cheers of the people. The procession passed through Middle Street, Broad Street, Court Street and Congress Street to Franklin Hall where the General alighted and was welcomed to Portsmouth by the chairman of the Selectmen who made him the following address:

"...We have nothing to lessen our esteem for the early friend of America".

Naturally, Lafayette had to respond:

"I thank you, gentlemen, for your constant concern in my behalf, during the vicissitudes you are pleased to allude the approbation of a free, virtuous and enlightened people will be the highest reward for anyone who knows how to value true glory — still more so when it is bestowed on an adopted son".

The gathering then broke up into small informal groups as General Lafayette and his son, George Washington Lafayette (died in 1849), were introduced to Govenor David Morrill, among other dignitaries. Morrill had been routed out of his Goffstown home, on short notice, to meet the General, but he made the journey as any true politician would.

Also on hand were "at least 30 soldiers of the Revolution who had served under him and many of whom had come from a great distance for the purpose of seeing him. The sight was very interesting, and we regret that we had no opportunity of learning their names — General Lafayette recognized General Smith of Portland who had served under him three years as a captain of light infantry and expressed the highest pleasure in meeting his old companion in arms. He took his hand again and again and declared himself 'very happy'. A Mr. Row of this neighborhood, a venerable old man, approached him, and while his eyes overflowed with tears, began to count over his battles and tell what 'the Marquis' had done for him. Our old friend Thomas Harvey found it difficult to restrain himself. The sight of Lafayette recalled the scenes of the Revolution and well nigh over came him. On retiring from the hall, General Lafayette withdrew to the mansion of the late President Langdon which had been prepared for his reception with great taste and elegance. After taking some rest, he was escorted to Jefferson Hall where a public dinner was provided and larger company assembled than ever before dined together in this town.

"The Honorable John F. Parrott presided, supported by Nathaniel A. Haven, Edward Cutts, Jr., Enoch G. Parrott, Langley Boardman, Benjamin Penhallow, Edmund Roberts, William Shackford and Samuel Larken, Esquires".

In the evening a ball was staged, more than 300 of the town's belles and beldames, were presented to the charming Frenchman, and over each he lingered long enough to offer an appropriate complpiment. But probably the greatest testimonial to the man's genuine emotional reaction to the exertions of the day was the fact that he stayed an hour past the time agreed upon, and at 10 p.m. repaired through brightly lighted streets, and a concourse of people, to the Langdon House, where he had "one for the road". Then, accompanied by his escort from Newburyport, and a deputation from the Committee of Arrangements, which went as far as Newburyport, Lafayette rode through the night back to Boston, arriving about 8 a.m., and at 2 p.m. he was on his way to New York. No one could complain, the man had fulfilled his commitment to the letter, although a long night ride was probably no strain on an old campaignor from the Revolution.

One closing note, one that shows that a crowd attracts all sorts of people:

"On Wednesday last there were no less than nine pocket-books stolen from the pockets of gentlemen from this town. One of the light-fingered gentry was detected and carried to prison".

More than 400 Portsmouth people went to Charlestown on the 17th of June, 1825, to attend the ceremonies at Bunker Hill at which General Lafayette was the highly honored guest. They were, incidentally, also treated to one of Daniel Webster's more famed orations. Later Lafayette came again to New Hampshire, visited the State House in Concord, where he sat down to dinner with the still surviving veterans of the Revolution. His travels then took him along the New Hampshire Turnpike to Durham and Dover; the next day to South Berwick where he breakfasted, and on to Portland. He turned around there and came back as far as Northwood, a distance of 70 miles, before going to Concord the next morning, and then leaving the state forever.

[58]. Perhaps it's just a newspaperman's fancy, but sometimes it seems possible to get a flavor of a town by looking at its police log. A couple of notes on police cases two weeks before the "Centenial Celebration", as it was called, tell us a lot. One reported the arrest of three young people for firing guns in the evening after a wedding. Two were fined lightly and the third, who fought the charges, more heavily. It's too bad the police don't pick up all the present-day hornblowers as they toot through town on a Saturday morning after a wedding.

The other case involved a young man who was charged with smoking "segars in the street and with disorderly conduct near the Baptist Meeting House on Sunday last. He pleaded guilty and was fined a small sum for the use of the Poor, with costs".

With two offenses like those above in mind, the reason for all the self-congratulations on the orderliness of the "Centennial Cele-bration" becomes evident. It started, as nearly always with a parade that had its assembly point at the South Meeting House (Meeting House Hill) and which moved along Pleasant to Broad (State) Street, Middle and then into Congress Street and to the North Church, predecessor of the one standing there today. Great fuss and protocol was marked in getting the proper seating arrangements in order that those participating could hear Nathaniel A. Haven, Jr., deliver the oration of the day. Wall pews, incidentally, were reserved for the use of ladies.

After the oration, the Masons moved out, under military escort, and went to Masons Hall (Congress Block). All those interested in attending the dinner in Jefferson Hall were directed to gather at the Academy at 2 p.m. There were some 200 on hand to eat, sing, hear speeches and offer toasts. After giving his directions, the secretary of the Centennial, Alexander Ladd, then announced that there would be a meeting of the committee at Wilde's Hotel.

"The completion of the second century from the first settlement of New Hampshire was celebrated in this town on Wednesday last". The Journal later said: "The exercises, the festivities of the day were such as had been previously announced in the papers. The dinner at Jefferson Hall was honored with the presence of several distinguished guests and the pleasures of the table were much increased by the number of original songs, well written and well sung. The company at Franklin Hall in the evening was the most numerous that had ever assembled at a ball in this town. Good order and kind feelings and innocent gaiety were everywhere displayed and nothing occurred during the whole proceedings to interrupt or diminish the enjoyments of the day".

And that, as far as first-hand reporting was concerned, is where The Journal dropped the matter. But the next week it picked up from the New Hampshire Republican of Concord an account of the party right in its own town. The Republican said Jefferson Hall had been painted by the town in honor of the occasion and was decorated with flags and paintings.

John F. Parrott, by then a U. S. Senator, presided at the dinner and on his committee were John Haven, Edward Cutts, Jr., Benjamin Penhallow, Enoch G. Parrott and Samuel Larkin, Esquires.

"The dinner was chiefly of fish, of all known names, and cooked in all possible variety. After the cloth was removed, the following toasts were drunk, and many fine songs finely sung".

Daniel Webster stood to offer a toast, reminding the company, "of what none had forgotten, that he was a native of New Hampshire. He briefly but eloquently remarked that this was the land of his birth, of his education and of his dearest associations". Webster used a quotation to describe his feelings:

"Where I ere roam, what ever rounds I see
My heart untraveled fondly turns to thee."

Let The Republican close out the picture of the "Centennial Celebration":

"In the evening a very supurb ball was given at Franklin Hall, at which it is supposed there were present nearly 400 ladies and gentlemen. The walls of the room were entirely covered with portraits of eminent persons who flourished in this state before the Revolution; the Wentworths, Jaffreys, Warners, Sparhawks, Atkinsons of old times. After spending the evening in innocent gaiety, the company separated at a reasonable hour. Everyone was pleased with the transactions of the day, the most perfect and good conduct that were manifest in every particular. There was no confusion and no disappointment. The sentiment was universal.

"Everything that could have been done was done, and everything that was done was well done".

[59]. The streets were formally named in 1778, when Nathaniel Adams and John Parker, Jr., did a survey and then asked for a committee to name them. For example, do you know where the original Market Square was? The 1778 street description puts it in the Spring Hill area, around the junction of Bow, Ceres and Market Streets. It was not until 1838, that the present Market Square was so called, and at that time the Board of Selectmen went through another ordeal of street-naming. That's an old Portsmouth trick. Take, just as an example, Daniel Street: Bridget Graffort, a daughter of Richard Cutt(s), a wealthy fisherman and merchant here and at the Isles of Shoals, gave not only the site of the present City Hall for a school, but also a strip of land, two rods wide through her property, which is now Daniel Street. At first, it terminated at a gate between Ted Lilakos' lunchroom and A. B. Duncan's, the jewelers. Much narrower than today, it was known as Graffort's Lane. Earliest reference to it as Daniel Street is in a probate record of 1726. For nearly two hundred years it bore that name, then, in World War I, to please a Secretary of the Navy, Josephus Daniels, the "s" was added. Daniels was the father of President Harry S. Truman's son-in-law, Clifton Daniels of The New York Times. During the tenure of the first city manager-council, Councilman Thomas H. Simes moved that it revert to Daniel Street, and it is today.

Deer and Bridge Streets are probably among the few in town that have not undergone name changes over the centuries. Various records seem to bear that out with the probate of George Vaughan's will, in 1724, giving "Deere" Street as a reference, and one of the oldest standing public inns was the Deer Street Tavern. This structure finally fell victim to urban renewal in June, 1972, but only because restoration was a hopeless proposition.

A little street like Chestnut has gone through several changes.

Once Prison Lane, it became Elm Street in 1838; then that name was tagged to that part of Maplewood Avenue that passes between the North Cemetery and the new home of The Portsmouth Herald. Elm Street is now the designation of a little stub of a thoroughfare off Islington. In 1838, using common sense for a change, the selectmen tried to make the highway from Market Square to Bartlett Street known as Islington all the way. The change did not "take". Local tendency to change street names at any old intersection still drives visitors out of their minds.

[60]. This is the building occupied today by Halprin Cleaners, and a stone inset into the brick, well above eye level, still testifies as to its former use. For a while, at least during the tenure of Joseph Whipple as collector, the Custom House was on his property on State Street, now the parking lot for the Portsmouth Savings Bank.

[61]. Present-day pollutant figures show Portsmouth as one of the state's more contaminated areas, thanks mainly to the smoke stacks of the two power plants. In May, 1972, the Public Service Company began installation of special smoke and pollution trapping gadgets on the chimneys of its Schiller Station, located at the river end of Gosling Road. Schiller Station was built shortly after World War II, with one unit an experimental mercury-type steam plant. That unit has since been pulled out and the operation is conventional steam. The Public Service Company has long-range plans to erect a nuclear plant in Seabrook, and is currently putting up a fossil fuel plant in Newington, a short distance upstream from Schiller Station.

For many years, Portsmouth was serviced by the New Hampshire Electric Company, a small utility with its main source of power at the Bow Street generators, buying additional power from Public Service. The Public Service Company gained control in the 1960s, and has since submerged New Hampshire Electric. It even abandoned the in-town offices and salesroom in the old National Block, for a new headquarters on Lafayette Road.

One of New Hampshire Electric's predecessors was the Rockingham Light and Power Company, chartered in 1901. But the first concern licensed to produce and sell electricity here was the Portsmouth Gas Company whose 1850 charter was amended in 1887 to allow it to expand its activities.

[62]. One of the peculiar things which "The Annalist" did throughout his work was to omit what he did not agree with or thought unessential. Suffice to say that there's no mention of the

1790 appearance here of the great Methodist missionary, the Reverend Jesse Lee. Nor did "The Annalist" recognize the formal organization of the society here in 1808. He did take note in 1790 that there had been a "wicked attempt" to burn the town when someone on July 13 tried to ignite the barn of Oliver Whipple in Jaffrey Street (Court). And in 1808 "The Annalist" took note of the founding of the Portsmouth Marine Society, intended for the relief of distressed mariners; the appropriation of a lot of land near the South School House for use by the United States as a "gun-house"; and he reported the ordination of the Reverend Nathan Parker by the South Church.

Be that as it may because the writer of this volume probably will be charged and found guilty of the same offenses.

The Methodists did organize at 12 Washington Street in the Hutching Home. Later they bought the Camenaeum on Camenaeum Avenue (A little way that ran where the back line of the Worth Corporation building, off Vaughn Street is.) from the Universalists for $2,000. In 1827, they built a church of their own on State Street, now Temple Isreal, which they used until they built their present church on Miller Avenue about 1906 on land they bought from Benjamin F. Webster for around $3,000. The lot was located between one owned by Calvin Page and another owned by Andrew P. Preston.

It was claimed that the old State Street church, built at a cost of $9,000, was becoming delapidated and not worth repairs. A few days before Temple Israel prepared to dedicate the building as a synagogue in 1912, a dispute flared between the two groups. The Jewish people felt the corner stone box belonged to them, but the Methodists were insistant that it should go to their new church. One of the real motivations in the controversy was that some coins had been found in the box which were immediately thought to be of great value. Tempers grew warm, litigation was in the offing when someone thought of having the treasure trove appraised. The coins were found to be worth less than $10, and the parties quickly and amiably settled their differences. The Methodists got the box.

[63]. The Reverend Timothy Alden, Jr., in "An Account of the Several Religious Societies in Portsmouth", written in 1808, says of the Sandemanian Society: "Mr. Robert Sandeman came to this country about the year 1764. His peculiar tenets attracted the attention of many, and gave rise to a new denomination in the christian world....One of these societies was formed in Portsmouth. A building was erected, for a place of worship, where,

since its demolishment, colonel Thomas Thompson (The Thayer House) has built his dwelling-house". The congregation was led by Daniel Humphreys.

In a note, Alden says that Sandeman's epitaph may be seen on a tombstone in Danbury, Connecticut, and reads: "Here lies until the resurrection, the body of Robert Sandeman, a native of Perth, Northbritain, who in the face of continual opposition from all sorts of men, long and boldly contended for the antient faith, that the bare work of Jesus Christ, without a deed or thought on the part of man, is sufficient to present the chief of sinners spotless before God". Sandeman died April 2, 1771, and it's not hard to think that his philosophy had great merit.

16

Portsmouth becomes a City

[1]. One of the most ardent of the Jacksonian Democrats, Levi Woodbury was born in Francestown in 1789. He served in the Legislature, was governor, U. S. senator, Secretary of the Navy, Secretary of the Treasury and a U. S. Supreme Court Justice. His home was located where the Woodbury Avenue housing project for the elderly is now, a big, three decker. Federal-type house. It was put up in 1811 by Captain Samuel Ham, who gave a party, on its completion, for all his friends and neighbors. When the guests departed, Ham went upstairs and quietly hanged himself. Woodbury bought the place in 1819. His career, long and distinguished, was apparently leading him to the presidency when he died September 4, 1851. By one of life's odd little touches, the man who did become the successful Democratic candidate in the next election was Franklin Pierce, Woodbury's one-time law student in his Portsmouth office. It's obvious that Woodbury Avenue took its name from this man. Originally Creek Street, it was renamed in 1899 when Frank Jones lined it with maples and had it almost for a private drive toward his home. Woodbury was the last Portsmouth man to serve in the Senate until Governor Wesley Powell appointed Maurice J. Murphy, Jr. to fill the seat left vacant by the death of Styles Bridges in 1961.

[2]. For years this was the expression used in describing trains.

[3]. The Powder House, still standing, was built in 1811 to get such dangerous materials away from the more heavily populated parts of the town. Previously there had been a magazine

near the school in the South End. Islington Street was opened up west of Bartlett in 1797, thus making access easy. For more than 70 years there has been agitation to demolish the old building, which is dwarfed by the standpipe behind it. This open air reservoir was finally capped in 1972, 80 years after its erection. In 1903, the city contracted for a powder magazine at Sagamore Creek. Built by Frank Newton, this structure was nine feet high, eight feet wide and ten feet long, and made of brick. Once completed, there was talk of removing the round building at the back of the George S. Robinson property and next door to Peter Collins, a labor official in the state government. Efforts have been made and are continuing to find someone to take an interest in preserving the magazine, but the repairs to it will be costly and no one appears willing, so the City Council may soon order its removal. In 1925, there was agitation for its removal. The Powder House was built from materials that came out of its predecessor.

[4]. Essex Avenue was part of a development set up in 1917.

[5]. Some of the freight sheds of the old terminal are used today by Goodwin Feed and Supply. The old station itself was the headquarters of William E. Dennett Tobacco for some years, under the proprietorship of Roy Peterson.

[6]. The Portsmouth and Concord Railroad was incorporated in July, 1845, but it was not until 1852 that "the cars" could run all the way to Concord. President in 1851 was Alfred W. Haven, with Andrew B. Vennard, treasurer. Portsmouth men on the board of directors at that time included Alexander Ladd and Josiah G. Hadley. As early as the summer of 1849, the directors were planning to join with the Eastern Railroad, then headed by Ichabod Goodwin, in constructing a depot. Money was always the paramount problem and a Portsmouth Loan Bill had rough sledding in the Legislature. This proposal would have allowed the city to use its credit to back up financing of the road. The Journal commented on July 21, 1849, "This road is a last resource for the preservation of Portsmouth, its ancient and legitimate trade having been much injured by the Boston Railroads. Capitalists are afraid it will not be a paying investment and keep aloof. And besides, many of them are directly interested by their connection with other roads, in holding this back". That perhaps is one of the most cogent comments available on the plight of Portsmouth as it fought to survive the diversion of its hinterland products into Boston. There was a further note that the road "is presently out of debt and earning". It was

expected that it would soon be in operation to Newmarket and Epping. On that same date, just to show the disparity in transport means, there is a note that T. L. Churchill was operating a stage between Portsmouth and Dover. On September 29, 1849, the P&C opened to Newmarket; the same week a committee was named to solicit funds for the Washington National Monument that had C. W. Cutler, James N. Tarlton, Ichabod Goodwin, Richard Jenness, Lory Odell and Augustus Jenkins as members. And it will always be wondered if the Robert Ham, 86, who walked home from Rockingham Junction, a distance of 12 miles, in six hours, because he missed the train, was the brother who took in "Shepard" Ham in the latter's last days. By December 8, the P&C was announcing that it would be open all the way to Epping on December 11, and that a big ball to celebrate would be held there with Flagg's Cotillion Band supplying the music. Tickets were half price to Epping for the event — 25 cents. On the 15th, The Journal reported that 350 stockholders had gone to Epping for the occasion behind the locomotive named "Epping". There they were welcomed by William Plumer, Jr. Those hardy souls who stayed for the ball arrived back in Portsmouth at 4 a.m. The 18 miles of track to Epping cost $313,000, and it was then expected that the cost of the total 47 miles to Concord would be in excess of $900,000.

[7]. The property owned by Mr. and Mrs. Alfred G. Ripley at 589 Middle Road is one such. This place was owned for generations by the Sheafe family. Because of a fire in 1931, only the two front rooms — with their Indian shutters, and the fireplace survive from the original farmhouse. A generation or more ago ice was cut on a pond — now a swamp — in back of the Ripley place, and later was a mink farm operated by William Bates. Muskrats still populate it, as the present city attorney, Peter Loughlin, knows from a boyhood spent near the pond.

[8]. St. Mary's Church was destroyed by fire on November 27, 1871, and the cornerstone of a new one was laid on November 5, 1872. Services were held in it on April 13, 1873 and it was dedicated on April 18, 1874. The Reverend Charles McCallion was the first pastor and was succeeded by the Reverend Patrick Cannovan.

[9]. A fascinating account of this fire came to light a few years ago in the form of a diary kept by Edward Augustus Ham, who was either an apprentice or a journeyman in the printing shop of The Portsmouth Journal. Ham tells of being awakened before 2 a.m. and going to the scene of the fire. "We found the house of Mrs. Lunt

(Mrs. Thomas) in Market Street in flames, and the adjacent block of five stores igniting. The heat was so intense and the smoke so suffocating, as to prevent anyone from remaining long in Mrs. L.'s house, but notwithstanding, many valuable articles of furniture were saved". The fire apparently started in a small dyehouse in the rear of a hat store operated by Daniel Knight and Company. Traveling fast, the fire spread northerly along Market Street, and jumped to the easterly side. Ham's narrative continues: "After satisfying myself that I could do but little for Mrs. L., I repaired to the Journal office where I found Mr. Brewster and Blake already on the spot. Mr. B. thought the danger imminent, and according to his wishes, we took all the valuable cases (type) from their racks carrying them to the lower floor, that in the event of conflagration we might the more easily save them....Mr. Miller, Mr. Moses, F. Miller, L. W. Brewster, Samuel Miller, C. W. Brewster, E. E. Blake, I. N. Fernald, G. G. Brewster and others worked like men, and although the building did not take fire as we feared, yet they showed a praiseworthy spirit".

He tells of going to the Farmer's Hotel (where the old P. O. stands now) and having a glass of lemonade before going back to the fire which covered an area "from C. W. Clark's tailor shop to Alexander Ladd's dwelling house, Fore (Lower Market) Street from S. I. Dodge's market to the corner of High Street, and from William Jones & Sons on Market to B. Swasey's paint shop on Penhallow Street, the flames had complete possession". Ham wound up his account: "We left the scene at 5 o'clock and found our way home, where we found our brother Joseph, Mother waiting our return with a fine pot of coffee under considerable agitation. We drank five large cups, ate some excellent fried 'nuts' and after listening to and relating sundry incidents, espied I. S. Haselton about to return to the fire....We then left for home, and retired. Had a quiet sleep of two hours, when we were obliged to answer a summons to breakfast, which we did without delay, for our appetite was unusally keen". The diary, 15 years ago, was in the possession of Leroy C. Moore of Rogers Street.

[10]. The old Franklin School is now an apartment house.

[11]. The New Franklin was built in 1919 and was enlarged and modernized in 1969-71, at far more expense than the original building. The site was on the old Town Farm, and in April of 1917, before the school was built, the City Council authorized plowing of the surrounding land for gardens to help residents raise extra food.

[12]. The Haven School was dedicated early in January, 1850, and one of the features was the reading of an ode by Miss Louisa Simes. The speaker was the Reverend A. P. Peabody, pastor of the South Church, ordained in 1833. The building was described as 67 feet square, first story 12 feet high; second, 14 feet; built at a cost of $11,000 for 200 scholars. Haven was later enlarged.

[13]. Little Harbour had drawn a lot of criticism because it's a radical departure from the old formal classroom concept. It's known as an "open school". Joyce Hanrahan, wife of the Bow Street book expert, Jack Hanrahan, was the first principal. The building also houses the administrative offices of the School Department, headed by School Superintendent James Cusick.

[14]. On April 5, 1708, the town voted to build a school. A free province school was also ordered for Portsmouth, for "righters, reeders, and Latiners". Spelling could have been used, too.

[15]. Town records are vague, but it's definite that a school was standing where the Gravelly Ridge School stood during the Revolution. The brick schoolhouse there now, named for Judge Levi Woodbury, was dedicated November 21, 1853, and Nathaniel D. Miller, Butterfield Carkin, Charles A. Wiggin and William H. Dennett were on the committee that supervised construction. Christopher S. Toppan was master of ceremonies at the dedication and an ode was presented by Miss Sarah A. Coffin. The first school on the spot came about through the efforts of Jeremy Dennett, John Shannon, Richard Pickering and Benjamin Miller. Pickering and Miller lived in Newington but they were concerned in establishing a school somewhere near their homes. Jonathan Warner and a Deacon Eliot owned the land.

The Reverend Tobias H. Miller, writing in the Morning Chronicle, left behind an account of that earlier school, as it was when he attended it about 1800. The building was about 20 feet square, and as the pupils entered he found boys and girls seated on benches, their backs to the wall. Charles Taft, a large man for the day, six feet tall, moved around the center of the room, keeping an eye on his pupils. There was a fireplace that nearly filled the west end of the building and only three windows, each with 12 panes of glass. These windows were set so low in the wall that bigger students blocked out light for the others. The school "yard" measured 7 by 9 feet, and in winter was used for the storage of wood.

Miller told of one day when the wood supply ran out, and the chill fingers of winter poked into the room. The girls were finally sent home and two older boys went home and borrowed axes; then all the boys and the teacher went into the swamps and cut wood with the bigger boys chopping and the little ones hauling it out. Pupils came to that school from Newington, Noble's Island, the Plains, Great Swamp and Gravelly Ridge itself. That building was found inadequate within a few years. So the fireplace was torn out; the room space doubled; more windows; and a stove was put in; plus plastering of the walls and ceiling. Miller gave the names of some of the teachers over the years: Alfred M. Hoyt, Samuel Hoyt, James Pickering, Winthrop Pickering, Hazen Pickering, John T. Tasker, and Mark A. Dennett, the son of one of the builders, who was in charge for a long time. There are still people living in Portsmouth who went to the Woodbury School as it closed its doors only 36 years ago.

[16]. The old Lafayette School is now a residence. The Lafayette Highway on which it sits was opened to travel in 1824, the year the Marquis de Lafayette visited the area. Until it opened up, all traffic toward the south was out through Greenland and then along the old Post Road (Route 151). School probably was first held in that area in 1828 or 1829.

[17]. This collection of glass photographic plates was the hobby for most of his adult years for the late Garland W. Patch, Sr.

[18]. This stood in the open field, probably back of the property line of the present houses on the east side of Richards Avenue.

[19]. Other than adoption of the charter, this was one of the last official acts of the town meeting. The voters agreed to buy this land, and bones have often been found in the vicinity of the New Franklin School, mute evidence that "strangers" had been buried on the Town Farm premises.

[20]. However, more investigation makes it obvious that "That Night" occurred prior to the Charter adoption. From the pen of Lewis W. Brewster comes the information that it involved an effort by Democrats to railroad their own candidate into the Legislature by keeping the voting open all through the night. The Democratic theory was that the Whigs would not stick around and eventually they would be able to overcome the Whig superiority because the rules then demanded that each candidate have a majority of the votes cast. The plot was conceived by Samuel A. Badger, William H. Rollins, Edward H. Sise and Charles D. Pillow. They put forward the names of Charles W. Cutter, Marcellus Bufford and Badger. The other candidates on the ticket were Andrew Hussey, James W. Emery, Horton D. Walker, and John Trundy.

Only Trundy, a mathematical instrument maker, won on the first ballot. The meeting adjourned until 7 in the evening, and at 11 p.m. another vote was counted but there was no choice. They started voting again at 11:30 p.m., closing the polls at 4:30 a.m. with 1,066 votes cast. The Whig ticket was elected by a majority of 30-odd, and the meeting adjourned at 5:45 a.m. until 2 p.m. The Whig victory represented the ability to get out their voters in the darkest hours of the night, something the Democrats ("Locos", their foes called them) did not think they could do. In the case of one reluctant Whig voter, he just did not want to get up, so half a dozen volunteers went to his house, kicked in his door and brought him. Another man, a banker, was aroused and, in his turn, went after another distinguished but reluctant voter. Pulled out of his bed, the man agreed to go to the polls, saying, "Yes, I will go with you — but I will move out of town tomorrow"! Such was the nature of affairs when Portsmouth's polls stayed open all through the night, and in Whig eyes symbolized the dim depths to which Democrats would go in trickery. Hence it was known to the Whigs as "That Night". The incident also led to legislation which would bar Portsmouth from having its polls open all night, and probably was the direct cause of the establishment of specified hours for voting.

[21]. The city's present charter also provides that meetings shall be open to the public and there shall be no secret votes. However, over the years various subterfuges have been tried. Once, during the regime of Mayor Andrew H. Jarvis, the City Council attempted to meet at Jarvis' summer place, Wallis Sands. Tipped off, a crew of reporters and photographers from The Herald were on hand to greet the councilmen as they arrived at the "Summer Council Chamber". On another occasion, the same council sought refuge at the Pannaway Club, a sylvan retreat on Sagamore Creek, then owned by Jarvis. The result was about the same.

Legend has it that in the days of railroading, many a secret meeting of the City Council was held in the old roundhouse off McDonough Street. And there was a report of a 7 o'clock meeting of the City Council in June, 1914, in the privacy of Mayor Harry B. Yeaton's office, before the formal meeting started at 10 p.m.

[22]. Abner Greenleaf was a brass founder by trade. A native of Newburyport, Massachusetts, born in 1785, he became a Mason in old Pythagorean Lodge in 1819. He died September 28, 1868. During the War of 1812, Greenleaf found employment at the Navy Yard and some of his copper work was in the fabric of the USS Washington. He taught school for a time; became postmaster; elected

mayor; served in both houses of the Legislature, presiding over the Senate in 1829. A lot of political writing flowed from his pen, and in 1815, he wrote for The People's Advocate, a political sheet published by William Weeks and Daniel P. Drown. The paper lasted only 26 weeks. When it expired, an "obit" was published in the New Hampshire Gazette, "Died in this town on Saturday last, much lamented! the Peoples Avocate. . . ." It was one of 40-0dd newspapers that have existed in Portsmouth since 1756. Greenleaf was one of the founders of the Democratic Party and later contributed to the New Hampshire Gazette.

[23]. The city built its second high school on the site of George Haven's house on Islington Street in 1904. After the new Portsmouth Senior High School was built and opened in 1956, this building for a time housed lower grades, and then, with the razing of the original Farragut School, it took that name, and was used until the opening of Little Harbour. The Haven house was sold at auction on May 9, 1903, to James R. Connell who paid $140 for it for salvage.

[24]. Thomas D. Bailey was the grandfather of Thomas Bailey Aldrich.

[25]. Aaron H. Hill became a prominent local businessman, a shoe dealer, partnered with James M. Carr. He was also a director of the Portsmouth & Concord Railroad.

[26]. Lyman D. Spalding was a shipmaster, later a dealer in iron and steel in partnership with James B. Parrott. This Spalding died in 1892. His father was Dr. Lyman D. Spalding who was born in Cornish and had a brilliant career both as a physician and a pharmacist. He held honorary doctorates from both Dartmouth and Harvard, helping to found the Dartmouth Medical School.

Spalding compiled the United States Pharmacopoeia, a definitive work in the field and really his lasting memorial. He also pioneered in the use of kine pox as a vaccine against the dreaded small pox. Dr. Edward Jenner made the discovery in 1799 in England, and yet by September 30, 1800, Spalding was advertising in the New Hampshire Gazette: "Dr. Spalding announces he has received inoculation of Kine Pox from Dr. Waterhouse.... Dr. Spalding gives information that he will attend to the inoculation for the Kine Pox.... at his lodgings at the Reverend Timothy Alden's near the South Meeting House". Spalding was 25 at the time, and had spent part of the year with Dr. Benjamin Waterhouse at Cambridge. Dr. Waterhouse's grandfather had a prosperous farm on Freeman's Point around 1700.

Despite progress with vaccination, the town and then the city kept Pest Houses ready. As late as 1903, a new one was built — under the polite name, "Contagious Disease Hospital — on city land near the old Jones Avenue dump. Willis J. Manson was the contractor, and, shortly after it was completed, it had its first patient. In the past 70 years all trace of the building has disappeared, and it would now be hard to find the site. As for Dr. Spalding, he died October 30, 1821, at the young age of 46.

[27]. This building did double duty until 1864 as town offices and County Court House. It had succeeded the old State House as a court house, and was itself supplanted in 1891 when the now-demolished County Court House was opened. The city offices were moved from it in 1864 when new "city rooms" were opened on the second floor of Jefferson Hall. The Rambler's discourse at the opening ceromonies is still in existence and needs no retelling here. This was "City Hall" until 1909 when it was decided to take over the old high school building on Daniel Street. Here most municipal functions have been quartered ever since.

Among the sites on which the County Court House stood was the home of Abraham Isaac, the first Jew known to have been a resident of Portsmouth. After Isaac's death, his widow moved to New Ipswich. This was before 1800. The well for Isaac's house was out in front, in State Street. While Isaac has the distinction of being the first of his faith known to have lived in the community, it's hard to believe others had not come here.

Even today there's no certainty as to what Jewish families followed Isaac into town. The first that can be pinpointed was Meyer Alkon, who arrived sometime in the 1870s. George W. Sherman, a local druggist, has made extensive search of old records but has yet to find anyone earlier than Alkon. Although it is believed several now Gentile families have Jewish antecedents. As Sherman explains it, "These men came early, married out of the faith and simply adopted the new ways. Who can blame them?" Another early Jewish family were the parents of Benjamin Green, who had an apothecary sho at 1 Market Square.

[28]. John McClintock, who served on a privateer in the Revolution, died November 13, 1855, at 94. Foss says of McClintock that he was the only one of four brothers to survive the Revolution, and that he was a lieutenant in the Continental Navy before the age of 20. Four of his war years were spent privateering, more profitable than naval service. Appointed naval officer for Portsmouth, he served under five presidents, starting with Fillmore.

When he died, he was the last of the Revolutionary War survivors.

[29]. Gideon Rundlett was often a moderator of the town meetings and was postmaster for a number of years. In the early 1850s he published the New Hampshire Gazette.

[30]. Abraham Q. Wendell founded Wendell's Hardware, which was, at the time of its closing about three years ago, one of the oldest business firms on Market Square. At the time of his death, The Chronicle observed that he was one of the "old businessmen of Portsmouth, having kept a hardware store on Market Square for over 40 years. Retiring a few years since, failing health and approaching old age inducing him to give up the business to his sons". (These were Andrew P. and Henry.) During his active life, Wendell engaged in politics and served in the General Court. When the 1904 high school building was under consideration by the city, Wendell was an earnest advocate of the measure and contributed materially to its adoption.

[31]. On October 24, 1904, a painting of Albert Ruyter Hatch, done by his granddaughter, Mary Astor Hatch, was presented to the county for hanging in the now-razed Court House on State Street. The eulogy, no other word is descriptive, was given by Judge Calvin Page, who had once served him as an office boy. Page's glowing words well cover the career of this prominent Rockingham County attorney. Born in 1817, he graduated from Bowdoin, in 1837, winning admission to the bar from the office of Colonel Ichabod Bartlett. For eight years he was county solicitor, and then found his growing civil practice made it impossible to continue in that office. In his years before the bar he contended with such legal luminaries as Daniel M. Christie, John S. Wells, James Bell, Amos Tuck, W. H. Y. Hackett and James W. Emery. For 25 years he was clerk of the U. S. District Court, resigning the post in 1873. He went to the Legislature and was speaker of the House in 1874. Hatch died on March 5, 1882.

[32]. Daniel H. Spinney was the intended victim of a stupid murder. As it was, his wife, Sarah, was slain, and that made Spinney the indirect victim, if nothing else. The slaying occurred at the door of their house on what was then called White's Road, but has since taken the name of Spinney Road in honor of Daniel's family. Preliminary to the killing, there was an argument in the house of a man named Nelson N. Downing of 17 Dennett Street.

Downing and Mrs. Spinney were cousins, and the Spinneys dropped in on the Downings while strolling on a March evening in 1858. An argument began between Spinney and Downing over the hiring practices at the Portsmouth Navy Yard, and the quarrel that ensued demonstrated how insecure a man's job was on the Yard. Downing was upset because a man named Theodore F. Rowe had been rehired, and Downing had to work under him. Spinney agreed that his brother Samuel and Charles Woodbury had been instrumental in Rowe's return.

The argument became nasty, and Spinney left, but not until after he and Downing had swapped a few punches. The Spinneys resumed their walk, going along to North Street (Maplewood), Vaughan, Congress and Islington Streets and so back to their home on White's Road. Downing found a gun and told everyone who would listen that he was "going to get Dan Spinney's meat". Elisha G. Ferguson, the city marshal, even heard about the threats and came to see what was going on, but he did nothing about it. Downing started for the Spinney place, met Samuel Spinney, and they walked along arguing over whether or not Downing should shoot Daniel.

They separated at the Joseph Akerman gateway, the entrace to White Road at Islington. Downing seemingly having given up his intent to kill Spinney, but Samuel still went on to his brother's house to warn him. Samuel found his brother and sister-in-law just entering their home. Daniel invited him inside while Sarah Spinney turned to say something to one of her children. In the softly falling darkness a gun blasted and Spinney yelled in an anguish of pain he quickly forgot because his wife was lying at his. feet — dead. Some of the shotgun pellets had hit him on the arm, but others caught her in the eye and she died before falling to the gound.

Downing ran off, forced a man named Joseph L. Gove to take him in for the night, but Gove eventually induced him to leave. He hid in an outbuilding back of his house where the police and neighbors found him. Coroner John Bennett, also city clerk, impaneled a jury of Augustus Jenkins, Phinehas Nichols and Horace Webster. The jury wasted no time in putting the blame directly on Downing who was tried the next October. The jury found him guilty of manslaughter, which led to a one-year term in prison. The Morning Chronicle had acrid comment for the "morbid women" who fawned over Downing. The crime faded from the public mind. Downing died here on February 15, 1884, and Daniel H. Spinney followed on August 14, while on a trip to South Berwick. He was 71. Daniel was the father of Ceylon Spinney who was sheriff of Rockingham County for many years, being succeeded by the late Simes Frink. Ceylon's daughter, Mrs. George B. Trefethen, still makes her home on Spinney Road, but not in the family homestead.

Instead she resides in a wing of the home of her daughter, Mrs. Frances Sanderson.

Daniel H. Spinney enjoyed in those years, a large reputation as an orchardist and farmer. The propagation of fruit trees was one of his specialities. The Journal said in 1849, "His nursery is systematically and handsomely arranged, and will in a few years afford enough for all the gardens and orchards in our city and neighborhood. He has already handled many orders". Where the North Church Parish House stands on Spinney Road, with its necessary adjunct, the parking lot, may well have been part of Daniel Spinney's prosperous orchard.

[33]. Robert Shillaber was subject of a Ramble, one of the few not written by Charles W. Brewster, by his brother Benjamin P. Shillaber, a well known New England newsman in the last half of the 19th Century. It's in Brewster's second Series.

[34]. Longfellow used a Portsmouth legend for one of his more familiar poems, "Lady Wentworth", which concerns the marriage of Benning Wentworth to the tavern maid, Martha Hilton.

17

The Glorious Days of the Clippers

[1]. Boots cost $26 a pair and shoes were $15, and this was not 1972.

[2]. At first the trains stopped in the vicinity of what was called Frenchman's Lane. So named because a sailor of that nationality, attached to the French fleet here in the Revolution (1782), was murdered near the mouth of Islington Creek. Frenchman's Lane wandered from the Bartlett Street area along the line of the B & M tracks to Boston and then swung southerly to cross the present Islington Street, and along the course of Spinney Road. The Brewster map of 1850 shows the Portsmouth and Concord Railroad depot near the foot of Bridge Street and the Eastern Railroad station was north and east of that, nearer Vaughan Street on Deer. The Rambler indicates that the French sailors did enjoy a rendezvous at the head of North Mill Pond; here they washed their clothes, did some drinking and carousing. The Rambler interviewed an aged man, Richard Fitzgerald, who, as a boy, saw the sailor's body. That was in 1856, and Fitzgerald was 85.

[3]. It's not known if this John Winkley is the same man who commanded privateer Fox during the War of 1812. Winkley, strictly speaking was not a Forty-Niner. He was already in California when the discovery was made, and had been there for several years.

[4]. The ship Norman was built on the Piscataqua by Samuel Badger, launched on March 26, 1836, from Badger's yard, and one of her local owners was Christopher S. Toppan. She sailed for Boston April 22, loaded with hay, for New Orleans, but ran on Carey's Reef from which she was pulled by wreckers out of Key West. They were given salvage of $5,000. Norman was on the Atlantic run for some years, probably being diverted to the profitable California trade.

[5]. Martha was built by Samuel Badger for a Boston firm, and she was launched in 1843. Account books for her are in the Portsmouth Athenaeum. Her total cost was $21,113.09, and she sold for $23,000, giving Badger a profit of $1,886.02.

[6]. Harriet Rockwell was built by John Mugridge on ways at the foot of Pickering Street. That was in 1835, and she was the first vessel built there since the 18th Century. She would be the last until 1856, when Sarah E. Pettigrew was launched. Harriet Rockwell was owned by Lewis Barnes and Theodore J. Harris, both local men. Perhaps it's coincidental but Mugridge's building ways were adjacent to a wharf owned by Barnes. The adventures of Harriet Rockwell, if space permitted their telling, would rival the adventures of Jason's Argosy. She was typical of her times, a tight little packet, operating mainly on the Atlantic run until a the smell of gold in California turned the commerce of the Unites States upside down. For example, in March of 1839, Harriet Rockwell cleared Liverpool for Boston and when next heard of, is in bad trouble off the coast of Ireland. She lost her skipper, Captain J. W. Jewett, when she was forced to anchor under the lee of Barra Head Lighthouse because of contrary winds. The captain, the second mate and four seamen were drowned when they tried to get ashore in the jolly boat to get a pilot. Charles Wattleworth, the first officer, worked the ship into Tobermoy Harbor, Isle of Mull. Captain Theodore J. Harris of Portsmouth had started the voyage, but had died, and Jewett had taken over. A newspaper note of the tragedy says that the vessel had been absent three years, and so probably none of the original crew were still on board. A ship called Wellington, under a Captain Melville, aided Harriet Rockwell so successfully that the captain and crew were awarded 500 pounds. Cargo and the Harriet Rockwell were estimated as worth 18,000 pounds.

[7]. One of the first companies from here was known as the New Hampshire Rockingham Mutual Mining and Trading Company. Those interested in this enterprise sailed from New York March 15, 1849, on the steamer Crescent City for Chagres to take what was termed the overland route — is across the Isthmus. John H. Jackson was president of the company and the members were George Gaines, R. F. Phiff, John S. Fabyan, Eben Dunells, Daniel Smith, G. Gee Pickering, Nathaniel Donnell, Benjamin W. Gannett, Haven Runnells, Edward J. Moulton, Benjamin Norton, James Rundlett, Enoch Coffin, Joseph B. Adams, James T. Brown, Alfred M. Berry, M. B. Goodrich, George L. Stockwell and B. F. Moses.

This party had a rough trip, and none of them was ever reported as having made a fortune in the gold fields.

However, as late as 1906, there were those who were still looking to California as the El Dorado. Not, it's good to note, through any illusion that there was a new gold rush but simply that business climate out there was healthier. In 1905, a former alderman, Elisha B. Newman, a painter by trade, sold out his business and moved to the Golden State. Shortly after that, Thomas Clark located in Los Angeles, also a young man named Quinlan. On top of these was the migration of William E. Peirce, a former city clerk, who closed up his insurance business and moved to Los Angeles.

[8]. George Raynes was born in 1799 and died April 12, 1855. The plain, towering granite shaft that honors him in the Union Cemetery is more impressive than his obituary. As a matter of fact, his death is not even recorded in the city clerk's office, at least the writer could not find it, not even with the aid of Mrs. Kay Thomits, the deputy city clerk.

This was not so of Raynes' competitor, and one time associate, Frederick W. Fernald, who died on the 30th of the same month. Fernald was 44. The Chronicle said, "It is worthy of remark that by this death, added to that of Mr. George Raynes, there are now three ships on the Piscataqua, which are to be finished or otherwise be disposed of on account of the estates of deceased persons, the loss of whose active enterprise will be severely felt". Fernald was the representative-elect from Ward 2.

[9]. Edward F. Sise, born September 23, 1799, was one of the local merchant princes. He fathered William H., Joseph and Edward H. Edward F. Sise died May 25, 1868.

[10]. A local merchant, Rollins lived at 69 Pleasant Street.

[11]. Cathedral is one of the great stories of seafaring. She was built for use as a Boston-Liverpool packet, launched under the supervision of Daniel Marcy on March 3, 1855. After her launch, a grand dinner was held at Piscataqua House, 9 Pleasant Street, of which Josiah G. Hadley was the proprietor.

Towed to Boston by the Enoch Train, Cathedral went into the Atlantic service and reports of her passages are frequent. On her very first, from Boston to Liverpool, her cargo was valued at $260,000, and she carried a large number of passengers. On another passage, inbound to Boston with 375 passengers, Cathedral reported immense icebergs at latitude 46, longitude 47 degrees 30 minutes; that was in July. Today icebergs are a pleasant diversion that transatlantic jet pilots call to the attention of their passengers to while away the boredom of that long seven-hour flight from London. But Cathedral, like so many others, finally went on to the Pacific runs, and was commanded by William H. Howard on her last passage. She was carrying coal to a Pacific port, and apparently had been poorly loaded and the cargo probably started shifting as she came around the Horn. Cathedral worked her way up into the 50s of latitude when she went, because of cargo movement, onto her beam ends. Captain Howard was in his cabin, a desperately ill man. With the ship badly in distress, the mate decided to abandon her, and manned the boats. On Cathedral, was a stewardess who had been with Captain Howard in Atlantic packet days. Apparently writing off his captain as a goner, the mate urged the stewardess to join him and the others as they abandoned ship. She refused to go and stayed with the stricken captain. The news account asks, probably unforgiveably in these days of equal rights for women, "How's that for woman's pluck"?

[12]. When people talk about Witch of the Wave, it's a question of which one they mean. There were two — both built by George Raynes. The first Witch was launched early in 1851, and set records never beaten. She went to Salem for registry, under tow of the steamer R. B. Forbes. She was rated at 1,494 tons, 202 feet long, 40 feet feet in breadth, with a depth of 21 feet. Her figurhead was of a young woman, clad in gossamer drapery of white and gold, with one shapely arm extended, and her small bare feet stepping on the crest of a wave. At a lunch on board, as she went to Salem, a toast was proposed, "Success to the newest and youngest of the Salem witches. Had they possessed a proportional share of her beauty, we are confident that the sternest tribunal before which any of them were arraigned, would never have had the heart to subject a single one to the trial to which their successor is designed — Trial by Water". Flowery? By today's standards, yes, but such was then the oratory. On that run, under tow, to Salem, Raynes induced Witch's captain to set a little sail, "just to assist the tow-boat a little". Topsails, jib and foretopmast stay sails were loosened by her crew of Portsmouth riggers on order from Captain John Bertram, and she soon ran up on the weather beam of the R. B. Forbes.

A news item in The Morning Chronicle of December 7, 1852, reports that Witch of the Wave had arrived at San Francisco in less time than on her maiden voyage, and discharged her cargo in as good condition as when taken aboard. Passengers on that run presented the captain with a silver pitcher and "resolved, that, although our expectations were much raised in the far-famed ship Witch of the Wave, we have not been disappointed in anyone particular, as she has not only proved herself a fast sailer, passing every ship seen on the voyage, but her qualities as a sea boat are all that can be desired". Shortly after that, the Witch, riding at her wharf in San Francisco was slightly damaged in a heavy gale. From San Francisco, Witch went to Hong Kong, and arrived with smallpox among her crew. On July 6, 1853, the Morning Chronicle reported that Witch arrived in Boston on July 3, from Calcutta, having left the Sand Heads on April 13, 81 days passage, one day shorter than that of Staffordshire, which arrived April 20, in 82 days. Up to that time, Staffordshire's passage was the shortest by five days. In an informal race in 1852, Witch set a mark from Canton to Deal of 90 days. Her freight rate on that run was eight dollars a ton, the highest yet paid. Again in 1854, Witch sailed from Boston on August 16, and Northern Light, a fast Clipper sailed on the 14th. Witch arrived in San Francisco on December 12 and Northern Light on December 16. In "Greyhounds of the Sea", it is reported that the brig Fox, 225 tons, ran from Calcutta to New York in 90 days, arriving home on December 26, 1809. "To fully appreciate what this meant, one need only recall that the record for all time is the 81-day passage of the extreme Clipper Witch of the Wave, a craft of many times her tonnage". About 1855, the first Witch was sold to Dutch shipping interests and took the name Electra.

On November 28, 1855, The Morning Chronicle reported that a new ship was being built by George Raynes & Son for C. H. Coffin of Newburyport, and is to be called Witch of the Wave. On January 28, 1856, the ship Witch of the Wave, 1,100 tons was launched in the midst of a cold snowstorm. The labors of the day closed "with a sumpuous repast, for all hands employed on the ship, provided by Charles W. Walker....It is a noteworthy fact that no liquor was to be had on the premises". On March 21, a boy named Andrew Moran, 12 years old, probably the son of John H. Moran, a joiner, fell from the deck to the hold on Witch of the Wave, fracturing his skull and one arm. Dr. William Laighton attended him. On May 10, 1856, Witch sailed from Charleston for Havre with 3,335 bales of Upland cotton and 605 bags of Sea Island cotton. Valued at $223,883, the most valuable cargo ever cleared from Charleston for Havre.

[13]. Sea Serpent, 1,402 tons, had for a figurehead a long slender serpent, "Whose life-like, slimy looking body, was picked out in shades of green and gold". She arrived in San Francisco on May 17, 1851, after putting into Valparaiso for repairs, having lost spars and sails off Cape Horn. Her time was 115 days, deducting time lost at Valparaiso. In 1853, she ran from New York to San Francisco in 107 days. She once went from Canton to New York in 88 days, and, on another occasion made the passage from New York

to the Equator in 17 days. A New York newspaper said of her when she first docked there: "The model of Sea Serpent is one that the greatest grumbler would be at a loss to find fault with. Head on she has a most rakish appearance, and her lines swell along the bow into their utmost fullness, and then taper off again into the clean run they show incontestably that 'the line of beauty' had been made the guide in her construction. They are as perfect as perfection itself. Her stern is most beautifully proportioned, and is tastefully decorated with two full long representations of the great American Sea Serpent". Sea Serpent once left Hong Kong on January 3, passed Amjier on the 11th and crossed 20 degrees in the North Atlantic on her 64th day out....From there she had light airs but reached Sandy Hook two days ahead of the Surprise, 78 days from Hong Kong, a mark only twice beaten. In 1859, Sea Serpent ran from China to Britain in three to fifteen days less than the time of the best British ships, although the monsoon was unfavorable.

[14]. Wild Pigeon, rated at 997 tons, was launched in 1851. In that year, she ran from New York to San Francisco in 109 days, under Captain George W. Putnam. But on another occasion she took 135 days, indicative of the variable times suffered by the windjammers. On July 25, 1854, The Morning Chronicle reported that "the celebrated Clipper ships Wild Pigeon...; the Sweepstakes, built by Westervelt, and the Flying Fish, built by Donald McKay, arrived in New York on Wednesday. These three ships passed the Straits of Sunda — the Sweepstakes and the Wild Pigeon in company and the Flying Fish four days previously; and, after repeatedly falling in with each other on passage, arrived within 14 hours of the same time. The Wild Pigeon in 1852 made the fastest October passage to San Francisco, 102 days. She went under the British flag in 1863, and was abandoned in the North Atlantic in 1892.

[15]. Wild Duck was launched on April 12, 1852, at 2:30 p.m., the 50th vessel built by George Raynes — the first was in 1828. Rated at 800 tons, she was 160 feet on the deck; 154 at the keel; with a beam of 34 feet, and depth of 22. She was copper-sheathed and commanded by Captain A. G. Hamilton. She cleared here on May 13, of and for New York, and a passenger wrote of the trip that started from Pray's Wharf (about opposite the line of Green Street) at 4:30 in the afternoon. "The Wild Duck in this trip proved herself a fast sailer, as she passed everything we came in sight of, although, on account of being light, she could not sail so close to the wind as most vessels she overtook. As the log was not thrown during the voyage, the number of knots she sailed is not known....She works

easy, is a fine sea boat and adds one more to the long list of first class ships built by G. Raynes, Esquire". On May 1854, The Morning Chronicle reported her at Woosung, China, ready for New York and getting $20 per ton for tea and $30 for silks. She was wrecked on October 1856, at Foo Chow Foo, in the River Min. The vessel and cargo were lost but the crew was saved. She was insured on Wall Street for about $270,000.

[16]. Tinqua was a small Clipper launched by Raynes in March, 1852. She was built for Oliphant & Sons, the big New York shipping firm, and intended for the China trade. Jacob D. Whitmore was the captain. Her maiden voyage apparently started in January for San Francisco. She was off the Horn seven days before making it around. In December she was back in New York from Canton and had been badly beaten in a gale in which she lost her jib boom, top gallant mast and entire suit of sails. She also lost all her water, but she was supplied by Captain Conway of ship Prince de Joinville. In 1854, on June 21, she left San Francisco for Shanghaii, and in October headed back to New York. She went ashore on Cape Hatteras on January 12. "When the crew left her, she was full of water, but with her masts still standing, and when last seen was drifting northeast, and if fallen in with would be found in the Gulf Stream. The stern was all under water. The captain had not sounded before the vessel struck, supposing himself to be 40 miles east of where he was". The 700-ton Tinqua was a total loss; her crew was saved by three different vessels. The ship was valued at $60,000 and her cargo, $290,000, which was insured in New York. Whitmore was a hard-driving captain, as proven by the fact that he forced his vessel so much that seven different times her rigging slacked off, even though it was made "of Russian hemp by men who knew their trade". On each occasion he was compelled to heave to and reset the rigging which experienced seamen believed cost him many hours on his run.

[17]. A model of Emily Farnum is in the Portsmouth Savings Bank. She was not a Clipper but was built as a freighter, weighing 1,200 tons. Her owners were local men, William Jones & Son, Richard Jenness and Captain William Parker, her skipper. The launching was on June 30, 1854. Her career was not glamorous; she did what she was built to do — haul freight — until lost on Cape Flattery, Washington in 1875.

[18]. On one run to Liverpool from New York, Webster carried 364 bales of cotton, 1,021 barrels of flour; 4,394 bushels of wheat; 31 barrels of pork; 400 tierces of beef; 50,000

pounds of bacon. She was strictly for the Liverpool trade, scooting back and forth like a ferry.

[19]. Coeur de Lion was built for George W. Tucker, a Portsmouth shipmaster, and Boston parties. The launching was on Tuesday, January 3, 1853, at 1 p.m. She was 182 feet long, 26 feet in breadth and 22 feet in depth. Tucker was her commander, and he boarded at the house of John Smith on Daniel Street. The Chronicle noted that the attendance at the launching was small because of the weather, and Captain Tucker entertained the mechanics at supper in the City Hotel. It's recorded in "Greyhounds of the Sea" that Coeur de Lion was one of seven Clippers to enter San Francisco in a single day, the only time it ever happened. The Alta Californian, a West Coast paper, was reported as saying: "The Clipper ship Coeur de Lion, now lying at Lombard Dock, in San Francisco, is one of the finest modeled and finished ships which we have ever seen in this port. In every place she had visited, her fine line, neat finish, finely proportioned spars, etc. have attracted universal attention and been the theme of praise by seafaring men, both American and foreign. She is the last ship built by George Raynes of Portsmouth, New Hampshire, and considered the best of the splendid fleet constructed by him....The Coeur De Lion is a medium-sized ship, carrying about 2,000 tons California cargo; has made thus far three voyages from the Atlantic States to this city, turning out her cargo each time in excellent order...."

[20]. Water Witch was another of Raynes' great ships, launched on May 7, 1853. With Boston owners, her captain was Washington Plumer of Portsmouth. The Chronicle reported on May 9: "The Clipper ship Water Witch of 1,200 tons burthen was launched promptly at the appointed time, 12 o'clock Saturday in fine style. The ship was fully masted and coppered on the stocks, being dressed with festoons of flags and parti-colored signals from truck to rail. The Union Jack was on the bowsprit, at the fore truck the ship's name, at the main a pennant, a private signal; and a complete set of Marryat's signals; at the mizzen the American ensign". Another note in the commentary on Water Witch gives a quick hint of the shipbuilding activity here: "Standing on one of our wharves on Wednesday, an observer could see four new ships on the stocks, one new ship (Water Witch) rigged and lying at the wharf". Further comment on Water Witch told of her departure from this port. When the tug hired to tow her did not show up, she breezed along under her topsails. Off Frost's Point, the tug tried to intercept and was nearly run down by the Clipper; so she was allowed to

proceed to Boston under sail. An open house had been held on her before she sailed and many went aboard to view "the spacious cabin". However, tragedy, as so often, was in the future for Water Witch. On June 15, 1855, she was blown on the rocks, off Ypala, Mexico, and was a total loss. First reports were that Captain Plumer had drowned, but these later proved untrue. This was on her second voyage to California. She was valued at $68,000 and was fully insured in Boston. All the men and officers were saved, and $500 was paid for the wreck itself.

[21]. In 1864, San Jacinto was at the Portsmouth Navy Yard for repairs and refitting.

[22]. Morning Light's dimensions were truly big. Her extreme length was 225 feet; at the keel, 206; beam, 43; depth of hold, 27½ feet. She was built for Maine interests, the Tuckers of Wiscasset.

[23]. The Portsmouth Morning Chronicle also was "launched" during this period, the city's first daily paper. It was founded by Frank W. Miller, Samuel Gray and Thomas W. Miller on August 2, 1852. The first issue describes the troubles the publishers had in making an engraving for the paper's banner. The scene depicted is Portsmouth Harbor. Charles M. Meinerth, a music teacher, did the drawing and engraving, charging $50 for his work. The paper's chief feature writer, or columnist, was T. H. Miller, who wrote under the name Uncle Toby. He was The Chronicle's answer to The Rambler, who was his close personal friend. F. W. Hartford bought The Chronicle in 1898, and published it until June 11, 1921, when it became obvious Portsmouth could not support both a morning and two afternoon papers.

[24]. Rated as the largest merchant ship yet built on the Piscataqua, Sierra Nevada was launched on May 30, 1854, and The Rockingham Messenger said, "She went off beautifully and sits upon the water like a duck". Her owners were the big firm Glidden and Williams of New York, and they intended her for California. "Clipper Ship Era" describes Sierra Nevada as one of the last of the extreme Clippers, and says she went into the Australian trade. In 1859, Sierra made the run to San Francisco in 97 days. Her dimensions were: Length, 225 feet; beam, 44 feet; hold, 27½. She originally was to have been called King of the Forest. Why it was changed is not known. Like a lot of others, Sierra Nevada was happy to pick up a cargo in 1855, as shown when she went into Chincha, Peru, for a load of guano. Her skipper at the time was a man named Penhallow, possibly Peirce W. Pennhallow of Portsmouth. Shortly

after that she ran into trouble at Liverpool when she grounded on the sill of Wellington Dock. On June 13, 1855, she was offered at auction at Liverpool. The bids failed to reach 6,000 pounds, so she was "bid in". With Penhallow still her captain, Sierra Nevada went ashore on Romer Shoal, below New York, on March 6, 1856, but got off at high water. According to "Greyhounds of the Sea", Sierra Nevada was lost on the coast of Chile in 1877.

[25]. These other Tobey and Littlefield vessels, in the Alice Ball model, were R. H. Tucker, Donati, Richard III, Liverpool Packet, Manchester, City of Montreal (a coal barge in 1906), Coronation and Semiramis. Liverpool Packet was built in 1863; she sailed from Shanghaii on September 15, 1863, and was never heard from again. Richard III was a barge in 1906.

[26]. Typhoon did the unusual in making a direct run from Portsmouth to Liverpool, an effort that won her lasting fame on the Atlantic. Four days out of Portsmouth, a young seaman, his first trip before the mast, was struck by lightning. William Badger of Newmarket was only 19, and lived until he reached Liverpool. There he died and was buried. On December 9, 1852, an item in The Chronicle reported that the Typhoon was in from Liverpool in 23 days. "This is a remarkably fast run for the season". Then there is an account from the San Francisco Herald: "It is a novel sight to see the Clipper ship Typhoon (August 11, 1853) lying flat upon her side at a wharf, with her vast spars hanging like the boughs of a tree over the heads of passers-by, and touching the eaves of the warehouse. The curious spectacle causes a universal halt to both the idle and the busy. But there she is, lying just as snugly as though in her natural position — a steam pump in a lighter puffing away on one side to relieve her of the water she has taken in, while on the other side is a swarm of busy workmen running under her keel, hammering away at her seams, and replacing the copper to keep the same element out". Typhoon had gotten into trouble by hitting some rocks when she was leaving the harbor. Typhoon's dimensions were given as 1,612 tons; 225 feet long; 41.5 feet, beam; hold, 23 feet. On the Liverpool run she frequently ran 15.5 knots and her best day was 346 miles. Typhoon once ran from New York to San Francisco in 106 days, beating both Raven and Sea Witch. In 1854, with Captain Samuel Goodhue in command, Typhoon ran from the Lizard to the Sand Heads, in 80 days, under a 12,000-pound charter. "She's now performing her third charter to the East Indies on English account, and from her uniform short passage and perfect delivery of cargo at London each previous time, she has become quite a favorite, and

received the round sum of 12,000 pounds sterling and back". When Typhoon was working in the Empire Line, out of New York for Liverpool, this note appeared in the New York Herald: "A great gale swept the coast on the 20th of January, accompanied by a blinding snowstorm. Many vessels went down with all on board, and more were wrecked with considerable loss of life. The day after the gale, the fast Clipper Typhoon limped in past Sandy Hook, 47 days from Liverpool, a mass of ice. Captain Salter had lost seven close-reefed topsails during the previous fortnight, and had only 10 men out of a crew of 40 able to stand watch". The crews of these runs were usually tough, illiterate Liverpool Irishmen. How many the captains killed in these raw ages, no one will ever know. Typhoon may not have been Portsmouth's greatest, but she was a good entry in any contest for the title.

[27]. Levi Woodbury, another workhorse of the North Atlantic, was built in 1851 for Daniel Marcy, James N. Tarlton, Frederick W. Fernald and William Pettigrew, all of Portsmouth, plus Peter Marcy of New Orleans. She was listed 988 tons, with a man named Grace, probably Joseph of 14 Gates Street, as master. She worked between New Orleans and Liverpool, and sometimes Boston, where she arrived, from Gottenburg, on July 21, 1854, with 440 passengers.

[28]. And still another of the hard-working Atlantic freighters was Frank Pierce "named in honor of the nominee of the Democratic party". She is to be owned in this city and New Orleans by the owners of the Levi Woodbury. Built entirely of New Hampshire white oak, the Frank Pierce, was listed at 1,400 tons, and her owners were Daniel Marcy, Washington Williams, James N. Tarlton, and Peter Marcy of New Orleans. Daniel Marcy was her captain. Richard Jenness later came in as an owner and Tarlton sold his interest to Captain Joseph Nickerson of Boston. Launched at 5 p.m. on October 21, 1852, the Frank Pierce sailed on November 26, with the captain's wife, and Captain D. D. Baker, formerly commander of the Marine detachment at the Navy Yard, and his family on board. Marcy later reported that she arrived at the Bar mouth of the Mississippi in 22 days. "We made the 'Hole in the Wall' in nine days from Portsmouth, although we had only 27 hours of fair wind, during which we ran 286 miles, with the main royal set. When within three miles of the Isaacs it fell calm, and we drifted out of the Gulf with a four-knot current....Finding there was no alternative but to return to the 'Hole in the Wall' again, we did so, thus making two passages for one. After passing the 'Hole in the Wall' the second time,

we were 80 hours to the Bar". In January, the Frank Pierce cleared New Orleans with 2,184,887 pounds of cotton on board, plus 102 tierces of beef. Frank Pierce was reported on June 7, 1853, as arriving in Boston with 710 passengers, which brought this comment from her captain: "The statement that Captain Marcy landed 710 passengers at Boston is correct, but the story about such a lot of babies is not true.

"Captain Marcy informs the Journal that through the excellent arrangement of the means of ventilation and the convenience of the ship, general health prevailed among the large company — not one death nor scarcely any case of sickness occurred. But he lays no claim in peculiar advantage on this score of bringing into port 11 more passengers than he took on at Liverpool as the papers are saying. There was no increase on the voyage". Shortly after she arrived, Captain Marcy was presented with a portrait of the President to hang in the cabin of the Frank Pierce. The Chronicle said on October 19, 1853, "We saw a beautiful oil painting at the home (57 Pleasant Street) of Captain Marcy, representing the ship Frank Pierce under full sail, up the Mersey River at Liverpool; in the distance the ship Levi Woodbury is seen coming around Bell Rock; and the Peter Marcy is just being taken into her dock". Shortly after that Marcy, as was his wont, yielded command to someone else and Frank Pierce kept on freighting.

[29]. Hope Goodwin, 1,199 tons, was built for Ichabod Goodwin and W. H. Parsons who commanded her. Launched in 1852, her career was short because she burned in Mobile Harbor on May 14, 1854, set on fire by her crew. Goodwin had $62,000 insurance on the ship and her freight money.

[30]. Red Rover's launching was October 27, 1852. Her commander was Captain William O. Putnam and Ichabod Goodwin was the agent for the owner, Robert Taylor of New York. During her launch, the British schooner McLellan, of Windsor, Nova Scotia, loaded with plaster, coming up river ran afoul of Red Rover and carried away one of her own davits. On coming into the wharf, Red Rover ran foul and broke the anchor stock. On November 17, while being fitted for sea, Red Rover nearly had a fatal accident as the workmen were setting up the masts. "The mizzen top mast was pointed and hoisted partly to its place, and the mast rope was belayed and seized. A rigger was standing on the top at work, when a laborer on deck, by some unaccountable blunder, cast off the rope and the top mast came down by the run, bruising and splitting the deck beam, then fell over the rail, breaking off. No one was hurt".

Rover finally sailed on November 24 for New York and thence to China. "A stiff nor'wester took her down the river and out of the harbor in grand style". The book "Clipper Ship Era" says Red Rover ultimately was sold or leased into the Australian trade about 1857, and once made the run from Liverpool to Melbourne in less than 75 days. Red Rover almost did not get to achieve this feat. In December 1853, when Donald McKay's ship Great Republic was destroyed by fire, Red Rover was near by and was towed out of her berth in flames. These were controlled and she survived to be at Chincha, Peru, in 1854 when one of her officers was abused and subjected to outrages by Peruvian officers. Other mariners at Chincha later memorialized Congress in protest and the memorials were at the Portsmouth Athenaeum and Exchange Building Reading Rooms for signatures.

[31]. Portsmouth men were the owners of Colorado, 1,200 tons, when she was launched on November 10, 1854. They were Jonathan M. Tredick, president of the Rockingham Bank; Samuel Sheafe, a merchant at 92 Market Street; and George W. Haven, who had offices at 21 Pleasant Street. John B. Haley was her captain and she left here in mid-February 1855. A news item on August 2, 1856, tells us that Colorado's master, Moses Ricker, "of this city", had been sun-struck in Calcutta. And in June 1857, she loaded 20,000 bags of rice at Calcutta for China.

[32]. According to the 1851 Directory, the Peter Marcy was built for Peter Marcy of New Orleans and his brother Daniel of Portsmouth. She was launched in July 1848, "a fine new ship of 900 tons....to the gratification of a large number of spectators". The Rockingham Messenger said on August 31, 1848, "This superb vessel went down our river on Tuesday morning with a light, favoring breeze, and was cheered as she left the wharf by a crowd of admiring spectators. She was built by Messrs. Fernald and Pettigrew for Messers. (Judah) Touro, R. D. Shepherd and Marcy, and is intended for the freighting business. It is calculated she will carry 3,000 bales of cotton. Her length on deck is 164 feet; beam, 34 feet; depth of hold, 23 feet. She is built of New Hampshire white oak, and although built with regard chiefly to strength and capacity, it is believed that her sailing qualities will be found inferior to few with which she may come in company....Her cabin is most beautiful, painted in fresco on pine, in imitation of birch, rose and zebra wood, and all bearing a polish equal to any of the fancy woods which it was intended to resemble....Her bow is ornamented with a full length statue of the gentleman whose name she bears, and on her stern is a

representation of a steamboat under full way, a ship just launched and workmen getting out timber for another". Edward Smith, 11 Hanover Street, did the painting; John Knowlton of 10 Islington Street was the blacksmith; Thomas Martin, 49 Islington, did the joiner work; Jeremiah Johnson, who had a rope walk at Johnson's Court, did the cordage; and her sails were made by Richard Boardman; Charles Harrat (there were two, father and son, both riggers) did the rigging. She sailed, under the command of Captain Daniel Marcy, for Boston to take on cargo for New Orleans. On June 26, 1855, the Peter Marcy did the unusual for big vessels built in Portsmouth — she returned here, bringing a cargo of salt — forerunner of Granite State Minerals, Inc. — to Frederick W. Rogers who had a grocery and wood business at 48 Hanover Street. The salt came from St. Ubes. When she came in from Calcutta in November 1856, the Peter Marcy had a seaman named John Frank in irons, charged with assaulting the mate, Bernard Thompson, with a knife. Frank had been held that way for 31 days and was turned over to the U. S. marshal on arrival in port.

[33]. A local syndicate had the Governor Langdon built. Members included Horton D. Walker, George W. Pendexter, John Knowlton, Thomas D. Bailey, Jonathan Barker, Samuel Adams, John Harratt, Nathaniel K. Walker, Frederick Fernald, William Pettigrew and Captain Thomas Weeks, her commander. H. D. Walker was a merchant and a mayor of the city; Pendexter, joiner; Knowlton, blacksmith; Bailey, a merchant; Barker (Jonathan) and Adams (Samuel) were in the lumber business as partners; Harratt was a grocer; and N. K. Walker had a hat store. Governor Langdon's launch was on August 15, 1854. Mrs. Elwyn of Philadelphia, only daughter of the late Governor John Langdon, presented the ship with a set of colors, and on September 18, the owners staged a party on board that shook the temperance people in attendance — wine was served "in the presence of ladies"! A letter was written to the editor of The Rockingham Messenger protesting the fact. Governor Langdon had one more adventure before leaving Portsmouth forever. One of the crew, having had an advance on his pay, decided to jump ship; he was seized and returned on board. When the ship was in the river, he got the idea his life was in danger and jumped overboard, picked up by a boat, he was put back in the ship. Governor Langdon went her way to ply the Atlantic run between southern ports and England.

[34]. Venice was a small ship built in 1841 by George Raynes for Edward F. Sise, Mark W. Peirce, John D. Simes, Jacob W.

Thompson and had James S. Salter for master in 1850. She made one run from New York to Liverpool that went unbeaten for years. But her life was primarily that of the toiling packet ship, back and forth across the Atlantic. With the gold rush, she, too, went on the West Coast run and in 1853 she took 10 men off a Spanish bark who had just been rescued from their floundering ship. She dropped them in Valparaiso, sailed again, and then spent 30 days trying to get around the Horn.

On another passage Venice, from India brought a Malay into New York who was tending an elephant. When he went ashore, the poor, bewildered fellow was arrested for indecent exposure because of his native costume.

[35]. Daniel Marcy served a term in Congress, 1863-65, and it was for his family that Marcy Street was named, finally including the notorious Water Street stretch between State Street and Liberty Bridge. Before and after his service in Congress, he was in the State Senate. Marcy was born in Portsmouth, November 7, 1809, but his family moved to Eliot while he was quite young. At 14, he did what so many Piscataqua youths did, he went to sea, an occupation he followed for 30 years.

Captain Marcy probably took more new ships, Clippers and work-horse freighters, out of Portsmouth than any other skipper. His first command was the brig Comet, owned by Judah Touro of New Orleans, a man with whom Marcy, his brother Peter, and R. D. Shepherd of Wiscasset, Maine, were closely associated for many years. So much so, that Daniel Marcy named one of his sons Judah Touro Marcy. In 1857, he gave up active sea life and went into ship construction, partnered with William Pettigrew, and their speciality was vessels for the syndicate named above.

Marcy was a Democrat of the old school, and he was a delegate to the famous Charleston convention that saw the way to political genocide. Although a Democrat, his service in the U. S. House came in the trying Civil War years. His bid for the governorship met rejection in 1876, but the esteem of his fellow citizens in Portsmouth must have offered some compensation. They made him an alderman in 1855-56; the New Hampshire National Bank honored him with its presidency; Portsmouth Savings made him a trustee; other such roles included Cottage Hospital, Chase Home and St. John's Church.

Twice married, his second wife, Katherine Tredick, was the mother of a Portsmouth mayor, George D. Marcy. Perhaps a little indication of the esteem in which Marcy was held can be found in the "Quiet Zone" that prevailed around his Pleasant Street home during his final illness. Not well in his last years, Marcy fell on October 10, and his condition worsened steadily. Even children walked by the house with muted voices, and heavy deposits of sawdust stilled the clatter of the wagon wheels in the street until he died on November 3, 1893.

[36]. John H. Yeaton died February 7, 1888, at 80.

[37]. Gleason and Henderson were Albert and Joseph, respectively. Their shop was at 34 Bow Street and the 1857 Directory described them as carvers. Gleason had disappeared by the time the 1860 Directory came out.

[38]. William Jones & Son consisted of William P. Jones and Albert L. Jones. Their offices were at 17 Market Square, and they were truly merchants, not shopkeepers. William P. entered business with his father, William Jones in 1832. The firm had a volume of nearly $300,000 on a site where George B. French's, now George H. Kimball's store is. Albert L., a brother to William P., came into the business of William H. Mendum. When William P. Jones died, July 2, 1872, newspaper gossip estimated his fortune as being between $400,000 and $800,000, quite respectable even in the time of the Nixon dollar.

Possibly a testimonial to Jones' good relations with the public, and/or those of lesser fortune was the experience of Andrew J. Penhallow who worked for him as an accountant in 1835, moved on to keep books for Hale (Samuel) & Rollins (William), then to the Portsmouth & Concord Railroad, but was welcomed back by Jones in 1855.

[39]. Daniel Moulton was a carpenter, living at 60 Islington Street.

[40]. William L. Dwight was a shipmaster living on Pleasant Street. A lineal descendant of an early New England family, Dwight was the son of Dr. Jacob Dwight who came here in 1799, and married the daughter of Colonel Thomas Thompson. Thompson, himself, was a native of England. He became grand master of the New Hampshire Masonic Lodge and laid the cornerstone for St. John's Church in 1806. One of his major building feats, as practical constructor, was the Piscataqua Bridge, a project in which he was agent for the stockholders. Thompson's grandson, William L. Dwight, went to sea at the age of 17, rose to captain in 1833, quitting the sea 19 years later. He married the daughter, Adeline, of another sea-going man, Captain William Rice. Their daughter, Susan Thompson Dwight, married a Captain Arthur Yates, USN.

[41]. This was probably Jacob Wendell, living in the Wendell House at 41 Pleasant. Later street numbering gave the house the No. 32 that can be seen, although 222 is the modern number.

[42]. A couple of items on Star of Hope tell a little more about Portsmouth shipbuilding in the 1850s. At first, Star of Hope was known as the St. Paul, then she was sold to C. H. Coffin of Newburyport and underwent a name change. From an advertisement in The Morning Chronicle we learn: "It gives me much pleasure to certify that Mr. A. K. P. Deering (Albion K. P. of 12 Gates Street and his rigging gang have performed the run from Portsmouth with me in the ship Star of Hope and I am happy to say that they, one and all, have performed their duty to my entire satisfaction...." This was signed by Abraham Somerby, skipper of Star of Hope, and the name would indicate that he, too, was of Newburyport. Once she reached New York, Star of Hope was chartered by the federal government to freight supplies out to the Pacific squadron, sailing for San Francisco on January 6, 1856. On her passage, in the spring and summer of 1856, Star of Hope caught fire on April 14. A news account says that "every effort was made to extinguish the fire without effect, the hatches were caulked down, and in 14 days she arrived at Montevideo. At the date of the letter, on taking off the hatches, great heat but no fire was discovered, and the vessel would be discharging to ascertain damage". She finally arrived at San Francisco on December 7. "Greyhounds" says she was abandoned at sea, June 13, 1861.

[43]. The Portsmouth Navy Yard's floating drydock was one of the great local engineering achievements of the century. For years it had been known that the Portsmouth Navy Yard needed a facility for complete overhaul of vessels. The Navy finally bought, for this Yard, the concept of a "floating or balance" dock. This device was 350 feet long, 105 feet wide, with walls 38 feet high. The technicalities of this contrivance were intricate, but involved the construction of a granite receiving basin, into which could be moved the floating dry dock, which, in turn, would receive the vessel to be repaired. Hydraulic engines were used to haul vessels out of the dock and onto the marine railway.

Once out of the water, the vessel could be followed by another. The timbered dock, the basic unit in docking, was done at Pierce Island and took most of a summer with more than a hundred carpenters employed. The Bureau of Ships tried out the new dock by putting the old warship Franklin in it. Franklin was rated at 2,257 tons, and getting it through the dock and up on the railway was considered a satisfactory test and was acceptable to the Navy. Total cost of the floating dry dock is hard to figure, but $765,202, though 1858, is probably reasonable. Although it demanded constant repair and upkeep the old dock stayed on active duty until the stone dock was installed. In June 1907, having been towed from Portsmouth, the old dock was burned at Revere Beach. In her "tour of duty" the dock probably serviced vessels on more than 200 different occasions.

[44]. Was this the Richard Walden who was mixed up in the Civil War riot? This Walden was a calker, living at 59 Water Street.

[45]. Swasey and Rowell were, respectively, Benjamin B. and Samuel, with a shop at 18 Penhallow Street.

[46]. Franklin House had Willis Barnabee as proprietor and was at 41 and 43 Congress Street. Barnabee, early in life, was the driver of the U. S. Mail Coach between Portsmouth and Boston, in the employ of the Eastern Stage Company. By 1840, he had become proprietor of the Franklin House, itself the focal point for many stage lines. Some of the drivers who came and went from Barnabee's establishment in 1840 were Oren Jackson, Gideon Walker, John Mendum and Aaron Conant. Sherburne Somerby and Charles Hoyt had a different run to Boston. There was also the mail stage, leaving at noon with Robert Annabel, Samuel Robinson and Elijah B. Young holding the reins on alternate days. It cost three dollars to get to Boston, whether you went directly by coach, or took the Haverhill route, changing to the "cars" at that point.

Besides all the runs south, there were stages inland and to Portland, most of them originating at Barnabee's, whose busy life came to an end on January 16, 1862, at the age of 73. Barnabee's son, Henry Clay Barnabee, born November 14, 1833, went on the theater stage, sometimes playing Portsmouth. One of these appearances was in the Music Hall in September 1903, when he played the role of sheriff of Nottingham in the light opera "Robin Hood". The man was then 70 but a news account said, "Mr. Barnabee...again demonstrated beyond question that he is one of the greatest comedians who ever tred the boards....Nothing quite like it has been seen in this city since Mr. Barnabee last appeared here....The Barnabee of today is better than the Barnabee of 10 years ago". The Herald has to be forgiven if it was extravagant in its praise, after all, the publisher also had an interest in Music Hall.

Shortly, however, after Barnabee's death, December 16, 1917, Dr. Edward B. Goodall, a local dentist, recalled Barnabee's early years, saying, "in about the year 1865, I should say, I commenced a series of concerts to be given every Fall under the auspices and cooperation of the Portsmouth Philharmonic Society, which was organized and established by Warren H. Day, organist, pianist and director; Dr. Goodall, assistant director and capitalist, and Frank Miller, editor of The Chronicle, looking after the advertising and the booming: "The first cantata was called "The Haymakers" and we made a big hit. I hired Henry Clay Barnabee two nights and paid him $50, $25 each night. That was really his first engagement for concert work here in his home town". Goodall also recalled that one of the highlights of the "Portsmouth Season", a century or so ago, included, "The Cantata of Esther" with Emma Jones Sinclair, Frank Jones' adopted daughter, singing the title role. In two nights that show at the Music Hall netted $1,200.

[47]. Once piled up on the rock and sinking as she did within three hours, it would be expected that would be the last that would ever be heard of Noonday, but such is not the case. In 1934, divers found what remained of Noonday on the rocks of the Farallone Islands, one of which is known today as Noonday Rock. One item they salvaged was the ship's bell, with "Noonday" engraved on it. Officers and men, according to the Morning Chronicle shipping note, escaped with their lives and personal baggage. Noonday crashed on the rock in broad daylight, under full sail — the rock was not on the charts — when she was 129 days out of Boston. Her freight, a total loss, was valued at $450,000. Noonday cost $72,000 after being completely fitted out. She made four complete circuits of the globe. Her first passage to California earned $18,000; she went on to Calcutta, where her captain, W. B. Gerry of Marblehead, died, and was paid $29,816 for freight from there, returning to the U. S. by the way of Liverpool. It took Noonday 14 months to make her first tour around the world. Much of the information about Noonday was given The Herald by Mrs. C. Waldo Pickett, then of 94 Pleasant Street, whose husband was a great-grandson of William Pettigrew, one of the builders. The papers are safely, but remotely deposited, in the Peabody Museum.

[48]. Columbus, built in 1847, was the first to top 1,300 tons. She was owned by D. C. and A. C. Kingsland of New York and went into the Atlantic trade. She was lost on the Irish coast in January 1852, with 12 of the passengers and crew being drowned. Captain Robert McCerran was master, and he may have been the same man who later had trouble in the Chincha Islands with the Peruvian government, that being in October 1853.

[49]. Danube was another of the many vessels built here which plied the oceans in search of a livelihood. She was owned

locally: Edward F. Sise, Joshua W. Peirce, John Chase and John D. Simes. Chase was listed as master. On June 1, 1860, she had the same owners, plus J. P. Lyman as master. The Rockingham Messenger described her launch, on August 31, 1848: "A beautiful new ship of 800 tons, from the yard of Fernald and Pettigrew....is generally acknowledged to have been the most pleasing exhibition of the kind presented this season. She threw spray in gallant style as she went down to her natural element for the first time, and, as her anchor checked her progress, she sat the water like a swan". Chase had previously commanded Athens, a Raynes-built ship (1839) of about 600 tons. Athens was locally owned, by many of the men listed above, and Charles H. Chase was the master in 1850. In 1856, the Morning Chronicle said Danube was a locally owned vessel engaged in the East Indian service. In 1851, she made a 16-day run from Harve to New York. Passengers brought by her from Lisbon in June 1857, included Joseph S. Simes and William S. Chase of Portsmouth.

[50]. Empire State was built for the Kingsland interests in New York for service in the Empire line. Her captain was Joseph G. Russell who had commanded Empire, a ship built by Raynes and Fernald in 1844, probably when Fernald was learning his craft as a shipbuilder. In October 1847, Empire, carrying soldiers for Vera Cruz, Mexico, was wrecked at Abaco. All hands saved except the helmsman. On board were Companies L and M, 1st Artillery, and L and M, 3rd Artillery, all under Captain Van Ness of the 1st.

[51]. Western World distinguished herself by going aground on Squam Beach, on October 12, 1853. She was a 1,354-ton packet, owned by the Kingslands of New York, The Chronicle reported on October 25, "The ship Western World, Captain (John G.) Moses, from Liverpool, went ashore on Friday night at Squam inlet. Her passengers, 600 in number, were all landed safely, the ship making no water and will probably be got off". A few days later the news was more grim, "On the 23rd, 4 p.m., the tide ebbed and flowed in the ship, and all her cargo was wet. It consists of 200 tons of dry goods; 400 tons of iron; 800 sacks of salt; 150 crates. She was much hogged, and it was feared that the steam pumps would not be able to free her. The steam tug Archilles, which returned to New York on Monday morning, reported that the ship had bilged, and had 10 feet of water in her hold. She has, ever since built, been run successfully between Liverpool and New York. How the accident happened we are at present unable to say, but probably the entire matter will be laid before the public in a few days. The vessel lies six miles north of where the Cornelius Grinnel was cast on shore. The

moon shone with great brilliancy and the wind, which was blowing from the southeast, was a fair one for vessels going into the port where the Western World was bound". Later it was reported that Western World was broken amidships, and, finally, that she had gone to pieces in the south-southeast blow of November 13. Some iron in the bottom was saved. The vessel was valued at $80,000, and insured for $70,000; the cargo, $180,000, almost all insured.

This item about Western World came from the pages of The Journal and concerns her launch:

"The above noble ship was launched from the yard of Messers. Fernald and Pettigrew in Portsmouth Harbor on Tuesday last, the 27th (November, 1849) a few minutes before 9 o'clock. She is owned by Messers. D. and A. Kingsland and Company of New York, and is intended for the Empire Line of New York and Liverpool packets and is to be commanded by Captain Charles Cheever, late of the ship Severn. She is 195 feet in length over all, 40 foot beam, 31 feet deep, has three regular decks and is 1,903 tons, carpenter's measurement, or 1,400 tons, custom house measurement. She is the largest merchant ship ever built on the river, being some 10 feet longer than the Empire State launched by the same builders in March last".

Probably no modern writer will ever come up with a really definitive explanation of the way ship tonnages were computed. As seen above, by one measurement, Western World would seem to have been a giantress of the river with her 1,903 tons, yet a few months later, local observers were saying that Sea Serpent, 1,402, was the biggest launched in the first half of the 19th Century. Which do you take for Western World? Custom House measurement of 1,400, or carpenter's measurement of 1,903? Each can be justified, and probably right, if each vessel was measured the same way, but they weren't.

[52]. Dashing Wave had a lot of adventures before she became a barge 50 or so years ago. On February 8, 1868, she struck on Barnegat Shoals; came off a few days later and sank in five fathoms of water. Later that year she was raised and sold for $6,150. "Greyhounds" records that so well did her builders "do their work that with the exception of the old Syren, she appears to have been the last of the Clippers in active service. It was stated that in 1920, while operating as a barge on the Pacific Coast, her hull was examined and found to be in sound condition, after nearly 70 years afloat". She was lost that year, but her career makes it obvious there was no "built-in obsolescense", as there is in our modern products.

[53]. William Badger first came to notice as a master craftsman at the Navy Yard when the Secretary of the Navy wrote that "Mr. William Badger had been mentioned to me as the most experienced and reputable shipbuilder in Portsmouth". On April 28, 1813, the secretary authorized the hiring of William Badger at the princely salary of $1,800 per annum.

[54]. Alabama's exact cost figures also are extant at the Portsmouth Athenaeum, even down to five pounds of mop yarn, costing $3.33. Alabama was not a particularly lucky craft. On the night of November 24, 1847, bound from Liverpool for Boston, she struck on Cohasset Rocks, backed off and sank immediately. Crewmen barely escaped in their skivvies. Christopher S. Toppan of Portsmouth was one of her owners. She was insured, but not her cargo.

[55]. Also among Sabine's passengers on the 1853 passage of Joshua W. Peirce from India was the Reverend J. Dulles, Mrs. Dulles, and three children. It's hard not to wonder if this family was connected to the J. Foster Dulles of the Eisenhower Administration. Her original captain, Henry Libbey, later transferred to the ship Orion. His wife died in Chelsea on November 26, 1855, at the age of 30, from tuberculosis; he had lost a child on October 3. That same Fall, Sabine was in dry dock at Fort Hill, Boston, and the shipkeeper, Ammi L. Knowlton of Portsmouth, was injured in a fall from her mainmast. Knowlton was taken to Massachusetts General Hospital, and later reports disclosed that he had fallen through the mast hole, and not from the mast. He returned to his home in Portsmouth, 3 Atkinson Street, to recuperate.

[56]. Granite State was in no hurry to begin her career. Her launch was delayed by a snowstorm on December 7, 1853, and she did not go down the ways until 6 a.m. the next day, with workmen burning fires all night to keep the grease on the stocks soft enough to let her slide. Captain Samuel Billings of Portsmouth was her first commander, and she was owned by Horton D. Walker, John N. Tarlton, William Simes, John T. French, Samuel Adams, G. W. Pendexter and Solomon Clark of Portsmouth. Granite State was launched fully rigged. Billings took her to sea, headed for Mobile, shortly after the New Year. She ran back and forth without incident until September 1855, when The Chronicle reported that Edward McNulty, a seaman on the Granite State went before W. H. Y. Hackett, the U. S. Commissioner, and swore to the complaint against Captain Billings and the second mate, William Valentine, for assult and a severe beating. The testimony showed that at sea, on August

27, Valentine "cruelly beat and abused" McNulty who was disabled by an injury to his hand. McNulty had refused to go aloft at night as ordered. The seaman ran to the captain for relief, but was given no redress. The commissioner freed the captain on the grounds that he was not fully aware of the extent of McNulty's injury. The mate was held in $200 bail for U. S. Court on October 2, and four witnesses were bound over in $50 bail each. J. Warren Towle of Portsmouth appeared in this case for McNulty and Albert R. Hatch and Samuel Storer for the defendants. The "bucko" mates of romantic tales did indeed exist, and it's also interesting to note that the item indicates that Granite State was in Portsmouth Harbor at the time of the hearing. Certainly the presence of W. H. Y. Hackett, Hatch and Storer must mean this. Granite State came home from Calcutta in October 1856, with John H. Sheafe as a passenger. Two years later she was lost at sea.

[57]. The second New Hampshire, built for James N. Tarlton, William Simes and others, was sold at Liverpool in 1857 for 6,000 pounds.

18

The Returns of the Sons

[1]. These emplacements were intended to house two different gun batteries, their fire control rooms and magazines. The more southerly of the installations, part of the defense-in-depth concept, was for a pair of six-inch guns, on barbette mounts. The biggest of the man-made hills is at the north end of the Odiorne's Point area, and was built for two, 16-inch, all electrically controlled rifles. The construction went on through the years of World War II, past the time when it was obvious to all that the weapons would have no function, until 1944 when the gun barrels — battleship type — arrived and were mounted. Sometime in that year, long after the bulk of the 22nd Coast Artillery troops had been shipped out, a detail from C. Battery of the 22nd Coast Artillery, fired three , settling shots from each gun. Two or three years after the war, the guns were cut up for scrap. The Parks Division of the Department of Resources and Economic Development is still making plans for the use of Fort Dearborn area, which it was given by the Federal government.

By June of 1972 these were far enough advanced to have the department seek a new name for the area, and it was decided to christen it "Odiorne's Park" in honor of the first family to really settle in the vicinity.

However, before the bunker gun installations were constructed, again defense-in-depth for Portsmouth Harbor, a battery of four 155mm rifles was located at the southern end. They were

French weapons, unchanged from World I except to be reshod with hard-rubber tires. The circular revetments built by Battery F of the 22nd Coast Artillery, under the command of Captain John J. Guy, are still visible (1972 photos) from the air.

[2]. Benjamin P. Shillaber was born in Portsmouth, July 12, 1814, went through local schools, worked on the old Boston Post, writing under the name of "Mrs. Partington", dying in Chelsea, Massachusetts, March 25, 1890.

[3]. The Reverend Charles W. Burroughs succeeded the Reverend Joseph Willard as pastor of what is now St. John's Church. Willard gave up his pastorate on March 20, 1806, but Burroughs did not appear here until 1809, and then it was as a reader. In the Fall of that year, he accepted an invitation to come as pastor. On December 10 he became a deacon, and, on May 20, 1812, he joined the priesthood, and the next day became rector, a tenure that lasted until 1857. He died March 8, 1868. Dr. Burroughs did much historical research here, and, with luck, some day his notes and papers may become available. Frequently he was a speaker at formal occasions, such as the opening of the Town Farm in 1834.

[4]. It was easy for Dr. Burroughs to recognize this philosophy, but it was a fact that for years was an anathema to the Puritan divines who tried to cope with a pragmatic people whose major concern was the next meal and not the next life. "They Came to Fish...." was the essence of their thinking.

[5]. In his "Indian Wars" Hubbard mentions that the fort, or house, was run down and that was in the 1680s. Much of what might have been of value to historians and archeologists was probably destroyed when workmen for the Town of Rye started a borrow pit on the site. Charles S. Gurney, compiler of the highly useful Portsmouth Historic and Picturesque, spoke of a personal visit to the area before his book came out in 1902. He told of watching vestiges of the ancient settlement being destroyed without being able to stop the vandalism. About this time, the coast road also was being pushed through, which put added pressure on the pit, an ugly scar still easily seen from the highway. However, across the way, Ralph L. Brown, who owns the property on which the ancient cemetery is located, is keeping these landmarks in excellent order. Poison ivy has been tamed, and foot paths lead to the sites.

[6]. Citizens named to work with the various committees organized by the City Council were Ichabod Goodwin, Christopher S. Toppan, William P. Jones, Jonathan M. Tredick, Henry F. Wendell, Albert R. Hatch, George N. Carlton, Samuel R.

Cleaves, Richard Jenness, William H. Sise, George L. Treadwell, Samuel Storer, John Buzzell and William P. Walker. (Wendell was an auctioneer, deputy sheriff and commission merchant; Carlton, a stove dealer; Cleaves, a soap and candle maker; Sise worked for E. F. Sise in the glass and crockery business; Treadwell, hardware; Buzzell, shoe store; Walker, a tailor.)

[7]. The Reverend Thomas Starr King was best known for his publications on the White Mountains. He was born in New York, December 17, 1824, and died at San Francisco, March 4, 1863. The Rambler refers to a boyhood incident locally in which King was involved, and a sketch in connection with his life indicates he was at one time the pupil of the Reverend Hosea Ballou, once pastor of the Universalist Church. His father, Thomas King, also served in the Portsmouth pulpit, coming here about 1827.

[8]. Charles Levi Woodbury was born here May 22, 1829, and, after graduating from Georgetown University, was a member of the Massachusetts bar and U. S. Attorney for Massachusetts by appointment of President Buchanan. He died July 1, 1898.

[9]. James T. Fields was the editor of Atlantic and a close friend of Charles Dickens. Born December 31, 1816, at 12 Gates Street, he died in Boston, April 24, 1881. Two lines of his we can use today:

"How sweet and gracious, even in common speech,
Is that fine sense which we call courtesy"!

[10]. Read the familiar Portsmouth family names on that Lowell committee: Hiram Dennett, Alfred Gilman, W. G. Wise, M. G. Howe, J. P. Walker, J. G. Peabody, Horatio Fogg, Joseph Raynes, R. N. Tullock, B. T. Hardy, L. R. Streeter, Leonard Huntress, J. L. Huntress, Samuel Kinsman, Joseph H. Towne, Thomas Ordway, J. A. Knowles and Charles H. Dennett.

[11]. Just to name a few: On Islington Street — Rufus K. Oxford, Hosea Crane, F. S. Jarvis, William Plaisted, Andrew H. Jones, Thomas Martin, Ichabod Goodwin, Mrs. Sarah A. Halliburton, Captain Lewis Barnes, Charles W. Brewster, James M. Carr, Ira Haselton, John Knowlton, Joseph M. Edmonds, Mrs. W. A. Thompson; Congress — William R. Preston; Daniel – Colonel John N. Sherburne, Abraham A. Staples; Deer — Peter Jenness, Mrs. Ellen Pray; Vaughan — Robert Gray; Pleasant — John K. Pickering, Jacob Wendell, Abraham Wendell, Ichabod Rollins; Water — Mrs. Rebecca Shaw; State — Samuel G. Folsom, J. Wesley Moses, Mrs. Ellen Hurd, Frederick Dodge, Mrs. Samuel Peirce, James F. Shores, Jr., Samuel

R. Cleaves, Colonel Samuel Gookin, Mrs. William Weeks; Court — George Melcher, Frederick W. Fernald, E. F. Sise; Dennett — Solomon Seymour.

[12]. Five years later, The Rambler had a letter from Moses who told a little of life in Portsmouth as a boy during the Revolution. He signed the letter "From a Portsmouth boy in his 93rd year".

[13]. At Gettysburg fell Henry L. Richards who was serving with the 2nd U. S. Sharpshooters. Richards and Dr. Robert O. Treadwell planted the elms that so long graced Richards Avenue, and are nearly gone in our time. That was in 1861. Like many other Portsmouth streets, Richards Avenue has borne other names — among them Cow Lane, Joshua Street and Auburn Street. It was named for Richards after his death.

[14]. Portsmouth 350, Inc., was organized in the Fall of 1971. On the afternoon and evening of November 10, more than a thousand Portsmouth and area people flocked to the Rockingham Hotel to sign the incorporation papers, paying one dollar each for the privilege. Three sets of papers were prepared, one for the Secretary of State, one for City Hall and the third for the Public Library. At the time of incorporation, the officers and directors were: Alice K. Sullivan, chairman; Charles L. Kaufmann, vice chairman; Catherine Jarvis, secretary, Edward C. Jackson, treasurer; Wyman P. Boynton, Kenneth A. Weiss and Raymond A. Brighton, directors; plus the executive secretary of the Chamber of Commerce, ex officio, presently James Hinchey; the president of the Chamber of Commerce, ex officio; and the Mayor of Portsmouth, ex officio. Mrs. Arthur F. Brady is representing her husband on the board. Formal celebration of the anniversary is planned for the week of August 11-19, 1973. The public relations agency of George W. Salzer had been retained by the committee to handle administrative details.

[15]. Frank W. Miller, besides being the guiding light that led to the establishment of Portsmouth's first daily paper, The Morning Chronicle, was also the developer of the Miller Avenue area. He began to open up this section of the city by buying two large lots on Lincoln Hill (the rise in ground in the vicinity of South and Union Streets) in April 1865.

Writing about Frank Miller in 1903, his boyhood friend, Lewis W. Brewster, said, "I knew Frank well, for we were brought up together. His father, Tobias Ham Miller, was of the firm of Miller and (Charles W.) Brewster, that assumed publication of The Portsmouth Journal when it was relinquished by Harrison Gray and E. L. Childs in 1825, and the Miller and Brewster boys naturally assimilated. We two sat together in the old brick Cabot Street School under the teaching of Miss Louisa Blaisdell of blessed memory though she was a terror when misbehavior or idleness came in contact with her awful authority". Brewster goes on to sketch the activities of Frank Miller, and from his pen emerges the picture of a vigorous, imaginative newspaperman who had a flair for making a dollar, not only from his paper but from outside operations as well. Brewster says, "Now Frank was full of business, with a light purse. How he managed to keep a horse (and we had many good rides with the old Doctor) was a little beyond our reckoning — just as his later enterprise of seizing a large slice of southwestern Portsmouth was a wonder to his friends.... He was always sanguine and venturesome and generally found means to accomplish his most fanciful schemes. Frank had in Concord, New Hampshire, a brother, Thomas W., who was one of the best type compositors and whose habits and disposition had enabled him to lay by a goodly portion of his not inconsiderable earnings".

That was Millers's start; his father, the Reverend Tobias H. Miller, helped out, and Samuel Gray was a partner. Eventually Frank Miller became sole owner. Later he sold to one of his contributors, George W. Marston, who was joined by Washington Freeman in publishing the paper. They were alone in the daily field until 1868 when Joshua L. Foster, "the acute and mordacious editor" of The States and the Union, started The Portsmouth Times as an afternoon Democratic daily. The two were sharp rivals and newspapers exchanged political insults with great zest. An incident relating to Frank Jones illustrates the point. For no apparent reason at all, one day in the 1870s the Republican-oriented Chronicle published a complete chronology of the life of Frank Jones, dressing it in the most flowery language possible. Why would it do a thing like that for a Democrat? Foster's needle-pointed pen, in The Portsmouth Times, later tells us that a horsewhipping had been in store for the editor of The Chronicle unless he made amends for some previous caustic remarks about the brewery king.

About a month after Brewster's anecdote appeared, a one-time printer wrote from the West Coast to tell of working in the offices of the New Hampshire Gazette when Gideon Rundlett was the editor (1850-53), Charles E. Blake, foreman; Frank Miller, journeyman; and Nathaniel Gunnison, journeyman; E. N. Fuller took Rundlett's post as editor. The Gazette office, 21 Daniel Street, was headquarters for the Pierce campaign in 1852, with Colonel John H. Jackson as a leading light. Frank Miller's home was later the residence of E. Curtis

Matthew's father and came, later still, into the ownership of Albert Hislop, mayor of Portsmouth in 1919-1920. Perhaps Miller's most permanent memorial are the trees in Langdon Park, off Junkins Avenue. More than 600 were given to the park after it was opened May 25, 1876, and Miller supervised their planting.

Miller was elected to the mayoralty in 1874 by a margin never before achieved, and was legislated out of office when the Democrats won control of both legislative bodies and had the governorship. It was, and no other word describes it, outright thievery. What they did was to file a bill calling for an amendment to the City Charter which would create seven wards, appoint Democratic registrars of voters, and require an immediate election of municipal officials. The bill was jammed through, and Mayor Miller was allowed to fill the mayoralty for only six months before being succeeded by Moses H. Goodrich.

Naturally the Republicans, as soon as they were back in the saddle, did away with the Democratic gerrymander by amending the City Charter for four wards, setting Ward 1 and 2 back much as they were before the gerrymander, creating a "Creek Ward" (Democratic), and keeping "Old Sebastapol" as Ward 4. Again in 1895, the Republicans struck, this time setting up five wards (much as they were until Ward 6 was created in 1959). The fifth ward came out of "Old Sebastapol" in the large part.

But to get back to Miller, he had left The Chronicle when he bought what was called "Packer's Pasture" — about 30 acres and started selling off house lots. Then, his time on the County Commission run out, and retiring from politics, he established and edited the newspaper Portsmouth Weekly, a work he was doing when he died in 1880.

[16]. As the name implies, the area is where the hay market, with scales, was set up in 1755.

[17]. In 1873, no unsightly cobweb of wires festooned the city streets, strung from pole to pole. It was six years later, May 9, 1879, that Wilbur I. Trafton, a jeweler at 57 Congress Street, set up the first telephone. And the charter of the Portsmouth Gas Company was amended to permit providing electric lighting in August of 1887. What the people of 100 years ago would make out of the forest of TV antennas on the roofs of the city is hard to guess, and it would amaze them as much to learn of cable TV, pictures piped in by wire from a remote point.

[18]. The tent at Wibird Hill was probably in the area nestling under the gentle slope that rises toward South Street on Wibird.

[19]. William H. Sise served four consecutive terms as mayor, 1878-1881, the only man ever to do so. Horton D. Walker went three straight, but his fourth term came 17 years later. Sise, a member of St. John's Lodge, was born August 5, 1827. dying August 5, 1896. The Chronicle described Sise as a "veritable compendium of local history and every inhabitant who had lived here long enough to become a part of our permanent population". The second son of Edward F. Sise, he loved the sea, and, like many another Portsmouth boy, shipped aboard a Portsmouth vessel, making several voyages and rising to the rank of mate when a very young man. Once he had his fill of the sea, Sise returned and joined his father in E. F. Sise & Company, taking over in 1868, when the father died, as senior partner to his brother Joseph.

During his service as mayor, Sise is credited with instituting many reforms, not the least of which is the present system of trash collection by the city, a service still enjoyed by the taxpayers, and certainly a welcome relief for householders who, a century ago, were almost buried under the ashes from their furnaces or fireplaces. President of the Board of Trade, Sise also had a hand in getting harbor improvements, the principal ones being the removal of Gangway and Pier rocks. An original member of the Portsmouth Police Commission, and its first chairman, Sise was also a trustee of the Public Library. In the Civil War years, Sise was commissary general, and also in charge of the state arsenal here, a job he held until 1895.

[20]. There will be further discussion of Thomas Entwistle, particularly his time as city marshal, in other parts of this work. Entwistle was born in Cheshire, England, January 12, 1840, and came to this country at an early age. Enlisting in the 3rd NHVR, June 21, 1861, Entwistle was twice wounded, taken prisoner and confined in the infamous Libbey and Andersonville Prison before escaping and making his way back to the Union lines. During his political and police career, he served as an alderman and councilman; succeeded Calvin Page in the State Senate, from 1905, with John Pender taking his place. In 1911-13, he had a seat on the Governor's Council.

[21].]. J. Horace Kent was born October 10, 1828, dying March 4, 1888, at Concord where he was warden of the State Prison. Kent came from Barnstead, went to school in Pittsfield and graduated from Portsmouth High, then taught by John P. Tasker. In 1845, he went to New York, yielding in 1849 to the excitement of the Gold Rush, arriving in San Francisco in October of that year. His

first vote was cast in California for the Consitution prohibiting slavery.

A little indication of the career he would later follow is to be had in his service on the first "Vigilance Committee" in San Francisco, an organization that brought law and order, of a kind, to the wild-living community. While on a trip East in 1852, he married Adeline Penniman, who went back to California with him. She, with their one son, Horace Penniman Kent, survived him. J. Horace Kent left California for good in 1860, returning East and enlisting in 1862 in a Massachusetts unit for service in the South. In 1863, he was discharged to take an appointment as a special agent for the provost marshal in New Hampshire. He became Portsmouth's city marshal in 1867, then went with the Secret Service until returning to Portsmouth as city marshal in 1871; then bouncing back to the Secret Service as New England chief until 1874. He became sheriff of Rockingham County in 1876. This job he held until 1886, when he was beaten, but then getting the wardenship at the State Prison, a job he held until he died.

19

The Civil War

[1]. On March 21, 1861, and Sumter's cannonade was less than a month away, a masquerade ball was staged in Union Hall, Market Street, and the committee lists many of the well known local names: Joshua E. Eldredge, J. Woodman Moses, George B. French, P. H. W. Fontani, William W. Cotton, J. H. Moses, Thomas H. Rider, Benjamin F. Chandler (USN), Charles L. Tidd, James F. Hartshorn, C. C. Coburn, S. P. Walker, Nathan P. Thatcher, Charles W. Marden, R. F. E. Dow, J. H. Jenness, J. Augustine Haseltine, Samuel G. Hooper, James A. Blaisdell, A. W. Fernald, C. C. Melcher, George T. Vaughan, Albert F. Merrill, James W. Bowles, John W. Stavers, William O. Sides, E. A. Tilton, A. P. Stevens, Benjamin B. Swasey, Lafayette V. Newell, G. C. Boardman, J. Albert Walker, John E. Rider, Edwin N. Mathes, James M. Carr, J. B. Adams, C. E. Rand, Charles C. Akerman, Levi Moulton, Marcellus Eldredge, D. Webster Barnabee, J. L. Lord, James H. Head, S. F. Lothrop, Frank Fuller, James W. Lord.

The ball was a "grand affair" and close scrutiny of the names on the committee lead quickly to the conclusion that these were the younger men in the Portsmouth social swim. For example, Marcellus Eldredge would become a leading brewer in less than 30 years and mayor in 1885-86. Music was provided by the Portsmouth Cornet Band, an ensemble of 17 pieces, and Turner's Quadrille, six pieces. There were 20 numbers on the program with the evening's pleasure "inaugurated by an introductory grand march and Sicilian Circle". It should be mentioned, New England weather being what it is, that while the ball was in progress, "A fierce snowstorm came up and those who remained until the end were unable to get home. Union Hall was directly over Mrs. Wells' (John H.) store (Market Street) and he invited the storm-bound pleasure seekers to partake of his hospitality. The invitation was accepted, and the party remained in the store all night, passing the time with singing and dancing". Wells told the story in 1903, when he was 81 years old.

[2]. Captain Robert Lefavour was long associated with these units. Lefavour's home is today part of the Portsmouth Public Library, connected to the old academy by a reading room built in the mid-1950s. Military units, independent companies, were long a part of Portsmouth. One, in 1840, was the Portsmouth Artillery with Theodore F. Rowe as captain; George W. Marshall (clerk at the Franklin House), Lieutenant; Meshach T. Muchmore (Ship carpenter for George Raynes), second lieutenant; John R. Hill (Ropemaker) standard bearer; William Shapley (Blacksmith at Portsmouth Iron Foundry) Clerk. The company was allowed a complement of 64. Then there was the outfit known as the Rockingham Guards with Phillips Currier (Butcher with a stall in the Brick Market), captain; Edward A. Smith (Painter), lieutenant; John H. Moran (Moulder Portsmouth Iron Foundry), ensign; John W. Moses (Draper and tailor), standard bearer; Henry F. Wendell (Clerk at Abraham Q. Wendell's), clerk. Sixty-four men allowed. Then there were (still 1840) some infantry units: Second Company — Augustus Jenkins (Calker), captain; Henry Whittemore (Mason), lieutenant; Samuel Spinney (Truckman), ensign. Third Company — William G. Nowell (Cabinet furniture in the firm of Jenness (George) & Nowell), captain; Joseph B. Currier (Butcher, stall, Spring Market), lieutenant; Benjamin D. Laighton (Grocer), ensign. Fourth Company — Joseph Marston (Farm, on South Road toward Pound), captain; Benjamin Marden (Barroom, 31 Penhallow), lieutenant; William Moses (Farmer, Rye Road), ensign. Fifth Company — Isaac Dow (Tin worker), captain; Mark Dennett (Farmer, North Road, near Gravelly Ridge School House), lieutenant; Alfred Pendexter (Joiner), ensign.

At the time, New Hampshire had 40 "regiments" of militia, so there were also staff, brigade and regimental officers around. Among them were Joseph Hill (Variety store), commissary general (This office was provided for in the State Constitution until 1950 in a referendum when it was removed at the instigation of the then State Representative Rae S. Laraba of Portsmouth.) Chandler E.

Potter was aide de camp and judge advocate of the 1st Division, 1st Brigade. Josiah G. Hadley (Farmers Hotel — site of old Post Office), lieutenant Colonel of the first regiment; Andrew J. Beck (Carriage maker when he was not city marshal), major; William P. Gookin, quartermaster. The militia in 1840 had a total (paper) strength of 30,232 men and officers. By 1851, as was inevitable, there were changes in the personnel of the companies. George W. Towle (Auctioneer) was in command of the City Greys; John Pepper (Machinist), first lieutenant; Joseph H. Pearson (Carpenter), second lieutenant; John W. Stavers (Dame (George W.) and Stavers, Tailors), third lieutenant; Charles F. Adams (Painter), fourth lieutenant; William W. Black (Mason), clerk. Rockingham Guards — Andrew J. Beck, captain; Alfred J. Hill (Carpenter), first lieutenant; John Dame (Ship smith), second lieutenant; Robert L. Emery (Miller, South Mill), third lieutenant; John E. Bailey (Book-binder), clerk.

In 1821 the first City Directory was published, Portsmouth was the headquarters of the 1st Division with Major-General Timothy Upham (Collector of customs among other things) commanding, and Charles W. Cutter and John N. Sherburne were aides. Edward J. Long commanded the first brigade; John Blunt, aide; Jacob Wendell, brigade quartermaster. Joshua W. Peirce commanded the 1st Regiment; John Goodrich, lieutenant colonel; David C. Foster, major; John K. Pickering, acting Adjutant; Samuel Cushman, paymaster; Rufus Kittredge, surgeon; William Norwood, surgeon's mate. Probably the most colorful military unit ever raised here was the "Governor's Horse Guards". Organized solely for the purpose of escorting Governor Ichabod Goodwin to his inaugural, it was an extravaganza in military splendor of a kind no longer seen. The uniforms for the unit were made by a military tailor in Boston. The men went through hours of drill for that one ceremony. There were 250 of them, and they came from all over the state and eventually all congregated at the Temple to do honor to the new governor. Odes were written by Thomas Bailey Aldrich and Albert Laighton, and then set to music by Carl Meinerth. After the services at the Temple, there was a banquet at City Hall. The shadows of war were gathering even as the Horse Guards honored their governor.

[3]. Business had not been good that spring in Portsmouth; as indicated in the chapter on the Clippers, the demand for West Coast vessels had slacked off, and without shipbuilding Portsmouth had economic problems. Then, too, the inauguration of Abraham Lincoln brought some changes in personnel at the Navy

Yard. The city budget was at the unprecedented total of $54,691, and $8,667 was the burden imposed by county government. April Fool's Day brought with it a New England caprice, a heavy snowstorm. Newspaper comment had been directed at the movement through town of a 6½-ton granite block, 17 feet long. Pulled by six yoke of oxen, it was intended for the Fisher Brewery (Michael Fisher) off Creek Street.

The Chronicle also was concerned with a public problem: "One of the most annoying nuisances to be encountered at this season, is the unrestricted running at large of cows about town. On Friday one of these wandering annoyances visited the premises of a gentleman on Middle Street who has spent much labor and money on a fine front yard". There were reports of drilling by the Goodwin Guards and Company C of the Govenor's Horse Guards. The Chronical commented, "And the opening of Spring will show more military spirit than has been exhibited in Portsmouth for some time". Washington Freeman opened his "spacious and inviting Oyster and Ice Cream Saloons (12 Congress Street). The ladies saloon is a perfect gem of a private parlor, carpeted in rich Brussels, to match in shade the green tints of the hangings there". At the foot of Salter Street, the burst of warm weather, which was drying the muddy streets, allowed the baptism of four converts in the river. But all the while, as Portsmouth tried to go about its regular business, the news from the South continued to be depressing. So much so, that Govenor Goodwin proclaimed April 11 a Fast Day, saying, "Never in our history has there been greater occasion for humility, penitence and prayer; never was our political horizon so darkened by the clouds of discord and rebellion; never were our dearest social and national interests in such imminent peril".

That day the Chronicle said, "If the truth of our dispatches from the South can be depended upon, there is scarcely a hope of averting a bloody struggle at Charlestown". Fast Day in Portsmouth was marked by religious services; baseball players gathered at Pierce Island and the Cricket Club played a match at the Plains. Even as they played, gunners were standing with lighted matches ready for the firing on Fort Sumter. On April 15, the town learned from its newspaper that war had begun. For Portsmouth, a way of life had ended, never to return, although no one then realized it.

[4]. How much rent was paid Jeremiah Johnson for the use of his ropewalk off Johnson's Court is not known. But he had a going business, so it must have been full recompense. Johnson, born in 1799, died in 1864.

[5]. This business of raising troops by the various states was one of President Lincoln's major problems. Too much depended on the governors, who, quite naturally, often favored their political henchmen for command roles. Governor Goodwin put Gilman Marston of Exeter in as colonel of the 2nd NHVR, and so it went. But a sample of the Portsmouth war fervor should be put upon the record. Everyone wanted in on the holy crusade — there's nothing like a little brotherly hate to bring out the worst in people. Josiah G. Hadley headed a veterans company, with Andrew J. Beck as second in command. Then there was an artillery unit with a Dr. Wesselhooft as commanding officer and Frank W. Ham (Probably Francis W. Ham, watchmaker) as second. Then there was a rifle outfit, commanded by James H. Head; E. A. Tilton and Benjamin F. Webster, a carpenter living at 2 Court Street who became one of Portsmouth's great builders in the last half of the 19th Century.

Robert Lefavour organized a unit for those over the age of combat efficiency. Then on May 17, the Chronicle said, "The workmen at our Navy Yard certainly do a large of amount of work in a short time. Either there has not been enough done there of late years for them 'to get the hang of the school-house', or, what is more probable, they make their object to do their duty, and not merely to draw their pay. At any rate, there are no laggards in their number now". The Chronicle went into ecstasies in describing the homeward progress of these workers, and all it makes a modern reader think of is that it's wise not to get in the way today when the Yard comes off shift at 4 p.m.

Through the month of May 1861, men flocked to Portsmouth, some of them from as far away as Peterborough. Before long a thousand of them were here, overtaxing the facilities, so 200 were barracked at Fort Constitution and the remaining 800 in the ropewalk. For their training ground, the troops had the open fields south of the Mill Pond in the area now occupied by Portsmouth Hospital and Langdon Park. Commented The Chronicle: "Portsmouth seems like a camp, with three full companies of Volunteers marching and countermarching in our streets, and the frequent roll of the drum and the whistle of the fife...."

The Goodwin Guards, a 70-man unit commaded by Captain William O. Sides was the center of local attention. Whenever the company had roll call, it must have read like the roster of the Sides family: John S. was first lieutenant; Andrew J. was first orderly sergeant; George E. was third orderly sergeant. Others in the unit were John S. Rand, second lieutenant; John H. Locke, second orderly sergeant; Charles W. Patch, first corporal; Daniel F. Hatch, second corporal; John H. Merrill, third corporal; Oliver F. Maxwell, fourth corporal. Nor should anyone get the impression that all was beer and skittles in the regimental camp. Soldiers are soldiers, no matter what war it is. Unlike our modern troops with their efficient quartermaster system, these poor devils were supplied by whatever politician was lucky enough to buy in the contract of regimental sutler. That lucrative deal fell to a Portsmouth livery stable operator by the name of William S. Hadley. Trouble started with the Abbott Guards, an upstate unit. They took a passionate dislike to the provender being peddled by Hadley. When they could make their feelings known no other way, they threw the "chow" back at the cooks. The Chronicle devoted considerable space to defending Hadley, but any ex-GI will still entertain suspicions that the men were probably right. After all, what would a liveryman know about food supply? The Abbott Guards, however, with utter Army logic, were restricted to Siberia — Fort Constitution — for giving voice to their opinions. Today their congressmen would take care of them.

The editor of The Chronicle himself went on an inspection trip and took a look at the cantonment. His description of the evening meal, a la Hadley, is glowing and does not sound all that bad, but the proof probably would be in the eating. Anyway, for the evening meal, the men were given a slice of "brick loaf", a slice of brown bread, a slice of cold beef, butter, cheese and a can of coffee. The editor thought it good fare, but does not mention "rapping" with the troops about it. But troops did not have rights then, the way they do today.

Another sore point with the men was the lack of clothing; many were still wearing the garments they had come to Portsmouth in, and these were getting a little seedy, to put it politely. Eventually they were issued blue blouses, but when they were ready to leave for the South they were all in grey (That's right!) uniforms. The editor also found 800 men doing various things, and not a single game of chance in sight. The editor was either naive or the "brass" was putting on a show. Soldiers are soldiers, and so it's also difficult to accept that there were no bottles of an alcoholic nature around! It was on May 20, that the men of the 2nd were asked to take discharges, and sign on for three years. Two-thirds of the men, after mulling things over for three days, decided to "re-up" and a "table of organization" for each company was set at a minimum of 83, maximum 101. Portsmouth had reason to be proud of its Goodwin Guards. Out of 70 in the company, 68 re-enlisted and became the nucleus of Company K, 2nd NHVR. To fill the depleted ranks — some 274 men had decided against a three-year bit — troops came in from all over the state. And yet, the reasons as stated are vague as to why a company of young Irishmen, recruited in Portsmouth by "the Reverend Mr. (Patrick) Canovan, the Catholic priest here" was not accepted.

When it became apparent the regiment would soon go South, various commissions were resigned. Thomas P. Pierce, the colonel commanding, stepped out and in his place, Governor Goodwin named a man who turned into a tough citizen-soldier, Gilman Marston. William O. Sides also resigned from Company K. It should not be thought that Portsmouth men were confined only to Company K. Robert C. Sides was with Company I, and became regimental adjutant; Charles H. Streeter was an officer with Company E; James A. Sanborn, Company C; James A. Hutton, Company C; Rufus L. Bean, Company B, later transferring to Company G; Oliver M. Dame, Company A; Charles A. Plaisted, adjutant; Nathaniel M. Ricker, principal musician. Charles N. Patch of Company K was killed at Gettysburg while serving as lieutenant. He left a wife and daughter at the age of 33. Finally on June 20, 1861, the regiment was ready for shipment. Of course, in the last flurry it was discovered there were not enough wagons, but these were made and brought in from Concord (The Deadwood Coach people) inside 10 days. At last the train came and the 2nd NHVR was on its way to the bloody battlefields of the Civil War. That same ropewalk which had housed it, had served that purpose in the War of 1812 when troops congregated here in anticipation of British attack. Before the war ended more than 3,000 names had been entered on the rolls of the 2nd; it had marched more than 6,000 miles; fought in 30 engagements; and lost more than a thousand men due to death, wounds or illness.

[6]. Thomas L. Tullock was secretary of state for three years, 1858-61. He went from that to naval agent at the Portsmouth Navy Yard where his reputation for integrity was unequalled. It was said at the time that Tullock was the only naval agent to come out of the war with an untarnished reputation. He went to Washington as secretary to the Republican congressional committee in Grant's first campaign for the presidency; he reorganized the collection forces in the treasury office and was later collector of internal revenue. Then he became postmaster of Washington. He died in the capital June 20, 1883. His son, Seymour W. Tullock, born in Portsmouth about 1858, became noted in Washington for his efforts to clean graft and

corruption out of the Postal Department.

[7]. Colonel John H. Jackson had combat experience in the Mexican War, and was cited for gallantry while a lieutenant with the 9th U. S. Infantry. Starting out a lieutenant colonel with the 3rd, he was promoted June 27, 1862, to colonel. Wounded in battle at Fort Wagner July 18, 1863, he was finally separated from the service for disability on February 24, 1864. He died in Boston, April 10, 1890, but is buried here.

Long after the war and Jackson's death, the story came to light of the "treasure box" possessed by his widow, Mrs. Lavinia G. Jackson, 1 Summer Street. One of the items found was a New Testament given Jackson by his sister, E. Dikerman. This little volume had saved Jackson's life during the Mexican War when, at Chapultepec, a bullet struck the breast pocket where he carried it and bounced off. Another curio was "an embossed cross of silver, 4 by 3 inches, and of Catholic production and quite heavy for its size. This Colonel Jackson wore all through the war, and which, too, seemed to immunize him from molestation". Jackson became a Mason in St. John's Lodge on September 4, 1856. Still another relic preserved by this veteran of two wars, was a silver cup, inscribed as being presented to John H. Jackson, May 7, 1839, for being the "best shot" at a target during a drill by the Rockingham Guards. And the final memento he had kept, as mortals do, was a poem written by Benjamin P. Shillaber, addressed to Jackson when he was serving in Mexico, entitled, "Soldier, Come Home".

[8]. For example, Company G of the 10th, Captain George W. Towle, was a Portsmouth outfit. As was Company B of the 4th, commanded by Captain George F. Towle. Company K of the 13th was led by Captain Matthew T. Betton with Portsmouth men as soldiers. Company B of the 17th was Portsmouth. Captain H. J. Sides had Company K of the 6th, with local men; Captain Joseph H. Thacher headed Company K of the 16th. Company G, 10th, also had George E. Hodgdon and Simon R. Marston, both of Portsmouth, as lieutenants. In Company B, 4th, was Lieutenant John W. Brewster, wounded May 20, 1864, and discharged. Enoch W. Goss of Portsmouth and Nathan J. Coffin, Portsmouth, were officers in Company K, 13th, as was William J. Ladd. In Captain Thacher's company, a nine-month outfit, George T. Wildes, who died at New Orleans, was first lieutenant and William A. Haven, second lieutenant.

One regiment, the 5th NHVR, reportedly suffered more casualties than any other unit in the Union Army. A Captain John Murray of Company D came from New Castle and was killed at

Fredericksburg, December 13,1862. Murray's career as a soldier is a book in itself, and everyone should hope that Joseph Copley of New Castle, a Civil War "buff" who has researched the man's life, will some day write about it.

[9]. Conscripting men for military service was far from a new concept. Sewall mentions it often in his diary. But it was the first time it had ever been tried on a national basis. In colonial times men were "impressed" for service either at Fort William and Mary, or on expeditions inland, or down Maine, against the Indians.

[10]. Mayor Jonathan Dearborn was not the first local official to use Marines. During the War of 1812, a detachment of "volunteers" for duty at Fort McClary, after creating some disturbance, were escorted across the river by a Marine detachment. Dearborn died November 2, 1880, as he was about to depart his house for the polls. Dearborn had gone through the throes of ill health in all his last years, spending summers at Poland Springs, Maine, searching for the elusive elixir that repairs all human frailties. Dearborn, a native of North Hampton, followed the trade of hatter for years, and was employed by the late Daniel Knight. Subsequently he entered partnership with Knight, and then later went into business on his own with his son, Frank E. Dearborn, as a partner. Elected mayor in 1862, he was re-elected in 1863, after the riots, and The Journal said he was one of the best city marshals Portsmouth ever had. For five years, during the Lincoln Administrations, a job later abolished, he was naval officer here. One of Dearborn's daughters became the wife of Portsmouth attorney C. E. Batchelder.

[11]. John Samuel Hatch Frink died on August 31, 1905, at the age of 73. He was then a resident of Greenland, but so much a part of the Portsmouth scene that he is worthy of mention. He held office as county solicitor, and for four years was U. S. district attorney. Twice he was nominated to the State Supreme Court, once even had the commission in his pocket, but refused to serve because the remuneration was too small.

[12]. Garland W. Patch, Sr., was a retired welder from the Portsmouth Naval Shipyard, an antique dealer and devoted student of Portsmouth's material history. At the time of his death, he was curator at the Portsmouth Athenaeum, a position voted him by the directors for his long service in cataloging much of the manuscript material in the Athenaum's collections. Another of his specialties was ship carpentering tools. For many years, with Mrs. Patch's help, he had been custodian of the Aldrich Memorial. He died in 1972.

[13]. Linden Street is no more, having been dug up and lost beneath the red-brick monstrosity called the Federal building, of which more later. The street sloped gently north and south from the crown of a small rise on which stood the fabled Jaffrey House. For years the thoroughfare was known as Jaffrey's Court. Here lived the King's counselor George Jaffrey, and his grounds ran east to the line of the present City Hall lot, north to Bow, and west to Penhallow. The property passed from the Jaffrey family to John and Amos Goodrich, and was lived in by their descendants for many years. As time went by, it was crowded in by smaller places until only the immediate yard remained.

[14]. Few immigrants to these shores went through more unnecessary torture than the Irish Catholics, except for those brought here as slaves. Forced to leave their homeland by famine in the 1840s, these exiles came crowding to America, the land of hope and promise. They died by the hundreds in the over-loaded Atlantic packets, owned by American and British shippers, and their plight has been described vividly in an article in American Heritage. Ultra-rabid fanatics, the radical conservatives of that day, did everything in their power to prevent the natural assimilation of the Irish; part of the cause was economic, fear that the newcomers would work better and more cheaply. Portsmouth was, perhaps, a little nicer than other communities in this respect. At least there was no rioting here against the Irish as there was in Manchester. But the reader can detect in the columns of The Morning Chronicle the prejudice of the day. If the "Several Irish families" burned out had been old-line Yankees, or the Scotch-Irish of 100 years earlier, they would have been named. Contemporary news items note that a drunk, "Irish, of course", was fined in court. Against these odds, the Irish-Catholics have come to a point where a descendant of immigrants has occupied the White House. But the early days show that prejudice is always latent within us.

[15]. The Portsmouth Aqueduct is discussed in more detail elsewhere, but in those days it was nothing to have lizards, frogs and snakes crawl out of the taps.

[16]. The reservoir is still there, but has not been used for a quarter of a century or more, according to Deputy Fire Chief Donald Lane. The hydrant system, with booster pumps, is now adequate.

[17]. Sagamore was the name given the first steam fire engine. Built in Portland at a cost of $5,000, it weighed 5,100 pounds with coal and water on board. Its arrival here was an event,

with Laconia Engine Co., No. 2, meeting it at the station and drawing it through the streets, accompanied by the Portsmouth Cornet Band, to Market Square. Five hundred feet of the new hose were laid and the new engine was demonstrated for about two hours. One can only guess that Oliver D. Ayres, manager of the Aqueduct Company and himself a fireman, must have had a fit seeing all that water wasted, but perhaps it came from the reservoir and had already been paid for by the city. That night a dinner was held in the Laconia fire house with Mayor Jonathan Dearborn, the aldermen and other dignitaries present. The city's second fire engine, the Dearborn, named to honor the mayor, arrived here on June 30, 1865, and was demonstrated on Portsmouth Pier. This one weighed 7,300 pounds, cost $4,500, and was built by Campbell, Whittier. Co., Roxbury, Mass. Dearborn and Sagamore were ordered at the same time. The third steam fire engine was the Kearsarge, bought from the Amokeag Co., Manchester, at a cost of $4,760. Kearsarge weighed 6,400 pounds on its delivery in June, 1870. Six years later the city bought another, the Moses H. Goodrich, named for a former mayor, and sold the Sagamore. Built in Burlington, Vt., the Goodrich weighed 7,400 pounds, and cost $4,230. The men who manned the Sagamore were reorganized into a company for the Goodrich. In 1880, the city accepted delivery of the Colonel Sise, weighing 7,500 pounds and costing $3,000. The fire company manning the Colonel Sise in 1903 — 70 years ago — had then been in continuous existence for 101 years, being originally the Laconia Co., then the Sagamore, and finally the Coloner Sise. And in 1903, the city was still using the three engines.

[18]. Fire Chief Ernest Weeks succeeded Frederick R. "Ted" Crompton, who had taken the place of Fire Chief George T. Cogan.

[19]. To build the original Congress Block, Samuel Coues sold off the lumber from the house that stood on the site. A goodly part of the lumber in this house was actually from the Old South Meeting House at the Mill Dam, which had been bought and moved uptown in 1738 by John Newmarch. Before Newmarch bought the land, a house and shop had stood there which had been occupied by baker Robert Macklin, who was burned out. After Newmarch's death, the property was occupied by Richard Billings, first clerk of the Brick Market. Coues sold the material to Frederick W. Rogers who used it in building a cottage on Jackson Street. This building was the first on the east side of the street, but was cleared away during the Vaughan Street Urban Renewal program. The

nearest building to that site is now the structure recently erected by The Portsmouth Herald.

[20]. Benjamin F. Webster was one of the great master carpenters of the 19th Century. Today he would be a "contractor", but, like Frank Miller, he was also a developer. Webster was born in Epsom, September 7, 1824, dying here on January 5, 1916. Still his memorial is the building that is now occupied by the J. Verne Wood Funeral Home, George B. Ward, proprietor, at 84 Broad Street. This is the oldest firm of its kind in the city. Ward himself is the successor to J. Verne Wood, former police commissioner, and Wood acquired the business from H. Wallace Nickerson, who operated from 5 Daniel Street. Wood moved the mortuary to the Buckminster House, and Ward later acquired the Webster House and moved there. The Webster House was the property of Miss Stella C. Webster, Benjamin's daughter, who lived into her 90's. The Rambler, First Series, gives a lengthy sketch of the history of Buckminster House, up to the time it was occupied by George Tompson, who had a wholesale grocery business at 24 Bow Street. It was in Tompson's ownership for a number of years before passing to Joseph H. Thacher, an apothecary at 12 Market Square. Mary Lane Bickford and Frank Bickford were the next occupants.

[21]. John R. Holbrook was a sailmaker, with a loft on Market Street, and lived on Court Street. Foss in his "Three Centuries of Freemasonry", says Holbrook was a past grand master of the New Hampshire lodge and he died October 2, 1883.

[22]. Washington Freeman's place of business was described in an earlier note in this chapter. There were other Freemans in town. Peyton R., a lawyer; Charles and John, both hosiery weavers. Peyton R. Freeman had a farm at Ham's Point, which, naturally, became Freeman's Point.

[23]. Charles G. Pickering was a flour dealer at 65 Market, and with a house on Pleasant. He died in Cleveland on February 1, 1885, at the age of 52.

[24]. Joseph Parry was a baker with a shop at 19 and 20 Fleet, and his home at 18 Fleet. One of the men who once worked for Joseph Parry was James W. Sowersby, a major victim of the fire of 1864. Sowersby was born here March 10, 1829, attended the public schools, and then apprenticed himself in the baking trade. Reaching the status of journeymen, he worked in Hudson, New York, then came back here and worked for Parry for eight years, before setting up on his own. In 1870, he bought the plant of John Nutter on Water Street.

[25]. Apparatus from several neighboring cities and towns came into Portsmouth to help battle that blaze which started somewhere in the two upper stories. Portsmouth's own ladder truck was in service, along with one from Dover, and there were pumpers from the Naval Shipyard, Kittery and other towns. Goods in the J. J. Newberry Store on the ground floor were badly damaged, but, curiously enough, goldfish swimming about in a basement tank seemed only to enjoy the unusual commotion. The late Joseph Eberle was then manager for Newberry and the building was owned by Andrew Jarvis, who carried out extensive repairs and put his own family name on the block. Eberle later had a stationer's business at 18 Market Square.

[26]. Wallace Hackett was born in Portsmouth, graduated Harvard Law, 1879; admitted to New Hampshire bar that year. Mayor of Portsmouth 1907-08; his home, 351 Middle Street, was bought by St. John's Lodge in 1920 and is now used for a Masonic Temple. Hackett died February 15, 1939, in Annapolis, Maryland.

[27]. Today the Holt family's work on the river is a story unto itself.

[28]. Dr. Benjamin S. Goodwin lived at 9 Market Street in 1861. It's left to the imagination whether or not he was connected to James W. Goodwin, Sr., a river pilot with a home at 2 Charles Street. He was not in Portsmouth by 1877.

[29]. Thomas Clapham was a baker by trade at 6 Cornwall Street.

[30]. Randall had a place of business at 2 Ceres Street.

[31]. On January 1, 1861, the Navy Yard had a work force of 140 men, a smaller number than had been employed there on any one day in the seven years preceding. This strength suffered a further "RIF" in February and again in March, so that on the first of April, 12 days before Fort Sumter, less than a hundred men were working on the Yard. On February 21, Congress passed a law — Summer was less than two months away — that not more than $3,000 should be expended in any Navy Yard in repairing the hull and spars of any vessel until the necessity has been ascertained and reported to the Navy Department.

[32]. Preble was launched on June 13, 1839. She was built in the Franklin Shiphouse, and the galleries in that building permitted a large crowd to watch the preliminaries to her launch. Thousands more watched outside. Preble was pierced for 20 guns but still carried only 16, fourteen 32-pounder carronades, and two long 12s; her complement of men and officers was 175. Cost of Preble

was $112,782, ready for sea. By 1850 repairs had totaled $44,949, and she underwent other repairs after that. Preble did the routine work of a vessel of her type. She cruised most of the foreign stations, worked as a training vessel for midshipmen, was in the Gulf Squadron in the Civil War, and was accidentally destroyed by fire April 27, 1863.

[33]. Keel of the USS Portsmouth was laid — the second sloop-of-war of that name — in 1843. Josiah Barker was the man in charge. He had relieved Samuel N. Pook whose home was at 1 Atkinson Street. Portsmouth was modeled along lines, much enlarged, of the privateer America. Portsmouth's dimensions were 151 feet in length; beam, 38 feet; depth of hold, 17 feet. When ready to go out to sea she had cost $170,586. Portsmouth sailed on her first foreign cruise in December 1844. In 1858 — June 13 — she came back to Portsmouth Harbor, the end of a cruise of 49,000 miles in which she took the bearer of the first treaty with Siam to Bangkok. She was part of Commodore Matthew C. Perry's fleet when he opened up Japan to the modern world in 1853. Repaired in 1858, she was back at sea in May.

In 1861 she was here again for repairs, but she was at sea again before Christmas. Again, in May, 1864, she came "home", but not really a welcome visitor because she had on board an unwelcome passenger — Yellow Fever. Three of her people were ill, and the sickest of the lot was her captain, Commodore William C. Wise. She had picked up the virus at St. Thomas, Virgin Islands, although the authorities in the Danish-owned islands said no fever was there.

During the time she was "down below" the Chronicle asked that reading material be supplied her people. She was allowed upriver in May, and it would appear came here only once more, and that was in July 1888. She spent a year here then and was put back in commission in July 1889. Portsmouth is getting so much attention here because she is one of the vessels that has carried the city's name to the far corners of the earth.

The last was a World War II cruiser, but that can be discussed later. Tradition has it that she helped the United States steal California when she hoisted the flag off that coast in 1846, and she is known to have been a mercy ship at the time of the San Francisco earthquake in 1906. In 1915 she was sold for junk and her wheel came to the Portsmouth Yacht Club but at some time before World War II, according to a former club commodore, Gerald G. Woods of 99 Bow Street, it was sold to the Bank of America — but whether the sale was on Bank Americard or not has not been reported. Portsmouth's end was dismal. She was burned in September of 1915 for the entertainment of a motion picture crew. That was in Boston Harbor, on a mudflat off Governor's Island.

[34]. USS Congress was launched, to a salute of 13 guns, on August 16, 1841, with the usual multitude on the neighboring river banks. Congress was the first vessel to be masted by the permanent shears on the wharf which had been erected at a cost of $2,240 by utilizing the lower masts of Alabama. That might help explain why Alabama was still on the stocks in 1864. The original Congress built here in 1799, was broken up at Norfolk in 1836.

[35]. "Baron Renfrew" never did set foot in the Portsmouth Navy Yard, but he did pass through Portsmouth on his way to Portland, where he boarded one of the vessels his mother, Queen Victoria, sent for him. However, the United States Navy is never reluctant to hand out honors when they are due, and so the battery began a 21-gun salute as the future ruler of the British Empire started across the old Portsmouth Bridge in his train. The train, a special, had stopped long enough in Portsmouth for a crowd of several thousand to be on hand to peek at the visiting "Royal". And he did show himself briefly, which is the closest Portsmouth ever came to a visit from a member of the British ruling house, although he was then 41 years away from the sceptre, to which he came as Edward VII.

[36]. Lieutenant David D. Porter, who had achieved fame in the War of 1812 as a midshipman, was to go on and become one of the Civil War's great naval leaders. USS Constitution would come back to Portsmouth Navy Yard. She returned in 1882, and was made into a museum piece, and receiving ship. April 30, 1891, Storer Post, GAR, held a reception and colonial party on board her. On September 20, 1897, after 15 years here, the Constitution was sent to Boston. She has not returned since.

[37]. The contract to build the Naval Prison was awarded to a New York firm, Snaire and Trieste, in December of 1903. Commissioning of the installation as the U. S. Naval Prison took place five years later. Prisoners were first housed on the site in 1898 when some 1,600 Spanish POWs were held there. At the tag end of World War II, the prison was used to house German submarine crews until it could be decided what to do with them. Fort Sullivan was first conceived at the time of the Revolution as means of commanding the river approach.

[38]. USS Franklin was one of those clever subterfuges used by the Navy to circumvent a penurious Congress. The technique

was known as "razeeing". When Congress allowed funds for the repair of a commissioned vessel, the Navy often kept the log open, had her torn apart, and the "repaired" ship would be virtually new from main to keel. Franklin was built as a "74" in Philadelphia, and came here in 1852 to test the new floating dry dock. The Yard crews ran her into the dock, and up the marine railway, back out again and in again. Finally she was put on the railway and the "repair" work started. A timber from her was carried over to the "new Shiphouse", known from that time on as the Franklin Shiphouse, and a new keel laid. "Repairing" Franklin made it necessary to lengthen the shiphouse and build a "pigeon coop" on top of it in order to accommodate Franklin, although "74s" once were built there. Over the next few years, as funds were available, "repairs" were continued, but when the Civil War started she was not ready. An engine had yet to be built for her, so she did not get into the water until 1864, but she had gained 65 feet of length over her original 200. When finally set for the sea in 1867, she was propelled by steam instead of wind, and was rated at 5,170 tons to her former 2,257. That 5,170 tons made her the largest vessel ever put into the water at the Portsmouth Navy Yard until the Polaris submarine Abraham Lincoln slid down the ways in 1960.

[39]. A note in Chapter XVI gives some detail of the Kearsarge story, although it has been told too many times to get lengthy consideration here. Captain Charles W. Pickering of Portsmouth was her commander when she began her long cruise.

[40]. John E. Rider was born July 22, 1837, and died on October 2, 1902, the day before his political mentor, Frank Jones.

[41]. Phinehas Nichols was principal of the Girls High School, in what is now City Hall, and had for an assistant Miss A. C. Morgan. Aurin M. Payson was principal of Boys High in the same building and Lewis F. Smith was his assistant. Other teachers and schools at this time included the Franklin School (1847), with the grammar classes conducted by Charles A. Shannon; intermediate, Miss Sarah A. Dodge; primary, Miss Lucy M. Patten. Bartlett School, School Street, grammar classes by Samuel M. DeMeritt; intermediate, Miss Mary F. Simes. Girls' Grammar, Hanover Street, Miss C. A. Mason. Primary, High Street, Miss Lusena B. Mullen. Woodbury, Gravelly Ridge, Tobias D. Foss. Cabot Street School, A.C. Hoyt and Miss Marion M. Ham. Academy (for girls), Academy building, corner of Middle and Islington, Miss Harriet L. Hill and Miss Susan J. Clapham. Boys Grammar, Court House, Court Street, John Durgin,

Principal, and Miss Sarah A. Whittem, assistant. Primary, State Street, Miss Charlotte A. Walker and Miss Sarah P. Clapham. Plains School, Samuel Hoyt. Haven School, South School Street, grammar, Alfred M. Hoyt, principal; Miss Ann C. and Miss Eliza M. Marshall, assistants; primary, Mrs. Dorothy N. Shackford and Miss Adaline Tucker; infant, Miss Sarah E. Moses and Martha H. Rand. Lafayette, J. Sullivan Rand (winter), and Miss Sarah M. Norton (summer).

Phinehas Nichols, "Our Teacher", died July 8, 1863, after 35 successive years of teaching in the local school system, beginning in 1828. Even earlier, with a stint as principal of Governor Dummer Academy before his return here, Nichols had taught in the Lafayette Road School. In the last half of his long career here, he was principal of the Girls High School, and was an alderman at the time of his death.

[42]. Charles A. Wiggin was then a clerk.

[43]. Joseph B. Adams, an auctioneer and commission merchant, was born in 1818 and died November 11, 1874.

[44]. William O. Sides was a stable keeper at 9 Vaughan Street. Postmaster William O. Sides died April 27, 1899, at his home on Middle Street. Sides was serving his second stint as postmaster when his chronic heart condition caused his death. Sides also turned his hand, or pen, to newspapering, editing The Evening Post until 1897, except for a year when John Pender had it. Sides was a veteran of the Civil War, gaining high honors.

[45]. Joshua Foster's descendant, Robert E. Foster, publishes Foster's Daily Dover Democrat, which was founded by Joshua Foster after he left Portsmouth in 1872.

[46]. A pamphlet, printed by C. W. Brewster & Son, has preserved for us a verbal picture of Portsmouth's mourning for President Lincoln. The day set for the ceremonies was Wednesday, April 19, and "the day was pleasant, and, but for wind and dust, was very favorable for the grand pageant. In this city the houses and stores were to a great extent trimmed with adornments of sorrow. . . ." A funeral procession, with Captain Robert Lefavour as chief marshal, was formed. (Lefavour derived his title from his captaincy of the Rockingham Guards, a ceremonial military unit which lasted from 1823 to 1853.)

Lefavour's assistants were Captain Daniel Hill and Colonel Samuel Webber, both mounted; and Colonel John H. Jackson, A. J. Hill, William O. Sides, Andrew J. Beck, Christopher C. Jackson and James A. Blaisdell, all on foot. In the parade's first division, the feature was a funeral car, symbolic of the occasion, drawn by six black horses. The car itself was 11 feet long, 4½ feet wide and 6 feet high. Pall bearers were W. H. Y. Hackett, William Shackford, Jonathan Dearborn, William Simes, Joseph B. Upham, William L. Dwight, James F. Shores and Ichabod Rollins. Shores and Rollins had been in the funeral procession for George Washington 65 years before.

Various fraternal bodies, craft unions, and The Portsmouth High School Cadets were components in the other divisions. One car carried disabled veterans, among them the brothers Rich, Henry C. and Robert E., each of whom had lost his left leg in combat; also James McKnight, Edmund Whalley, Washington Sweat and Daniel Hatch, who had also lost limbs in the war; then there was John Perkins, left arm gone; and Henry Palmer, William Lolley, C. Dwight Hanscom, John Dooley, Patrick Sullivan, James Burnham and Robert C. Ranson. In Market Square there was a religious service with Mayor John H. Bailey presiding. The Rev. James DeNormandie, pastor of the South Church, offered a prayer; Albert Laighton, read one of his poems. The Rev. Adoniram J. Patterson, pastor of the Universalist Church, delivered the eulogy which was reproduced in full by the Brewsters. Three volleys were fired at the conclusion and the audience drifted quietly away after a benediction by the Rev. Holman.

20

The Age of Frank Jones

[1]. Joshua Wentworth lived in a house that stood where the brick house presently is at 180 Middle Street. He moved there after living many years in the house on Hanover Street which was recently given to Strawbery Banke by Harry Winebaum. For reasons which make no sense, it's hard to find any rapport with this man. From somewhere, a touch of the occult perhaps, comes the feeling that he was an opportunist of the first water. Wentworth played a prominent role in the Revolution, being a commissary and naval agent. In 1776 he was colonel of the 1st New Hampshire Regiment, and in 1785 he was in the State Senate. Washington appointed him supervisor for New Hampshire in 1791. He was such a close friend to the wealthy George Jaffrey that he expected to inherit the man's estate. Probably gambling on that intimacy, Wentworth left Jaffrey to make good on some of his notes. That soured the relationship. Jaffrey turned to nephew George Jeffries of Boston and offered to leave him his estate, so The Rambler said, on three conditions: (1) that he became a permanent resident of Portsmouth; (2) that he assume the name of Jaffrey; (3) that he follow no occupation but that of gentleman. As they would in this day, the conditions created no obstacles to the inheritance.

[2]. This would have been south and east of the locale known as Gravelly Ridge, but the Directory of 1840 does not list such an inn, nor does the 1851 issue. However, it's more than possible that what would be defined as an inn might have been only a farm where travelers from up-country could find accommodations without having to pay the outrageous prices prevalent in the town.

Hotels listed in 1840, and their proprietors, were Bell Tavern, Samuel Rea, 20 Congress Street; Danielson House, Hamilton G. Locke, Middle Street; Farmers' Hotel, Josiah G. Hadley and Alice

Clark, 9 Pleasant Street, corner of Warren (Porter) Street; Franklin House, Willis Barnabee, 27 Congress Street; Globe Tavern, John H. Jackson, at the Plains; Mansion House, Enoch Tilton, 22 Congress Street; Market Street House, Jonathan Walker, 114 Market Street; Pound Tavern, at the Pound, Asa Watson (Poundkeeper), off South, near Spinney Road; Rockingham House, Thomas J. Coburn, 97 State Street.

In 1851, a year or two before Jones' advent, the hotels were: Rockingham House, 97 State Street, S. A. Coburn; Franklin House, 43 Congress, Willis Barnabee; Piscataqua House, 9 Pleasant Street, Josiah G. Hadley; Market Street House, 114 Market Street, Charles W. Walker. And in 1857, after the advent of Jones, Rockingham House, Thomas J. Coburn, 97 State Street; Franklin House, 43 Congress, Willis Barnabee; Piscataqua House, 9 Pleasant, Josiah G. Hadley; Market Street House, 114 Market, C. W. Walker; and Granite State, 5 Pleasant, William S. Hadley.

[3]. The cellar hole of the Thomas Jones' home in Barrington may still be seen on U. S. Rt. 4 to Concord. It is now used as a combination of emergency supply of water against fire and as a swimming pool, and is about two miles west of the Lee traffic circle. The family cemetery is also in the vicinity.

[4]. This quartet, of whom three are still living, includes two of the town's better known residents, Colonel Henry B. Margeson, USA, Ret., a West Pointer and professional soldier for 30 years. On leaving the service, he engaged in banking at the Portsmouth Trust Co., but is now retired. Donald H. is the youngest of the four, a partner in Margeson Bros.; three times a city councilman; a founder and inveterate worker for Strawbery Banke, of which he has been president. He makes his home in the Oracle House, Marcy Street. This building originally stood at the northwest corner of Middle and Court Streets was moved to make way for the brick building offices owned by the United Federation of Postal Clerks Benefit Association of which Orrin L. Bradshaw is the secretary-treasurer. A third brother, Ralph C., makes his home in New Castle. He saw service in World War II as a major in the Marine Corps, and at one time, was on the Portsmouth Board of Education. The fourth, and oldest of the brothers, Richman S. Margeson, died in 1972, having made his home in New Castle. While he was Mayor, his wife, Miriam, was on the Board of Education, an office-holding feat unique to the city.

[5]. One tradition has it that it was while on his rounds as a tin peddler, Frank Jones found the recipe for his ale. Supposedly

Jones, who was a ladies man of the first water, was given it by a smitten South Berwick housewife. That will never be known, but the late Ira Newick, again according to tradition, was the last man to know the secret formula.

[6]. The school was dedicated in 1856 for secondary education. For the first time, boys and girls were taught under the same roof, but in separate classrooms. This non-mixing of the sexes was abandoned in 1873. According to The Rambler, the house of Mark Hunking Wentworth stood on the site, and it was to his father's house that Governor John Wentworth repaired on his return to Portsmouth in 1767. The Rambler was disappointed when the house was torn down because so little could be found to date it accurately.

[7]. After long and bitter hassling, such as always accompanies such proposals, this building, now owned by City Councilman Richard S. Levy, and used by him as a store for auto parts and electronic goods, was erected in 1858 and dedicated in 1860. The site had been occupied by the Rockingham Bank and Farmer's Hotel. When the new federal building was opened on Daniel Street in 1967, the old one was put up for bids and bought by Levy for $37,500.

[8]. Is it possible Jones might have been on hand the day they pulled down the steeple of the Old North Church? That was on May 12, 1854, after the lofty spire had been reaching toward heaven about 140 years. The decision to tear down the old church building came only after long soul searching, but the state of disrepair was such that something had to be done. However, there were those who met it with protests, as witness this letter to the editor of The Chronicle:

"The lot on which the church now stands would be valuable to the town, would add much to the spaciousness of the central portion termed the "Parade". It could be disposed of for a sufficient sum to enable the society to purchase a spot large enough for such surroundings as shall be a credit to the taste, and manifest a proper respect for the great purpose to which it is to be consecrated. We would suggest the lot opposite the Post Office, (prior to 1858) on the corner of Daniel and Penhallow Streets, if it can be purchased, or the one which has already been mentioned, opposite the Academy; any spot indeed will be preferable to that now contemplated". A retired place, "where the voice of prayer may at all times be understood . . . ." was urged.

The editor's response to this sums up well the attitude of the North Parish, both then and now:

"We can answer all these suggestions and queries, very readily. The people who have worshipped in the old meeting house, and who mean to worship in the new, have an exceedingly strong attachment to the old site, and whatever associations of holy things they have, belong to this particular spot whereon their fathers worshipped".

This probably answers modern conjecture as to why the North Church does not remove entirely from Market Square to the land off Spinney and Middle Roads where its parish house and church activities center are located.

"We have heard many suggestions similar to those above, not only at the present time, but also 17 years ago when the old house was repaired; and because *** writes well, we give him (or her?) a hearing. But a great majority of the parishioners, then as now, pertinaciously clung to the 'old ground', and would hardly hear of any other".

Other letters indicate that the old building, was disappearing piece by piece, until the climatic day arrived, May 12, 1854, when the fine old steeple itself would come down. On May 13, The Chronicle reported, "The heavenward pointing spire of the old North Meeting House points upward no more; it was beleaguered with ropes on Friday morning, by Mr. Albion K. P. Deering, a bold mariner, who ascended by the lightening rod, to a point chosen by himself, where he fastened his guys. Then descending to the bell deck, he and his assistants cut off the eight posts that supported the several corners of the octagonal crown which sustained the heavy steeple. At one o'clock the hawser leading to Market Street was hauled taut, and at 12 minutes past one, the steeple toppled over and fell into Market Square, pointing towards the Athenaeum, and being dashed into a thousand pieces by the concussion. The spectators were very numerous, and apparently delighted that the spectacle was at noonday and exhibited according to the programme.

"The steeple was the largest and most noble specimen of its kind which we had ever happened to see. But it has given way before the onward march of progress, and now we expect to see one not less noble nor less substantial in its place. And perhaps it has not come down to soon, for it was much decayed — the pine timber actually being in better preservation than the oak.

"The builder's name was seen plainly chalked on the kingpost — 'Joseph Libbey, 1730', and the same date is on the Vane. The venerable vane, was somewhat injured, but will be straightened out and preserved as a relic inside the new steeple. It is of copper, mostly cast, from the head to the fork, which is iron. It is pointed to the South, the land of sunshine, till rudely cast down to earth".

Deering undoubtedly brought his own rigging gang along with him to do the job and the names of two of them have come down. One was John Campbell of 37 Water Street. Another was Alfred Moore, painter and rigger who lived on Pleasant Street, who "fell from the ridgepole, about 40 feet into the celler". This was a few days after the steeple had been pulled down. Moore was able to walk out of the wreckage to the street where a carriage was waiting to take him home.

With the leveling of the North Meeting House, the face of the intown area was really changed, the beginning of other sharp changes, to the point where only a few structures remain around Market Square that have not undergone marked alterations. One is the Portsmouth Athenaeum, probably the least damaged by time, and another the structure that houses the Warwick Club and A. B. Duncan's Jewelry (now Alies). Even the Glebe Building, on the south end of the church, has lost its top deck. Fires and rebuilding programs have taken heavy toll.

[9]. An example of Father Brennan's sense of humor is contained in a little anecdote involving him and the late Charles Donovan, at one time a lineman for New England Telephone. During the time the new church was being built, the Immaculate Conception parishioners used what is now the Civic Theater for Masses. Until only a few years ago the DeWitt Hotel stood on what has been until recently a parking lot used by the employees of The Portsmouth Herald. Donovan, a bachelor, was one of proprietor Charles Pike's more or less permanent guests. Donovan also was a non-too-faithful member of Father Brennan's parish; his attendance at Mass being honored more in the breach than the observance. One day, shortly after Mass started in the theater building, Father Brennan chanced to meet Donovan on the street. With a bit more than a twinkle, the priest said, "Well, Charlie, the Mountain has finally come to Mohammed! I'll be expecting you at Mass on Sunday". For once, Donovan, a noted wit, was speechless.

[10]. This paper, with the late True L. Norris as editor, was a frequent critic of the founding editor and publisher of The Portsmouth Herald, the late F. W. Hartford, who served the city seven times as mayor. Hartford acquired The Times and merged it with The Herald on June 6, 1925. Previously he had bought The Chronicle and had run that for a number of years as the city's morning paper. This, too, was "folded" when it became econ-

omically unfeasible to publish two papers a day in the city. In 1902, Hartford purchased and eventually closed out The Portsmouth Journal of Literature and Politics, thus ending the Brewster era in newspapering here.

[11]. The "Creek" — pronounced "Crick" — takes its name from the tiny stream, Islington Creek, that flows into the North Mill Pond. Ethnically, particularly in Jones Brewery days, it was the Irish section of the city, back when people were apt to acquired nicknames like "Big Stone Thrower" or "Bag of Cats". Saturday nights were not the best of times to have the police patrol the Creek. One of the most treasured institutions – there's no other word to describe it — at the Creek is the "Creek A. C.". Once it was the sponsor, as the name implies, of athletic teams that went forth to do honor for the Creek, but now it's a social club in all but formal organization. Headquarters are still in the old fire sub station, with the city providing the fuel to heat the place in winter. Here for years was the polling place for the voters of Ward 3, and it's easy to recall the late Patrick Duffy patroling in the Ward Room on Election night, watching for reporters and Democrats. Duffy, so the legend goes, was one of those in the Creek who believed that the late George H. Moses, a U. S. senator and a bit of a medicine show pitchman, could carry out his promise "to free Ireland", so he became a Republican.

"Pat" Duffy will be remembered by many Portsmouth people for years to come for that erect, military carriage he showed in leading parades throughout the city. Probably the last surviving veteran here of the Spanish-American War, Duffy died February 20, 1971, at the age of 90. Almost to the day of his death, his raven black hair was his badge of defiance against the inroads of time.

[12]. These springs, some now contaminated, still exist and can be seen out on the Pease AFB Golf Course; Jones was forced to extremes of building his own water system by the inadequacy of the Portsmouth Aqueduct. At one time, there were even plans for a rival firm, the Portsmouth Water Company, which intended to pipe water into the city from across the Piscataqua. Actually, as indicated elsewhere, Jones' primary intent for this water was to wash his equipment. Portsmouth water was still preferred for the actual brewing process. Geologically speaking, the water for the Jones' system came out of a white sand strata in what is called a "bowl".

[13]. While this company used the name of "Frank Jones Ale", it had no real relation to the former concern. It started the brewing of ale in 1936, after Repeal, when land and buildings, off Bartlett Street were acquired from the Eldredge Brewing Company.

The late Albert Hislop, a former mayor, was the proprietor, with his son Gordon as brewmaster. Right after World War II, a poker game was assembled weekly in one of the city's then most historic houses. The game had as one of its feature attractions a small keg of Frank Jones Ale, furnished by the younger Hislop, who, along with John R. Wiggin, the late Richard Hartford, "Wally" Dunn, the writer and a lawyer or two were the usual participants. Not much money was won or lost, but not much ale went to waste either. The house is, unfortunately, now gone — relocated in Sturbridge Village, Sturbridge, Massachusetts.

[14]. The Rambler once said of Jonathan Warner that he was "the last of the cocked hats", that is, the three-corner style of Revolutionary days. And it might be said of Judge Simes that he was probably the last man in town to wear spats, and to the end of his days he attempted an English accent, although born here. The judge also had a remarkable capacity for liquor, and there is a story, that should not be lost to posterity, of the night he and the late J. D. Hartford, then editor and publisher of The Herald, sat down to talk over their differences. The two men had been close in working for civic betterment; fell into disagreement and were quite estranged. Mutual friends had brought them together at the Rockingham — naturally — and left them together with a bottle on the table. When the dawn came, more bottles of whiskey were gone, but the two men had reconciled their differences. The judge went to the Municipal Court to sit on some cases as special justice. Hartford went about his day's newspaper duties, although he did leave a little earlier than usual. The judge, incidentally, later was on the first city manager council.

[15]. Legend again has it that the only reason that Jones brought that load of wood to the city was that, despite a hired man's objections, he insisted on putting a wild pair of oxen into the traces. So the hired man left him to come alone.

[16]. Granite State established a national reputation in 1906 when San Francisco was damaged by an earthquake. The company's agent treated the quake victims so well that word of its integrity spread across the country. Granite State was for years managed by John Emery and then by the late Orel C. Dexter, who was a former mayor and also a police commissioner. Martin C. Cherry was manager when the parent company, New Hampshire Fire Insurance, moved Granite State to Manchester. The first secretary was Alfred F. Howard, a former partner of John Pender's in the insurance business.

[17]. The course of ownership of the two hotels cannot be traced here. The Wentworth was purchased by James B. Smith, who had been a major in the Army Air Corps, shortly after World War II. Subsequently he bought the Rockingham from Andrew Jarvis, a former mayor, city councilman and governor's councilor. Smith kept the two under his ownership until 1962 when he sold the Rockingham to Miss Hazel Woods. Smith operates the Wentworth in a much different manner than the custom in Jones' day when the hotel catered to the "carriage trade" exclusively. July and August were the fashionable months then for such a hotel, and the Wentworth is, sadly enough, one of the last of its kind to be still in operation in the Northeast.

The writer remembers, in his chauffeuring days, swinging under the Wentworth's portals, in a 12-cylinder Packard, and unloading his passengers as their yacht waited for them at the dock. That's only 30-odd years ago.

Some conception of what Frank Jones did to make that hotel one of the most prominent summer resorts in the northeast may be found in an item published in 1903. At that time the trustees of the Frank Jones' estate sold to the City of Portsmouth 11,000 feet of water main Jones had laid from the corner of Spring Street and Miller Avenue to the Wentworth. The main was put down in 1898, and the city bought it for $3,121. At the same time, the city won the concession to be able to lay a water main from Sagamore Creek (Sagamore Bridge was opened to traffic in 1850), through the hotel grounds, "to New Castle village", although it was stipulated that the line could not cross "the ornamental grounds in front". Further it was agreed that the City of Portsmouth had to supply water to the Wentworth, as desired, at a rate of six cents per thousand gallons until June 4, 1908.

The grounds of the Wentworth were under the supervision of a man named Robert Paterson, a native of Nova Scotia, who came to Portsmouth about 1880 when he was 21 to visit a half-brother, William G. Paterson, a gardener at the Jones Estate. Induced to work for Jones, he was five years a journeyman gardener, then assistant, and, finally, head gardener after his brother's death in 1890. Thirty-five men were on the staff in the gardens at the Wentworth.

One of the high spots of Smith's regime at the hotel came quite early in his tenure when the National Governors' Conference, under the aegis of ex-Governor Charles M. Dale of New Hampshire and ex-Governor Horace Hildreth of Maine, convened there in June 1948. That was the year the late Thomas E. Dewey — the "Little

Man on the Wedding Cake" — came to New Hampshire so completely the man of the hour that he was only waiting for the formality of the election before moving to Washington. The only man with doubts was the incumbent, President Harry S. Truman, who was given another four-year lease on the White House — to Dewey's great shock. Another luminary in that assortment of 40-odd governors was the man who did more to guide the U. S. Supreme Court into the 20th Century than any other — Earl Warren, a great chief justice. Irascible, even then, was Strom Thurmond of South Carolina, now a "Republican" senator from that state, but who was then governor and in attendance, and arguing with Jim Smith's clerks over a sixty-cent charge.

[18]. The National Block for years was the head-quarters of the New Hampshire Electric Co., a small utility eventually absorbed by the Public Service Company of New Hampshire. Part of it is now occupied by Continental Cablevision, the firm that supplies cable TV to homes and businesses in the city from a towering antenna near the old Jones Avenue dump. A fire early in 1972 put out of business a store operated by Kenneth A. Weiss. Before New Hampshire Electric, the building had housed Granite State Fire Insurance until it moved to its new building at State and Middle Streets about 1924. The eastern half of the first floor is now the store of Andrew's Electric, an appliance firm.

[19]. The fire-ravaged building that had to be removed had been known before its change into a hotel, as the Cutter House because of its ownership by Dr. Ammi R. Cutter, one of the leading local physicians in the 18th Century. That house, and two others in the immediate area — only one of them still standing, but not on its original site — tell a powerful story of mother love, and ruthless determination to succeed.

Mary (Kelley) Treadwell, the heroine of this note, built a house for each of her three children. This was in the 1750's, and the wherewithal to accomplish it came from her own small income from a little shop she operated on King (Congress) Street. Her husband was one of those unfortunate men, and too many still populate the world, for whom nothing went right. Early in their married life, having no intention of returning to the poverty she had known in her New Castle girlhood, she became the leader. Her store policy was one we could still use a lot of in downtown Portsmouth: Her customers were made to feel welcome.

Daughter Hannah was the first one to get a house, the one that preceded the National Block. Here she lived with her husband,

Dr. Cutter, next door to her mother's home and shop. That was in 1745; in 1750, Mary Treadwell built a second house, this time for son Jacob. This house, which stood across from the Library at the corner of Middle and Congress, was torn down in 1956 by ex-Governor Charles M. Dale because he said it could not be properly maintained. An outbuilding that stood at the rear is at Dale's home in North Hampton. A block of shops and offices, including the successor to Vincent Mattison's barber shop, now occupy the site. The third house, when it was built for son Nathaniel in 1758, had a yard that backed up to sister Hannah's Congress Street property, although the house faced south on State Street where the First National Bank is now located. Porter Street was not then opened up between Fleet and Pleasant and Mary Treadwell owned a goodly share of the land in the area.

This third house is the only one extant. For years it served as the YWCA building and later was owned by the Walker and Waldron families. When the First National Bank acquired it, once again taking up a location near its long-time neighbor on Market Square — the Portsmouth Savings Bank — it was moved to a vacant lot on Court Street, No. 70, where it provides offices for the law firm of Boynton, Waldron, Dill, Nadeau and Aeschliman. This is a successor partnership to the old firm of Waldron, Boynton and Waldron, founded by the late Jeremy R. Waldron, Sr., for many years presiding justice of the Municipal Court, and the man who, as attorney general, finally managed to get the New Hampshire-Vermont boundary settled. This concluded litigation that had been going on for 150 years. His son, Jeremy, a World War II combat veteran, is the Waldron in the firm now.

[20]. The Morley Button went under construction in June 1893, and opened for business in October. The Morley Company, with John Taylor as president, still operates in part of the original building. Jones' son-in-law, Charles A. Sinclair, was active in this company, besides his myriad of other interests.

[21]. When he was resident in these apartments, owned by his family, Maurice J. Murphy learned that by the caprice of the then governor, Wesley Powell, he had been designated U. S. senator to succeed Styles Bridges. Murphy, scion of an old Dover family, was attorney general when this honor came. In a later primary contest to continue in the office, Murphy was defeated by Perkins Bass of Peterborough, who lost, subsequently, to the incumbent, Democrat Tom McIntyre of Laconia. Another resident of these apartments for many years has been Miss Katherine Brady, a fine teacher of history

at Portsmouth High School for many years.

When the original owner of the apartments, Charles A. Sinclair, died in April, 1899, The Herald managed to make it sound as though one of the Heavenly Host had departed. Three and a half columns of ghastly obituary were poured into its front page on April 27, extolling the virtues of the man. For example:

"The sudden death of Hon. Charles A. Sinclair will be a personal grief to the many people of New Hampshire who were drawn to him by the cordiality of his personal greeting, the warmth of his sympathy and the generosity of his nature. He made friends everywhere, and none were more devoted to him than those of his native state."

Sinclair died in Brookline, Mass. He came to Portsmouth in 1873, wooed and won the only daughter of Frank Jones. He saw service in both houses of the Legislature, three terms in the Senate, and Governor James A. Weston made him a colonel on his staff. A life-long Democrat, Sinclair entered the railroading field in 1881, and had control of the Worcester & Nashua Railroad by 1884; in 1886 bought into the Manchester & Lawrence Railroad, getting control that same year, and then leasing to the Boston & Maine. Teaming up with his father-in-law, in 1887 Sinclair built the Upper Cohos and Hereford Railroad. The B&M's stockholders elected him a director in 1890, but he retired in 1898.

Frank Jones was at Sorrento, Maine, when he heard, as The Herald described it, that his "beloved son-in-law" was dying. Justin V. Hanscom was the man who reached Jones with the news, and Jones ordered a special train to take him to Boston. A record run ensued, and the train passed through Portsmouth at 5:38 a.m.

[22]. Work on Portsmouth Shoe began in 1878, on a location in the vicinity of present-day Anchor Buick, and it was ready for operation on October 2, 1880, and enlarged eight years later to dimensions of 55 by 350 feet. Charles Berry, plant manager, moved to Laconia and in 1905 his home at 40 Islington was sold, through C. Dwight Hanscom's real estate agency, to Justin V. Hanscom. "This is," The Herald said, "one of the finest locations in the vicinity. Overlooking as it does the charming Goodwin Park, the view can never be obstructed." Portsmouth Shoe Company, for a time, was the largest in the world.

[23]. Now an apartment house, the mansion is owned by Milton Pappas of 213 Aldrich Road. The Jones estate trustees sold the "farm" part of the property in December 1906, to a Doctor M. L. Chamberlain of Boston, and then to Charles Badger. The Herald

said of it: "This is the farm made famous by Mr. Jones who spent hundreds of thousands of dollars in its development. There are extensive gardens, large greenhouses, and all the details of a big establishment which a country gentleman could desire." Then it added a description of it:

"The entire farm consists of one field of about 30 acres, laid down to grass, and which grew this year 500 tons of first quality hay. Probably there is not another field of equal area in New England devoted to one crop. There goes with the farm a large and expensively built cow stable, a palatial stable of: 2 large box stalls for horses, three other barns, a new boarding house of 28 rooms, furnished, two other houses, a piggery, a hennery, creamery, silo, steel grist mill, hay press, and farming implements. There are three trout ponds, a half-mile trotting track, seven knolls of beautiful spruce trees and scores of stately elms. The farm fronts on Woodbury and Rockingham Avenues, enclosed by a split granite wall, and bordered by thrifty maple trees, set out by Mr. Jones many years ago. The mansion house and private stables are not conveyed."

[24.] Woodbury Avenue, originally conceived as a way to Newington, really became almost a drive to the Jones Mansion. The granite-walled frog pond, on the left as the motorist heads in town, was the turn table for the old Eastern Railroad.

[25]. Anyone who would like a fictionalized but probably quite authentic account of the dictatorial control the railroads had over New Hampshire's fortunes is urged to read Winston S. Churchill's "Coniston". Jethroe Bass is an unforgettable character.

[26]. The old railroad station off Deer Street, familiar to several generations of Portsmouth travelers, was built in 1863. One last remodeling took place in the 1950s at the behest of the Portsmouth Chamber of Commerce, and in 1960 was sold to the W. E. Dennett Tobacco Company for a sales room and warehouse. The freight offices, extensively renovated in parts, are now occupied by Goodwin Feed and Supply Co., managed by John Goodwin, after the death of his father, Chester. It has since been sold.

[27]. The abutments of this long span lie south of the bridge across the "Race Horses" from Bloody Point. In the early years of motoring, traffic used a sort of jerry-built addition to the old P&D Bridge at this point. Then in 1934 the General Sullivan Bridge was opened to traffic as a toll span. The P&D in 1873 was the first usable bridge across in 20 years. The old Piscataqua Bridge, farther to the south, became a total loss in the early 1850's, and the

owners, the Frink family, could not see further investment in trying to keep it operative. The General Sullivan was a toll bridge until November 1, 1949, when it went "free". Last man to hand over a toll ticket was the late John E. Holden of Newington, whose truckers, out of the family-owned oil depot - - now known as Atlantic Terminal, with Henry Downey of Rye as executive officer - - paid out a lot of tolls over the years. In later years, with the advent of Pease AFB, Holden, a Newington selectman and the fire chief, became known, to the news media anyway, as the "Little General," because of the manner in which Air Force officers at Pease kow-towed to him. This was due to some belief in their minds that Holden held a "hot" line to the late Senator Styles Bridges, patron saint of the military due to his position on the Senate Armed Services Committee. It's probably only a legend, but the story is told that each new field officer at Pease was assigned to the problem of eliminating Holden. At one point, a genius with an electronic and satanic twist of mind, had worked out a booby-trapped toilet seat; it was never put to the test.

[28]. These tales of Frank Jones are legion, and it's easy to remember the late James T. Whitman telling of being dandled on the great man's lap. Whitman, building inspector here shortly after World War II, was then no young man. But another woman here in Portsmouth, in her late 80s, remembers the great ale baron with no affection. She recalls when many a family — her own included — went hungry in the Creek because the family bread winner spent all his pay on the beverage Jones brewed before he arrived home.

There is a story that if the late John J. Leary's father had not carried many of these people on the books of his Islington Street grocery store they would have starved to death. "Johnny" Leary, for whom the field at South Playground is named, became mayor, and went to the State Legislature for several terms.

One story told of Jones involves his wife's church and the brewery. She belonged to the Middle Street Baptist, an edifice torn down a few years ago and rebuilt across the way, to designs by the late Maurice E. Witmer, a leading architect and at one time on the Portsmouth Planning Board. Louis L. Dow's Atlantic station is on the site, although the city probably lost a good bet in handling traffic at that point when it did not buy it from the Baptists. Jones did many things for this church, not the least of which was providing warm water, in the brewery barrels, for baptisms. The barrels — with water — would be carted through the streets, fresh from the brewery any Sunday morning that baptism, by the Baptist rite, was to take place, and it was a lot more pleasant, undoubtedly, on a cold winter Sunday than a ducking in a cold font would have been. The Middle Street Baptist Society, for years known locally as the "Welcome Church" - - because of the sign over the doors — was organized September 29, 1826, by James Day, Samuel Bowles, Samuel Cleaves, George Janvrin, John Durgin, John Oxford, Jr., E. C. Crane, John Pearson, Ezekiel Frye, William C. Parks and S. B. Lord.

They acquired the land from Robert Ham, nephew of the famed eccentric "Shephard" Ham, who had run a "church" — probably as religious as most — on the site for many years; i.e., his cronies were accustomed to meeting in his rickety stable on a Sabbath instead of in the more orthodox and prayerful establishments. "Shephard" did have some really weird habits, according to The Rambler. For instance, he kept the skins of his departed horses with him for years. He was finally prevailed upon by his brother to give up his eremitic existence, but only on the promise that he could keep some of his treasures. William Tucker, a noted carpenter, built the church, using rock blasted out of the ledge in front of the North Church for foundation stone. Jonathan Barker executed the brick work. Dedication of the old church was held on September 24, 1828, and, within two days, two-thirds of the pews had been sold for $4000. Extensive renovations were carried out in 1868 with Frank Jones a member of the committee. There were renovations in 1898, and again Jones was a benefactor, pledging $5,000 annually for three years to help meet the costs.

At that time, the church also sold the residence of Deacon Samuel Cleaves on Vaughan Street which had been willed to it. While there is little point in dwelling on a building long torn down, it must be noted that when the parish moved across the way, the old Peirce House, built in 1799, was acquired for a parish house. Moved back 50 feet from its original, cozy position near the street, it's now an integral part of the church complex, spiral staircase and all.

Another story told of Jones is that on one occasion he saw a Jones Brewery drayman whipping his horses as he passed through Market Square. Jones walked over and fired the man on the spot. The teamster went back to the brewery and turned in his wagon and animals. But when Jones' brother-in-law, Josiah Morrison, heard what had happened he rehired the man and made it stick. And still another one: Jones thought the time had come to repaint the Wentworth, a thought, under today's prices, which must give the present owners the shudders. Jones invited a local master painter to take a ride with him, and their way took them past the Wentworth.

As they passed, Jones looked at his hotel casually and asked, "How much to paint it?" The artisan could not, or would not give a price, hemming and hawing himself out of a deal. Jones later admitted to friends that any estimate the man made would have been acceptable.

[29]. Jones' estate was tied up for years in litigation brought by this woman. Judge Calvin Page, with the complete complacency of the usual estate lawyer, said, "The papers in the suit brought by Mrs. Curtis of Manchester (Mrs. Delana B. (Harrington) Curtis) have been served on me. It is nothing more than a raid on the estate by a woman who has no claim on us . . . . They then offered to sell us letters she had received from Mr. Jones, but we refused to do this. We did, however, offer to buy back from her the house at Sorrento given to her by Mr. Jones. She refused to do this, but offered to let us have the letters and the house if a settlement was made. We, of course, refused to do this . . . . We, of course, will fight the case to the limit. We don't intend to pay anything until the courts say so, and that is not at all probable." The Herald reported on December 29, 1903, that Kirk D. Peirce, a grand-nephew of the late President, Franklin Pierce, and former Attorney General Eastman "are among the counsel for Mrs. Curtis."

Mrs. Curtis was further identified as being the daughter of Captain Edwin D. Harrington, mayor of Manchester in 1859, and later the Democratic candidate for governor. The Herald said that "many years ago she was married to Samuel F. Curtis, manager of a big clothing establishment. About 15 years ago Curtis left Manchester . . . . and Mrs. Curtis divorced him . . . .

"Delana B. Curtis, who was known in her girlhood as Lena Harrington, is a handsome woman now in the prime of life . . . She is said to be not more than 45 . . . . Her father was one of the pioneers of the city . . . . In the present generation her brother, the managing owner of the opera house, divides with nobody the title of most popular citizen . . . .

"It is said that Mrs. Curtis' acquaintance with Frank Jones began when she was a girl of thirteen years, in the heyday of her father's prominence in this state . . . . It is said that Mrs. Curtis was in Washington a good deal of the time during Mr. Jones' stay there . . . .

"Her daughter, Miss Margaret Curtis, a charming young woman of 20, and her sister, Mrs. Harrington, said to inquiries that Mrs. Curtis would see no one and very positively she would not talk with reporters . . . Mrs. Curtis' friends and many who knew her only by name and repute knew that she and Mr. Jones were very friendly . . The friendship was open. Neither tried to conceal it."

[30]. The visitor cannot mistake this tombstone - - it's the tallest in the cemetery, about opposite Jones Avenue, in a cemetery road called "Rum Row." Local wags so designated it because Jones and some other makers of alcoholic beverages are interred along its sides.

21

Moving Toward the 20th Century

[1]. Way back in June 1814, the Legislature threw out the whole Portsmouth vote in an election because the voting lists contained 500 more names than those present and voting. The object was really to unseat Councilor Elijah Hall, the Revolutionary War hero, and it succeeded for the moment. Before criticizing the Legislature, however, it should be realized that it could not have done what it did if there had not been hanky-panky with the Portsmouth lists. Hall managed to scramble back into office through legislative election but it was close. Hall, who served under John Paul Jones, and lived in what we know as Stoodley's Tavern, died June 22, 1830.

[2]. Portsmouth was the first community in the state to adopt voting machines. The writer recalls being at the Rockingham Hotel where the demonstration machines were set up and watching various local politicians make deliberate attempts to manipulate the machines in a check to see how foolproof they were. The machines came into use shortly after the city manager referendum vote in 1947, when wide discrepancies were found in the Ward 2 vote, just as then Mayor Mary C. Dondero predicted to the writer that there would be. It led to a public hearing, at which the late Harry H. Foote, former mailman and then a long-time member of the House, confessed his own sins in the Ward 2 count. Ironically, The Portsmouth Herald had brought in special agents of the Honest Ballot Association to see to it that very thing did not happen. Party politics in Portsmouth have never really been the same since the adoption of the manager-council plan because the parties no longer have City Yard jobs to hand out to the faithful. The late city marshal, William J. Linchey, and former County Commissioner Ira A. Brown used to delight in regaling "carpetbaggers" with tales of election trickery here more than 50 years ago, when ballot box stuffing was ordinary practice and people in South Cemetery were more apt to vote in death than in life.

For example, they told of a Republican mayoralty caucus — back in the early 1920s — when the late Fernanco W. Hartford was in contention against some candidate sponsored by Ernest L. Guptill, local court judge and Republican political boss. The caucus was in the Probate Courtroom of the old County Court Building. The ballet box was so set up that it was partially screened from view and a man, on hands and knees, could maneuver behind it. Whenever Guptill saw that he needed a few more votes for his man, one of his henchmen would take some "spare" ballots, sneak along and drop them in the box. When the counting was done, Hartford was also done.

[3]. Old Sebastapol was the area taken in by the Meeting House Hill polling place for Ward 4. The name derived from the tough fortress of Crimean War fame because the ward was so long a stronghold of Republican Party orthodoxy. The Meeting House itself is today used by Strawbery Banke, and only a few years ago John Elwyn Stone donated $50,000 to bring about its renovation. Stone still owns property along Elwyn Road that was part of the ancestral Langdon farm.

[4]. Richard Jenness served only one term as mayor. President of the Mechanics and Traders Bank, in 1857 he was among the city's largest taxpayers with a bill of $621, quite substantial 115 years ago. Jenness made his home at 30 Pleasant Street, the building occupied by the Portsmouth Lodge of Elks. Before his mayoralty, he had two terms in the State Senate, one of them as president. He died in 1872.

[5]. Today's gross valuation is $142,644,478, but that is subject to change before the end of 1972 when the revaluation of the city, now in progress, is completed.

[6]. The city debt in 1972 is $7.8 million.

[7]. Arthur F. Brady, Jr. makes his home on Pleasant Street and is proprietor of the local Ford Agency. In November 1971, he won election as mayor by running at the top of the field of candidates for City Council; former Mayor John J. Wholey finished second. Wholey throughout his career in local politics has been a consistent battler for intellectual and social liberalism in this city.

[8]. A more kindly gentleman than Arthur I. Harriman never lived here. He was especially patient with a new-comer reporter for The Herald who asked a lot of questions about ward lines. Why he had the nickname "Buckshot" was never explained. In 1932 he wrote and published a delightful little monograph on the North Cemetery, entitled, "Praises on Tombs".

[9]. Frank Jones became a Republican in 1896 after attending the Democratic Convention and hearing William Jennings Bryan make his famous "Cross of Gold" speech. He was quoted on his return as saying, "My right hand shall wither before I cast a ballot for Bryan and the other nominees of the Chicago convention". He

meant it. Throughout the campaign he was bitter in his attacks on Bryan, and, just before the election, spent many dollars illuminating the Rockingham for a Republican victory rally. In 1900 he supported McKinley's bid for re-election.

[10]. Probably a misnomer in a day when women wear pantyhose. However, years ago the back fence line along the west side of Middle Street, from Cass Street south, was the ward bound. Twenty-five years ago the writer was told by a member of the House, Representative John J. Leary, "You can't expect those people to vote in Ward 3". Changes in the lines were made then (1947), not affecting the "Bulge" and again in 1959. Because of the Supreme Court's mandate of "one-man, one-vote" the wards have been again redistricted, and through the spring of 1972 a re-registration of voters was held. This is a fairly common occurrence because the military influence is strong in the ever-changing population, and the checklists soon go out of date.

[11]. This was the first major local effort to break away from the old school of thought in education. Major Samuel Hale's Latin Grammar School, preceded by Dr. Samuel Langdon's, had set the pattern through much of the 18th Century, and was strictly "classical" in curriculum. Hale's efforts had been continued by men such as the father of Salmon P. Chase (Abraham Lincoln's Secretary of the Treasury). Chase ended his career here in 1789. In 1815, the town decided to switch to a district school system, with the boys and girls on equal footing. Then, in 1818, $1,000 was voted to put the schools on the Lancasterian Plan.

From the pages of The Portsmouth Journal comes a bit of information as to the criteria involved in eligibility for the Lancasterian system: "Notice is hereby given to the inhabitants of this town that boys of the age of seven years old and upwards may be admitted into the Lancasterian School from all parts of the town except Christian Shore District, provided that they are sent during the present months and that the rule established is when found to be duly qualified they are admitted from the Lancasterian School into the school taught by Mr. Bicknell. By order of the Selectman, Thomas P. Drown, Sectetary."

About seven years after the Lancasterian School was launched, a typical boating tragedy happened. On Wednesday, June 22, 1825, a small craft was coming in from the Isles of Shoals when it ran into a flaw in the wind which caused it to upset and founder immediately. Among the victims was Edwin B. Stevens, principal of the Lancasterian School; Horace B. Morse, the instructor of the Latin

School at the academy; Samuel Gardner; John Veazey; a lad named Moses Long; and two sons of attorney Samuel Cushman, Esquire (John S. in his 12th year and George in his 11th).

"The deaths of Messers Steevens and Morse," The Journal said, "has cast gloom over the town which will not soon be dissipated. They were young men of uncommon worth and of fine talents, cultivated minds and agreeable manners. From their employment as instructors, they were known to most of the families in town. Wherever known they were respected and beloved. It will be difficult to supply the place of either of them". A later news item reported that a Mr. Magoun had been chosen to succeed Steevens in the Lancasterian School.

This was a system in which there was one master who instructed an able student in the art of teaching and then allowed him to administer to a small group of his fellows. At this time the hours for school attendance, from April 1 to October 1, were 8 a.m. to noon, 2 p.m. to 6; October 1 to April 1, 9 a.m. to noon, 2 p.m. to sunset.

[12]. In 1886, the Board of Instruction appointed Charles H. Morse as the first superintendent of schools under a state law of 1885. Five years later came the law ordering free textbooks in the schools. In 1895, the superintendent was instructed to establish an experimental kindergarten at the Haven School. Classes for this grade have been maintained ever since, despite a close call in 1972.

Other events for the Portsmouth School Department include:

Introduction of drawing here in 1889; opening of a Central School Office in 1900 in the old State Street School building. This stood next east of the former St. John's Rectory, 214 State Street, with a sign that says Yankee Clipper. The old school housed the Salvation Army for a number of years.

The present parochial school opened in 1906. The first one began in 1868 at 50 State Street.

Miss A. C. Morgan opened her private school at the corner of Rockland Street and Miller Avenue in September 1874.

In October 1874, the Spalding School on Cambridge (Bartlett) Street opened; also in 1874 the study of vocal music was introduced in the local schools.

Cabot Street School was opened in 1860 on the site of the old brick school house. For many years in this century this fine old structure sheltered St. Nicholas Greek Orthodox Church.

In 1808 the Portsmouth Female Asylum was incorporated and helped bring about in May, 1844, the teaching of sewing in the

273

Portsmouth school system, and then, in 1856 society funds were devoted to paying the salary of a sewing teacher in ten public schools.

[13]. Twice within recent years, the more recently in the fall of 1971, a proposal to repeal the Police Commission Law has been on the local ballot. Agitation was particularly bitter several years ago when two Democrats, the late John L. Loughlin and Henry Gerber, were on the board. Presently the members are J. Paul Griffin, a contractor, who has served for 25 years; George B. Ward, proprietor of J. Verne Wood Funeral Home and a leading figure in New Hampshire Masonic circles; and George Amergian, the lone Democrat, proprietor of Pic 'n Pay Supermarket. Most of the criticism directed at the commission derives from the fact that its members are appointed by Governor and Council and that it does not have to account for its appropriations to the City Council.

[14]. Edward Hart was the son of the Colonel John Hart who commanded one of the New Hampshire regiments at Lake Champlain in 1758, He was subsequently court-martialed on charges of failing to cut off an expedition of French and Indians. The Rambler seems to feel that most of the odium for this should be attached to Colonel John Goff who was the senior officer. Until the court proceedings can be studied in the Public Record Office, London, the rights and wrongs will have to wait. Edward Hart built the Pickering House on Vaughan Street, since removed. When it was put up, reeds in the North Mill Pond stood nearly as high as a man's head. Hart was a baker by trade and had his shop, as so often the custom, in his house. From here he ran a delivery route for his products.

At one time, Hart was a deputy sheriff, and, as the law then required, was personally liable for any persons thrown into jail for debt. One man who would not meet his obligations was a General Nathaniel Peabody of Exeter. Hart served a writ on him. "Money, jail, or bail", was the rule in such cases, but Peabody had neither money nor a way of raising bail. He asked that he be jailed in Exeter as that would be more convenient and the kindly Hart agreed. On the way to the Exeter jail, the wily Peabody talked Hart out of making the trip, agreeing to surrender himself the next day. The next part seems a little far-fetched, but it's The Rambler's story so it is accepted. Anyway, when Hart went for Peabody he refused to give himself up or to come out of his house, so Hart was liable for the debt. His bondsmen, Judge John Pickering and Dr. William Cutter, paid the debt, but promptly collected against Hart, Pickering taking the house and Cutter some land adjacent to the North Cemetery.

[15]. City Marshal Stanton G. Remick, who succeeded

City Marshal Martin O. Betz, is a career police officer. He is a descendant of the ancient Remick family, and first went on the police force in 1941, moving through the ranks until he attained his present post in September 1964. One of the first Remick (Remark) houses in the city was on Islington Street where Samuel Kline's furniture store now stands. In fact, it was removed in 1955 to make room for that building.

On September 17, 1890, it was the scene of a tragedy when a distraught father shot his three daughters to death before taking his own life. Frederick H. J. Hein, a native of Germany, was a cooper for the Eldredge Brewing Company, and apparently had an entangled relationship with his wife who walked out on him. She took up a liaison with a man named Charles W. Taylor, local stove dealer. Years ago the late Frederick W. Harrington told the writer of knowing the Hein girls and of viewing their dead bodies after the shootings.

Hein, it would seem, was resolved to do a thorough job of the whole thing. Before killing his daughters, he paid a visit to Taylor, shot him and left him for dead. Reports flooded to the Police Station, then under Jefferson Hall in Market Square, and Dr. Samuel G. Whittier, the coroner, assumed control of the case almost before the police could move. It took no great detective reasoning to know that Hein was responsible, although no one yet knew to what extent. And, in Portsmouth, where mobs have always been popular, the man was soon the quarry in a search.

Going to his house, the mob found one daughter dead on the walk outside the building, another was found dying inside, and a third, also dying, was found outside. A typical Portsmouth mob, ready to execute its own brand of justice, had lynching in mind, but Hein had anticipated such thoughts. His body was found in a bedroom.

Dr. Whittier impaneled George E. Hodgdon, a carpenter; Richard H. Beacham, a liveryman; and Dr. H. F. Clark as a coroner's jury. The trio had little difficulty in reaching a verdict. As for Taylor, he recovered, left town, and went to Chicago where he met and married the widow Hein.

For the superstitious reader it might be pointed out that Taylor had once lived in a house at the Creek in which had lived James Palmer, the Portsmouth man who was hanged in 1889 for murdering Henry Whitehouse on the ole Portsmouth Bridge, probably the last local man to pay such a price for bumping off a buddy — in New Hampshire anyway.

Or it may be that James Palmer did not see Whitehouse as a

"Buddy". Although they had worked together at the Bow Street plant of the Portsmouth Electric Light Company they were probably not particularly friendly. Whitehouse was the younger man, the underling, and was instrumental in bringing about Palmer's final undoing, when a search for stolen tools led to Palmer's house.

That was early in 1888, and on May 28 of that year, two men, Charles H. Kent and Albert H. Hammond, walking on the Portsmouth Bridge to work saw something that was to change their whole day. Below them, at the water's edge, was a body, and it did not take a medical degree to tell the pair that murder had been done. It took the authorities little time to establish identity of the dead man. He was Henry Whitehouse, about 22, an employee of the power company who was well-known to be courting a girl on the Kittery side of the river. It looked to be the work of a madman, and yet, before the morning was out, the police had under arrest the man who was to hang for the crime, James Palmer.

Coroner Samuel C. Whittier impaneled a jury consisting of Jerome C. Butler, John Knowlton and C. Dwight Hanscom. These worthies were helped considerably in reaching a finding against Palmer when Melvin Staples testified to finding a hammer, unique to the power plant, only 60 feet from the body. Actually it was with little threads like that, that the prosecution wove the circumstantial case against Palmer into a hangman's halter. Nothing apparently could have bothered Palmer less. From the day of his arrest until the foreman of the trial jury announced the guilty finding, Palmer was nothing if not care free. He took the stand in his trial as his own best witness, and did a fairly adequate job in explaining many things, but he could not beat off the grim attack his nemesis, County Solicitor Samuel W. Emery, kept throwing at him. Palmer could never have claimed his counsel was incompetent. He had as good as they come, Calvin Page and General Gilman Marston. They tried every trick in the book, but there was simply too much on the other side.

Witness after witness kept digging Palmer's hole deeper. Fred S. Palmer, his former boss at the power plant, but no relation, was one; Dennis Reagan, the coal passer, was another; Freeman H. Peverly, deputy marshal; Daniel J. Hurley, another deputy; Professor Edwin R. Angell, a chemist, was another thread in the State's skein of guilt. All told, they did the deadly task assigned to them: They convinced a jury of Palmer's guilt.

On May 1, 1890, Sheriff E. D. Coffin went to Concord and carried out the macabre duty that is still vested in New Hampshire's county sheriffs — taking a man's life. All Palmer asked of him was that he do it "as quickly as you can".

[16]. Andrew J. Beck was a carriagemaker by trade with a shop at 82 State Street and his home on Rogers Street. His assistants and police officers in the first year as a city were Phineas J. Goodrich, Joseph G. Todd, Thomas S. Gammon, Albert Hayes and John Shaw.

[17]. One man, an incumbent, expressed the hope to incoming Mayor Mary C. Dondero — this was in 1945 — that there would be "something on the tree" for him at the City Hall Christmas Party. There was not. The mayor, just elected with a Democratic Council, had other ideas in mind.

[18]. Jefferson C. Rowe undoubtedly was one of the most colorful of all the men who have headed Portsmouth's police. Before he took the marshalship, he had lost an arm in an Eastern Railroad wreck at Revere in 1871. When he finally yielded his badge, he drove hansom cabs for a while and went to the Navy Yard as captain of the watch. Retiring as the Yard's chief of police in 1921, he died in 1935 at the age of 92.

[19]. John E. Dimick was at one time wharf agent for the B & M.

[20]. Colonel Simon Marston was born here February 24, 1832, and died May 5, 1920. Educated in the public schools and at Dartmouth (Class of 1853), he was, at the time of his death, the oldest New England alumnus of the institution. Marston managed to get some adventurous living into his long life, and one of his favorite anecdotes related to a Civil War experience, when as a major and paymaster, he was charged with getting $600,000 in cash from St. Louis, Missouri to Santa Fe, New Mexico to meet the payrolls. Earlier he had been at Vicksburg when that shell-torn, starved city surrendered.

"October 1, 1864, he was ordered to St. Louis to receive $600,000 and to take it at the first safe opportunity to Santa Fe. He left St. Louis during the last days of November and succeeded in getting the money safely to its destination on December 17". That was Apache country in those days.

Marston's first war service was with Company G in the 10th NHVR, and ended with his discharge at Santa Fe in 1866. Returning to civilian life, he followed the profession of civil engineer and in the 1880s was responsible for construction of the New Castle breakwater.

[21]. Edwin B. Prime at one time served as city treasurer. He was one of the city officials in 1903 who refused to yield his books for audit until compelled by the court. Prime was the father of Herbert O. Prime who was associated in the coal business

with Charles W. Gray, and they were successors to E. F. Sise Company, the first large-scale importer of coal. Gray and Prime were in turn bought out by Consolidation Coal Company, and Gray was the manager of the coal pockets where Granite State Minerals, Inc., now bunkers highway salt at the foot of Market Street.

For years, Gray and Prime displayed ship models and half-models in their offices, which are now one of the feature attractions at the Portsmouth Athenaeum, of which one of C. W. Gray's sons, Dr. Frederick S. Gray, is a proprietor and director. Another son, Charles W. Gray, is a real estate man with his home and office on Wentworth Road, Rye.

[22]. Sherman Newton, operator of the Kearsarge Hotel, was also involved in the fish business with his father Elvin Newton. The late city councilman, Sherman "Mike" Newton, was his son and followed him in ownership of the Kearsarge, a business now under the management of Sherman Newton, Jr., who makes his home in Rye. "Mike" Newton was a member of one of Portsmouth's more active youth groups, the Wenehasa Club, which, in the days before Portsmouth High sponsored basketball teams, competed against schools around the state. The club name incorporated the first two letters in the surnames of Burleigh Wendell, Newton, John Hassett and Philip F. Sanderson. All of them are deceased as is their coach, Heinie Cragin. Theodore R. Butler, former mayor and postmaster, is one of the last survivors of these ball clubs. Wenehasa also staged many social affairs.

"Mike" Newton's father, Sherman T., was born at the Isles of Shoals on September 5, 1865, coming to Portsmouth at the age of eight. The father and son, under the firm name of E. Newton & Company developed a highly successful fishing business, and at one time had 28 vessels in their employ. These were unloaded at the Newton warehouse on Commercial Wharf (now vanished under Prescott Park). In 1912, the warehouse was destroyed by fire and the elder Newton decided to retire because the son had to devote so much time to the Hotel Kearsarge.

[23. Ira C. Seymour was a blacksmith by trade. Born in 1842, he died February 20, 1920.

[24]. Frank L. Marks died in 1899, age 60. A native of Penebscot, Marks came here in 1863. For two years he was a police officer, 1863-65, quitting the force to go to work on the Navy Yard as a ships carpenter. This line of work he followed for some years before going on the road as a salesman for a Cambridge firm. The latter part of his life he was clerk to Street Commissioner Joseph Hett.

[25]. Appointed to the new force were E. H. Marden, Michael Hurley (late city marshal), Michael Kelley, Frank West, Willie Franklin Weeks, William N. Hodgdon, Jacob S. Burns, Lamont Hilton, James F. Shannon, William H. Seymour, Henry B. Holbrook, William H. Anderson, James A. McCaffery, Clement March Waterhouse, Charles Quinn, George E. Robinson and Dennis Murphy. Of these, five were Democrats — Hurley, Kelley, Murphy, Seymour and Holbrook. Not all of the men named, of course, were regulars; there were only five of those, among them Hurley and Kelley.

"Big Mike" Kelley was the father of two Portsmouth officers of a later day, the late Inspector Dennis Kelley and the late Patrolman Joseph Kelley; the latter had wide fame with summer visitors as the guardian angel of Market Square. He also had considerable renown for his ability to acquire cigars. Theirs was a different day of police work; when, informed of some misdoing in the North End, Denny Kelley, for example, would go straight to the house of the wrongdoer and matters would soon be ironed out. It was "Big Mike" who used to give erring drunks "two churses: Ayther ye goes home, me bhoy, ye comes along with me".

[26]. Calvin Page, an attorney, was one of the men closest to Frank Jones. His daughter married John Henry Bartlett, who was governor of New Hampshire in 1918. Bartlett, it is said, was once in Florida and hired a man to drive his car to Portsmouth while he came by train. His instructions were simple: "Follow U. S. Route 1 until you get to Portsmouth, turn right at the second traffic light, and then into the first driveway on the left". Such would not work today for several reasons, the major one being that where Bartlett's house stood is a parking lot owned by the Masons. Page's grandson, Calvin Page Bartlett, today is chairman of the board of the Portsmouth Trust Company, Market Square, founded in 1871. Jarvis Stokes is president. Calvin Page, incidentally, has always been regarded as one of the authors of The Chronicles of Portsmouth, an allegorical satire on political life here right after World War I. His co-author, as indicated elsewhere, was the late True L. Norris, editor of The Portsmouth Times. The late John Frary, then a linotype operator at The Times, used to tell of hearing the two men laughing and chortling as they composed some new lampoon of the political dignitaries of the day.

[27]. Charles P. Berry was twice mayor of Portsmouth and another of Frank Jones' close henchmen. Berry was born in Lynn in 1840, quit school at an early age to help support a fatherless family, and came to Portsmouth in 1885 to be associated with Frank

Jones, Charles A. Sinclair and Charles H. Mendum in the shoe company. He had one son, Frank Jones Berry.

Having sons of men he had befriended named for him was not unusual for Frank Jones. For example, although known throughout his life as Justin Downing Hartford, the publisher of The Herald for 25 years (1938-63), really was on the city clerk's records as Frank Jones Hartford. This fact he discovered when he applied for a birth certificate for identification on a planned trip out of the country. Frank Jones had put up the money ($2,000) that Hartford's father, Fernando W. Hartford, needed to buy The Penny Post, and change it into The Portsmouth Herald. After Jones' death, the Hartfords simply changed their son's given name to Justin, honoring Justin V. Hanscom, Jones' administrator, and the Downing was Mrs. Hartford's maiden name. Another who carries the Frank Jones label is Frank Jones Massey who operated the George B. French store for some years before selling the business to George H. Kimball.

[28]. Chief Justice Charles Doe, and that really was his name, was one of New Hampshire's most respected jurists. Opinions written by Judge Doe are still cited in courts across the country. However, some of these rulings displeased too many people for him to gain the seat on the U. S. Supreme Court that might have made his name ring with that of Brandeis or Warren. He was considered for it, but the appointment was blocked by Doe's enemies. He even incurred displeasure because he once said good morning to a man being tried before him for murder, calling the accused, "Mr. Sawtelle". This courtesy did not stop Doe from sentencing the man to death, and on Christmas Day, at that. Sawtelle died before the hangman got him.

[29]. Walter S. Gray was born December 26, 1843. At the age of 14, he enlisted in the Navy, and was on board the sloop USS Cumberland when she foundered in 1862. Discharged from the Navy, he enlisted in Company G, 10th NHVR, under George W. Towle. After the war he worked as a brick mason at the Navy Yard for 10 years; and then went to work for C. E. Boynton in his brewery. He left that business to become deputy city marshal in 1895.

[30]. "Cappy" Stewart achieved a fame of his own in the Portsmouth of 70 years ago, and his name comes down through the years for his association with Marcy Street when it was Water Street, notorious everywhere for loose women and booze joints. The writer remembers coming to Portsmouth to a "Y" conference in the fall of 1930, and the host took his guests on a drive along what is now Marcy Street, trying to tell what the area had once been.

Sixteen-year olds were not then as well informed as they are today, so most of it went right over the heads of his audience. But the effort is still appreciated. Stewart, in his later, more legitimate years, went into the antique business, and some valuable Portsmouth materials were acquired from him by the late Garland W. Patch, Sr.

[31]. The County Jail, now the Portsmouth Police Station, was opened for business in May 1892, replacing the old jail on Islington Street. During World War II, the county gave up its use of the building and in 1950 it was acquired by the city for a police station, a function it is still serving. Credit for obtaining these improved quarters over those occupied in the rear of City Hall, must go to City Marshal William J. Linchey, now deceased, who worked persistently in his four-year tenure to improve the lot of the Portsmouth Police Department. Linchey was brought in "from the outside" in 1949 to head the police when City Marshal Leonard H. Hewitt retired. Hewitt was a tough-minded man, obsessed with the idea that the old days and ways would still work. "Uncle Leonard", as newsmen irreverently called him, had served in the regular Army, was stationed at the Harbor Forts in World War I, as was former Governor Charles M. Dale. That the present police station is no longer adequate is an oft-voiced complaint and will have to be left to future years for resolution.

[32]. Work was begun on the County Courthouse, State Street, in 1891. When opened for the October term, 1892, it replaced the Courthouse on Court Street which was built in 1836 on the lot now occupied by the Portsmouth Fire Station. Before being moved to a site facing Parrott Avenue, the old structure was used for an armory by Company B, 2nd Regiment, New Hampshire National Guard, and for a practice hall for the Portsmouth City Band.

In 1919, the old Courthouse was moved southerly and turned to face the other way. Its last service to the community was as headquarters for the Emerson Hovey Post, Veterans of Foreign Wars. Fire destroyed it on May 1, 1953.

[33]. Samuel W. Emery was born here on March 30, 1863; attended the public schools; studied law with Walter C. Harriman and was admitted to the bar, April 24, 1884. A Republican, he was city solicitor, 1885-90; county solicitor, 1887-91; and became judge of the Police Court on December 1, 1894.

Just before Emery had gone on the bench, on April 19, 1894, had come the death of Marcellus Bufford, who had served a 30-year span as associate justice. Bufford was born November 4, 1817, on Summer Street, in a house that had been built by his father, Henry, in 1806. He graduated from Portsmouth High at 15 and worked in Henry B. Brewster's printing office until it failed. Then he left town for a few years, returning when he reached his majority. For a while he worked with his father in the latter's sign and carriage painting business at 2 Chestnut Street. He was there when he first went to the Legislature in 1849; in 1856, he served in the State Senate; and in 1860 went on the Board of Aldermen. During the 1850s, he served as chief engineer (fire chief) in the Fire Department, not then a full-time job, finally becoming city clerk in 1862, a post he held until 1874. His service with the court started in 1863 and lasted until 1893.

[34]. Ernest L. Guptill was born in Berwick, March 9, 1867, the son of Albert W. Guptill. Reading The Herald's obituary, it's hard to realize that this man and Fernando W. Hartford, according to Hartford's son, J. D. Hartford, and others, were mortal political enemies. However, J. D. Hartford used to tell of a reconciliation between the two men in "Gup's" late years. Guptill came to Portsmouth in 1888, after being admitted to the Maine bar, following study in a Somersworth law office. The city solicitorship fell to him in 1890 and he held it until 1894, returning again to the office in 1903-04. He went to the House, served as county solicitor for three terms. When the District Court was abolished in 1916, he was named judge of the new Municipal Court. He died April 13, 1931.

[35]. The Associated Mechanics and Manufacturers Association began an Apprentices Library in 1823 with gifts of books and money from local persons. On August 1, 1865, the Association opened a reading room for members and apprentices at the corner of State and Pleasant Streets. In 1868, the Association went out of existence, giving its books, with one small "hooker" to the Portsmouth Public Library. The condition set was that the Association could, even though defunct, name two trustees to the Public Library's board. By just what alchemy this responsibility fell on the shoulders of E. Curtis Matthews, former president of the Piscataqua Savings Bank, is still baffling. It was ended by City Manager Robert Violette.

[36]. One of the great Portsmouth myths for years has been the belief that the immortal architect Charles Bulfinch provided the plans for the Portsmouth Academy, a structure which has housed the Portsmouth Public Library since 1896. Nothing could be further from the truth. In recent years, it has been established that the design was actually by a man named James Nutter, although the Library persists in hanging an unsightly, fast-deteriorating sign from its premises that perpetuates the legend about Bulfinch.

Nutter was a highly skilled craftsman, or master builder. Teaming with another man, he is credited with finishing the interior of St. John's Church, a labor that probably brought much attention to him when the academy trustees were talking about their project. He also did much of the work on the Exchange Buildings on Pleasant Street. For part of his career he was in the direct employ of James Sheafe. Early in manhood, he became a convert to Methodism and practiced that faith, as it was then interpreted, strictly to the letter, even turning down work if he did not approve of the character or philosophy of a prospective employer.

The academy was proposed about 1806, and was intended entirely as a profit-making institution, its founders wanting to take advantage of the ever-increasing demand for better educational facilities. Funds to build it were raised by assessments on the stockholders as in any other business enterprise. Daniel Webster was on its board of trustees from 1810 to 1816. It operated as a private school until 1868 when the city took the building over and brought it into the public school system. However, the city did not buy the building until 1906, after the Library had occupied it for 10 years on a lease. The city paid $9,875.

[37]. Robert E. Rich died February 25, 1908, at 62. Rich had a brilliant record as a soldier in the Civil War, serving with the 19th Massachusetts. A native of Newburyport, he enlisted in a militia company for Civil War service. Shortly after he made sergeant, he was wounded at South Mountain, a musket ball striking him in the center of the knee. He laid on the field for a day, between the lines, and at one time was in Confederate hands. Nine days after the wound, he was hospitalized, and a month later the leg was amputated above the knee. By strange coincidence, on another battlefield, his older brother Henry was also wounded in the left knee, and suffered the same kind of amputation. Their father died of war injuries in their Newburyport home.

[38]. Hannah Fernald was born October 23, 1875. She was a graduate of the Pratt Library Institute and was employed in Buffalo before coming to Portsmouth where she worked in the Public Library for 38 years, retiring as librarian in the early 1950s. She died in 1967.

[39]. Dorothy M. Vaughan is a native of Concord, but graduated from Portsmouth High in 1920. Her life-long interest has been Portsmouth, its history and the genealogies of the founding families. As suggested in the preface, no one person is better qualified to write a history of Portsmouth, but no one person is any

busier, so she has never done it. Dorothy Vaughan provided the spark, leadership, or what you will, that touched off the phenomena we call Strawbery Banke, which entertained 34,000 patrons in 1971, and will exceed that number in 1972.

[40]. Benedict House adjoins the Public Library, and, thanks to a passage created a few years ago, is attached to it. This house was the home, for more than 20 years, of Captain Robert Lefavour, commander of the Rockingham Guards, a crack local military unit.

[41]. The Reverend James DeNormandie was ordained and installed over the South Church October 1, 1862. He resigned in 1883, and on October 15, 1884, the Reverend Alfred Gooding was installed. Dr. Gooding was a native of Brookline, Massachusetts, born May 10, 1856; he graduated from Harvard in 1877, and came here from Brunswick, Maine, his first pastorate, in 1884. When he was installed, he became the eighth minister to preside over the parish since 1714. He preached his farewell sermon, becoming pastor emeritus, on December 25, 1921. For 43 years, he served on the Board of Instruction; was president of the Portsmouth Historical Society; and gave the address on the city's tercentenary in 1923 at the Portsmouth Theater. He died October 17, 1934.

[42]. In the Goodwin House, the governor's daughter Susie was married in October 1867 to Lieutenant George Dewey, USN. Dewey was to win lasting fame as the victor over the Spanish fleet at Manila Bay in the Spanish-American War. Their son, who died in Chicago in February 1963, was not interested in preservation of the house. His mother, Susan Goodwin Dewey, died in 1872, at the age of 28.

[43]. At that time Merrill H. Smith was local manager, but he now works out of store headquarters in Haverhill.

[44]. Dr. Haven died March 3, 1806, and his wife the next day. They were buried under the altar of the church. Under terms of the wills of descendants of Dr. Haven, it was provided that, when the last member of the family died, the home was to be taken down, and the grounds, along with the Parry and Hatch estates on either side, were to be purchased and given to the city, for a tract to be known as Haven Park. Dr. Haven was settled with the South Parish — Meeting House Hill — on May 6, 1752. He was born in Framingham, Massachusetts, August 4, 1727, graduating from Harvard in 1749. His doctorate of divinity was conferred on him by the University of Edinburgh in 1770. On land next door, later the site of the Parry House, Dr. Haven's patriotic zeal led him to the

manufacture of salt petre for gunpowder during the Revolution. The Rambler quotes from an agreement between Dr. Haven and two men named Melcher and Lang arranging for operation of the works. Dr. Haven's product passed an inspection in 1776 conducted by Drs. Hall Jackson and Joshua Brackett. Dr. Haven's son, Nathaniel, Sr., and later grandson, Nathaniel, Jr., lived in the house after his death.

[45]. The presence of Dr. Haven and of Dr. Langdon on this street leading to the South Mill Dam for so many years led to it being called Divinity Street before the present name of Pleasant Street was given in 1778.

[46]. The Edward Parry who lived in this house was not the Parry who had the tea troubles during the Revolution. This was learned some years ago by Miss Dorothy M. Vaughan in conversation with a descendant. What connection there was between the two men, if any, is not yet known. This second Parry had a store on Market Street where Coleman Pearson's clothing store was, a building that he had erected, according to an inscription on a stone let into the brick work, after the fire of 1802. Parry maintained an elegant garden and grounds all the way to the banks of the Mill Pond. Here, so the map of 1813 shows, Parry erected a fortification and called it Fort Anglesey, and fired its "guns" on the Fourth of July. His reasons for such a construction project were probably much the same as those of English gentlemen of the time who put up buildings called "follies". Parry's house stood at the corner of Edward and Pleasant Streets, across the way from the home of Mrs. William G. Wendell. Parry eventually left Portsmouth and died in Philadelphia. The house was moved from its site in 1900 to what is now the municipal parking lot. It was later torn down.

[47]. Fitz-John Porter was born in a house that once stood in the park where his own statue is today. That was in 1822. In 1862, he was a major general of volunteers and was court-martialled for misconduct. Dismissed from the Army, Porter fought for reinstatement and finally won. He retired in 1886, and died May 21, 1901, leaving another memorial to himself in the name of Porter Street. That thoroughfare has born several names. From Middle to Fleet it was called Fetter Lane, and, when opened up, the stretch from Fleet to Pleasant was called Pond Lane. In 1838, the selectmen renamed the whole length Warren Street in honor of Dr. Joseph Warren who fell at Bunker Hill. Then after Porter's death, it took his name, but somehow we feel that Warren was the man more worthy of honoring. Apparently, even in Portsmouth there are mixed sentiments on Fitz-John Porter. The Portsmouth Times of September

8, 1904, lets a present-day world know a little of the controversy that surrounded the unveiling of the statue. "At the break of day this morning, the famous general, as he sits there in Haven Park, upon his famous charger unmoved and without a word to say regarding his feelings toward the committee who had the dedication exercise in charge, was allowed to view his pleasant surroundings. The flag, which had draped his noble head for some weeks — and which, by the way, was preceded by a meal bag — was removed sometime during the dark hours of last night". If we are to read between the lines, it would seem that we are to conclude that the committee in charge of the Porter affair was a little bit out in its arrangements. It waited to hear if the President was coming, or General Miles or Admiral Dewey, and ultimately it was stuck trying to find anyone it could hire for the job. Public indignation made the committee take the meal bag off the statue's head and put an American flag in its place, but still the committee dillyed and dallyed. The Times said, "Thus for two months it remained a disgrace to the City of Portsmouth, a disgrace to the memory of the man who gave it, and a disgrace to the widow of General Porter and her family".

[48]. With Puddle Dock filled in, it is hard to realize that its headwater ran right up to the back grounds of the Langdon and Thayer Houses, which made it so close to the South Mill Pond that it created a pennisula or neck of land. Filling of Puddle Dock, once with soundings deep enough to accommodate ocean-going vessels, started when people began using it for a dump. Ultimately, the area, dock webbing and all, was covered in and the city created Newton Avenue. Strawbery Banke has plans to excavate the area, not to its original depths, thus giving some idea of what Puddle Dock originally was. Some archeological digging has been carried out with many artifacts recovered. A petition by Elvin Newton to create a street the length of Puddle Dock was granted May 11, 1903. Mayor George D. Marcy set up a committee to assess damages.

[49]. Thatcher Emery was one of Portsmouth's most gifted mechanics. It was he who made the first piano ever built here.

[50]. Proposals for a mall at South Mill Pond are still made. One of the more recent was put forward by then Mayor Robert A. Shaines (1960-61), and came at a time when stench from the pond was attracting much unfavorable attention.

[51]. Aldermen Plumer D. Norton and George A. Perkins teamed with Mayor Sise in trying to do something about the South Mill Pond.

[52]. Major David Urch was an owner of the New

Castle Toll Bridge. At the Toll House (right at the abutment of the first bridge) he had an aquarium which attracted people from miles around. The Major was also something of an inventor, designing and building, among other things a bicycle on which he rode out to the Isles of Shoals. One of these Urch-type water bicycles was found a dozen years ago and restored by George Burke who was photographed riding around on it in the quieter waters of the harbor.

One of Urch's riding companions was C. A. Hazlett who wrote an article on his experiences for the July and August issues of "The Wheelman" in 1883. On one of his expeditions, Hazlett, who did much research in local history, had both Major Urch and his sister for companions on a water tour around New Castle. Urch was a native of Newport, Wales, and came here at the age of four. The family soon moved on to Chicago and it was there that Urch went to school. He saw service with an Illinois regiment in the Civil War, and, after leaving the Army, he came to Fort Constitution, then still active, as a civilian worker. From there he went to New London, returned and again went to work at the Fort. In 1876, he took over management of the toll bridges to New Castle, and operated his aquarium both as a hobby and a source of income. The aquarium was stocked with all native fish, and the Major trained seals for exhibitions. A newspaper item in 1880 records that more than a thousand visited the aquarium on one summer day.

In September, 1876, the bridges were posted, "This Bridge is dangerous and will be closed until funds can be raised for repairs".

[53]. Thomas E. Call was born October 2, 1846, and spent his active business life in lumber retailing, first with his father and brother, Richard T., while another brother, Howe, was engaged in practice as a counsellor at law. Thomas Call died August 28, 1918.

[54]. James A. Sanborn lived at 41 South Street, and was described as a mining prospector. He died in 1913 at 72.

[55]. Christopher Smart was the grandson of Richard D. Smart, captain of the first privateer to leave Portsmouth in the War of 1812 — the Nancy. With the money he made from that prize, Richard Smart built the house which is occupied today by his great-grandson, at 64 Mt. Vernon Street. Richard's wife was French, a Mary LaRose, and he was lost at sea while a young man, but his son George J. Smart, was born in the "Nancy House", and George's son, Christopher, was born there, George Smart was a stone mason by trade, a life-long Democrat, and 36 years sexton of the Unitarian Church.

Christopher was the youngest and started out in life working for Abraham Q. Wendell, moving later to John H. Bailey's. Finally he went in business for himself, starting with a cart and then opening up a store at 24½ Pleasant Street as manager for the Chicago Meat Company. About 1912, he was a clerk at Thomas Loughlin & Sons. He died in 1932. Christopher was the father of the well known former Portsmouth Police Officer Roland Smart, who was the third generation of Smarts to be born in the house built by the Nancy. After ex-Patrolman Smart retired, he went to work for the First National Bank, handling its parking lot. He has since retired from that post, and now devotes his time to the care of the "Nancy House". Remarking on his great-grandfather's feat only the other day, Smart said, "I guess that makes me a native almost, doesn't it"?

[56]. Freeman Pearson and his son, John N., ran a confectioner business on State Street. He died in 1921.

[57]. Langdon M. Perkins, a carpenter by trade, was born here April 25, 1834, but left town for a number of years, working in New Orleans and Buffalo. For a while he was in business with Joseph Whidden, then he bought out John Stokell. His health failed, and he went south and then later to Vermont. Returning to Portsmouth five years later, he organized, with his brother George, an effort to gain control of the city's ice business. Another of his ventures was the purchase of Joseph Parry's bakery, and moving it from Fleet to Daniel Street. In his latter years he returned to carpentering and died October 3, 1917.

[58]. Years ago the county commissioners had much more power in relation to roads than they do today. They did the work of laying out roads and so forth, now the job of the State Public Works and Highway Departments. Agitation over this particular strip of road went back almost 20 years to when W. H. Y. Hackett petitioned for such a way to be built to afford readier access to the newly laid out Langdon Park.

[59]. Marginal Road was renamed Parrott Avenue in honor of Rear Admiral Enoch G. Parrott who invented the famed Parrott rifle, a groove-barreled artillery piece used in the Civil War. The Parrott families made their homes in the double house owned by Dr. Maurice Dinnerman and Irving Bratter, 132 and 134 middle Street. Dr. Dinnerman has the western half with his offices on the lower floor and apartments upstairs. In World War I days, this part was occupied by a Dr. Edward Cowles for a mental home.

[60]. Mark H. Wentworth owned the property now Dr. Thayer's. Born here in 1813, he was the son of the man, Ebenezer Wentworth, whose house is now the Mark H. Wentworth Home, 346 Pleasant Street, one of the city's finest and most useful institutions.

Mark H. Wentworth married twice, each time to a daughter of William Jones. In 1843, he migrated to Cincinnati but returned in 1855 after piling up a fortune in the dry goods business.

On his return he associated himself with his father-in-law and brothers-in-law in William Jones & Son. He particularly distinguished himself in representing the shipping industry in the forwarding of suits before the Alabama Claims Commission. Wentworth died in 1902. His daughter, Susan, lived on for years, becoming, according to Dorothy M. Vaughan, a fine source of local genealogical and historical lore.

[61]. Dr. Charles Thayer is a surgeon with extensive practice and has his consulting rooms on the premises.

[62]. A major fund raising campaign was staged throughout the Seacoast, taking in all communities served by the hospital.

[63]. Harriet Kimball literally was a slave to what she conceived to be her duty. While she finally went off the Board of Trustees, her interest in the hospital ended only with her death in 1917.

[64]. The Reverend Henry Emerson Hovey was born in Lowell in 1844. He graduated from Trinity College in 1866, was made a deacon in 1869, and had his first pastorate at Fall River, moving from there to Brooklyn, New York, where he spent the period from 1872 to 1882, and came to Portsmouth in 1883. He was a member of the Board of Instruction in 1883.

[65]. This house is the one we know today as the Aldrich Memorial. The building was erected in 1790, and was owned and occupied by the grandfather of Thomas Bailey Aldrich, Thomas D. Bailey, until his death in 1870. Aldrich, who won undying local fame by penning "The Story of a Bad Boy" and "Little Old Town by the Sea", really lived in the house for only a short time in his boyhood. There are even those who look somewhat askance at some of the boyhood adventures he relates. When T. D. Bailey died, the house was sold to George Bilbruck who at first rented it and then gave it to the Children's Home Society. That organization was there until 1883, when the children were moved to what is called the Chase House, now a part of Strawbery Banke, Inc., and open to the public after extensive renovations. The children had barely left the Aldrich House when it was converted to a hospital. When its service as a hospital was done, F. W. Hartford, then publisher of The Portsmouth Herald, sponsored a successful campaign to have it organized as a memorial to Thomas Bailey Aldrich. It was dedicated in 1907. In the rear of the building today is a brick strongroom

which contains many of the treasures accumulated by Aldrich in his lifetime. Numbers can still be seen on the doors of the rooms in the main house, mute reminders of the days when it was a hospital. It is probably one of the best furnished houses in the style of the mid-19th Century that can be found. Thomas B. Aldrich's grandson, Judge Bailey Aldrich, in on the U. S. Court of Appeals at Boston.

[66]. Known even today as the Chase House, this structure sheltered the Chase Home for Children until 1916 when the institution moved to new quarters off Middle Road where it is today. Chase Home had its start in 1877, when a man named William H. Parks, a mariner, had to solve the problem of what to do with his motherless children while he was at sea. His answer was to set up a "home" on Mt. Vernon Street. In 1879, George W. Bilbruck presented the "home" with the Bailey House. But the institution outgrew that and moved into a house given it by George B. Chase of Boston, who asked only that a plaque, commemorating a visit of President Washington to his grandfather, the Reverend Stephen Chase, be erected, and that the pastor of St. John's Church always have a seat on the Board of Trustees, ex officio. There the "home" stayed for 32 years.

The house was built in 1730, as part of the development along what was known locally as the "New Highway". Later the town called it Low Street, then it became Pitt, and finally Court Street throughout its length. The Chase House does have the distinction of being one of the few homes in America that once sheltered a Lord Mayor of London. Barlow Trecothick, probably not a native because a baptismal record in London shows him to have been born there, was elected Lord Mayor in 1769, a time of political dispute, and his years of life in America prompted some adverse comments during the election. The Guild Hall in London has a complete file on this man, with newspaper clippings of letters for and against his election. Copies of this file are now in the Portsmouth Public Library.

[67]. Hospitalization, even here in Portsmouth, was not a new concept. One of the first efforts known along that line was Dr. Hall Jackson who went to Boston in 1764 to learn the technique being used there to combat that deadly killer — smallpox. On his return, he was given the use of Pest Island for a hospital in which to house those who voluntarily submitted to inoculation with the virus itself. The theory being that these people would have light cases under controlled conditions, becoming immune. Jackson was a pioneer in many medical fields, being one of the first surgeons to

operate for cataracts on the eye. He did a lot of medical work with the troops around Boston in the early days of the Revolution. One of his fights to collect a bill was with the Town of Hampton, which attempted to renege on paying him for his services to a boy who lost both legs to exposure during the winter. Court records at Exeter show that Hampton was ordered to pay the doctor his three pounds. That fee was for the amputations and treating the stumps.

[68]. He's forgotten now, but George A. Bilbruck's name should forever have a place of honor in this community for his philanthropy. Born in England November 11, 1818, Bilbruck came to America shortly after reaching his majority, and the fact he achieved material success here, perhaps prompted him to be generous with his adopted city. Chief beneficiaries of his largesse were the Cottage Hospital and the Chase Home, but others also benefited.

He arrived in Portsmouth in 1852, and lived out his days here until his death in 1894, "having been for a number of years head brewer for Messers Fisher and Eldredge. For 10 or more years past he had not been in active business, but has lived quietly at his handsome estate on Woodbury Avenue, having acquired a competence, by his industry and frugality".

[69]. William A. Hodgdon, the unlucky low bidder on the Cottage Hospital job, was a local man, born December 9, 1849, and learned the carpenter trade under Moses Yeaton. He later studied architecture in New York City and came back here to practice his two crafts. He served on the County Commission. His granddaughter married Clark Clifford, noted in the Roosevelt administration.

[70]. Every Portsmouth visitor to Sturbridge Village should be delighted with one of the show places there because it began its existence in Portsmouth. For 203 years it stood on Pleasant Street, erected by the Reverend Samuel Langdon in 1749. Dr. Langdon administered to the North Church from 1747 to 1774 when he took the presidency of Harvard College. For various reasons Langdon and the Harvard Corporation did not get along. When the arrangement was terminated, Langdon took the pastorate at Hampton Falls which he held until his death in 1797. John Goddard who is distinguished if only because he declined a seat in the U. S. Senate, and sired a full quiver of children, lived in it in 1813.

Dr. Langdon is probably the only New Hampshire man ever awarded a doctorate for making a map. In partnership with Joseph Blanchard, a surveyor, the eminent divine published a map of the province in 1761, and the University of Aberdeen honored him for the project. Approximately on the site of the Langdon House was the first religious edifice in town, a Church of England chapel with house attached. The town took it over in 1657, remoldeled it into a parsonage for the minister. This building burned in 1704, killing the mother of the Reverend Nathaniel Rogers, one of his daughters and a Negro woman slave. The Reverend William W. Lewis and his family were the last local occupants of the mansion.

[71]. Josiah F. Adams was one of those indispensable fellows: A diaryist. He notes when he first began service in a store, one owned by William Rand, on November 30, 1845, at the princely wage of $72 annually, and it was a two-year indenture. Later he went to work in a periodical store operated by Joseph P. Morse for $7 a month. Adams, on April 26, 1852, made history of a kind when he became the first merchant to sell ale; he had a dozen barrels brought here from New York in the schooner Amelia. This was an introduction of what was to be a major Portsmouth product, created a large demand locally. On October 5, 1855, Adams became sexton of the Universalist Church, a post he was to hold for 46 years. At one time, he was an undertaker with an establishment on Daniel Street. Adams lived to the age of 86, dying April 27, 1916. His undertaking business was bought by H. W. Nickerson, who later sold out to J. Verne Wood.

[72]. An electric Gamewell Fire Alarm System was installed in Portsmouth in 1885, at an expense of $2,860. Six and three quarter miles of wire were originally used, upon which were 11 signal boxes, an automatic bell striker, one indicator, one gong, and two mechanical tappers, charged with a 24-cell battery. In 1886, the "No School" signal was added. It should be noted that this Gamewell apparatus was largely inspired, if not created, by an inventive genius from Eliot, Moses Farmer. If Farmer had lived in this age, his name would be on many electronic items. He fought Alexander Graham Bell's claims to invention of the telephone, but finally lost. His was the first home ever wired and lit by electricity and that was in Eliot. His daughter was Sarah J. Farmer.

Before the Gamewell equipment was introduced, a fire alarm was given by yelling. According to Frank W. Hackett, a son of W. H. Y. Hackett, the old system of giving an alarm for a fire was really quite simple. The first person to spot a red glow in the sky immediately opened windows and started yelling "Fire"! He repeated his stenatorian clamor until he heard it repeated somewhere in the distance, then he closed his window — especially in winter -- and climbed into his clothes, grabbed his buckets, fire hook and bed wrench and off he went. By that time the alarm had spread all over town, and some one living near the North Church would get the key, open it up and start pealing the bell.

These sounds would be taken up until every church bell in town was clanging. One of the "engine houses", the Torrent was located opposite the jail on Islington Street; later, when the company acquired a new engine, the Sagamore, it moved to the top of Mason's Hill, under the command of Captain Bob Shillaber. One father and son team that served with it were the Treadwells, City Treasurer Samuel P. and his father Thomas.

[73]. John G. Randall was chief from 1895 to March of 1903 when he was relieved by Herbert A. Marden. Chief engineers in the Fire Department changed, in those days, with the swing of politics. Marden, a Democrat, was born here February 4, 1849. He became a member of the department in 1874 with the Dearborn Engine Company, and continued with it until it was reorganized into the Moses H. Goodrich Company in 1876. Elected to the board of engineers, Marden made chief in 1884, a job he held until 1890 when J. Frank Stanton, a Republican, was elected. Marden won the job back the next year, but Randall took over in 1895. Marden went back to the ranks as a member of Goodrich Company until he succeeded Randall as chief. Marden's father, George J., worked as a carpenter for Eldredge Brewing, the son became a journeyman in two different trades, blacksmithing and carpentering. At one time the younger Marden worked for the Laightons at the Isles of Shoals.

[74]. Every fire produces its share of heroes and heroines. One of these at the Universalist Church blaze was a blind pianist, Miss Emma Watkins, who filled buckets of water for use in keeping sparks from igniting other properties. Another was William Ashe, an employee of the Portsmouth Gas and Electric Light and Power Company, who went into the cellar and turned off the gas. The plant for this company was at 66-68 State Street, and managed by A. E. McReel.

[75]. Among the properties damaged were those of Mrs. Thomas A. Harris, Mark H. Wentworth, Sidney Wentworth, George Hill, William P. Robinson, John S. Wendell, Major E. A. Tilton and E. E. Colcord.

[76]. It cost the City of Portsmoth $150,300 to acquire the Aqueduct, the stockholders being paid off, with the exception of three shares, at a rate of $1,500 per share. The estate of Mrs. Ichabod Goodwin, daughter of Captain William Rice, and mother-in-law of Admiral George Dewey, was paid $22,500 for 15 shares. Oliver Ayers had 12, worth $18,000; James Rundlett, 10,

$15,000. A major living stockholder was Peter Peduzzi, son of Dominick, who held seven shares and was paid $10,500. Marcellus Eldredge, the brewer, who had long been a major trouble maker for the Aqueduct Company, was holding out for $2,100 a share but accepted $1,600, it being worth the extra to get rid of him. The company had agreed to sell only when it became obvious to all concerned that the good return on the investment was not worth the headaches involved.

For instance, Eldredge was constantly seeking preferential treatment in water rates, and did get them reduced in 1888. Both he and Frank Jones were involved in the final push that induced the Aqueduct to sell.

The first approach was made by the Portsmouth Water Company which proposed development of a source over in Maine. But the two could not get together on a price. John O. Ayers, John J. Pickering and William A. Peirce met with Jones and Eldredge but the negotiations came to nothing. And, while they were dickering, sentiment in the city grew steadily for public ownership of the water system. So intense did the public pressure become that the City Council at last asked for a price. The directors set $175,000. Every meeting of the City Council was marked by acrid discussion of the Aqueduct. On May 14, the city fathers, Aqueduct officials, two English engineers and Frank Jones made a tour of the system, which provoked Alderman George D. Marcy into remarking that it was "a lot of rotten logs". The company, it should be said, had done some modernization but not nearly enough to cope with the growing demand.

A month later a petition from 2,000 citizens was presented to the Board of Aldermen and the Common Council urging that the Aqueduct be bought. Alderman True W. Priest was quoted as saying he would not vote for the purchase "if every damned person in town" signed the petition.

But the City Council committee recommended buying at the $150,000 figure and that price was accepted. The story of the Aqueduct should not be closed without some mention of what the investment had meant to the stockholders, because it is in itself a study in 19th Century economics. Originally, it was intended to have 107 shares outstanding, but for some reason John Langdon refused his allocation of five, and these were never issued. Two others were bought in by the company and so that left an even 100 outstanding at the time it was sold.

Each share, during the years, had been assessed $83 for

construction or improvements and an additional $20 was assessed in 1891 to pay off the outstanding debts, so total investment was $103 a share. By 1876, the company had returned $1,102, and an additional $545 per share in dividends was added between 1877 and 1891, for a total of $1,647. The cost of each share was $103. which reduces the profit per share to $1,544, and each sold for $1,500, so the net gain across the 94 years the company lasted was $3,044. Not bad at all in a day when Internal Revenue was a mild-mannered organization. On January 7, 1891, the proprietors voted to adjourn until March 25. Of that meeting the notation, and the last in the record books, was, "No stockholder appeared". The City of Portsmouth was in the water business as it is today.

[77]. Local organizer of the Universalist Church was Noah Parker, a man untutored in formal theological pursuits. In 1777, four years after the appearance of the Reverend John Murray here, Parker began services in a school house on Market Street. Then they moved to "Brimstone Hill", the high land off Pleasant Street, at last building a church of their own in 1784 on a site in the old Vaughan Street parking lot. Noah Parker died on August 17, 1787, and for a while there was no pastor. The Reverend George Richards began preaching in 1793 and was the occupant of the pulpit in 1807 when the church was built.

[78]. The Reverend William W. Lewis left here to take a pastorate in Arlington, Massachusetts. He was succeeded by the Reverend John Papandrew, who became a stormy figure in the civil rights movement, later taking a parish in Florida. The Reverend John S. McPhee came here from Utica, New York, and is the present pastor. The Reverend Mr. Lewis has left the ministry and is living at Spofford Lake.

[79]. George T. Cogan never married, and put most of his active life into the Fire Department. In his will he created a fund for scholarships which is administered by attorney Wyman P. Boynton, ex-Fire Chief Frederick R. Crompton, Cogan's successor, and Maurice Pike.

[80]. Building of the Stone Church represented surrender by the South Parish of the "up-town" movement initiated 115 years before by the North Church. Rather than capitulate at the time of the big schism, the stand-patters had continued meeting in the church south of the Mill Dam. Then about 1730, they built a new church for themselves on Meeting House Hill. It was in the tomb under the pulpit here that they buried several of their pastors, among them Job Strong, William Shurtliff and Samuel Langdon. These

remains were removed to the South Cemetery when the old church was sold and the congregation went to the Stone Church. The old building was used by various groups until 1863, when it was torn down and the lumber sold off at auction. The present structure went up shortly thereafter.

[81]. The Temple was built on the site where the Portsmouth Almshouse was erected in 1716, a use that maintained until 1755. In 1803, the Temple was built by the Free Will Baptist Society which had formed only the previous year under the urging of Elder Elias Smith. The Baptists used it until 1844 and then it was taken over by the Washingtonian Temperance Society, which remodeled it into a lecture hall. After the fire, Christmas Eve, a building called Music Hall was erected, one which we know today as the Civic Theater. This was remodeled in 1901. It opened on January 29, 1878, with the inevitable address by W. H. Y. Hackett and presentation of a play, "Caste". In 1903, Frank W. Hackett and John H. Bartlett were the speakers when the city observed the quarter millennial of its change of name from Strawbery Banke to Portsmouth.

[82]. These buildings were the old Portsmouth Steam Factory.

[83]. Edward F. Sise was the first large-scale importer of coal. Through the 18th Century, merchants often advertised New Castle (England) coals but it was Sise who started bringing in native products. This was in 1831. In 1905, 358,918 tons of coal passed through the Boston and Maine coal pocket alone.

[84]. For instance there is record of the ship Piscataqua, built by Fernald and Pettigrew in 1852, arriving in Madras, India, in 1854 with a cargo of ice from Boston. Part of the ice had melted and she had a heavy list when she made port. She was later sold at Calcutta and her master, Captain George B. Wendell, came back to Portsmouth in the ship Lotus. Another example, more pertinent perhaps, was the ship Express, built also by Fernald and Pettigrew, which was launched January 28, 1854. In February she was loaded with ice for New Orleans at Pray's Wharf (upper end of Market Street) by the Portsmouth and South Berwick Ice Company. It was the first ship so loaded here and the ice was cut in South Berwick. Express was taken to sea by Captain Thomas Weeks, who had at one time commanded Piscataqua. That she went ashore on Hart's Island, Long Island Sound, on her maiden voyage, and had to be towed into New York for repairs, has nothing to do with the story of the boom in the ice business. The late Dr. Lucius H. Thayer, after graduation from Amherst College, was not in good health. He

shipped as supercargo on one of the vessels running from Maine to Calcutta with ice.

[85]. Harris lived here for some years at what was then 14 Chapel Street. In the 1903 Directory his address was given as New York, although he was still president of the brewing company.

[86]. George Ansley Mudge was born in Portsmouth March 16, 1833, the son of Aaron and Lucy (Jones) Mudge. He attended local schools and then went to Boston to enter the jewelry business. Located on Washington Street at the time of the great fire in 1872, he sold out to one of the firms that had been wiped out and came back to Portsmouth. He became vice president and treasurer of the brewing company, joined the Mechanics Fire Society. He died at his home, at the corner of Sheafe and Penahllow Streets, March 9, 1913. Incidentally at the time of the great fire in Boston, Portsmouth repaid some of the kindnesses she had been shown in her times of trouble. Equipment and a large contingent of men went down by train to help battle that blaze.

[87]. Henry H. Ham, Jr., was the son of Henry H. Ham, one of Portsmouth's most respected watchmakers. Henry, Jr., left Portsmouth Brewing and went to the Navy Yard as a clerk. The elder Henry was born here in 1814, and apprenticed as a watchmaker in Lowell. When he became a journeyman, he returned to Portsmouth and followed his trade until Thanksgiving, 1892. He died February 17, 1893.

[88]. Patrick Harrington, father of William F. Harrington, Sr., was grandfather to Judge William F. Harrington, Jr., of New Castle.

[89]. William F. Harrington, Sr., who made his home in Manchester and whose normal occupation was that of banker, came to Portsmouth when Portsmouth Brewing ran into financial troubles and had to be bailed out, but he never lived here, although the family had summer places in Rye. Judge Harrington says his father acted quickly to get the business moving, going to Germany and hiring a brewmaster and a refrigeration specialist for the brewery. These two men were instrumental in stepping up the pace to a point where Frank Jones knew he had competition, enough so that he offered Harrington a job in his organization. Harrington commuted daily from Manchester for many years, and was shrewd enough to see the advent of Prohibition and persuaded his bank to sell out ahead of that disaster. He died in 1955 at the age of 84. Judge Harrington, who lives on Wild Rose Lane, New Castle, is a partner in the law firm of Griffin (Charles J.), Harrington and Brigham (Lindsey R.).

[90]. Thomas Leary was vice president and brewmaster at the Portsmouth Brewing Company. A native of Ireland, he was trained in brewing by Mark A. Scott, a gardener by trade who boarded at 2 Elm Street when the company was founded. Leary came to the United States with his parents at the age of 13 in 1866. He lived his teen years here, served three years on the police force, before beginning training at the Eldredge Brewing Company in 1875. He was elected an alderman and died April 1, 1903.

[91]. Edward L. Butler was the father of the former Portsmouth postmaster and former mayor, Theodore R. Butler. Born here in 1873, he was the son of Lafayette and Harriet (Rand) Butler. He was only 18 when he began keeping books for the Portsmouth Brewing Company. He died October 2, 1937, as a retired leadingman electrician at the Portsmouth Navy Yard.

[92]. The Eldredges were all natives of Chatham, Massachusetts. Heman, the father, came here some time after the birth of H. Fisher, his younger son, April 13, 1852. H. Fisher Eldredge was active in community affairs, served in the Legislature in 1899. He died May 13, 1919. Marcellus, whose Miller Avenue mansion is now an apartment house and his stable the home of the Portsmouth YWCA, died in Boston, Massachusetts, on March 15, 1898. Eldredge left an estate of $450,000, and bequeathed $5,000 each to Cottage Hospital, Chase Home, Portsmouth Public Library and the Unitarian Church. Eldredge had two terms as Mayor, 1885-86, and was in the State Senate 1877-78.

[93]. It was from this building, as told earlier, that the last barrel of Frank Jones Ale was shipped. That's sort of ironic, when it is remembered that Eldredge tried desperately to compete with Frank Jones, not only in brewing, but in life style as well. The difference in the size of their estates tells how that came out.

[94]. John H. Cheever was born here May 5, 1841, the son of Benjamin and Mary (Holbrook) Cheever. For more than 30 years he was cashier and general factotum of the Eldredge Brewing Company. His son was Dr. Benjamin Cheever and his daughter, Mary, married a Dr. Kingman. The Cheever family owned land which is now the South Cemetery and used it for a pasture. As both the Cotton and Proprietors' Cemeteries "filled up", they started selling off their land in additional cemeteries — Harmony Grove and Sagamore — until the old cow pasture became the vast expanse of stone monuments to the departed that this generation knows.

Their interest in the cemetery lands was sold many years ago to the Michael J. Griffin family, one that has become increasingly influential with the years. A grandson of Michael Griffin, the son of a J. Paul Griffin, is Police Commissioner J. Paul Griffin. His brother John is presently superintendent of cemeteries, and his wife, Ruth is in the House of Representatives. They have two sisters, Mrs. Eleanor (Griffin) Adams, a teacher at Portsmouth High, and Mrs. Mary (Griffin) Ritzo.

But that's only the beginning: Old Michael had a son Michael, who was the father of Charles J. Griffin, attorney, former city solicitor, Democratic leader for many years; Mrs. Margaret (Griffin) Googins, Portland; William M., works at the Portsmouth Naval Shipyard; Virginia, Nashua, Sisters of Mercy; and the Reverend Michael J. Griffin, pastor of St. Kieran's Church, Berlin. Then there was William T., whose son, Frederick, lives on Hillside Drive. And then Dr. Samuel, the dentist, who was the father of Dr. S. Gerard Griffin, city health officer; Bradley of Eliot, a postal worker; the Reverend Robert Griffin, pastor of St. Peter's, Peterborough; and Sister Robert, dean at Mount St. Mary's, Hooksett. No attempt will be made to trace the next generations.

[95]. John Newick was born in Sussex, England, December 9, 1841, and, on first coming to this country, located in Syracuse, New York. He came to Portsmouth in 1880, and was superintendent of the Eldredge Brewing Company until 1914. Active politically, he was in the Legislature in 1904 and 1905, on the City Council, 1907-09. He was the father of four sons, William H., who went to Hartford, Connecticut; Ira A. and Frank F., both of Portsmouth; and Albert E. of York. There were also two daughters, Mrs. William Shuttlesworth and Miss Laura Newick. Ira A. Newick, a noted brewmaster in his own right, was an uncle to "Johnny" who operated for a number of years the best lobster eatery in town down at the Ceres Street landing, and then removed to Dover Point to go into business with his son, and has since died.

[96]. Justin V. Hanscom was closer to Frank Jones than his right hand. Born in Eliot November 11, 1829, Hanscom first started his working life with the shipbuilding firm of Tobey and Littlefield. In 1867, he started an association with Jones that was to last the rest of Jones' life. Hanscom survived Jones by only three years, dying May 4, 1905.

[97]. William Moat built the house which has been the property of the Wyman P. Boynton family at 668 Middle Street for many years.

[98]. No one today can imagine the utter misery that incarceration in the Portsmouth Jail might involve, not even if they

have been in Sheriff George Sampson's "Brentwood Hilton", where prisoners are given "haircuts". The Jail referred to here actually stood at the corner of Brewster and Islington Streets, spreading east to take in the lot where the Knights of Columbus Home stands. Our knowledge of this tragic place comes, as so often, from The Rambler who lived the years of his life in the vicinity.

Oddly, and here it gives pause to wonder about The Rambler; he never discussed the savagery at the Jail in his columns so familiar and dear to Portsmouth readers. Before getting into that, it should be remembered that as late as 1829, in New Hampshire, there were several crimes punishable by the whip and branding. And the U. S. Navy, some years later, was permitting a ship captain the discretionary use of 12 lashes. Of course, the early authorities were really stimulated by the thought that the whip would save almost any brand from the burning. They saw it as a way of getting their point across to anyone who might have "wrong" thoughts then, or in the future. Not many accounts are extant of the whippings that were frequent in that long-ago Portsmouth, so many hail with almost nauseating nostalgia.

In the early days, they used the Town Pump, near the North Church, as a whipping post and women really had "equal rights". They were lashed on the bare back, along with the men. These whippings were public, but, with the coming of the "new jail" on Islington Street they became somewhat more private. Incidentally, the part of the jail complex that housed the jailer stands at the foot of Summer Street. Space limitations prevent getting into the circumstances that provoked The Rambler into descriptions of what went on in the Jail during his boyhood: "Our residence being next door to the Jail, our young blood was often chilled by the frequent exhibition of clotted gore on the bare backs of naked culprits, who were tied up to the public whipping post, or pinioned on the jail door for branding".

During his boyhood, Brewster said, hardly a year passed but someone was soundly lashed at the jail. Deputy Sheriffs Low, Eastman and Timothy Gerrish represented the strong arm of the law at these functions. Gerrish was keeper of the jail from 1800 to 1815. One of the victims listed by The Rambler was a man named Morse, who was between 60 and 70 years of age when he was strung up to get 39 lashes for counterfeiting, rather rough on a man past his middle years. In 1804, Samuel Hogg was whipped and branded. Nehemiah Clam was the victim in 1806, along with a man named John Wilson. 1808 saw James Brown, "an Irishman", whipped and branded. Brewster said that the last man he knew to be branded was John Bickford and that this barbarism was carried out after 1810 when a man named Butler had ceased to be sheriff.

For those so fond of the "good old days", that they wish their return forthwith, Brewster's description of the scene is included:

"We saw him undergoing the barbarous punishment in front of the jail. With several needles projecting from a piece of cork, the India ink was, agreeable to the words of the law, 'well and deeply inserted, above the eye-brow from the hair of the temple on one side, to the hair of the temple on the other side of the forehead, and by a line in the same manner inserted from the line aforesaid to the end of the nose'. He was not permitted to wipe the blood from his face for some time, that the ink might not be disturbed: a friend, however, afterwards rubbed with a shoe brush so effectually, that the marks were completely eradicated from the nose, and those on the forehead much effaced. The instrument used for whipping was a 'cat-o-nine-tails', a whip with nine lashes, each of which was knotted and terminated with iron wire". To add a little sting to the punishment, the prisoner's wounds were sometimes treated with salt brine. Ah yes, those were indeed the "good old days"!

[99]. On December 8, 1895, Portsmouth Council, Knights of Columbus, fourth in the state, was established. In the first suite of officers were William J. Kelly, grand knight; John Griffin, deputy grand knight; the Reverend John B. Delaney, chaplain; F. A. Fagan, chancellor; William T. Morrisey, financial secretary; John E. Meegan, recording secretary; Daniel Casey, treasurer; Patrick McGann, treasurer; Henry Donnelly, outer guard; John H. Kirvan, inner guard. Father Delaney, the first chaplain, was later consecrated as the second bishop of Manchester.

During World War I, the Council held daily open houses for servicemen and staged weekly dances. The slogan was "Everybody Welcome and Everything Free". The first meetings of the Council were held in Red Men's Hall, High Street, where the American Legion now stages Bingo games. In 1902, and this material is taken from historical notes prepared by the late John C. Dolan, a former city clerk; "The Red Men vacated these quarters and the Council moved to Congress Street and purchased furnishings for a club room. A year later the Council moved to State Street in the Hartford Building adjacent to the Times Building directly across from the Post Office...in 1911, it was decided to open new quarters in the Old Custom House at the corner of Daniel and Penhallow Streets, and the furniture purchased at that time is still in service in the Council

Chamber....As the Council cannot hold property, a holding corporation under the name of the Knights of Columbus Home Corporation, was incorporated in 1913 and a majority of the members of the Council purchased stock in sufficient amounts to obtain a loan from the bank and the present building on Islington Street was purchased....The mortgage having been considerably reduced in 1923, the stock was called in and all members of the Council became members of a new corporation of the same name".

In 1931, the Council expanded the building, and paid off its mortgage in 1938 with Mrs. Julia Kelly, widow of the first grand knight, supplying the match for the burning ceremony. Charter members, in addition to those named were John Casey, Dr. William H. Lyons, T. J. Kelly, Patrick E. Kane, John Killoren, Patrick J. Flanigan, William T. Morrisey, T. F. Mulcahy, Joseph E. Kelly, James Whitaker, James Whitman, Frank Whitman, Timothy Donovan, Michael Hurley, William Ballard, Patrick Gallagher, Charles Chase, Jeremiah Lyons, Thomas McCarthy, M. A. Monahan, B. J. Malloy and E. J. Sullivan. At the time of the 1945 anniversary celebration these sons of charter members were saluted: Dr. Justin E. Flanigan, Frederick A. Griffin and Gerald Lyons. So far has the city gone along the road to better understanding that the Masonic order and the Knights of Columbus now hold a joint dinner on an annual basis, an event that would not have been even dreamed of when the Knights of Columbus Council was formed. Shortly after it was opened, the Masons offered use of their parking lot on the old Bartlett house site to members of Immaculate Conception Parish on Sunday mornings.

[100]. The Franklin Shiphouse was a familiar landmark on Portsmouth's eastern skyline for almost a century. Under construction in 1838, the building was not finished when the keel of USS Preble was laid and work started on her. The building was 343 feet long, 84 feet wide, 52 feet hight. Fifty feet of the length was added in 1854 to accommodate the 74 Franklin. That old vessel gave the Shiphouse its name. It cost $71,000 to build and one man, Daniel LeGrow, was killed in the course of the work. The winds and suns of nearly one hundred years had dried the building to the point where all it needed was a spark and that happened on March 5, 1936. The fire started in an upper gallery around 5 a.m. and spread like an explosion. Despite the early hour, hundreds were attracted to the waterfront to see the old building end its existence in one firey burst.

[101]. Miss Helen L. Drury, daughter of Hiram E. Drury, general storekeeper at the Yard, was sponsor. George H. Rock, supervised Boxer's construction. Some of the men who

worked on her were Thomas P. Connors, John Grant, Frank Kuse, shipfitters; I. B. Davis, Charles M. Sheppard, outside shipfitters; Augustus Stevenson and M. C. Fernald, shipwrights; George W. Muchemore, C. C. Muchemore, shipsmiths; James K. Boyle, Warren Pryor, joiners; Walter L. Ball, leadingman painter; Charles W. Coleman, calker; C. F. Drake, plumber; J. A. Drake, patternmaker. The Portsmouth Herald said: "The Boxer is a graceful craft, built on fine lines and carefully constructed. Her model is probably the best of any ship of her class in the Navy".

[102]. A dry dock is an essential installation at any operating shipyard. This was recognized here as far back as the 17th Century when commissioners sent to America by King Charles II in 1665 said of Piscataqua: "...which is a very good harbor, always free from ice and very capable of fortification; and here dry docks might be made". It was not until the United States was a young Republic that study was given to a dry dock at the local yard. More than two decades passed before anything was done and finally in 1848, work was started on the floating dry dock described earlier. That functioned well for a number of years after its completion in 1852, but was soon found inadequate when the Navy went to larger, steel-hulled vessels. So on June 4, 1900, work was begun on the familiar stone dry dock. Five years later the work was done and the men involved in the first docking were Thomas P. Connor, Frank Kuse, Samuel Caswell, Samuel Grant, Frank Bond, John Pethic, Thomas F. Flanigan, Harry McKenney, H. S. Swett, John Byrne and George H. Rock.

[103]. River legends are numerous among the men who navigate it as part of their daily toil. One story that persists is of Captain "Billy" Patch, a river pilot more than 70 years ago, great-grandfather to Garland W. Patch, Jr. One day "Billy" was taking a ship downriver when someone remarked to him that he "must know every rock in the river". No sooner were the words out than the vessel grated on a rock. On which, "Billy" observed, "I sure do and there's one right now". Most famous of the river piloting families in recent years have been the Holts, Shirley, Shirley, Jr., and Shirley, III, along with Warren White of New Castle. Employed by the Portsmouth Navigation Company, a subsidiary of Moran, these men are entrusted with the tankers that enter and depart this river.

[104]. It is hard to judge from the old news accounts which was the greater volume: The (1) stream of Portsmouth people trying to escape what they believed would be the lethal effects of the blast, or (2) the curious who came in from the outside to see it.

Whichever way it might have been, it was one of the causes of the first serious street car accident ever recorded here. Two electric cars, one outbound from Portsmouth, the other inbound from Stratham, met in head-on collision on Middle Road at the foot of Schurman's Hill (approximately where the Interstate By-Pass Bridge is now). The in-bound car from Stratham was loaded with Portsmouth people returning home after the blast at Henderson's Point, and the outbound car had Haverhill sightseers aboard, going home. More than 40 persons were injured when the overloaded cars crashed together. Most severely injured was Mrs. George H. Pahls. The electric railway had come here in 1898. At first, it was a local line, looping around Islington Street, Middle Road, Dennett Street and the Creek. First spike in the rails for this line was driven by Morris C. Foye, on September 8, 1898, on the Raynes Avenue section of the track. Inevitably it became part of the thousands of miles of inter-urban electric railways that once fanned through the nation's countryside. The writer, on his first trip to Portsmouth, remembers arriving here with his father, Albert Brighton, one day in early August 1920, from their home in Peterborough, after an all-day ride on the steam train, and then catching the electric car to Hampton Beach. Leaving the beach a few days later, the journey was on an electric car to Boston. The electric railways, with their fixed road-beds, were forced into oblivion by the gasoline engine before World War II, but Portsmouth motorists were for years reminded of them when they used Middle Street, until it was resurfaced and widened several years ago. Schurman, incidentally, had an ice pond where the Rehabilitation Center is now.

[105]. It was because his son, Robert Todd Lincoln, was a student at Phillips Exeter Academy that Abraham Lincoln, soon to be elected President of the United States, paid his only visit to New Hampshire. The younger Lincoln made his first public appearance as a speaker at Stratham Hill on the Fourth of July during his student days in Exeter.

[106]. USS Kearsarge was probably the most famous vessel ever built in the Portsmouth Navy Yard. Other famed ships, like USS Constitution, have been here, but Kearsarge was a local product. Kearsarge's keel was laid on June 17, 1861. The work was done on level land back of the old floating dry dock, and when work was far enough along, Kearsarge was pushed by hydraulic jacks into the dry dock, which then flooded, thus launching Kearsarge. She sailed February 5, 1862, on her mission to find and destroy Alabama. It took her more than two years to accomplish this task

but on June 19, 1864, there was warm work for her 30-pound Parrott rifle and two Dahlgren smoothbores. It was an 80-minute engagement which left Alabama with 40 dead and destroyed her. The cost to Kearsarge was the life of only one man. Almost 30 years later, February 2, 1894, Kearsarge met her own end on Roncador Reef in the Caribbean.

A local man, the late James E. Whalley, was chief yeoman engineer on Kearsarge on that last cruise. She was running under sail, with no heat at all in her boilers when the warning of "breakers on the port bow" came. After striking, they coaxed steam into the boilers and tried to huff and puff her off, but the rocks clung fast. The crew scrambled onto the Roncador Key, and an officer took a boat crew to find help. Two weeks later, a steamer came by and picked up those still on the key, although one man had drowned.

When Kearsarge fought Alabama, a Portsmouth man, True W. Priest, was first engineer. For more than a quarter century, Priest, who served on the Board of Aldermen, ran a saloon at 20 Market Square, in a building between Eberle's and Portsmouth Trust Company. Later he moved his business to 5 Ladd Street, which his son, Oliver W. Priest later operated. True W. Priest died February 20, 1909, and his widow, Elizabeth (Wendell) Priest, died March 27, 1912. After he left Kearsarge, Priest worked at the Navy Yard until 1868. He left the city for a while, returning in 1876 and setting up his bar.

[107]. Peirce Hall was a much frequented place for years, between dances and civic functions. Today it's used by the Frank E. Booma Post, American Legion, for Bingo games. Even the night of President Kenndey's death at an assassin's hand, a game was held in Peirce Hall.

[108]. Edward E. McIntire was the son of Jefferson and Eliza McIntire, born in 1850. At the age of 12 he went to work on the Yard as a coppersmith in the copper shop. When he died on July 20, 1916, he had been working at the Yard for 54 years, being in charge of the shop in which he began his service. McIntire was a member of the old Dearborn Fire Company; served two terms as mayor, two as alderman; and was a state representative in 1890. The day he died, the Navy Yard had its biggest payroll in 50 years with $20,000 being paid to 1,526 workers.

[109]. Frank W. Hackett, in his late years, contributed often to the local newspapers on old-time topics. At the time his father's portrait was hung in the old Courthouse, Hackett gave a vivid description of local law offices as they existed when the old State

House in front of the North Church still served as a Courthouse.

[110]. Two of these newsmen were the late Richard McDonough and the late Fernando W. Hartford, owner of The Herald. McDonough, father of John, who lives on Miller Avenue, and the late Commander Richard McDonough of New Castle, was a photographer, with a lively interest in sports — especially golf. For years he was secretary of the New Hampshire Golf Association, and a scholarship fund for caddies has been named in his honor. At one time, McDonough was probation officer in the local municipal court.

22

A New Century Dawns

[1]. Alderman Wallace D. Smith was cashier at the Granite State Insurance Company. Born in Lempster, April 14, 1856, his family moved early in his life to Hillsboro. In 1873 he went to Concord where he entered the insurance business. Portsmouth became his home in 1889 when he entered the employ of Granite State. His wife was a Concord girl; they married January 12, 1879. Smith served twice as an alderman and was a member of the Portsmouth Athletic Club. For more than forty years he was a key official with Granite State. Each payday he would give every girl in the office an orange. A story is told about Alderman Smith that should be preserved. The automobile became popular in his middle years, but he had reservations about its permanency, although he bought one and built a garage in which to house it. Neither he nor his wife would learn to drive. Perhaps she was more devoted to the fabulous stamp collection she had than to chauffeuring. When the Smiths (whose disagreements on the command deck of the ship of matrimony were more frequent than their agreements) wanted to go anywhere, they hired a driver. But Smith liked his auto, and its care became the hobby to him that stamps were to his wife. Because he could not drive he would get a youngster in the neighborhood of his home, 126 Wibird Street, to back the vehicle out of the garage so he could wash and polish it. One day he went through this routine, but when the car was ready for garaging, he counld not find a boy to put it away for him.

Not daunted, Smith decided that this was the time to prove his mastery. He got in, started the beast, put it in gear and started toward the garage. But he stalled it on the wooden ramp into the garage. Still not shaken, he let it roll back to the foot of the driveway and restarted it. Utterly determined, he gave it the gas. Up the driveway Smith and his horseless carriage roared, ascending the ramp with ridiculous ease. Unfortunately he could not remember how his drivers managed to stop the thing. On Smith and his auto moved, plowing into the back wall of the garage which lifted majestically like a well hinged gate. They plunged through, the back wall closed, and there was Alderman Smith and his juggernaut sitting in the middle of the garden. When the garage people came, it was beyond their understanding how it had been accomplished. The carpenters tacked the back wall down again, put in a shingle or two, and the adventure was over.

[2]. The special committee consisted of Alderman Fred L. Martin, Clarence H. Paul and Herbert E. Fernald. Martin was a watchmaker on Congress Street; Paul was a master mechanic with the Frank Jones Brewing Co. and also partnered with Fred L. Leach and George D. Richardson in Portsmouth Plumbing and Heating Co. Fernald was a ship's carpenter by trade.

[3]. It is a matter of familiar note that Market Street between Bow Street and the Square was the first (1767) paved thoroughfare in Portsmouth, but that paving was cobblestone. The first sidewalks were put down about 1808, as City Attorney Peter J. Loughlin learned after some research not long ago.

[4]. George A. Wood's career was closely intertwined with that of his wife, Mary I. Wood, one of the really early fighters in the battle for women's rights. During World War I this was to be her forte, standing in the forefront of the struggle to have women recognized as human beings. A generation or two ahead of her time, but still a necessary person. George A. Wood, at the time of his death on December 18, 1930, had been active in the New Hampshire Chamber of Commerce. He spent four terms in the House. His workaday life began as a railway mail clerk; becoming active in their organization, he became secretary in 1897 of the National Postal Clerks. He came to Portsmouth in 1898 as chief deputy collector for Internal Revenue. He had his own insurance office in 1913 in Market Square. His wife, who attained a fame wider than his, was the former Mary I. Stevens, a native of Saxton's River, Vermont.

[5]. George D. Marcy died at the comparatively young age of fifty. His death closed out the Marcy family in this city. At one time he was associated with William E. Peirce in the insurance business and was a field deputy with Internal Revenue. Marcy saw service in both the Common Council and the State Legislature. His

mayoralty service spanned 1903-04, and he was a past president of the Portsmouth Athletic Club.

[6]. To Emma J. W. Magraw goes the distinction of being one of Portsmouth's better known teachers. Many still remember her, as she retired in 1928 after 45 years of service, as a teacher and then as school librarian. She began her career in 1873, and before she left the school system she was teaching the grandchildren of her original pupils. In 1905 she won a statewide contest as teacher of the year, gaining from it an expense-paid trip to Oregon for the Lewis and Clark Exposition.

A charter member of the Graffort Club, she lived out her years with her younger sister, Miss Annie Magraw, and on that rests another of life's little ironies. The writer happened to be a witness to Miss Emma Magraw's last will and testament, and throughout the witnessing formalities she kept reiterating that her purpose in executing a will (she was then about 94) was to make sure that her cousin, Charles H. Magraw, a retired carpenter, did not inherit her estate. She did not like the man, although the writer had found him a pleasant old chap. But families are families, so what's the use of arguing? Under her will Miss Annie, a youngster of ninety or so, was the beneficiary. Everything went off as scheduled. Miss Emma died, but, unfortunately for her plans, Miss Annie also died three weeks later, saying with satisfied resignation, "Now my work is done". The only trouble was she died intestate, and the cousin inherited Emma's little nest egg. The moral being that everyone, even young people of nine decades, should have a will — just ask your lawyer.

[7]. Dr. Andrew B. Sherburne was typical of another day, a general practitioner who cared about the families he served. Early in his life he was an Army surgeon out West. He died in 1917 at the age of 70.

[8]. Leon F. Scruton was a civil engineer in this area for a number of years after the asphalt case. He worked on the entrances to Portsmouth Harbor, among other projects.

[9]. August Hett would in this day rate as a "contractor", but he advertised himself as a "teamster", saying that he had "Twenty years experience in the business. Forwarder of all government freight to and from the Navy Yard. . ." Hett also published a "Sanitary Notice" in which he offered to service cesspools and drains. His tool for this highly essential function, in a day before wide-flung sewerage, was the "New Odorless Excavator".

[10]. The asphalt case, if it did nothing else, solidified opinion in Portsmouth that the time had come for change. For those

trying to make head or tail out of the issues nearly seventy years later, it's difficult to tell the players without a score card. Column after column of testimony appeared in the pages of The Portsmouth Herald. Who was lying? Who was not is probably the better question.

From what the reader can glean, the original contract was executed to everyone's satisfaction, although privately there may have been those who felt they did not get quite enough out of it. Certainly no more was heard about the chipping and wearing issue after December of 1903 when the first $30,000 contract was finished. The fun started in the summer of 1904 when it was proposed that additional asphalting be done, and paid for out of license fees, a form of state tax returned to cities and towns, some $17,200. Two issues became paramount: (1) Had these fees already been converted to general funds and, therefore, expended? and/or (2) Was the appropriation made at a legal meeting of the Board of Aldermen? Underlying it all was the ugly word, corruption.

Even Judge Charles F. Stone himself introduced the word, saying in the course of the hearing that the issue at large seemed to be the charge of corrupt proceedings.

Mayor George D. Marcy was questioned as to whether or not he had promised Alderman Philip T. McWilliams, a blacksmith, a place on the committee to buy horses for the chemical fire engine. It was claimed that this deal had been made to win McWilliams' vote for the second Barber contract. Marcy, naturally, denied the allegation.

City Clerk William E. Peirce was on and off the witness stand like a puppet pulled by legal strings. A major part of the controversy centered around the role played by Peirce who, it was charged, had candidly admitted that he was agent for the Barber Co. This Peirce denied. Alderman R. Clyde Margeson testified that Peirce told him that there was $100 in it for him, as "easy as taking candy from a child" if he voted for the asphalt deal. Margeson was recalled to the stand and closely questioned as to whether or not he had said that the first thing he was going to do when he got into office was "furnish the Pest House". Margeson heatedly denied this, and as far as Peirce's offer was concerned, he said that he had told Peirce that he made his living at the store and did not need that kind of money.

Margeson was also a key figure in the case because of the arguments over whether or not he had received notice of the meeting. The city Clerk maintained that he had sent a message, but the weight of the evidence — included that of the alderman's brother, Richman P. Margeson — seems to indicate that Margeson was not told, that the asphalt bloc knew he would vote against them and that would kill the appropriation.

Alderman John Parkin said he voted for the asphalt resolution, that no improper influence was used, nor was there any attempt to bribe him. The president of the Common Council, Arthur F. Rutledge, testified that he had not been offered any bribe. Rutledge said August Hett had told him that the six councilmen from Ward 1 who had voted against asphalt had better watch out because his brother, Joseph Hett, had said that the Hetts would be back again next year. Rutledge said that August Hett told him that he got $75 out of the "horse deal". Rutledge said he had voted for asphalt although opposed to "Joe Hett and his dealings". Rutledge said he had so notified Hett, and he added that it was Joseph Hett's custom to attend meetings of the Common Council and shake his head one way or the other as to how he wanted his followers to vote. Rutledge said he told Hett that he did not want him in the Council Chamber, and that Hett said he would be there, that he would talk with councilmen, and would do as he pleased. "Not while I'm here", Rutledge said he told Hett. August Hett, so Rutledge said, remonstrated with Rutledge saying, "It isn't right to call Joe down that way...He's all right".

August Hett was called in rebuttal to the Rutledge story and promptly denied the whole thing. The exchange between lawyers and witnesses indicates the bitterness of the feeling:

Judge Calvin Page: "Did he lie when he said you were a member of the Common Council"?

Hett: "I mean that his account of what occured was false".

Judge Page: "It's true that you're a brother of Joe Hett, isn't it"?

Judge Samuel W. Emery: "Can't you get along without insulting Joe Hett"?

Judge Page: "Pshaw, you can't insult him".

Judge Emery: "As easily as one can insult you, I think".

Judge Page: "You can't insult me for I care nothing for what you say".

Before moving on with the asphalt case, it might be well to digress a moment and talk about this man, Joe Hett. The sketch that follows is taken from the Portsmouth Times of April 18, 1903:

". . . For a half dozen or more years, Joseph Hett has been a power in his city's political affairs. A nod of his head or a snap of his fingers has made or unmade men seeking political preferment. He has lifted into office scores of men, and other scores who have had ambition have had that ambition throttled by him. There was a time, however, when Joseph Hett was without influence, and when he walked our streets a poor man, working early and late, untiringly and unceasingly. Of this he is not ashamed, and there is no reason why he should be.

"On the contrary he takes pride in telling it. He has worked himself up to his present position of power by indomitable perseverance and pluck. His friends will also tell you that no small measure of his success has been achieved because he never turned his back to friend or foe. They will tell you that Joe Hett takes care of his friends and never forgets an enemy . . . Now, just a word or two of the colonel's personal history. He was born in Hamburg, Germany, in 1849. He got what education he possesses in the public schools there and then learned the carpenter's trade. In 1868 he came to this country and went to work on a farm in Newington . . . He next went to work for Honorable John H. Broughton and some twenty-two years ago he went into the job teaming business on his own account . . . . It is only in politics that he is viewed as a being of satanic mould. But then that depends upon which side of the fence you view him from . . . . ." Such was a contemporary description of a man whose name appeared frequently throughout the asphalt hearings.

Getting back to that political charade, another witness was Leon F. Scruton, a civil engineer, the man who directed the installation of the city's high-pressure water line after the Aquaduct was acquired. He was the man who supervised the asphalt work done under the original contract. Scruton was a key witness because the basic premise of the Hett argument was that Judge Stone should grant a temporary injunction to stop work on State Street in the Rockingham Hotel area. Hett's counsel was contending that unless the court acted to stop the ripping up of State Street irremedial harm would be done the old log water pipe system. With or without graft, Emery's argument seems sort of fatuous, and Scruton put it in that perspective. He said it did not matter whether the lines went down State or Court. He said the eight-inch log line was lying in a trench from which all ledge had been removed. Earlier J. Albert Sanborn, one of the water commissioners, probably in some sincerity (it is difficult to know) had voiced concern over the security of the eight-inch log main which carried Peverly Brook water into the city. But Scruton was unconcerned, and he was a highly competent engineer. That estimation of him comes from John W. Durgin, Sr., who has been for forty years "Mr. Surveyor" around Portsmouth. Durgin explains that in Scruton's later years he was a little inclined toward the pleasures afforded by the cider he laid down each fall, but when allowed to sit down on an engineering project he maintained his competency for a long time.

Judge Stone, and it is impossible for anyone to envy him, finally ruled that the city treasurer could not pay the Barber Co. until everything had been thrashed out in the courts. The Superior Court rulings in the winter term, 1905, went against Hett. He appealed to the Supreme Court. On June 30, 1905, the Supreme Court overruled the Hett exceptions, and, as the text says "the Asphalt Case is history".

Lest anyone should want to shed tears for the Barber Asphalt Company, let it be known that it was one of the early classic examples of monopolistic trusts. Remember Teddy Roosevelt and his "big stick"? Barber was one of the outfits he was talking about. Citations about it fill every legal textbook that comes anywhere near the subject.

[11]. William E. Peirce was really out of another era. His philosophy was simple and forthright. He believed that the city's books were his private business and no one else had any business inquiring about them. What a battle he would have had with the "Right-to-Know Law" that is now the weapon of all citizens.

[12]. The 1908 listings will suffice. Starting with the brewers, there were Charles E. Boynton, 16 Bow Street, brewer of "small beer" and agent for two of the big local brewers, plus Schlitz; then there was Frank Jones Brewery Co. The only distiller in town was William Ward & Sons, with a distillery at 23 Dennett Street and offices on Market Street. They described themselves as distillers of "Pure Molasses Rum".

The list of those dispensing wines, liquors and beers begins with Atwell & Co. at 28 Market Street. Benjamin Atwell was the owner. Allen W. Baker, proprietor of the Gloucester House, at 2 and 4 State Street, was next in the listing. This place, which figured in other investigations, was torn down to make way for the lawn to the home now owned by Donald H. Margeson. Harry M. Bullard operated at 4 Water Street. Mrs. Anna T. Dixon, living on Court Street, sold liquor at 13 Water Street.

Dennis E. Drislane had a bar at 9 Water Street; he lived at 31 Vaughan Street. Another barroom at 25 Water Street was owned by William H. Dunn who lived at No. 17. Patrick J. Flanigan's place was another dispenser of the cup that cheers; his place of business was at 41 Penhallow Street. Alexander J. Frazier, spelled Fraser in another part of the same directory, has a bar at 39 Bridge Street. John H.

Galloway had a bar at 6 McDonough Street. And Nathan J. Goss was operating a bar in the vicinity of Flynn's at 26 Penhallow.

Charles W. Ham was offering wines and liquors at 6 High Street and, at 6½ High, Ham was proprietor of a restaurant which as recently as a generation ago had the reputation of being one of the finest in New England. People came from miles around for the pleasure of eating at Ham's. An attempt was made to move the name and reputation out to Lafayette Road, but it was not successful. The building, under the name of Dragon Inn, was destroyed by fire on December 16, 1949. The building had started life in 1928 as Foyecliff, a fine restaurant with a chef that had come from the Adams House in Boston. The Foye family founded it, and then sold out to Albert McLane. Then a man named Melvin Warren operated the General Warren Lobster House on the premises. Just before World War II it became Ham's Inn under the proprietorship of T. Wesley Ham and Harold J. Ham. T. Wesley Ham, right after World War II, was a city assessor. From that the name switched to St. John's Inn, under the management of John Christides. Then it was Mal's Hotel and Restaurant, run by Albert Petrillo. In those days immediately after World War II it was often hired for commissioning and launching parties by Navy personnel. The outcropping of ledge upon which it stood was flattened by dynamite and bulldozers when the Lafayette Plaza, housing King's, Woolworth's, Dan's, and the Radio Shack was created.

Fred E. Henderson had a bar at 83 Islington Street, and Emma Jordan, widow of C. N. Jordan, was licensed for a bar at 28 High Street, the Haven Hotel, of which Casper K. Jordan was manager. This establishment later came into the possession of Elwyn H. Libby and Gordon B. Ladd who operated it under the name of the National Hotel, which should not be confused with the one on Congress Street. Later the National Hotel became the Dolphin, owned by the Coussoule family who operated it for some years. In 1968 they converted the lower floor of the establishment to a well-appointed dining room called the Red Lion Steakhouse. On December 11, 1969, the old hotel and restaurant were destroyed in a fire. Ironically City Electrical Inspector Walter B. Redden had ordered the electricity to the restaurant cut off for what he believed were violations of the electrical code. This had been countered by the Coussoule lawyer, Thomas E. Flynn, who obtained a temporary injunction, levied on all the rolling equipment of the Public Service Company of N. H., thus forcing it to restore power to the restaurant which burned shortly thereafter.

A Mrs. Ellen Kilroe, widow of Peter, was licensed at 3 Bartlett Street. Joseph F. Lamb sold liquor and operated a poolroom at 27 Fleet Street. There were two Learys running bars; Ellen, widow of Thomas, at 122 Market Street, and Daniel at 23 Fleet Street. Also on Fleet Street, No. 8, was Oliver E. Locke. Thomas Loughlin had a wholesale liquor business at 98 Islington Street and a retail outlet at 90 Market Street. Bartholomew Mahoney had a bar at the same address as his home, 116 Islington Street. Charles McCarthy not only had a liquor business on Market Street but he also clerked at Hett's Hotel, "formerly the Dewitt Hotel". Fred V. Hett was operating this Chestnut Street establishment, but he did not last long. By 1912 he was a driver for Hett Bros., and Hett's Hotel was again the Hotel Dewitt with Cornelius Quinn as proprietor. In its last years the Dewitt was managed by Charles Pike who sold out to the Herald Publishing Co. Justin D. Hartford, president and publisher, had the building torn down, and the site was converted to a parking lot for employees. Quinn advertised that he had a "first class innholder's license" and that it was the only hotel in the city using Tungsten electric bulbs. The brass rail from the old bar is still in existence, installed by Richard Blalock, former editor of The Herald, in front of his basement bar counter in his Brackett Road home.

Mitchell & Co. did business at 9 McDonough Street, Thomas E. and John W. Mitchell as partners with John B. Flanagan. Benjamin F. Mugridge dealt as a liquor wholesaler next door to a provision business managed by Benjamin F. Jr., at 51 Market Street. A sister to Benjamin, Jr., Carrie was a reporter for the Portsmouth Times. Sherman T. Newton, grandfather of Sherman Newton, Jr., the present proprietor of the Kearsarge Hotel at Chestnut and Congress Streets, was licensed for a bar at the Kearsarge. Sherman T. Newton was also a collector at the Custom House.

Maurice O'Leary was a piper at the Frank Jones Brewery, and he moonlighted by operating a saloon at 23 Daniel Street with Patrick O'Leary as clerk. Henry P. Payne was a dealer in liquors at his grocery in the Exchange Building. His was a successor firm to Charles E. Laighton & Son, established in 1822. True W. Priest's place in Market Square has already been mentioned. When Priest moved to Ladd Street, one of his competitors was Daniel J. Regan, who, in addition to his saloon on Ladd Street, had a cigar manufactory at 73 Congress Street. Alta Roberts ran a saloon at 14 Water Street; she lived at No. 16. Ernest Robinson had a saloon at 4 Vaughan Street; Percy Rowe was nearby at No. 8. Edward Russell's place was at 24

Water Street, and James J. Ryan was at 18 Penhallow.

Richard Seeley operated a saloon at 38 Deer Street and lived on nearby Maplewood Avenue. Lester W. Thompson was proprietor of the Portsmouth House at 5 Maplewood Avenue, and he also had a license for 25 Bridge Street. Bertram Tilton's store was at the corner of Market and Ladd; the site was later occupied for years by John S. Tilton for a news agency. Harry A Titus ran a saloon in the vicinity of the old Arcadia Theater building. C. Frank Wells had a saloon at 56 Market Street, the same address that John H. Wells had for his grocery; the residence of both men was 43 Islington Street. John H. Wiggin had his home and a saloon at the extreme western end of Deer Street. Samuel T. Young had a saloon on Ceres Street.

In addition three liquor wholesalers are listed. Samuel E. Ross was at 24 Penhallow; he boarded at 1 Chestnut Street (about where the newsroom door of The Portsmouth Herald used to be) with a Charles A. Smith who was a fish packer for E. Newton and Co. Joseph Sacco had a place of business at 218 Market Street, and William Ward & Sons were at 93 Market.

[13]. Something similar to this hassle took place in 1946 when the late Justin D. Hartford, publisher of The Portsmouth Herald, sought to have the South Playground enclosed in canvas so that a baseball team he was sponsoring could play without a lot of "freebies" watching. The issue was researched to some extent by the writer's brother, Peterborough District Court Judge, Kenneth A. Brighton, then a student at Michigan University Law School, who was spending a summer studying under now Superior Court Judge Thomas J. Morris of Rye. It was decided that the playground could be shielded from public view, and Hartford's baseball team, managed by Horace Powell, brother to the ex-Governor S. Wesley Powell, played in the privacy it sought.

[14]. Attorney John W. Kelley died while a comparatively young man at the age of 48. Born here in 1865, he attended Haven School and graduated from Portsmouth High in 1883. At Dartmouth he starred in football for three years. He entered the law office of Frink and Batchelder to read law at the same time teaching school in order to support himself. For four years he was principal at the Whipple School, then was admitted to the bar in 1894. He became city solicitor in 1896 and three years later won election as county solicitor.

Kelley, appointed to the Board of Water Commissioners, was the man who took the City of Portsmouth, at least its Board of Aldermen, to the mat and won a legal fight that established that the city had to pay hydrant rental. Kelley was counsel for the Boston and Maine Railroad and, probably a corollary, for the Frank Jones Brewery. He figured in large degree in the bitter fight over the will of Mary Baker Eddy, the founder of Christian Science.

[15]. When the baseball controversy broke in the news, everyone wanted to say something. The Plains is something special to Portsmouth people, long associated with frontier days, with military drills, with picnics, with presidential receptions, with days when The Plains seemed almost as remote as Exeter. And so the letters to the Editor began to appear, and they give some insight into boundaries and life at The Plains long ago. One of the letters was from a T. M. Jackson who gave his address at Brooklyn, N. Y. He said he had been born in the old Globe Tavern, and he added, "The Plains has a history that it would take a big book to give in full. The land titles are of interest just now. The Gazette of December 7, 1901, has a report to the Common Council by City Solicitor S. Peter Emery relative to The Plains and recites that 'the General Assembly of the Province of New Hampshire on the 21st of July, 1716, made a grant to Thomas Westbrook to keep the only public house by himself or another at the Plains to the Town of Portsmouth, in the consideration that the said Westbrook should lay out six acres of land at said Plains for an accommodation of drawing up the militia of the town or province. Westbrook, to enable him to do this, made an agreement with Henry Sherburne whereby he sold one half of his privilege to run a public house, for three acres of land and other considerations. Later on Joseph Akerman deeded an acre of land at the Plains to the city free from restrictions, which was afterward added to the training field . . . .

"'As to the Akerman deed, here is the real story. Rockingham County deeds, Vol. 157, p. 277, 4 April, 1799, Joseph Akerman of Portsmouth, cordwainer, and wife Elizabeth for $22 convey to the selectmen of Portsmouth for a public road and an addition to the Training Field at the Plains, about one acre of land, fronting southerly on the old Post Road leading from Portsmouth to Greenland, west and north on the land of Samuel Sherburne and east on the common Trainfield, being land that was formerly Richard Leander Nelson's, late of Portsmouth, schoolmaster, deceased, and the same that I purchased of his administrator 3rd April 1799.' Apparently the land was conveyed by George Gains, administrator to Richard Leander Nelson to Akerman. Perhaps Akerman was only a means of getting the land to the Town of Portsmouth because Gains, the administrator, was a selectman."

Jackson goes on, "Now it happens that previously another strip was added to the Plains, and on the opposite side by Samuel Tucker, owner of the Globe Tavern and the 41 acres adjoining. Richard Leander Nelson and Samuel Tucker married the granddaughters of Joshua Brewster, who owned land at the Plains, eight acres as by his inventory, August 1779". Nelson, himself, in April of 1789 advertised for sale "that pleasantly situated place nearly opposite the Globe Tavern, containing one acre of land with house and barn thereon".

A Daniel Waldron apparently conveyed to Tucker the 41 acres mentioned previously, bordering on property owned by Catherine Whipple and Thomas Manning. Waldron also set forth in a mortgage that a strip of land at the Plains, on the south side of the road leading to Greenland, 48¼ rods long, 18 feet wide at the west end and 26 feet wide on the east, "running by the northwestern corner of my dwelling house commonly called the Globe Tavern. The premises conveyed to be a public highway forever".

One resident of the Plains area, with whom the writer has talked but promised not to name, recalled that before the general area of the Globe Tavern became Calvary Cemetery the Globe Tavern was standing just to the west and nearer the road than the Frank C. Ricklefs house, and the tavern barn was a bit to the rear of the Ricklefs house. "The Exeter electric car tracks used to run almost at the edge of the building, but the tavern was falling apart when I was a teenager, and sold for the lumber, but I don't remember who bought it". The Ricklefs house was built about 1920. Two centuries earlier Judge Samuel Sewall of Boston used to stop off in the area to break his journey into Maine for court sessions.

Donald F. Ricklefs, born in 1918, a local carpenter and contractor, remembers playing in the cellar hole of the old tavern as a little boy. "My Dad was so afraid that we'd get hurt that he kept filling it in", Ricklefs recalls. And he mentioned that he has in his possession an unusual bottle that he found in the vicinity many years ago. Also he said that a stair rail from the tavern was installed in the house of his grandmother, Mrs. Michael E. McCarthy, at 871 Middle Road, on a stairway leading to the attic. "As far as I know, it's still there", said Ricklefs.

[16]. This dispute, as so many do, had its roots in the distant past. Because of the way the original bank building was constructed, and photos still extant make this apparent, the two banks would have to agree to changes in the exterior to maintain any symmetry whatsoever. In 1870 they executed such a pact. Some

years later major alterations were made, with uniformity being the watchword. This held good for some years, but about 1901, the Portsmouth Savings Bank started a major remodeling job, claiming that the previous renovations had nullified the agreement of 1870. To this the First National took exception and the legal battle was on. Ultimately the courts agreed with the Savings Bank, and the 1870 pact was ended. The bank let a contract to a Providence firm and took up temporary quarters in the old Portsmouth Athletic Club quarters on Market Street. A little more than a year later Portsmouth Savings moved into the renovated building it had created out of an old friendship.

[17]. Dennis J. Leahy, who died September 14, 1958, was born in Ireland in 1870. He came to America when he was eleven years old. In 1933 he retired from the Portsmouth Navy Yard as a quarterman.

[18]. Let The Herald's story tell it: "Two things are very apparent — this sweeper should be run with the wind, and at night, so that the traveling public will not have to eat the dust that it kicks up. The trial today (Saturday, December 19, 1903) seemed to indicate that when the sweeper goes one way, shoving the dirt to one side, the wind has the greater part of it back in the path before the machine gets back again".

[19]. When Dr. Andrew Preston died unexpectedly on December 6, 1906, it meant the winding up of an unusual business and a close association with the city. Dr. Preston was born here in 1856, the son of William R. Preston. The elder Preston came here about 1840 at the behest of his relative, the Rev. Andrew P. Peabody, pastor of the South Church. Contemporary accounts have it that Preston stayed here only because of a rainstorm. He had come from Salem in the days before "the cars", so it meant he traveled by stage while the goods for his apothecary shop were brought up by a teamster. Preston was unimpressed by the quarters Peabody had found for his business, directly across the street from the stone church — just west of where McCaffery's filling station is today. These quarters were later occupied by the well remembered and well liked Dr. Herbert L. Taylor until he moved to Middle Street in 1920. Preston, who had really wanted to move west to Illinois, was about to pack up and pull out when the rains hit, threatening to ruin his goods. He moved them from the teamster's wagon to the store and there he stayed, prospering as the years went by. He moved from there to the Congress Block, being one of its first tenants, and was one of the first tenants to return to it when it was rebuilt after the

fire of 1865. Dr. Andrew Preston was running his retail drug business from there when he sold out in 1903. The Preston name, however, was visible on the Bow Street building until comparatively recent times.

[20]. Grandson of the John Pickering who married the intended bride of James McDonough, the man who disappeared on his wedding night, John J. Pickering spent his entire life in banking and mercantile pursuits. The scion of money, he married more money when he took as his bride Sarah Jenness, the daughter of Peter Jenness, president of the New Hampshire Bank. At the time of his death in 1904 he was president of the Portsmouth and Concord Railroad, the SPCA, and a director of the Portsmouth Athenaeum.

[21]. Albert C. Anderson, although dead since July 3, 1906, figured in the news again in May of this year. Workmen making alterations in the building at 54 Court Street owned by Irenee Lebel uncovered a chalked inscription on the south outside wall which read: "Albert C. Anderson and Frank Kiernan, Wood Butchers, May 8, 1872". Lebel is a public accountant and treasurer of the Portsmouth Historical Society. At that time Anderson lived at 56 Union Street, and Kiernan and Willis F. Kiernan lived at 46 Union. Anderson, at public auction in 1903, paid a little over $10,000 for the Pickering property. He acted as a "straw" for Agnes Page Bartlett, wife of John H. Bartlett. It is now a parking lot. Death came to Anderson in the shape of electrocution in 1906. Emerging from his home at 39 Middle Street and planning to walk to Albert E. Rand's store next door at No. 43 — now the Stop-n-Go Food Market — he turned the switch on the pole in front of his home and something went wrong. Anderson was still breathing when found by Morris C. Foye and Patrolman Charles Quinn.

Five years after he had scribbled his name on the wall of the house he was building for True M. Ball at 5 Court Street (now No. 54), Anderson went into partnership with his brother-in-law, Albert R. Junkins. They built a house for Charles E. Walker, father to Mrs. Jeremy R. Waldron, Sr., who lived diagonally across the street. Also the G. Ralph Laighton house, now the residence of former U. S. Senator Maurice J. Murphy, Jr., at 660 Middle Street. They also built a house at 37 Middle Street, next door to Anderson's, for Morris C. Foye.

[22]. The Herald said, "This meeting is unique in the political annals of Portsmouth and many of the politicians are guessing in consequence. They all recognize the importance of the gathering." A woman leader told a reporter, "Politics as politics do

not enter into the situation as we view it. Our actions will be guided entirely for the good of the schools". Previous to this meeting, many Portsmouth women had attended a session in Red Men's Hall in which their new right was explained to them by a couple of Concord women. But the rally on November 24 was indeed different because it was the first such affair in which Portsmouth women rallied to elect a candidate.

[23]. William E. Marvin was a nephew of a previous Portsmouth mayor, T. E. O. Marvin, and bears the distinction of being probably one of the few men, if not the only one, ever to serve both as mayor of Portsmouth and a selectman of New Castle. Born here in 1872, he attended Harvard Law and then joined the firm of Frink, Batchelder and Marvin. Later he was the senior partner in the firm of Marvin, (Harry) Peyser, (F. Garland) Tucker and (Robert) Marvin, which has been succeeded by the firm of David Sanderson and Thomas M. Dudley, Jr. In 1885 Marvin moved to New Castle and was elected a selectman in 1890, serving until 1896. Four years after he returned to Portsmouth to live, he was elected mayor and was the first mayor under the new City Charter. He died in 1938.

[24]. Concurrent with the asphalt scandal, and quite probably an incidental phase of it, was the stink kicked up when the city clerk, William E. Peirce, and the ex-treasurer, E. B. Prime, refused to turn their books over to an outside auditor for examination. Why they took this stance is hard to understand because the auditor, Chester Marr, could find a discrepancy of only $400 or so, not really serious.

But they did fight it. J. H. S. Frink, acting for a special aldermanic committee consisting of John G. Parsons, Frank M. Dennett and Elisha B. Newman, sought a court ruling. The dispute before Judge Charles F. Stone was concurrent with the hearing the jurist was holding into a petition for an injunction against continued paving under a contract with the Barber Asphalt Co. Judge Stone told the litigants that as far as he was concerned, the only question was whether or not the city should pay the outside auditor.

Frink said he really did not care on that point. What he wanted was a thorough examination of the books. John W. Kelley, city solicitor, appearing for the two beleaguered officials, insisted he would fight payment all the way because only the city auditor was authorized by law to see the books, and the City Council had no power in the matter. Arguments like that sound odd today because audits by outside accountants are a matter of annual routine in City Hall.

The court finally ordered the books turned over, and Prime then told accountant Marr that his books were in the city auditor's hands. When Marr completed his audit, his criticism of Portsmouth accounting procedures was damning:

"In short, I am of the opinion that what is needed in your city is the establishment of a system of methods which will prevent such confusion in the future, a system not too elaborate — no fancy bookkeeping — but plain, simple and concise . . . . My investigation may have seemed somewhat time consuming, but, could I have had the books at the start, I might have concluded my examination, which, under the circumstances, has proved puzzling and ofttimes provoking".

[25]. The first City Council under the new charter is worth a bit of study. The Democrats held a 6 to 3 edge. The Herald, with a Republican bias under publisher F. W. Hartford, listed the three minority members first:

Charles H. Colbeth: Teamster. Has been in business 17 years, and for a few years previous was connected with Valentine Hett, as Hett and Colbeth. When elected, he was agent for the National Biscuit Co. Had been a ward officer, served on the Common Council.

Michael E. Long: Alderman Long was a foreman boilermaker at the Navy Yard. Long had no fraternal affiliations other than the Grand Army, of which he had been president.

Harry E. Boynton: When elected he was serving his first term in public office on the Common Council. He was treasurer of the Portsmouth Savings Bank and managing the business founded by his father C. E. Boynton.

John J. Molloy: A cooper by trade, he was employed by the Frank Jones Brewing Co. Had lived in Portsmouth twenty years. Was a member of the Elks, active in athletics, a member of the Portsmouth Athletic Club and Portsmouth Council, Knights of Columbus.

Stanton M. Trueman: A cooper at Frank Jones brewery, serving a first term as alderman, previously on the Common Council.

James T. Whitman: A cooper by trade; had previous service on both bodies at City Hall; a member of the Coopers' Union, the Knights of Columbus, and the Ancient Order of Hibernians.

William A. A. Cullen: Cooper, expert with tools of the trade.

Henry Wendell: Merchant; since 1874 had conducted a hardware business with his brother, Andrew P. Wendell, founded by their father, Abraham Q. Wendell in 1834.

Ira C. Seymour: A highly successful blacksmith; with the Fire

Department twenty years, two years as chief engineer; Democratic member of first Police Commission.

[26]. Annie H. Hewitt apparently was not much appreciated by The Herald for her pioneering role. Despite the fact that she was the first woman ever elected to public office in the City of Portsmouth, her obituary was minimal and mentioned only that she served eight years on the Board of Instruction. She was already widowed when elected, and lived with her sister-in-law, Florence Hewitt, a teacher. Her husband, Henry C. Hewitt, had run a haberdashery where Liggett's drug store used to be on Congress Street. If there is any Women's Lib organization in Portsmouth, Annie H. Hewitt should be its official saint.

[27]. Alfred F. Howard was secretary of the Granite State Fire Insurance Company from the time of its founding in 1885 until the day of his death in 1919. A native of Marlow, he came here early in life and was admitted to the bar. He served as city solicitor and was on the Police Commission prior to the scandal of 1912, resigning and being replaced by Morris C. Foye. In addition to his insurance work, he practiced law, was a vice president of Portsmouth Trust and Guarantee. During President William Howard Taft's visit to Portsmouth in October 1912, Howard was introduced to the President, and they exchanged pleasantries on a possible family connection. Howard died in 1919 at the age of 77.

[28]. Some indication of the prospects the women faced when they turned out on the morning of December 12 to cast their first votes can be gleaned from what The Herald said was NOT going on. Mrs. Sarah Foote was the first of her sex ever to vote in the city, casting her ballot at 6:20 a.m. in Ward 5. It's too bad that a photographic record could not have been made. The Herald's reporter, after a round of the polls election morning — even as Herald reporters do today — said:

"On the whole Portsmouth has never known a quieter election day. It is hardly possible that the vote will reach the expected figures, although it will not be as light as the early hours led many to believe. It may be stated positively that the man with the roll is conspicuous entirely by his absence. There is no money in sight. Everywhere the same conditions prevail. The voter who wishes to barter his right of franchise for coin of the realm finds absolutely nothing doing. There is no market at all for his ballot. He may exercise the privilege of the American citizen if he wishes, but he must do it without cash return. Everyone of the polling places might serve as a model for Sunday School. Order, with the biggest O in the type case, reigns throughout the city. Portsmouth was never a city in which election outrages were committed but it is a Puritan town today. All the men who used to regard Election Day as a proper one on which to celebrate are apparently occupying seats on the water wagon. If they are not, they are certainly giving rein to their joy in some places other than the wardrooms.

"Perhaps the women voters are in a measure responsible for this idyllic state of affairs. It may be that their influence calmed the first wild, untamed political enthusiast and made him a Chesterfield".

This advent of the women must have been really earthshaking because the reader can almost sense the awe in The Herald reporter's pen when he reported, "Whenever a woman appears in the ward-room, every man doffs his hat."

[29]. The Farragut School obviously was named in honor of Admiral David G. Farragut who died at the Portsmouth Navy Yard.

[30]. The Rev. Lucius H. Thayer cast a long shadow. Certainly his successor at the North Church, the Rev. Arthur Acy Rouner, was never able to establish himself in nineteen years as worthy of coming out from under that shadow. The Rev. Mr. Rouner, a member of the Board of Education, and one of the last local ministers to wear a stiff high-winged collar, never was formally installed as pastor over the North Church.

[31]. Daniel F. Borthwick served several terms as a police commissioner. He was one of those people who preferred the background in the operation of their good works, whether civic or charitable. For nearly fifty years, he was treasurer of the Howard Benevolent Society, a post later taken over by the late Albert H. Hunt, the husband of his niece, Susan Borthwick. He founded a store that he operated as D. F. Borthwick's, 19 Market Street, for many years. He was succeeded in it by his brother, James F. Borthwick. He was born in 1858 and died December 20, 1936.

[32]. The fire that destroyed in a large part Walker's wharf bothered local authorities more than they let it be known at the time. It followed, in less than 24 hours, a spectacular blaze at Littlefield Lumber Co. Walker's, because of the high tower, probably was the more spectacular, and literally thousands watched from various vantage points when it finally crumpled and crashed. Today, as the visitor views the parking lot created for Prescott Park, it is hard to visualize the old, coal-grimed Walker wharf.

Damage was estimated at $200,000. The fire also destroyed a

building owned by Charles H. Walker that housed the Portsmouth Fish Co., a business owned by Paul Desjardins and Earl Chandler.

Arson had been suspected at the Littlefield fire the night before, and arson was again suspected when Littlefield's was afire on October 7, 1951. All three fires were fought from both water and land, as the Navy, under the mutual aid pact, had sent its fireboat over to help battle the flames.

[33]. George H. Ducker will be heard from later. He became city marshal.

[34]. Dr. Fred Seales Towle was to die a tragic death during World War I. That was on October 10, 1918 when he was killed in a blaze that swept the BOQ at the General Base Hospital, Colonial, N. J., where he was serving as a captain in the Medical Corps.

[35]. Sperry H. Locke was one of the more colorful of latter-day Portsmouth politicians. A native of North Hampton, he attained early fame as a baseball pitcher in the rugged sand lot ball prevalent early in this century. Locke graduated from Phillips Exeter and attended Dartmouth. He was a police commissioner in 1913. Almost into the last days of his long life, he could be seen along Congress Street talking politics with anyone who would spare him a second. One of the great heroes of his life was James Farley, Postmaster General under Franklin D. Roosevelt, a consummate politician whose great stock-in-trade was a phenomenal memory for names and faces.

More than twenty years ago, Richard Blalock, former editor of The Herald, was attending a newspaper convention at the Waldorf Astoria in New York. Farley was a luncheon speaker, and, as was his wont, he left the podium, like a Protestant pastor, to get to the doors to greet as many as possible. When Blalock shook hands, he said he was from Portsmouth. Farley, without a second's hesitation, asked, "How's my old friend, Sperry Locke?" A startled Blalock indicated that Locke, considering his age, was in fine health and found Locke completely unsurprised when informed of the incident on his return to Portsmouth. After all, he was a friend of Jim Farley's.

However, Locke was not that successful with one of his other pet projects: A water line to Merrymeeting Lake. This pipedream of Locke's was, and is, more practical than many would believe because water supplies are going to be a critical matter in Portsmouth and the seacoast in the next few years. This is being made increasingly apparent as city officials, desperate for property to tax, continue to turn all the cities in the coastal area into boundary-to-boundary concrete and hottop. It is all part of the price New Hampshire pays for dependence almost entirely on the property tax as a source of revenue. But there will be more on water later.

[36]. Guy E. Corey practiced law here for many years, was active in Republican politics, serving in the Legislature in 1904, 1942 and 1946. At one time he was city solicitor and also did a stint as city clerk. He was graduated from Portsmouth High in 1895 and from Dartmouth with the Class of 1899.

[37]. Willis F. Kiernan died in North Kittery in 1922 after a long career as a carpenter and contractor.

[38]. Cornelius Quinn died in May 1931.

[39]. Into this house moved Sarah Purcell, owner of the boarding house at which John Paul Jones stayed during his two Portsmouth sojourns. She followed Governor John Langdon in her residency, having sold the present-day John Paul Jones House to Woodbury Langdon, the governor's brother. Langdon himself moved into the beautiful home that bears his name even today. In 1786, the Rambler says she swapped houses with Colonel William Brewster, landlord of the Bell Tavern, and so Brewster became host to President Washington.

[40]. E. Percy Stoddard died August 9, 1941, after a long illness. A native of Portsmouth, he had for some years operated a real estate and insurance business. In 1903 he was appointed a deputy U. S. Marshal and was at that time in his 27th year. Portsmouth's public schools gave him his basic education, and he was graduated from Portsmouth High in 1897, president of the class. He entered Dartmouth College but left in 1899 to follow a newspaper career in the offices of The Portsmouth Times, under True L. Norris. Stoddard belonged to the Portsmouth Athletic Club, Masonic groups, the Portsmouth Yacht Club and the John Langdon Club.

[41]. Of the ninth generation from the first immigrant, Henry Adams, Edward H. Adams died on October 30, 1939, while on a daily excursion into the downtown area. At the time of his death he was the oldest of the ex-mayors. Adams was admitted to the bar in 1897. He had served, as an associate, on the bench of the local courts since 1895. Adams' judicial career followed the bent of the court. He was an associate under Judge Thomas H. Simes and when that court was abolished in favor of a district court under Harry K. Torrey, Adams became the associate. Two years later that system was abolished, but Adams became the associate under a new municipal court format and held that post until 1934 when age caught up with him. Adams served on the Board of Instruction from

1895 until 1902 when he moved to the Board of Aldermen. Elected mayor twice, 1909 and 1910, Adams was still civic minded enough to accept a term on the City Council in 1913.

His son, the late Woodbury S. Adams, a retired captain in the U. S. Navy had been a close associate of Gerald D. Foss in the compilation of the definitive work in Masonic history. Adams was extremely active in Masonic work, a past master of St. John's Lodge. He served as treasurer of the Portsmouth Athenaeum.

[42]. Conner was postmaster until a change of administrations put him out of office. He was succeeded by Joseph H. Dowd. Conner was the father of Mrs. Morris C. Foye, Mrs. Chester P. Hartford and Joseph Conner, Jr.

[43]. A native of Somersworth, Fred E. Hasty spent all his working life in the employ of the Henry W. Peyser firm, the clothiers on Market Street. His life centered around his work and the Portsmouth Athletic Club of which he was a founder and the first president. A few months before his death in 1935, the P.A.C. presented Hasty and four other charter members, the only living ones, with canes in recognition of their services.

[44]. James H. Dow was one of Portsmouth's most outstanding athletes and played a prominent role in the development of baseball locally. Dow had the reputation of being one of the longest hitters and of having the best throwing arm in this section of the country. Unfortunately for Dow, he came along a century too soon. With that sort of ability he could probably at least make the present-day Boston Red Sox. His working life was in the employ of the G. B. French Company. He was 78 when he died in 1918.

[45]. William J. Cater's name lives on, perpetuated by the playground on Columbia Street that he gave to the city in 1947. A native of Ontario, Canada, he was active politically. He was a member of the State Legislature in 1913, served two terms on the City Council, and also served on the staff of Governor John H. Bartlett. He died in December 1954.

[46]. There was no shortage of volunteers; there never is in Portsmouth when it comes to a "fun thing". The executive committee for the 1910 Return had alread been named, and "pot luck" is the best that can be done with listing some of the many others. Space limitations will force the exclusion of some, probably even more deserving than those on the roster.

On the Finance Committee were Frank J. Philbrick, Wallace Hackett, Gustave Peyser, William N. Norton, Edward E. McIntire, Eben Blaisdell, I. H. Washburn, Arthur M. Clark, Joseph W.

Akerman, S. F. A. Pickering, Morgan Dade, Frederick Gardner, Ralph B. Flynn, Ceylon Spinney, Lawrence G. Peyser, Stanton M. Trueman, Fred L. Trask, Ernest L. Channey, Cater and John H. Bartlett.

As was inevitable, a lot of these committee assignments were doubled up. Postmaster Joseph P. Conner was on the Finance and General Committees; Charles W. Gray's name was on several; in fact, nearly everyone in the city was on the General Committee so a few chairmen of other groups will be named: Badge, E. Percy Stoddard; Band Concerts, Fred E. Hasty; Ladies, Mrs. Charles W. Brewster; Decoration, Arthur E. Richardson; Collation, George H. McCauley; Procession, J. Albert Sanborn; Transportation, Dana B. Cutter; Carriages, Ira A. Newick; Literary Exercises, Wallace Hackett; Fireworks, Chauncey B. Hoyt; Athletics, J. William Newell; Information, Alfred O. Booth (YMCA secretary); Press Committee, True L. Norris, chairman, and F. W. Hartford, Lewis W. Brewster, Arthur G. Brewster, Richard I. Walden, Samuel Dodge, Richard D. McDonough, John T. Lambert, Patrick E. Kane, Fred E. Drew, Percival Moulton, George H. Sanderson and D. C. Clark.

[47]. J. Albert Sanborn had a Civil War record of almost unequalled gallantry. He was, apparently, one of those citizen-soldiers who rise to the occasion when America calls. His obituary in The Herald, the day after his death, April 21, 1913, was a column in length, detailing the man's military career. One outstanding incident describes how Sanborn, accompanied by another soldier, piled up bodies of their fallen comrades and used them as a shield in driving back determined Confederate assaults. They were finally relieved by the arrival of a Massachusetts company. Sanborn entered the service as a private in Co. G, 10th NHVR, and came out a captain, the rank he bore until his death.

Sanborn was born in Portland in 1841 and came to Portsmouth as a boy. He was educated in the local schools and enlisted at the age of twenty. He was wounded twice.

[48]. The Portsmouth Athletic Club was organized on September 10, 1885. It was in existence about 50 years, its last quarters being at 130 Court Street — the Folsom-Salter house — which was taken over by the American Legion in 1937 before the Frank E. Booma Post moved to its present quarters on Islington Street. During the half century of its life, no organization appeared more active in community life than the P. A. C.

[49]. One of the great Portsmouth stories is the burning of the Stagecoach about 1846. Even in this violent age, it

does not seem as amusing, from the point of view of the police, as it did to Thomas Bailey Aldrich. Writing about the event in 1892, a "Bad Boy" — not Aldrich — said the whole incident had its start on July 4, 1846, in the far off Pacific. Generally a holiday like the Fourth would be observed with only must-work on board ship. But on this occasion two Portsmouth boys were ordered to slush down the masts. "Sitting in the main and foretopmast cross-trees they vowed a vow that if they arrived home safe to old Portsmouth by the next Fourth of July, they would make up for the unpatriotic duty they were then doing, by painting the old town red — such a Fourth as Adams said there always should be, for time and forever".

Imagine their consternation the next year to learn that the selectmen of Portsmouth, because President James K. Polk was visiting the town on that day, had ordained that no bells were to be rung, nor bonfires built, as "from the first Fourth of July it had been the custom to usher in the day we celebrate ". Why it is that public officials have always persisted in bringing so many troubles on their own heads is past understanding. The town fathers, if they ever had any boyhoods, should have known such a ban, President or no President, would only spark more mischief than a legion of police could handle. And it did.

But let the story teller spin his own yarn:

"This (the ban) fired their youthful patriotism and they were more than resolved to paint the town red, and many now with us can vouch for their good works. Hardly had the old North bell pealed forth the midnight hour and the advent of the glorious natal day of our beloved country, than the painting began. Such a salvo of all kinds of firearms the old Parade had never heard before. Then the churches were visited and all found guarded by the police, but it was not long before by some sleight of hand the bell ropes were in the boys' hands, or else a bad boy was in the belfry. The last bell to be captured was the Methodist (now Temple Israel). Then after such devotion to the spirit of patriotism, a visit to the saloon of Benn - - - - (Whitcomb) was made, and quenching their thirst with pop beer, they marched out armed with muskets, horse pistols, etc., forming in front of the saloon, where stood five of the leaders, two of whom were the two who registered the vow one year before as they sat in the cross-trees, sailing over the broad Pacific".

It should be mentioned here that the saloon referred to was actually a confectioner's shop and ice cream "saloon". It stood where the eastern wall of Portsmouth Savings now rests, and was a building with romantic traditions. Here lived the famed Molly Pitman whose beauty attracted the eye of old Benning Wentworth. He proposed, so the legend goes, was rejected, and was so angered that soon thereafter, Miss Pitman's beloved Richard Shortridge was "pressed" into the Royal Navy, and it was seven years before he could return to claim his bride. Captain George Turner, an enterprising ship captain and merchant, occupied the building for some years. Sometime after 1840 Whitcomb took it over and sold confections. According to C. S. Gurney, one of the ringleaders in the stage coach affair, returned every year on the night before the Fourth and ate ice cream there even when he was serving four terms as mayor.

Then the "bad boys" gave thought as to what to do next. With the two chief conspirators in the lead, they went to the carriage makers shop operated by Hill and Safford in the rear of the Pierce block at Market Square and High Street. In the shadows they "confiscated" a stage coach called the "Plow Boy". Where the vigilant police were all this time is hard to guess. Many willing hands made short work of pulling the stage to the Parade where it was soon put to the torch. The letter gives credit to Aldrich for telling the story except that he insisted that Aldrich was wrong in thinking that the burning of the coach occasioned the arrest of the "bad boys".

" . . . . It was not so. They were arrested for breaking and entering the Methodist Church, and thus securing the possession of the bell. An entrance was made by breaking out with a musket one of the door panels and shoving in a small boy whose escape the officer (guarding the inside of the church) tried to prevent by standing, lantern in hand, in front of the broken panel. A vigorous blow on his legs from a musket in the hands of one boy on the outside caused the officer to lie down, and the boy came out with the bell rope.

"For this only were they arrested, and brought before Justice William H. Rollins, our present honored citizen of that name, and notwithstanding the eloquent pleading of that one of their number who had studied law with Colonel (Ichabod) Bartlett, they were sentenced to pay a fine of $5 and costs, total $7.37½, which was paid.

"Then it was that the "bad boys" blocked their persecutors by purchasing that cremated stage coach while the officers were out getting a warrant, and when the officers attempted to arrest them for that act they coolly asked, as they shoved the receipted bill in their faces, "can't we burn our own property"?"

Before closing this note, it should be recorded that

President Polk, despite the worries of the selectmen, did arrive in Portsmouth on the Fourth and paid his visit without untoward incident. He arrived at 10:15 a.m., leaving "the cars" on the Kittery side and walking across Portsmouth Bridge where he was met by city and state officials and escorted to the center of town to the old Congress Block where a platform had been built out from the second story. President Polk spoke as did James Buchanan, soon to come to the presidency himself. The crowd saved its cheers for a wounded veteran of the Mexican War who was in the party. In the audience were Mark Green and George Fishley, both of whom had been soldiers in the Revolution. From the Congress Block the President was taken to the old Rockingham House where there was a reception. Then he went out to Judge Levi Woodbury's home, off present-day Woodbury Avenue, and had dinner, leaving town about 3 p.m. for Newburyport.

On July 4, 1879, one of those who had been at the burning of the "Plow Boy" left a stage coach in front of the house of one of the ringleaders as a practical joke and reminder of the occasion of 32 years before. The "bad boy" had it taken to the Parade and burned.

The Morning Chronicle on July 7, 1879, reported:

"The cricket match on the grounds at the Creek between the Portsmouth and Boston Cricket Clubs was won by the local organization. In the evening the American Band of Rochester occupied the bandstand on Market Square, and for something over two hours made music for a large audience. During the evening an ancient stage coach was burned on the Square. The band playing "Departed Days" and "Auld Lang Syne" as the cremation progressed. This coach was deposited in front of William H. Sise's house at 2 o'clock on the morning of the Fourth, having been sent from Boston on a freight train by Mr. William H. Thompson of the Kearsarge mills as a present to our respected mayor, who, 32 years ago, with Mr. Thompson and other boys who have since filled responsible positions in the world, confiscated and burned an old mail coach one Fourth of July morning and got into a scrape thereby. . . ."

331

23

The Red Lights are Turned Off

[1]. Charles H. Stewart died August 31, 1945. He was described as an antique dealer. Some indication of his interest in this and kindred lines can be found in the fact that he was one of a syndicate who bought the Old Almshouse at public auction. That was on January 25, 1917; the building was bought for $1,655 by Harry Wood, Joseph Sacco and Stewart. Their sole purpose was to wreck the building for the material. In fact they sold off the copper and other easily removed pieces before leaving the site. Stewart later sold out to Sacco and Wood. Also in the winter of 1917, Stewart bought in the John Paul Jones House for $1,500 with the intent to wreck it and salvage the paneling, mantel shelves and planking. The Granite State Fire Insurance Company had acquired the land and buildings for the site of a new office building, but agreed to erect a structure on the other side of the street. Fernando W. Hartford, thanks to Woodbury Langdon's $10,000 gift, bought the house from Stewart. Some time afterward, the Portsmouth Historical Society was able to obtain the land itself from Granite State and the whole property is now the museum of the Portsmouth Historical Society. Stewart and others, including Garland W. Patch, Sr., frequently bought buildings that were about to be razed, saving in that way the best of the cabinet work, doors and such.

[2]. The Gloucester Hotel disappeared when ex-Governor Charles M. Dale started carrying out the wishes of the Prescott sisters, Miss Mary and Miss Josie, to improve Portsmouth's waterfront area. This will be developed in more detail in a subsequent chapter.

[3]. Eva White's Elm House disappeared under the approaches to the Memorial Bridge when construction started. Part of this old house still exists, a fact largely unknown to the passerby.

If a stroller along Bow Street will glance upward when he passes No. 35, he will note a second floor bay window. That window came from the Elm House. Eva White had it salvaged when the old place was being leveled, had it brought to her apartment on Bow Street and installed, perhaps as a memento of "better days".

[4]. Crank's letter is a graphic outline of the problem as the Navy saw it, and was addressed to the editor of The Herald:

"A great deal of criticism and discussion has been heard regarding the partial quarantine established by the commanding officers of the ships at this Navy Yard against the City of Portsmouth, the injustice done thereby to the shopkeepers, the absence of any good reasons for the quarantine, etc.

"While I am of the opinion that the greater portion of this criticsm and protest is inspired by the keepers of the brothels and gin mills which abound in town and who miss sadly the toll which they collect from the younger enlisted men. I have heard criticism from other quarters which impels me to request that you give me sufficient space in your paper to set forth the view and attitude of an officer who has endeavored to regulate the shore going of the men with a view solely to their health and welfare, both physical and spiritual. As far as this ship is concerned the partial quarantine of the ship was established solely on the recommendation of the medical officer of the ship because of the health conditions on shore, conditions which made advisable the closing of the public schools, the non-attendance of children at Sunday School and the taking of other precautions. Is the commanding officer of a ship to be any less solicitous of the health of the men under his command and care than others? If anyone in authority on shore replies that there was no condition on shore to warrant the steps taken at this yard, I will say that in my opinion that even if there was no epidemic of any sort ashore there are other remediable conditions which would warrant a commanding officer placing certain restrictions on the shore-going of the men.

"If there is any doubt as to what is meant, let any interested person visit that portion of Water Street which lies between State and Hancock on the sixth of any month after the men have been given their monthly money, or certain portions of Court and Penhallow Streets. Lest we condemn the men themselves for going to such places, let it be considered that they are just released from the close confinement and restriction of ship routine and turned loose in a place which offers little or nothing in the way of diversion or entertainment and that the very first street that they cross after landing is lined with places of a sort that offer a dangerous lure to our young.

"Portsmouth is, presumably, interested in this Navy Yard. Portsmouth can do a great deal towards making it more attractive and agreeable for the hundreds who are sent there. Let Portsmouth do a little sanitary housecleaning; let someone make an effort to provide a decent place of resort for the men when they go ashore, and a little concerted action will accomplish much. Let someone put a shoulder to the wheel to aid the officers of the ships sent here to help the men of the Navy. Let the people realize that the officers are actuated by no feeling of prejudice against the town but by a desire to help and protect the men against the existing conditions. Then there will be no cause for anyone to protest against any action on the part of the officers. Some of the effective politics which have been used here from time to time might be employed in getting for the men at this yard a place of resort where they might be employed in getting recreation and change. The sale of vile liquor on shore, and the income of the harlot would be sadly reduced, but the men and the service would profit thereby".

[5]. It hardly needs to be said that this group of feminine battlers for decency was headed by the indefatigable Annie L. Hewitt, the first woman ever to hold public office here. Some of her compatriots were Mattie I. Kimball, Mary I. Wood and Ida A. Urch. The group's purpose was the furtherance of civic improvements.

[6]. Daniel W. Badger was one of Portsmouth's sharpest businessmen, and founder of the Portsmouth Creamery in 1918 which became Badger Farms Creamery on Bow Street, a firm which prided itself on the modernity of its equipment and the fact that it introduced pasteurization. Badger was born on August 18, 1865. He had worked on a farm in Newington and had represented that town in the State Legislature in 1903.

At the time of mayoralty, a post he held for three one-year terms, Badger was in business as a milk dealer with his son, Ralph W. Badger, on Boyd Road. Another of the odd ways in which life works - - Badger succeeded his foe City Marshal Thomas Entwistle on the Governor's Council for 1913-1914, and his ward sent him to the Legislature in 1917-1918. In 1923 he again served the city as a police commissioner. Besides his son, Badger fathered five daughters, among them Mrs. John E. Seybolt and Mrs. Albert Fagan.

[7]. True L. Norris was typical of the newspaper editors of the time. To them the newspaper was merely a vehicle

employed in the furtherance of their personal political ambitions or those of the party with which they were affiliated. Membership in a political party was a passion equaled only by religious dogma. The Herald described Norris as "a newspaperman of the old school". Norris was brought here by Charles A. Sinclair, Frank Jones' son-in-law, after he bought The Portsmouth Times. Norris' mission was simple: To expound the tenets of the Democratic Party. This he did throughout his career.

Norris was well grounded in his profession. A graduate of Harvard, he enlisted in Company K, 5th Massachusetts Regiment, in the Civil War. He studied law, was admitted to the bar, and bounced around a wide variety of governmental offices in Washington, including a stint under the notorious Ben Butler. From there he went to the New York Herald and two years later he moved to the Boston Globe. In 1888, at the age of forty, he returned to his native New Hampshire, settling in Concord where he practiced law and did work as a stringer for the Boston Globe and the New York Herald. Ultimately he bought The Portsmouth Times from Sinclair and retained it until two years before his death in 1920. What happened to the bound files of The Times is still a mystery. Some early volumes are in the Portsmouth Public Library, but all those that would interest the student of the late 19th and 20th Century local politics apparently have vanished, unless a set is in the Library of Congress.

[8]. Morris C. Foye, I, died on August 30, 1932, bringing an end to a long career in merchandising here. Foye started in the dry goods business in 1878 and was active until a few days before his death. He was born at Foye's Corner, Rye, in 1853. Foye represented his adopted town in the legislature twice, and served on the Police Commission through the harassing days of the cleanup when he and True L. Norris were under fire from all sides. Dimick had died, and the two of them were the board until Sperry H. Locke came on to finish Dimick's term, but that was after it was all over.

[9]. One of the really amazing things about this period was Charles H. "Cappy" Stewart's relative immunity to arrest. True, he was caught selling liquor after hours in 1895, but it was not until February of 1910 that he was again in court, and that for keeping liquor for sale, a complaint that was discharged. Another in July was nol prossed. When all the madams were being taken to jail in 1912 to do ninety days, Stewart's name was not on the list. Perhaps it was because he really did run a well behaved joint, and the police were glad to afford him any protection he needed.

[10]. Richard M. Hughes, captain of the USS Washington, was the first to let his men free to run the perils of Water Street. To the "girls" and their keepers, and to the Portsmouth merchants, it must have been a beautiful sight when boatload after boatload of liberty-bound, blue-clad sailors poured across the river from the battleship. The Wisconsin's men, however, although chafing to get in on the action, were kept restricted for a while longer. Incidentally, a bulkhead door from the Wisconsin is on display in the John Paul Jones House.

[11]. Captain Paul F. Connors is probably as big a man as any who ever wore the local police uniform. The writer's first introduction to this gargantuan upholder of law and order came in the spring of 1946 at a small, night-time fire in Ladd Street. An eager beaver reporter in those days, the writer went through the fire line and entered the burning structure. His presence there was brief; suddenly he felt himself grasped in the rear-most portion of his pants, and an ungentle hand on his collar aided his swift exodus from the building. The propulsive force came from then Patrolman Paul F. Connors, and once taking a good look at his size, who would argue?

[12]. The Edisonian had many names, before and afterward. At one point it was called "Your Theater". Then it was the Gaiety, and ultimately, until television put so many theaters out of business, The Arcadia. Others in town included the Portsmouth Theater, where the Civic now is. The Portsmouth also ran variety acts and vaudeville.

[13]. With almost daily burglaries, it was decided on August 3 that it would be impolitic if the entire Police Department took the day off for a picnic.

[14]. While indebted to many persons for what little he knows about this fine old city, the writer had the honor and pleasure of knowing Mrs. Helen P. Boynton, and from her gleaned no small part of the information he does have about a Portsmouth that is gone, even as the Portsmouth of only yesterday has vanished into the Limbo of time. Mrs. Boynton was well equipped for the task, being the daughter of Colonel John E. Pender. Before her marriage to banker Harry E. Boynton, she worked for her father in the office of The Penny Post. Where better to learn the lore of a community than in a newspaper office and from the lips of one of the participants in the thriving local scene.

[15]. On May 5, 1931, the McIntosh Furniture Store was destroyed by fire. This building was on the site of the structure now owned by Robert A. Shaines. It was built by McIntosh as a

successor to his early store building. The structure ruined by fire had been erected in 1919-1920.

[16]. Deputy Sheriff Wilbur B. Shaw was also, at this time, keeper of the County Jail, Penhallow Street, now the Portsmouth Police Station. A native of Boston, Shaw was educated in Kittery, attended Phillips Exeter Academy, and then was apprenticed as a printer. He finished his training in Lynn, Mass. While in Lynn, he worked for shoe companies. With the outbreak of the Spanish War, he enlisted in Co. A, 1st NHVR. After military service, he came to Portsmouth and was a printer for a time, then went into the restaurant business, and finally joined the police force.

Sheriff Marcus Collis hired him as jailer; Sheriff Ceylon Spinney promoted him to keeper in 1909. As another line of business, Shaw was clerk of the municipal court, a job he took over from Stanton M. Trueman. Shaw died September 18, 1934, at the age of 59.

[17]. Oliver W. Ham's establishment was at 122 Market Street. It was the successor to a furniture and undertaking business operated by Samuel S. Fletcher and Harry G. Tanton. Ham came to the funeral trade by a roundabout route. Early in his life his father died, and he helped his mother support a family of six. This he did by working on a farm off Maplewood Avenue, near his home, rising early to milk cows and tend a drove of 100 hogs. Four years of this and he went to work in Horton D. Walker's tallow factory for seven years. Gradually he made himself of use in the Fletcher & Tanton firm and took over the business on Fletcher's death in 1894. He sold out to Thurston Parker in 1916 but resumed the business when Parker died a year later. Albert Trottier finally bought him out. Ham belonged to the fire department and was assigned to the Atlantic handtub which was sheltered in the now-gone Veteran Firemen's building at the North Cemetery. He died in 1925 at the age of 75.

[18]. "Editor of The Herald —

"On Wednesday night a party of soldiers disturbed the residents of the South End in the vicinity of the South Mill Bridge for upwards of an hour by indulging in a free fight as well as indulging in some of the choicest of profanity.

"The brawl began at 11:30 o'clock and continued for upwards of one hour.

"During this time one of the soldiers was knocked insensible and for a time looked as though he would not recover. It was then that some of his comrades became alarmed, and it was suggested that if he did not come to, the proper thing to do would be to throw the body overboard. When the disturbance was at its height, a resident of this district threw open his window and spoke to the belligerents, saying that he would notify the police. With an oath, one of the soldiers yelled that if he did not close the window at once, he would blow his head off.

"For upwards of an hour we were kept awake by the fighting and the foul talk of these men who, judging by their talk, came from the forts at Portland, Maine. Then they moved down the road to the toll gate, and I suppose the people lower down the road got their share of it. The residents of the South End pay their taxes and naturally expect to have some police protection, but I'm sorry to say that they have none whatever. Two policemen are kept on the upper end of Water Street for the protection of the 'dens of infamy' that are allowed to flourish. They are given police protection but the residents of this section of the city are forced to be annoyed by their dumpings after closing up time. It has been no uncommon thing of late for a party of soldiers as soon as they reach the South Mill Bridge to commence their work of carousal and annoy the people along on the road from there to the toll gate.

"I am told that Major Urch has frequently made reports to the police that men in uniform were lying in the roadway and on his lawn in an intoxicated condition, but no heed was paid to these reports. It would, however, seem as though the people of this section of the town were entitled to some consideration at the hands of the police authorities.

"South End Taxpayer"

[19]. For John Falvey it is easier to feel a respect not given the fisherman who hooked a cod and handed the line to President Washington. Falvey — and the world needs more like him — did the job he was given to do. That is a rarity in this day and age, when state legislators push bills through the General Court exempting themselves from paying on the state's toll roads. Today, of course, poor John Falvey would be pushed out of the way, first by the TV camermen, and then by the Secret Service, the FBI, the State Police, and anyone else who could get in on the act. Falvey died January 4, 1913, after long service with the B & M, part of it as baggage master at the depot here.

[20]. Harold H. Bennett was superintendent of the Morley Button Company at the time.

[21]. If only for laughs, it would still be fun to know who it was that Charles H. "Cappy" Stewart knew who kept him out of the mess.

[22]. Michael J. Hurley had been a long time with the police force. He had an unusual avocation even when he became deputy in 1902. After leaving school, Hurley worked for a time for a grocer named W. E. Dennett, but that existence palled on him so he trained as a diver. One of the major jobs on which he worked was the blasting of Gangway Rock. Probably the grimmest, and most tragic, as well as difficult, came in August of 1904 when his services were needed to retrieve the bodies of 14 girls.

The drowning victims were all waitresses at the Isles of Shoals, enjoying a sail when their boat capsized. Working in considerable depths, Hurley recovered the bodies of those entangled in the wreckage. On another occasion he brought up the bodies of two people who had gone down in their boat after it struck Portsmouth Bridge. Hurley's police career started under the old system when the mayor and aldermen ran the Police Department. Edmund S. Fay was mayor when his service began on April 2, 1895. Hurley died January 30, 1924, and the tributes to him ran more than two columns in The Herald. His deputy, George H. Ducker, took over on March 3 with Leonard H. Hewitt as deputy.

[23]. George H. Ducker died October 7, 1937, ending a career of nearly 35 years in the Police Department, during thirteen of which he was marshal. Born in Portsmouth November 17, 1872, he was graduated from Portsmouth High School, then went into the printing trade briefly with The Portsmouth Times, and then into sign painting with Joseph E. Hoxie. At one time he was a member of the Portsmouth Fire Department.

Marshal Ducker broke into police work as a "special" at Peirce Hall, then became a patrolman in November 1902 and law enforcement became his life work. From 1904 until 1936 Ducker never missed being a member of the Portsmouth Police Platoon in the annual Memorial Day parade. Ducker was succeeded as marshal by his deputy, Leonard H. Hewitt.

24

An Era Ends

[1]. Probably it depends on how you count such events. The first presidential visit, already discussed, was that George Washington who made what might almost be described as a royal progress up the coast. Next came James Monroe who made a tour of the northern states and arrived in Portsmouth on July 12, 1817. While here, he stayed in the building we know as the Folsom-Salter House, although it is no longer on the site Monroe knew. President Monroe was given the full treatment, being met at Greenland and escorted to Portsmouth Plains where military units were drawn up. He visited Forts Sullivan, Constitution and McClary, besides attending services in St. John's Church. He dined with U. S. Senator Jeremiah Mason.

Next to come was James K. Polk whose visit also has been discussed. President Franklin Pierce came to Portsmouth on October 8, 1856 and was received at the Portsmouth & Concord Railroad depot by city authorities. Mayor Richard Jenness made a speech of welcome and Pierce responded. Under escort by the Buchanan Guards, the President wended his way to the Rockingham House where local citizens, many of whom had known him in his days as a law student here, called on him, but "there was little enthusiasm". The next day he boarded the steamer Wabash in the lower harbor, getting all due courtesies from the fort. The Wabash then weighed anchor and took the President to Annapolis, Md. On Friday evening, September 8, 1882, President Chester A. Arthur arrived in the lower harbor on the USS Despatch. Saturday morning he went ashore at the Wentworth to which he had been invited by ex-Congressman Frank Jones. Later that day he was met on Lafayette Road by Alfred L. Howard, William H. Hackett and Senator Edward H.Rollins of Concord. As the party drove into town, the chimes of Christ Church (not dedicated until July 3, 1883) sounded patriotic airs, and householders along the way opened their doors to hail the chief executive. At the Rockingham House he was greeted by Mayor John S. Treat and members of the city government.

It should be noted that a seventh president, prior to Taft's visit, had been in the city, albeit he did not get beyond the Eastern Railroad depot. That was President Ulysses S. Grant who was en route to Augusta on August 12, 1873. There was no formal ceremony; the President's train stopped; General Benjamin F. Butler hurried off it and scurried across the platform to enter a Boston-bound train on the other side. Apparently he had ridden on the Presidential Special to talk with the President and was then returning. However, while his train was stopped, Grant chatted with the crowd and shook hands with all who could reach him, a freedom of movement that a president would dearly love to be permitted, today.

[2]. Dr. John H. Neal was the father of former Mayor Cecil M. Neal, who was mayor under the council-manager charter in 1948-49.

[3]. John H. Bartlett died March 19, 1952, at the age of 83. Death culminated a long and eventful life which began in Sunapee, led to the governorship of New Hampshire, and to key offices in Washington, such as assistant postmaster general and a seat on the International Boundary Commission. He served for thirty years as president of the Societies for the Prevention of Cruelty to Children and Animals. During much of that long tenure his brother, Mott L. Bartlett, was agent. He began his life here as a school teacher. He was principal of the Whipple, Haven and Portsmouth High Schools. While teaching he read law with Judge Calvin Page and married the judge's daughter, Miss Agnes Page, in 1900. During the presidencies of William McKinley and Theodore Roosevelt, his Republican orthodoxy won him the postmastership, but he abandoned the Republican party to back Franklin D. Roosevelt's New Deal. Bartlett was governor in 1919-21. His son, Calvin Page Bartlett, still takes some interest in Portsmouth affairs, being chairman of the board at Portsmouth Trust Company.

[4]. John H. Broughton must have held a record of sorts — he worked in the same office for 75 years. On July 11, 1920, this still active gentleman attained the age of 90, and, although retired, he made it a point to go to his old office once a day. Broughton's lumber wharf, which he sold to C. E. Walker & Co., stood where the Memorial Bridge piers are now, and disappeared during the old man's last days. In 1845, at the age of 15, Broughton

began work in the lumber business of Barker (Jonathan) & Adams (Samuel of Kittery), and a few years later he was put in charge of the company books. In 1863, the firm name was changed to Samuel Adams & Co., and in 1881, Broughton bought it. Broughton, who served a term in the House, was the first Portsmouth man elected to the State Senate after that body was doubled in size to its present strength of twenty-four in 1879. Service in the Senate followed two terms as mayor, 1876-77. Broughton was one of the original water commissioners.

[5]. This was quite an honor for the old native of the Isles of Shoals and showed how far he had come in the esteem of his fellows. Already retired from his fishing business, he died shortly after Taft's visit.

[6]. Probably few presidents have had a faster tour of the Naval Prison area than did Harry S. Truman who visited it in October of 1952 while stumping for Adlai Stevenson for president. Maine and New Hampshire State Police cruisers whipped the presidential party through the grounds at just about all the speed the road would take and whirled Truman back to the Mall where he climbed the Squalus Memorial before making a mad dash for Somersworth to see an old Senate colleague, Fred H. Brown. Then the cavalcade swept through Dover to the City Hall and then to Rockingham Junction where the President's special train awaited.

[7]. One cannot help but wonder if anyone told Senator Robert A. Taft on March 8, 1952, of his father's visit forty years before. The senator was in Portsmouth hunting for votes to assist him in his fight to get the Republican presidential nomination. His hopes vanished as the Eisenhower juggernaut rolled over him, but the reception given Taft at the Rockingham was enthusiastic.

[8]. Charles "Rubberlegs" Marotta battled the authorities all the way when they tried to put him out of business early in 1913. His trial at Exeter, on charges of keeping a disorderly house, resulted in a hung jury. One prosecution witness was City Marshal Michael Hurley who said he was "in Marotta's place when the Water Street people were ordered out of the city" and he saw two girls in the parlor dressed in their street clothes, who were apparently ready to leave the city. Patrolman James Doherty said he frequently saw sailors and soldiers and all classes of people going and coming from the place. He was asked if beer was sold in the place, and he said one per cent, or "Uno Beer", and that he reported it to his superior, former Marshal Thomas Entwistle who said he knew about it. Another prosecution witness was Patrolman Frank H. West who said

that he frequently saw people coming and going. Marotta went on the stand in his own defense and said that he had been a resident of the United States for twenty-one years, coming here from Naples, Italy, and had lived in Portsmouth about ten years. Marotta claimed that he never sold intoxicating liquors or kept any girls. He admitted selling "Uno Beer" and said the police knew it. Cross-examined by Attorney General James P. Tuttle, he said there were seven furnished bedrooms upstairs.

Marotta brought two distinguished businessmen as defense witnesses. One of them was Charles W. Gray, superintendent of the Consolidated Coal Company who testified that he frequently went into Marotta's place for meals and that he never saw anything out of the way. Herbert G. Prime, Gray's former partner, also testified for the defense. Thomas W. Mullen, a stevedore at the coal wharf; Lawrence H. Dowling of Kittery, a coal company employee; Frank Lougee, coal company employee and Thomas F. Malloy, a bartender for Joseph Sacco whose saloon was nearby, all testified on Marotta's behalf. The jury could not agree, and Marotta was bailed to the next term of court. However, there can be no doubt that Marotta was always under police surveillance. On September 6, 1913, they raided his place and confiscated liquor which they had found buried out in the back yard.

The City Council, as is often the failing of legislative bodies, tried to regulate morality early in 1914 by banning certain kinds of dances, such as the turkey hop. The ordinance had the endorsement of City Marshal Hurley and the Civic Association; it was intended to "eliminate the objectionable dances which have been the cause of so much comment all over the world". The bill was similar to one enacted and then in force in Boston.

[9]. Harry K. Torrey later moved to Portland.

[10]. Samuel W. Emery, Jr., was mixed up in the bitter fight to break his father's will which had cut both him and his sister off with the proverbial dollar. Emery, before the realization of a promising career, took his own life.

[11]. Judge Gerald F. Giles is partnered with former Senator Maurice J. Murphy in the practice of law. At one time he was in the offices of Boynton, Waldron and Dill. His term on the Rye bench does not expire until December 17, 1999, his 70th birthday.

[12]. The Armory was turned over to the city by the state when the National Guard obtained a new facility on Circuit Road. It is managed at present by the Recreation Department under the direction of Joseph Fate who is also charged with the respon-

sibility for the Community Center (former Army and Navy Building and former USO) and the city playgrounds including the swimming pool at Pierce Island.

[13]. Naylor had the unusual experience, while at work in a power plant, of surviving a jolt of 30,000 volts of electricity.

[14]. This structure, pictured in Gurney's "Portsmouth, Historic and Picturesque", was built on land ceded to the state in 1808. It was removed shortly before the United States entered the first World War. Senator Calvin Page's resolutions in March 1916 may have helped bring its end, but not for another four years. In the first week of December 1920, the old building was finally razed. It would seem as though the end was simple after all the debate. The city asked the state adjutant general for permission to tear the building down; he told the city to clear the matter with the War Department. The War Department said it had no further use for the "Gun House", and the adjutant general said the city could tear it down as long as there was no expense to the state. This was done, the bricks being used in city projects. The relief to parents and teachers in the South End was great because the old structure had become a hazard to the life and limb of the youngsters who played around it.

[15]. Norman H. Beane, busy politically, ran a clothing store at 5 Congress Street.

[16]. Frank W. Knight ran a shoe store next door to the Portsmouth Athenaeum.

[17]. One night a meeting of the Democratic City Committee was being held back in the days when the late Mary C. Dondero, a highly adroit politician, was running it. The former mayor, with a large distrust of the local news media, closed the doors. Three members of the Fourth Estate, "Charlie" Gray, a news man for Station WHEB, and Richard Blalock and the writer, both from The Herald, stood under the open window to find out what was going on. Unfortunately, the trio forgot that cigarette smoke can be seen, and there it was, spiraling upward and in the window. Oh, well, the Democrats had to simmer in the hot courtroom that night after the window was slammed down.

[18]. It would not be fair to close out the career of the venerable Courthouse without mentioning the Christmas parties County Commissioner Ira A. Brown used to hold there in the early 1950's. They were held down in the cellar; the food was good and the beverages plentiful, with people in the legal profession, off-duty policemen, deputy sheriffs, politicians and newsmen as guests.

[19]. Harry J. Freeman operated a real estate business on Islington Street. In addition he operated a soap and tallow business in the vicinity of the Jones Brewery. Reportedly his objective in crowding in so close to the brewery was to be able to demand a good price should the brewery decide to expand. His last plant was 100 yards south of Islington, about where Thaxter Road is now. Wyman P. Boynton recalls Freeman as the man who paid him the first money he ever "earned": Fifty cents for a day of haying.

[20]. Fred A. Gray ran a paint and wallpapering business on Daniel Street where the store is still under the management of G. Morris Gray.

[21]. Dr. Boylston was a dentist, living in New Castle.

[22]. From the temper of the meeting, the reader would gather that acquisition of the bridges was only weeks, or at worst a few months away, but such was not the case. The freeing of the New Castle bridges came nearly thirteen years later, on August 2, 1926, and will be discussed in more detail later. But Major Urch did make one big effort to keep the public happy; he set up what was perhaps the first bus line in this vicinity. He acquired two seven--passenger Studebaker touring cars and fixed up a tow rig which would pull a basket type trailer, this making it possible to take twelve persons to New Castle on a trip. The "bus" left Market Square at 10 past the hour until 10:10 P. M.

In his effort to please, Urch replanked the bridges length-wise in order to give a smoother ride, and a planked track was built up on the grade at the hill near the cemetery on New Castle Island. In case of rain, the basket trailers could be enclosed to keep the passengers dry. The Studebaker cars were obtained from Arthur W. Horton, the dealer for this line. The Herald gave considerable space to the work done on the New Castle end for the ascent of Cemetery Hill: "The grading for a planked railway, curved and gradual, in ascent some 600 feet up Cemetery Hill beyond the breakwater roadway, was begun that month (September 1914) and continued until cold weather. This new and novel rise for a hill ascension has been completed and an attractive though costly piece of engineering road work. The incline is the same per cent of degree from bottom to top and cannot fail to prove a delight to every motor car operator, and no less to his passengers. This hill is the only one of consequence between this city, over the toll bridge route, to the island town. The perpendicular height gained by this novel planking way is 42 feet and will be made by almost every motor without change of gears. The plank way is as smooth and solid as any railway can be constructed and will always be dustless and being on the extreme right, the ascending motor will always have the right of way, although the planks can be taken or left at any point along the incline . . .

"On Tuesday afternoon the following were guests of Major Urch: Mayor Harry B. Yeaton, City Clerk Frederick E. Drew, Oliver B. Marvin, Arthur W. Horton, F. W. Hartford, and George B. Meloon." It was reported that the Studebaker well demonstrated the ease with which it could climb hills without change of gear.

[23]. Bridge projects are not easily pushed through legislatures. It is usually called lobbying when special interests try to influence legislation and that was what Judge Calvin Page did in February of 1917 when he brought 200 members of the House here as his guests to inspect the old Portsmouth Bridge. He had a bit of help from William F. Harrington of the Portsmouth Brewing Company, who entertained more than half of the visitors for lunch at the brewery. Everyone in this area was thoroughly aware of the inadequacies of the Portsmouth Bridge. The Boston & Maine, the owners, had a full time gang working on the bridge, constantly repairing it in one way or another. The railroad even had a steam piledriver on permanent duty. At night a watchman made a trip across every half-hour to make sure that the bridge was intact; trains were limited to a speed of 15 m.p.h. Such was the power in those days of the Boston & Maine that the bridge came under regulation of no one except the Legislature itself. Two plans were being constantly pushed. The most favored was "for a bridge further down the river, from Church Hill Point to Badger's Island, and this to be for highway and electric cars, leaving the railroad to provide a bridge either where it is now or further up the river. The other is to build a combination highway and railroad bridge at a point a short distance below the present structure, the state and railroad jointly to stand the expense." This was 1917 and the new bridge was ever nearing reality.

[24]. The Portsmouth Driving Club elected officers on November 24, 1914, the presidency going to Hamilton H. Burton, manager of the restaurant at the B & M depot; Charles Allen and W. P. Eldredge, vice presidents; Dr. Samuel Griffin, Secretary; Norman H. Beane, treasurer. Directors included the Rev. Edward J. Walsh, pastor of the Immaculate Conception parish, Edwin Seybolt, Daniel Mahoney, Albert Hislop, Arthur E. Freeman, Arthur Schurman, Mayor H. B. Yeaton, Dr. John H. Neal, William McGinnis, Philip T. McWilliams, James Quill, Dr. E. S. Cowles, William A. Bragdon and Harry E. Philbrook. One of the problems facing the membership was whether or not it should take over the old Rockingham track at the

fairgrounds off Sherburne Road, or the track once owned by Frank Jones; the former was thought to be the better spot and would one day be the general site of the airport. Barnstormers started coming there shortly after the First World War, one of the first being a Lieutenant Sturgis who landed there and was refueled by the late Earl R. Elsea who once operated Portsmouth Motor Mart.

A month later, on Christmas afternoon, the club held its first winter race meeting of the season on Lafayette Road. The starting line was at the Harry C. Caswell farm and the finish at the residence of William Ballard (until recently, owned by his daughter, retired Portsmouth High teacher Margaret G. Ballard). The "track" was a quarter mile. Some of the match races included Arthur Schurman's "Mudlake" against William McGinnis' "Miss McClure"; Wolfe Eldredge entered the bay mare "Easter Lily" against Joseph Mott's grey mare, "Bessie Herrick"; Arthur Freeman had a brown gelding against Charles M. Blaisdell's "Teddy Roosevelt." In January of 1914, there was horse racing on the North Mill Pond.

[25]. Patrolman Christopher Smart was the older brother of retired Police Officer Roland Smart. He died in the flu epidemic of 1918 on September 18 in Boston while serving in the Navy. He was 26 years old. His police work began on November 23, 1915, as a driver of the patrol wagon; later he became a patrolman.

[26]. Attorney Ralph C. Gray died in 1919.

[27]. Even that late, Portsmouth patrolmen wore the helmet type headgear made familiar by the London bobbies.

[28]. Few men ever served the U. S. Navy longer than Chief Boatswain William L. Hill, who later was given the commissioned rank of lieutenant. Hill retired in October of 1919 after 46 years of service, having reached the age of 64. He enlisted in 1873 when the wooden Navy was still afloat, serving his first three years on the USS Juhlata. His next period of sea duty was on the USS Minnesota from 1876 to 1877. From 1907 to 1917, Hill commanded the USS Southery and the USS Topeka at the Portsmouth Navy Yard, both ships being used as receiving vessels and prison ships. All prisoners arriving at the Yard passed through his hands and he kept the two ships models of disciplined cleanliness. Hill instituted techniques aimed at restoring men to duty, techniques that were later put into effect by the celebrated Thomas Mott Osborne, former warden of Sing Sing, when he took command of the Naval Prison. Hill was awarded the Congressional Medal of Honor in 1881; the standards demanding high personal valor were not then in effect. Not that Hill was wanting in that respect; his official record carried

citations for hazardous peace time rescues of people in distress. He was on the USS Brooklyn in the Spanish War, and took part in the Santiago operation. After he retired he was brought back to active duty to assist Osborne's successor.

While discussing the handling of prisoners, one story is still hard to understand. It concerns the handcuffing of the men being brought to Portsmouth during the days of World War I for confinement in "The Castle." The source is a former chief gunner's mate who had the detail of bringing men here after courts martial in Boston. The guards would take the man to the Daniel Street ferry to the Navy Yard. Half way across the river, the handcuffs were always taken off the prisoner. Why it was done this way was never explained, so Christian E. Nelson, retired sheetmetalsmith, recalls.

[29]. Harriet W. Potter was the widow of Frederick E. Potter, a physician.

[30]. Mrs. Kimball was Martha J., the widow of Edward P., who had been president of the First National and Piscataqua Savings Banks. They lived in the big house at the corner of South and Union Streets, now owned by Mrs. Charles Gouse.

[31]. Back in 1949, The Portsmouth Herald's managing editor, Richard Blalock, hired two reporters for the express purpose of investigating the activities of horse racing bookies. These two men, Robert H. Morrison and Edward G. McGrath, did not report to the paper. They lived at the Community Center, and were men about town with nothing to do. Ultimately raids on four different bookie places were staged by the State Police under the direction of the late William J. Linchey, city marshal. The raids were led by State Police Major Herbert F. Gray of Portsmouth. Morrison and McGrath were key witnesses, arrested during the raids for "being present" where gaming took place. Imagine their surprise when they learned that Portsmouth Police Inspector Dennis Kelley knew all about them. He had been tipped off that a couple of suspicious characters were hanging around, so much were the ways in the old days, he looked through their rooms on the Center's third floor. McGrath today is Captain McGrath, USN, chief of naval information, Europe, based in Naples.

[32]. On November 2, 1914, The Herald carried a news item concerning the Colonial Paper Company. The article is a concise outline of the paper-making complex developed at Freeman's Point between 1900 and 1915. Even today it is difficult to know how much the problems were created by high-wheeling financial manipulators and how much by the fact that the product was

questionable and the raw material sources doubtful. But let the Herald tell it:

"A receiver has been appointed for the Colonial Paper Co. - - Theodore W. Law of this city. The appointment of a receiver was in response to a petition by the Old Colony Trust Co. of Boston, which instituted foreclosure proceedings in consequence of the alleged default of interest payments on a bond issue of $1.5 million made in March 1910.

"The Colonial Paper Co. about five years ago absorbed the Publishers Paper Co., an $8 million corporation which consisted of many of the leading newspaper publishers in the country for whom paper was to be manufactured in Portsmouth in one of the largest paper mills in the world. The mill was built at heavy cost but never turned out any product. The company also constructed water power plants at Buxton and South Berwick, Maine, which are now idle.

"It controlled water power on the Saco River, aggregating 300,000 horse power, which was to have been extensively developed as well as along the Connecticut River in New Hampshire, and was in possession of approximately 200,000 acres of land, representing the holdings of George B. Gaines of Boston and the New Hampshire Land Co. in western Maine and New Hampshire.

"The Publishers Paper Co., by a special act of the Maine Legislature in 1905, controlled the franchise and property of the Eastern Timber Co., an $8 million Maine corporation, which was organized earlier that year to assume the assets and the property of the $25 million White Mountain Paper Co., for which receivers were appointed in July 1903."

Back in June 1903, everything had looked good for the plant at Freeman's Point. Some top names in the world of business were in the management. Its securities were being marketed without question. Then suddenly there were questions, such as demands as to who furnished the information on the value of the timber lands. Then someone wanted to know about the financial standing of the men backing the enterprise.

"It was then declared that the lands had been previously offered for sale and that a purchaser could not be found. Someone prepared a table which was alleged to show that while the White Mountain Paper Co. was being organized with securities with a supposed value of $25 million, the promoters were giving to the company itself $7 million and reserving for themselves $18 million. Another question led to the investigation of the industry of paper making and it was contended that the profits had been overstated, and that the demand is being readily supplied by mills now in existence.

"Friends of White Mountain Paper Co. asserted that a splendid investment had been provided and that more money was needed. They explained that the paper mill was more than 40 per cent completed. That was a year ago (1902). Troubles began to miltiply, and some of the men who had advanced cash made investigations and discovered that the Portsmouth plant is not yet 40 per cent completed. An expert was sent to Portsmouth a few weeks ago, and from his report the following is quoted"

"'The only two buildings which have been completed face toward Portsmouth, and at first sight it appears as though the mill were progressing in good shape. These buildings are the office (which looks like a Carnegie gift) and is said to have cost $50,000; the other the shipping, storing and finishing room. Behind this all is confusion, and the policy seems to have been to make a start on everything and to complete nothing. Very little is completed beyond the foundations. Some few buildings are bricked up as far as the lower windows. One chimney is up 20 feet and another 10. No men are at work except a few Italians. It will be impossible to complete the plant inside of a year if no more time is lost. But many investors are determined to make no further attempt to go with the company unless new men are in control.'"

In the cold light of retrospect, it is easy to see that investors should have been a bit wary. One of White Mountain Paper's manufacturing principles entailed the use of salt water (Piscataqua) in the manufacture of paper. As far as is known, this is still not done.

[33]. In a gesture of real civic-mindedness, the late Albert H. Hunt sold to the commission a large tract of land owned by himself and his wife, the late Susan Borthwick Hunt. This has the advantage of bordering both the Greenland Road and Interstate 95 with ready access to either. The first company to take advantage of the site was the machine shop of Chadwick and Trefethen. Then came Booth Fisheries with a multi-million dollar plant which is managed by Robert J. Malone. Now, on the northern extremes of the tract, Liberty Mutual Insurance is putting up a multi-story branch office building. At present, Liberty's offices in the city are located in several different buildings.

[34]. 1913 saw the first election in which a voter was given the privacy of a booth in which to mark his ballot, and "the bosses" usually knew who had gone with them and who against. The new law spelled out the requirement of a voting booth, directed the

setting up of a controlled area into which only properly elected officials could go, and the amount of distance that would safeguard the ballot box from possible interference.

[35]. Former Bay State Governor Alvin T. Fuller was for many years a summer resident in North Hampton. His son, Peter Fuller, still has a home there and maintains farm facilities for his string of race horses.

[36]. The "Portsmouth Stone" today is on the grounds of the Wentworth-Coolidge Mansion. Its manner of arrival there is another story. When it was finally decided that the Vaughan and Congress corner simply had to be widened, the stone was loaded into a cart and hauled away. However, a city councilman stopped the wagon on the way to the dump and had the stone dropped off on his property to keep people from cutting across a corner of his land. Eventually he tired of it and sent it to the dump. There it was spotted by a carter for J. Templeman Coolidge who told his boss about the "funny stone" he had seen. He was instructed to bring it back with him on his next trip. And so the "Portsmouth Stone" reposes there, far out of harm's way.

[37]. Thomas Ward was a partner, with his brother Fred H. Ward, in the distilling firm of William Ward and Sons. Before his house was leveled to make way for the Lafayette Professional Park owned by a syndicate of doctors — it was the property of Bartolomeo Guiducci who was the proprietor of the Deer Street Market. The house stood on the southwest corner of the intersection, an imposing wooden pile of Victorian mold, painted yellow in its last days. Guiducci was an uncle to Principal Joseph Grilli of the Pease School.

That attempt to improve his city was not Thomas Ward's only gesture. In September 1920 the City Council accepted his gift of a triangle of land just west of the Lafayette School, which was named Ward Park in his honor. It is bounded on the west by Middle Road, east by Monroe Street and south by Ward Place.

25

The First World War

[1]. The Herald said, "Fifteen men, representing several branches of work at the Navy Yard, appeared before Secretary Daniels of the Navy in the office of the Yard commandant, Captain Charles C. Rogers, at 5:30 on Tuesday. Each man presented papers of any grievance that existed among the men of their trade. Secretary Daniels promised that he would look them all over carefully and study each one. In regard to the planning system, the men voiced the sentiments of the force in general by asking that the old system of surveying the work and then sending it to the shops be adopted. The secretary informed them that this same request had been made by other yards and that he would put it up to the department. He thought the old system the better of the two. He wanted the conditions as good here as at the Charlestown Yard and could see no reason why this station could not build ships as well as other yards".

[2]. That inspection and the report were carried in full in The Herald. It boiled down in essence to an expression of the board's belief that Portsmouth did have a place in the Navy's scheme of things, that it possessed certain definite assets. Captain Rumble's digest of them is the easiest on the reader:

a. Greatest depth of water of any Navy Yard.

b. Can furnish 5,000 or more skilled mechanics.

c. Is a working Navy Yard.

d. Harbor never crowded with shipping. (The board probably did not know on one occasion late in the 19th Century a storm sent 500 sail into this harbor.)

e. Harbor never freezes and always free of ice.

f. Unlimited space for development.

g. Near the sea.

h. Well protected and easily defended. (The reader should recall Commodore Isaac Hull's protests back in the War of 1812.)

i. A dry dock excavated from solid rock, 750 feet long.

j. Ample room for a long dry dock.

k. Largest boiler shop (new) in New England.

l. New shipsmith building, new equipment buildings, fine steam machinery and pattern shop and foundry.

m. Portsmouth Yard has built ships since 1600. (A bit exaggerated, but not really when it is realized that Piscataqua mechanics had been doing that almost since the beginning.)

o. Portsmouth is imbued with the right kind of naval spirit.

p. Ships can be built here as advantageously and with as little cost as anywhere on earth.

The board also recommended actions that did not take place until after World War II — the acquisition of Clarke and Jamaica Islands.

[3]. It is impossible to get into any discussion of the Navy Yard without further mention of the old floating dry dock which wound up a blazing pyre in the Revere Beach area in 1907. Apparently the buyers of the dry dock did not get the bargain they anticipated. They bought it expecting to clean up on the scrap metal. Samuel Butter Co. of Boston was the purchaser but, not long after burning it, found out that there was far from the metal content that the $26,000 price tag justified. Butter was able to sell Congress and the Navy Department on the claim that he based his bid on a semi-official book, Stuart's "History of Dry Docks". In March of 1913 Congress passed a relief bill, paying Butter $12,000 to ease the sting of his bad guess. Butter had to live with his regret at having bought the Portsmouth floating dry dock which had been, back in the 1850's, one of the marvels of the day.

[4]. The L-8 was phased out in 1925.

[5]. On April 4, 1917, The Herald announced, "The first women to enter the services of Uncle Sam for duty at the Portsmouth Navy Yard, following the appointment of the three telephone operators, reported for duty today in the enrollment office in the military department. Five of them came from Manchester and one from this city". They were rated as yeomen. The woman from Portsmouth was Miss May Warren.

[6]. James N. Pringle later became the top figure in New Hampshire education.

[7]. To list all of those lively Portsmouth people of more than a half-century ago who participated in that Preparedness Parade is impossible, but the names of some of them are available and are part of the annals of the city. Starting with the first groups, the names come echoing back over the decades: Chief Marshal,

Chauncey M. Hoyt; chief of staff, Arthur L. Smith, adjutant, 1st Battalion, New Hampshire National Guard, Coast Artillery; assistants, Horace W. Locklin, I. Henry Washburn; mounted aides, R. A. Mitchell, Russell McCue, Stuart Humphreys, Oliver B. Marvin, Morris Hurd, John Mooney, Orville Badger, John C. Dolan; dismounted aides, William H. White, Richard D. McDonough, Philip H. White, Patrick E. Kane, Mark W. Anthony, William B. Marvin and Harry K. Torrey. That was the command group. Next came the first division with Marines, Coast Artillerymen and sailors in the front units; somewhere back in automobile No. 6 came Mayor Samuel T. Ladd and the commandant of the Navy Yard, Captain W. L. Howard; then back of auto No. 10 came the Sons of Veterans under former Mayor Edward H. Adams; Camp Schley, Spanish War veterans, James P. Kelley, commanding; Spirit of '76, drum corps, Portsmouth Athletic Club, J. William Newell; Court Tripoli, Foresters of America, Joseph Sacco; Portsmouth Hebrew Community, Maurice Silverman, Louis Shapiro, Harry Cohen.

Immediately following, was the second division with R. T. Roberts in command. Under Roberts' immediate supervision was the New Hampshire College Cadet Corps, with 10 autos closely following; Mrs. Arthur C. Heffenger, wife of a local doctor, headed the women's section of the Navy League; providing martial tempo for the units ahead was the Portsmouth City Band, directed by Howard S. Kneeland. Arthur W. Horton, a garage operator and proprietor of the Sinclair Inn, headed the Elks; the Portsmouth Council, K. of C., was led by Thomas H. Palmer. Then came the Portsmouth Ministerial Association with Lucius H. Thayer, D. D., North Church; Rev. William P. Stanley, Middle Street Baptist; Rev. Nelson Kellogg, St. John's; Rev. Percy Warren Caswell, Court Street Christian; Rev. Freeman J. Scott, Methodist; Chaplain E. W. Scott, USN; Rev. Charles leV. Brine, Christ Church; Rev. John L. Davis, People's Church. Some units to the rear were the Christ Church Cadets under E. P. Wyatt, with the Boy Scouts under Harold M. Smith following closely. Chief Engineer William F. Woods led the Fire Department; then Division No. 1, AOH, Paul Howard. That section of the parade included the Gale Shoe Company, with H. L. Taylor; the Warwick Club, George A. Wood, president; Fred H. Ward, vice president; Jeremy R. Waldron, secretary-treasurer.

The third division was led by the naval construction superintendent, R. P. Schlabach, marshal; Morris Hurd, a mounted aide; then Lucullus Company, Knights of Pythias, led by Fred W. Harrington, Charles K. Butler, Hiram B. Merrifield, and Frank W. Horrocks.

Inevitably there were speeches. Capacity houses were on hand to greet these orators in both the Colonial and Portsmouth (Civic) Theaters. The theater managers had to cut off admissions. Mayor Samuel T. Ladd presided at the Portsmouth Theater and Exalted Ruler James W. Barrett, B.P.O.E., No. 97, in the Colonial. As might be expected, The Times devoted its major attention to the remarks of John H. Bartlett, its owner. His oratorical fancy covered a wild gamut of patriotic fervor. One phrase from his remarks is memorable, particularly for those who remember when Franklin Delano Roosevelt delivered an address, the key phrase of which still lives in memory . . . "I hate war", Bartlett said, "but I hate worse seeing defenseless Americans killed. That is our only alternative now. It is not whether we will declare war or not, it is whether we will defend ourselves or not. Shall we have war, or shall we be slain without war . . . . We are dwelling here in Portsmouth on historic soil. The nation expects to find strong men here. To this town Paul Revere galloped his steed to warn General Sullivan (To such extents can oratory carry the speaker!) to capture the powder at New Castle before it was too late. Sullivan, alert and brave, seized the powder, carried it to Boston (Distortion, thy name is patriotism.) to win the battle of Bunker Hill . . ." Before he finished, Bartlett even had John Paul Jones as a "resident" of the community.

[8]. Former Commodore Gerald G. Woods of the Portsmouth Yacht Club, who makes his home at 99 Bow Street where he is proprietor of the Martingale Apartments, says that the old Yacht Club building "stood a little on the down slope, the Mechanic Street side", of the abutments to the present bridge across to Pierce Island. It moved to quarters in New Castle in 1938. According to Woods, the present site was bought by the late John E. Seybolt and the late Robert Marvin in anticipation that their action would be approved by the club membership. It was then known as Drowne Landing.

[9]. One of the most memorable nights in the writer's recollection of this now gone building was in 1946 when the Late Mary C. Dondero lost the State Senate contest to Rae S. Laraba by a vote or two. It was then the polling place for Ward 1 and notorious for getting in its returns late in the dawn. That night was marked by the late John R. McIntire's attempt to stage a real, old-time election with empty whiskey bottles rolling across the floor. As the night hours tightened the Senate race, the Republicans, usually dominant in such things, began to panic. Among the first arrivals was Wyman P. Boynton, rolled out of bed when GOP ward heelers called Jeremy R.

Waldron, Sr., one of the elder statesmen of the party, who immediately sent his junior, Boynton, to safeguard Republican and, incidentally, Laraba's interests. There are still those who wonder if the recount apparatus was not cocked in favor of the Republicans.

[10]. "The Dean Murder" was a tale that kept children awake in the long ago around Peterborough. Oddly enough, or it would have no place in this volume, it had Portsmouth connections because some of the people investigated at the time worked at the Atlantic Shipyard. Still unsolved, the Dean case even touches on a cousin of one of Portsmouth's elder statesmen, Ralph May. This man was Horace Morrison, then a captain in Army intelligence, near whose Peterborough home, Terrace Hill Farm, the Dean murder took place. Dr. Dean was an eccentric - - - any man who milks his cows at midnight would be so considered. His farm was sheltered on the southeastern slope of Grand Monadnock Mountain. Widely prevalent in those days were tales of signal lights from the peak of the mountain, the first point of land to catch the eye coming into Boston harbor. Dr. Dean supposedly knew the story of the signal lights. Failing to return from a Tuesday night shopping visit to Jaffrey, his wife reported him missing. The old doctor — he was a retired dentist from Boston — was found in his well, head bashed in and bound with wire. Of such things as the Dean murder were World War I suspicions raised. For a time his wife was a prime suspect, but, poor ailing soul, it was finally laid to persons unknown, tied partly into Morrison testimony that Dean had wanted to talk with counter-intelligence people.

[11]. Costello was a dealer in poultry feeds and garden seeds at 115 Congress Street. His neighbors included Francisco Cacciatori, a shoe merchant; George P. Jones, second hand clothing; Bernard Michaelson, the B & M Dye House; and William P. Miskell, undertaker.

[12]. These early members of the Chamber of Commerce included William L. Hill, USN, Hartford, Sweetser, John G. Tobey, H. J. Freeman, Charles P. Carroll, Belden, Gray, Charles H. Brackett, C. Dwight Hanscom (Hanscom had been badly wounded at Chancellorsville on May 3, 1863), Richman P. Margeson, Willis E. Underhill (for many years a real guiding hand in the Portsmouth Trust Co., and a kindly gentleman), John C. Batchelder, John M. McPhee, George E. Cox, Joseph Sacco, Robert Clyde Margeson, Edward Seybolt, Robert I. Sugden, Edward L. Paterson, E. Curtis Matthews, Jr., Frank F. Dunfield (PHS principal), James N. Pringle, J. True Davis (fruit wholesaler), Miles Standish Watson, Orville J.

Allinson, Elmer J. F. Littlefield, George B. Davis, Ernest A. Tucker, Frank W. Randall, Richard P. Bridle, William McEvoy, Henry P. Payne, Harry T. Wendell, Charles H. Walker, Albert Hislop, George H. Clark, Edward E. Rowell, Norman H. Beane, John H. Neal, William E. Marvin, Gustave Peyser, Laurence G. Peyser, Costello, Lydston, Eugene B. Eastman, Ralph C. Dickey, Sise and Bates.

[13]. Griffin was the son of Michael J. Griffin, Sr., a local political leader, whose major business was the care of the cemeteries. The son was employed with Internal Revenue for many years and was the father of Attorney Charles J. Griffin. The senior Griffin died December 21, 1924.

[14]. The registration officer in Ward 1 was Louis Soule, assisted by Walter Badger, Harry Dowdell and Thomas Timmons; Ward 2, Charles E. Batchelder, assisted by George B. Lord, Mark W. Anthony, Charles H. Long and Richard D. McDonough; Ward 3, Clinton Trueman, assisted by Stanton M. Trueman, Thomas M. Marden; Ward 4, John W. Newell, aided by John G. Tobey, Harold M. "Beauty" Smith, the Rev. Evan W. Scott (Navy Chaplain) and Arthur H. Locke; Ward 5, Elmer E. Clark, assisted by Robert E. Lear.

[15]. The name appears in Longfellow's "Hiawatha".

[16]. The ultimate fate of this fleet of vessels is not known. Long after the war, the government was trying to sell its wooden ships but found no takers. So probably they eventually went to the scrap piles. However, the Roy H. Beattie burned at sea late in April 1919, on her way to Brazil with coal. She caught fire between Bermuda and Barbados and was abandonded with the loss of one man, the third officer. The Milton also was lost at sea. In October, the Ammonoosic, while on a passage to Rotterdam with a load of coal, was reported leaking badly. A few hundred miles off the Atlantic coast was the report, but no one seemed to know precisely where. A Coast Guard Cutter, Acushnet, and an English steamer, Port Chalmers, were on their way to her, according to a news report. A few days later the Ammonoosic was abandoned at sea, a sinking, smoldering ruin. Perhaps only coincidence, but in each instance the lost Piscataqua-built freighters were hauling coal when trouble struck. Could it have been a combination of coal dust and the probably green timber in the hull? There were reports that the government planned to investigate, but it is doubtful that it was ever done. One other of the Newington freighters had an unusual adventure. During the first week of January 1920, the Wasagya was on her way south when mutiny broke out. She had to put into

Bermuda when the crew jammed the rudder. The Wasagya was owned by Standard Oil. A Portsmouth man, Bernard Linchey, was her first officer.

[17]. These ships were Haverhill, August 24, 1918; Ammonoosic, September 21, 1918; Yawah, November 7, 1918; Woyaca, December 7, 1918; Newton, January 4, 1919; Sylvanus, April 14, 1919; Winapie, May 3, 1919; Wasagya, May 25, 1919; Yustan, June 2, 1919; Ulak, June 28, 1919; Dover, July 24, 1919; Newburyport, August 14, 1919. The Ulak had the only Portsmouth person involved in the launchings as sponsor. Mary I. Wood, prominent feminist, did the honors for that one.

[18]. L. H. Shattuck, Inc., was a bit fortunate. For one thing the company, although L. H. Shattuck had died in Manchester a few weeks before, bid in the contract to build the New Franklin School, a project which absorbed some of its surplus material. Then it was able to unload the shipyard itself on the Atlantic Dyestuff Co.

In fact, the cornerstone laying for the school preceded by a few days the announcement of the disposal of the Newington property. The cornerstone laying ran the gamut of such affairs. The traditional box with documents, newspapers, contemporary coins is still in place at the school. Present for the affair were Mayor Albert Hislop, the Rev. Alfred Gooding, Councilman Harry B. Yeaton, William H. Slayton (superintendent of schools), Judge Calvin Page, the Rev. Lucius H. Thayer, Frank W. Knight, Councilman E. Curtis Matthews, Jr., Fernando W. Hartford, R. Clyde Margeson, Miss Alice S. Mildran (Farragut School principal). For the sake of posterity, it should be mentioned that when it is decided to open that copper box a French coin will be found therein. That coin was picked up by an unidentified Portsmouth soldier on a battlefield in France in 1918. This morsel of information is intended to keep archeologists a century or two hence from undue perplexity.

Right on the heels of the ceremonies at the New Franklin School came the announcement that the Atlantic Chemical Dyestuff Co. had taken over Shattuck's Newington plant, and "they will begin work almost immediately on the building of a plant that will be a permanent fixture and an important addition to the industries of this section. Atlantic Dyestuff Co. stemmed from a firm started in 1916 in Boston. The company made coal tar dyes. Six oddly shaped buildings were erected, with high pitched, one-sided roofs. Because it is still important to Portsmouth's economy, it is necessary to explain that after Atlantic Dyestuff finished with the plant in Newington, Atlantic Terminal Corp., and probably a myriad of others, were involved there in making it an oil storage terminal. Presently the owner of record is the C. H. Sprague Co.; that firm bought the property from the late John E. Holden, former Newington selectman and fire chief, the "Little General". Today Atlantic Terminal distributes through northern New England the oil that average householder pipes into his furnace. In direct charge of the operation is Henry Downey. C. H. Sprague itself is owned by a Swedish combine, Axel Johnson. The sales operation is managed by Robert W. Hill, Sr., formerly of Portsmouth, but now a resident of Newington. Downey's Atlantic Terminal organization early in June of 1972 removed the last vestiges of the old L. H. Shattuck Shipyard. When Herald photographer, Wade Burnette, took the last pictures of that World War I installation in June 1972, contractors were fast moving in for the building of one of the largest oil storage tanks in the northeast. Atlantic already had a tank with a rated capacity of 217,000 barrels. To it is being added, if not already completed, a tank that will store 252,914 barrels; this steel cylinder at 194 feet in diameter is 14 feet larger than its gigantic companion. Both tanks are 48 feet in depth. An item in an article on the tank farm which appeared in The Herald prompts the mention that a man named Valentine Pickering, a descendant of the Portsmouth clan, is buried out there in that cluster of Atlantic's oil tanks. Pickering wanted to be buried on his property and he is. He is buried today on the family lands. How many today can understand what that means?

[19]. Harry C. Raynes was a nephew of the famed Clipper builder, George Raynes.

[20]. Ground was actually broken for the ways at Atlantic Shipyard on February 22, 1918, and the keel of the first ship, the Kisnop, was laid on May 29, 1918. Kisnop was 427 feet overall, between perpendiculars 410 feet; beam, 54 feet; draft, 23 feet, tonnage, 8,800, full displacement, 11,300 tons; and a single screw. She was driven by reciprocating engines of 2,800 horse power and required a crew of 60 men and officers. As the yard workmen improved their techniques they became capable of launching these vessels with fire under the boilers and steam available for power to assist in getting them back to the dock immediately after launching. After the Kisnop in January 1919, nine others went down the ways, all built to the same general specifications: Baboosic, May 3, 1919; Portsmouth, June 28, 1919; Nipmuc, October 28, 1919. In 1920 there were Norumbeaga, January 10; Brookline, May 1; Springfield, May 26; Tolosa, July 17; Pachet, August 28, and Pagasset, October 9. Out of the lot, only the Portsmouth had a local sponsor. The naming

of the ship and the sponsor were honors conferred on the city for leading in subscriptions to a Liberty Loan drive. The sponsor was Mrs. Albert Hislop, wife of the mayor.

[21]. Simply getting the Freeman's Point area ready for shipbuilding was no inexpensive task. Steam shovels were brought in to excavate the material for the ways, and this surplus was trucked to the south end of the yard, a process that added several acres to the area of the yard where shipbuilding materials could be stored handy to the outfitting dock which was built in the cove at that end. Five ways were built, numbered from one to five beginning on the upriver side. Some rock formation was found in the sites for ways one and two, so it was decided to shift the ways further south where the ground was easier to prepare. This forced the moving of the office building from in front of way 4, to a point 200 yards west. Atlantic converted the Colonial Paper Company's machine shop into a steel plate shop and throughout utilized whatever it could that was on the ground.

[22]. Concerned citizens present included Frank A. Belden, Frederick M. Sise, Raphael L. Costello, R. Clyde Margeson, Fernando W. Hartford, John P. Sweetser, C. E. Downton, M. L. Bullard, James H. Dixon, Lucius H. Thayer, Norman H. Beane, Edward H. Baker, Louis W. Ewald, Thomas C. Leckey, Fred A. Gray and Charles Long. Leckey was famed as the operator of a cigar store on Congress Street. He was a political dealer of no small ability.

[23]. Now occupied by the Salvation Army, this building was first planned in Civil War days. In 1864, a Box Club was formed to earn funds for a new chapel. The club dissolved February 23, 1871, once the objective was achieved. This building was preceded by the brick vestry on Fleet Street to which John Langdon had given $1,000 in 1817. He later bequeathed $1,000 to the North Church itself. By 1900 it became apparent that the 1871 chapel was no longer adequate, and a fund drive was started to build a new one, still on the land given by Mary Rogers. Part of the fund campaign consisted of organizing a new "Box Club". This group is one to which researchers will be forever indebted, tabulating, as it did, by the day of the month, events in the city's history. The committee was a distinguished one. Editors of the compilation were Frances A. Mathes and Charles A. Hazlett; their assistants were Mrs. Andrew B. Sherburne, Mrs. Sarah L. Simpson, Miss Olive A. Akerman, Mrs. Robert L. Ellery, Mrs. Annie J. Connell. Miss Katharine A. Sweetser was chairman of the "Box Club", and Helen C. Harvey was treasurer. The "Calendar", as the club called it, was printed by Randall Press

(John D. Randall). The new Parish House was dedicated, September 12, 1962, on Spinney Road on land given to the church by Mrs. George A. Trefethen.

[24]. The Daniells owned a farm in Greenland where the Portsmouth Country Club is now located. The present mayor of Franklin, Eugene Daniell, Jr., is Mrs. Daniell's son. The Country Club property had been farmed for more than 300 years, originally being the property of Francis Champernowne who is buried on Gerrish Island in Kittery. The Portsmouth Country Club was founded in 1901, one of the oldest in this area. The location is now occupied by the Pease Golf Club. The Air Force took the old Country Club property shortly after Pease AFB was built, on the grounds that it needed a navigational easement across it. The government put $114,000 in escrow as part of the eminent domain proceedings, but the club appealed to the courts and was awarded more than $300,000 by the jury. The present course, one of the longest in New Hampshire and one of the more difficult, was designed by the famed Robert Trent Jones, an architect noted for the severity of his courses. Tony Loch, formerly of Exeter, is the resident professional.

[25]. Portsmouth commemorated its war dead with a common marker at the Plains, and individual stones and maple trees. The roster — in verdigris-coated bronze — includes Carl A. Pearson, Evelyn Petrie, Edward J. Mack, Christopher Smart, Frederick S. Towle, Frank E. Booma, Harold L. Dennett, Paul C. Dutton, Sydney R. Pickles, John P. White, Hugh C. Hill, Michael Lynch, John Tanco, Arthur T. Patch, Frank H. N. Grant, Chester A. Bock, Floyd Barker, John J. Connors, George Durand, Faye E. Hatt, Henry Taylor, Theodore D. Schmidt, Francis A. Scott, and Amedio Priori.

[26]. As earlier noted, Portsmouth Brewing was founded in 1870 by Arthur Harris, Reorganized in 1875 as the Portsmouth Brewing Company, it underwent further reorganization when William F. Harrington moved in as financial advisor. Stock outstanding when it was sold totaled 160 shares, and the shares had sold as high as $800 but not below $500 for many years. The company was taken over by McVey Brothers of Boston, which proposed to found a fleet of fishing vessels and operate out of this port. The new firm became known as the Portsmouth Cold Storage Company. Major A. White was president; John K. Bates, Treasurer; Edward S. Downs, manager.

[27]. This first victim of a bad law was Samuel H. Grossman of Penhallow Street. He was arrested May 16, 1918.

[28]. One of the first of these stories involved a large

furniture van owned by Wood Brothers (Rufus). The Herald said, "The largest seizure of liquor ever made in this city, at least for many years, was made by the local police on Wednesday evening January 22, 1919, when they captured a truckload of stuff which included about 100 cases. The capture was made on Middle Street, and the police were on the watch for the truck. It appears that they received information that a truckload of booze had been shipped into this city and was on its way in one of Wood Brothers big furniture vans. Men were stationed on Middle Street, and they attempted to stop the truck as it came in over Lafayette Road. The driver refused to stop and started his big truck down the street at full speed, hoping to get away. The police secured an automobile and followed, at the same time firing shots to stop him. Down the street they came tearing, with a noise that brought people to their doors. On Haymarket Square the driver, seeing that he would be cornered, stopped his machine and jumped out and went over the Peirce Estate fence and disappeared down over the open land to the playgrounds. The machine swung around sharp and ran up on the center lot where it stopped. The police were soon up to the truck, and securing a driver they proceeded to the police station. Chief Hurley ordered the stuff unloaded, and it was stored in the cell block under lock and the truck was also kept at the police station. The consignment was all high grade goods including Gordon gin, Italian vermouth, a good grade of brandy and also many cases of a good grade whiskey. The total valuation at wholesale, or at least case lots, would be at least $3,000. Later in the evening the driver, Carl Beetle, was arrested by Chief Hurley, but either he did not know who it was consigned to or "he would not tell". Thereafter, the saga of the booze truck dragged on for weeks while city, county, state and federal government wrangled over the ownership of the liquor.

As observed earlier, strange tales came out of the Prohibition era, and some of the people who participated still walk the streets. One man, well known, used to make regular runs to a place on Plum Island, Newburyport, pick up a few cases in his car and return to Portsmouth. He gave up the practice when, he said, "I could see that the people I was getting mixed up with were apt to get rough". Apocryphal perhaps, but the story still persists that one of the city's more prominent citizens built a small fortune out of running booze in Portsmouth on his boat from the Isles of Shoals. He had the freedom of a certain dock for his landings, the police staying away. But he became forgetful about showing proper appreciation for this privilege. So one night when approaching the dock, he was met with pistol shots and forced to stand off until a new agreement had been reached. A catalogue of adventures during the Prohibition era would itself be a fair sized book. It suffices to say that smuggling liquor was an old Portsmouth custom, dating from colonial times.

26

The Roaring Twenties

[1]. So great was the consternation over the Census figures that The Herald began agitating for a recount. It was quickly established that entire streets had been left out of the nose count. Portsmouth people felt that the growth of the city should reach 17,000 or more. "There is every reason to believe that the city would show a great increase because the 1910 Census was at the time when there were about 1,100 men at work on the Navy Yard, the breweries were running on reduced force, and there were no new industries. At that time there were five to ten houses for every new tenant. This year when the Census was taken, the Navy Yard had over 4,000 workmen; the Atlantic Shipyard, 2,300; the Gale Shoe Company, the Morley Button Company more men than ever, and there were twenty to thirty applicants for every house. In addition to the houses where there was one family there are now three and four, and the number of people to each house in the city is greatly increased. The school population in 1910 was about 1,500, now it is 3,000. These are but a few of the reasons why the general public thought the population would show an increase of at least 5,000 over ten years ago. The Census was badly taken; it was not so much the fault of the young men who took it, as the system and the lack of supervision. In 1910 it was the supervisor for the city who laid out the zones for each enumerator and checked it up. This year a young man from Rochester was given the supervision over this city. After the Census was reported to have been completed, this paper made an investigation and discovered that whole streets had been skipped. The matter was referred to the department who sent a man from Washington here and the returns placed in his hands quickly

convinced him that the Census had not been taken properly. As a result of the publicity given the matter by this paper, upwards of 800 additional names were placed on the list in the revision. For instance, the whole of Maplewood Avenue was not taken; in various parts of the city entire streets were skipped. This was due to the fact that the enumerators did not know the districts and left out streets. Even up to this week, complaints have been received in this office of houses missed even in the rechecking of the city. Another condition which cut down the returns was the instructions to the enumerators not to take people who work here and go home weekends or once in two weeks. There are hundreds of these in all parts of the city living in rooms, and they should have been taken here. A great many of the people report that they have not been taken anywhere. In most cases when they returned home they found that the enumerators thought they were working in Portsmouth; as a result other towns did not take them, so as a result they were counted in neither place."

[2]. The 1920 Directory lists Andrew Jarvis as the proprietor of the Apollo Lunch. Jarvis, a native of Greece who realized the American dream, is happy to explain it. Now 80 years of age, he is still a faithful winter smelt fisherman. Jarvis says his relationship with Hislop was possible because "Hislop was a gambler". Back in the hectic World War I era Jarvis watched one day as Hislop and Clifford P. Bass, the druggist, at the back of Bass' store on Congress Street, were hitting golf shots using egg shells for balls. When they finished, Jarvis said to Hislop, "Al, you're a gambler. I have a proposition for you. This town needs a self-service restaurant". According to Jarvis, Hislop had to make a trip to Boston with him before he understood what a cafeteria could do. Hislop put $4,000 into the new business; Jarvis $5,000, and they borrowed the rest. In the first year, Hislop made $7,000 on his investment, and the business grew from there. Jarvis agrees there was a little bit of "heing and sheing" going on but it was "nothing like the articles The American reported" and he readily agreed that "Harry Winebaum was railroaded" by the local political machine headed by John H. Bartlett. "Al Hislop got mixed up in one of Bartlett's deals in Washington and lost his investment", Jarvis says. Jarvis himself once was a partner with Bartlett in the Congress Block.

Another man for whom Jarvis has nothing but praise was Chauncey B. Hoyt who operated a stationer's store with Herbert B. Dow near the Apollo. Jarvis eventually bought the block and paid Hoyt's moving expenses to Market Street where the firm is still in business at No. 47.

Jarvis is the man who has attained the highest elective office in this state of anyone of Greek background - - Governor's Councilor. He is a walking compendium of Congress Street lore from a half-century ago. He remembers when Norman H. Beane, political figure and businessman, had a clothing store at 5 Congress Street. Beane, who died July 1, 1921, was an uncle of the several Margeson brothers. He was born in Newington and began his business career in this city in 1907 in association with George Macauley. Together they bought out the store that had been operated by Edmond S. Fay and then William H. Fay. After Beane's death, the store was acquired by Albert J. Trottier who took his own life in 1928. For several years Trottier sponsored a basketball team in the tough City League.

[3]. The Portsmouth News Agency at this time was operated by J. Adams deRochmont who made his home at 266 Middle Street. The place was later owned by Leroy Harmon whose wife, Agnes, has been in the past few years the guardian of Portsmouth's green life. One of Mrs. Harmon's pet projects for a number of years has been the Christmas lighting contest. She has long been active in garden club work.

[4]. Edward J. Gallagher is the highly respected publisher of the Laconia Citizen, the father of Alma J. Gallagher, a noted airplane pilot. When The Herald modernized its plant, the old press went to Laconia and was used by the Citizen for some years.

[5]. The Republican caucus in December of 1920, when the mayorality candidate was chosen, must have presented a scene almost impossible for those unfamiliar with the Courthouse to believe. For weeks Guptill and Bartlett had pushed their campaign; being no fools, they knew that the advent of Fernando W. Hartford would mean the passing of party control from their hands. With Albert Hislop as mayor, and Bartlett in the governor's chair, the organization appeared potent enough to run things for some time to come. Hartford was subjected to a smear campaign of virulent proportions. So stinging was it that on December 3, 1920, he felt compelled to publish an elaborate defense of his honesty. This involved getting sworn statements from officials of companies like L. H. Shattuck to bear witness that he had not derived any personal benefit from offices he held. Atlantic Corporation people made written statements that Hartford's only benefit from his association with them came during a period when they were recruiting help and he advised them on advertising. No shrinking violet, Hartford also, obtained testimonials from national Republican figures as to his GOP regularity. Hartford said, "My attention has been invited to a savage

and unwarranted attack made in a paper controlled by the man who has been endeavoring for many years to injure me in any way possible. I have always ignored these attacks because I have trusted the people to know that it was their game and what inspired them. In this particular case certain statements are made affecting my honesty and integrity. This I cannot let go unchallenged, although I feel that the men and women of Portsmouth (where I have lived so long among them) know them to be false and only a repetition of the work of this one-man ruler. The statement that I have in any way benefited from the L. H. Shattuck Shipyard, Inc., financially or otherwise, is absolutely false."

Years ago, Charles W. Brewster wrote of "That Night", beseeching his fellow Whigs never to forget the ordeal of an all-night election. After the 1920 Republican caucus, Hartford could have spent the rest of his political career exhorting his own followers never to forget "That Night". The description in The Herald tested credulity, yet from conversations with those who were there, it is apparent that the report was all too true, and some of the details are being printed here to illustrate what elections were often like in Portsmouth 50 years ago:

"The Republicans of Portsmouth took things in their own hands Monday night and, in the largest caucus ever held in this city, nominated Fernando W. Hartford for mayor over Eugene B. Eastman by a vote of 858 to 797. It was the most outrageous exhibition of the misuse of power by the City Committee ever seen in this section of the state. It beat any of the famous old-time caucuses when everything was fixed beforehand and incidentally it sounded the death knell of the ring in this city. Never was there such open expressions of disgust for the arrangements that had been made for voting and for the high-handed manner in which the City Committee carried out orders. The jam was so bad that women fainted in the corridor and strong men grew faint in the crushes of people seeking to express their choice.

"Everything was done that possibly could be done to throw the caucus, but the people turned out in such a mass that it could not be done, although there were things that savored of the old days when packing the ballot box was a favorite diversion. In the first place the ballot was printed so that Major Hartford's name was under a column all by itself, under the heading, "Independent". It was a Republican caucus; there was no such thing as an "Independent", except that he was independent of the big boss. Motions from the floor were absolutely ignored by the chairman, even the motion to have the ballot box examined before proceeding to ballot. The caucus was opened at 5 o'clock in the Probate Courtroom, and at that time there were several hundred people waiting in the line and rather a jam out in the corridors and on the steps of the building. This crowd increased as time went on and by 6 o'clock it was impossible to get into the building. The women were out in great force and while a majority of them stuck to their guns and hung onto their places, there were many who fainted or grew so faint that they had to work their way out of the building without even getting into the courtroom. Strong men caught in the jam gave up the battle and climbed through the windows and dropped to the ground outside. Some relief was given a number of people marooned in a room by opening the upper courtroom and allowing them to go out of another entrance. At first it required only a short time to vote, but after a time an hour was a good time to make it, and from seven on it required two solid hours to work one's way in from the street and cast a ballot.

"Judge Ernest L. Guptill presided at the caucus and the members of the City Committee as a rule were the checkers for each ward. The checklists for the November election were used and these had been carefully pruned so that many names were scratched off. Many persons who voted the Republican ticket in the September primary found their names scratched off and some people who had never been in a primary and expressed their choice were scratched. . . Mr. Hartford, one of the candidates, was summarily ordered removed from standing where he could watch the proceedings and later even prohibited from standing in the door. It was 10:40 before the last of the voters had passed through and the polls were declared closed. A motion by Dr. Neal that two representatives of each candidate be allowed to watch the counting of the ballots was ignored, and the chair appointed Bernard J. Magraw and John Long as tellers. They were some time counting the ballots, but the big crowd who packed the room and the corridors, including a good number of women, remained until the last. It was shortly before 12 o'clock when the tellers completed their count and the chairman announced the results, which were as follows, Hartford, 858; Eastman, 797." And that is the way a caucus could be held in Portsmouth about 50 years ago.

[6]. This man was a Sam Smith and he, too, was booked and bailed for distributing libelous matter.

[7]. One of the confiscation orders was signed by Jeremy R. Waldron, Sr., later a judge of the Municipal Court, a rather

brusque man, who once fined a motorist $15 after the man had driven three hours through a snowstorm in order to get to court.

[8]. In June of this year, he gave to Strawbery Banke the Joshua Wentworth House, Hanover Street, long the headquarters of his news agency.

[9]. The "quick hitch", a means of dropping onto the backs of horses as they stood in their stalls, was first employed when John D. Randall was fire chief. Later it was abolished for economy reasons but afterward reinstated. San Juan Gray was the first driver when the "quick hitch" was instituted in 1897. Gray was transferred from the Street Department to handle it, and he was the only regular driver it had had when abolished in 1906. Dennis J. Lynch was driver of Hose Wagon 3 while John H. Ham was the first driver of the hook and ladder, later moving to the chemical wagon and being succeeded on the hook and ladder by Charles H. Colson. The first call answered by the "quick hitch" came on March 1, 1897, for a fire that destroyed the West End Hotel, Columbia Street, opposite the Portsmouth Shoe Company. The "quick hitch" was re-established in March 1907. Perhaps the last feat of the "quick hitch" is what induced the economy-minded city fathers to bring it back. On the day it was to phase out, April 4, 1906, Box 19 was rung for the Liberty Bridge Laundry operated by William H. Phinney. Lynch, not the usual driver, Gray, had the hose wagon on the scene within three minutes, an incredible performance, with Colson pounding on his heels. The old laundry building was a mass of flames and the firemen, according to Chief J. Morrison Varrell, were lucky to save the adjoining structures.

[10]. A small central station had been maintained on Hanover Street, just west of John Welch's Auto Service at 195 Hanover. Here were kept the Moses H. Goodrich engine and a chemical company. With the advent of the telephone, fire calls were made into this center.

[11]. The Frank E. Booma Post, American Legion, held an organizational meeting on June 2, 1919, adopted its name, voted to apply for a charter and elected officers. Jeremy R. Waldron, Sr., became the first commander; vice commander, Edward J. Neville; post adjutant, Arthur L. McCaffrey; finance officer, Charles H. Walker; historian, Lyman F. MacDonald (moved to Pittsfield, Massachusetts, shortly thereafter); chaplain, C. Waldo Pickett.

[12]. The Charles Emerson Hovey Post, Veterans of Foreign Wars, had its inception at a meeting held August 10, 1919, in Woodworkers and Helpers Hall, Congress Street. The name honors a

naval officer, son of the pastor of St. John's Church, who was killed fighting the Moros in the Philippines in 1911. A fountain honoring his memory still stands at the old Post Office. Officers elected were: Commander, George Hill; aide-de-camp, Maurice Riney; senior vice commander, Walter J. Griffin; junior vice commander, Albert H. Cruse; adjutant, Charles L. Prince; quartermaster, Charles H. Foster; officer of the day, Martin Damm; chaplain, Thomas W. Gibbons; sergeant major, Walter Carkins; color bearers, Frank W. York and Everett C. Gatchell; color guards, George Wilson and Eugene Piche; bugler, Harry R. Larose; sentry, Winsford Stuart.

[13]. On the committee were Mayor Albert D. Hislop and Councilmen Norman H. Beane, Harry B. Yeaton and Frink.

[14]. While the name of any man willing to risk his neck fighting fires on behalf of his fellow citizens is worthy of mention, the name of one man from those long-ago days still persists - - that of George N. Jones. Few men ever served the department any longer, and none more faithfully. Jones started with the fire department on January 1, 1866, and he lived to see the department move into the new quarters. His first service was on the old handtub, Granite State, then he was assigned to Dearborn, the first steam pumper. When permanent men were decided upon, about 1897, Jones was one of them. On November 10, 1872, Jones was with Mayor T. E. O. Marvin and the crew which went to Boston to help stop the blaze that threatened the entire city. The Boston firemen called them "The Haymakers" but they are credited with saving the old South Meeting House.

[15]. One of these steel freighters gave Portsmouth a different sort of thrill on its maiden trip down river on May 18, 1920, when it crashed into the wharves along Ceres Street. The Herald said: "The long old-fashioned brick block on Market Street, between Bow Street and Fernald's Landing, came within an ace of being crumbled to the ground shortly after noon today when the big steel freighter Brookline, starting on her maiden ocean trip, was allowed to crash with great force into Lindsey's Wharf on Ceres Street on the rear of the block."

The tugs apparently had just let the Brookline run free and she swung out of the channel (Memorial Bridge was still on the drawing boards.) and headed for the wharves. "She rammed her bow with great force into the Lindsey Wharf, making splinters of the planking and her nose went deep into the dirt of the street. Quick presence of mind in reversing her engines is all that saved the big boat from hitting the brick block fronting on Market Street. The river tugs were soon to the rescue, and they quickly had her back in midstream and headed for the harbor. The big boat was not injured." Later the skipper explained that a sudden eddy in the current had swung the Brookline before he could get her under control.

[16]. Present were R. W. Wilson, George Wilson, Walter Miller, Richard Brennan, A. F. Borrell, Guy E. Corey, L. Stanley Thompson, John T. Carroll, William Taylor, John Sullivan, Michael Chandler, John Wiseman, Carl Hedblom, Theodore R. Almy, Dr. John D. Carty, Arthur Bullard, Frank Kiel, John Fitzgerald, F. A. Carr, S. G. McClintock, Fred Peckham, Arthur Dawson, Mr. Foensen, Thomas Brooks, Wesley Grogan, William Berg, C. T. Fernald, C. H. Jewett, Ira A. Newick and John Craig. Horace Rowe played musical selections and Newick led the singing.

In March of 1922, Raynes came under considerable criticism when auditors filed reports showing that instead of a surplus there was actually a deficit of $996,728 in Atlantic accounts. The investigator, whose report was entered into the congressional records by Senator George H. Moses, savagely critized Raynes' management. Especially under fire were records of petty cash disbursemants and the restaurant inventory. "The report", The Herald said, "deals extensively with the suits brought by H. C. Raynes and the National Engineering Company against the corporation (Emergency Fleet). In his analysis of the Raynes' claims, as stated by counsel, relating to the credits and assets of the Atlantic Corporation, the investigator conclusively shows the futile negative character of his suit. Raynes' total assets claimed amounted to $3,287,000." The report concludes, "Upon the foregoing analysis of the claims of Rayne's counsel and other data furnished in this investigation I do not hesitate to report that in any event . . . . . the Atlantic Corporation is absolutely bankrupt. There is not and cannot be a dollar for any share of stock of any stockholder."

Only highly skilled accountants could ever follow the ins and outs of this litigation. At one time an $18 million suit was brought against Atlantic by Emergency Fleet, which was explained as being motivated by a desire to get the tangled affairs straightened out. During this period it was made public that Raynes had been hired by Atlantic as manager at a salary of $2,000 a month, fabulous wages in the days of World War I. This the Emergency Fleet refused to allow and it was reduced to $1,000.

[17]. These workmen included John J. Rafferty, Chana ("Chick") Robbins, John Tibbets, Ernest Collins, Leo Collins, Ernest

Petral, John Wallach, Jack Driscoll, Eddie Grady, Joseph Flinn, F. Ertman, Jack Meldrum, Robert Wiseman, Wallace Boyd, Sam Whittaker, Jim Brown and Jack Wheeler.

[18]. An unidentified writer in The Herald of November 23, 1903, has left behind a sketch of the Jaffrey House, to which nothing can be added: "Come with me for a little walk and I will show you right in the heart of our quaint old town the oddest, quaintest bit of colonial history you have seen for many a day. On the top of a hill, the old strawberry bank from which this town derived its name, is perched the old Jaffrey mansion, with a record extending back into the pages of history to 1730. Back to the days when on the green hill overlooking the river and the surrounding country for miles, George Jaffrey, the king's counselor, built in this newly settled land, a big gambrel roof house set in the midst of gardens and fields, and there it stands today covered with vines, shaded by trees, dark with age but little changed, the old house with its wonderful life history.

"Turn into Linden Street with me and up by the modern residences which have crowded back and taken up the original site until only a door yard remains, step over the worn granite block which serves as a door stone, and you stand in front of the massive front door, solid and firm as if a fortress, and wide enough to admit its guests four abreast. Tiny brass knobs adorn the old-fashioned latch, and on the panel is the place where the old knocker used to rest. The door is opened and we find that the hospitality and courtesy of the old mansion in by gone days is not lacking now. We step into the big wide hall with its rich hand carvings, dark with age. At one side ascends the stairway and in those days certainly stairs were built for comfort as well as use, for they are low, wide and easy, and as we look up we almost see the guests of colonial days as they gracefully ascended and descended for the balls, banquets or festivities which were part of the life of the house. From room to room we pass; each one is as a treasure. On one is paper known to be over a century old, of Japanese manufacture. There are doors made of one enormously wide panel, odd closets, which seem a part of the wainscoating or window frames until you discover the fastening. In the dining room is an old wine closet, shell shape and of most exquisite workmanship in the carvings which adorn it, and the beautiful design of shelves. . . .In one of the two parlors are two magnificent card tables of highly polished inlaid wood; these were the property of Daniel Webster. Several of the fireplaces have tiles which were put in when the house was built almost two centuries ago. . . .In all the house has sixteen rooms, besides two attics, enough surely for even an old-fashioned family Thanksgiving party.

"At the death of the original owner he bequeathed it to his nephew on condition he 'always lived a gentleman'; as to whether he did or not is not known, but at his death the old house was offered for sale and purchased by the late John and Amos Goodrich and occupied ever since by their descendants, the present occupants being Mr. John Goodrich and his sister, Miss (Robelina) Goodrich, and Mr. and Mrs. Albert Goldthwaite, the latter formerly Miss Ida Goodrich. The old place has received no material alterations; an addition was put on, but as far as possible everything has been kept. But the city has crowded it on all sides until its gardens and grounds have almost disappeared. It has been called 'haunted', and mysterious stories of hidden treasure have been told . . ."

[19]. Mrs. Clarke, on February 6, 1923, found out that when it comes to politics men have no sense of chivalry. She was voted out of office because the Democrats had captured City Hall, but another spot was found for her.

[20]. Ex-Governor Charles M. Dale is one of the many men who came to Portsmouth on military duty and remained to make it their permanent home. This has been true in every war and also in times of peace. Governor Dale was an artillery officer assigned to Fort Constitution and he served there three years. He married Marian Marvin. Even while on military duty, he was admitted to the New Hampshire bar, and began a local practice after leaving the service in 1920. He was city solicitor and then elected to his first term as mayor in 1926. Dale's career was given major impetus when he succeeded in breaking the will of a brother of the Prescott sisters, Miss Mary and Miss Josephine, local school teachers. The money the sisters derived as their share of the brother's estate has in large measure been devoted to the betterment of Portsmouth. More than a million dollars is in the Prescott Trust, a part of the city trust funds.

Dale had four terms as Portsmouth's mayor, the last in 1944 immediately preceding the first of his two terms as governor. The last part of his administration was plagued with the investigation into the wrong-doings of two key officials. When he left the governorship, Dale retired to the private practice of law and has not been overtly active politically since. Despite a serious illness a year ago, he is back again in his office, practicing law.

[21]. The resolution read:

"The City Council of Portsmouth, conscious of the value of the unselfish service rendered by the late Councilman Harry E.

Boynton over a period of many years in this community which he loved and labored for so earnestly and sincerely desires to place on record a lasting appreciation of his public service and to establish a permanent memorial to his name.

"Be it further resolved, that we believe as time passes the citizens of this city will be more fully conscious of the value of the work which he so faithfully and loyally performed and will appreciate in an increasing degree his high ideals of civic virtues and the unstinted service he gave in all his dealings with his fellow men.

"Be it, therefore, resolved, that the property now owned by the City commonly known as Pierce Island which came into the possession of the City through his efforts shall hereafter be designated as 'Boynton Park', as a permanent memorial to Harry E. Boynton and a token of appreciation for the efficiency and faithfulness of his long period of public service, with the hope that this memorial and the memory of his work, which alone will ever be a monument to him, may forever be an inspiration to the people of this communtiy".

[22]. Neil C. Bierce's long police career ended with his death on April 14, 1960. At that time he held the rank of deputy marshal.

[23]. One item, amusing now, was the act in 1912 to ban dogs from the use of the bridge in order to make it safer for pedestrians. In July, 1828, it was decided to let the fifteen men and officers at Fort Constitution pay a $50 annual fee for use of the bridge. At one time Rufus Amazeen, the toll collector, was paid an annual wage of $125, a ton of coal and free oil for the only lamp on the bridge. Workmen on the bridge were paid in rum, but the collector was expressly barred from sharing in the alcoholic emolument.

Another record, undated but old, gives some specifications of the bridge: "Length of bridge No. 1, from Portsmouth to New Castle, 844 feet; No. 2, 648 feet; No. 3, 800 feet - - total, 2,292 feet. Length of road, No. 1, 604 feet, No. 2, 1,271 feet - - total, 1,875 feet of road. Bridge 20 feet wide and railed; 119 capsill, 119 sections, three piles each, and 357 piles from 40 to 75 feet in length. It requires 360 stringers, and 11,460 feet of plank to cover the same, board measure, three-inch plank."

[24]. Harry W. Peyser practiced law here for many years, was associate justice of the Municipal Court, and a member of the School Board.

[25]. Committee members from the Chamber were

George A. Wood, John H. Neal, Chauncey B. Hoyt, Raphael L. Costello, Samuel D. Eastman, Max Goodman, Fred E. Hasty, Volney Badger, G. D. Boulter, Edward H. Drew, Flagg F. Grant, Ray B. Foye and Frederick Gardner. Efforts of both the city and Chamber were coordinated with the New Castle selectmen, Charles F. Prohaska, Jr., Fred P. Green and William Haywood.

[26]. Mrs. Urch had been elected proprietors' clerk in June 1921 to succeed the major who had died in April. The directors of the bridge, on July 6, 1925, sold to Mrs. Urch for $100 the toll house which had been occupied by the Urch family for forty years. Elmer P. Tucker, president, and Mrs. Urch, clerk, were designated as lawful attorneys to sell for $28,000 the bridge, and the City Council of Portsmouth, on April 20, 1926, empowered Mayor Dale to act for the city while the town meetings of New Castle and Rye gave similar power to their boards of selectmen.

[27]. Although a previous chapter note also tells of the part played by former Mayor Eileen Dondero Foley in cutting the ribbon to open the bridge, it is not generally known that she did it ahead of schedule as a report in the August 18, 1923, issue of The Herald indicates: "One of the pretty incidents of the opening ceremony was the cutting of the silken bond that held the bridge closed. This was a ribbon across the bridge which little Miss Eileen Dondero, with a pair of shears almost as large as herself, cut before the two governors could meet". Asked about this not long ago, the ex-mayor chortled delightedly, "Did I really do that? I remember those scissors, but no one ever told me I cut the ribbon too soon", and she went off into another gale of laughter. She then suggested that Portsmouth 350 ought to make note of the fact that August 17, 1973, will mark 50 years of service for the Memorial Bridge, and again the irrepressible humor came bubbling out, "Perhaps I could find the dress I wore that time. . ."

[28]. Kittery residents hailed the opening of the bridge as "the emancipation of Kittery", declaring that once more they were "free, just like other people". News accounts report that more than 5,000 people waited on both sides and that a line of automobiles three miles long was waiting on the Maine side to move over it. The first weekend it was in operation, 10,000 cars crossed, coming from 34 states, an indication of the traffic the streets of Portsmouth were already beginning to carry. Even at that, the old Portsmouth Bridge collected tolls from a thousand motorists on that same Sunday. During Labor Day weekend in 1923 the Memorial Bridge was used by 28,000 motorists.

[29]. Portsmouth's First Annual Fair was held July 15, 1915, off Sherburne Road and attracted 7,000 people. Six years later the fairgrounds were bought by Fred L. Shaw. Previously there had been a Rockingham County Fair of early origin.

[30]. The late Frank W. Randall was for many years the strong right arm of the University of New Hampshire, serving as chairman of the Board of Trustees. Boardman M. Randall, was at that time a member of the City Council, and appointed as Council member of the Airport Commission.

[31]. Along with presumably many others, Vincent "Bud" Taccetta can recall flying out of this strip. State Representative C. Cecil Dame remembers the summer that three barnstormers spent there, flying the old OX-5s. The takeoff pattern was usually in an easterly line from the new Christ Church building.

[32]. These flight strips are now buried under the giant complex of Pease AFB, and it would be difficult for the most knowledgeable to orient themselves on the ground. The old airport served in a couple of ways not envisioned by the City Council when it was built. For one thing it became for local residents the best place to learn to drive an automobile. Its other function was best described by former Herald reporter Robert Norling, now managing editor of The Concord Monitor, as "the place where Pa courted Ma".

[33]. The team roster, besides Scarponi, included Manuel Cohen, Frederick Howell, Lincoln Ferrini, Charles Flanagan, Cornelius Quinn, William Bradbard and Richard Jameson. Team Manager was Finnbar Corcoran. Ralph D. Brackett was coach and E. Bliss Marriner, faculty manager. The Clippers played Raton, N. M., in their opener and were beaten by the score of 24 to 23. They were beaten in a consolation game, 33 to 27, by Winnemuga High of Nevada. They won the trip to Chicago by winning the New Hampshire title, the third in a long string of such triumphs by PHS basketball teams. The first two came in 1923 and 1925.

27

Portsmouth Marks Three Centuries

[1]. Many more of the historic houses were yet to be torn down before an agonized public called a halt. Today it is a civic virtue to have participated in the renovation of some old house or other. The absolute wantoness of the past has been checked. In fact one of the outstanding features of the Tercentenary was a guided "Ramble" about the city, led by Dr. John H. Neal and Miss Dorothy M. Vaughan, presently Portsmouth's librarian. Miss Vaughan, if prevailed upon to make a similar tour one day for Portsmouth 350, will find, as she knows all too well, that many of the most familiar of those places she talked about that day in 1923 are long gone, victims of fire, urban renewal and other forms of "progress".

[2]. Commission members were Harry L. Lord of Manchester, Charles S. Emerson of Milford, Arthur G. Whittemore of Dover, J. Winslow Peirce of Portsmouth and Henry H. Metcalf of Concord.

[3]. Ernest L. Chaney was transferred to Washington by the Navy Department.

[4]. F. W. Hartford, Fred E. Drew, Patrick E. Kane, Philip H. Sanderson, R. D. McDonough and F. Irish were the publicity men.

[5]. Portsmouth 350 plans to wind up its week-long celebration with a parade which is budgeted for more than $12,000, an item which cost only $1,116.65 in 1923, although in fairness it must be explained that many of the expenses were covered under different headings at that time.

[6]. Portsmouth Country Club players shared first place both in low net and low gross. J. P. H. Chandler, a 14-handicapper, with an 85, net 71 tied with a man from Rochester. John Hassett was second, 86-14, net 72. F. B. Ives of Portsmouth Country Club had an 84 for low gross.

[7]. Archie McEachern is still going strong, a former State representative. He is famed for the annual sale of Christmas trees with the whole family participating in the merchandising, and with his son-in-law Newell Keenan as co-manager. He had five sons and three daughters. Three of the sons are lawyers, state representative and ex-City Councilman Paul, John and Duncan. Raymond is a newspaperman in Quincy and William, a Ph.D. candidate at the University of Virginia. The daughters are Mary Keenan who resides in Portsmouth, Kathryn D'Amour, a nurse, of Manchester, and Margaret, a student at Plymouth State College.

[8]. Vincent Taccetta is deceased. For many years he operated Taccetta Chevrolet, now managed by his son, Vincent "Bud" Taccetta. The firm's headquarters has crossed the city line into Newington, from the old Albany Street quarters.

[9]. As far as "Mickey" Whalen is concerned he would have finished the race, "and probably won it" if he had not fallen down on Hospital Hill and skinned his knees and legs. "Mickey" opened up the United Cigar store, the shop where Harold J. Silverman is now proprietor. He later worked in a creamery, and then went into the trucking business which now bears his name, "M. J. Whalen Co." His son, Robert E. Whalen, former city councilman, assistant mayor, and now governor's councilor, is the active head of the business now. The Whalens make their home in Rye.

[10]. Reginald P. Reed served for some years on the Board of Education and is the holder of a silver pass to all state basketball tournaments, awarded on the 25th anniversary of the tourneys in the state because he had not missed a tournament since the first one in 1923. Also honored on that occasion for the same feat were Leon "Speedy" West and the late George O. Lane.

[11]. The living ex-mayors included Fernando W. Hartford, Albert Hislop, Harry B. Yeaton, Edward H. Adams, Daniel W. Badger, Wallace Hackett, William E. Marvin, John Pender, John W. Emery and William O. Junkins.

Portsmouth 350 President Alice K. Sullivan, in keeping with precedent, named the living ex-mayors to be the committee for the opening dinner. The list was headed by the dean of them all, ex-Governor Charles M. Dale, 1926-27; 1943-44; Kennard E. Goldsmith, 1937-40; Cecil M. Neal, 1948-49; Theodore R. Butler, 1952-55; ex-Governor's Councilor Andrew Jarvis, 1958-59; Robert A. Shaines, 1960-61; City Councilman John J. Wholey, 1962-63; Racing Commissioner Timothy J. Connors, 1963-67, and State Senator Eileen D. Foley, 1967-71. Expected to attend the 1973 dinner are the Lord Mayor of Portsmouth, England, the mayors of Portsmouth, Ohio, Portsmouth, Virginia, and the chief administrative officer of Portsmouth, Rhode Island.

[12]. Dennett & McCarthy were Frank M. Dennett and George W. McCarthy, dry goods merchants. One of their neighbors was the F. W. Woolworth Company. Another was Robert M. Herrick who once worked at the Navy Yard. He was active in city politics and was a motor vehicle license examiner. His last public office was city assessor, before the council-manager plan was adopted in 1947. Herrick died on January 14, 1951, at the age of 84. Across the way was the shop of Costas Giftakis, a confectioner. Roy J. Varotsis, a confectioner, and Arthur H. Green, barber, were also in the vicinity.

[13]. The Pines was Portsmouth's great recreational area, particularly for winter sports. Three ponds afforded skating. There was a toboggan chute and a ski jump. Charles W. Gray of Rye recalls jumping 55 feet on that slope in his college days, prior to 1930. Generally people entered the area for skating about where the new nursing home is now situated off South Street.

[14]. Frank W. Hackett was the gadfly type, flitting in and out of the pages of Portsmouth history as the fancy took him. He was one of the sons of William H. Y. Hackett, a prominent local lawyer in the middle 50 years of the 19th century. Hackett was a frequent writer to the local papers on historical subjects, and there can be no doubt he often used his influence on behalf of his native city in the nation's capital. Hackett died at the Portsmouth Naval Hospital on August 10, 1926, at the age of 85. He is buried in Arlington National Cemetery.

[15]. The bookkeeping gets a bit involved because the committee put the state's contribution of $5,000, and some other gifts, to the direct benefit of the pageant. Some other income was also added.

[16]. Besides Mayor Ladd, the committee had Ernest L. Chaney, secretary; E. Curtis Matthews, Jr., assistant secretary; Charles L. Kimball, treasurer, and Robert J. Eustace, manager. Members were Frank A. Belden, Raphael L. Costello, Thomas E. Collins, Captain D. E. Dismukes, Mrs. Rollin L. Dixon, Edward S. Downs, John W. Emery, Oliver L. Frisbee, Rev. Alfred Gooding, Fernando W. Hartford, Rev. Isaac Higginbotham, Lt. E. P. Jolls, Dr. William O. Junkins, Martha S. Kimball, R. Clyde Margeson, William E. Marvin, William McEvoy, Walter N. Meloon, Gustave Peyser, Harry E. Philbrook, Captain S. R. Sands, Edward Seybolt, William H. Slayton, E. Percy Stoddard, Reverend D. Alex Sullivan, Edmund C.

Tarbell, Rev. L. H. Thayer, Mrs. L. H. Thayer, James T. Whitman and Mary I. Wood.

A lot of the lift of the Tercentenary had come originally from the Chamber of Commerce which in 1923 had Seybolt as president; Albert J. Trottier and Harry W. Peyser, vice presidents; Matthews, treasurer; and Eustace, secretary. Directors were Belden, George D. Boulter, Harry E. Boynton, Joseph P. Conner, Costello, Charles W. Gray, Frank W. Knight, Philbrook, Robert I. Sugden and Trottier.

[17]. Portsmouth 350, Inc., has already been involved in one move to enjoin a local merchant, Richard Doloff, State Street coin dealer, from exploiting the 350 motif in the sale of an unofficial coin. It resulted in Doloff agreeing to cease and desist.

[18]. Among the concessionaires licensed were Anthony Leras, O'Brien and Burns, James Rutledge (2 permits), George A. Anderson, Edgar E. Brown, James E. White (2), Samuel Applebaum, Fred Warner, E. E. Heagan, Maurice Andreol (2), G. Burke and J. Shaw, Fred Hurley (3), Louis Byer, C. S. Locke, Benjamin Suslovits, Philip DeCicco, William Levine, Hyman Waxman, Mario Massa and Sam Katz. The 25 permits actually issued netted the Tercentenary $870.

28

The Terrible Thirties

[1]. Today the old grain store is in the tenancy of Roger Kennedy, who operates an electric appliance business out of it. Walter F. Beevers, who runs a second hand furniture store at 175 Market Street, calls Kennedy the "Mayor of Market Street", and, while he may be speaking in fun, the fact remains that the ancient thoroughfare, in all probability, is coming back into style. The new access way from the complex of superhighways to Maine could give Market Street a significance it has not possessed since the days of Portsmouth Bridge. One entrepreneur, ever careful with his investment dollars, is Richard Morton, a vice president of Strawbery Banke, Inc., and president of Portsmouth Preservation. He has invested heavily in real estate along the street, renovating it into modern apartments. Another investor in the area is Judge Thomas E. Flynn.

[2]. A recital of Rae S. Laraba's accomplishments, in spite of the terrible handicap of failing eyesight, could take up a fair sized biography in itself. Laraba has been a legislator of great acumen, executive secretary of the Judicial Council - - a task to which he has devoted long hours and many weary unrepaid miles. Sometimes, perhaps more seriously than in jest, Laraba, a former able member of the Public Utilities Commission, has remarked, "If I had my political life to do over, I'd be a Democrat. Then the Republicans would give me a good job just to get rid of me." Laraba was a highly efficient member of the PUC but was chopped up in the political shuffles that plague such organizations. Laraba's wife, Margaret, was one of the most efficient stenographers in the state's

Superior Court system. Many times the writer has gone back to Margaret Laraba to find out what lawyers like Tom Morris, Sam Levy, Charles J. Griffin, Ralph McCarthy, Harold "Beauty" Smith, Wyman P. Boynton, Lindsey R. Brigham, William Sleeper, et al were muttering in their little asides.

[3]. The local Municipal Court had other officers at this time in the persons of Edward H. Adams, associate justice; F. Garland Tucker, city solicitor; and Edgar J. True, probation officer.

[4]. Two Portsmouth firms and one in Manchester were ready to swing into action once they could be assured that beer was really here to stay.

[5]. If nothing else, the Prohibition law put brewers where they had not been for many years - - in private homes. Going back into colonial times, one reads in Judge Sewall's diary of how he "brewed his wife's 'groaning beer'." meaning the poor woman was bearing their umpteenth child and the beer was intended for the period of labor and the regaling of the midwives afterward. It was not, however, labored pregnancies for which Portsmouth and the rest of the nation brewed beer in the 1920's - - it was intended to slake thirst.

[6]. Freak storms are not rare. In August 1926 a hailstorm hit Portsmouth, leaving chunks of ice big enough, according to Alvah C. Card, to be stored in the ice boxes of the day. The fabric roofs of automobiles were riddled. Then there was the famous year, 1816, without any summer.

[7]. F. Clyde Keefe, at the hands of the Republicans and Charles M. Dale, was to take the worst drubbing ever administered to a Democrat in a contest for the governorship. This was in 1946.

[8]. Members of that original Control Commission were Ralph W. Caswell of Dover (later head of the New Hampshire State Police), James Tufts of Exeter and Henri LeDoux of Nashua.

[9]. Perhaps some day more of a character will come along to figure in Portsmouth's public life, but until he does, Stewart E. Rowe will suffice. Older lawyers say that one of the objects that bothered them when they entered Rowe's offices was the noose that swung from the chandelier. This gruesome instrument of death was the one knotted for Sidney Thorp, but unused. It was Rowe's symbol of triumph over adversity. Rowe was drafted as the Republican candidate for mayor in 1941. J. Verne Wood, local undertaker, used to chortle over how "they brought 'Stewie' over for a fitting" - - J. Verne provided the suit - - so he could be inaugurated. The writer

has been told by a local lawyer of seeing in Rowe's office the cud of gum he was chewing when he pitched Dartmouth to victory over an Ivy League opponent. The building where Rowe lived and practiced law was at one time the rectory for St. John's Church. While in such occupancy the Rev. Henry Hovey and his family even assumed that their tenancy gave them the privilege of using the County Courthouse lawn, across the street, as a croquet court. One of the sheriffs happened to be a man named John Pender who threw wickets, posts, mallets and the like into the street -- but then he was a member of the North Church.

[10]. Thorp was right. Under still existing New Hampshire law, a condemned man has a year and a day for appeals and other legal redress. It remains to be seen what will happen to this statute if the U. S. Supreme Court's recent ruling on the death penalty still stands.

[11]. Another point which shows Thorp knew much about New Hampshire law. Until the death penalty was ruled out by the U. S. Supreme Court, New Hampshire followed the pattern of ancient days by making the high sheriffs responsible for the execution of the death penalty. This was, of course, a preservation of colonial law when Sheriff Thomas Packer saw to the hanging of four persons - - more than any other New Hampshire official. Three of them were women, Penelope Kinney and Sarah Simpson on December 27, 1739; Ruth Blay, December 1768; and Eliphaz Dow, 1756. These four were actually the only hangings in provincial New Hampshire. In 1770, the colony was sub-divided into five counties and the hanging of record took place in Dover after the Revolution. New Hampshire, when the number of really good murders is considered, has never been partial to the infliction of captial punishment.

[12]. See Note 9, this chapter. The observation should be made that the tying of a hangman's knot is an art unto itself, and one wonders who tied the one for Thorp. The proper knot is supposed to kill before strangulation takes place.

[13]. Roosevelt had been here in connection with the operation of the Portsmouth Naval Prison under Thomas Mott Osborne, the former warden of Sing Sing. He also had shown up on several occasions before and during World War I when vacationing on the coast. He came here to campaign in 1932 before his election to the presidency.

[14]. One of the properties eventually acquired from Charles H. "Cappy" Stewart was Four Tree Island. It had been

owned at one time by Charles E. Gray, who left behind him legal problems in inheritance unparalleled in Rockingham County jurisdiction. The Herald, for some reason of its own, on June 11, 1920, published a picture of the island, and this is the caption below it: "This is Four Tree Island which was famous in the days of Charles E. Gray and now owned by Charles H. Stewart. This island, after Gray's death, was the cause of many legal questions and brought out the queerest cases in the history of Rockingham County Superior Court, owing to Gray's matrimonial mixups. Here (on Four Tree Island) he conducted a dance hall and maintained a curio hall which contained everything in the freak line from a stuffed cow to the shoes of Jesse James. His resort was widely known among the Navy men, and every ship leaving the Navy Yard always received a salute from a small brass cannon which he had mounted in the yard. He made all kinds of money, but gave it away to needy people and died a poor man. Shortly after his death, a sister, Mrs. John Sullivan, and a niece claimed the entire island as the heirs of Gray. This started a general all around legal fight which really opened when Mrs. Annie Gray came along as the widow of Charles and demanded her share. The question came out whether or not she was the real widow. One thing led to another and it finally developed that Gray had five women to his credit as wives during his 56 years of life and it was many years before the courts and the several lawyers settled the fight for and against the petition for partition".

Why The Herald happened to publish that when it did cannot be determined now, but it was well timed. For generations the islet had been known as Four Tree but the ravages of time had disposed of two of the trees, really making it Two Tree Island. Then on July 16, 1920, The Herald reported, "There is not a tree standing now on the once famous spot in the Piscataqua. The two remaining trees were struck by lightning during the storm on Thursday afternoon and badly wrecked. The lightning jumped from one tree to the other and tore the elms to pieces. Charles Marston, a well known fisherman and clam dealer who makes his home on the island, had a narrow escape from being fatally injured during the storm and more than once he wished he was somewhere on the mainland. He has no desire to be as near again to any discharges of atomospheric electricity".

[15]. Why they chose to spend their fortune this way was prompted for the most part by a desire to see Portsmouth's waterfront restored to its old-time place of prestige. In 1934 Miss Josie Prescott told an interviewer, "We have always been interested in doing what we considered the right thing towards charities.

Beyond that I do not care to discuss it. You will realize of course that when stories are published of persons having great wealth they are besieged with requests for aid. They come from all parts of the country. Strangely enough, few people in our home city bother us. It is the outsiders who send us the letters asking aid, and ask for appointments." In the essence, these two gallant women stayed with that credo, and their charities remained their own business.

[16]. When Dale moved the "Oracle House", it was the second journey undertaken by that venerable structure. At one time it had stood south of the North Church, and in it was published Charles W. Pierce's "Oracle of the Day", later succeeded by "The Portsmouth Journal of Literature and Politics".

[17]. Ex-Governor Dale bought this property from Alta Roberts who died in 1940. He then sold it to the Marconi family where title still rests. Mrs. Roberts moved to another Prescott property at 17 Liberty Street where she died. Dale says her rent "came out from under her pillow every month in cash". Alta Roberts, through those last years, was an ill woman, but she had made a bargain and she kept it.

[18]. The bounds of the Prescott Trust are carefully spelled out in her will. They are State, Washington, Gates to Marcy Streets; Marcy to Pickering, Pickering to the Piscataqua River.

[19]. Members at that time were John J. Wholey, Mary C. Dondero, Eugene P. Soles, Andrew Jarvis, Sherman P. Newton, Donald H. Margeson, Edward C. Peterson, John J. Leary and Mayor Theodore R. Butler. Peterson was Portsmouth's first city manager. He left that post after a hassle with the City Council and won election to the Council himself. Newton, Leary and Mrs. Dondero are deceased, as well as the then city clerk Amerigo Bellucci. Leary, Wholey and Jarvis were later to serve as Portsmouth mayors.

[20]. This group administers funds left for the benefit of the City of Portsmouth. At the present time membership consists of Robert E. McLaughlin, chairman; James R. Kelly and Arthur E. Splaine.

[21]. The city itself and the Chamber of Commerce tried to stimulate action, and in November 1931 a local committee on unemployment was in operation. The Herald said, "A finance committee was appointed, completing the organization of the relief body, and the definite plans for the raising of funds were formulated". There was a proposal that those lucky enough to have jobs should help others, at a rate of perhaps a day's pay a month. If a worker was making four dollars a day, then his donation would be

four dollars spread across the paydays in the month. The finance committee included Frank W. Randall, Laurence G. Peyser, Harry Winebaum, Thomas Flanagan, Clayton E. Osborn, Joseph P. Conner, Frederick M. Gardner, Andrew Jarvis, E. Curtis Matthews, George B. Lord, the Rev. H. W. Curtis, B. H. Crowell, Phillips B. Badger, State Senator Charles H. Brackett and Dr. Philip H. Greeley.

This was a strictly no-nonsense matter. The Unemployment Committee made a statement to "Our Citizens" which admitted that due to the "economic conditions now existing in the country a large number of deserving citizens are without employment. This condition exists in our city as well as elsewhere and without doubt will become increasingly acute as the winter goes on . . . . . Contributions or pledges to the local committee may be forwarded to Orel A. Dexter, treasurer, or will be received by any of the local banks". General chairman of this committee was Fernando W. Hartford; Henry B. Tilton, chairman of the executive committee; Norman E. Rand, auditor. H. Clinton Taylor, Edward Seybolt and Peter J. Hickey made up the committee on plans; E. H. Drew was investigator. Tilton headed the executive committee, the other members of which were Hartford, Taylor, Jarvis, Flanagan, R. C. L. Greer, William C. Walton, John W. Emery, Morris Silverman, Hickey, Rand, Frank E. Brooks, Seybolt, Drew, Randall, Dexter, William B. Hirshberg and Ralph W. Eaton.

Various kinds of pledge cards were in circulation. There was one that authorized the superintendent for the Board of Public Works to put a given individual to work, and the subscriber would pick up the bill for it. Another was a flat pledge to support the committee's efforts with a weekly or monthly pledge of a certain amount of money. A football game between the Marines and UNH freshmen was staged on Armistice Day, and Robert M. Bruce reported that it raised $128.49. Do not laugh; at 40 cents an hour that would help a lot of people. On December 14, 1931, Treasurer Dexter reported a collection of $4,537.15, and an outgoing payroll of $2,303.75. A week later statistics were given for six weeks of the committee's operation, reporting payrolls of $225.25 the first week; $403.75, the second; $591.25, the third; $563.25, the fourth; dropping to $519.75, the fifth week; and jumping to $1,867.50 for the sixth week. The committee at the end of its summary challenged: "Portsmouth faces this question - - will we, its citizens, permit men, women and children to the number of 1,448 to go through this winter without sufficient food, clothing and fuel? The answer will be NO, we will not permit this condition. We will get back of the

Unemployment Committee and give as we are able to assure the maximum amount of employment to these deserving men. And in the spirit of Christmas, we will start our payment now".

These reports went on with a deadly monotony that only those who lived through the grim years of 1932 and 1933 can recall. It should be understood that these were not handouts, that honest labor was performed in order to get paid, and that the funds did not come from overflowing government chests but out of the pockets of fellow citizens. The program was in operation from November 1931 through May 1932; a final report was filed on July 7, 1932.

The project created for the unemployed by the Planning Board of the committee was beautification work around the South Mill Pond and the adjacent parks. It was agreed the city would supply all materials, this leaving the funds contributed for distribution as wages. A total of $24,237.03 was collected and the payrolls amounted to $24,158.57, the remaining $78.36 being spent on postage and printing. Before the project ended 511 men had signed up. The amount of work time they were given depended on the number of their dependents. For example, men with 2, 3 or 4 in the family were given three days work out of every 12, while a man with 9 had the chance to work six out of nine days. There were 127 working days and 48,317 man hours were put in. Actual survey work and laying out of the project was done by John W. Durgin, Sr. All in all, it was a notable effort by Portsmouth residents to help neighbors over a rough patch in life's road.

Completion of the Unemployment Committee's project, however, did not mean that the struggle with the Depression was over and that employment was back to normal. Dr. S. F. A. Pickering took over administration of the city government in January 1933, and at a joint meeting of the Rotary and Kiwanis Clubs and the Chamber of Commerce at the Rockingham Hotel, he outlined the steps the city was taking to provide community relief. Pickering said, ". . . . The first meeting of the city government was the inauguration. Following this meeting I was at a meeting of the Board of Public Works, of which I automatically became chairman, and we immediately proceeded to reduce salaries. We staggered the work by giving all of those employed three days work each. That allowed us to increase the payroll from about 37 members less than four weeks ago to 80 on the payroll Monday night which would be about 40 extra earning $12 a week to live on.

"The donations from the several departments have been wonderful," Pickering continued. "The members of the departments have signed their names to an agreement to the amount set opposite their names to be taken out of the 1933 payroll. The School Department has agreed, from the superintendent down to the teachers earning above $1,200; the police court, from the judge down, all signed it. In the Police Department, from the chief down, every man volunteered his contribution. In the city officials every man has signed. The Fire Department, with two exceptions, to a man; and the teachers all contributed very generously, and they have for over a year. . . . . . "

Others taking part in the long program that night included Richard B. Shelton, managing secretary of the Chamber, and the Rev. Arthur Acy Rouner. Ernest L. Cook led community singing with Leon Robinson at the piano and John L. Phelps doing a solo. Frank W. Randall, chairman of the Community Citizens Committee, gave a lengthy report, keying it to the observation, "In building for the future the first necessary step is to face and analyze the existing conditions of the present". He explained the operations of this second privately financed self-help program..

A little more than a year later another such meeting was held at the Rockingham with Randall, then president of the Portsmouth Civic Council and the Chamber of Commerce, as toastmaster. It brought together people like Mrs. William E. Marvin, Mr. and Mrs. Charles H. Walker, the Rev. and Mrs. William Safford Jones, Mr. and Mrs. Frank E. Brooks, Governor's Councilor Charles H. Brackett of Greenland, Mayor Robert Marvin, Mrs. Vida Randall, R. C. L. Greer, Albert H. Woolfson, Mr. and Mrs. Andrew Graves, Richard B. Shelton, Mrs. Lillian Albee, Frank C. Remick, Mr. and Mrs. E. Curtis Matthews and the Rev. Mr. Rouner. Mayor Marvin gave a status report on some of the Civil Works Administration projects which were under way, citing the Council's appropriation of $5,650 for the purchase of materials to build a swimming pool at Pierce Island, "a project that will keep 60 men at work until the first day of May. Another project which I filed", Marvin said, "was one to paint the City Hall. That will put nine or more painters to work".

"The project for painting the Central Fire Station has been approved and we wait only the arrival of the paint to begin the work. A new project to take care of almost 150 men has been submitted. This is the creation of new runways at the airport. Still another project submitted to the federal Civil Works Administration which will be of invaluable aid to the City of Portsmouth at the present time, and looking into the future, is that of construction of a city map with a view to future planning". Then Marvin mentioned that

10 architects had been commissioned by the government to make detailed drawings of the old houses, so that even were they destroyed, they could be reproduced. If nothing else, these interminably long meetings established that Portsmouth was willing to do almost anything to improve the lot of its citizens. The giant federal agencies such as CWA, WPA, CCC and a host of others were, however, taking up the slack that public gifts could not meet. In 1934 Charles H. Walker touched on this by tracing the original local effort in 1931 and how the need for outside monies had become obvious. The agency chiefly involved was the CWA, with Walker serving on the local CWA committee. The sustained effort continued through the 1930's until war clouds in Europe brought American industry back into full swing. Here in Portsmouth, from the nadir of 1,475 in 1932, the employment rolls at the Navy Yard inched steadily upward to a point where in the first year of the new decade more than 7,000 were working.

[22]. One well known local woman has told of swimming in the pool in 1936 and coming down with a severe case of impetigo.

[23]. Few people in Portsmouth were better known than Clayton E. Osborn, who at one time served as Public Works superintendent, was a member of the City Council and an active legislator. Osborn had the faculty of being able to cut through to the heart of practical problems while others were still in perplexity. With a piece of chalk, for example, he created on a blackboard the layout of the present Parrott Avenue parking spaces as they are today while his fellow councilmen were still in complete befuddlement.

[24]. The sessions of this conference were held in the North Church Parish House, Middle Street, now Salvation Army headquarters. Registration was in the YMCA building where Mel Goodman's haberdashery now flourishes. One of the big treats of the occasion was the chance to ride up on the Memorial Bridge lift.

[25]. Chief Boatswain's Mate Hill's life ended on a tragic note when he took his own life by gunshot in the little cemetery at the Navy Yard he had cared for for so long. That was in August 1922.

[26]. S-4 was in collision with the USCG Paulding off Provincetown on December 17, 1927. An entire nation waited sickly and anxiously as the Navy tried to reach six living men trapped in the submarine. The fact that she had been in a collision enabled men to locate her quickly. She had gone down like a proverbial rock at the point where she collided with Paulding. Even the weather conspired

against efforts to reach the hulk. The accident had happened on Saturday afternoon; enough help had been rounded up to get the USS Bushnell, S-4's mother ship, ready to sail by 5 P.M., but by Monday afternoon no vessel could stay in place over the wreck. Divers had been able to cut airlines into the hull, but the tapped out signals became fainter and finally ceased. In the spring, the S-4 was brought to the surface, the men's bodies were removed, and the S-4 was taken into Charlestown Navy Yard. She was later brought to Portsmouth where she was cut in two, lengthened and used in experimenting with escape techniques.

[27]. S-48 ran into trouble by going aground on the bar at Jeffrey's Point and then drifting onto the mud flats off Frost Point. She had come from New London in company with S-51 and the sub tender Chewink. The skippers of these two vessels stayed outside the harbor all night because of the wild snowstorm that was raging, a storm so severe that it obliterated all lights and landmarks. It was Janaury 29, 1925, still in the early evening, when the SOS reached the Yard about 7:30. The radio people decided the calls were coming from a submarine aground at Whale Back Light and that is where the search started. S-48 was finally found but tugs, because of the storm, could not reach her. The Coast Guard was asked to bring a breeches buoy rig from Wallis Sands because, while no one in the crew had been lost, there was some danger from chlorine gas leaking out of her battery room. Eventually the crew was taken off.

A week after she went aground S-48 was floated, brought to the Navy Yard drydock where it could be seen that the rocks had ripped her hull badly. She was decommissioned and the Yard waited for almost two years for the funds to recondition the submarine. Once the funds were in hand, the Yard decided on a bold course: An effort would be made to get S-48 up onto the ways in the Franklin Shiphouse, almost the reverse of a launching. Three B & M railroad engines were brought onto the Yard to provide the pulling power. They were hooked up in line by cables, chains and shackles to S-48. It took three pulls to bring S-48 out of the river. The first two were short in duration, intended to get all slack out of the lines. Then came the true haul which lasted 16 minutes. A newspaper estimated that the three locomotives generated 85,700 pounds of power in getting the 600-ton sub up the ways. Once positioned on the ways, the men went about the task of cutting her in two and piecing in a 30-foot section.

[28]. The Navy's official decision to put down these horses produced a lot of protest. They were finally reprieved and

lived out their natural lives in green pastures at the University of New Hampshire.

[29]. Councilman Thomas E. Collins made the motion and the City Council voted on May 23, 1923, to change the name of Daniel Street to Daniels Street in honor of the Portsmouth Navy Yard's great friend, former Navy secretary Josephus Daniels. The response from Daniels came quickly in a letter to the mayor: "Councilman Collins had done me the kindness to convey the information that you have done me the honor to name the street in Portsmouth leading to the Memorial Bridge in my honor. I wish to express to you my grateful appreciation of this honor and my deep interest in the welfare of the Portsmouth Navy Yard and its skilled employees, and my congratulations at the completion of the bridge which will be of lasting benefit, not only to those working for Uncle Sam on the Navy Yard but to all who live in Maine and New Hampshire and all of the thousands of Americans who visit Maine and New Hampshire every summer. I hope one of these days to give myself the pleasure of visiting your city and seeing the bridge."

[30]. Kay Akerley, secretary to the yard commandant and wife of District Conservation Officer Carl Akerley, was kind enough to dig out from the files some interesting correspondence on the matter. For an official letter, there are some humorous overtones. Because the material covering the subject of the submerged logs is pertinent to the sometimes weird operation of government, it has been included as appendix VII.

[31]. The old Franklin Shiphouse dominated the Navy Yard waterfront for nearly a century and was part of Portsmouth's easterly skyline for that period of time. On March 10, 1936, the wooden structure, dried out by nearly a hundred summers, caught fire; those who stirred from their beds at 5:10 a. m. saw a spectacular blaze. The building was 343 feet long, 84 feet wide, and 52 feet in height. Fifty feet of that length was added when it was decided to rebuild the USS Franklin under its cover, hence the name it bore.

[32]. Plunger was Portsmouth's 23rd submarine when she went down the ways at 15:50 hours on July 8, 1936. Her constructors had set a remarkably fast time with her, her keel having been laid on July 17, 1935, a little less than a year before. Portsmouth's pace was beginning to pick up.

[33]. Later Preble, under the non-partisan aspects of a new City Charter, was a candidate for the City Council.

[34]. Perhaps this is not the place to relate the saga of the USS Portsmouth, but it will have to do. Portsmouth, a new

cruiser, came into port after the war was over and was given a royal welcome. The Portsmouth's first cruise had been in the Caribbean and the Portsmouth Herald had sent reporter Robert G. Kennedy along on the trip. James M. Langley, later ambassador to Pakistan, and publisher of The Concord Monitor, also was aboard. Portsmouth came into port and her crew and officers were feted, dined and wined for one solid week. It was so much fun that the night before she sailed Kennedy and Langley, deep in idyllic bliss, came up with a great idea. Why not keep Portsmouth for another week? Easy enough to do. After all, Langley knew John Sullivan, Secretary of the Navy. So the two conspirators called Sullivan in Washington. The Secretary, who had once aspired to New Hampshire's governorship, was agreeable to doing Langley a favor. Before anyone in official Portsmouth, or official anywhere else, knew what was going on, the orders were cut, and the USS Portsmouth stayed on for another weary week. Kennedy never could understand why J. D. Hartford, Annapolis graduate and publisher of The Portsmouth Herald, was still seething 10 years later at this breach of naval protocol. "Did I ever tell you," Hartford would ask, "what those two did?" Without waiting for an answer he would continue, "They called up the Secretary of the Navy and got a ship's orders changed. Can you imagine it?" The suspicion still lingers that over its 200 years of life, the Navy could have used more Kennedys and Langleys, but it is only a feeling that has never been put to the test.

[35]. No matter how casual you get in the news business about dignitaries, there is still something awesome about covering the President of the United States. On that particular day President Truman swiftly climbed the steps of the Squalus monument and The Herald's photographer lingered far behind. Suddenly a Secret Serviceman near the President said, "Hey, look, Mac, if you want a picture you'd better get up here where you can do something."

[36]. Vetter is no longer in the Portsmouth Police Department. He is a deputy sheriff serving under Sheriff George Sampson. For some time Vetter, a police lieutenant, headed the plain clothes section of the police.

[37]. William J. Linchey, one of the most honest men to walk Portsmouth's crooked streets, became marshal on the retirement of City Marshal Leonard H. Hewitt. Linchey sponsored one of the most spectacular raids on gambling establishments ever pulled off in this city when on a Saturday afternoon in July 1949, twenty-five green uniformed State Police officers, under the leader-

ship of State Police Major Herbert F. Gray of Portsmouth, came into town and cleaned out four bookie joints. Linchey used that day only his most trusted men, veterans like "Denny" Kelley, Lloyd McGraw and Captain Timothy J. Connors, father of former Mayor Timothy J. Connors. The rest of the raiders were state troopers. The raids were based on information supplied by a couple of reporters for The Herald who lived under cover here for weeks. They were Edward G. McGrath and Robert Morrison.

[38]. Sheriff Simes Frink, stocky and almost as wide as he was tall, was one of the most powerful men the writer ever knew. One day, hopefully in jest, the sheriff bear-hugged the writer, demonstrating his physical strength, and the lesson was never forgotten. Frink succeeded Ceylon Spinney; Sheriff George Sampson, the incumbent, followed him.

[39]. McGraw's later suicide by gunshot still defies explanation - - the man was always so critical of those who chose to take their own lives.

29

The Second World War

[1]. Staff Sergeant James Copley retired in 1943 in that grade after 33 years of faithful service to the United States and the United States Army. There were pleas in the Harbor Defenses of Portsmouth that he be promoted to master sergeant in recognition of that service but Camp Langdon politicians prevailed against that. Staff Sergeant Copley was the father of Joseph Copley, antiquarian, Civil War student, gun buff and antique dealer.

[2]. An auction of the furnishings of the Jones Mansion was held on July 25, 1940. The Herald said: "He came to Portsmouth a penniless young man and he died owning the city. His home was elaborate and the expensive showplace of the state. Its palatial interior was filled with elegant furnishings, crystal chandeliers and enormous gilt framed paintings. The walls were decorated with gold and the fireplaces were of marble. Today his possessions are being sold at auction. The estate of Frank Jones, millionaire founder of the Portsmouth brewing company bearing his name, is soon to be turned into a residential section and his massive house will be made over into apartments. Magnificent furniture, the finest pieces brought from all parts of the world to adorn his mansion, is up for public bid. The house is being stripped, piece by piece, of its former beauty. An exquisite dining room cabinet, purchased in France by Mr. Jones, for over $5,000, couldn't be sold for $300. This morning the jovial auctioneer stood on the side steps and shouted the attributes of his wares.

"'What am I bid for this gorgeous hand-carved chair?' he queried. Voices from the fair-sized crowd carried on the bidding until the article was sold probably for half its former value. Another part of the atmospphere of the old house is gone never to be replaced. Thirty coats of gold leaf embellished the walls of one room where handsome leather-trimed furniture and rich, soft brown rugs were piled in a shambles in the middle. The grand house seems impassive to the hum of activity filling its rooms. High in the turret, far from the noise of the auction, the dust lies thick and an old truck stands alone...''

[3]. His first visit was discussed at length earlier. He was also off the coast in the summer of 1939 to visit the scene of the Squalus salvage.

[4]. The nine previous presidential visitors were Washington, Adams, Monroe, Polk, Pierce, Grant, Arthur, Harrison and Taft. Since that time, President Harry S. Truman, FDR's successor has been here. Herbert Hoover was here, but that was after he had left the presidency. John F. Kennedy, a successful candidate, came here in March of 1960 and held a conference in the Rockingham Hotel. That conference had been preceded by attacks on him by Dolores Bridges, wife of Senator Styles Bridges, and Governor Wesley Powell, both of whom initimated that JFK was "weak on communism".

[5]. State Senator Eileen D. Foley remembers a couple of her sisters running into the Street and touching the presidential coat sleeve as his car turned from Vaughan into Congress Street. To Alvah C. Card it was a privilege to stand on the City Hall steps and watch the President pass.

[6]. Portsmouth Police Department had a large contingent of officers on hand under Deputy Marshal Frank H. Demars. Included were Officers James A. McCaffrey, John McCann, Lawrence T. Dow, Joseph L. Thomson, Paul F. Connors, Francis J. Hurley, E. Edward Scarponi, John J. Sullivan, Roland T. Smart, Harold J. Trueman, Neil C. Bierce, Lloyd N. McGraw, Martin O. Betz, Joseph Kelley, Dennis J. Kelley and Captain Dougal D. McLean. Of these, only Scarponi (deputy marshal) and Connors (captain) are still on the force.

[7]. The president was Ory S. Connery; treasurer, Jack Fenwick; secretary, John W. Howe.

[8]. In civilian life, Smith followed a career in the Post Office and retired while serving as Superintendent of Mails.

[9]. Boynton had, a few years before, done a 150-page paper (since read by the writer) on the Portsmouth Water Works as part of the requirements for a degree in civil engineering from Massachusetts Institute of Technology. That experience, coupled with a later degree in law, convinced J. D. Hartford, that Boynton was the man to raise pertinent questions at hearings on the water matter. Boynton did, and Jeremy R. Waldron, Sr., and Boynton subsequently were active in the court proceedings.

[10]. Ralph H. Atwell is presently the proprietor of the Randall Press, a long-established printing firm at 19 Daniel Street. The firm name derived from John D. Randall whose original shop

was at 3 Congress Street. Associated with him was his brother William B. Randall. John D. Randall was the father of William I. and Frank W. Randall. William I. was city electrician for many years, while Frank was following a career as an electrical engineer. John D. Randall, in the years before it became a full-time job, was also chief engineer at times in the Fire Department. Frank W. Randall was once general manager of New Hampshire Gas and Electric. Incidentally, Boardman M. Randall, for many years with the St. Croix Paper Co., and who lived at the corner of Lincoln Avenue and Broad Street, was no relation to Frank W. Randall.

[11]. Amerigo Fransoso is familiar to present-day-Portsmouth as Councilman Rick Fransoso. For many years, he worked for Charles M. Dale, later ran a painting business and is now retired. Fransoso served on the Board of Street Commissioners into the post-war period. At one time, his fellow members were David R. Smith and Fred V. ("Val") Hett, Jr. During the mayoralty of Mary C. Dondoero, meetings of the commission were apt to get heated, usually with Smith in the minority.

At one such session, with Mayor Dondero presiding, the vote on some long-since forgotten issue was 2 to 1, and not the way the indomitable mayor wanted it. Forthwith she announced her "vote" was with Smith, which made it, she said, a "2 to 2" vote and the motion failed to pass. With that, she adjourned the meeting and left the room; leaving Fransoso and Hett talking to themselves. Mayor Dondero's understanding of Roberts' Rules of Order, or any other regulatory code, it seemed, went only as far as it suited her convenience.

[12]. Dale resigned the post on October 1, 1941, due to the pressure of personal business.

[13]. John W. Perkins retired August 13, 1972, from the bench of the Hampton District Court, the judgeship of which he had held since January 10, 1945.

[14]. Ralph G. McCarthy served in various civic posts, and in the latter years of World War II was county solicitor. Wyman P. Boynton succeeded him in that post in 1946.

[15]. Alvah C. Card reads meters for the Portsmouth Water Department for a living, but his hobby is Portsmouth. Knowing about the weather of his native city, its major fires, its notable people, its scandals, its murders and all grist for Card's mill. The city had many years service from him as a call fireman. It might be said that, over the years, without dozens of men like Card, the city's firefighting ability would have been of low order.

[16]. Miss Vivian Brown retired a year or two ago as a commander in the Naval Reserve, but is still on the faculty of Portsmouth Senior High School.

[17]. Francis T. ("Babe") Malloy is the "senior deacon" at PHS. His teaching career in the Portsmouth school system spans four decades. At present, and he threatens retirement every year, he is master of one of the high school's four "houses".

[18]. Harrison H. Workman today lives on Sagamore Avenue. His military service never took him overseas. Like many another in the early callup, he was shifted from place to place, outfit to outfit. At one time, he guarded aluminum plants in Tennessee; he served in North Carolina; then, in one of those miracles rare in Army circles, the square peg was put in the square hole. Workman, a boat builder by trade and a lover of the sea by avocation, came to Battery A of the 22nd Coast Artillery, Portsmouth Harbor Defenses. Battery A had responsibility for mining Portsmouth Harbor and maintaining the field. Workman wound up as skipper of one of the L-boats and plied Portsmouth Harbor waters. One of his most miserable duties was towing targets for the various gun batteries. His opinion of some of the gunnery he saw is caustic. "You guys", he said not long ago, after learning the writer was in one of the gun batteries, "couldn't have hit anything if it had stood still. All you did was hit my boat one day". Workman, in the normal course of events, left the Army and returned to the Portsmouth Naval Shipyard, and retired on May 31, 1972.

[19]. "The March of Time"! Admittedly those who remember those words are in the Senior Citizen grouping but their thrill lingers on. The producer, Louis deRochemont, maintains a home in Newington.

[20]. A. Richard Chase was from Keene and returned there.

[21]. The first event of that day was the "departure of Kittery refugees" to Portsmouth's welcoming shore. They were to leave Warren's Wharf, under the escort of Ralph T. Wood, and arrive at Prescott Park where a Red Cross Motor Corps unit, under the direction of Mrs. J. B. Longstaff, "rushed the victims" to Salvation Army headquarters where Captain Clair Lowman was in command . . . . While these people were arriving the first division of the parade, under James E. Barnett, was forming. The parade route was down Congress Street, Islington, to Cabot, Middle, Miller, Rockland, Richards and Parrott Avenue. At Prescott Park, Goodwin Park and the Playground, Chairman John Mooney of the Portsmouth Chapter,

American Red Cross, had first aid tents, with Miss Irma Rintz in charge. Then, in the Parrott Avenue area, various demonstrations took place with Dr. Elijah L. Levine, supervising. Raymond I. Beal (later superintendent of the Portsmouth school system) headed the children's day nursery; a communications center, directed by Harry Winebaum, and Andrew Jarvis' emergency canteen were opposite the VFW home.

[22]. Ralph T. Wood, with Ira A. Newick, operated for some years Newick and Wood, a garage at 145 Fleet Street, which had previously been under the proprietorship of Albert Hislop and Wood as partners. One of their salesmen at one time was former County Commissioner Ira A. Brown.

[23]. The State Employment Service, as it was known to the returning veterans of World War II, had its offices in the old quarters of the Ham Cafe on High Street.

[24]. Andrew C. Graves is the father of City Councilman Bruce Graves. The son works for Iafolla Industries, and used as a campaign slogan in 1971, "I Dig Graves", the play being on slang use of the word "dig", meaning to like.

[25]. On October 21, 1941, the Portsmouth Board of Street Commissioners agreed "to furnish water to the PBA 800-home development (Wentworth Acres, presently Sea Crest Village), the work to start as soon as the board is informed money has been made available under the federal grant. The guarantee of supply is for six months". Commissioner Fred V. Hett, Jr., and Ralph H. Atwell voted favorably and Amerigo Fransoso opposed.

[26]. Fire swept through this old home almost unimpeded, having too much of a start by the time the chemical truck could run out from the Central Fire Station. The second oldest house in the city, built in 1681, the Wentworth Farm was owned by the American Agriculture and Chemical Company and "is used as an experiment farm". The house was occupied by head farmer H. Haye Eldridge and family. Shortly after two o'clock, the house was discovered on fire and a telephone message was sent to Chief Randall and he ordered the auto chemical out, going along himself. They made good time (The property stood opposite the Woodbury Avenue entrance to Echo Avenue.) and when they arrived the house was beyond saving, inasmuch as there was no water and the two tanks of the chemical would not have checked the flames, but they did save the barns. The fire started in an upper room and had spread to the entire upper part of the house. The furniture, with the exception of the room where the fire started, was saved. The auto chemical having

arrived, the firemen did the greater part of this.

"Several times the sparks from the burning building set fire to the stables but the chemical put them out and saved the building. Had a fire engine been sent out, it would not have been of any use as there was no water even if it had arrived in good season. The loss is about $3,500 with insurance on the house but none on the furniture".

Madam Ursula Cutt built the house after being willed the farm by her husband John Cutt, president of the Governors Council. She built well and the house at the time of the fire was reportedly in a good state of preservation. Madam Cutt lost her life, and her scalp, in an Indian raid, July 17, 1694, when some of the aborigines made their way across the river. They did not destroy the property because an alarm sounded too soon. In the 19th Century, the property passed into the possession of Ichabod Bartlett, and then to Mark H. Wentworth, from whom Wentworth Acres acquired its name. A couple of cherubim that had been put on the house by Madam Cutt were taken off at the time of one of the sales and still exist in the hallway of the John Paul Jones House, perhaps waiting for another Indian raid.

[27]. "Thousands of Portsmouth citizens watched apprehensively as the plane, coming in from the direction of Hampton, circled the city, zoomed over Kittery and then over the airport and finally dropped a bright yellow distress flare which floated slowly down into a tree on Woodbury Avenue near the home of Policeman Joseph L. Thomson . . .

"Meanwhile listening and observation posts along the coast had spotted the plane and identified it. Word was sent to the Army Base at Boston, the Navy and the Harbor Defenses, who were notified by radio and no blackout was ordered so the ship was not fired on . . . . At the airport volunteer observers, Ben Slom and Neil Schiot, who were manning the Greenland observation post under Police Chief Earl W. Caswell, spotted the plane and reported it. Meanwhile Warren Scholz of Coastal Airways had spotted the distress signal and called the fire department, the police department and everybody else", The Herald reported.

Edison Carroll and another man went to the far end of the field with their cars and lighted that end. Other cars were strung out along the unlighted runway, then Carl B. Akerly and Rex Kennard, poured a straight line of gasoline along the side of the runway and touched it off. With that for a guideline, the aircraft came in, bounced once, and stopped. Traffic converged rapidly on the airport and City Marshal Leonard H. Hewitt took over control, aided by Motor Vehicle Inspector Kennard E. Goldsmith who had come in from Dover way and State Trooper Delwyn E. Philbrick (Now Rye's postmaster) came up from Seabrook "in record time". The plane immediately had an Army guard placed over it with Lieutenant Albert G. Welch in command and Sergeants Michael Fiore and John Caldwell heading a 16-man detail. Because of the short runway, the plane took on only enough fuel to get it to Portland, although excessive weight problems forced three of the crew to go to that city by bus.

[28]. Although efforts to create a permanent memorial to the women and men of World War II began before the war's end, nothing has really been done. The Hanscom Memorial at Atlantic Heights specifically honors men who lived in that neighborhood. During the summer of 1945, a wooden tablet honoring the city's 2,657 service people was placed on the Court House lawn.

On September 16, 1945, after V-J Day, the scroll was dedicated to the then known 48 dead whose names were preceded by a gold star. So designated were Robert A. Anderson, Ralph C. Alberger, Herbert W. Baird, Edward J. Barton, Harry W. Blaisdell, Raymond F. Burns, John Carey, Francis H. Danielson, Paul A. Doble, William A. Dorney, Jr., Alexander Drobisewski, Robert L. Fetter, Robert A. Harrison, Russell A. Hanscom, Kenneth C. Hersey, Percy Hodgson, Jr., John W. Horner, Guy E. House, Jr., Carlton S. Howe, Howard A. Hunt, John Ianuzzo, Norman Ives, Frank J. LaCava, James J. Leary, Thomas Meagher, Raymond A. Mieure, William J. Monagle, Jr., Hermand E. Pettigrew, Jr., Robert Pontbriand, Gordon V. Renner, Harold Sandford, Forrest E. Schultz, Alva E. Shatto, Everett H. Smith, Bernard T. Stradley, Hugh E. Sullivan, Norman D. Thorne, Paul H. Valley, Edgar P. Wallace, James A. Whitmore, Jr., Richard E. Day, Herbert C. Hartford, James J. Joyce, Jr., John Ryan, Napoleon E. Ledoux, Louis R. Fitzgerald, Ray R. Winn and Richard L. Hazel.

Since that time the Legion and the VFW have added other names. They now include Donald G. Allen, James E. Birt, Christos G. Bratiotis, John W. Chamberlain, Joseph Chatigny, Charles Drowne, Henry Eaton, Peter H. Finck, Roger L. Foss, Frederick H. Gamester, Quinton T. Gregory, Charles H. Hayden, George Laderbush, Leonard R. Ledoux, Ernest V. Locke, Benjamin Martin, Lee G. McCann, Pierce Morrisey, Richard V. Nichols, Iver H. Nodine, Peter L. Phillippe, Harvey C. Regan, Robert Sanford, Robert W. Smith, William J. P. Whicher and Paul Wiseman. Each of those names should be as much honored as any who fell at Bunker Hill, Gettysburg or Belleau Wood.

John C. Gamble, past commander of the Booma Post, was co-chairman with Mayor Mary C. Dondero, with Booma Post Commander Charles S. Conlon, as master of ceremonies. The Rev. Thomas F. Duffy, a curate at Immaculate Conception, gave the invocation. A. Roland Hinckley directed the band with World War I vet Thomas J. Downs delivering the dedicatory address, and a prominent Legionnaire, Ralph G. McCarthy, led the flag salute. Joseph H. Cullen, Sr., acted as chaplain and prayers were offered by Rabbi Arthur Oleshinsky of Temple Israel. Mrs. Leroy Burns, mother of Raymond F. Burns, killed in an explosion on the USS Juneau early in the war, represented the Gold Star Mothers, 15 of whom were on the platform. Mrs. Burns laid a wreath while a bugler sounded the doleful notes of "Taps".

Mayor Dondero continued her fight for a suitable, permanent memorial, and the next spring presented a plan for a gymnasium that would honor Portsmouth's dead of World War II. That proposal remains exactly that - - a plan; perhaps only because Mrs. Dondero was a "dangerous" Democrat in a town that really wanted to be Republican. Mrs. Dondero persisted in her efforts to recognize the war dead. In 1946, she was instrumental in the replanting of the poppy bed in Haymarket Square with poppy seeds brought from Flanders. That one-time Low Country province had been the source of the original plants, growning from seeds brought to the U. S. by Mrs. Hulda Thomas who, in 1930, made a trip to France to visit the grave of her son, Gunnard, killed in World War I. She gave the seeds to Mrs. Leah O'Brien, who was one of those who arranged for the flower bed in Haymarket Square, which has been replaced, if an editorial note may be permitted, by a contrivance that should yet be successful in killing off some unwary motorist. The Memorial that stood on a post in the middle of the flower bed has been removed to Goodwin Park.

Portsmouth still has no real World War II memorial, and not much has been heard of it since 1951. That last note was sounded in October by Franklin Butler of Piscataqua Chapter, DAV, during a meeting in the Community Center. Mayor Richman S. Margeson presided, and Butler urged that the wooden memorial and the others "have outlived their usefulness. The Haymarket Square memorial and the one on Wright Avenue were ideal in their day, but they're now a traffic hazard to people who have to cross the busy streets to visit the memorials". Rep. Mary C. Dondero, Richard A. Pinkham,

Benjamin Thurlow, John Bechard, Guy Gregg, and Arlo Pierce all had suggestions for a fitting memorial. Today, what memorials there are, stand in Goodwin Park, mostly ignored by a hurrying world, except on the official days of remembrance.

[29]. A similar situation existed down the coast at Odiorne's Point where a construction firm labored mightily to create the mammoth gun emplacements which are there yet. Not even a match could legally be struck along the beaches, but these well lighted installations made perfect landmarks for ships at sea; Such are the wonder-working ways of a government at war.

[30]. One of these times was the never-to-be-forgotten visit by the British cruiser HMS Capetown, under the command of Captain W. E. C. Tait. It was really a full week of fun and frolic for everyone as Portsmouth took the Capetown's crew to its heart. Friendships made at the time continued for years. She came on August 13, 1929, although fog delayed her for a few hours off the coast. "The arrival of this spic and span craft", The Herald said, "marks an epoch in history that will be chronicled in the annals of Portsmouth along with the visit of Martin Pring, the first known person to sail into Portsmouth Harbor and up Piscataqua River.

"Agleam with brilliant lights, the handsome English cruiser, HMS Capetown, steamed up Portsmouth Harbor last evening receiving a hearty tumultuous welcome from the cheering crowds that lined the shores of New Castle and Portsmouth. It was indeed a striking entrance the warship made in Portsmouth Harbor, riding along through the dusk of the evening, aglow from stem to stern with lights, presenting a picture that will remain long in the memory of those who witnessed it. The Capetown docked at the Navy Yard about 7:15 o'clock. On her way in, the ship remained outside of Whalesback Light about half an hour, and passed the Wood Island Coast Guard Station about 6:30. The tugs James Wolley of the Navy Yard and Mitchell Davis of the Piscataqua Towing Company picked up the ship off Fort Point and did an excellent job in placing her alongside the Flatiron Pier.

"Regardless of the approaching darkness the crowds of people waited for several hours on Memorial Bridge, Pierce Island and along the shores of New Castle and on the South End wharves for her arrival. And they were well repaid and thrilled as they gazed upon this fine ship moving through the harbor and up the river to dock at the Portsmouth Navy Yard...."

"Next morning Capetown and the American cruiser USS Richmond exchanged salutes and a week of festivities began. There were dances, receptions, cookouts, clambakes, trips to Hampton Beach, dinners and one real community luncheon at the Army and Navy Building (Community Center) for which the food was cooked in the kitchens of homes throughout the city. Mrs. Elizabeth Garrett, wife of Wallace H. Garrett, managed the affair which mingled dignitaries and crew. It's almost needless to say, that at that point in Portsmouth history, the stage manager for the entire affair was the late Fernando W. Hartford, then serving one of his six terms as mayor, and it's only fair to say also that Portsmouth never had a more persistent promoter of its virtues than F. W. Hartford. He could get stirred to enthusiasm over anything that might make the name of Portsmouth large in the land. To be sure he had hard-working committee people helping, but Hartford was, as retired Army Colonel Henry B. Margeson would put it, "in command". For instance, a dinner-dance at the Hotel Wentworth had Frederick M. Sise as chairman. Assisting him were Fred Hayes, H. Clinton Taylor, George B. Lord, Dennis Long, Dr. William A. Dorney, Rufus E. Ross, Major I. H. Washburn, Albert Hislop, Major Arthur L. Smith, Dr. J. D. Carty, Dr. Samuel T. Ladd, Jeremy R. Waldron, Sr., Laurence G. Peyser, Andrew Jarvis, Thomas H. Simes, H. E. Philbrick, Fred Oldfield, Major Boardman M. Randall, Patrick J. Reardon, George E. Cox, W. E. Goodrich and Ira A. Brown.

The Masons, headed by Edward H. Adams, father of the late Captain Woodbury Adams, welcomed some of their fellow travelers. Dr. E. C. Blaisdell welcomed Capetown's officers to a Rotary Club meeting at the Rockingham. Ira A. Brown headed the excursion to Hampton Beach, aided by Frederick Gardner of the Chamber of Commerce and Dr. Dorney and Richard B. Shelton. Fire Chief William F. Woods took charge of the clambake at Pierce Island which was put on by Simpson of Dover. On the committee were Ralph T. Brackett, Daniel O'Brien, James A. McCarthy, Jr., Richard D. McDonough, Jackson M. Washburn and Walter S. Woods. A "smoker" was held in the Portsmouth Theater (Civic) under the direction of Fred E. Hasty, aided by Ira A. Brown, Frederick P. Payne and Thomas Mullen.

And, of course, there was a parade. In Portsmouth, what else? The Herald said: "The forces of Great Britain and the United States joined this morning (August 17) in a colorful parade. One of the most impressive military spectacles ever seen in this city and a happening which marked another outstanding event in the history of Portsmouth. To the strains of martial music, with banners flying in the breeze, the Army and Navy forces, with steady tread, garbed in spic and span uniforms, marched proudly through the streets in historic old Portsmouth while thousands of people from all parts of New England greeted them with rousing cheers and hearty applause as they passed by. The parade moved from Pleasant Street on Congress, to Islington, to Cabot, to Middle, to Court, to Pleasant, to State, passing before the reviewing party at the Hotel Rockingham".

[31]. This man was a cousin to Dr. John T. Guy, now deceased.

[32]. The 10-inch was an unusual battery in having three guns, the barrels being numbered 1, 13, and 14, from Watervliet Arsenal. They were "disappearing" in model, meaning that they were behind a revetment for loading and counterweights hoisted them into firing position. At the first target practice, No. 1 gun bounced up and down a few times, stripping parts as it went, and was never again in service. One of its gun crew was found hiding under a barracks after the turmoil was over. Battery E of the 22nd CA manned these guns until 1943, when it was sent to Biddeford Pool to man a 155 mm gun battery there.

[33]. Ross Stevens was advertising director at The Herald, and was succeeded by C. Andrew Bartlett, now on the staff of the Dover Democrat. Bartlett was followed by Joseph R. Bradt, now of Exeter, and then the late Jeremiah R. Morrissey, who held the post until his retirement December 31, 1968. Harold L. Clark is the present advertising director.

[34]. Hopley is the brother of three well known local men: Arthur H. P. Hopley, William H. P. Hopley, and Robert Hopley. They were the sons of the late John W. Hopley who worked many years for New Hampshire Gas and Electric Co., and then, in his latter years, became a familiar figure to a generation of PHS students by acting as security officer at the high school. Arthur Hopley retired from the Post Office June 30, 1972, after moving up through the ranks from clerk to postmaster, succeeding Theodore R. Butler. Alfred V. Cashman is presently the officer in charge.

[35]. Edward I. Shaines for years operated a shoe store on Congress Street. He is the father of Robert A. Shaines, an attorney and former mayor, and of Stuart Shaines, a merchant here and in Dover.

[36]. One of the worst fires in years visited Portsmouth March 15, 1943, wiping out a whole business block from the Hotel Kearsarge to Montgomery Ward's. Damage was estimated at $200,000. Two men suffered injuries in conncection with the fire -- Robert P. Murphy, now Fire Captain Murphy, and James Scott was

injured on his way to the fire when his car struck a tree on Richards Avenue. Shaines' shoe shop suffered heavy loss as did the tailoring establishment operated by Louis Sherman and Abraham Grossman, the spot where the fire probably started. The Katherine G. Connor hat shop was ruined; as was the store of Portsmouth Hardware and Plumbing which lost many valuable merchandise items, irreplacable because of the war. Hubbard's store, managed by Helen Reikard, next door to the hotel, was badly hit.

Another note of the times had been struck a few months earlier, in a Market Square speech, by Mayor Stewart E. Rowe, when he warned against any thought of adopting the city manager form of government. Rowe expressed the conviction that the people would never stand for having their government operated by a manager.

[37]. Before his service as Postmaster, Hickey had been city clerk.

[38]. This building is now occupied by Margeson Brothers on old Vaughan Street. The Margesons acquired it when the phone company moved its exchange to new quarters on Islington Street next to the Farragut School.

[39]. American experts learned a lot about the art of building "unterseebooten" when they examined these German craft with their snorkel devices for undersea breathing. One of the submarines brought in here was the U-505, and that vessel still exists, a war memorial in the City of Chicago. U-505 is the only submarine to make the journey from the Atlantic, through the St. Lawrence, to the Great Lakes. Germans taken prisoner were housed for a while in "The Castle", and two or three of them have come back to Portsmouth to show their families the place in which they were incarcerated.

[40]. "Angie" Barrett was quite a famous runner in his youth. In his latter years, he operated a taxi and dabbled in politics, and also delivered "singing telegrams" as a sideline. During one Democratic Primary in old Ward 1, "Angie" offered free rides in his cab to all voters. He hauled 17 people to the polls and received 14 votes. He died still wondering who the three ingrates were.

30

A Generation of Upheaval (1945–1972)

[1]. Back in the early 1930s, those young people who seemingly were thwarted by the Depression were called the "Lost Generation", However, it's doubtful if their plight ever neared the pathos offered by the present-day "drop outs" from normal society seen in the streets of every American city and many of those in Europe. These young people are "doing their own thing" and where exactly that will fit them into the constantly evolving society of our day is beyond guess. Certainly, the men and women who built the North Church 12 decades ago did not have the steps of their house of worship in mind as a summer-time roost for these cormorants.

[2]. Teddy's Lunch is quartered in the spot familiar to two generations of Portsmouth people as Moulton's. Albert W. Moulton retired after selling his business to Teddy Lilakos, a son of Mr. and Mrs. Arthur Lilakos, long-time local residents, although natives of Greece. Moulton himself took over a candy business operated by Frank B. Johnson, after working as manager for several years. A senior at Keene High School when World War I broke out in April 1917, Moulton quit school to enlist in the Navy and settled here after the war.

[3]. Erminio A. Ricci is one of Portsmouth's more active contractors. Associated with him is his son Robert who is the developer of an apartment complex off Lafayette Road near the Rye line. The father is a former city councilman.

[4]. Frank E. Paterson is a prominent local contractor, who is associated with his two sons, John and David. The Patersons were the prime contractors in Strawbery Banke's first restoration, the Chase House. Frank Paterson was on the first city manager council, and he and the late Roland I. Noyes, once, before a Council meeting, treated the Council Chamber to the spectacle of two councilmen literally rolling around on the floor in a friendly wrestling match.

406

[5]. Firms like J. M. Fields, able to operate on Sundays under a liberal Newington ordinance, brought about a change in Portsmouth's Blue Laws. The City Council, during Mayor Eileen D. Foley's regime, repealed restrictions on Sunday openings by grocery and department stores.

[6]. The Portsmouth Herald offers its visitors a mimeographed thumb-nailed history of Portsmouth newspapering. which reads in part:

"The Portsmouth Herald is the collateral descendant of one of America's oldest newspapers, the New Hampshire Gazette."

The Herald was founded on September 23, 1886, as The Penny Post. Files of bound copies of the old Penny Post are now at Strawbery Banke, presented to that institution in 1972, by Kenneth K. Burke on behalf of The Herald. Primarily a political organ, Fernando W. Hartford acquired The Penny Post and changed its name to The Portsmouth Herald. That was in 1897. The Herald's information sheet goes on to say, "As he prospered with The Herald, he acquired opposition newspapers in the town. One of them, The Morning Chronicle, he published for many years before it became an economic liability. Another, The Portsmouth Times, was purchased in 1925 and merged with The Herald. Earlier, Hartford had bought The Portsmouth Journal of Literature and Politics, a weekly, which was quietly folded. As it appears today, The Herald is the sole survivor of some 40 newspapering ventures in the city that have been launched, prospered, faded and died in the course of more than two centuries. Many of them came into being for purely political reasons, to serve the purposes of a particular campaign".

One anecdote about the age of The Portsmouth Herald can now be told. In the upper left side of the paper's mast head is given the "volume number". For example, the current year it reads "LXXXVI". It really should read two years older, "LXXXVIII". The error was found during the life time of the late J. D. Hartford, and traced back to the years of his personal supervision of the paper, a simple typographical error in 1945. However, Hartford would not admit that it could have happened, so the volume number continues to be two years younger than the paper actually is.

[7]. Hartford published The Portsmouth Herald and The Morning Chronicle in the Exchange Buildings for nearly 30 years. In 1921, not long before he had to move to a new plant, Hartford proudly announced that he had purchased a new press for The Herald. The building in which it was housed, off the alley beside the Indian Head National Bank, was torn down in early summer of

1972. Hartford's announcement about the press, a Goss product, said:

"That the editor and publisher of The Herald has faith in the future of Portsmouth is evidenced in the purchase of this high speed press, with a capacity of 20,000 16-page papers per hour. It will serve (1) to advance the interests of the Portsmouth Navy Yard and keep its advantages ever before Congress; (2) to back the Chamber of Commerce in every effort to build up the business of the city; (3) a square deal for capital and labor with a purpose to help the underdog in life's battles; (4) the people of Rockingham and York Counties must be brought in closer touch with this city and with this big press and The Associated Press news service we can give them a paper in every way equal to any big city paper. . .It even has a color attachment, something no other press in the state has. The new press room is being fitted up in the First National Bank building annex and if all goes well it will be in operation the first of the New Year. The present press equipment of The Herald is indequate and has been for some time. Portsmouth in 1922 must regain some of the business that has been lost".

The press described above served The Herald for nearly two decades. In 1939, Hartford's son, Justin D. Hartford, traded it in on a 16-page, high speed Hoe Duplex. The Herald today is being printed on a 40-page Goss.

Another odd note about The Herald is in its April 1 issue in 1922. The paper announced it was buying one of the finest of radio sets, and would use it in its news work. About this time, The Herald began the practice of publishing radio station programming. Many - 50ish - readers will remember spending hours at night twisting the dials of their Atwater Kents so they could brag the next day of bringing in such distant points as Chicago, and Cincinnati's WLW which claimed to be the world's most powerful station.

[8]. Wood Bros. trucking was headed by Rufus Wood with Cedric L. Wood as bookkeeper. For many years Cedric L. Wood, out of a sense of compassion lacking in most of us and not because he needed the money, had the job of removing dead animals from streets and highways. Also going with the land package bought by Hartford was the restaurant of W. Harry Chick at 82 Congress, and the Portsmouth Ice Cream Company, operated by Samuel D. Eastham, at No. 86. Cedric also had the habit of packing temperance tracts in with people's dishes when he moved them. He made it a custom to pack a client's liquor himself so his men wouldn't be tempted into having a snort or two.

[9]. The first owner was F. W. Hartford; then the property passed to his widow, two daughters and son, the late J. D. Hartford. After Mrs. F. W. Hartford's death, the paper went through some shuffling among the children and, ultimately, ownership came into the hands of J. D. Hartford. On his death in March 1963, he willed it to his widow and seven of the company's executives: Richard Blalock, William E. Colwell, the late Jeremiah R. Morrissey, Roger R. Thompson, David A. Tober, Azio J. Ferrini and Raymond A. Brighton. After the widow, Margaret Manson Hartford, left the company, Thomson Newspapers bought it in October 1968. The present publisher is Kenneth K. Burke, a former executive with the Gannett Company, who makes his home in Rye.

[10]. Flames destroyed the original Christ Church building on June 19, 1963. A lowering, dark structure, built out of stone, the funds for its construction were provided in the will of George Massey Marsh who died in 1878. Trustees were appointed in 1879, and work started in 1881. St. John's Day, June 24, 1881, saw the laying of the cornerstone in approved Masonic ceremony. Stone used to build the church was quarried on Leach's Island, barged to the mainland and dragged by oxen to the site. Formal dedication came on July 3, 1883, nearly 90 years ago. One of the most memorable occasions in Christ Church history took place on Tuesday, September 5, 1905, when the Russian delegates to the Portsmouth Peace Conference held a service, after signing the document so humiliating to the Russia of the Czars. Never before nor since have so many dignitaries crowded their way into the church. In fact, that was often the problem with Christ Church: too few parishioners and too little money. In 1954, a southeast wing was torn down. This at one time had been used as a hospital by the Rev. Charles Brine and Dr. Fred S. Towle. Mrs. Robert Cutter Pierce provided the funds for the wing. For years, the Rev. Sheafe Walker served the church's ministerial needs, although he lived in Concord.

Christ Church, under the ministry of the highly controversial John D. Swanson, a highly idealistic man, dedicated to the cause of humanity, started making a comeback and then suffered the loss of its building. The Rev. Mr. Swanson brought about construction of the new church on Lafayette Road on land given to the parish by John Elwyn Stone. Dedicated on May 8, 1966, the present rector is the Rev. Canon Gordon Gillett.

[11]. The Cabot Street School was built in 1860 on the site of "the old brick schoolhouse." The Greek Orthodox Church bought the building 40 years ago when the steadily increasing

number of families brought about the need for larger quarters than the hall rented from the Paras brothers. Not until 1914 did members of the Greek Orthodox faith worship in one place, previously, services had been in various homes. In that year, on the Orthodox Easter Sunday, they held services in Christ Church as guests of that parish. But that was not enough. More and more demand grew for a church. In 1932, Andrew Jarvis, representing St. Nicholas Greek Orthodox Church, offered to buy the vacant Cabot Street School for $1,000. The city accepted the bid and a committee went to work to adapt the 70-year-old school building for religious use. The workers included George Soteros, Christ Sagris, George Scliris, Christ Roylos, Paul Chuliaris, Peter Stabrow and Jarvis. For many years, the old school served well but fire in 1966 did severe damage, and the members ruled out spending any more money on the old building. They decided on a new structure on Alumni Drive.

Andrew Jarvis headed the general committee which planned and built the church for 185 families. Those active in the work included John Soteros, Harry Jarvis, Ted Lilakos, Charles Raizes, Phil Soris, Harry Berates, Menio Giovanis, George Paras, Catherine Jarvis, Kiki Sotis, Sophie Roylos, Ernest Natcho and George Georgacopoulos.

[12]. One of these hearings, held at the Junior High School, produced what will probably be always thought of as Andrew Jarvis' finest hour in public service. The matter under discussion was a proposed bond issue of $300,000 to finance the city's share of Washington-Marcy Streets Urban Renewal Project. That it would be a colonial restoration project was already known and also well-known was the fact that opposition to the plan centered around Evelyn Ladrie Marconi, a Marcy Street housewife, highly opinionated and articulate. She dominated, at that time, a daily radio "talk show" on Station WHEB. The night of the hearing, Mrs. Marconi's carefully staged opposition went into full swing, running the gamut of the emotional and ethnic scales. Then the lady, herself, advanced to the podium to deliver the killing blow. She was well into her tirade, with the Council squirming in its seats, but Mayor Andrew Jarvis was of serious mien, and listening carefully. Mrs. Marconi began to relate all the troubles the foreign-born were having in face of the proposed upheaval; the trials they had had in the New World.

Solemnly, his glasses flashing in the stage lights, Mayor Jarvis softly interrupted her, "I know, Mrs. Marconi, I was an immigrant boy myself". A hushed moment prevailed, then applause swept over the Portsmouth Junior High School auditorium, as it suddenly dawned on the Strawbery Banke supporters that the opposition had reached its high-water mark and had failed. A key man in this opposition, incidently was ex-Governor Charles M. Dale, legal advisor to Mrs. Marconi. Dale, ironically, had been one of the first, while managing the Prescott monies, to attempt revitalization of the area, but his feeling toward Strawbery Banke appeared one of bitter aversion.

[13]. Another great moment in the life story of Strawbery Banke came on June 10, 1967, when Mrs. Lyndon B. Johnson, who happened to be "Ladybird" Johnson, wife of the President of the United States, visited Strawbery Banke. With Secretary of the Interior Steward B. Udall, she toured the project and apparently enjoyed what she saw. That she came at all was due largely to the good offices of Senator Tom McIntyre, who had been persuaded by a staff member, John Barker, ex-Herald reporter, that Strawbery Banke was well worth quarrying in a political sense. Barker, now teaching school in England, came back to New Hampshire in 1968 to manage the ill-starred LBJ campaign for the presidency.

[14]. Captain Carl A. Johnson, USN, Retired, commanded the Portsmouth Naval Base in the final days of his long career. When he went "ashore", he interested himself in Strawbery Banke, first as a volunteer, then later as a paid administrator. He is married to a daughter of Dr. Herbert L. Taylor.

[15]. Charles L. "Chuck" Kaufmann and wife Jane are refugees from the urban swirl of Chicago. While vacationing on the coast of Maine at Black Point Inn, they went exploring. They came to Portsmouth, went to the Hotel Rockingham when the Strawbery Banke belles were operating out of there thanks to the generosity of Miss Hazel Wood, the owner. This guide service to Strawbery Banke in the early days, under the direction of Eleanor Larkin, did much to build interest in Strawbery Banke. To the Kaufmanns, Strawbery Banke became a challenge. They bought property on Gates Street, "for a vacation home" but found Chicago and their life there less meaningful. Sooner than he ever planned, Kaufmann retired. Today, the family makes its home on Gates Street. Since that first purchase, the Kaufmanns have acquired two other houses in the area, each now enjoying badly needed restoration. In this, they are fellows with Dr. Ronald Buchan and his wife Maureen who have worked miracles with One Walton Alley. Probably nowhere in Portsmouth is the mood of change more apparent than in the South End. Strawbery Banke had stimulated a desire for neighborhood improvements.

[16]. Captain Carl A. Johnson's major failing, as newsmen saw it anyway, was that he could never overcome the handicap of a lifetime of service in the Navy. At one point, he wanted to put a chain-link fence around "Strawbery Banke Compound". In one sense the man may have been justified because vandalism is always a problem at Strawbery Banke.

[17]. A successor building to the one in "Rogers' Rangers".

[18]. One of the portraits in this stately old mansion, which is still incongruous in a colonial village, is that of ex-Governor Wesley Powell's mother, who once worked in the house. Powell was governor at the time the state bought and moved the house.

[19]. This production was "The Tooth-Ache", a farce first staged in Portsmouth in 1818. Producer for the modern version was Helen Winebaum, wife of Sumner Winebaum. He manages the local Winebaum interests.

[20]. The trustees are Robert E. McLaughlin, chairman; James R. Kelly and Arthur E. Splaine. McLaughlin, a resident of Rye, centers his interest in the Prescott Fund. Kelly is the proprietor of the Colonial Laundry on Bartlett Street and Splaine is on the staff of the First National Bank.

[21]. In the area where the Josie Prescott Garden grows, once bloomed the ugly storage tanks of the Allied New Hampshire Gas Co.

[22]. "A friendly suit", more or less acquiesced in by the former trustees, Charles M. Dale and Edwin Buck. It tested the limitations imposed by Miss Josie Prescott. While the court did not permit large-scale enlargements on the bounds, it did visualize the waterfront as extending to Pierce Island Bridge.

[23]. Justin Downing Hartford probably was one of the most extraordinary men ever to hold a position of influence in the City of Portsmouth. Son of Fernando W. Hartford, and one of the really "rich kids" around town, Hartford used to tell of fighting his way home in grade school days from the Whipple School to the Hartford House at 133 Miller Avenue when the St. Pat's boys were waging a vendetta against local WASPs. Hartford graduated from the Naval Academy in 1919, tried naval aviation, later served in submarines. In the mid-20's he went to work for International Paper, a job he held until 1937 when his father became ill.

After the father's death, he assumed a management role at The Herald, and became a tough-minded crusader for civic betterment. He echoed his father's creed in wanting a more perfect

Portsmouth, but was far less inclined to yield to the importuning of an advertiser when it came to public matters. Hartford exposued some of Portsmouth's great causes, and the people who worked for him were trained to accept them as their own. In the early days, it did not matter how late the Council meeting ran, the reporter had to call "J. D." and tell him what happened before he could go to bed. For a long time, unfortunately, he completely lost interest in civic matters, except to annoy his staff with night calls which were, luckily, mostly forgotten the next day. The man knew no "grey areas" in anything. The issue was either black or white; nor, did he ever accept the fast-shuffled loyalties of political types who were against a man in one election and for him in the next. The enmity that existed between Hartford and Charles M. Dale undoubtedly had a real effect on the whole city, although few people understood the pulling and hauling that went on. Hartford was that rare human creation, "a rugged individualist" who was fortunate enough to be able to afford to be one, and he played life that way. Four times married, he fathered a daughter, Mrs. Frank Fate of Rye, and a son, Justin D. Hartford, Jr. His widow, Margaret M. Hartford, lives in New Castle.

[24]. The Herald was angered because the City Council could not arrive at a budget for the year.

[25]. Frederick D. Gardner operated the Gardner Agency, a going business which he sold, shortly after the manager victory, to Forrest M. Eaton, and then moved to California. Eaton, who managed the New Hampshire Electric Company after the retirement of R. C. L. Greer, took Philip F. Gray into the Gardner Agency and Gray manages it today. Eaton lived for many years at 1381 South Street, a property now owned by Mr. and Mrs. Teddy Lilakos. Gray, a graduate of Hobart, is a former member of the Portsmouth School Board.

[26]. The "New Face" ticket in 1947 was headed by Cecil M. Neal, the mayoralty candidate; Richman S. Margeson, William J. Linchey, Vito P. Massaro and Leslie C. Manning were the designated candidates for councilman at large. Starting with Ward 1, the hand-picked candidates were Leland W. "Snooky" Davis, Porter McIntire, Arthur A. Bean, Jr., Kenneth Littlefield and Neil Dusseault. This was the approved ticket, but State Representative John R. McIntire and Councilman Fred R. Hoffmann were equally determined they should be the mayoralty candidates.

John R. McIntire, who was to die virtually broke and living on a family dole, should have consideration if a title is ever awarded for being one of Portsmouth's most fantastic characters. Scion of the York lumbering family, McIntire came here after World War II after inheriting a substantial sum of money. This he invested in McIntire Enterprises, a construction firm, although the large pieces of equipment he bought sat shiny and new on a lot across the street from his Woodbury Avenue home. In the venture, he was aided and abetted by two Portsmouth lawyers, Harold M. "Beauty" Smith, who had once been Speaker of the State House of Representatives, and Ralph G. McCarthy. The adventures of this trio, on McIntire's first and second fortunes, also would fill the pages of a book.

The McIntire Saga probably had its high point the night that he put a crew of construction workers to the task of ripping up the city Sidewalk in front of Joseph Geiger's American Cafe. Geiger's only offense was that McIntire had bought the building after an argument over a beer or two and wanted Geiger out. Geiger, having no place to go, fought him in the courts, appealing every notice of eviction but this was too slow to suit McIntire. In the dark of early morning, McIntire's hired men — where the police were is a good question — descended on Geiger's Market Street beer parlor. Jackhammers made short work of the concrete sidewalk, and, just to add to the harrassment, Geiger's windows were covered over with black paint. McIntire proudly made no secret of his role, and threatened to come back the next night and finish the job. Joe Geiger seldom had as busy an evening trade as he did the next night when all his friends waited to tangle with McIntire's gang if and when it showed up. Public outcry over the sidewalk episode forced police action and McIntire appeared before the court, paying a fine, that, to John, was merely a "cost of doing business".

He fought Mayor Mary C. Dondero through the courts over the expenditure of the Comfort Station that is located at Church and Porter Streets. That was the location determined on, after the alley back of the North Church was barred as a possible site.

These were merely episodes in the life of John McIntire. One night when John was deep in consultation with one of his favorite Bourbons, he called a major airline and ordered an airplane to take him to visit the battlefield he had known only a few years before. Chartered aircraft were a bit cheaper in the days of the prop planes, so it only cost John $2,500 to have the airplane come to Portsmouth Airport and wait for him to board. He did not.

Somehow, mostly through spending an awful lot of money, McIntire won election to the House of Representatives. His Cadillac, equipped with its forbidden police siren, used to shake up old

Portsmouth as John and some of his "friends" who surrounded him, would howl their way through town. John certainly put up the money that turned the Ward 1 polling place, the old Eureka Fire House, into one of the drunkenest places in town election night in 1946. Bottles literally rolled across the floor.

There was a lot of protest about such goings on but no one did anything until John threw away the last of his money. After all, he used to buy a turkey for each member of the Police Department on Thanksgiving, and who can look the giver of birds in the eye and tell him "No"? Ultimately, John tossed it all away, and lived out his short life, a sick man on the family dole. If alive today, he would not yet be 60.

Today, looking back, it's realized that some of John R. McIntire's thinking was not all that weird. Ex-Governor Wesley Powell, without anyone asking, will claim credit for the State Pier, but John McIntire was battling for that facility long before Powell had been weaned by Senator Styles Bridges. McIntire would persist, with anyone who would listen, in explaining his visions of a Port of Portsmouth, under the New Hampshire Port Authority, which could attract some of the freight business going into the St. Lawrence, and argued constantly that the state should compel the railroads to provide the feeder lines. John eventually paid the price of having sipped too often and too deeply from the cup of life, but the city could use some of his ideas today.

The other contestant in the three-way mayoralty field, Fred R. Hoffmann, had teamed with two other Republicans, in Mayor Dondero's years, to try to frustrate each of her projects, whether good or bad. His cohorts were Winfield S. Call and Laurence G. Peyser, both deceased. Hoffmann and McIntire were repudiated in the Republican caucus, leaving Neal alone to run against Mrs. Dondero, who was the widow of Charles A. Dondero, an employee at the Internal Revenue.

Neal bested Mayor Dondero in the election by 15 votes. The only Democrat survivor in this GOP deluge was Mrs. Hilda Hundley, a close friend of Mayor Dondero's who had served on the first woman mayor's City Council. Mrs. Hundley defeated Leland W. Davis in Ward 1. Davis is today a highly respected lay expert in the field of forensic medicine. Affluent local physicians refused to meet the rigors of the job of being medical referee after the retirement of Dr. Wendell P. "Cowboy" Clare, has made it necessary that laymen take on the function in deputy status, trusting they will have the competency to call in trained medical people should doubt arise as to the cause of any unattended death.

Dr. Clare derived his nickname from his propensity for wearing black, five-gallon hats, plus a pistol in holster at the hip. The writer has watched the doctor going over a newly created "stiff", stripped to shirtsleeves, pistol in sight, and wondered what the late departed would have thought had he been able to arise, like Lazarus, from the slab and take notice of his surroundings. It should be said that Dr. Clare was a thorough workman. There was no danger, as once happened, that a cadaver would be called a heart attack victim, only to have the undertaker find he had two bullet holes in the back.

Mrs. Hundley, active in USO work, went to the Shipyard and later returned to city government as overseer of the poor. She has since retired.

[27]. The manager fight was spearheaded by an organization known as the Good Government Association to its members and friends and as the "Goo-Goos" to the anti-manager people. The working executive was Franklin E. Jordan, formerly managing editor of The Portsmouth Herald, a post assumed by Richard Blalock in March 1947. Mary R. Healy assisted Jordan in office administration, and the association had headquarters in the Chestnut Street store where Teddy Bosen now sells popcorn — across the street from the former Herald newsroom. Volunteers did yeoman service on telephones in getting out the vote.

Managership opponents had been successful in so wording the referendum that the voters had to say "No" in order to mean they favored the plan. Despite that deceitful maneuvering in the Legislature, there were 3,529 out of the 7,250 voting who wanted a city manager, but this was 97 votes short of the majority required because 1,496 did not vote on the question. The act authorizing the referendum not only had a tricky question, but also demanded that the proponents get a majority of those voting in the election. The outcome made it apparent that the people's will had been stymied.

Mayor Dondero, loser to Neal by a mere 15 votes, appeared before the City Council asking a recount, and, in an unprecedented move, Jordan demanded a recount of the manager question. There was considerable palavering but the upshot was that Jordan's request was granted. Both Mrs. Dondero and Neal were on hand, with their lawyers, to watch the recount of the managerial fight. That recount bore out what Mayor Dondero had said on election night. In Ward 2, there were 93 switches, mostly among the straight ballots which had been counted by the late Harry H. Foote and Thomas J. Downs. Those changes from "Yes" to "No" gave victory to the manager forces, and canceled out a recount of the mayoralty vote. Charles T. Durell, Ward 2 moderator and later a member of the Governor's Council, put the finger directly on Foote and Downs by saying, "I just stand around. I don't push the pencils". Several years later, when Portsmouth became the first community in the state to buy voting machines, Foote stood up at a public hearing and made full confession of the errors on "That Night" and urged that voting machines would solve the problem.

Active members of the "Goo-Goos" refused to run for the new City Council, lest there be charges that they had merely sought their own political preferment. Elected to that first city manager council was former Mayor Mary C. Dondero, who topped the ticket, close behind her were Cecil M. Neal, Richman S. Margeson, Lester R. Whitaker, Thomas H. Simes, John J. Leary, William J. Linchey, Frank E. Paterson and Roland I. Noyes. Only Neal and Paterson are now living, out of that roster. The Council elected Neal mayor, after secret meetings in the Rockingham, and, as soon as the new regime was sworn in, Neal, Paterson and two or three others rushed to City Hall to change the locks on the mayor's office door. Today, of course, Mrs. Dondero would, as top vote-getter, automatically be mayor, but 25 years ago Mrs. Dondero struck terror in all good Republican hearts. She had all the ruthlessness of any of the tough male politicians around town, and her feminity gave them fits because they never quite knew how to strike back.

In her youth, as her later-in-life protraits show, Mrs. Dondero must have been one of the most beautiful women ever born here. She won a Miss Portsmouth pageant in 1918, although already the mother of three children. One of the first of her sex to go to the State Legislature, she became known as the "Sweetheart of the House", but that cognomen merely paid tribute to her looks. She was tough; she had to be to survive in her chosen career. The writer was one of the reporters who covered her administration during the last years. Let it be said, and Charles W. Gray of Rye, then WHEB's star reporter, under the ownership of Charles M. Dale, will agree that there were few dull moments in Mary's time.

While Mary Carey Dondero lived no one in this city made the final trip to any of the cemeteries — WASP, Catholic or Jewish — without her in attendance. When Charles J. Griffin, her own chosen city solicitor, ruled against her views of a tricky question, she remarked, "That's only one man's opinion", and proceeded with what she wanted to do. As far as is known, no one ever took it any further. Fred R. Hoffmann, a member of the City Council and one of

417

her deadly foes, felt the lash of her scorn on one occasion, even contemplated suit, but decided against it.

Love her or hate her, Mary Carey Dondero was one of the great Portsmouth personalities of the 20th Century. The writer is privileged to have known her.

[28]. C. Cecil Dame is an authentic descendant of the "Dams" who settled Portsmouth and the Seacoast 350 years ago; the family had a garrison house, one of those barricades against Indian assault so greatly prized by anyone who comes into the ownership of one.

[29]. James J. Joyce had retired from the Navy. Right after World War II, when golf first started to zoom into popularity, Joyce operated a driving range out beside Route 101, where the old 101 stems off the modern bypass of Greenland. Tom "Tipperary" Marshal was one of the frequent customers because, right over Joyce's fence, were the sacred precincts of the old Portsmouth Country Club.

[30]. One of the areas to benefit under this expanded city program was Essex Avenue, first laid out in 1917.

[31]. Dick Zoffoli for some years operated the local Oldsmobile agency off Myrtle Avenue. During his term in the House, he set a record for absenteeism.

[32]. Marcia Adams, an outgoing, dedicated Democrat when the word was an epithet in Portsmouth, is a devoted worker in Ward 1, although her original base of operations was old Ward 4 where former Mayor Kennard E. Goldsmith held sway. In 1946 the polling place was then in the Old Meeting House. Ward 4 probably had the tightest Republican organization in the city with Ivene Severance Patch and others its hierarchy. The control was still there a few years later when ex-Representative Rae S. Laraba decided to try for a vacancy in the House from that Ward. Laraba and his political sponsors failed to consult with Ivene Patch — Mrs. Garland W. Patch, Jr. They paid the price. Mrs. Patch put her candidate, Theodore F. Munz, into the House, to the chagrin of the veteran Laraba.

[33]. William F. Keefe is another of Portsmouth's more controversial people. "Bill" Keefe is a politician who has always had the happy faculty of knowing about the things that were bothering people, and responding. One of these is the Bellamy River water, a source of supply the Army Engineers tapped for city benefit after drilled wells in Madbury proved inadequate as a replacement for the wells covered over by the parking apron at Pease AFB. Probably the two men most instrumental in winning from the Air Force the

agreement to build the Bellamy Dam were attorneys John J. Wholey and Wyman P. Boynton. They, along with former City Solicitor John C. Driscoll fought the issue, after it had been lost, and finally won.

However, this is where "Bill" Keefe comes in. The Bellamy, pure though the water may be after it has gone through the plant at Madbury, is surface water, and it does not taste like that from the old Haven Springs. When the Bellamy water is poured into the archaic system of mains that prevails throughout the city's North End and the Creek, it makes for a foul-tasting beverage at times, enough to ruin the flavor of the best of whiskeys. To the calls of his constituents on this matter, "Bill" has ever been responsive, although he knows full well that it is not entirely the water that is to blame.

With "Bill," the city has had a lot of hilarious moments. For example, there was a time when The Herald discovered that the City Yard boys were mowing his lawn, as part of their regular chores. City Manager Violette sent him a bill to cover the labor charges in that escapade. As recently as this year, as a member of the current City Council, Keefe has been in a hassle with the Police Department, claiming harassment because he was arrested for going through a traffic light in one instance, then in a row with Patrolman Richard Pearson over a parking ticket. At one time, "Bill" was ardently "anti-establishment", but nowadays is in the forefront of every fight to gain advantages for the schools. He embraces a liberal approach to city affairs that deeply angers the ever-carping right wing. "Bill's" wife, "Molly" is a politician in her own right, and is a representative from Ward 1 in the House.

[34]. State Representative Ernest Stafford, as an official in Ward 2, then a Republican stronghold, played a key role in a vote-count slowdown when John F. Kennedy won the presidency. Because the Electronic Age has created a whole new world of communications, there was a paralyzing fear in local Republican circles that Portsmouth's voting machine results — going, as everyone knew they would, for Kennedy — might influence voters in distant California, three hours behind in time. Three Republican plotters, Jeremy R. Waldron, Jr., Raimond Bowles and Robert E. Whalen, allegedly hatched a scheme to stall the counting as long as possible in the three wards controlled by Republican officials. The plan succeeded, at least in Ward 2. Stafford and Ward Moderator Edward M. Paterson carried out someone's instructions to the letter. They delayed, counting absentee ballots without opening the machines, until well after the California deadline. The more they diddle-daddled, the greater the glee of Waldron and Bowles as they watched

the mounting anger of the pro-Kennedy people, among them was the writer.

[35]. Forrest M. Eaton, known as "Marty" to his college friends, served on the UNH Board of Trustees.

[36]. E. Harry "Tiny" Boothby, a "little chap" who stood about 6 feet, 4 inches, and weighed more than 250 pounds, presided over Portsmouth High for several years. He left after a conflict with the equally strong-minded Herbert R. Hagstrom, now deceased, who was then school superintendent. Hagstrom, shortly after his retirement due to ill health, died tragically in February of 1971 when coals from his pipe set his clothing on fire. His successor is James J. Cusick. Boothby's replacement was Gordon Thorburn who lost out in a power struggle with Superintendent Cusick, an issue which split the city emotionally in 1972, and appeared before the State Board of Education for review and final determination.

[37]. Edward H. Lawrence, who trained for the priesthood, is one of the city's more consistent protestors against taxes. He sells real estate for a living.

[38]. The city employees union was organized on March 1, 1951, and one of the leading spirits has been Arthur W. Tobey.

[39]. Bowen persisted in living in Andover, Massachusetts, although required by the Charter to live in the city. He even went to the extreme of registering, in Massachusetts, the car which is made available to the city manager. Really a man of ideas, imagination, he quickly ran afoul of the City Council. Bowen was irreverently known to Herald reporters as "Superchief."

[40]. Dr. Lester R. Whitaker for some years was among the city's top surgeons. Dr. Whitaker had an unusual medical background in that he had first trained as an osteopathic physician and then retrained in more conventional medical channels.

[41]. Winfield W. "Bill" Scott during his working life at New Hampshire Electric was one of Congress Street's best known figures and sharpest wits. He still strolls it nearly every day greeting friends with his same keen interest in the life of the community.

[42]. Cecil M. Neal is a veteran of both World Wars. Part of his duty in WWII saw him in command of POW trains. Mrs. Dorothy Neal, his wife, became familiar to a generation of PHS students through her work as dietician in the school cafeteria.

[43]. General LeMay, who ran in 1968 as George C. Wallace's vice presidential candidate, struck terror throughout the Strategic Air Command. Pease AFB officers never knew when he

420

might drop in on the base unheralded. He once caught the then commanding officer, Brigadier General Walter J. "Pop" Arnold at eventide out in his garden weeding tomatoes. Life was rigorous in SAC in those days because LeMay was "always at war". In fact, he even terrified George C. Wallace with his ultra-militarism during a speech in Pittsburgh.

[44]. Thanks to the efforts of U. S. Senator Tom McIntyre, the town won approval for the construction of a road, roughly parallel to the old one, as requested by the Board of Selectmen whose membership consisted of Paul deRochemont, Sydney Frink and Paul Kent. One of the most unusual parties ever staged in the Seacoast took place in celebration of "Unity Day". Senator McIntyre, whose name was given to the new road, came with Mrs. Myrtle McIntyre, and gave a short talk. Then there was a "social hour" in the woods back of the Langdon Library, followed by dinner under tents on the recreation area. But, what made the affair unique was the fact that the town itself paid for the whole party out of tax revenues, a rarity indeed in this day of "Tax Fighters".

[45]. Louis deRochemont, an impressive figure of a man, waged all-out war against the base. So convinced was he that he would win, that he once told Herald reporter Richard J. Connolly, now a Pulitzer prize-winner with the Boston Globe, that he would give him a case of scotch if the military ever flew a plane out of Portsmouth Air Base. DeRochemont at this time was engaged in filming semi-documentaries, the most outstanding of which were "Lost Boundaries", "Walk East on Beacon Street" and "The Whistle at Eaton Falls", all of which were made in this vicinity.

[46]. Norcor, a manufacturer of school furniture, unfortunately, lived a short life in Portsmouth. One of the executives with Norcor was the late James E. "Jesse" Morrissey, older brother to Jeremiah R. Morrissey and to Pierce Morrissey, a World War II airman who went down on a bombing mission. One of their sisters is Mrs. Franklin Jackson.

[47]. The Robinsons farmed extensively in the Sherburne Road area more than 130 years ago.

[48]. The agreement was drafted by City Solicitor Thomas E. Flynn, Jr., and the other signer was City Manager Edward C. Peterson.

[49]. At that time, associated with the John Sise and Company, an insurance agency headed by Stowe Wilder. Soles now lives in New Castle and works for the Dunfey organization. His wife, Jeanne for many years owner of Portsmouth Travel Agency, Daniel

Street, is now the manager for an out-of-town owner.

[50]. John Frink Rowe has been prominent in Newington affairs for a generation. He is a former commissioner of the Department of Resources and Economic Development for the State of New Hampshire, a post now held by George T. "Gus" Gilman.

[51]. For all his fervor, John E. Holden was a late convert to the air base proposal. After he had visited an air base or two in Florida, he became convinced that the air base was in Newington and Holden's best interests.

[52]. Benjamin A. Tober, who died while at the height of a business career, was the eldest son of Louis Tober, who is today "dean" among Portsmouth merchants, a fact that bothered him not at all when in August of 1972, he opened a new store in a Lafayette Road shopping center, assisted by his sons David and Irving. Another son, Edward, is a surgeon.

[53]. J. Paul Griffin was a partner in the firm then known as Landers and Griffin, contractors. That company, associated with a giant in business, Morrison-Knudsen, became the prime contractor for the base construction for the past 25 years.

[54]. The Reverend William Stafford Jones was a sincere friend of the City of Portsmouth. For years, he was president of the Portsmouth Athenaeum when it was struggling to stay alive. Aside from his ministry, his greatest service to the community was as a member of the School Board. For some years, whenever a couple appeared at City Hall for a license and wanted something more than a JP wedding, they were referred to Dr. Jones. After the ceremony, Mrs. Jones would serve tea and cakes and the good divine would deliver a few homilies. One day, Dr. Jones was in the Portsmouth Motor Mart and ran into his friend, Msgr. James McCooey of Immaculate Conception. The Dr. was complaining a bit about the hardships of life, when Father McCooey, with a big grin, interrupted to say, "But, Dr. Jones, you have a wife to help you with your problems". The subject was changed. It's a situation somewhat improved today, but Dr. Jones was one of the practitioners of the ministry who retired literally on a starvation pension — $600 annually. He was one of the fine gentlemanly persons who have made Portsmouth a better place in which to live. Dr. Jones was succeeded in the South Parish by Reverend William W. Lewis. The Reverend John Papandrew followed the Reverend Mr. Lewis and the present pastor is the Reverend John S. MacPhee. The Reverend Mr. Lewis is now an antique dealer in Stoddard, New Hampshire, and Florida, and the Reverend Mr. Papandrew has a church in Florida.

[55]. The committee listing for that event, nearly 20 years ago, are long and carefully preserved in the souvenir program. The general committee had Holden as chairman and Mayor Theodore R. Butler, City Manager Robert C. Violette, Andrew Jarvis, Eugene P. Soles, Lawrence E. Mulooney, Lieutenant Colonel Andreas A. Andreae and Reginald P. Kennard as members. Andreae is today retired from the Air Force and associated with the Portsmouth Motor Mart.

[56]. As above, the details of the dedication on June 30, 1956, have been well preserved in souvenir booklets published for the occasion. The 20,000-odd who attended saw a real military show, as the Air Force trotted out its best for the ceremonies, including SAC's commander, General Curtis LeMay. John E. Holden, "The Little General", again was chairman. Andrew Jarvis headed the entertainment committee, and the late Joseph Eberle, Jr., was chairman of the Portsmouth city committee. Two wings of B47s, plus KC97s were assigned. Herald reporter, Bob Norling, rode triumphantly into the base aboard the first aircraft officially detailed for duty, a Beechcraft Bonanza. As the B47s reached the age of phaseout, they were replaced by B52s, the giant bombers which have seen yeoman service in Vietnam, many of these are home-based here. Today, the primary aircraft is the FB111A, and, in addition, the New Hampshire Air Guard, is also based at Pease. Personnel, at one time, probably topped the 7,000-figure This has since dropped, although the Air Force continues to be coy about population data. There is a growing sentiment that the air base should be shared with civilian air services, a proposal meeting stubborn resistance from the Air Force.

[57]. The base is named in honor of Captain Harl Pease of Plymouth, New Hampshire, an Army Air Corps pilot killed during World War II.

[58]. The major components were the Naval Disciplinary Command (the Prison), the Naval Hospital and the Naval Shipyard. The hospital is a fine, 300-bed facility which is to be closed so the Air Force can justify construction of an 80-bed unit at Pease at a cost of $8 million. While the Naval Hospital was founded in 1834, it has constantly undergone modernization, and the present main building dates back only to 1931. It served the Air Force, Marines, Coast Guard and the Navy in this immediate area and Naval personnel from Brunswick Naval Air Station also come to Portsmouth, via helicopter. For this service, a "pad" has been hard-topped on the flat land below the rise on which the hospital sits. Two distinguished admirals have died on the base, on of them in the

hospital. Fleet Admiral Ernest J. King, the Navy's highest rank, died in the hospital, and Admiral David Farragut died in the base commander's house. King's local funeral rites were virtually non-existent but Farragut's obsequies were a full-dress rehearsal for a ceremony in Washington, where final honors were paid. Farragut died August 14, 1870, and the services were held at St. John's Church on the 17th. The original Farragut School, on School Street, was named for him.

[59]. Four vessels, intended for World War II service, slid into the river in the year after V-J Day. They were Pomodon, Remora, Sarda and Spinax.

[60]. USS Dolphin, one of the most sophisticated of Portsmouth submarines, exemplified the wave of the future except she did not have nuclear power. Dolphin qualified for dives the depths of which are still secret, and all the rest of her capabilities are in the same category.

[61]. Tom Prentiss, after a lengthy career in the cable business, on September 1, 1972, assumed full-time duties as town manager in Exeter, thus returning to a community he had liked well during his Simplex years. Simplex itself had been started in Newington in 1953. Since then, Simplex's Cambridge, Massachusetts, operations have been moved to North Berwick, but this division met business reverses, and, on August 18, 1972, its eventual closing became public knowledge. More than 600 persons in the Seacoast were expected to lose employment when the $11 million plant is phased out.

[62]. Jerauld McDermott, quite active in the community for a number of years, served as executive secretary to the United Federation of Postal Clerks Benefit Association. The post is now held by Orrin Bradshaw.

[63]. Harry I. Caswell became one of Portsmouth's best known insurance agents and real estate handlers. His son, Harry, was an outstanding golfer, and his widow is the former Katherine McGee, sister to Probation Officer John McGee. Quite a few years ago, the younger Caswell sold out his local interests and moved to Newmarket. Katherine Caswell for many years has been secretary to the steady succession of Pease AFB commanders.

[64]. John Iafolla retired to Portsmouth after years in the highway construction business in Massachusetts. Unable to be idle, he founded one of the city's major business firms, Iafolla Industries. This extensive plant on Peverly Hill Road, is operated by his sons, Robert and Michael, and his stepson, Ferris G. Bavicchi.

Both Robert Iafolla and Bavicchi are active in Portsmouth civic affaris. Bavicchi's major interest has been Portsmouth Hospital, while Iafolla is presently a member of the Portsmouth School Board.

[65]. For years Orman R. Paul operated one of Portsmouth's finest grocery and meat markets at 31 Daniel Street. When he finally retired, he sold his business to Louis Card, a long-time employee. However, in Portsmouth's tradition of elder statesmen, Paul continues to keep an eye on the business that made him a wealthy man.

[66]. Lawrence E. "Larry" Mulloney managed C. H. Sprague, the major oil distributing firm which has offices in the vicinity of Schiller Station on Gosling Road. After his retirement he was succeeded by Robert W. Hill, Sr., a resident of Little Bay Road in Newington. Hill formerly lived in Portsmouth.

[67]. As a city assessor, a job he first obtained during City Manager Edward C. Peterson's tenure, Lucien O. Geoffrion was a man who ever had an answer to questions asked by those who thought his assessing philosophy was somewhat fallible. The writer remembers asking Geoffrion why he was assessed so much in comparison to a far superior property next door. To which, Geoffrion replied, with great equanimity, "Your property drags that one down". A fair enough answer, if sufficient thought is given to it.

[68]. One of Portsmouth's finest days took place in late Spring, 1972, with a reunion in the North End. Miss Lucy Pray, who had taught school in the area many years before — and for many years — called it, in a letter to The Herald, "The Italian Reunion". Perhaps she was right. They met, these exiles from their beloved North End, at the VFW building. What else was standing? Just to name a few, there were Alessis, Vinciguerras, Tosis, Ferrinis, Perinis, Marcellos, Caninos, Lemarcas, Finandacas, Fusegnis, Fransosos and Caminatis, among the city's fine families who kept that affection for the North End.

From the pen of one of these wonderful people came the following letter to the editor of The Herald, a description of life as it was lived in the North End for at least two generations. It should be preserved in the city's archives exactly as Rose (De Stefano) Lemarca wrote it:

"All that is left of our 'North End' are empty roads with dirt-filled basement holes where homes once stood.

"Urban Renewal is what they call it.

"As I wander over this very special ground, I remember the intimacy of a people away from their own native land, grouped together to find comfort and assurance from the foreign customs and language barrier which surrounded them. I pause in retrospect of the distant visions and sounds of my childhood.

"Where else on this earth could a child have found a better place to grow than on this spot?

"What affluent neighborhood had a built-in swimming pool to compare with our fresh flowing river and the many graduated diving boards, provided by the railroad's trestled beams and stopped freight train. We would sit on the fence where we could ski; with our custom-made skis, made from slats of broken wooden barrels.

"The boys would get together and make sleds from an assortment of pieces of wood and junkyard recoveries, tie them all together and then with shouts of 'all aboard' down the hill we would glide, screaming with delight, some spilling off and others frantically holding on till the end.

"Summer nights were filled with happy sounds. The toot of the locomotive would warn us of the approaching long freight train. We would sit on the fence bordering the railroad tracks and oblivious to all our surroundings, would stare intently at the passing freight cars and soon the lulling noise of the heavy wheels rolling on the steel tracks and the movement of the frieght cars gave us a trip all our own.

"After supper and chores finished, it was time to get out doors. The street was our own playground and meeting place. We would build a bonfire and the sound of harmonicas, accordion, guitar strumming and singing voices filled the warm evening air. At the close of our day, the warm mantle of mother's voice, 'Come home now, it's getting late.'

"I can still feel the presence of all these sounds which, once uttered, seem forever in the air above and need only a memory to bring them all back to life.

"We were the fortunate ones to have grown up in the 'North End'."

[69]. On August 16, 1972, authorization came from HUD for the expenditure of $1.3 million on the development planned by Portsmouth Preservation, Inc., and Aldrich Associates. The announcement was published in The Herald on August 19, 1972.

[70]. If you were to mention public benefactors in Portsmouth, the name of Frank Jones would probably be the first to pop up, and yet he stands pale and forlorn compared to Woodbury Langdon. This man's largesse made many projects possible, and he often put $5,000 into this or that scheme. If the Portsmouth City

426

Council at one point had not been more pigheaded than usual, the entire South Mill Pond complex might well have a different appearance today. Langdon offered to put up $10,000 for beautification if the city would match his gift. He took several insults from councilmen before he withdrew his proposal.

Woodbury Langdon was a descendant in the sixth generation of Judge Woodbury Langdon, Governor John Langdon's brother. That kinship perhaps stimulated his interest in the present-day John Paul Jones House because it was at one time owned by Judge Woodbury Langdon. Certainly it was Woodbury Langdon who put up the money needed to buy the house and land when the area was in danger of becoming a site for Granite State Insurance Company. The Portsmouth Historical Society still benefits from his legacy. A native of Portsmouth, Langdon's business life was concentrated in New York between 1863 and 1911. In the latter year, he returned to Portsmouth to live. He died in October 1921.

[71]. The dedication was on February 16, 1964. At that time, Mrs. Warren Delano, the present president of Strawbery Banke, Inc., was president of the Board of Trustees. Paul V. Brown, Sr., led the building committee. Vernon L. Ballard, as he does today, held the post of administrator. Guests of honor at the affair were Mayor Timothy J. Connors, Miss Rosamond Thaxter, Mrs. Louis B. McCarthy. The clerical delegation had the Rev. John N. Feaster, D.D., the late Rabbi Aaron Goldin and the late James F. Happny, pastor of the Immaculate Conception with the rank of monsignor, as members. Rabbi Goldin loved his little joke and Father Happny, as he preferred to be called, knew no equal as a pastoral leader.

On the Board of Trustees, besides Mrs. Delano, Brown and Dr. Feaster, were Mrs. Parkhurst H. Blood, secretary; the late Richman S. Margeson, Treasurer; Ferris G. Bavicchi, Frank E. Brooks, Frank Butterworth, Jr., the late Burnell E. Frisbee, Bradford M. Kingman, Robert E. McLaughlin, the late John E. Seybolt, Charles H. Walker and Harry Winebaum. McLaughlin headed the steering committee for the dedication and assisting were Mrs. Peter Beck, Henry W. Berounsky, Mrs. Wendell P. Clare, Jr., Mrs. Justin E. Flanigan, Dr. Stanley W. Machaj and Mrs. McCarthy.

[72]. Anthony R. "Tony" Jarrett, as noted elsewhere contributed to these volumes. An Englishman, Jarrett has followed a career in industry and is now involved in the field of industrial development.

Appendix I
Portsmouth's Mayors

Arthur F. Brady is the 55th person to serve as mayor of the City of Portsmouth, two of them have been women, mother and daughter. For a brief moment during the tenure of Robert A. Shaines, his brother, Stuart Shaines, was serving as mayor of Dover. Shaines also was involved in what is probably the only instance when the mayoralty was decided by the flip of a coin. Shaines won. At that time it was not stipulated in the City Charter that the highest vote-getter would automatically be mayor, and election was in the hands of the City Council itself. Both Shaines and Wholey, ambitious young lawyers, wanted the honor — the Council vote split between them on poll after poll.

The reason for the even division of the votes was that former Mayor Mary C. Dondero, a member of the Council, was fatally ill, and the first vote went four for Shaines, two for Mrs. Dondero and two for Donald H. Margeson. Then the vote swung four for Shaines, three for Wholey and one for Margeson. Margeson urged his supporter to vote for Wholey, and the Council went through several four-to-four votes before Herald reporter George S. Robinson remarked, "Why don't you fellows flip for it?" This the principals agreed to, but it was decided not to desecrate the Council Chambers with such a performance, and so the party adjourned to the cellar. Here attorney John C. Driscoll tossed the coin with Shaines calling heads. After bouncing off Councilman Erminio A. Ricci's knee, the coin landed heads and Shaines became mayor.

Below is a complete listing of all those who have served as this city's chief executive:

Abner Greenleaf	1850	Edward E. McIntire	1900-01
John Laighton	1851	John Pender	1902
Christopher S. Toppan	1852	George D. Marcy	1903-04
Horton D. Walker	1853-55	William E. Marvin	1905-06
	1872	Wallace Hackett	1907-08
Richard Jenness	1856	Edward H. Adams	1909-10
Robert Morrison	1857-59	Daniel W. Badger	1911-13
John R. Reding	1860	Harry B. Yeaton	1914-15
William Simes	1861	Samuel T. Ladd	1916-18
Jonathan Dearborn	1862-63		1923
	1867	Albert Hislop	1919-20
John H. Bailey	1864-66	F. W. Hartford	1921-22
Frank Jones	1868-69		1928-32
Joseph B. Adams	1870-71	Orel A. Dexter	1924-25
Thomas E. O. Marvin	1873	Charles M. Dale	1926-27
Frank W. Miller	1874		1943-44
*Moses H. Goodrich	1874-75	S. F. A. Pickering	1933
John H. Broughton	1876-77	Robert Marvin	1934-36
William H. Sise	1878-81	Kennard E. Goldsmith	1937-40
John S. Treat	1882-83	Stewart E. Rowe	1941-42
Calvin Page	1884	Mary C. Dondero	1945-47
	1889	**Cecil M. Neal	1948-50
Marcellus Eldredge	1885-86	Richman S. Margeson	1950-52
George E. Hodgdon	1887-88	Theodore R. Butler	1952-56
Edmund S. Fay	1889-90	John J. Leary	1956-58
John J. Laskey	1891-92	Andrew Jarvis	1958-60
Charles P. Berry	1893-94	Robert A. Shaines	1960-62
William O. Junkins	1895-96	John J. Wholey	1962-64
John W. Emery	1897	Timothy J. Connors	1964-68
John S. Tilton	1898	Eileen D. Foley	1968-72
		Arthur F. Brady, Jr.	1972

* Moses Goodrich became mayor in a special election after the State Legislature put Frank W. Miller out of office.

** Cecil M. Neal was the first mayor under the city manager system, and with him started the two-year regimes for city administrations. Heretofore, elections had been held annually, which means that Mayor Jonathan Dearborn, for example, served a total of three years as mayor.

Appendix II
Portsmouth's City Managers

Five men have held the office of city manager in Portsmouth. Edward C. Peterson was the first, and Calvin A. Canney the present.

Edward C. Peterson	1948-53
Jack Fenwick	1952
*Robert C. Violette	1952-69
Richard J. Bowen	1970
Calvin A. Canney	1971-

* As an aftermath of the time when the Council found the City Charter did not permit employment of acting managers, a change was made in 1959. When Robert C. Violette died, Arthur H. Castelazo, a retired naval captain, who was serving as city engineer, acted as manager for some months before Richard J. Bowen took over.

Appendix III
Portsmouth's City Marshals

For what little information we do have about Portsmouth's city marshals, we are indebted to the late Reginald Goldsmith who, during his tenure as a police commissioner, did extensive research into the Police Department.

As indicated in the main text, Andrew J. Beck was the first city marshal, serving in 1850 and 1851. Beck also served in the years 1853, 1854, 1856, 1857, 1858, 1859, 1860.

Jonathan Dearborn	1852-53
Oliver Hanscom	1855-56
Elisha G. Ferguson	1858
Benjamin Norton	1861
Oren Bragdon	1861-63
Emery A. Dresser	1863-65
J. Horace Kent	1866, 1871-73
Frank B. Johnson	1874-75
Israel Marden	1874, 1876
John Dame	1876-77
Thomas Entwistle	1877-84, 1895-1912
Charles W. Norton	1884-86
Jefferson C. Rowe	1887-89, 1892-95
Charles H. Joy	1890-91
Finley R. Butterfield	1895
Michael Hurley	1913-24
George H. Ducker	1924-37
Leonard H. Hewitt	1937-49
William J. Linchey	1949-53
Martin O. Betz	1953-60
Stanton G. Remick	1960-

Appendix IV
Portsmouth's Fire Chiefs

It's only in the last few years that Portsmouth's fire chiefs have had that title. Prior to that the man charged with the responsibility in marshaling the firefighting forces was called the chief engineer. And that title did not come into being until Portsmouth became a city. In the early years, the firewards, supervising various city districts, were under the supervision of the chief of firewards.

Fire Department records run back to 1806 and these make it possible to determine the names of the chief firewards, or as they would be now called, the fire chiefs. The town records, dating back to the beginning, are available in City Clerk Peter O'Donnell's office, but these do not designate chief firewards, apparently a matter of choice among the firewards themselves.

The roster starts with Daniel Austin in 1806, and runs through to Fire Chief Ernest W. Weeks, the incumbent.

Chief Fire Wards

William Boyd	1807-08, 1811
Clement Storer	1809, 1813
John F. Parrott	1810, 1814-16
Abel Harris	1812
Samuel Larkin	1817-24
John Rice	1825-28
Alexander Ladd	1829
Francis Wingate	1830
James Bartlett	1831
Robert Neal	1832-33
Ichabod Goodwin	1834, 1837
Sampson B. Lord	1835
Josiah G. Hadley	1836
Jacob Wendell	1838-39
Leonard Cotton	1840-45
Oliver Ayers	1846-49

Chief Engineers

Oliver Ayers	1850-52
John Trundy	1853
Marcellus Bufford	1854
Alfred T. Joy	1855
Thomas Norton	1856
Josiah G. Hadley	1857, 1859
Leonard Cotton	1858
Charles E. Main	1860-61
John H. Moran	1862-66
William Grogan	1867
James A. Waterhouse	1868-69
Stephen L. Marston	1870-74, 1876-77, 1879-83
Ira C. Seymour	1874-76
Samuel S. Fletcher	1877-79
Willard Sears	1883-84
Herbert A. Marden	1884-90, 1891-95, 1903-04
J. Frank Shannon	1890-91
John D. Randall	1895-99, 1900-03, 1905, 1909-12
Eugene J. Sullivan	1899-1900
Charles Varrell	1906
David Junkins	1907-08
William F. Woods	1913-38
George T. Cogne	1938-52
Frederick R. Crompton	1952-66
Ernest W. Weeks	1966-

Over the years, to augment the water supply in case of major fire, the city has built and maintained several reservoirs. Among these are Market Square, brick construction, 20,000 gallons capacity; School Street, brick, 18,000; Pleasant Street, brick (now filled in), 15,000; Austin Street, brick, 12,000; Haymarket Square, brick (now filled in), 30,000; Hanover Street — engine house yard, brick (now filled in), 63,000; Boston & Maine Railroad, brick (now filled in), 37,000; Union Street, wood, 8,000.

Appendix V
Portsmouth's Postmasters

No one knows who Portsmouth's first postmaster might have been. He probably lived at Great Island, and it would not be surprising if he often was dependent on ships stopping at the Isles of Shoals for any letters that might be coming to New England. The Shoals were often the first landfall for inward-bound vessels and letters could be put off there for people in the Piscataqua country.

That's all conjecture, but it is known that Benjamin Franklin came through here in 1762 in his role as Deputy Postmaster General for North America.

A listing of those who can be said to have served as postmaster since the founding of the Republic has been made available by Alfred V. Cashman, officer-in-charge at the Portsmouth Post Office, although the original request went to his predecessor, Arthur H. P. Hopley, who retired on June 30, 1972.

Samuel Penhallow, whose first report as postmaster was dated January 5, 1776, apparently heads the listing. Others followed:

Jeremiah Libbey	December 14, 1776
Mark Simes	April 1, 1798
	first report
Nathan Payson	February 10, 1812
John F. Parrott	February 24, 1826
Abner Greenleaf	April 22, 1829
Samuel Cushman	June 26, 1840
Samuel Gookin	May 19, 1841
Nehemiah Moses	March 22, 1845
Thomas L. Tullock	April 4, 1849
Gideon H. Rundlett	April 4, 1853
Joseph P. Morse	March 27, 1861
Joseph B. Adams	April 11, 1865

Elbridge G. Pierce, Jr.	April 21, 1869
Samuel J. Gerrish	March 30, 1885
John H. Locke	June 4, 1889
William O. Sides	July 27, 1897
John H. Bartlett	July 11, 1899
Joseph P. Conner	December 10, 1907
John H. Dowd	February 11, 1916
Fred C. Tucker	August 1, 1918
Joseph P. Conner	February 18, 1920
Peter J. Hickey	confirmed March 12, 1937
Mary C. Dondero	assumed charge March 15, 1952
	acting, April 8, 1952
Frederick J. Rowe	assumed charge June 15, 1953
	acting, July 2, 1953
	confirmed, July 31, 1954
Theodore R. Butler	assumed charge April 15, 1955
	acting, May 5, 1955
	confirmed, June 4, 1956
Arthur H. P. Hopley	assumed charge February 20, 1971
Alfred V. Cashman	appointed officer-in-charge, July 1, 1972

The Portsmouth Post Office plays a large regional function with 80-odd area offices under its direct management. Cashman is responsible for the performance of more than 600 employees. This new role was created when the United State Postal Service came into being as a government corporation.

Appendix VI
Portsmouth's Major Fires

From the very beginning, colonial New England's major enemy was fire. It's impossible to know today what this dreaded scourge took in the way of lives in earlier times. Thanks to Fire Captain Robert Murphy, a listing of some of the major fires over more than 270 years has been made available.

Minister's House, Pleasant Street, October 31, 1704, three perished.

Robert Macklin's House, King (Congress) Street, January 22, 1728; bake shop also lost.

Stoodley's Tavern, Daniel Street, January 25, 1761; all buildings on property, plus damage to adjacent structures.

John Wendell's House, Canoe Bridge, April 3, 1763, about midnight. House destroyed, firefighters used the town's three "engines" in combatting the blaze.

Woodbury Langdon's House, March 15, 1781. Fire started in barn of Nathaniel Treadwell's destroyed his house, spread across the lane to the jail, then to Langdon's property. Almost ignited Joseph Whipple House which is now standing at Middle and Park Streets.

Fire of 1802, started on day after Christmas at 4 a.m.; every building on Parade destroyed except North Church and Court House; Daniel Street swept to Stoodley's Tavern; buildings on Market Street as far as Fore Street leveled, also structures on Bow and Ladd.

Queen's Chapel, Church Hill (Chapel Street), December 24, 1806, about 5 a.m. Fire started in store owned by Stephen Little. Destroyed 15 buildings, including Queen's Chapel.

Fire of 1813, most destructive in city history, 300 buildings, started on December 22, at 7 p.m. Destroyed State Street on both sides from just west of Pleasant Street to the river.

Market Street Fire, May, 1845.

Penhallow Street Fire, July 18, 1864.

Congress Block, November 30, 1865.

Bell Tavern, Congress Street, February 25, 1867.

St. Mary's Church, November 27, 1871.

Came Brothers Carriage Factory, McDonough Street, July 12, 1872, two killed.

Melcher Block, Congress Street, January 30, 1874. The Hartford Building now stands on the site.

Sowersby's Bake Shop, Marcy Street, August 1, 1875.

Old Temple, Chestnut Street, December 24, 1876. Site of Present Civic Theater.

Franklin Block, Congress Street, May 8, 1879.

Kearsarge Mill, a six-story cotton mill, December 4, 1880. Formerly Brooks Garage, it is now occupied by a plumbing supply firm, Peerless-Finberg.

Creosote Works, Nobles Island, April 23, 1880.

Gibson House and Stoddard's Stable, Vaughan Street, July 23, 1883.

Rockingham House, State Street, September 17, 1884.

Old Piscataqua House, April 5, 1886.

Tenement, Atkinson Street, March 15, 1888, at the height of the Great Blizzard, a Mrs. Harrington was killed.

Universalist Church, Pleasant Street, March 28, 1896.

Wendell Block, Market Street, February 7, 1897.

West End Hotel, Islington Street, March 1, 1897.

Times Building, State and Church Streets, February 3, 1902.

Glebe Building, Porter and Pleasant Streets, 10:45 p.m., February 1, 1904.

Malt House, Jones Brewery, 8:30 a.m.

Portsmouth Coal Co. Stable, Market Street, 12:35 a.m., March 10, 1909.

John Broughton Lumber, State Street, 11:57 a.m., December 26, 1909.

Coal Pocket, Noble's Island, April 30, 1911.

Chadwick and Trefethen Machine Shop, 10:20 a.m., July 8, 1911.

Times Publishing Co., 2:30 a.m., December 1913.

Walden Block, Congress Street, 11:45 p.m., November 23, 1914.

B. F. Canney, Vaughan Street, 5:32 a.m., February 8, 1916.

Maplewood Garage, Vaughan Street, 10:45 p.m., March 2, 1926.

Airplane Crash, Sherburne Road, 1:20 p.m., April 27, 1930, two killed.

Atlantic Gypsum Co., 12:05 p.m., November 9, 1930.

McIntosh Furniture Store, Congress Street, 2:03 p.m., May 5, 1931.

Phinney's Laundry, Marcy Street, May 18, 1934.

N. H. Provision Co., Market Street, 4:40 a.m., January 8, 1937.

Montgomery Ward storehouse, Albany Street, 10:55 a.m., July 6, 1938.

Diamond Match Co. and Brooks Garage, 8:20 p.m., February 20, 1939.

B & M Roundhouse, 11:45 p.m., June 27, 1941.

Shaines Shoe Store, Congress Street, 1:08 a.m., March 15, 1943.

Tank Car, B & M Rail Yards, 7:31 a.m., October 14, 1943. (Richard V. Parnham's photograph won New-England wide recognition.)

Bow Street Apartments, 11:24 p.m., June 15, 1944. Kenneth Mason killed.

Carpenters Hall, High Street, 6 a.m., February 9, 1945, a day of extremely stormy weather.

Frank D. Perkins Tire, Market Street, 3:37 a.m., March 3, 1945.

Hislop Block, Fleet Street, 6:31 p.m., February 3, 1946. Fireman Eliot Staples injured.

Universalist Church, Pleasant Street, 2:44 a.m., January 11, 1947. Total loss.

Frank D. Perkins Tire, Market Street, 12:05 a.m., September 14, 1947.

Frank D. Perkins Tire, Market Street, 6:01 a.m., January 11, 1948.

Kray's Store and Shaines Store, Congress Street, 9:15 p.m., January 17, 1948.

Dragon Inn, Lafayette Road, 12:35 a.m., December 16, 1949.

L. V. Regan Wharehouse, Vaughan Street, 4:21 a.m., August 19, 1950. Two Alarms.

Littlefield Lumber Co., Vaughan Street, 1:20 a.m., June 8, 1951.

C. E. Walker Co. coal pocket, foot of State Street, 12:25 a.m., June 9, 1951. Two Alarms.

Littlefield Lumber Co., Vaughan Street, 3:19 a.m., October 7, 1951. Two Alarms.

Michael J. Whalen Warehouse, Albany Street, 11:44 p.m.,

November 25, 1952.

Ricci Warehouse, Albany Street, 11:23 a.m., April 18, 1953.

VFW Home (Old Courthouse), Parrott Avenue, 1:59 a.m., May 1, 1953.

Dinnerman Block, Pleasant Street (Glebe Building), 4:50 a.m., December 25, 1953.

Dawson's Paint Store, Lafayette Road, 10:10 a.m., March 29, 1955. Susan Ayer, age 2, killed.

Kearsarge Hotel, Congress Street, 9:20 p.m., January 1, 1956. Two Alarms.

J. J. Newberry Company, Congress Street, 6:25 p.m., February 29, 1956. Two Alarms.

N. H. Provision Co., 698 Islington Street, 10:31 p.m., October 21, 1957. Two Alarms.

Peirce Block, High Street, 1:55 a.m., December 14, 1960. Two Alarms.

Kearsarge Hotel, Congress Street, 3:25 p.m., September 5, 1961. Two Alarms.

Radio Station WHEB, Lafayette Road, 11:45 a.m., March 8, 1962. Two Alarms. Destroyed.

Hillcrest Trailer Park, Lafayette Road, 2:30 a.m., June 12, 1962. Three burned to death.

Michael J. Whalen Warehouse, 674 Islington Street, 8:20 p.m., June 14, 1960. Two Alarms.

Christ Episcopal Church, Madison Street, 1:05 p.m., June 19, 1963. Two alarms. The New England Association of Fire Chiefs was in convention at the Hotel Wentworth at the time. Deputy Chief Ernest W. Weeks, in command in the absence of Chief Frederick R. Crompton, had a lot of high-ranking supervision from the visiting fire chiefs, many of whom pitched in and worked as firefighters.

Colonial Theater Block, Congress Street, 11:07 p.m., March 13, 1964. Two alarms. This fire destroyed what remained of the ancient Rogers House, next door to the theater. This building had been built in 1704 after the minister was burned out on Pleasant Street. At some time in its life the old house had been jacked up and an new ground floor built underneath it.

Jones Avenue Dump, 10:44 a.m., November 4, 1965. The fire spread through the woods to Sagamore Avenue and to Walker Bungalow Road, destroying at least one home.

Iafolla Co., Peverly Hill Road, 5:30 p.m., September 20, 1966, a Seybolt oil truck and the asphalt plant. Lawrence Bromfield was badly burned and has since died.

440

Radio Station WBBX, Islington Street, 12:45 a.m., November 2, 1966. Destroyed.

House, 83 Russell Street, 8:29 p.m., November 11, 1967. David Scott, 2, killed.

House, 31 Sudbury Street, 1:49 a.m., March 6, 1968. Two killed, Samuel Faulkner and Clair E. French.

House, 765 Islington, 1:05 a.m., December 22, 1968. Five children were killed. Seething flames kept firemen from reaching any of the youngsters, the children of Frederick McLaughlin.

Rockingham Electric, 345 Court Street, 8:12 p.m., December 28, 1968. The company has since built a store in Newington.

Mark Wentworth Home, 346 Pleasant Street, 5:06 p.m., November 27. 1969. A fire confined wholly to his room took the life of former Portsmouth tax collector J. Warren Somerby, 88 years old.

Red Coach Steak House, 28 High Street, 9:13 p.m., December 11, 1969. The restaurant was in what had once been the Dolphin Hotel, and before that the National House. it was owned by members of the Coussoule family who have since opened a new Red Coach Steak House on Lafayette Road, North Hampton.

Not included, although noted by firemen, are two crashes of B47 bombers from Pease AFB, which took the lives of six men, and a KC97 crash on Rt. 101, just east of the golf course which killed seven.

Appendix VII
The USS Constitution Timbers

        Included here is the correspondence pertaining to the storage of logs for use in any rebuilding of the USS Constitution. The restraint of the official language makes the letters all the more enjoyable, and they should put an end to the illusion that The Constitution might ever come here for rebuilding because of the timbers.

500
10300/NY1
(07291)
8 June 1971

MEMORANDUM

From: 500
To: 400

Subj: Live Oak Timbers Stored in Meade Pond

Ref: (a) 400 memo 400:mep 10300 of 4 June 1971

Encl: (1) Copy of 500 memo of 24 May 1962

1. Reference (a) requested confirmation that the live oak timbers in Meade Pond were not carried on the stock records of the Supply Department.

2. The timbers in Meade Pond are not on the Supply Department records. For information, however, there have been previous projects to recoup some of the live oak remaining in Meade Pond for various purposes. In each case, the effort was a failure in that the wood was so tough that it did considerable damage to the tools used to work with and it generated a stench which was offensive to those working with the material. To quote a report we have on hand, written in 1962, an attempt was made in 1945 "To ascertain suitability......... The saw was severely damaged, millworkers were nauseated by the stench and the Master Joiner stated (with certain pertinent and pithy comment) that the job could not be undertaken under any circumstances."

3. Enclosure (1) is forwarded for information.

W. C. WILLIAMS

cc:
200
440
508B
500/501
591/591A

ENCLOSURE (1)
24 May 1962

MEMORANDUM

From: 500
To: 100

Subj: Oak, The USF Constitution, and related facts and fallacies

1. Records on the subject material are voluminous and cover a period of thirty-two years. A concise digest of these records is here presented.
    After the 1930-31 reconditioning of the USF Constitution at Boston Navy Yard, arrangements were made to store some 285 pieces of excess oak of various shapes and sizes in the Ice Pond in the rear of Bldg. 136. Boston later added "seventy or eighty" pieces to this figure and shipment was made by barge and the

material was placed in the pond in early fall of 1930. In June 1931 Public Works prepared sketches MC-170 and MC-170a which showed shapes and locations of 329 pieces of oak. It was pointed out that discrepancies in quantities existed and that it was impossible to correlate the sketches furnished by Boston with individual pieces. The two sketches, MC-170 and MC-170a, were factual at the time but the quantity discrepancies would indicate that not all the oak came from Boston. It is very likely that some pieces came from the old sawmill pond.

In August 1938 at the request of Navy Yard, Charleston, S. C. seventeen pieces were removed from the pond and shipped to that activity. Considerable difficulty was experienced at that time in identifying the individual pieces since no identification had been attached at the time of submersion. The irregular shapes made comparison with sketches difficult but the seventeen pieces were tentatively identified to particular numbers.

In December 1941 Boston again requested submerged storage for two carloads of oak logs and in May 1942 for 147 pieces consisting of knees and heavy dimension pieces. Arrival on the Yard is not confirmed, but in January of 1942 twenty-seven pieces from Boston were placed in the pond. There is definite record of receipt of 250 pieces of salvaged oak knees and timbers from Navy Yard, New York in September 1942.

In 1945 the material was declared surplus and reported to Buships and Busanda. Busanda suggested possible use by the Prison in their Pallet Program. To ascertain suitability, two pieces were sent to the sawmill. The saw was severely damaged, millworkers were nauseated by the stench, and the Master Joiner stated (with certain pertinent and pithy comment) that the job could not be undertaken under any circumstances. Consequently, 592 peices were offered for bid and were sold to the Industrial Lumber Co., Jersey City, N. J.

These facts are relevant in that they point out that by this time due to uncertain origins, in and out movements, settling in the ooze, etc., that identification became more and more of a problem.

In 1948 the possible restoration of USF Constellation created a whole new wave of interest in our oak. Numerous letters went between Buships, Boston, and Portsmouth. It became obvious that definite facts be established. Accordingly, Public Works did an exhaustive job of removing, measuring, and sketching each piece and returned same to the pond. Two hundred seventy-two pieces were itemized and a Booklet of Dimensions and Shapes of Live Oak dated Aug 1949 was prepared and forwarded to interested activities. The

Industrial Lumber Co. was even contacted to ascertain if any of the amount they had bought was still available. This situation held "hot and cold" until Aug 1954 when it was determined that USF Constellation would not be repaired by the Navy and Buships recommended tha the material be retained "pending possible future demands."

During 1955 and 1956 several communications passed between the Shipyard, Buships, and the Constellation Commission in the hope that some use might be made with negative results. In 1955 the Inspector General recommended that disposition action be initiated. In May 1957 the Shipyard Commander appointed an officer to conduct a "thorough investigation" to determine proper action. Two pieces, No.70 and No.106, of the 1949 listing were removed to the sawmill. Piece No.106 was split and sawed into planks. It appeared to be in fair condition but within 24 hours began to split, check, and crack. Pieces were sawed, planed, turned, and soaked in linseed oil, all of which showed progressively serious cracking. As it dried it became harder with more tool damage. The stench was even "riper" than before and the comments more pithy.

As a result of the investigation the recommendation was made that the entire lot be abandoned, that it has no commercial value, is not donable, and that it remain "as is" and "where is." This was concurred in by the Review Board and on the instructions of the Commander, abandonment was accomplished on 29 July 1957.

The logs are still there and likely to remain if removal expense is considered. Many have sunk out of sight in the mud and can only be found by probing. In the interest of accuracy two fallacies which have crept into the records should be noted. None of this oak was ever bought for the USF Constellation. None of it was ever bought with contributions of school children.

W. F. HARVEY, JR.

Bibliography

Newspapers:

Boston Evening Transcript

Boston Globe

Boston Post

Boston Post Boy

Federal Observer (William Treadwell and Samuel G. Hart)

Freeman's Journal (Benjamin Dearborn continuing the New Hampshire Gazette, 1776-78)

Herald of Gospel Liberty (Elias Smith)

Manchester Mirror

New Hampshire Gazette (1756-1820)

New Hampshire Patriot (Concord)

New Hampshire Spy (George Jerry Osborne, 1786-1793)

Oracle of the Day (Charles Peirce, 1793-99)

Portsmouth Herald (1897 to the present)

Portsmouth Journal of Literature and Politics (C. W. Brewster)

Portsmouth Mercury (Thomas Furber and Ezekiel Russell, 1765-1767)

Portsmouth Morning Chronicle (August 2, 1852 to 1925)

Portsmouth Oracle (William and Daniel Treadwell, 1803 until it became Portsmouth Journal of Literature and Politics)

Portsmouth Times

Republican Ledger (George Jerry Osborne, 1799-1803)

Rockingham Messenger

States and the Union (Joshua Foster)

United States Oracle (Continued the Oracle of the Day to 1803)

War Journal (Gideon Beck and Daniel C. Foster, 1813)

Pamphlets:

        Dunn, Robert H., Old St. John's, 1947

        Foster, Joseph, Graves We Decorate, 1917

        Foster, Joseph, Some Revolutionary Veterans, 1929

        Fuller, W. O., "An Old Town by the Sea", 1912

        Harriman, Arthur I., "Praises on Tombs", 1932

        Jarvis, Andrew, St. Nicholas Church, 40th Anniversary, 1971

        Locke, Arthur H., Cemetery Inscriptions, Portsmouth and New Castle, 1907

        Montgomery, H. P., Portsmouth Guide Book, 1901

        Penrose, Charles, Ichabod Goodwin, 1956

        Penrose, Charles, "They Live on a Rock", 1957

        Rutledge, Lyman V., Moonlight Murder at Smuttynose, 1958

        Tanner, Virginia, Pageant of Portsmouth, 1923

        Wendell, William G., Jonathan Warner, 1950

        Air Force Guide, 1956

        Golden Jubilee Banquet, Knights of Columbus, 1945

        Ground Breaking Program, Pease AFB, 1954

        Historical Souvenir, Portsmouth, 1923

        Pease AFB Dedication, Souvenir Booklet, 1956

        Portsmouth Athenaeum History, 1967

        Portsmouth Chamber of Commerce brochure, 1969

        Portsmouth Press Club, 1896

        St. John's Lodge, Trestleboard, Gerald D. Foss, editor

Magazines:

        American Heritage

        Granite State Monthlies, 57 vols., 1877-1925

        Historical New Hampshire

        New Hampshire Profiles

        U. S. Naval Institute Proceedings, February, 1961

Portsmouth Histories:

        Adams, Nathaniel, "Annals of Portsmouth", 1825

        Alden, Timothy G., "An Account of the Several Religious Societies in Portsmouth", 1808

        Aldrich, Thomas Bailey, "Old Town by the Sea", 1893
                         "The Story of a Bad Boy"

        Brewster, Charles W., editor, Portsmouth Jubilee, 1853
            "Rambles About Portsmouth", 2 vols., 1859, 1869

        Brighton, Ray, "The Portsmouth Savings Bank", 1958

        Chamberlain, Samuel, "Portsmouth, New Hampshire, a Camera Impression", 1935

        Foster, Joseph, "Portsmouth Guide Book", 1884

Gurney, C. S., "An Historical Calendar of Portsmouth, (The Box Book), copyrighted 1907 by C.A.H.

May, Ralph, "Among Old Portsmouth Houses", 1946

"Early Portsmouth", 1926

Universalism in Portsmouth, "Centennial Anniversary of the Planting", 1874

Pearson, Helen, "Vignettes of Portsmouth", 1913

Portsmouth Navy Yard Histories:

Fentress, Walter E. H., "Centennial History of the Portsmouth Navy Yard", 1876

Preble, George H., "History of the United States Navy Yard", 1892

Rumble, Henry N., "History of the Portsmouth Naval Shipyard", 1958 (paper bound)

County Histories:

Hazlett, Charles A., "Rockingham County", 1915

Hurd, D. Hamilton, "Rockingham and Strafford Counties",1885

Town and Area Histories:

Albee, John, "New Castle, Historic and Picturesque", 1884

Dow, Joseph, "History of Hampton", 1893

Howells, John Meade, "Architectural Heritage of the Piscataqua", 1937

Rutledge, Lyman V., "The Isles of Shoals", 1965

Saltonstall, William G., "Ports of the Piscataqua", 1941

Thaxter, Rosamond, "Sandpiper"

Varrell, William, "Rye on the Rocks"

State Histories:

Belknap, Jeremy, "History of New Hampshire", 3 vols. 1784-1792; also John Farmer edition, Vol. 1, 1831

Foss, Gerald D., "Three Centuries of Freemasonry in New Hampshire", 1972

Hunt, Elmer, Munson, "New Hampshire Town Names", 1970

Jenness, John S., "Notes on the First Planting of New Hampshire", 1878

"Transcripts of Original Documents in the English Archives Relating to the Early History

of the State of New Hampshire", 1876

McClintock, John N., "History of New Hampshire", 1888

Page, Judge Elwin, "Judicial Beginnings in New Hampshire", 1959

Robinson, Maurice H., "A History of Taxation in New Hampshire", 1902

Squires, Duane, "The Granite State", 4 vols., 1956

Stackpole, Everett G., "History of New Hampshire", 4 vols., 1916

Tuttle, Charles W., "Historical Papers", 1889

General Reading:

Bell, Charles H., "Bench and Bar of New Hampshire", 1894

Bradford, William, "Plimouth Plantation", edited by Charles Deane, 1856

Briggs, Martin S., "The Homes of the Pilgrim Fathers in England and America", 1932

Chapelle, Howard, "History of the American Sailing Navy", 1949

Chastellux, Marquis le, "Travels in North America", translated by Howard C. Rice, Jr., University of North Carolina, 1963

Chatterton, E. K., "The Ship Under Sail"

Cole, Donald B., "Jacksonian Democracy in New Hampshire", 1970

Daniell, Jere R., "Experiment in Republicanism", 1971

Drake, Samuel G., editor, "Hubbard's Indian Wars", 1865

Freeman, Douglas, "George Washington", a biography

Hutchinson, Thomas, "History of Massachusetts Bay", 3 vols., 1749-74

Jossalyn, John, "An Account of Two Voyages to New England", edited by William Veazie, 1865

Lipscomb, F. W., "The Heritage of Sea Power" (Portsmouth, England) 1967

Leach, Douglas, E., "The Northern Colonial Frontier", 1966

Randolph, Edward, "Memoir, Prince Society", 7 vols., 1898-1909

Rogers, Stanley, "The Book of the Sailing Ship", 1931

Sewall, Samuel, "Diary, Collections of the Massachusetts Historical Society"

Sherburne, Andrew, "Memoir of Andrew Sherburne", 1831

Smith, John, "A Description of New England", William Veazie, editor, 1865

Tuttle, Charles W., "Captain John Mason", 1887

Winthrop, John, "History of New England", 2 vols., edited by James Savage, 1853

Reference Books:
 Bibliography of American Newspapers Before 1820, Brigham, 1947
 Checklist of N. H. History, Otis G. Hammond, 1925
 Civil War Regimental Histories, 1st through 18th
 Dictionary of American Biography
 History of Harvard University, Josiah Quincy, 1840
 Naval Documents of the American Revolution
 New England Historical and Genealogical Register, vols., 1-123
 New Hampshire Manual for the General Court, 1943-1971
 New Hampshire Registers, 1943, 1963, 1971
 Portsmouth City Reports, various years
 Portsmouth Town and City Directories, 1821-1972
 Province and State Papers, 40 vols.
 Province and State Laws, 10 vols.
 Unites States Census Report, 1790

Manuscript Materials:
 Colonial Documents, Public Record Office, London, England
 Larkin Papers, Portsmouth Athenaeum
 Marine Railway Records
 Minutes of the Committee of Safety, 1775-83
 Peirce Papers, Portsmouth Athenaeum
 Portsmouth Aqueduct Records
 Portsmouth Athenaeum Records
 Portsmouth Town and City Records (both manuscript and WPA abstracts)
 Rockingham County Deeds
 Rockingham County Court Records in Civil and Criminal Cases
 Rockingham County Probate Records
 Ruth Blay Trial Proceedings, New Hampshire Historical Society Archives
 Tower of London Records, Edward Gove Case, 1683-86
 York County Deeds

INDEX

453

454

455

457

460

461

462

466

467

470

471

472

474

479

489

490

492

493

495

496

502

503